W9-ARB-339

Nationalism and Revolution in Indonesia

Nationalism and Revolution

in Indonesia

GEORGE McTURNAN KAHIN

Assistant Professor of Government and
Executive Director, Southeast Asia Program, Cornell University

PUBLISHED UNDER THE AUSPICES OF THE INTERNATIONAL
SECRETARIAT OF THE INSTITUTE OF PACIFIC RELATIONS
AND THE SOUTHEAST ASIA PROGRAM, CORNELL UNIVERSITY

Cornell University Press

ITHACA, NEW YORK

To Maggie

Preface

THIS book has grown out of a year's study of political developments in Indonesia undertaken there by the author from mid-1948 to mid-1949. The study was made possible by a fellowship from the Social Science Research Council. The author wishes to thank the Council for this much appreciated assistance as well as to indicate appreciation to the Institute of Pacific Relations and the Cornell University Southeast Asia Program for support enabling him to devote three subsequent summers to research and writing related to this book.

The author particularly wishes to express his gratitude to three men who throughout the writing of this book have given him their warm encouragement and helpful criticism—Professor Rupert Emerson, Chairman of the Department of Government of Harvard University; William L. Holland, Secretary-General of the Institute of Pacific Relations; and Professor Owen Lattimore, Director of the Walter Hines Page School of International Relations at the Johns Hopkins University. The author wishes to make clear that he personally is responsible for all statements appearing in the book and for all its inadequacies.

In preparing the book the author is also indebted to a policy pioneered by Professor Owen Lattimore of the Johns Hopkins University and supported by its late President, Isaiah Bowman, and his successor, Detlev Bronk. Under this plan the graduate student who has completed all work toward his doctorate except the dissertation goes out into the field to do research with the understanding that upon his return he will have a year's academic appointment during which his only duty will be to give a seminar relating to the general subject of which the topic of his dissertation is a major constituent. Thereby, in preparing for the seminar, he contributes indirectly to his dissertation; the remaining major part of his time he is free to devote to the organization and writing of the material he has gathered in the field while it is still fresh. As the grateful recipient of such an appointment, the author was able to devote most of the academic year following his return from Indonesia to work on this book.

To a major extent the book is based upon the author's personal observations in Indonesia and upon extensive conversations with people there, political leaders as well as members of the rank and file. A list of persons both in Indonesia and the United States to whom the author is particularly indebted for help in gathering information will be found in the Acknowledgments. Much of this information would not have been obtained by the writer had it not been for the candor of many of these people and other leaders and officials with whom he spoke. A great deal of what they told him had, and still retains, important significance with respect to Indonesia's domestic politics or relationship with other countries. Because of this fact, many of them requested that their names not be mentioned should the author use this information in his writing. Thus, frequently where information supplied him by these persons is incorporated into this book, the author has had to refrain from citing the sources.

A Note on the Spelling of Indonesian Places and Names

Early in the course of the revolution it was officially decided that all place names which had used the letters "oe" to express the sound ū (as in flute) should substitute the letter "u" for "oe." (Thus Soerakarta became Surakarta.) This spelling has been adopted throughout this book.

It was optional whether or not this change in spelling was carried over to the names of people. Some adopted the change; some did not; some adopted it and then later changed back to the previous method, while some incorporated this change for one of their names and not for the other. Frequently news dispatches and periodical articles give the "u" spelling rather than the "oe" even though the individual in question has kept the old way of spelling and so writes his name. The writer has endeavored to spell names according to the manner which, to the best of his knowledge, the individual in question now prefers.

For a time during the course of the revolution there was a tendency with both place names and personal names to abandon "dj" in favor of "j" and "j" in favor of "y," using these letters as in English rather than according to the previously adopted Dutch system. In general this change was abandoned after a year or two. However, since in English-language newspapers the present capital of Indonesia and its former revolutionary capital are generally spelled with a "j" rather than a "dj," in this book, for the convenience of the reader, they both appear with a similar spelling: i.e. Jakarta and Jogjakarta.

Indonesian Names and Titles

Many Indonesians have only one name, and in such cases it usually has no relation to that of their father. In particular this is frequent among Javanese. Thus the only name of the President of Indonesia is "Soekarno." (It was an enterprising American newspaperman who wanted his dispatches to look more complete and first tacked on "Achmed" as a first name.)

With the revolution the majority of Indonesians with aristocratic titles (such as *Raden* and *Raden Mas*) have dropped them. On the other hand, academic titles are still much prized. These conform with those in use in the Netherlands. Most frequent is the title "Mr." (*Meester in Rechten,* Master of Laws), which indicates that the person has a law degree, usually involving three to four years of university study in the Netherlands or five in Indonesia. Second in frequency is the title "Ir." (*Ingénieur,* Engineer), which indicates that the individual has a degree in engineering, usually involving five to six years of work at the university level. Much less frequent is the title "Drs." (*Doctorandus*). This indicates that the individual has completed all work toward his doctorate with the exception of the dissertation. Finally there is the title "Dr." (Doctor), indicating as elsewhere that the individual is either a Doctor of Medicine or the holder of a Ph.D. Recently the situation has become confused with the tendency of many holders of the *Meester in Rechten* to use the title "Dr." instead of "Mr."

GEORGE McT. KAHIN

Cornell University
July, 1952

Contents

Maps

Nationalism and Revolution in Indonesia

CHAPTER I

The Social Environment
of Indonesian Nationalism

THE ENVIRONMENT which has conditioned the growth of Indonesian nationalism will undoubtedly appear somewhat unique to those whose understanding of the dynamics of nationalism is based primarily upon its history in the West. This quality of uniqueness remains even when comparisons are made with such colonial-conditioned nationalisms as have emerged in India and the Philippines. Indeed, even rough congruence in the pattern of conditioning background is found only when comparison is made with Burma and Indochina.

In order to understand the nature of Indonesian nationalism and the revolutionary movement into which it developed it is particularly necessary, therefore, to have some knowledge of the most important features of the social milieu in which it was generated. The twentieth-century colonial environment which conditioned the modern, articulate, and discernible phase of Indonesian nationalism is one demanding fullest analysis. This cannot, however, be undertaken satisfactorily without some prior understanding of the previous historical conditioning of the more salient features of that environment. For, though the thickest roots of contemporary Indonesian nationalism are nourished principally by the soil of the twentieth century, some of their most critical tentacles reach down further into much older strata of history.

It has been a frequently made observation that during their more than three centuries of colonial rule in the Indies the policy of the Dutch was to maintain the existing structure of native society, and that

1

during this period the basic characteristics of that society, except for a grafting upon it of European and Chinese economic enterprise, remained virtually unchanged.

Though considerable popular writing has concerned itself with the question of whether the maintenance of the old native society was good or bad for the Indonesians, very little attention has been paid as to whether the basic postulate itself is correct. With respect to Java—which long before and throughout the period of Dutch rule was the political and cultural center of Indonesia and the supporter of most of its population [1]—modern scholarship has increasingly demonstrated the incorrectness of this postulate. In fact, the impact of Dutch rule substantially altered the basic structure of Javanese social organization.[2] Apparently to an appreciable extent it also altered the political and economic attitudes of much of the population of Java.

During three centuries of colonial rule a Javanese society whose political articulation had been for the most part only moderately authoritarian became generally strongly authoritarian in character. A Javanese peasantry which in most areas had been able to force the indigenous nobility to respect its rights became weakened in its relationship with this nobility, which was then able to secure greatly increased power and rights over it. In addition, the peasantry, which on the whole had possessed substantial economic strength and among whom generally there had been only a relatively moderate degree of communalistic economic organization, became economically as well as politically weak, much more communalistic in economic organization, and so dulled in its economic sense as to bring some Dutch scholars to describe its twentieth-century mentality as still "precapitalistic."[3] To

[1] Department van Economische Zaken (Dept. of Economic Affairs), *Volkstelling* ("Census") *1930* (Batavia, 1936), VIII, 7. The first official estimate of population for the whole of Indonesia was in 1890. It reckoned the population of the areas outside Java and Madura (a small island adjacent to the northeastern coast of Java and included with it for administrative purposes) as approximately 10,000,000 as against a population of 23,609,312 for Java and Madura. The last census, that of 1930, counted the population of Java and Madura as 40,891,093 as against 18,246,974 for all the rest of Indonesia.

[2] The structure of social organization in some areas outside Java—as in some of the most important spice-producing islands of the Moluccas (e.g., Banda and Amboina) and much later in the East Coast residency of Sumatra—was also greatly altered under the impact of Dutch rule, though in different ways than occurred in Java.

[3] Cf. Nicolaas Dirk Ploegsma, *Oorspronkelijkheid en Economisch Aspect van het Dorp op Java en Madoera* (Leiden, 1937), pp. 179–181. In some areas the tendency towards increased communalistic organization in the village had been significant even before the arrival of the Dutch as a reaction to the pressure of the demands

the limited extent that pre-Dutch Indonesian society could be described as having had a middle class, that class was almost completely eliminated during the course of Dutch rule, the once-flourishing Javanese merchant class all but disappearing.

The impact of the Dutch on the Indonesian social structure commenced shortly after the founding of their East India Company in 1602. The objective of the Company was to make maximum profits in trade, and to realize this aim it was felt necessary to monopolize exports and imports. The Company's attention, which initially had been absorbed by the spice of the Moluccas,[4] was soon attracted to the well-established and extensive trade centering on Java. Here it obtained trading privileges, at first of a relatively limited character, from the native wielders of political power.

The objective of the Company being trading privileges, it had no inclination to sink its limited resources into developing political control over Javanese territory, except insofar as this was necessary to secure and maintain such privileges. But it soon became clear that unless these could be exercised as monopolies vis-à-vis competing traders from other countries they were of little value. In order to eliminate competition from Javanese, Arab, Chinese, and non-Dutch European traders and to ensure an implementation of agreements made with local rulers most suited to its own interests, the Company gradually found it necessary to intervene politically more and more decisively over wider and wider areas of Java.

Fortunately for the Dutch, Java in the seventeenth and eighteenth centuries was politically unintegrated. Moreover, Mataram, the largest

---

of the native rulers. The effect of Dutch rule was to increase this tendency, spreading its operation much more widely.

Prior to the arrival of the Dutch, the political and economic autonomy of the peasantry was greatest in the areas of the native states lying some distance from their capitals (the *mantjanegara*). In the area centering around the capital (the *negara-gung*) the peasantry was obliged to give part of its crops to the capital's ruler or to those whom he granted apanage rights. However, even in this area the land was considered to belong to the peasant, although he kept but 40 per cent of the crop (*Berita Panitya Tanah Konversi* [Report of the Conversion Land Commission to the Working Committee of the Parliament (KNIP) of the Republic of Indonesia], [Jogjakarta, April, 1948], ch. iii).

4 The native spice production of these small islands was restricted by the Dutch to Amboina and a few small neighboring islands. Elsewhere it was forcibly forbidden. On Amboina the Dutch were able to restrict and expand production according to market demand and to enforce a low purchase price (G. H. van der Kolff, "European Influences on Native Agriculture," in Schrieke, *The Effect of Western Influence on Native Civilizations in the Malay Archipelago* [Batavia, 1929], p. 104).

of the Javanese states, was during much of this period seriously weakened by civil wars. Initially, only by playing off the Sultanate of Bantam against Mataram were the Dutch able to maintain their trading post at Batavia. It was to an important extent because of the division and mutual enmity of the chief Javanese states that they were thereafter, by playing one state against the other, eventually able to dominate the island completely.

Between 1677 and 1777, the Company extended its political and economic control over two-thirds of Java,[5] while it dominated, for the most part, the economic life of the remainder of the island, the truncated and nominally independent state of Mataram. Mataram was totally excluded from commercial relations with the outer world. Its commerce was vigorously suppressed; ". . . merchants, and shipbuilders lost their occupation, and the fisheries and forests were no longer profitable. The Javanese became a people of cultivators and the economic content of their social life was stunted." [6]

Commanding very limited resources and expected to show a high annual profit on its small capital, the Dutch East India Company was not in a position to pay the high costs that a system of direct administration would have entailed. Sufficient to secure the political control necessary for attainment of its economic objectives was the inexpensive system of indirect rule that it came to follow. The essence of this system consisted in the utilization of the indigenous power structure for its own interests. More precisely this meant the maintenance and reinforcement of the position and power of the amenable elements of the Javanese aristocracy. Their power had to be enlarged, for the Company's interests called for new and additional burdens being placed on the peasantry.[7] The power of this aristocracy was strengthened by Dutch military force, which stood ready to back it against the populace so long as it controlled the economic activities of the latter in accordance with the interests of the Company.

Thereby Javanese society was thrown seriously out of balance. The formerly strong peasantry could no longer curb the arbitrary actions

[5] For an account in English of these conquests see B.H.M. Vlekke, *Nusantara, A History of the East Indian Archipelago* (Cambridge, Mass., 1945), especially pp. 146–163. By 1777, the Company's conquests had also brought the Moluccas, Bangka, Billiton, south Sumatra, and the more important parts of Celebes and southern and eastern Borneo under its control.

[6] J. S. Furnivall, *Netherlands India, A Study of Plural Economy* (New York, 1941), pp. 39, 43–44.

[7] H. D. Burger, *De Ontsluiting van Java's Binneland voor het Wereld Verkeer* (Wageningen, 1934), p. 36.

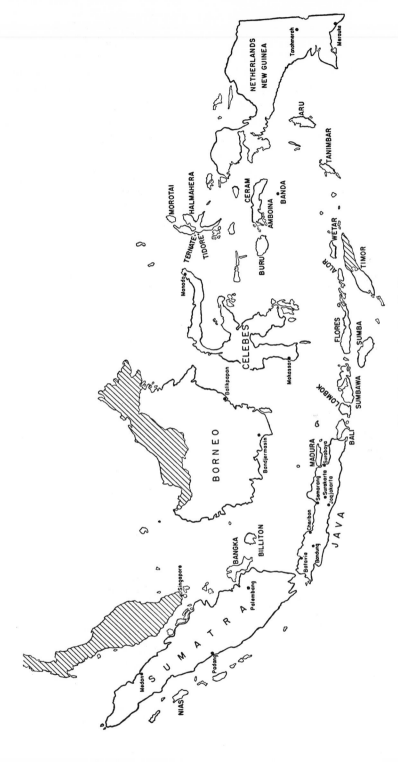

Map 1. The Netherlands East Indies.

of the aristocratic elite; the balance that previously had given its interests protection could not be maintained, for the aristocrats, backed as
they were by the Dutch, could now muster overwhelming force against
it. "The center of gravity of power moved to the party which received
the support from the foreign power, so that the position of the native
ruler in his own jurisdiction became stronger, but on the contrary in
his relations with the foreign military power, the ruler became less
and less independent." [8] As a result, in all the Javanese states the administration of the local rulers tended to develop in a despotic direction.[9] As a consequence the pattern of social relationships among the
population of Java underwent important changes, and the structure
of Javanese society became strongly distorted.

To carry out its program of economic exploitation, the Company
shaped the formerly loosely integrated and relatively balanced indigenous power apparatus into an integrated, hierarchic system, strongly
authoritarian in character.[10] At the apex of the hierarchy stood the
Company. The second echelon in the hierarchy was composed largely
of those members of the native aristocracy who were appointed by
the Company; some of these top appointments, however, during the
later period of Company rule were given to Chinese. Except in a few
places the development of political relationships between this level
and the village was entirely in the hands of these appointees and was
rarely interfered with by the Company.

In those areas taken over by the Company which still retained much
of the administrative apparatus of no-longer-sovereign native states,
even in pseudoindependent Mataram, the existing small-scale development of apanage was greatly expanded by their Company-buttressed
rulers. Under this system the native lord granted authority over a certain area to the apanage holder, usually a relative, court servant, or
official of his. The holder then frequently leased his rights over the
area to another Indonesian or to a Chinese.[11] Otherwise, in the
Company-controlled princely states and generally in more directly administered areas such as Priangan the practice was for the Company's
aristocratic employee, usually known as "regent," [12] to appoint either

[8] *Berita Panitya Tanah Konversi*, ch. iii, p. 1.   [9] Burger, *op. cit.*, p. 37.

[10] Dutch scholars generally refer to this system as "feudal." Only in a very rough
sense does the writer believe the system can be so described.

[11] C. van Vollenhoven, *Het Adatrecht van Nederlandsch-Indie* (Leiden, 1916–1918),
pp. 559, 569.

[12] "The Regents of the Company's lands had an all powerful position in which
the Company, though cooperating with them, seldom interfered" (Burger, *op. cit.*,
p. 32).

Indonesian or Chinese subordinates who administered subdivisions in his and their own behalf. Finally, at the bottom was the village headman who exercised control over the village in behalf of his supervisors.

The functioning of amenable elements of the native aristocracy as effective vassal-agents in the Company's system of economic exploitation necessitated that it endow them with wide powers over the peasant in the economic sphere that they previously had not possessed. "Nearly all the threads of economic life therefore came together in the lords, who derived from this enormous power." [13]

The over-all system operated to exploit as much from the villages as was possible. Their populations were compelled to make forced deliveries of a large portion of their crops and to perform nonagricultural forced labor on an extensive scale. Theoretically these deliveries in kind were paid for, but actually they amounted to sustained tribute levies on an immense scale, the village generally being allowed to keep just enough of its produce to sustain its inhabitants as a labor force.

It must be emphasized that not only the Company but the native aristocracy upon which the functioning of the system was dependent likewise benefited. The quid pro quo for its serving as the instrument of the Company's policy was not only political, the strengthening and expansion of its powers vis-à-vis the native population made possible by the Company's backing; in addition, it shared with the Company the direct economic benefits of the system. Over and above the amount they were charged with delivering to the Company in return for its backing, these aristocrats were generally free to add to these demands as much more as could be squeezed out of the villages in the areas under their control. Thus "the demand for these products by the Company in the interior frequently was made heavier by the Indonesian lords to their own advantage." [14]

The key position occupied by the native aristocracy in the Company's system of economic exploitation soon came to be equaled by that of the Chinese, who likewise came to be indispensable to its successful functioning. Neither the system developed by the Company and continued along roughly similar lines after its demise under the

[13] *Ibid.*

[14] Burger, *op. cit.*, p. 8. As an example of the working of this system, in 1791 the native cultivator was allowed to keep just 14 lbs. of every 240–270 lbs. of coffee that he was charged with delivering to the Company. Nearly 100 lbs. was absorbed by the administrative hierarchy between the village and the Company's warehouses, while the Company's underpaid officials squeezed another 34 lbs. out of the total (Furnivall, *op. cit.*, p. 40).

name of "the Cultivation System" nor the social legacy of Dutch rule as a whole can be clearly understood without some account of the building up of the economic role of the Chinese in Indonesia.

Prior to the arrival of the Dutch, Chinese merchants were active in the Indies and had established several trading settlements on the north coast of Java.[15] However, the local princes severely limited the areas of their settlement,[16] and their principal activity was as intermediaries in the exchange of Indies and Chinese goods, largely on a wholesale basis.[17]

With the establishment of the Company's power over Java, however, the scope of the activity of the Chinese greatly expanded. This expansion was made possible by the Company, which initially looked upon the Chinese as its special protégés and strove to protect and favor them because of its conviction that its own exploitation of the Indies could be most efficiently achieved with their help.[18] The Dutch East India Company's policy is well expressed by its first governor, J. P. Coen, who stated: "There is no people in the world which serves us better than the Chinese; too many of them cannot be brought to Batavia." [19] Coen held that the Company should limit its trade to that of a "mighty wholesale dealer," with the Dutch active as middlemen. Retail trade was to be left to the Chinese, "retailers who in this connection, and even as merchants, far exceed ours in ability." [20] The role of the Chinese in Java thus changed from that of intermediaries between the big China-based merchants and the population of Java to that of intermediaries between the Company and the latter.[21]

At first the activities of the Chinese in Company-controlled territory were largely confined to the retailing of imports, and this sector of the economy they soon came to dominate. Increasingly, however, despite the Company's initial unwillingness to have them enter the field, they came to participate in the gathering of native produce for

15 Jz. Moerman, *In en om de Chineesche Kamp* (Batavia, 1932), p. 13.

16 B. Hoetink, "So Bing Kong, het Eerste Hoofd der Chineezen te Batavia," *Bijdrage tot de Taal-Land-en Volkenkunde van Nederlandsch-Indie*, LXXIII (1917), 346–347.

17 Phoa Liong Gie, "De Economische Positie der Chinezen in Nederlandsch-Indie," *Koloniale Studien*, XX (Dec. 1936), 100–102.

18 *Ibid.*, pp. 104–105.   19 *Ibid.*, p. 104.

20 Quoted in W. J. Cator, *The Economic Position of the Chinese in Netherlands Indies* (Chicago, 1936), p. 7. Coen was so convinced of the necessity for a wide-scale use of Chinese in this capacity that, upon leaving in 1623, he urged his successor to send a fleet to China for the purpose of capturing as many of its inhabitants as possible for the peopling of the Indies (H. F. MacNair, *The Chinese Abroad* [Shanghai, 1925], p. 52).

21 Liem Twan Djie, *De Distribueernde Tusschenhandel der Chineezen op Java* (The Hague, 1947), p. 27.

export by the Company.[22] In essence this meant that they were absorbed into the system of political relationships developed by the Company. There they came to occupy an extremely important position, holding to an increasing extent positions at first reserved only for members of the Indonesian aristocracy.

Such Chinese actually stood on a contractual basis with the Company or the Indonesian lords from whom, for a stipulated payment in gold or produce, they leased political and economic authority over one or more villages or whole districts for a certain number of years. However, the relationship of these Chinese with the inhabitants of the areas they leased was not contractual but semifeudal in the same degree as obtained between the Company and the native nobility and the areas under their control.[23] "In nearly all these cases," states Cator, "the lessee acted as the new feudal lord, who kept an unwilling population in check, if need be by force of arms. The result of this system was that the lessees, 'like bloodsuckers, took as much as they could get.' "[24] The power of these Chinese was very widely conceived. Not only did the system allow them to squeeze as much as they could in the way of agricultural produce and forced labor from the population; in addition, "they found in it at the same time the opportunity for the practice of usury, because in the villages they had the village authority in their hands and thus could be assured of repayment."[25]

The Company took the initiative in the leasing of villages to Chinese, but its example was soon followed by the regents (the top aristocratic leaders in the areas directly controlled by the Company),[26] and in varying degrees by the native rulers of Java, including Mataram.[27] By the end of the eighteenth century in the Company's lands on the north coast of Java alone 1,134 villages (out of a total of about 16,000 for all Java) were leased to the Chinese. Not only villages, but three entire districts had been leased by it to the Chinese, who thereby held about the same position as the regents did elsewhere.[28]

[22] Hoetink, op. cit., p. 348.

[23] Burger, op. cit., p. 7. Burger terms the relationship "feudal."

[24] Cator, op. cit., p. 21.

[25] Burger, op. cit., p. 15. Sometimes the burdens imposed on the peasant were so onerous that he gave up his land and went elsewhere. This was frequently the case in Bantam (ibid., p. 16).

[26] Furnivall, op. cit., p. 46. Regents who leased villages to Chinese had to make good their tribute to the Company from their remaining villages.

[27] Burger, op. cit., p. 15. In the principalities the leasing was done mostly through the apanage holders.

[28] Ibid., p. 16.

In addition to these area leases the Company farmed out to the Chinese various monopolies, such as the right to collect road tolls, levy bazaar fees, sell salt, and even the right to collect the customs duty. Through these, particularly their control of the bazaars and their strong hold on the rice trade arising out of their control of the economies of their leased villages, the Chinese came to govern almost completely the internal commerce of Java,[29] the indigenous merchant class being nearly eliminated.[30]

Widespread corruption in its administration in the Indies and a reckless financial policy which paid stockholders an average rate of 18 per cent per year between 1602 and 1800 led to the collapse of the Dutch East India Company in 1798.[31] The area controlled by it was then placed under the direct authority of the Dutch Government. However, as Vandenbosch states, "there was no sharp break with the Company system; indeed, nearly all the old institutions, such as forced labor, deliveries in kind, feudalism, and monopolies in certain crops were retained." [32] With the brief interlude of British rule (1811–1816) under Sir Stamford Raffles, an impressive program of reforms was started, but most of them were only partially realized, and much of what was accomplished was abandoned by the Dutch after their return.[33]

Between 1816 and 1830 the policy of the Dutch government was

[29] Cator, *op. cit.,* p. 19; see also Furnivall, *op. cit.,* pp. 47–48, and Burger, *op. cit.,* pp. 15, 21, 26, 27.

[30] For an account of the role and importance of the Javanese merchant class prior to the arrival of the Dutch, see B.J.O. Schrieke, *Het Boek van Bonang* (Utrecht, 1916), especially pp. 25–28. For this and for a fuller description of the extent and character of the pre-Dutch trade centering on Indonesia, see J. C. van Leur, *Eenige Beschouwingen Betreffende den Ouden Aziatischen Handel* (Middleburg, 1934), especially pp. 157–180. Only in Mataram did the Javanese merchants manage to maintain a position of some consequence.

[31] Furnivall, *op. cit.,* p. 49. See also Amry Vandenbosch, *The Dutch East Indies* (Berkeley, 1944), p. 53. Vandenbosch points out that "the salaries paid to its personnel were so slight that the Company failed to attract honest people. . . . Illicit trade with Arabians and the English was so brisk in the latter part of the 18th century that more linen of foreign than Dutch origin was sold in Batavia."

[32] Vandenbosch, *op. cit.,* p. 54.

[33] The British occupation of Java arose out of the war with Napoleon, who had imposed his control over Holland. Raffles' program called for the abolishment of compulsory deliveries of crops and the substituting of a tax (payable in kind or money) which left the peasant in possession of a larger proportion of his crop than previously had been the case. It also aimed at the elimination of autocratic characteristics of the administration. To this end the powers of the regents and the rulers of the native states were sharply reduced, the European administration coming directly in contact with the village. The leasing of political authority by the Chinese was halted and their economic monopolies curtailed.

indecisive and wavered between opening up the Indies to individual enterprise and reverting to a system of government monopoly closely parallel to that followed by the Company. Ultimately, financial considerations arising out of the large-scale rebellion in Java between 1825 and 1830,[34] and the unsuccessful war with Belgium induced the government to embark on the latter course. The new system, known as the Cultivation System ("Cultuur Stelsel"),[35] lasted as a whole until 1877, after which it was progressively restricted until in 1915 it was completely abolished. The success of the new system from the standpoint of the Dutch can be measured by the fact that by 1877 it had paid off the East India Company's debts of 35,500,000 guilders and in addition brought into the Netherlands home treasury a tribute totaling 664,500,000 guilders.[36]

Essentially the Cultivation System had much in common with the system of the Company. Though it utilized a considerable number of European employees, the basic elements of the partially destroyed system of political relations developed by the Company were resuscitated in order to make it operative. Indeed, these elements provided the warp and woof of its pattern of exploitation.[37] Fromberg feels that the new system could not have succeeded without the support of the top element in the Javanese aristocratic hierarchy, the regents,[38] and it is generally conceded that under it their powers actually increased.[39] In order to secure the effective support of the regents, the government gave them grants of land and made their office hereditary. In addition it gave them, as well as lesser native officials and the new European officials, a direct financial interest in the system's operation, a percentage of the crops collected from the peasantry.[40] "Over against his subordinate civil servants and the population," states Fromberg, "the regent was elevated to become a feudal prince, who in turn, however, had to carry out the will of the resident [the top territorial Dutch

[34] A revolt against the Dutch by a prince of the central Java state of Jogjakarta and supported by a considerable number of aristocrats and peasants. For an excellent account in English see: Justus M. van der Kroef, "Prince Diponegoro, Progenitor of Indonesian Nationalism," *The Far Eastern Quarterly*, Aug., 1949, pp. 424–450.

[35] Though not originally so envisaged, this system was confined to Java.

[36] Furnivall, *op. cit.*, p. 210. Of this sum 236,000,000 guilders was applied to the reduction of the Netherlands public debt, 115,000,000 for reduction of Dutch taxes, 153,000,000 to the construction of the Dutch State Railways, and 146,000,000 to the improvement of fortifications in the Netherlands.

[37] See Burger, *op. cit.*, pp. 117–160, especially p. 123.

[38] P. H. Fromberg, "De Inlandsche Beweging," *Verspreide Geschriften* (Leiden, 1926), p. 558.

[39] Burger, *op. cit.*, p. 123.   [40] Van der Kolff, *op. cit.*, p. 109.

official]. From the population servile submission was demanded and even the village leadership, by nature identical with the interests of the people, was made a tool in the hands of the regents and their subordinate district heads." [41]

In theory the Cultivation System called for only one-fifth of the peasant's rice fields being planted with a commercial crop designated by the government. He was to spend no more time cultivating this crop than he would have spent if the ground upon which it grew had been planted in rice. Upon delivery of the designated crop to the government he was to be exempted from paying a tax.[42]

In practice, the peasant was not only forced to continue payment of the land tax, but the restriction calling for the limitation of the government's crop area to one-fifth of the peasant's rice land was rarely observed. According to Van der Kolff, "One-third, one-half, and even the whole of these irrigated fields were used for that purpose." [43] The demands on the peasant's labor for the cultivation of dry as well as irrigated land far exceeded the limit that the government had announced. "Instead of 66 days per year, which originally was the normal period, the interests of certain government cultures necessitated those liable to service working 240 days and even more." [44] In short, the peasant paid his former land tax plus whatever amount of crops the various financially interested elements in the hierarchy operating the system could squeeze out of him. He had no choice as to the crops he grew; and the amount of coffee, sugar, indigo, etc. left to him from what he produced was frequently not enough for him to purchase sufficient food for his family, so that in some areas serious famines resulted. As a result of a succession of famines between 1843 and 1848 the population of one regency fell from 336,000 to 120,000 and that of another from 89,500 to 9,000.[45]

Though territorial leases appear to have been discontinued under the Cultivation System, functional monopoly leases were considerably expanded, so that the economic position of the Chinese who controlled these leases became further consolidated. By about 1850 the principal leased monopolies included levying of the poll tax, bridge tolls, slaughtering tax, and gaming tax; the sale of fish, opium, and alcoholic liquors; the operation of pawnshops; and the levying of tax fees on all goods brought to public market.[46] A few of these monopolies, the

[41] Fromberg, *op. cit.*, p. 558.   [42] Van der Kolff, *op. cit.*, p. 108.
[43] *Ibid.*, pp. 109–111.   [44] *Ibid.*, p. 110.
[45] Furnivall, *op. cit.*, p. 138.   [46] Cator, *op. cit.*, p. 98.

market tax monopoly being the most important, were abolished before the ending of the Cultivation System in 1877, but other important ones such as the opium,[47] pawnshop, and slaughtering monopolies ran until the turn of the century or slightly after.

These monopolies frequently brought indirect as well as direct benefits and powers to the Chinese. For instance, a French observer writing in 1899 noted the Javanese was forced to pay a slaughtering tax of three guilders on each animal, the Chinese keeping spies in each village to report slaughterings. Generally, however, the native did not have the three guilders, so the Chinese took the hide of the animal instead, the native not knowing its value was more than three guilders. This practice among the Chinese was so general that they had contracts with the principal tanners in which they guaranteed delivery of a fixed number of hides.[48]

The system of economic exploitation followed under the Cultivation System was, therefore, in its basic elements roughly the same as that pursued earlier by the Company. It thus tended to solidify the pattern of Java's social structure and emphasize among the indigenous inhabitants the socio-psychological penchants that had begun to develop under the rule of the Company. The functioning of these systems necessitated that the authoritarian content of native society be not only maintained but considerably increased. The village headman came more and more to owe his position to the Dutch and the Dutch-backed aristocratic hierarchy above him, the interests of which he came increasingly to represent rather than those of the villagers. The relationship between the village and the political structure above it assumed a substantially more authoritarian character than had obtained in most parts of Java prior to the arrival of the Dutch.

A continuation of the development of native society along communal lines had been increased under the Company and was an outstanding feature of the Cultivation System. "So great were the demands on landholders," states Furnivall, "that landholding was no longer a privilege but a burden which occupants tried to share with others." [49]

[47] A certain amount of political power accrued to those Chinese holding opium leases by virtue of their right to use a sort of private opium police. Through these police they were able to exercise considerable control over native opium smokers (see Chen Ta, *Chinese Migrations with Special Reference to Labor Conditions*, Bull. of the U.S. Bureau of Labor Statistics, No. 340 [Washington, D.C., 1923], p. 59). This data was extracted from a memorandum sent him by the Volksraad (People's Council) of the N.E.I. government.

[48] J. Chailley-Bert, *Java et ses habitants* (Paris, 1907), p. 113.

[49] Furnivall, *op. cit.*, p. 140.

Moreover, from the standpoint of government supervision of crop growing and the most efficient use of irrigation facilities, Van der Kolff
notes, "It was much easier to deal with compact blocs of land" and to
regulate such matters "with a powerful village council rather than with
the individual landowners." [50] In addition, "In many parts of Java the
liability of service on public works was confined by custom to landholders; and as the officials wished to increase the number of hands available
for public works, and the people themselves wished to distribute and
reduce the burden of service on such works, it was to the interest of
both officials and landholders that the occupation of land should be
widely shared. This encouraged communal possession and obliterated
hereditary social distinctions." [51]

Again parallel with development under Company rule was the isolation of the Javanese population from contact with a market economy.
The economic function of the population was restricted to that of
agricultural laborer in the service of the government, and it was unable to acquire trading experience.[52] As was the case during the Company's rule, the monopoly policy of the Cultivation System "caused a
gap between the producer and the market whereby there was no knowledge of the market, no outlet for enterprise, and no possibility of developing a native trading class." [53] Moreover, the system apparently
tended to develop an enduring economic psychology among the Javanese population. In the words of Van der Kolff:

The long degradation of the tani [peasant] to an underpaid labourer in compulsory service on the large estate which the government of the Netherlands
Indies, as it were, exploited in Java, coupled with the uncertainty of being able
to dispose of his own ground and energy, killed all his creative qualities and
initiative as a farmer. This social-psychological factor did not immediately disappear on the abolition of the forced labour system and with this there were
strong influences continuing which did much towards retarding development
of the native along agrarian lines.[54]

It must be emphasized that the effects of the political and economic
organization of the Company and Cultivation systems were not transitory. They were strongly in evidence until the end of Dutch rule in
early 1942 and are still very much felt. The contours of the mold
in which they cast Indonesian society were eroded only partially by
changes in Dutch policy subsequent to their abolishment. Likewise,

---

[50] Van der Kolff, *op. cit.*, p. 111.   [51] Furnivall, *op. cit.*, p. 141.
[52] Van der Kolff, *op. cit.*, pp. 111, 115.   [53] *Ibid.*, p. 116.
[54] *Ibid.*, p. 111.

much of the social psychology induced by that rule appears to have lingered on. As a matter of fact its survival in some respects tended to be preserved by the character of certain of the facets of subsequent Dutch rule.

In the first place, the ending of the government's export monopoly in 1877 and the throwing open of the Indies to exploitation by private capital did not mean the immediate end of forced cultivation in behalf of the government. This was only gradually abolished; the forced cultivation of coffee (the most important of the crops) did not completely disappear until 1918–1919.[55] Moreover, for a considerable period the power of the village headman, still backed by the government, was used to organize forcibly the supply of native labor needed by Dutch private capital. Not until 1890 did the government begin to oppose this practice with vigor.[56]

For a considerable time after this the government's needs for forced labor for roads and other public works necessitated its maintenance of authoritarian rule in the village through its agent, the village headman. In Java such compulsory labor by the village population was not completely ended until 1916, and outside Java it was never abolished, though in 1941 a law was passed making it possible to avoid liability for such labor by the payment of a tax.[57]

However, though the forced labor for the government for which the Indonesian was liable was ended in Java and much reduced elsewhere, he remained obligated to perform forced labor for his village. Under the authority of an arbitrary headman this could often be a severe burden. The autocratic power of the government-backed village headman only began to be reduced after 1906, when a new and more enlightened colonial policy appreciated the necessity of building up the village's lapsed democratic institutions, if the government's policy of increasing native welfare was to be achieved.[58]

Although the powers of the village headman were sharply limited in some directions (for instance, his authority to exact forced labor

[55] The law calling for the ending of forced cultivation for the state was passed in 1915. Furnivall, *op. cit.*, p. 183. Forced cultivation of sugar was not entirely discontinued until 1891. Van der Kolff, *op. cit.*, p. 113.

[56] Burger, *op. cit.*, pp. 185–186.

[57] *Ibid.*, p. 167; Vandenbosch, *op. cit.*, p. 297. Liability for such labor in Java was 42 days per year in 1882, from 12–36 days in 1893, and 10–30 days in 1912, though by the latter date the average actually worked was only 5 days. In 1905 the population was given the alternative of making a money payment in lieu of labor (Burger, *op. cit.*, p. 167).

[58] Furnivall, *op. cit.*, pp. 294–295.

from the villagers), the needs of the government demanded that they be expanded in others (collection of the land rent, police functions, co-operation with the civil service in carrying out new measures designed to benefit the village, etc.). By virtue of these functions and the fact that his responsibility was primarily to the Netherlands Indies civil service hierarchy rather than to the people of his village, the authoritarian nature of his relationship with the village remained dominant. As late as 1941, it was observed in the report of a government commission that the village headman in Java was "almost exclusively an instrument of the government . . . his concern for the interests of the village itself remaining completely in the background." [59]

Moreover, quite apart from the authoritarian role which he played as agent of the government, the village headman frequently abused his government-backed authority by independent activity. This developed partly in response to the needs generated among the peasantry by the penetration of money economy; but partly it was for his personal benefit. Sometimes this resulted in the leasing of village rice lands to European plantations and often in the division of the communal holdings among individuals exercising private rights of ownership. Writing in 1929, Schrieke stated:

Genealogical headmen—the traditional administrators of the undivided family possessions—assume the disposition over them. Supported by the administration of which they are the instruments they begin to exhibit feudal tendencies insofar as the presence of an autocratic administration allows. Mortgaging of the ground is on the increase for purposes which the old customary law never recognized. Even the sale of ground—which was forbidden by customary law—is becoming more and more usual. The division of family lands, of which the members of the family receive individual shares to look after, assumes a more permanent character.[60]

Increasingly, and particularly after about 1910, the European personnel in the civil service sought to protect the Indonesian peasant from the village headman, the Chinese, and Dutch capital. However, despite this and the protection given him by the new agrarian laws introduced in 1875,[61] it was difficult for the peasant to better his status in the new

[59] I. J. Brugmans and Mr. Soenario, "Enkele Gegevens van Socialen Aard," *Verslag van de Commissie tot Bestudeering van Staatsrechtelijke Hervormingen* ("Report of the Commission for Study of Constitutional Reform"), (Batavia, 1941), I, 73. This government report will hereafter be cited as *Rapport Visman* ("Visman Report," Visman being chairman of the commission making this report for the government).

[60] B. Schrieke, "Native Society in the Transformation Period," in *The Effect of Western Influence on Native Civilizations in the Malay Archipelago*, p. 240.

[61] These forbade the sale of native agricultural land to non-natives and protected

economic environment which began to develop around him. The need for money to pay taxes and to buy commodities no longer produced in the village, often combined with the personal interests of the headman, brought many Javanese villages in the richest rice areas of the island to lease their land to European entrepreneurs in return for advances paid by the latter. The major crop grown on such land was sugar cane, and the pattern of agricultural relations involved in its growth tended to maintain and reinforce communal land ownership and blocked the possibility of developing a strong peasantry. In 1929 it was estimated that from 20 to 25 per cent of the total rice field area of Java was thus affected, with no prospect existing "for the development of a strong and prosperous peasantry." [62]

In the areas of Java not affected by Western estates the discontinuance of forced cultivation and the influence of such factors as individual liability for taxation and the increasing pressure of the population on the available arable land gradually broke down the communal landownership that the Company and Cultivation systems had fostered. By 1932, of all native agricultural land, 83 per cent was privately owned. The diminishing of the village's right to dispose of land is brought out by the figures in Table 1, showing agricultural holdings for Java.

Table 1. LAND HOLDINGS IN JAVA (in thousands of hectares).*

Year	Individual ownership	Communal ownership	Fields for support of village officials
1882	1760 (47%)	1590 (42%)	340 (11%)
1907	3150 (64%)	1545 (31%)	205 (4%)
1932	5459 (83%)	894 (13%)	242 (4%)

* Figures quoted by Burger from J. W. Stoppelaar, "De Aard van het Inlandsch Bezitrecht op Java en Madura," *Kolonial Tijdschrift,* (1937), p. 398. Much of this change in proportion of individually owned land arose through the clearing of new land which tended to remain outside the ambit of communal control (Burger, *op. cit.,* p. 210).

the native's title to new land which he cleared. Private enterprise was given ample opportunity for development by being granted the right to lease uncleared land in Java from the government for a period of 75 years and lease cultivated lands from the native owner for short periods. Outside of Java and Madura such legislation was not introduced into directly governed territory until 1914 and until 1919 in self-governing areas. Previously in these areas non-Indonesian agricultural operations were governed by concessions, a long-term hire contract allowing use of unused land for agricultural purposes (Van der Kolff, *op. cit.,* pp. 113–114).

[62] *Ibid.,* pp. 123–124. See also J. van Gelderen, "Western Enterprises and the

The over-all result of the increasingly individualistic basis of land ownership was the concomitant development of social differentiation in a society that previously, under the leveling impact of enforced communalism, had been marked by a signal absence of differentiation.[63]

The pattern of Indonesian, particularly Javanese, society of the 1920's and 1930's was still remarkably balanced and free of the distortion of socio-economic extremes characteristic of most other Asian agrarian societies, but it was less so than the Indonesian pattern that had obtained during the previous few decades. Though the percentage of agricultural families on Java and Madura that owned land was estimated at over 49 per cent in 1925, an increase of about 4 per cent over 1905,[64] this must not obscure the fact that the absolute number of landless peasants must have been increasing during this period. Moreover, because of the rapidly diminishing margin of noncultivated reserves of arable land and the growing disparity between the agricultural base of the village and the population dependent on it, the number of landless peasants undoubtedly increased greatly during the 1930's. Very likely this resulted in a substantial increase in the proportion of landless peasants to peasant-owners.

The widespread supplanting of communal by individual land ownership did not, however, entail a commensurate disintegration of the communal pattern of social relationships. This remained surprisingly strong almost everywhere in Java and throughout much of the rest of Indonesia as well. Though the chief objective characteristic of agrarian communalism—common ownership and/or disposition of land—had for the most part disappeared, the communalistic psychology induced by its previous long period of operation remained. Such activities as house building and harvesting were still widely carried out on a co-operative basis. The village as a whole continued to support not only all its orphans, aged, and sick, but its unemployed as well.

The number of landless agricultural workers was increasing rapidly

---

Density of the Population in the Netherlands Indies," in Schrieke, *op. cit.,* p. 99. Only about one-third of this area was actually planted in sugar cane at any one time, the law holding that no more than one-third of a village's land could at any one time be devoted to that crop. However, the whole of the village's socio-economic organization was affected.

[63] In 1929 this differentiation was extreme enough to bring Schrieke to speak of "symptoms of an agrarian revolution" (Schrieke, *op. cit.,* p. 240) .

[64] J. W. Meijer Ranneft and W. Huender, *Onderzoek naar de Belasting Druk op de Inlandsche Bevolking* (Weltevreden, 1926), pp. 11–12. So far as the writer knows, reliable ownership statistics for later periods do not exist.

during the last decades of Dutch rule, but the great "revolutionary agrarian proletariat" that some Indonesian Communist leaders had been counting on did not emerge. Though the economic insecurity of this "proletariat" was great enough to develop within it a considerable degree of political consciousness, the minimum social security still provided in most cases by the village restrained most of this group from manifesting any serious political restiveness. In both the depression of the early 1920's [65] and that of the 1930's, most of the economically destitute were succored by the village.

Boeke, regarding this continuing communalism as a strong barrier to the development of capitalism, has in what are possibly somewhat exaggerated terms thus described the system:

Every person in need—from whatever cause—can count on help; such is the nature of the communal life. But the advantage of this is offset by a disadvantage in which lurks the weakness of this communal solidarity: every little windfall must be distributed without delay. The village community tolerates no economic difference but acts as a leveller in this respect, regarding the individual as part of the community.[66]

In some areas, at least, it could undoubtedly be argued that this continuing communal relationship was more a consequence than a cause of the weak economic position of the peasant. At any rate this phenomenon was certainly not the only important factor working against the development of an agrarian-based Indonesian capitalism.

In the first place, the possibilities of accomplishing this were not particularly bright in an area such as Java where the per capita income of the 70 per cent of the population dependent upon agriculture for a living [67] was in 1939 estimated to be only $8.32, including the value of crops consumed as food, only $4.45 being actual cash income. (Outside Java the respective figures averaged about 65 per cent greater.) [68] In the relatively prosperous year of 1925, of the Indonesian families on Java and Madura dependent on agriculture for a living and dwell-

[65] Meijer Ranneft and Huender, *op. cit.,* pp. 11–12.

[66] J. H. Boeke, *The Structure of Netherlands Indian Economy* (New York, 1942), p. 26.

[67] Of the 20,279,644 Indonesian workers indicated by the 1930 census, 11,996,800 were listed as being engaged in native agriculture and 1,351,134 as working for nonnative agricultural enterprises, 529,157 of the latter category working on sugar-cane plantations (*Volkstelling, 1930,* p. 123).

[68] E. de Vries, "Het Economisch Leven," *Rapport Visman,* I, 17. Figures here given by the writer are derived from the figures on family income in guilders supplied by de Vries on the basis of a guilder value of 40 cents to the United States dollar and assuming de Vries' calculation of 4.5 persons per family to be correct.

ing outside municipalities, about 2½ per cent were classified (according to a rough government survey based on a sampling technique) as "rich peasants" and had an average money income equivalent to $436. The next highest category of landowners, "ordinary landowners," constituted 19.8 per cent of this population and averaged $120 yearly per family, while the remaining landowning group, "poor landowners," constituting 27.1 per cent, averaged $59 per family.[69] According to this survey the remainder of the population of Java and Madura dwelling outside municipalities was classified as shown in Table 2.

Table 2. INCOME OF VARIOUS SOCIAL GROUPS IN 1925.

Social Classification	% of total	Average money income per family	
		guilders	
Sharecroppers (owning no land)	3.4	119	($ 49)
Agricultural laborers (working in native agriculture)	12.4	101	($ 41)
Laborers on plantations, in factories, or European and Chinese businesses	2.4	370	($148)
Casual laborers	19.6	120	($ 48)
Village chiefs and officials	2.4	485	($192)
Independent artisans (*toekangs*) and retailers	5.9	248	($ 99)

Secondly, though the general pattern of Indonesian landownership during the last decades of Dutch rule appeared to be relatively balanced and free from extremes [70] with relatively little concentration of land into large holdings and almost half the families on Java and Madura dependent on agriculture owning all or part of the land which they worked,[71] this pattern of legal ownership gives very little

[69] Meijer Ranneft and Huender, *op. cit.*, app. viii and p. 10. For the Indonesian population as a whole in Java and Madura in 1925, an average of 56 per cent of their income was actually money income. The percentage was less, of course, for those primarily dependent upon agriculture.

[70] Ploegsma, *op. cit.*, pp. 60, 67; Boeke, *op. cit.*, pp. 42–44.

[71] Meijer Ranneft and Huender, *op. cit.*, p. 11. Though their numbers rapidly increased between 1905 and 1925, there were few large landholders, only 3,387 Indonesians holding legal title to more than 17.7 hectares on Java and Madura in 1925; and during this period the percentage of peasants owning land increased from about 44% to 48%.

insight into the actual economic position of the peasantry. In fact, though important to the peasant in a social sense, legal ownership often had little relevance to economic status, for it did not ensure economic control of the land owned. Frequently, and very possibly in the majority of cases, the Javanese peasant did not exercise economic control over the land to which he held legal title.

Though the government's agrarian legislation afforded the peasant protection that his counterpart in other colonial countries did not enjoy, it gave him only a limited protection. The penetration of a money economy, in particular the liability for various taxes payable in money,[72] unaccompanied by any spread of reasonable credit facilities, forced the peasant to borrow from the local moneylender, usually a Chinese and in most cases his only source of credit.[73] Often because of inability to repay these loans, the peasant was forced to grow crops designated by his creditor, selling them to him at a price set by the latter. Thereby he became a tenant on his own land, with the profits of his labor going to his creditor.[74]

Not until after the initiation of its Ethical Policy in 1900 did the government take steps to make credit facilities available to the peasant, and its efforts were entirely inadequate to meet this situation.[75] Par-

[72] Possibly of equal importance was the necessity of paying money for consumer goods which formerly had been manufactured by village handicraft industry, much of which was eliminated during the first quarter of the twentieth century when the market was flooded by cheap factory-produced articles from the West and from Japan.

[73] Cator, op. cit., p. 82. According to Cator, the average rate of interest for loans by village moneylenders, almost all of whom were Chinese, averaged 20% on a loan of one-month duration.

[74] Moerman, op. cit., pp. 27–28. With respect to this situation see in particular Karl J. Pelzer, Pioneer Settlement in the Asiatic Tropics (New York, 1945), pp. 169–172. Pelzer notes that generally such tenancy contracts were unregistered and were not known to the authorities unless special surveys were made. He cites one such survey made in 1939 in the regency of Toeloengagoeng in East Java where it was disclosed that "out of a total of 2,740 landowning peasants 74.2% had been forced to lease some of their land in order to obtain cash and as many as 33.9% had been forced to lease all of their land."

[75] The chief source of government credit (in 1930, 194,000,000 out of a total of 318,000,000 guilders extended through all government-controlled credit institutions) was the State Pawnshop system established in 1900. For all Indonesia, however, there were established only 500 government pawnshops. Because of the distance involved, many peasants were unable to make use of these shops. But even more important, their rates were often not sufficiently lower than those of the Chinese to induce the peasants to comply with the unfamiliar red tape which their loans entailed. Though the government's operation of this credit source was at first based exclusively on the desire to help the peasant, it soon became concerned to an important extent with bringing revenue into the state treasury. During one period the interest charged was

ticularly during the 1930's, when they profited by the money scarcity of the depression years, the Chinese came to control more and more native crop land. As in previous years they did not obtain legal title to it, but they did obtain functional control over it. In the words of Boeke, "Their aim was not to appropriate land, but to have at their disposal the marketable products derived from the land—the rice from the sawahs . . ." as well as export crops. Taking advantage of the peasant's critical need of money, they supplied him with "buyers' credit against an undertaking to repay by handing over produce after harvesting and they manage to acquire ever-increasing rights by imposing onerous conditions when issuing the loan." [76]

Finally, it must be noted that the increasing volume of export crops grown by the Indonesian population [77] during the last decades of Dutch rule did not mean a proportionate increase in the welfare of the Indonesian peasant. A substantial part of the value of these exports went to Chinese—and to a lesser extent to Arab—entrepreneurs, who absorbed a major share of the prices earned by these commodities. Because of their credit relationship with the indebted Indonesian grower, they could purchase his products at considerably under the local market prices.

Moreover, though many government officials strove hard to raise the economic status of the Indonesian population, it must be noted that their efforts were considerably handicapped because of the apparently greater feeling of obligation for the welfare of Dutch capital displayed in critical periods by the government. This became especially clear during the great depression of the 1930's and was manifested in the government's penalizing the 600,000 Indonesian producers of rubber (by far the most important export crop grown by the native population) for the benefit of the Western-owned rubber estates.

"twice the amount needed to cover expenses plus the interest due the state." In 1938, the rate charged was still "higher than would be necessary in an institution which could afford to be nonprofit-making" (Th. A. Fruin, "Popular and Rural Credit in the Netherlands Indies, Part II," *Bulletin of the Colonial Institute of Amsterdam,* I [May, 1938], 162–163). Between 1904 and 1934, government pawnshops yielded a total net profit of 146,000,000 guilders (J. S. Furnivall, *State Pawnshops in Netherlands India* [Rangoon, 1935], p. 11). In 1938 the government was left with a net surplus of 5,231,000 guilders from the operation of these pawnshops (*Indisch Verslag* [Netherlands Indian Report, official statistical yearbook of the Netherlands Indies government], *1939,* II [Batavia, 1940], 449).

[76] Boeke, *op. cit.,* p. 44.

[77] Not only on Java, but also extensively on Sumatra (rubber) and to an important extent on Celebes and some of the smaller adjacent islands (copra).

Though the annual rate of production by Indonesian growers had been 300,000 tons as against 220,000 by the Western-owned estates, the government in 1934 (in meeting the quota assigned it under the international rubber control regulation to which it was a party) restricted the native producers to a quota of 145,000 tons while allowing the estates to produce 205,000 tons.[78] Between June, 1934, and December, 1936, native rubber exports were kept in check through "a special export tax designed to depress local prices sufficiently to keep native exports within the permissible level." [79] In order to keep this production by Indonesians down the government imposed a progressively stiffer tax, so that in 1936 over 95 per cent of the export value of the rubber produced by them was absorbed by the tax.[80] Estate rubber was subjected to a much smaller tax. The minimum disparity in this taxation allowed the estate owner to realize thirty cents on each kilo produced and the Indonesian twenty cents, while the maximum reached was sixty-two cents for the estate owner and five cents for the Indonesian producer.[81] The consequences for the Indonesian population were so severe that in some areas famine and hunger riots resulted.[82]

Of the 20,279,642 Indonesian workers indicated by the 1930 census, 1,351,134 were listed as working for non-Indonesian agricultural enterprises (509,759 of this number being women and 529,157 being male and female workers employed by sugar plantations) [83] and 2,105,129

[78] P. T. Bauer, *The Rubber Industry, A Study in Competition and Monopoly* (Cambridge, Mass., 1948), p. 102. Output for the 12 months ending May, 1934, had been 185,000 tons for Indonesian producers and 180,000 tons for estates; in the latter months of the period, however, the disparity increased sharply in favor of the native producers.

[79] *Ibid.*, p. 38.   [80] *Ibid.*, p. 118.

[81] Baron C.C.M.M. van Suchtelen, "Parallellen," *Kolonial Tijdschrift* (Sept., 1938), p. 578. Ostensibly the extra tax collected from the Indonesian producers was to be used on government projects designed to promote their welfare. During the two-and-a-half years of its operation this tax netted 82,000,000 guilders from the Indonesian rubber producer. However, "these large sums proved too strong a temptation for the N.E.I. authorities, and part of the funds were diverted to general expenditure," while in 1935 at least 6,000,000 of the guilders derived from the special tax on the Indonesian producer were used by the government to pay the estate producers for their rubber (Bauer, *op. cit.*, pp. 142, 143, 118). As of 1938, 30,000,000 of the total so collected was reported to be still in the Netherlands Indies Treasury (Van Suchtelen, *op. cit.*, p. 585).

[82] Van Suchtelen, *op. cit.*, pp. 580, 584.

[83] Though in the latter quarter of the nineteenth century almost all plantation workers outside of Java were Chinese, during the last decade of Dutch rule Javanese labor had come to replace the Chinese almost entirely. At the end of 1940 on all plantations outside of Java there were only 22,101 Chinese as against 308,610 Javanese plantation laborers (*Indisch Verslag, 1941*, p. 250).

were listed as industrial workers, 628,272 of this number being women.[84] A large part of Indonesian labor working outside of the village, much nonvillage-based plantation labor as well as probably the majority of urban labor, maintained close contact with the village through former domicile and/or blood relationship with its members and in time of economic crisis was able to rely to an important extent on the social security that the village provided. The fact that these groups could look to the agriculturally based village for minimum food and shelter in times of prolonged industrial and plantation unemployment is essential in understanding the political orientation and activity of Indonesian labor. The still strongly communalistically inclined village must be considered as having provided for a major portion of industrial and plantation labor a cushion of social security which tended to obviate the violent political reactions that might otherwise have been generated during the considerable periods of unemployment experienced by this group in times of economic depression. Thus though discontent with wage levels and working conditions certainly developed the political consciousness of urban and plantation labor, because of the social security offered by the village most members of these groups fell far short of developing the revolutionary mentality that some Communist leaders were counting on.

Some indication of rural wage levels is provided by the statistics concerning daily wages given in Table 3.

There does not appear to be sufficient reliable data to warrant conclusions as to the progress or retrogression of the economic welfare of the native population of Indonesia during the whole of the last four decades of Dutch rule.[85] However, enough is available concerning the

[84] *Volkstelling, 1930*, pp. 122–123. The foregoing figures are based on data relating to 58,214,877 persons out of a native population of 59,138,067 in 1930. The remaining 923,190 lived in areas where data was not obtained. The compilers of the census warn concerning statistics relating to labor designated as engaged in other than native agriculture: "The reader who thinks that all those enumerated as doing other sorts of work than agriculture had freed themselves entirely from the trammels of agriculture is making a great mistake. In this respect the figures of the census give no true picture of the 'differentiation' of occupations among natives. For instance, in Jogjakarta industry is an important branch of occupation, but a very large percentage of those working at 'industrial' occupations are women who earn a meager crumb for their families by household piece work such as weaving or batikking, while the principal source of income of the family remains agriculture. . . . Even among those working in the European estate agriculture . . . there are some who do not stand entirely free from the native agriculture" (*ibid.*, p. 56).

[85] Furnivall has collected data suggesting that the economic welfare of the native population around the turn of the century was substantially less than it had been in the decade 1875–1884 (Furnivall, *op. cit.*, pp. 214–216.)

Table 3. WAGES OF VARIOUS GROUPS OF WORKERS.

	Daily wage in U.S. dollars
Regular workmen on sugar plantations	.22 (1940)
Seasonal laborers on sugar plantations (male workers)	.11 (1940)
Male workers on tobacco plantations of Deli Planter's Union (East Coast of Sumatra)	.23 (1939)
Average daily wage of workers in sugar factories in Java *	.11 (1940)
Skilled laborers in metal industry (Java and Madura)	.24–.32 (1939)
Male workers in tile and pottery factories (Java and Madura)	.12–.24 (1939)
Male and female workers in textile factories (Java and Madura)	.06–.13 (1939)
Male workers in batik enterprises (Java and Madura) †	.07–.17 (1939)

* The above data is from *Indisch Verslag, 1941*, II, 248–249.

† Virginia Thompson, *Labor Problems in Southeast Asia* (New Haven, 1947), pp. 142–143.

period from 1913 until the great economic depression of the 1930's to suggest why during the course of that period Indonesians came to develop a degree of political consciousness not previously manifest. The evidence indicates that even prior to the depression the general level of economic welfare of the native population was declining, while at the same time it was being obliged to shoulder a heavier burden of taxes.

After a short period of diminishing economic welfare during the first years of this century there was a general increase in the real income of the native population of Java up until World War I, during and after which it declined until 1924.[86] Total real income of this population during the critical period 1920–1923 was estimated as ranging from 5 to 10 per cent less than in 1913 and in 1924 only slightly exceeding that of 1913[87] despite the fact that the population had increased by at least 10 per cent during this period.[88] Meijer Ranneft and Huender, on the basis of their government-sponsored investigation of 1925, concluded that "everywhere in recent years there has been an

[86] Meijer Ranneft and Huender, *op. cit.*, pp. 5–6, 160–166.

[87] *Ibid.*, pp. 6, 166.

[88] This population estimate is derived from the author's interpolation of census data. *Volkstelling, 1930*, VIII, 84–85. The native population of Java was calculated as 29,978,588 in 1905; 34,428,711 in 1920; and 40,891,093 in 1930.

unmistakable decline in the welfare of the native population." [89]
Analysis of the income data collected by them, when viewed in conjunction with the population increase, allows no conclusion but that
between 1913 and 1923 there was a very considerable and apparently
rather steady decline in the real per capita income of the population
of Java and that even in 1924 it was still well under what it had been
in 1913.[90]

Statistics for the years 1926–1932 indicate that during that period
the native population of Indonesia as a whole experienced a further
decline in economic welfare. Between these years the average income
per person declined steadily from 47.6 guilders to 20.3 guilders in Java
and Madura and from 52.5 to 18.8 guilders in the rest of Indonesia.[91]
Over the course of these years the relative decrease in the over-all cost of
living for Indonesians lagged slightly behind such income decrease.[92]
During the same period the percentage of taxes in relation to income
paid by the whole native population increased from 7.64 per cent to
10.95 per cent.[93]

The head of a government-sponsored investigation of the economic
position of the Indonesian population of Java and Madura made in
1920–1921, concluded that this population had "been taxed to the
furthest limits of its ability" and read "with a shudder" plans to increase the native land and head taxes.[94] Despite his warning, during
the next seven years the amount of land tax paid by the peasant was
steeply increased,[95] and, though in 1925 the capitation tax was ended,

[89] Meijer Ranneft and Huender, *op. cit.*, p. 11.

[90] This conclusion, derived from income figures, is lent substantiation by figures
concerning imports of basic native consumer's goods—cotton cloth, thread, and
sarongs. These show a distinct decrease in per capita imports between 1913 and
1923 (*ibid.*, p. 96). An independent government survey noted that wages in 1924
were much lower than in 1920 and that 1924 showed a continued increase in living
costs over real wages (N.E.I. Government, *Verslag van de Economischen Toestand der
Inlandsche Bevolking* [Weltevreden, 1926], I, 240–241, 229).

[91] L. Götzen, "Volksinkomen en Belasting," *Koloniale Studien* (Oct. 1933), p. 479.

[92] *Indisch Verslag, 1933*, II, 280. This conclusion is based on the assumption that
food was the chief and governing item in the native's cost of living. The price index
of food consumed by the native population dropped from 173.8 in 1926 to 75.5 in
1932.

[93] Götzen, *op. cit.*, p. 473.

[94] W. Huender, *Overzicht van den Economischen Toestand der Inheemsche Bevolking van Java en Madoera* (The Hague, 1921), p. 246. Huender concluded that the
Indonesian was paying on an average 13.2% of his income in taxes (*ibid.*, p. 244).

[95] A.D.A. de Kat Angelino, *Colonial Policy*, tr. from the Dutch by G. J. Renier
(Chicago, 1931), II, 291. During this period the land tax paid by the Indonesian population rose from 21,000,000 to 31,000,000 guilders.

the proportion of taxes to income paid by the native population continued to increase.

In 1932, though taxes collected from the native population were but 65 per cent of 1926, its income was only 45 per cent as large as in the earlier year. Thus its tax burden increased by 44.4 per cent between 1926 and 1932.[96] During the depression years of the mid-1930's, the over-all Netherlands Indies tax burden increased by 50 per cent over 1928 and by 1940 had reached 250 per cent of the 1928 figure.[97] Undoubtedly, these general increases entailed a considerable additional growth in the tax burden borne by the Indonesian population.

The tiny remnant of the Javanese commercial class which still survived at the end of the Cultivation System may have received some initial benefit from the ending of that system and the introduction of a laissez faire economy. But there was little or no increase in its numbers. The conditioning of the Company and Cultivation systems had blunted the people's sensitivity to the urges of capitalist economics. In Java, at least, there was no significant response among the Indonesian population toward taking advantage of the entrepreneurial opportunities which the new system opened up. Into the resulting vacuum crowded the aggressive, already-established, resident Chinese merchant class supplemented by thousands of immigrants from southeast China,[98] armed with the industriousness and commercial know-how they had acquired in the fiercely competitive society of their own country, to exploit opportunities which the native population was no longer equipped to dispute with them and which did not tempt most Netherlanders.

At first, Chinese credit buyers, retailers, moneylenders, and indus-

---

[96] Götzen, op. cit., p. 479. It should be noted, as Indonesian nationalists did note, that though the non-native population paid taxes in 1932 equal to 85% of 1926, its income stood at 75% of the earlier year, so that its tax burden increased by only 13.3%.

[97] C. Ch. W. Uffelie and W. H. J. Elias, "De Landsfinancien," Rapport Visman, I, 42. The writer has been unable to secure information as to whether the increase of tax pressure on the Indonesian population after 1932 was more or less than the over-all increase, but in any case it must have been considerable.

[98] By no means all of these immigrants undertook entrepreneurial functions. Almost all incoming Chinese started out as laborers, but by extreme thrift many were able in a very short time to fill such positions. Between 1860 and 1890, the Chinese population of Indonesia increased from 221,438 to 461,089, reaching a total of 1,233,214 in 1930 (Volkstelling, 1930, VIII, 86). To an important, though much lesser, extent, the Arab population and immigrants from Arabia undertook similar functions. The Arab population increased from 8,909 to 21,640 between 1860 and 1890, reaching 71,335 in 1930 (ibid.).

trial entrepreneurs were restricted by government regulations to coastal areas; or if they were allowed to operate in the interior, they had to obtain passes from the Dutch authorities, whose aim it was to protect the Indonesians from their exploitation. Between 1904 and 1910, however, the government, under growing pressure from a rising and organized Chinese nationalist movement among Indonesia-domiciled Chinese, acceded to its demands and lifted most travel and residence restrictions pertaining to Chinese.[99] The considerable amount of Chinese capital set free by the government's cancellation, shortly before, of the Chinese-held opium and pawnshop monopolies was able to operate in the interior without hindrance. Remaining Indonesian merchants and industrialists of the interior, who had been relatively unmolested previously were thereby subjected to the full brunt of aggressive Chinese competition.

As a reaction, and in order to resist this competition, Javanese batik merchants in Surakarta in 1911 formed a co-operative association, Sarekat Dagang Islam (Islamic Trading Society). This soon changed its primary orientation from commerce to politics and was for a long time the most important Indonesian nationalist organization.[100] But as a means of stopping Chinese penetration into the last preserves of the Javanese merchant and industrial class its success was limited. Increasingly the Chinese penetrated the two chief remaining native industries, batik (a highly specialized indigenous process for affixing color designs to cloth) and *kretek* (Indonesian cigarettes). Often, though an Indonesian remained nominally the owner of such enterprises, a Chinese came to control them, and the former was merely "a wage slave in the service of a Chinese creditor." [101]

Not only did the remnant Indonesian entrepreneurial groups suffer from the now unimpeded competition of the Chinese. Equally disastrous to their survival was the disappearance during the first quarter of this century of much of the indigenous village industry that had provided a large part of the economic opportunities which nourished these groups. Much of such industry and the trade arising from it was destroyed by the heavy import of cheap, mass-produced articles from the West and Japan.[102]

[99] See Fromberg, "De Chineesche Beweging op Java," *Verspreide Geschriften,* pp. 426–428. By 1915 all such restrictions were ended.

[100] As such its name was Sarekat Islam (Islamic Association) and later Partai Sarekat Islam Indonesia (Indonesian Islamic Association Party).

[101] Cator, *op. cit.,* pp. 115, 118–120.

[102] Van Gelderen, *op. cit.,* p. 99. It is worth noting that in 1936 in the batik in-

Bearing in mind the fact that many nominally Indonesian-owned industries were actually controlled by non-Indonesians, particularly Chinese, some additional comprehension of the weak position of the Indonesian entrepreneurial group is given by the figures of a government survey showing ownership of industries in Indonesia employing more than six persons in 1925. Of all such enterprises, 2,816 were owned by Europeans, 1,516 by Chinese, and only 865 by Indonesians, Arabs, and all other non-Europeans and non-Chinese combined.[103]

If one can speak of an Indonesian middle class, its entrepreneurial element had been almost eliminated by the circumstances attending three centuries of Dutch rule. If the term "middle class" can be used as pertaining to those nonaristocratic members of Indonesian society whose economic position was well above the average, it can then be said that the Indonesian middle class that existed during the last two decades of Dutch rule was predominantly noncapitalistic. If the term can be employed in an equally loose but more restricted sense as meaning all such elements whose income was not directly derived from agriculture, it can be said that this middle class was not only predominantly noncapitalistic, but that for the most part it consisted of salaried employees, most of whom were civil servants.

The last three decades of Dutch rule resulted in a rapid change in the over-all character of the tiny native middle class, its capitalist element becoming smaller in proportion to a new and soon much larger group made up of government clerks, administrative officials (mostly of a junior grade), and teachers, basing their positions on the newly available Western education, and in particular on their command of the Dutch language. It is of importance to note that Western education resulted in almost no increase in the native capitalist element. The educated elements of that group continued to be preponderantly educated in Islamic schools.

A government survey in 1928–1929 of urban areas showed that less than 2 per cent of Western-educated Indonesians were self-employed; over 83 per cent worked for wages (only 2.1 per cent of their employers

---

dustry, of total working expenses 73% went in payment to non-native importers for such commodities as cloth, wax, and dyes, and only 23% was left for the Indonesian as a producer (Boeke, *op. cit.*, p. 164).

[103] These figures are compiled from statistics appearing on pp. 280–287 of the report of the governmental survey headed by J. L. Vleming, *Het Chineesche Zakenleven in Nederlandsch-Indie* (Weltevreden, 1926). Of these 865 enterprises, 224 manufactured batik.

being Indonesians), while the remainder was unemployed.[104] These figures, the survey noted, did not indicate that Western education was augmenting the economic development of native society. To the extent that it led to employment for Indonesians it was to jobs with the Netherlands Indies government and Western business enterprise.[105] The opportunities opened up by the latter were, however, extremely limited. Of the Western-educated (able to use the Dutch language) Indonesians employed in the offices of Western firms, only 816 Indonesians received 100 guilders ($40) or more per month, and of these only 126 were receiving more than 200 guilders ($80) per month. This compared with 833 "foreign orientals" (mostly Chinese) and 3,300 Europeans receiving 100 guilders or more per month, of whom 212 and 1,841 respectively were receiving more than 200 guilders per month.[106]

Most Western-educated Indonesians able to find employment found it in the government service. Of the 33,044 employment-seeking Indonesians who had received at least a primary education along Western lines, 45 per cent were in 1928 employed as civil servants.[107] Since only 75 per cent of all such graduates managed to obtain jobs where the use of the Dutch language was required,[108] this meant that of those Indonesians able to find employment where their education was used about 60 per cent found it with the colonial government. A somewhat clearer picture of the character of the Indonesian middle class is gained by an inspection of income tax statistics for 1925. These indicate that almost 53 per cent of the 4,016 Indonesians assessed as having incomes between 3,000 guilders ($1,200) and 20,000 guilders ($8,000) were civil servants.[109]

[104] Hollandsch-Inlandsch Onderwijs-Commissie (Dutch-Native Education Commission) Publication 6a, *De Werkgelegenheid in Nederlandsch-Indie voor Nederlandsch Sprekenden* (Opportunities for Employment in the Netherlands Indies for Speakers of Dutch), (Weltevreden, 1931), p. 46.

[105] *Ibid.*

[106] Computed from figures appearing in *ibid.*, pp. 28–29.

[107] *Ibid.*, p. 16. There was a total of 36,207 Indonesian graduates from schools offering a Western education between 1900 and 1927, compared with 46,646 Europeans and 7,324 "foreign orientals" (*ibid.*, p. 15).

[108] *Ibid.*, p. 73.

[109] Computed from figures appearing in *Mededeelingen van het Centraal Kantoor voor de Statistiek, 69, Eenige Bijzonderheden Betreffende het Aantal Aangeslagen in de Inkomstbelasting en hun Belastbaar Inkomen over het Jaar 1925* ("Bulletin of the Central Bureau of Statistics, 69, Some Particulars Concerning the Number of Persons Assessed in the Income Tax and Their Assessable Incomes for the Year 1925"), (Weltevreden, 1929), p. 23. (These figures exclude persons whose source of income was from native agriculture. The income tax was not assessed on incomes deriving from this source; a land tax was collected.)

The development of this noncapitalistic sector of the Indonesian middle class got well under way only during the last two decades of Dutch rule and was made possible through the introduction of Western education, particularly secondary education and beyond.[110] The slow initial growth of such educational facilities is shown in Table 4.

Table 4. NUMBERS OF INDONESIANS OBTAINING WESTERN EDUCATION, 1900–1928.*

Years	Average number of Indonesians in schools giving Western primary education	Average number of Indonesians in schools giving Western secondary education (incl. Mulo [grades 7–9])
1900–1904	2,987	25
1905–1909	5,175	45
1910–1914	23,910	135
1915–1919	33,516	675
1920–1924	51,308	2,602
1925	61,425	4,431
1926	64,721	4,799
1927	66,824	5,692
1928	74,697	6,468

* Hollandsch-Inlandsch Onderwijs Commissie, no. 12, *Resumé* (Batavia, 1931), pp. 24–25.

By 1940, there were 88,223 Indonesians enrolled in all schools giving a Western primary education, 8,235 in Mulo schools (Western education, grades 7–9), and 1,786 in all high schools. From these three types of schools respectively 7,790, 1,130, and 240 Indonesian students graduated in 1940. It is important to note, as Indonesian nationalists certainly did, that in 1940 high school education (that is, secondary education above the Mulo level) was still largely reserved for the European population, 5,688 of the students in such schools being Europeans as against 1,786 Indonesians.[111] Graduates of high school in Indonesia are listed in Table 5.

The establishment in Indonesia of a technical college in 1919, a law college in 1924, and a medical college in 1926, all open to Indonesians, created additional, though exceedingly tiny, channels for the develop-

[110] Government secondary education was given only in the Dutch language.

[111] These figures are computed from statistics appearing in *Indisch Verslag, 1941,* II, pp. 103, 107. (This statistical abstract was put out yearly by the Central Statistical Bureau of the Department of Economic Affairs of the Netherlands Indies Government.)

Table 5. RACIAL ORIGINS OF HIGH-SCHOOL GRADUATES.*

Year (Average)	Europeans	Indonesians	Foreign Orientals (mostly Chinese)
1910/14	49	4	3
1920/21	141	11	17
1924/25	161	32	32
1929/30	252	157	53
1934/35	374	204	124
1938/39	457	204	116

* Brugmans and Soenario, "Enkele Gegevens van Socialen Aard," *op. cit.,* p. 62.

ment of an Indonesian middle class. By 1940 there were 637 Indonesians attending the various colleges, with 37 being graduated in that year.[112]

At first Western education was available only to a few children of the Indonesian aristocracy who were being trained for the top ranks of the native branch of the civil service. Thus as late as the school year 1912–1913, in one of the chief secondary schools, the law school, all of the forty Indonesian students were sons of the native aristocracy.[113] During the First World War and thereafter secondary education became open to talent as well as to birth. For Indonesian society this approximated a small-scale social revolution. By academic training and ability a man could rise in the civil service to a rank close to that of regent (a group who continued to be recruited exclusively from the top aristocracy). The social position of these newcomers in Indonesian society tended to approximate their heightened economic position. Even in the Javanese principalities the princely nobility commenced to grant high social positions to intellectuals.[114] It must be emphasized, however, that the social mobility induced by this new situation was limited, owing to the fact that schooling for Indonesians was not free and only the relatively wealthy could afford to educate their children in secondary schools or even in Western primary schools.[115] Moreover,

[112] *Indisch Verslag, 1941,* II, 103, 107. A considerably smaller number of Indonesians were enrolled in Dutch universities.

[113] Fromberg, "De Inlandsche Beweging op Java," *op. cit.,* p. 558.

[114] Brugmans and Soenario, *op. cit.,* p. 72.

[115] Minimum tuition for Western primary education in government schools for Indonesians was 36 guilders. It is worth noting that the annual income of the parents of 102 out of 14,105 Indonesian students in schools giving such an education in 1929 was between 120 and 150 guilders. Dutch children whose parents' income was under

children of the aristocracy continued to be strongly favored over others. The intelligent son of an aristocrat could usually gain admittance, while the equally intelligent son of a nonaristocrat, even though able to provide tuition, very frequently could not.

Expansion of this new sector of the Indonesian middle class was sharply limited by the paucity of secondary and higher educational opportunities open to it. The government's announced hiring policy was that function must be dependent upon education, and few Indonesians were in a position to apply for civil service positions higher than the rank of clerk. So limited were the opportunities for an Indonesian to acquire a secondary education, much less a college education, that few were able to equip themselves to compete with the Netherlands-trained and Indies-trained Dutch and Eurasians.[116] Moreover, Indonesians who had the required education for the jobs they sought found that they were subject to discrimination in favor of Dutch and Eurasian applicants. Private enterprise discriminated against Eurasians as well as Indonesians in favor of Dutch applicants,[117] while in a number of departments the government's hiring policy favored both the Eurasian and the Hollander over the Indonesian as the competition for its positions became keener.[118]

An extensive survey made by a government commission in the still prosperous years of 1928–1929 [119] showed that 25 per cent of all Indonesians who had graduated from Western schools were unable to find jobs where their education could be utilized. Members of this group found their diplomas "devalued" and were only able to get "jobs that were more on the periphery of economic life" with salaries well below

---

1,200 guilders were tuition-free (Hollandsch-Inlandsch Onderwijs Commissie 4, *De Kosten van het Westersch Onderwijs in Verhouding tot de Draagkracht der Bevolking* ["The Cost of Western Education in Proportion to the Carrying Capacity of the Population"], [Weltevreden, 1930], pp. 21, 27). For many parents geography as well as tuition raised financial obstacles. At least as late as 1938 there were only 8 towns in all Indonesia where secondary education was available, and 7 of these were in Java (Department van Economische Zaken, *Onderwijs Statistiek Schooljaar 1937–1938* [Batavia, 1941], p. 354).

[116] Legally the status of Eurasians (persons of mixed European and Indonesian ancestry) was equal to that of the Dutch and socially it was very close. Probably at least one-half of the quarter-million "Europeans" in Indonesia were Eurasians.

[117] Meijer Ranneft, "The Economic Structure of Java," in Schrieke, *op. cit.*, pp. 81, 83; Furnivall, *op. cit.*, pp. 374–375; W. F. Wertheim, "The Indo-European Problem," *Pacific Affairs* (Sept. 1947), p. 294.

[118] See Brugmans and Soenario, in *Rapport Visman*, I, 57.

[119] The great depression hit Indonesia slightly after the United States and Europe.

those earned in jobs calling for a knowledge of Dutch. In private enterprise the increased supply of Indonesians educated along Western
lines forced down the wage scale of those Indonesians employed by
such concerns. The commission stated, "about twice as many pupils
graduate with a Western education as jobs can be found for." It envisaged the situation growing much worse and anticipated that even
in prosperous times over-all government employment could not increase more than 2 per cent yearly, while instruction of the Indonesian
population in Western education was increasing at a yearly rate of
6.7 per cent. Thus, it concluded that the "tempo of expansion exceeds
the scope of social development." [120]

The degree of economic devaluation of Western education and the
disparity between Western-trained Indonesians and jobs available
kept rapidly increasing. Thus between 1928 and 1932 the number of
Indonesians graduating from primary schools giving a Western education was 22,980 and from secondary schools 598,[121] while the number
of Indonesians employed in the Class B civil service category rose only
from 4,872 to 6,054 and in Class C, the highest of the three categories,
from 190 to 277.[122] Between 1932 and 1941 there was some increase in
the number and proportion of Indonesians holding middle-rank positions in the government service. However, despite the decrease in
growth of educational opportunities for the Indonesian population
attendant upon the government's retrenchment of expenditure during the depression years, the disparity between government jobs open
to Indonesians and the Indonesians qualified to fill them continued to
grow. As late as October, 1940, out of the 3,039 higher-rank civil service positions only 221 were held by Indonesians.[123] Indonesians in 1940
held 5,023 out of the 13,172 upper-middle civil service positions and
8,830 out of 14,212 lower-middle rank positions. These figures cannot
be compared with categories B and C above; since 1938 new categories
were in use. However, both sets of categories embrace the large majority of positions requiring a Western education. A breakdown of statistics relating to government employment as of October 1938 showed a
distribution of the four civil service categories as given in Table 6.

[120] Hollandsch-Inlandsch Onderwijs Commissie, 6a, pp. 73–78.
[121] Deple Department van Economische Zaken, *Onderwijs Statistiek Schooljaar 1937–1938*, pp. 316–320.
[122] *Indisch Verslag, 1931*, II, 422; *Indisch-Verslag, 1939*, II, 430. European (Dutch
and Eurasians) Class B personnel numbered 11,164 in 1928 and 8,761 in 1932; European Class C personnel numbered 7,944 in 1928 and 7,951 in 1932.
[123] *Indisch Verslag, 1941*, II, p. 466.

Table 6. CIVIL SERVICE EMPLOYMENT (BY PERCENTAGE).*

Nationality	Lower Personnel	Lower-middle	Middle	Higher
European	0.6	33.3	57.6	92.2
Indonesian	98.9	60.6	38.0	6.4
Assimilated Indonesians †	0.2	3.4	2.0	0.5
Chinese	0.3	2.3	1.5	0.3
Assimilated Chinese		0.4	0.8	0.5

* Brugmans and Soenario, *op. cit.,* p. 56.

† "Assimilated Indonesians" means persons assimilated to European legal status, an extremely difficult thing for an Indonesian to achieve.

Except as teachers in private schools there were almost no openings within Indonesian society itself for Indonesians with a Western education. The tremendous growth in the number of highly nationalistic private Indonesian "wild schools" during the last twenty years of Dutch rule is certainly related to this situation.[124]

Some impression of the relative strength of the nonagricultural Indonesian middle class as compared to similar groups among the European and Chinese population as well as of the over-all pattern of the plural society that existed in colonial Indonesia can be gained by an inspection of income tax statistics for 1939,[125] as shown in Table 7.

These statistics clearly reflect the minuteness of the Indonesian nonagricultural middle and upper classes in proportion to the whole Indonesian population and their small size in comparison with European and Chinese middle and upper-class sectors of the colonial society. Likewise, they suggest how few were the Indonesians, other than the

[124] By 1938 there were 1,961 such schools excluding the considerable number of Taman Siswa and other private Indonesian schools. Of these, 1,388 were Western primary schools (Brugmans and Soenario, *op. cit.,* p. 65).

[125] *Indisch Verslag, 1941,* II, 181, 184–185. The income of Indonesians from native agriculture is not shown in these statistics, such income being subject to the land tax rather than to the income tax. (Land tax statistics of a comprehensive nature are not in existence.)

Some additional insight can be gained from the following statistics showing real-estate ownership (other than native agricultural land) in 1940 in terms of assessed value in guilders: limited liability companies and other bodies (mostly European-owned), 1,860,756,000; European, 1,119,200,000; Chinese, 1,428,522,000; other foreign Asiatics, 427,201,000; Indonesian, 191,839,000 (*ibid.,* pp. 198–199).

remaining Dutch-backed aristocratic elements and the handful of large landholders, who on material grounds might be deemed to have an interest in the maintenance of the colonial *status quo*. Finally, they help explain the Indonesian's growing conviction that economic position in colonial society was determined along ethnic lines.

Table 7. INCOME TAX STATISTICS, 1939.

	Europeans	Indonesians	Chinese	Other foreign Asiatics
Population (1930) *	240,162	59,138,067	1,190,014	114,637
Total assessed income (guilders)	350,718,953	446,506,343	171,171,181	16,842,078
Total assd. inc. of those whose inc. (other than wages) † was less than 200 guilders	148,163	210,111,753	3,845,833	585,061
Total of those whose assd. inc. (nonwage) was between 200 and 900 guilders	5,613,391	166,421,780	58,204,573	5,475,368
Number of persons assd. at less than 200 guilders	1,000	1,434,077	25,647	4,053
Number assd. with incomes between 200 and 900 guilders	10,375	562,155	147,127	14,564
Total income of those assd. at over 900 guilders	344,981,646	69,972,810	109,120,765	10,780,649
Number whose assd. income was over 900 guilders	73,247	36,112	44,342	3,714
Number assd. with income between 900 and 2500 guilders	25,701	28,932	32,244	2,517
Number assd. with income between 2,500 and 5,000 guilders	24,643	5,940	8,726	765
Number assd. with income between 5,000 and 10,000 guilders	17,226	1,034	2,556	286
Number assd. with income between 10,000 and 20,000 guilders	4,622	189	610	114
Number assd. with income between 20,000 and 40,000 guilders	831	17	158	27
Number assd. whose income was above 40,000 guilders	224	4	48	5

* *Volkstelling, 1930,* VIII, 88–90. Of the European population 208,269 were Netherlanders (of whom more than half were Eurasians); 6,867 were Germans; 7,195 were Japanese (the criterion of European being legal status); 2,414 were British. Of the 114,637 "other foreign Asiatics," 71,335 were Arabs and 30,018 were British Indians. The last completed census was that of 1930.

† The wage income of those receiving total incomes of less than 900 guilders was not subject to the income tax. The value of the guilder (or florin) was U.S. 40 cents or British 1s. 8d.

❧ CHAPTER II ❧

Genesis of the Indonesian
Nationalist Movement

IT HAS often been noted that political frontiers tend to establish national consciousness, and it is certain that the arbitrary frontier delineating the area of Dutch political control in the East Indies was decisive in determining the boundaries of the Indonesia which absorbed the attention of Indonesian nationalists. Dutch administration welded together peoples of various tongues and cultures into one political unit and in so doing tended to develop in them a "consciousness of kind." Thereby the Dutch helped join the archipelago's many local patriotisms together into one all-embracing patriotism. Thereby they helped open up one great channel into which the many local-based antagonisms and grievances resulting from contact with the alien ruler could flow—a channel into which the countless little currents of local dissatisfaction could merge and maintain themselves in collectivity, rather than dissipate themselves singly in the sands of their own isolated parochialism.

However, the geographical limits of the territory of Indonesian nationalism were not exclusively determined by the boundaries of Dutch political control. Prior to the coming of the Dutch, Indonesia was no mere geographical expression. To an important, though subsidiary, extent these limits were determined by the fact that the area administered by the Dutch was roughly congruent with the two great Indonesian empires of the ninth and fourteenth centuries, Shrivijaya and Majapahit.[1] Moreover, the tradition of this mighty past was important also in the development of the community pride that is basic to the development of nationalism. In this respect, the awareness of former political might as exemplified by the area controlled by Indonesian states of the past and such incidents as the defeat of Kublai Khan's invading army by the Javanese, along with remembrances of past cultural glory such as Shrivijaya's having been an international center of Buddhist studies, were all important.

One of the most important factors contributing to the growth of an integrated nationalism was the high degree of religious homogeneity that prevailed in Indonesia, over 90 per cent of the population being Mohammedan. As the nationalist movement spread out from its original and principal base on Java to the other islands of the Dutch-controlled portion of the archipelago, the parochial tendencies that might otherwise have become strong among their communities tended to be counteracted because of the solidarity induced by a common religion.

The Mohammedan religion was not just a common bond; it was, indeed, a sort, of in-group symbol as against an alien intruder and oppressor of a different religion. Thus Wertheim states: "One can, indeed, sustain the paradox that the extension of Islam in the Indonesian archipelago was due to the Westerners." The arrival of Portuguese power in the area, he says, "induced a large number of Indonesian princes to embrace the Islamic faith as a political move to counter Christian penetration." [2] The subsequent impingement of Dutch power undoubtedly sustained, if it did not actually accelerate, the latter stages of this process.

---

[1] Shrivijaya at its height exerted varying degrees of control over most of the Indies, the South China Sea, part of India, and waged successful wars against Cambodia. See Vlekke, *op. cit.,* pp. 30–32. Majapahit, based on East and Central Java, though not controlling West Java, controlled almost all the rest of the Indies (including North Borneo), and Malaya as well. The hard-headed French colonial administrator and observer of Dutch policy, Bousquet, expressed his agreement with Snouck Hurgronje "that Indonesia is more than a geographical expression" and goes on to remark, "There is historical relation between its different parts. It is not merely an accident that the Netherlands Indies as we know them include almost exactly the territory of the Hindu kingdom of Madjapahit at the time of its most extensive power in the 14th century" (G. H. Bousquet, *A French View of the Netherlands Indies,* tr. from the French by Philip E. Lilienthal [New York and London, 1940], pp. 30–31) .

[2] W. F. Wertheim, *Effects of Western Civilization on Indonesian Society* (New York, 1950), p. 52. Professor Wertheim states that his hypothesis is derived from the posthumous writings of B. J. O. Schrieke.

Another important integrative factor was the development of the old *lingua franca* of the Indies, bazaar Malay, into a national language, transcending the bazaar and serving with Mohammedanism to break down parochial penchants in Indonesian nationalism. To an important extent this happened because the Dutch frequently used Malay in administration, some of them insisting that Dutch prestige and the Indonesian's feeling of inferiority could best be maintained by refusing to allow him to use Dutch in addressing a Netherlander. In 1938, Bousquet observed: "The real truth is that the Dutch *desired and still desire to establish their superiority on a basis of native ignorance.* The use of Dutch diminishes the gap between inferior and superior—and this must be avoided at all costs." [3] He concluded:

By opposing him [the Indonesian] with a language intended to mark the distance which sets him apart from the European, the Dutch have striven and still strive, though vainly, to deprive their ward of contact with the outside world. . . . Since the Dutch did not allow the use of their language to spread before the birth of nationalism, nationalists now employ Malay as a weapon against Dutch influence. . . . They believed themselves to be forging a chain for their subjects, but they see now that they have given him a weapon, that terrible psychological weapon, a common national language with which to express their common national aspirations.[4]

In addition, the integration of Indonesian nationalism is generally recognized to be to some extent indebted to the existence of the Volksraad (People's Council), the top representative council for all Indonesia. In bringing together Indonesians from various parts of the archipelago and making them more aware of their common problems and common relationship with the Dutch, this body tended to develop in them a more conscious unity which integrated their nationalism more closely.[5] The degree of the Volksraad's importance in the development of organized nationalism is somewhat harder to determine.[6] Established in 1917 with purely advisory powers, the Volksraad

[3] Bousquet, *op. cit.*, p. 88 (italics are Bousquet's).

[4] *Ibid.*, p. 89. Probably Bousquet somewhat overstates the case.

[5] H. Colijn, who was later to become Prime Minister of the Netherlands, was acutely aware of this and urged replacement of the Volksraad by several local bodies (H. Colijn, *Koloniale Vraagstukken van Heden en Morgen* ["Colonial Questions of Today and Tomorrow"], (Amsterdam, 1928), p. 47 ff. Prior to writing, Colijn had been chairman of the Batavia Petroleum Co. In the 1930's he was Netherlands Prime Minister and later Colonial Minister.

[6] In certain respects it may have retarded the movement. Some Indonesians argue that it was an important force in splitting the movement into "co-operative" and "nonco-operative" elements and thereby weakening it. The "co-operative" felt that

was in 1927 granted co-legislative powers with the Netherlands-appointed Governor General. Principally because of the latter's right of veto, however, this power was not of great consequence.[7] Actually, the Volksraad was chiefly a sounding board, useful to the government in determining the views of the Netherlands Indies community. It provided limited means for those Indonesian nationalists who were members of it to educate the literate public in the more moderate aims of the nationalist movement and to keep a number of nationalist grievances before its eye. However, during most of the period of the Volksraad's existence, the majority of the important nationalist leaders refused to work through it. Its membership usually represented the views of a minority of the nationalist movement, and many of its Indonesian members aimed openly no higher than limited self-government to be reached by an evolutionary process on the basis of co-operation with the government.

In any case, the Volksraad was not an institution designed to provide contact between the nationalist leaders and the masses. The mechanics of the indirect electoral process leading to its membership effectively precluded this possibility. Whether or not, as some Indonesians allege, intimidation by Dutch civil and police officers played a part in the latter stages of the indirect electoral process whereby the 10 per cent of the Indonesian population allowed to vote chose its 937 electors, it is certain that these electors did not have full freedom of selection. For the selections were not made by them alone, but in conjunction with 515 Indonesian electors appointed by the government.[8] This method of election may partially explain why eleven of the nineteen elected Indonesian members of the sixty-man Volksraad were active or retired-and-pensioned government officials.[9]

----

worthwhile progress might be made towards nationalist objectives by working legally through the Volksraad; the "nonco-operative" denied this possibility. Others maintain that membership in it tended to satisfy the desire for dignity and prestige in some Indonesians who would otherwise have been more aggressive in their nationalism and more valuable to the nationalist movement.

[7] Between 1927 and 1941 a considerable number of government bills were altered by Volksraad amendment and in some cases withdrawn in the face of its criticism. During this entire period, however, on only six occasions did the Volksraad initiate legislation and only three of these bills were accepted by the government (Amry Vandenbosch, *The Dutch East Indies* [Berkeley, 1944], p. 125).

[8] These statistics are for 1939. See C. T. De Booy and L. F. Jansen, "De Volksraad," *Rapport Visman*, I, 95.

[9] *Indisch Verslag, 1941*, II, 540. Of the 11 Indonesian members who were appointed, 9 were either active or retired-and-pensioned government officials. Indonesians had

Finally, the growth and spread of nationalism was considerably abetted by the means of idea dissemination provided by the development of a vernacular press and the radio, as well as by the great increase in the geographical mobility of people and ideas which was a consequence of the twentieth-century pattern of economic organization in Indonesia and the transportation facilities which it entailed.

The beginnings of Indonesian nationalism cannot be precisely or even roughly dated. Its clearly articulate and organized phase began only in the second decade of the twentieth century, but many of its most essential constituent elements go back much further, some probably to the period when the impact of Dutch rule was first felt. It might be argued that latent nationalisms of an embryonic character have existed within the chief Indonesian societies since then and that their active manifestation was kept so long in abeyance primarily because of lack of leadership, their traditional aristocracies refusing to be identified with them since their personal interests were best served by supporting the Dutch. On most of the few occasions when the Indonesian aristocracy did assert itself against Dutch rule, it found a ready and strong support from the Indonesian peasantry.

However, the structure of colonial society was such that the peasantry, without the guidance of an indigenous elite, was generally unable to understand the relationship between its deteriorated position and Dutch power. Interposed between it and that power stood the traditional Indonesian aristocracy by which it remained governed, albeit more thoroughly and harshly than before. The political buffer between the Dutch and the Indonesian masses provided by this aristocracy was matched by the buffer in economic relationships provided by the aristocracy and the Chinese jointly and subsequently by the Chinese alone. By virtue of their indirect political rule and indirect economic exploitation, the Dutch for three centuries were able to avoid collision with the reaction and opposition of the general Indonesian population to the conditions for which in an ultimate sense the Dutch were responsible. Indonesian opposition was almost entirely absorbed by or vented upon the indigenous aristocracy, the visible rulers; and upon the Chinese, the visible economic exploiters. With the abandonment of the Cultivation System these buffers were gradually broken down. However, they never entirely disappeared, despite the political education of the

---

30 seats (19 elected and 11 appointed); Europeans 25 (15 elected and 10 appointed); Chinese 4 (3 elected and 1 appointed); and Arabs 1 appointed seat.

masses attempted by the new Indonesian leadership that began to emerge just before the First World War.

With the replacement of the indirectly administered system of economic exploitation of the Cultivation System by the directly administered system of free enterprise which succeeded it, considerable sectors of the agricultural population began to come into immediate contact with Dutch persons and Dutch economic power. At first on the sugar plantations in Java and later on the plantations of Sumatra, when Javanese labor replaced Chinese contract coolies, large numbers of Indonesian peasants came to develop some comprehension of their subordinate and dependent economic position vis-à-vis the Dutch. In periods of economic crisis and unemployment this discernment tended to become sharper. A clearer understanding of colonial economics, or at least a more acute awareness of the disparity in economic welfare between the Dutch and the Indonesian population, was developed among the oil field workers, railway men, and the urban laborers whose numbers began to expand rapidly during and after the First World War.

In general, the increasing erosion of communalistic relationships and the concomitant emergence of individualistic social orientations developed a receptivity among the peasantry to nationalistic ideas that would not have existed had their horizons continued to be limited to the introversive communal village. This receptivity was, of course, greatest among workers on plantations and among those landless, casual laborers most marginal to the village core. However, the social security provided to such elements by the village in the post-World War I depression and the longer depression of the 1930's greatly mitigated the economic distress they would otherwise have encountered and thereby tended to counteract the growth of a more militant type of nationalism among them. On the other hand, they came back to the haven of the village as proselytizers of the nationalistic ideas that their experience outside had already developed in them, ideas still somewhat inchoate but much stronger and more precise than the embryonic or even latent nationalistic concepts of the villagers.

With the abandonment of much of the structure of indirect government in Java and parts of Sumatra that followed the ending of the Cultivation System and the large increase of Dutch personnel in the civil service, the Indonesian's awareness of political control by the Dutch was heightened. To an increasing extent he became conscious of the relationship between Dutch power and the economic and political conditions which he was experiencing. Particularly was this true after 1900, when Dutch civil servants—frequently altruistic and zealous for the welfare of the Indonesian, but often overly paternalistic—came into direct contact with the village and sought to introduce reforms by methods of "gentle pressure" depending ultimately on economic sanctions or actual force. Equally important in developing the peasant's awareness of his subordination to Dutch power and arousing his antipathy to it was the increasing burden of money taxes demanded of him by the government.

The peasantry's frequent negative reaction to this change in the pattern of political control over it was often strong and at first spontaneous without prompting by the emerging nationalist leadership. Its acts of protest, both violent and nonviolent, were not in a strict sense manifestations of nationalism. But they did represent a politics of protest against the Dutch Indies government which nationalist leaders soon undertook to exploit, attempting to direct these energies into more clearly nationalistic channels.

One of the best examples of such spontaneous peasant protest is furnished by the Saminist movement, which began about 1890 in the Blora area of northeast Middle Java. By 1907 when the government arrested and exiled Samin and eight other peasant leaders the movement enrolled 3,000 family heads. Thereafter it continued to spread, and, though in general relying on passive resistance to governmental authority, led to serious disturbances in 1914 in the Pati area. These the government had to put down with armed force, and the leader of the resistance, Pak Karsijah, was exiled in October, 1917.[10]

The essential character of the Saminist movement was the desire of the peasants to be left free to lead their own lives unmolested by government interference and to return to a communalistic social organization based upon the economic equality of individuals and upon possession of the land and its products in common. As it progressed the movement developed increasingly anarchistic tendencies; many members refused to pay taxes or to perform *corvée* or the multitude of new legally required village services, and all members sought to avoid any contact with the government's employees. According to the government investigation of 1917, the chief grievances of the Saminists were the obligation to pay a head tax, the introduction of new land tax regu-

---

[10] J. J. Schrieke, *De Indlandsche Politiek* (Amsterdam, 1929), pp. 14–15; *Encyclopaedie van Nederlandsch-Indie* (2nd ed.; The Hague and Leiden, 1919), art. "Saminisme," III, 683–684.

lations and later increase in that tax, slaughtering taxes, and the host of new and enforced duties—designed to benefit them but not so appreciated by them—which the government's Ethical Policy after 1900 progressively demanded. (These new duties included taxes to support the establishment of village banks, schools, night watchmen, bull studs, and irrigation regulations, as well as surrender of land for the support of the village schoolteacher, and forestry regulations making procurement of traditional wood requirements more difficult.)

The government's investigation of the causes of the movement is instructive in that the conditions it found responsible for the attitudes of the peasant followers of Samin were also responsible for roughly similar, though less articulate and more passive, attitudes on the part of much of the Indonesian peasantry at the time. It is also enlightening to note the many basic similarities between the conditions provoking the Saminist movement and those which later government investigations found to have underlain peasant support of the Communist-led rebellions of 1926–1927 in Java and the West Coast Residency of Sumatra.

Translation of the peasantry's grievances and increased political consciousness into an articulate nationalism awaited only the emergence of a nationalist Indonesian elite to lead it. This elite the Dutch themselves were largely—though unconsciously—responsible for producing. The preoccupation of the Dutch with the dangers of Pan-Islam caused them to underestimate the dangers to their regime inherent in the Islamic Modernist movement,[11] while the weapon with which they chose to fight Pan-Islam—Western education—soon developed a second edge which cut the other way. It is the supreme irony of Dutch rule that the means chosen to defend the colonial regime from the overrated threat of Pan-Islam developed into one of the most potent of the forces undermining that regime.

In retrospect it seems surprising to find Snouck Hurgronje, the outstanding Dutch authority on the Mohammedan religion and its practice in the Indies,[12] regretting in 1911 that the apparently minatory

[11] H. A. R. Gibb, one of the foremost modern authorities on Islam, defines the "modernists" as "those who do care, and sometimes care deeply, about their religion but who are, in various degrees, offended by the traditional dogmatics and by the insistence of the conservatives upon the sanctity of the traditional institutions in the Muslim world. For the majority the issues in dispute are mainly those relating to the practical duties and the social institutions of Islam" (H. A. R. Gibb, *Modern Trends in Islam* [Chicago, 1947], p. 11).

[12] At that time he was Counselor for Native Affairs to the Netherlands Ministry of Colonies.

Pan-Islamic movement [13] was "not counterbalanced by a powerful national sentiment among the natives. . . ." [14] For, given the advantage of hindsight, it seems clear that the Mohammedan religion in Indonesia, and the Pan-Islamic movement in particular, had absorbed and become energized by the very national sentiment which Snouck Hurgronje sought.[15]

The Mohammedan religion did not passively absorb impulses of a nationalist character. It came to provide the earliest channel of development of modern, mature Indonesian nationalism, a channel which is still of great importance. The unique character of the Mohammedan religion professed by most of the 90 per cent of the Indonesian population of that faith helped make this possible. Probably in no other Moslem country does one find the high degree of religious tolerance, lack of bigotry, and openness to new ideas that one finds in most of Indonesia. In Java, at least, this is partly due to the fact that Islam has usually been only a relatively thin frosting on top of thick cakes of Hindu-Buddhism and the older indigenous Javanese mysticism. But there and throughout most of the rest of Mohammedan Indonesia this also arises from the fact that—unlike the situation in the Near East—the Moslem religion has not been tied in with either the political or the socio-economic order or interpreted so as to maintain their *status quo.*

Thus the Modernist Islamic teachings as they developed during the first decades of this century in Cairo found a response in Indonesia out of all proportion to that which they elicited in other Islamic countries. Danger to Dutch ascendancy in the Indies came not so much

13 Pan-Islamism, according to Gibb, "preached the doctrine of loyalty to the Ottoman caliph primarily as the head of the most powerful Muslim state, and therefore the authority most fitted to direct and to coordinate the political forces of the Muslim peoples" (Gibb, *op. cit.,* p. 11).

14 C. Snouck Hurgronje, *Politique Musulmane de la Hollande* (Paris, 1911), p. 98.

15 A few people did appear to sense this connection between Islam and nationalism. Thus Fromberg, a member of the Supreme Court of the Netherlands East Indies, wrote in 1914: "Islam is for the Javanese not only a point of religious conviction, but also formed of nationality. For with respect to Islam the ruler had not interfered; religion is therefore that part which remains of the dormant nationalism suppressed by the ruler, the sign whereby men recognize each other as nationalists" (P. H. Fromberg, "De Inlandsche Beweging Op Java," *Verspreide Geschriften* [Leiden, 1926], p. 545). Some Indonesian Communist leaders likewise came to be aware of this connection. Thus at the 4th Congress of the Comintern in 1922 Tan Malaka, representing Indonesia, made a speech in which he maintained that Pan-Islamism meant "the national struggle for freedom. . . ." (*Protokoll des Vierten Kongresses der Kommunistischen Internationale,* vom. 5 Nov.bis 5 Dezember, 1922, Petrograd-Moscow, Verlag der Kommunistischen Internationale [Hamburg, 1923], p. 189).

from the Pan-Islamic ideas that Indonesian students at Mecca brought back with them, of which Snouck Hurgronje and the Netherlands Indies Government were so much afraid, as from the Modernist Islamic ideas being taught in Cairo, in particular those stemming from the teaching of Mohammed Abduh.[16]

The Abduh movement emerged to prominence about the turn of the century and has continued as a potent force ever since. Islam, its followers [17] believed, could be defended only by their understanding Western knowledge and methods and the reasons for the progress of the West, while purifying the Mohammedan religion of its accumulated corrupt and superstitious influences and practices. Moslem higher education was to be reformed by inclusion of study of the modern sciences, European history, and Christianity. Political and social justice were emphasized. This emphasis quite naturally reinforced the already awakened nationalist feelings harbored by its adherents.

It was the important Al Manar branch [18] of the movement, with its attempt "to restate the principles of Islamic ethics in terms of social values" [19] and its particular concern for social and political justice, which exercised the chief attraction for Indonesians. At least, they so interpreted its emphasis. As Manarist ideas filtered down to Indonesia, at first principally through members of the communalistically oriented Menangkabou society of west-central Sumatra, their nationalistic content took on strongly anti-imperialist overtones, and in general they were so interpreted as to render them more easily reconcilable with socialist economic principles than appears to have been the case in any other Islamic country.

Though gradually the government became alerted to the danger

[16] For discussion of the ideas of Mohammed Abduh and of his background see Gibb, *op. cit.*, especially pp. 33–43; and C. C. Adams, *Islam and Modernism in Egypt* (London, 1933), pp. 18–176.

[17] With reference to Mohammed Abduh, Gibb states: "He and his writings formed, and still form, a shield, a support, and a weapon for [the] social and political reformers. . . . By the authority of his name 'they were able to gain acceptance among the people for those of the new principles for which they could not have gained a hearing before.' In the second place he bridged, at least temporarily, the widening gap between the traditional learning and the new rationalism introduced from the West, and made it possible for the Muslim graduate of the Western universities to prosecute his studies without being conscious of a fear, or inciting the reproach, that he had abjured his faith" (Gibb, *op. cit.*, pp. 42–43).

[18] This group was formed c.1905 after the death of Mohammed Abduh by one of his chief disciples, Rashid Rida, who edited an influential magazine, *Al Manar* (The Lighthouse), from c.1900 to c.1930.

[19] Gibb, *op. cit.*, p. 52.

of the Modernist movement in general and banned much of its litera-
ture, its initial and dominant concern was with the threat to the political *status quo* that it believed Pan-Islam constituted. Snouck
Hurgronje's assessment of the problem and his advice as to its solution were particularly influential in determining the government's
policy, and it is therefore worth while to note them in some detail.
Speaking in 1911, he observed that Indonesians then studying in the
international Mohammedan milieu of Mecca were absorbing Pan-
Islamic ideas "which can make their disposition towards the European
administration of their fatherland unfavorable." [20] "Happily," he
continued:

These germs of fanaticism become completely developed among only a minority of the Indonesians who study in Arabia. No one has so far found the means
of stopping this flow. The only procedure which can be recommended is slow
and indirect. It consists in influencing the character of the natives in another
direction. All that develops the education of the people can serve it. Each step
of the native along the path of our culture leads him away from the desire
for the pilgrimage. [21]

By giving the Indonesian population, at least its elite, a Western education, it would be turned away from the path of Islam toward cultural
association with the Dutch, and this would "remove all political and
social significance from the difference of religion." If this association
were not made, he held, "the inevitable impulse of the civilization of
the Indonesians," would be, "to move further and further away from
us, for then others than we will control the direction of their intellectual evolution." [22] While providing the Indonesians with a Western
education, the government was to control Mohammedan education,
watching against all Pan-Islamic propaganda, and be "completely intransigent" against admission of all political elements of Mohammedan
doctrine and law. [23]

Snouck Hurgronje particularly emphasized that these Indonesians
who acquired a Western education should be guaranteed positions in
the service of the state worthy of their education. "In multiplying the
opportunities for natives of superior development," he held, "the gov-

[20] C. Snouck Hurgronje, *Nederland en de Islam* (Leiden, 1915), p. 58. This work
renders in Dutch his speeches before the Nederlandsch-Indisch Bestuurs-Academie
of March, 1911, somewhat more accurately in places than the previously quoted
French rendition. His analysis and proposals can also be found in *Verspreide Geschriften* (Bonn and Leipzig, 1923), I, 365–380; see especially pp. 378–380.

[21] *Politique Musulmane de la Hollande,* p. 81.

[22] *Ibid.,* p. 113.   [23] *Ibid.;* pp. 98–99, 107, 129–130.

ernment must revise the division of official functions so as to reserve a large part to the natives of modern culture." [24] If his suggestions were fully carried out, Snouck Hurgronje anticipated that:

The Pan-Islamic idea, which has not yet taken a great hold on the native aristocracy of Java and the other islands, will lose all chance of existence within this milieu, when those who compose it have become the free associates of our civilization. If it then happens that a part of the millions of native Indonesians, whose daily labor as small peasants does not permit their spirits to rise above the level of their fields of rice, find themselves attacked by the epidemic of Pan Islamism, their compatriots, who have become our associates and equals, will themselves have the greatest interest to ward off this menacing danger. In order to emancipate the other classes from the Islamic creed, it is only a question of time, without application of force, if we know how to enlarge liberally our political and national frontiers. . . . (We add that it will also furnish, in other respects, the solution of the problem of future relations between the population of the Indonesian archipelago and the mother country.) From the point of view of general politics, it is to our vital interest not to wait until unexpected circumstances compel us to give that which we can grant to the Indonesians voluntarily and in the form which seems to us the best.[25]

Cogent as Snouck Hurgronje's ideas were, they were only partially carried out, and the results he anticipated were only partially achieved. The spread of Pan-Islamic ideas was largely checked, but the government was not successful in keeping out all political elements of Mohammedan teaching. Modernist political and social ideas entered the country and exerted a tremendous influence, finally manifesting themselves in the first powerful Indonesian nationalist movement, the Sarekat Islam. It was the nationalistic, anti-imperialist, and socialistically inclined program of this movement, rather than the ideas of Pan-Islam, which was the "epidemic" that attacked so considerable a part of the Indonesian population.

However, undoubtedly the most important reason for the nonfulfillment of Snouck Hurgronje's expectations was the government's failure to carry out his recommendation that Indonesians to whom it provided a Western education be guaranteed an important place in the service of the state. Many of those who were given such posts upheld his thesis and did tend to identify themselves with the colonial political order.

[24] *Ibid.*, p. 125. The Dutch edition of his address states that the government must divide the work of civil servants "so as to ensure that all the work they [the Indonesians] are capable of doing is actually entrusted to them" (*Nederland en de Islam*, p. 94).

[25] *Politique Musulmane de la Hollande*, pp. 130–131.

But the large majority of Western-educated Indonesians were either given posts which they felt to be inferior to their educational training or were unable to get governmental or any other employment where their training was utilized. It was this group which was to emerge as the chief force behind the Indonesian nationalist movement and which soon produced leaders much more numerous than those coming from the slightly older Modernist Islamic root of the nationalist movement.

In conjunction with, but to a much greater extent than, the Modernist movement in Islam, Western education was responsible for the development of a new Indonesian elite, the interests of which were at variance with colonial rule. (In addition, the tendency was for Indonesians of strong Mohammedan convictions who received Western education to be attracted to the Modernist movement.) This new elite was a dissatisfied elite, and it was endowed with Western and Modernist Islamic social and political ideas which could not be harmonized with colonial social and political relationships. With its emergence the Indonesian masses were provided with what they had so long lacked, and what the traditional Indonesian aristocratic elite had not given them— political leadership.

Under the impetus of the counsel of Snouck Hurgronje and his numerous following among liberal circles in the Netherlands, and because of the demand for cheap clerical help by the government and private enterprise in the Indies, Western education was increasingly made available to Indonesians during the first four decades of this century, though the number allowed access to it, particularly at the secondary level and above, remained extremely small. Even the student who limited his reading to the curriculum could not help noting that the dominant strain in the Dutch national ideology was independence from outside control and found it hard not to see a parallel between an upholder of Dutch power in the Indies, such as Van Heutz, and the Duke of Alba. Likewise he found it difficult, in view of Dutch national history, to understand why the history books on Indonesia which he was given painted Diponegoro and other leaders of resistance to the Dutch as worthless traitors and selfish opportunists. A large number utilized their command of the Dutch language to explore extracurricular subjects, especially of a political nature, many of those receiving a secondary or higher education being strongly attracted to the writings of Rousseau, Locke, Mazzini, Sorel, and the Utopian and Marxist socialists. Their dominantly Western channel of approach to political

and social problems is emphasized by the fact that the attention given
to Sun Yat-sen, Gandhi, and Tagore, though important, was much less.

In general, the social and political ideas of the West justified, garbed
with authority, and greatly intensified the broadly social impulse of
Indonesians to resist political and economic subjection and exploitation by the Dutch. In a similar manner these ideas reacted upon their
more subjective and individual desires for dignity and assertion of
equality against the numb feeling of inferiority that subjection to alien
domination had developed in them.

The long-inculcated idea that the Indonesian was inferior to the
Netherlander and needed his guidance and protection was rapidly
eroded not only by Western political ideas, but likewise by the political events in Asia that roughly paralleled the introduction of Western
education and which also affected large numbers of people not exposed
to it. The struggle of the Filipinos against Spain and the early American occupation, the successes of Kemal Ataturk against Western military power, the activities of the Congress party in India, the rising tide
of anti-Western Chinese nationalism especially as represented by Sun
Yat-sen, the industrialization of Japan, and most of all that country's
victory over Russia—all combined to make the Indonesians doubt that
they were inferior to the Dutch or unable to govern themselves without
Dutch help.[26]

The few Indonesian students able to study in the Netherlands were
strongly influenced by the political conditions as well as the political
ideas which they encountered there. The civil liberties and democratic
government which they found in Holland contrasted so sharply with
conditions in Indonesia that they were bound to make a strong impression on these students. Likewise, they could not fail to be impressed
by the fact that up until 1929 the only political party which advocated
complete independence for Indonesia was the Communist Party. Later,
equally impressive for them was the fact that gradually thereafter the
Dutch socialists (Social Democratic Party) came out for independence
rather than limited self-government as they had previously advocated,
while in 1938 the Communist Party, as part of its over-all United Front
policy, took a stand against independence and supported the Dutch

[26] The former head of the Netherlands Indies government's Department of Public
Instruction wrote in 1921, "It is above all since the war between Japan and Russia,
that the idea that an Asiatic population can govern itself without the necessity of
otra Europa has penetrated." J. H. Abendanon, *Las Indias neerlandesas* (Madrid,
1921), p. 2.

government.[27] The Communist Party undertook to justify its *volte-face* by what seemed to many Indonesian intellectuals to be a specious and hypocritical rationalization, namely, that an independent Indonesia would be too weak to withstand the advance of "Japanese Imperialist Fascism." [28]

The appeal of Leninist Marxism was especially strong, for to many it alone seemed to posit a satisfactory solution to the antithesis presented by Western political concepts of liberty and equality and Western colonialism. Of particular influence were the writings of Bukharin and Lenin concerning imperialism, and to them the handful of Indonesian students able to study in continental Europe was especially attracted. Had they been able to study in England they might rather have looked primarily to Hobson, for their attraction to Marxism was predominantly because of its anti-imperialist content. Indeed, as events were to prove, the majority approached it in an extremely eclectic manner.[29] The high degree of religious and politico-ideological tolerance possessed by many Indonesians allowed many sincere Mohammedans to develop a working synthesis of important constituent elements of Marxism and their religion. The noncapitalist background of the overwhelming majority of Indonesian secondary and college students meant that on personal, material grounds they were not alienated by the socialist economics of Marxism. Very few had any vested interest in capitalism. The only important development of capitalism in Indonesia was in the colonial economic sphere, the benefits of which, they were convinced, completely by-passed them and their families.

[27] This change in attitude stemmed from the so-called "Dimitrov Doctrine" announced at the 7th Comintern Conference (July–Aug., 1935). Dimitrov in his speech did not specifically counsel shelving policies of colonial emancipation, but his broad statements allowed such an inference and this soon became the very definite policy of the Comintern. Independence for Indonesia was dropped from the program of the Communist Party of the Netherlands beginning with its 1938 Congress and did not again become part of it until 1947.

[28] See S. Krause, "Trotskyism in Indonesia," *International Press Correspondence*, XVIII, no. 32 (June 25, 1938), 770. This publication was the principal news organ of the Comintern.

[29] A small but important minority hewed to a narrower and more orthodox approach, a few studying at the Lenin Institute in Moscow, and one, Darsono, apparently was judged by the Executive Committee of the Comintern to be so sound that he was made the Comintern's representative in Germany during a period in the mid-1920's. In the late 1930's, in large part because of disgust with opportunistic shifts in Comintern policy which he was convinced had become subservient to the national interests of Russia, he severed his connection with the Comintern and the Netherlands Communist Party.

Capitalism and imperialism were to them equated, and hostility to imperialism quite naturally entailed hostility to capitalism.

In addition, the conviction was common among educated Indonesians that any future political independence would mean little unless accompanied by economic independence. In a society where almost all capital was possessed by nonindigenous elements it was essential, they felt, that the government of an independent Indonesia control economic life and operate critical sectors of the economy. Even among those who did not consider themselves to be socialists, most agreed that, since there were virtually no Indonesian capitalist class and no Indonesian capital accumulation, it would necessarily devolve upon any future government of their own to fill much of the economic void that the Indonesian's lack of training and capital left. Moreover, as we have seen, of those obtaining a Western education who were able to find employment utilizing it, three-fourths worked as government employees, a type of employment unlikely to engender hostility to socialist ideas. Also the ever-increasing number of Western-educated Indonesians unable to find employment that utilized their education could not easily avoid begetting nationalistic reactions having a strongly socialistic content.

But apart from the ideological orientation which it induced, the most important consequence of Western education was undoubtedly its development of an indigenous elite which colonial society could not absorb—an acutely dissatisfied, cramped, and frustrated elite. For only a small proportion of those Indonesians equipped with Western education were able to get jobs commensurate with their training and ability. A majority experienced sharp discontent because the positions they obtained were inferior to what they were convinced their qualifications entitled them. The conviction that discriminatory employment policies were responsible for giving the better positions to Netherlanders and Eurasians increased the bitterness. A substantial minority were unemployed or forced to accept inferior positions requiring no Western training, and that group experienced even greater discontent. Finally, a group of considerable size, embittered because unsuccessful in finding employment with either the government or Western business enterprise, led a precarious economic existence as poorly paid teachers in the numerous strongly nationalist Indonesian private schools which burgeoned largely because of this group's economic plight. Thereby was developed a propagator of Indonesian nationalism, and often of socialist ideas as well, the potency of which has generally been un-noticed or underestimated.

Aside from this widespread and basic dissatisfaction there were a number of other grievances important in nourishing Indonesian nationalism. These were not confined to the Western-educated majority of the new Indonesian intelligentsia and the miniscule Indonesian middle class, but were held by these groups as a whole, as well as by most white-collar workers and the more politically conscious and better educated sectors of the rapidly growing skilled labor element. Of substantial importance was the social discrimination which many Netherlanders and Eurasians practiced toward Indonesians and the blatant attitude of superiority which some of them manifested toward the latter even though the former's educational backgrounds, manners, and abilities were, as Colijn remarked, often quite inferior.[30] Despite some mitigation, this discrimination and attitude of superiority continued to be important in generating nationalistic feelings as late as 1949.[31]

A continual source of grievance was that judicial administration and penal legislation discriminated sharply against Indonesians. The courts to which they had access were of much poorer quality than those provided for the European population, and, because of the participation of executive officers in them, offered much less protection. Whereas legally trained judges sat in the courts for Europeans, Indonesians were forced to rely on courts half of whose members combined both executive and legal functions, two of the members being active or retired (and pensioned) members of the Indonesian administrative civil service. Indonesians, as opposed to Europeans, could be held in jail under "preventive detention," even though no judicial authorization had been made.

Discrimination in the economic sphere was of greater and more widespread importance. The new Western-educated elite in particular, but also educated Indonesians in general, felt strongly that the paucity of jobs and the few good positions open to them in the civil service and private enterprise were a result of employment practices which dis-

[30] Colijn, op. cit., pp. 43–44. This was deplored by Colijn and recognized by him as important in influencing the course of the nationalist movement.

[31] In mid-1949 this discrimination was still so much in evidence that Dr. van Royen, chairman of the Netherlands delegation in Indonesia, felt obliged to take a strong public stand against it, stating that such discrimination "reflects unfavorably on the political situation and is not in accordance with the Netherlands task in this country" (Sin Po, June 10, 1949).

criminated against Indonesians. Almost every Indonesian nationalist experienced the bitterness and frustration born of this realization. Typical of this was the experience related to the writer by an Indonesian successful in passing the examination for entrance to a government school leading to middle-rank civil service positions. In 1939 there were 400 Indonesians and 100 Dutch (including Eurasians) who took the examination for entrance to the school. Twenty-three Dutch and 3 Indonesians were accepted. He later discovered that 15 of the Dutch applicants knew before the examination that they had been accepted and that a quota of 3 had been set for Indonesians. His discovery of this, he felt, was one of the events in his life most important in turning him into a nationalist.

Indonesian aspirants for professional positions were keenly aware of the efforts of Netherlanders to monopolize these positions and the government's compliance with the opposition of Dutch professional men trying to avoid Indonesian competition. The lawyers were able to resist the projected opening of a law school in 1909 and the Medical Association the opening of a medical school in 1913, such schools being established only in 1924 and 1926, respectively. However, the lawyers continued to make Indonesian competition difficult. To get a degree from Batavia Law School it was necessary to study five years as against three or four in Holland, and the school was considered by Indonesians to be more difficult than Dutch law schools.

Acute dissatisfaction developed because of the lower rate of pay of Indonesian government employees in comparison with Dutch and Eurasians doing similar work. For instance, in the Indonesian branch of the civil service those who had passed the clerkship examination (*kleine ambtenaar*) started at 25 guilders per month, while Europeans (mostly Eurasians) passing the same examination started at 60 guilders in the European branch. Similarly in the army, Indonesian privates received either 15 or 25 guilders per month (the latter sum if they came from the Christian areas of Ambon, Menado, and Timor), while privates who were Netherlanders or Eurasians received 60 guilders.

Probably the most widespread grievance was that resulting from the very limited educational facilities provided Indonesians and the fact that so large a proportion of such facilities was reserved for European children.[32] Particular bitterness was felt over the fact that

[32] A fact of wide currency among Indonesians was that per capita educational expenditure by the government for European (including Eurasian) children was 87

while almost all Indonesians (except for a meager handful able to obtain scholarships) had to pay substantial tuition fees, Dutch and Eurasian children were tuition-free unless the yearly income of their parents was more than 1,200 guilders.[33] Nationalist sensitivities were further aroused by the unofficial but widely known government attitude that began to develop during the 1930's that too much education was politically dangerous and that Western education, especially secondary education, should be curtailed at least to the point where the colonial economy could absorb all those individuals who received it. Thus Colijn in 1928 saw in the quick growth of Western education for Indonesians "a danger for the peaceful development of the course of affairs in Indonesia." Such education had been too much expanded, he felt, and should be limited to the point where the indigenous economy itself (as opposed to employment with the government and Western enterprise), could absorb it.[34]

Finally, note must be taken of the fact that during the last twenty-five years of Dutch rule an increasing conviction developed among politically conscious Indonesians that their country was being milked by the Dutch. Some, particularly those under the influence of Communist indoctrination, conceived of this as a simple syphoning off of Indonesian wealth to Dutch coffers. Others admitted that Dutch capital developed the over-all economy in a manner which provided some incidental benefits to Indonesians but maintained that their benefit was miniscule compared to that of the Dutch. Moreover, they maintained that this capital had been for the most part originally created by the tribute levies on Indonesia inherent in the Company and Cultivation systems. Regardless of the extent of their understanding of the colonial economic system that operated in Indonesia, most were cognizant of certain available economic facts which gained an ever-widening currency and which tended increasingly to be given a political interpretation. Prominent among these was the wide margin of

---

times that provided for Indonesian children. Cf. Sri Soewarni Pringgodigdo, "Soal Peladjaran Dan Pendidikan Nasional," *Sedar* (the foremost women's nationalist magazine), (July, 1932), pp. 20–24. The writer concluded that the government's per capita expenditure on education for Indonesian children was 0.55 guilders per year as against 47.86 for European children.

[33] Income tax statistics for 1939 listed 24,059 Indonesians as having incomes over 1,200 guilders ($480) per year as against 67,229 Europeans. Among Europeans 17,453 had incomes of less than 1,200 guilders. *Indisch Verslag, 1941*, II, 184–185. (See fn. 115 in Ch. I.)

[34] Colijn, *op. cit.*, pp. 14, 17, 34, 35.

exports over imports. The value of Indonesia's imports and exports in private trade (merchandise) in guilders ($.40) is shown in Table 8.

Table 8. VALUE OF IMPORTS AND EXPORTS.*

Year	Imports	Exports
1913	436,682,000	614,203,000
1920	1,116,213,000	2,224,999,000
1925	818,372,000	1,784,798,000
1930	855,425,000	1,159,601,000
1936	278,908,000	589,637,000
1940	430,160,000	940,256,000

* *Indisch Verslag, 1941*, II, p. 343. These figures include merchandise exports in private trade only. They do not include coined and uncoined gold and silver shipments in private trade or for government account, and they do not include merchandise shipments for government account. Such exports and imports were negligible in comparison with private trade exports and imports in merchandise and change the over-all picture very little.

Also important were the price differential between the government rubber monopoly's price to European and Indonesian growers,[35] the heavy tax burden borne by the Indonesian population and its greater relative increase as compared to that borne by European residents of Indonesia,[36] and the high percentage (30 per cent according to government estimates) of Indonesia's wealth that went to non-Indonesians.[37]

Opposed to the growth of Indonesian nationalism—and to the political and social revolution for which it came to stand—were a number of factors which in their combination were effective in limiting its growth and preventing the force it was able to muster during the period of Dutch rule from reaching its objectives. One of the most important of these factors was the general system of indirect rule which, through a multiplicity of patterns, the Dutch applied to the different areas of Indonesia and which, Rupert Emerson observed in 1937, served "as a

[35] See Ch. I.

[36] See Ch. I. Meijer Ranneft and W. Huender in their government-sponsored investigation of the tax pressure on the Indonesian population concluded that between 1915 and 1925 a broad group of Indonesian intellectuals had become conscious that the tax burden borne by that population was too heavy, particularly in comparison with that borne by non-Indonesian elements and that this had generated "a distinct political current" (*Onderzoek naar de Belasting Druk op de Inlandsche Bevolking*, p. 26).

[37] The latest confirmation of this estimate is provided by C. Ch. W. Uffelie and W. H. J. Elias, "De Landsfinancien," *Rapport Visman* (Batavia, 1941), I, 42.

highly efficient device for breaking up and segregating potential nationalist movements and as something of a moral justification for de-
nying the claims to power of the more advanced elements of native
society." [38]

Even in the areas formally designated as "directly ruled" (93 per
cent of Java and somewhat less than half of the rest of Indonesia), the
formula of indirect rule, though less thorough than previously, continued through the last decades of Dutch rule to be of great importance.
In these areas the upper ranks of the Indonesian aristocratic hierarchy
(in Java the regents and to a lesser extent their principal subordinates,
the Wedonos and Assistant Wedonos) during this period had lost many
of their powers and much of their effectiveness as instruments of indirect
rule. However, the lowest strata, comprised of the village headmen, had
been reinforced in its power and, where it did not too much abuse it,
was effective in serving as a buffer between the Dutch civil service and
a substantial, though diminishing, sector of the agrarian population.

Taken as a whole, this aristocratic hierarchy continued to play an
important part in the over-all pattern of Dutch political control, so
much so that as late as 1928 Colijn, though recognizing its decreased
capacity, referred to it as "the backbone" of Dutch authority.[39] Its effectiveness, particularly that of its upper strata, progressively declined
after that date. But up until the end of Dutch rule, it still commanded
a considerable support from a major part of the Indonesian masses
and continued to constitute one of the most important pillars supporting the Dutch regime.

To an important extent this decline in the effectiveness of the upper
ranks of the aristocratic Indonesian administrative element was a result of Western education. A strong and widespread tendency was for
the Western-educated sons of its members to refuse to fill the positions
of their fathers. More and more of these, because of their awakened
nationalism, sought to disassociate themselves from the old aristocracy
which they correctly saw as supporter of the colonial regime. Sometimes
all the sons of an aristocrat would refuse to fill the administrative
posts of their fathers, seeking to equip themselves for other jobs, the
tendency often being to seek positions which would give them as much
economic independence as possible from the colonial regime. (Thus
the surprising number of Indonesian nationalist leaders who have been

[38] Rupert Emerson, *Malaysia, A Study in Direct and Indirect Rule* (New York,
1937), p. 518. He is here referring to Malaya as well.
[39] Colijn, *op. cit.*, p. 33.

and are doctors and who often entered that profession as much from
a desire to obtain the economic independence necessary for effective
participation in the nationalist movement as from a desire to practice
medicine.) Increasingly the ablest sons of Indonesian aristocratic officials sought such positions, leaving the least educated and generally
least competent sons to fill the posts of their fathers. The result was
not only to lower the caliber of the aristocratic elements that continued
to serve the Dutch, but also the government was obliged to draft nonaristocratic Indonesians to fill these positions. Because of this as well
as because of sustained attack by the nationalist leaders, the prestige
of the indirect ruler in the eyes of the Indonesian population was
greatly lowered, and as a consequence his effectiveness as an instrument
of indirect rule diminished. Colijn noted that while in 1909 72.3 per
cent of the students in the government's school for Indonesian administrators were the sons of Assistant Wedonos (administrators of sub-
districts) or higher, by 1926 this was true for only 44.7 per cent and that
only two of the fourteen admitted to the school in 1927 were sons of
such aristocratic administrators.[40]

In those areas officially designated as "indirectly ruled," that is, in
the 269 native states [41] maintained by the Dutch,[42] the character of their
rule continued to be a good deal less direct in most cases than in the
nominally "directly ruled" areas, but the effectiveness of Netherlands
control was no less. In those areas the contact between the population
and the Dutch administration was less, and the conviction of the
population that it was being governed by its own traditional ruling
elements greater than in the relatively directly ruled areas. The maintenance of these states by the Dutch as a bulwark against nationalism
was strongly sensed in 1937 by Emerson, who wrote:

Their present maintenance by the Dutch . . . is to be explained less in terms
of a concern for the spiritual and material ease of their people than in terms

[40] *Ibid.,* pp. 40–41.

[41] These states embraced more than half the area of Indonesia outside Java, and
7 per cent of that island where Surakarta and Jogjakarta, the two largest native
states, were located. They ranged in population from 350 to 1,704,000 and totaled
12,372,000 inhabitants as against 48,355,000 living in the nominally directly ruled
areas (1930 census; Emerson, *op. cit.,* p. 55).

[42] Emerson notes: "That there is nothing sacrosanct about the native State as such
the Dutch have amply demonstrated by the cavalier fashion in which they built up
States here and killed them off there with no better argument than expediency or
historical accident to justify this choice; and those that have survived to the present
day have done so only at the cost of transferring large segments of their powers
directly to the Dutch" (*ibid.,* p. 464).

of Dutch dread of Indonesian communism and nationalism. Originally encouraged for the sake of imperial convenience in controlling vast territories and heterogeneous peoples, the States have now increasingly come to be regarded as essential bulwarks against the spread of dissension and as partially isolated backwaters in which the old loyalties to well-subsidized rulers are exploited in the interests of the new masters.[43]

It is likely that the much earlier and more potent development of the nationalist movement in Java and other relatively directly administered parts of the Indies as compared to the native states [44] was to some extent due to the relatively greater directness of rule in those areas and the consequently more-pronounced anti-Dutch reaction that it provoked. It does not seem altogether unjustified to suggest that realization of this fact may have played some part in the policy of administrative decentralization and augmentation of the powers of the native states which the Dutch embarked upon in 1938 in Borneo, Celebes, the Lesser Sundas, and the Moluccas.[45]

The plural nature of colonial society in Indonesia, in particular the correspondence of ethnic and socio-economic groups, constituted a major limitation in the growth of Indonesian nationalism. Its European ruling class felt its welfare tied up with the political and economic *status quo* and with few exceptions opposed the nationalist movement. The middle class of that society was predominantly non-Indonesian, being largely Chinese and Eurasian, and was likewise wedded to the political and economic *status quo* and strongly hostile to the nationalist movement. From the previous chapter the stake of the Chinese in the maintenance of the colonial regime should be obvious. As for the Eurasians, Wertheim observes, "Together with the feudal chiefs and the Amboinese and Menandonese Christians [mostly in the army] they became pillars of Dutch authority in the Indies. They soon constituted the core of the army, the police, the civil servants and the judiciary." Moreover, a number were in the apex of the government structure.[46] In their access to these positions the Eurasians had in general been strongly favored by the Dutch over the Indonesians, and by the middle 1920's it was apparent that the overwhelming majority of them was not only effectively detached from the nationalist movement, but as strongly if

---

[43] *Ibid.*, pp. 464–465.

[44] With a few exceptions, Jogjakarta in central Java in particular.

[45] See "Vastelling van de Zelfbestuursregelen, 1938," *Staatsblad van Nederlandsch-Indie* (1938), no. 529.

[46] W. F. Wertheim, "The Indo-European Problem in Indonesia," *Pacific Affairs* (Sept. 1947), p. 294.

not more strongly opposed to it than were the Dutch. "More Dutch than the Dutch," many nationalists characterized them. With respect to the Eurasians, Wertheim concludes:

As the pillars of Dutch rule, they believed their privileges depended on that authority. Hence their main political association—the IEV (*Indo-Europeesch Verbond*)—was conspicuously conservative in character; wholeheartedly loyal to Dutch rule, it sought to preserve the numerous privileges concerned with the European status of its members.[47]

As Furnivall has remarked, "Nationalism within a plural society is itself a disruptive force, tending to shatter and not to consolidate its social order." [48] The gulf between Indonesians and non-Indonesians continued to increase through the last years of Dutch rule.[49] Indonesian nationalists could not, as their European counterparts have done, count upon the middle class as their principal basis of support, only a tiny fraction of that class being Indonesian. This meant that the only possible basis for a successful Indonesian nationalist movement, that is, one powerful enough to achieve its political objectives, lay in the establishment of effective liaison between the nationalist leadership, drawn particularly from the intellectual elements of the tiny Indonesian sector of the middle class, and the Indonesian masses.

Opposed to the achievement of this end was the near monopoly of force at the disposal of the Dutch. Possessed of this, they were able to obstruct almost completely the efforts of the nationalist leaders and the fractional Indonesian middle class as a whole to establish effective political contact with the Indonesian agrarian population. An army and a police force almost wholly officered by Dutch and Eurasians with a major proportion of their rank and file drawn from these elements and from Christian Indonesians from the Minahassa (Menado area),

[47] *Ibid.*, p. 296. Wertheim notes: "However, some Indos [Eurasians] had a more Asiatic outlook. Resentment towards the whites, felt in some measure by many Indos, led certain of them to join the Indonesian nationalist movement. Before the first world war it looked for a time as if the Indos would become the leaders of the colored races. . . . In cooperation with Indonesians, a number of Indos founded a powerful nationalist movement [see Ch. III] directed against white domination. In the long run, however, the reactionary view of the I.E.V. gained ascendancy" (*ibid.*, pp. 296–297).

[48] J. S. Furnivall, *Netherlands India, A Study of Plural Economy* (New York, 1944), p. 468.

[49] J. W. Meijer Ranneft, "The Economic Structure of Java," in Schrieke, ed., *The Effect of Western Influence on Native Civilizations of the Malay Archipelago* (Batavia, 1929), p. 83; *Rapport Visman*, II (1941) , 85, 89–90.

Ambon, and Timor [50] were the chief instruments of the Dutch repressive power. This police and military power was supplemented by and intermeshed with government regulations which narrowly circumscribed and often almost completely cut off legal organization and prosecution of the nationalist movement. The strength of the army and the police force and their nonsympathetic attitude toward the nationalistic movement in conjunction with the general ability of the PID (Politieke Inlichtingen Dienst, Political Intelligence Service), the government's secret service, made it extremely difficult to develop the movement effectively on the extralegal plane.

One of the government's strongest legal weapons against the nationalist movement—it was not always averse to applying extralegal force against the movement—was the power of the governor-general to exile a person to any particular part of Indonesia whenever he deemed this necessary "in the interests of peace and order." [51] This power was invoked frequently and on a wide scale and was largely responsible for the rapid turnover in leadership of the nationalist movement. This impermanence of leadership greatly weakened the movement; for in a society such as the Indonesian, where political organization from the top down was the traditional norm, an almost sustained disruption of that leadership was disastrous. Also frequently invoked and bearing similar consequences was the government's power to arrest without previous authorization by a court any Indonesian suspected of an offense and to keep him under "provisional arrest." [52] This was used particularly against second- and third-echelon nationalist leaders. The widespread fear of being observed by the omnipresent agents of the PID and being subjected to an indefinite period of provisional arrest was sufficient to suppress even informal proselytizing efforts by the less courageous nationalists.

Attempts at organizational proselytizing by leaders courageous enough to disregard these prospects were rendered extremely difficult

[50] Many Indonesian leaders insist that it was a calculated policy of the Dutch to attempt to detach Christian Indonesians of these areas from the nationalist movement by telling them that nationalism's victory would mean a Mohammedan political ascendancy deleterious to their interests. The higher pay which soldiers from these areas received as compared to other Indonesian soldiers was in any case a substantial reason for their identifying their interests with the Dutch and being reliable when used in opposition to nationalists.

[51] *Indische Staatsregeling*, arts. 36, 37. See *De Nederlandsch-Indische Wetboeken*, W. A. Engelbrecht, ed. (Leiden, 1939), pp. 44–45.

[52] *Indische Staatsregeling*, art. 73 (1).

because the rights of association and assembly were tightly controlled and their exercise narrowly restricted by the government.[53] One of the severest handicaps encountered by the nationalists was Article 155 of the Penal Code which provided a maximum imprisonment of four years for anyone who "publicly [orally or in writing] manifests hostility, dislike or contempt for one or more of the population groups of the Indies." The governor-general's power to suspend the publication of all periodicals whose content was deemed by him to be contrary to the interests of public security [54] was an additional limitation on the value of the press as a means of furthering the nationalist movement. The effectiveness of the press was, of course, already restricted because only 6.4 per cent of the Indonesian population were literate.[55]

Until 1927, despite severe legal restrictions, the trade union movement constituted an important means for prosecuting the nationalist struggle. Thereafter, and particularly after 1929, the government's policy and legislation were so hostile toward it that it was no longer of great effectiveness.[56] Labor legislation of 1923 incorporated limitations on the right to strike into the Penal Code. Respecting this Virginia Thompson observes:

Any labor agitation that tended to disturb public order or contravene a labor contract was liable to penalization. Theoretically this legislation aimed to prevent political agitators from vitiating economic issues, but in practice its terms could be applied to prohibiting any organization of strikes.[57]

[53] The governor-general was empowered to declare any association illegal which he deemed "in contravention of public security." Open air public meetings were prohibited unless previous permission had been secured from the head of the local administration. Indoors meetings "of a political nature" were forbidden unless notice was served to the chief local administrative officer 24 hours in advance in Java and Madura and 48 hours in advance elsewhere. To such meetings "and to all meetings which are open to the public, officers and employees of the police" were to have freedom of admission. For the above regulations on association and assembly see *Staatsblad van Nederlandsch-Indie*, 1919, no. 17, as amended, *ibid.*, 1935, no. 18. Commencing with the State of War and Siege instituted in 1939, all private meetings of a political nature were forbidden unless notice had been served five days previously, and permission could be denied by the military authorities (*Staatsblad*, 1939, no. 382).

[54] *Staatsblad*, 1931, no. 394 (Ordinance of Sept. 7, 1931). Between 1906 and 1931, freedom of the press was somewhat greater.

[55] As of the last census, that of 1930.

[56] Virginia Thompson, *Labor Problems in Southeast Asia* (New Haven, 1947), p. 160. She notes that official statistics indicate the effectiveness of this legislation. The total number of strikers in the whole of Indonesia during 1940 was only 2,115, a number greater than that of any of the previous 4 years.

[57] *Ibid.*, p. 160. Indonesian labor leaders informed the writer that with the procla-

Because of the overwhelming power possessed by the Dutch and the extremely restricted channels of development which their power allowed the nationalist leaders and their organizations, these leaders were never during the course of Dutch rule able to come into sufficient contact with the peasantry to organize it effectively into the nationalist movement. Extensive ideological and considerable organizational contact was consummated with urban labor, particularly its skilled elements; but it, in conjunction with Indonesian white-collar workers and the tiny Indonesian middle class, constituted almost the entire organized social weight behind the nationalist movement. A limited ideological contact was made with the peasantry, a considerable portion of which, because of its changing social environment, had been developing an incipient nationalist orientation of its own. Fitful and incomplete organizational contact was established with some marginal elements of peasant society, such as plantation workers and some of those casual laborers most loosely tied to the village. But attempts at organizational contact with the mass of the peasantry were almost completely frustrated. Without the organized backing of this mass, the Indonesian nationalist movement stood little chance of success against the repressive power which the Dutch regime was able to marshal against it.

---

mation of a State of War and Siege in 1939, antistrike regulations were even more severe than before.

⚜ CHAPTER III ⚜

History of the Nationalist

Movement until 1942

BEFORE 1912 the emphasis of Indonesian nationalism except for its Pan-Islamic and incipient Modernist Islamic currents was cultural rather than political, though political overtones were often present. Education was the chief vehicle for this phase of the nationalist movement. The most important early effort along these lines was launched by Raden Adjeng Kartini, the young daughter of a Javanese regent. She felt that the condition of her people could be raised through education which was Western as well as Indonesian in content. In 1902 by founding a school for the daughters of Indonesian officials, she gave the initial impetus to modern female education and was important in stimulating the cultural-nationalist movement as a whole. Her activity marked the first manifestation of the important role which women came to play in the Indonesian nationalist movement. (The Mohammedan religion had been unable to make an appreciable inroad upon the strong social position of Indonesian women, particularly among the Javanese and Menangkabau.)

The first organized cultural-nationalist movement was launched between 1906 and 1908 through the efforts of a retired Javanese physician, Mas Wahidin Soediro Hoesodo, who sought to elevate the Javanese people through study of Western knowledge as well as their own cultural heritage. He tried with almost no success to collect funds to be used for such education from the aristocratic Indonesians in the government's administrative service. Finally he met with success among the sons of these aristocrats attending the medical school at Batavia. Particularly through the efforts of two of these students, Raden Soetomo and Raden Goenawan Mangoenkoesoemo, who were later to emerge as important nationalist leaders, there was founded in October, 1908, an organization called Boedi Oetomo (Pure Endeavor). Its initial program was essentially nonpolitical and called for the development of traditional and Western education among the peoples of Java and Madura, the advancement of agriculture, industry and commerce among them, and finally "everything that will guarantee them the life of a dignified people."[1] Despite the circumstances of its launching, older and relatively conservative men emerged as its first leaders, all coming from the top echelon of the Javanese aristocracy. The organization's early policy was that: "The youth should remain 'the motor which drives forward'; the elders should be 'the steersmen, who with dextrous hand know how to avoid dangerous rocks in order to bring the boat to safe harbor.'"[2] By the end of 1909, Boedi Oetomo numbered almost 10,000 members, made up largely of Indonesian civil servants as well as nearly all the students above the sixth grade in Java and Madura. Its numerical strength was short-lived, however, for as politically oriented nationalist organizations began to arise, almost all its members except the politically conservative aristocratic elements, mostly civil servants, drifted away. This loss of membership to political-nationalist organizations was so great that after 1913 the organization went into a period of stagnation and an over-all decline from which it never fully recovered despite its establishment of a political program in 1917[3] and its even later attempt to develop a mass following.

The first politically-based Indonesian nationalist organization— Sarekat Islam—burst upon the heretofore tranquil colonial scene with a suddenness and a force which quite astonished not only the Dutch but many Indonesians as well. Within four years of its founding in 1912 it had developed a membership of 360,000 and was embarked upon a

[1] L. M. Sitorus, *Sedjarah Pergerakan Kebangsaan Indonesia* ("History of the Indonesian Nationalist Movement"), (Jakarta, 1947), pp. 10–11.

[2] J. Th. Petrus Blumberger, *De Nationalistische Beweging in Nederlandsch-Indie* (Haarlem, 1931), p. 19.

[3] *Ibid.*, pp. 19–23. Commenting on the leadership of Boedi Oetomo, Fromberg states: "They were able to arouse support, but they were unable to exercise driving power, because they did not know how to reach the people and therefore got little power behind them" (P. H. Fromberg, "De Inlandsche Beweging op Java," reprinted from *De Gids*, 1914, in the collection of Fromberg's writings, *Verspreide Geschriften* [Leiden, 1926], p. 540).

political program calling for self-government. By 1919, its membership had reached almost two and a half million, and its militant nationalist program was boldly dedicated to complete independence, to be attained by force if necessary.

The spectacular burgeoning of Sarekat Islam can in a negative sense be explained by the fact that the colonial administration was caught off guard. The Dutch had neither the experience nor the well-organized repressive apparatus with which they were later armed and which they later used with such success against the political-nationalist movement. In a positive sense it can be explained by the previously mentioned social conditions obtaining in Indonesia and the grievances which they were developing among the population. More particularly the rise of Sarekat Islam was a demonstration of the tremendous nationalist response which could be expected of a large sector of the Indonesian masses once it was provided with political leadership. When such leadership emerged, the rallying of the people behind it was inevitable.

Though the general circumstances responsible for the latent political-nationalism of the masses were important in the over-all social conditioning that activated this leadership, there were other salient factors involved as well. Of great importance was the impact of Modernist Islamic thought. This tended to find an enhanced receptivity among literate Indonesians due to the increasingly aggressive character of Christian missionary activity that developed during the first decade of this century in Indonesia. Also of importance was the strong reaction generated by Indonesian contact with the hauteur and political aggressiveness manifested by Indies Chinese as a result of the contagion of the ideas of Chinese nationalism. The surge of Chinese nationalism among them, particularly in the revolutionary year of 1911, tended to generate additional friction in their already none-too-cordial relations with Indonesians and to beget an Indonesian nationalist reaction amongst many of those with whom they came in contact.[4] Moreover, the numerous political and economic concessions won from the Netherlands Indies government between 1904 and 1911 by the organized Chinese national movement of Indies Chinese not only excited the envy of many Indonesians but awakened them to the possibilities offered by organized political action.[5]

---

[4] Sitorus, *op. cit.*, pp. 14–15; Blumberger, *op. cit.*, p. 55.

[5] Pressure against the government by the Chinese community in conjunction with the former's desire to remove grievances which might make stronger the growing entente between Indonesian Chinese and China resulted in the lifting of travel and

However, the outstanding immediate cause for the emergence of an Indonesian political-nationalist leadership resulted from the suddenly increased impingement of aggressively competitive Chinese entrepreneurs upon the interests of the vestigial Javanese merchant class that attended the gradual lifting of travel restrictions on the Chinese in the interior of Java between 1904 and 1911. The political-nationalist organization, Sarekat Islam, stemmed from an Indonesian trading society, Sarekat Dagang Islam (Islamic Trading Association) formed in 1909 by Raden Mas Tirtoadisoerjo, an aristocratic Javanese merchant and manager of a trading company then in process of liquidation. Sharp Chinese trading practices brought him and other Javanese merchants to form a co-operative trading organization for protection against Chinese dealers, whom they were prepared to boycott if necessary. In 1911, support was obtained from a great Javanese merchant and batik manufacturer of Surakarta, Hadji Samanhoedi, who was also a Moslem religious leader of considerable stature. The venture was reorganized on a co-operative basis and geared to launch boycotts against the Chinese in defense of the interests of the large number of Javanese merchants it had attracted.

The new organization was seen by Indonesians in general, regardless of their economic function, as a symbol of religious—and thereby of Indonesian—unity against foreigners, at first especially Chinese. Its basis of mutual assistance and advancement of the interests of all Mohammedans was easily interpreted in terms of strong nationalism, and its religious and nationalist character soon overshadowed its original economic emphasis. Not only did it attract an avalanche of members,[6] but its program also served to stir and embolden outsiders. There resulted widespread boycotts against the Chinese as well as a number of physical attacks upon them culminating early in 1912 in anti-Chinese riots in Surakarta and Surabaja. Though its leadership was not in itself responsible for this violence, the organization was for a few months

---

residence restrictions on Chinese which had been in force in the interior of Java. Likewise it resulted in certain legal reforms beneficial to the Chinese, government subsidies to Chinese schools and the establishment in 1908 of a Dutch-Chinese school, the latter being created before any similar school for Indonesians (P. H. Fromberg, "De Chineesche Beweging op Java," *Verspreide Geschriften,* pp. 426–430).

[6] Contrasting the leadership of Sarekat Islam with that of Boedi Oetomo, Fromberg wrote in 1914: "The new men on the contrary have gone down to the people, have known how to reach the people through the medium of religion, the national bond, and through it have obtained the connection. They have got a mass behind them to whose feelings and dreams they can give expression" ("De Inlandsche Beweging op Java," *op. cit.,* p. 540).

banned by the government.[7] In September, 1912, the Sarekat Dagang
Islam re-emerged as Sarekat Islam (Islamic Association) under the
leadership of non-merchant intellectuals and religious leaders as well
as merchants and was chairmaned by Oemar Said Tjokroaminoto, employee of a commercial firm in Surabaya, and a man possessed of considerable Western education. At the association's first congress in January, 1913, Tjokroaminoto emphasized that it was not a political party
and that it would maintain absolute loyalty to the government. Its announced program was: [8] (a) promoting commerce among Indonesians;
(b) mutual support of members who encounter economic difficulties;
(c) promotion of the intellectual development and material interests of
the Indonesians; and (d) opposition to wrong religious concepts concerning the Mohammedan religion, and promotion of religious life
among Indonesians.

The non-political appearance of this program is rather deceptive. It
was necessary because of Government Regulation 111 which Supreme
Court Justice Fromberg, writing in 1914, noted, "absolutely forbids
organizations and meetings of a political character." [9]

Certainly the rapidly expanding organization had interests wider
than its announced program, as speeches made at its early meetings
testify. Thus, the president of the important Semarang branch of
Sarekat Islam stated in March, 1914, before a large meeting there:
" 'The Sarekat Islam already existed in the hearts of the natives before it was established. This is not only a movement of an economic and
moral nature, but means also that the natives seek justice, which
they have never yet found.' " He then pointed out that the Indonesians
did not understand why they were poor, and that to understand the
cause of their poverty, it was necessary for them to be united.[10]

The antithesis between the traditional Indonesian aristocracy and
the interests of the people was emphasized by the movement's leaders
and generally felt by its mounting membership. This feeling was intensified by the strong opposition to Sarekat Islam shown by aristocratic
Indonesian administrative officers of the Dutch regime. They felt that
it attacked their privileges and opposed it as a matter of self-
preservation.[11] Early in 1914, Fromberg observed:

[7] Blumberger, op. cit., pp. 56–57.

[8] Blumberger in Encyc. Nederlandsch-Indie (2nd ed.; The Hague and Leiden, 1919), III, 695.

[9] Fromberg, "De Inlandsche Beweging op Java," op. cit., p. 562.

[10] Ibid., p. 543.   [11] Ibid., p. 554.

One characteristic of the Sarekat Islam movement is that it blames the native government officials for a large part of the misery of the people; in them and the emancipation of the people opposing elements are seen. The non-native is seen making off with the profits of the country, and these native officials are found to be no protectors; people feel themselves repressed and obstructed by the oppressive customary laws; every attempt to raise themselves is frustrated, and the native officials are seen as the star maintainers of these laws.[12]

In this vein Tjokroaminoto referred to the people as "the servants of the regent" [13] and in March, 1914, Raden Achmad, another of the Sarekat Islam leaders, stated:

The people have joined Sarekat Islam en masse because they seek their rights! They have sought them in vain from their legal chiefs [the Indonesian aristocracy]. . . . It is the people that sees its rights continually threatened; that is why there is the great cry for them to unite themselves in order to defend and resist with more power those who rob them of their rights.[14]

Increasingly the outwardly religious emphasis of the organization yielded place to a political one, some leaders frankly acknowledging religion to be principally a means to the political ends sought by the movement. Thus at the Semarang meeting of 1914, Tjokroaminoto openly stated: "Sarekat Islam uses religion as a bond, as a means of cohesion, and the progress which it wants is not going to be hampered by this religion." [15]

The wide basis of support that Sarekat Islam's leaders were bent on developing was already emerging at the beginning of 1914, when Fromberg noted that it was made up of the most heterogeneous elements, "educated young Javanese, religious leaders, merchants, peasants, and laborers." [16] The tremendous growth of the movement and its already apparent ability to attract wide mass support alarmed the government. It does not seem unreasonable to assume, as has Sitorus, that the government's leaders reasoned that a frontal attempt to crush Sarekat Islam might beget a reaction among Indonesians that would be dangerous.[17] Whether or not that was their reasoning, their policy was not one of frontal assault but rather an indirect one based on weakening the movement and attempting to control it through refusal to countenance its organizational integration. It is highly probable that government leaders understood what Fromberg in 1914 credited the leaders of

12 *Ibid.*, p. 557. 13 *Ibid.* 14 *Ibid.*, p. 543. 15 *Ibid.*, p. 545.
16 *Ibid.*, p. 544. 17 Sitorus, *op. cit.*, pp. 15–16.

Sarekat Islam with realizing, that the power of the movement lay "not in disconnected groups, but in united mass; that local organizations which are thrown on their own resources with nothing behind them have every chance of coming under the influence of the conservative Native Administration and thereby being rendered powerless. . . ." [18]

The government's policy found expression in an act of March, 1914, wherein it conferred legal status on the various *branches* of Sarekat Islam only, refusing such status for the organization as a corporate whole.[19] Thereby its central headquarters was cut off from the local branches. Effective central direction of policy and co-ordination of activity were rendered extremely difficult, while control over the activities of any particular branch was made almost impossible. That the immediate effect of this policy was to weaken Sarekat Islam and to decrease whatever threat it may have constituted to the colonial regime there is no doubt. The irony is that its long-term result—one that began to emerge within less than three years—was the development of the movement in a much more radical direction. By undermining the authority of the relatively moderate exponents of Modernist Islamic ideas who preponderated in its central leadership over the constituent branches of Sarekat Islam, the Dutch made it a great deal easier for much more radical elements, basically Communist rather than Islamic in character, to infiltrate and finally capture control of a major number of those branches.

A short-lived attempt to found a political party advocating racial equality, socio-economic justice, and ultimate independence, and based upon Eurasian-Indonesian co-operation was launched in December, 1912, as the Nationale Indische Partij (National Indies party). Its motto was "The Indies for those who make their home there," and in addition to some 1,300 Indonesians it soon attracted about 6,000 Eurasians, particularly those who resented the growing competition of an increased influx of Netherlanders who generally retired to Holland upon ending their careers in the Indies. Within a year's time the party was suppressed, and its leaders—Douwes Dekker, a Eurasian, and Dr. Tjipto Mangoenkoesoemo and Soewardi Soeryaningrat (afterwards known as Ki Hadjar Dewantoro), both Indonesians were exiled, but permitted to go to Holland.[20] Therewith the first and last threat of

---

[18] Fromberg, *op. cit.*, p. 550.   [19] *Ibid.*, pp. 549–550.

[20] D. M. G. Koch, *Om de Vrijheid* (Jakarta, 1950), pp. 30–43; also Sitorus, *op. cit.*, pp. 11–13. The increased radicalness of the party finally manifested itself in an article

Indonesian-Eurasian combination against Dutch rule came to an end.

Most of the Eurasian following of Douwes Dekker then joined Insulinde, a purely Eurasian party, with a relatively moderate program. However, the minority of the Nationale Indische Partij's membership which had already developed an interest in Marxist ideas was attracted, along with a small but growing group of similarly inclined people, mostly Eurasians and Netherlanders, to the new and forceful leadership provided by Hendrik Sneevliet. He was a former member of the Social Democratic Labor Party in the Netherlands who in 1914, shortly after his arrival in the Indies, founded the Indies Social Democratic Association with the help of the Dutch socialists, H. W. Dekker,[21] Bergsma, and Brandsteder. Despite defection of some of its more moderate members, Sneevliet's organization grew rapidly in numbers and in the radicalism of its Marxism. However, it soon became apparent that its European leadership would be able to acquire little Indonesian and, therefore, little mass support. Without such support, Sneevliet realized, a successful revolution aiming at political independence and socialist economic organization could never succeed. Acquisition of this backing necessitated winning Indonesian support for the basic tenets of his revolutionary Marxism. Contact was made with socialistically inclined Indonesian leaders from the Semarang branch of Sarekat Islam who, while remaining active in that organization, joined the Social Democratic Association and became energetic proselytizers in its behalf throughout the ranks of Sarekat Islam. By 1917 a revolutionary current was visible in Sarekat Islam, with Semaoen and Darsono, leaders of its Semarang branch and the ablest of these proselytizers, as its spokesmen.[22]

There was nothing casual in the infiltration of the Sarekat Islam branches by Sneevliet's organization, which, it should be noted, became increasingly influenced by events in Russia. Sneevliet recognized that the rapidly growing mass-based Sarekat Islam was the ideal medium for his group to work through in order to establish contact with and capture support of the Indonesian masses. The government's legislation forcing Sarekat Islam's organizational disintegration made the conditions for infiltration ideal. So successful was the infiltration

---

by Dekker in which he likened twentieth-century Dutch rule in Indonesia to that in the Netherlands under Napoleon.

[21] Not to be confused with Douwes Dekker.

[22] Sitorus, *op. cit.*, p. 23; see also Bernard H. M. Vlekke, *Nusantara, A History of the East Indian Archipelago* (Cambridge, Mass., 1945), p. 339.

by Sneevliet's organization that in 1922, a little over three years after his expulsion from Indonesia, Sneevliet (Maring) as the Comintern's first delegate to China, primarily on the basis of his experience with Sarekat Islam, proposed to the Chinese Communist Central Committee that "the Communists join the Kuomintang and utilize its broad loose organization structure as a means for developing their propaganda and contacts among the masses." According to Sneevliet, Harold Isaacs states, "the majority of the Chinese Central Committee accepted these views." [23]

Under mounting pressure from the growing number of increasingly Marxist-oriented local branches of Sarekat Islam, the organization's central leadership, possessed of no effective means of disciplining such dissident elements, was progressively forced to compromise its original Modernist Islamic tenets in the direction of revolutionary Marxism. The effect of this pressure was noticeable as early as October, 1917, in the program drawn up by its second national congress. This called for independence, as contrasted to the self-government previously demanded, and indicated that if nonviolent efforts to obtain this goal were fruitless, another approach might be necessary. Actually neither this nor the extensive social reforms which the program called for were incompatible with the Modernist Islamic ideas which had given impetus to the organization's genesis and which had at first exerted a preponderating influence upon its leadership.[24] But the explicit condemnation of "sinful capitalism," though by no means diametrically in opposition to these ideas, was undoubtedly prompted by pressure from Communist-dominated branches. It is understandable that the Indonesian merchants who backed the movement and were particularly important because of the financial support which they gave it might well have taken strong exception to this point. It is probable that Tjokroaminoto's public elucidation of the term a short time later was occasioned by their resentment. The explanation which he gave shows

---

[23] Harold R. Isaacs, *The Tragedy of the Chinese Revolution* (London, 1938), p. 61. This information is based on Isaacs' conversation with Sneevliet in 1935. Sneevliet's Comintern name was "Maring." Of the three factors upon which Sneevliet based his proposal, the first, he told Isaacs, was his own experience in Java. He based it secondly on the strategic and tactical conclusions of the Second Congress of the Comintern and thirdly on the fact that connections had already been established between the Kuomintang and the labor movement in south China. (The reasons for the looseness in organization of the Kuomintang and Sarekat Islam were, of course, not identical.)

[24] For an account of the program drawn up by this congress see Blumberger in *Encyc. Nederlandsch-Indie,* pp. 699–700; and Sitorus, *op. cit.,* pp. 17–18.

clearly how he was being forced to straddle basic social issues in order to maintain the support of his original followers, while meeting the minimum demands of the fast-growing Marxist influence in many of the most important local branches. Temporarily Tjokroaminoto resolved this antithesis by describing "sinful capitalism" as foreign capitalism and inferring that Indonesian capitalism was acceptable.

Not only because of the necessity to control its Marxist-oriented branches, but also because it was conscious of the sympathetic response that Marxist slogans were eliciting from urban laborers and the poorer peasants, the central leadership of Sarekat Islam felt impelled to move further towards an espousal of a revolutionary political program and Marxist ideas. Moreover, the widespread revolutionary movements in Europe in 1917–1918, which in the latter year for a moment seemed to threaten even Holland, emboldened the organization's leadership by suggesting to it that traditional political relationships all over the world were being or were about to be overturned.

Thus in the third national congress of Sarekat Islam in October, 1918, where a membership of 450,000 was represented, its potentially revolutionary character and increased socialistic emphasis were clearly apparent. Despite this and Tjokroaminoto's statement that if the government did not speedily undertake wide social reforms Sarekat Islam would do so by itself, the powerful Marxist faction led by Semaoen was far from satisfied. In the first sessions of the newly established Volksraad (People's Council) in May, 1918, the Sarekat Islam representation voiced strong criticism of the government. At its second meeting in December, 1918, Cramer, a Dutch socialist, organized the "Radical Concentration," which included his own moderate socialist organization, Sarekat Islam, the Indies Social Democratic Association, Insulinde, and even Boedi Oetomo. This coalition displayed a strongly critical attitude toward the government,[25] culminating in a revolutionary speech by a Eurasian of the Insulinde party. A few days later the Governor-General learned by cable of the heightened revolutionary disturbances in Europe and their threatened spread to the Netherlands. Thoroughly alarmed, he appeared before the Volksraad and made far-reaching promises for rapid and extensive reforms in the structure of the Netherlands Indies government. The apparent weakness and willingness to appease displayed by the government at this time of crisis

[25] Among other things the Radical Concentration demanded a responsible parliamentary government for Indonesia based on elections. See Blumberger in *Encyc. Nederlandsch-Indie*, p. 702.

strongly impressed Indonesian leaders and emboldened them to embark upon more extreme nationalistic programs.

Sneevliet was arrested by the government and forced to leave Indonesia in December, 1918, but this did not retard the process of infiltration of Indonesian members of the Social Democratic Association into positions of leadership in local branches of Sarekat Islam. Despite the growing strength of these elements, they were unable to get control of the Fourth Congress of Sarekat Islam, held in 1919, by which time the organization's total membership had reached almost two and a half million. Following the central leadership of Sarekat Islam's refusal at this congress to accept the extreme proposals of Semaoen's faction, he and the other leaders of the Social Democratic Association undertook to convert their organization into the Communist Party of the Indies (Perserikaten Kommunist di India), or PKI, as it was generally known. In this new party launched at the Semarang office of Sarekat Islam on May 23, 1920, Semaoen was elected as president, Darsono as vice-president, Bergsma as secretary, and H. W. Dekker as treasurer.[26]

The new party developed a close relationship with the Comintern, joining that organization at the end of 1920. Sneevliet, who had undertaken on his own to represent Indonesia at the Second Congress of the Comintern (summer of 1920), later established contact with the Indonesian party via Shanghai,[27] and in 1921 Darsono went to Moscow to represent Indonesia at the Third Congress.[28] Tan Malaka, one of the party's top leaders, represented Indonesia at the Fourth Congress in the subsequent year and took an active part in framing its policies.[29] In August, 1923, Semaoen was arrested and forced to leave the country or face exile to Timor, and by the end of the year all Dutch leaders of the party had also been forced to leave. According to Semaoen, the departure of the Dutch leaders from the party "raised the prestige of the party in the eyes of the masses" because of existing prejudice against the Dutch, whatever their attitude towards colonialism.[30] Certainly thereafter during the 1920's there was little rapport with the Communist Party in the Netherlands. Indonesian Communists looked

---

[26] Sitorus, *op. cit.*, p. 25; Blumberger, *Le Communisme aux Indes Néerlandaises* (Paris, 1929), p. 18. In the meantime the Social Democratic Labor party in the Netherlands had changed its name to the "Netherlands Communist party" and in 1919 joined the Comintern.

[27] Blumberger, *op. cit.*, pp. 23, 17.   [28] Sitorus, *op. cit.*, p. 26.

[29] Blumberger, *op. cit.*, pp. 27–28.

[30] Samin (Semaoen) "The Situation in Indonesia," Co-report to the 6th Congress of the Comintern (30th Session, Aug. 15, 1928), *International Press Correspondence*, VIII, No. 68 (Oct. 4, 1928), 1245.

to the Comintern for guidance but not to the Netherlands Communist Party. Indeed at the Fifth Congress of the Comintern in 1924, Semaoen bluntly indicated that the Netherlands Communist party was more of a liability than an asset to the Indonesian Communists.[31]

In the meantime the central leadership of Sarekat Islam undertook an increasingly active policy and for a time kept the initiative in its struggle with the Semaoen faction. Its leaders, Abdoel Moeis in particular, made violent attacks against the government which stirred up the population and at one place, Toli Toli in the Celebes, in the middle of 1919 led to a short insurrection. Shortly thereafter a local Sarekat Islam leader in Tjimareme, West Java, acting on his own authority, led a small insurrection against the government in protest against its collection of rice.[32]

Considerable success had been encountered in organizing labor unions, and at the end of December, 1919, the Sarekat Islam's central leadership managed to unite twenty-two Indonesian trade unions, totaling 77,000 members, under one of its leaders, R. M. Soerjopranoto. Semaoen's group immediately attempted to get control of this organization, the Trade Union Central (Pergeraken Kaoem Boeroeh).[33] At its first congress in August, 1920, Semaoen was elected chairman; Soerjopranoto, vice-chairman; and Hadji Agoes Salim, a young and able leader of Tjokroaminoto's group, secretary.[34] It was particularly due to the efforts of Salim that Semaoen and his faction were unable to wrest control of the organization from Sarekat Islam's central leadership.[35] Defeated in this effort, in June of the next year Semaoen was successful in setting up a rival association of trade unions, the "Revolutionary Trade Union Central," and in the process was able to detach considerable strength from the older organization.[36]

The increasingly bitter struggle between the central leadership of Sarekat Islam and the Communists for control of the organization's branches and the growing Indonesian trade union movement, in conjunction with their differences over questions such as class warfare

[31] Ve Congrès de L'Internationale Communiste (17 Juin–8 Juillet 1924), Compte Rendu Analytique (Paris, 1924), p. 117.

[32] Sitorus, op. cit., p. 19. [33] Literally "Worker's Movement."

[34] Blumberger in Encyc. Nederlandsch-Indie, supp. no. 31 (June, 1932), pp. 961–962.

[35] According to the Communists: "It is true that up to 1921 the Sarekat Islam was the only political movement which was giving a revolutionary lead to the trade unions" (Musso, "The National Parties and the Worker's Organizations in Indonesia," International Press Correspondence, IX, No. 27 (June 7, 1929), 588).

[36] Blumberger in op. cit., p. 962; Koch, op. cit., p. 64.

and religion, made a formal rupture between them inevitable. At the Sixth National Congress of Sarekat Islam in October, 1921, the struggle came to a head. Here the offensive was taken by Hadji Agoes Salim, who introduced a motion backed by Abdoel Moeis calling for party discipline and requiring that no member of Sarekat Islam could at the same time hold membership in any other party. A bitter debate followed wherein Semaoen and Tan Malaka, leading the opposition to the motion, sought to ridicule the central leadership's refusal to recognize the class struggle and accused it of being capitalist and anti-socialist. After a spirited answer by Hadji Salim, in which he maintained that Mohammed had preached socialist economics twelve centuries before Marx was born, a vote was taken with a large majority of delegates favoring party discipline. Thereupon the Communists present resigned, and with that the Communist-controlled branches of Semarang and its vicinity seceded.

The intense struggle that followed for control of the local branches of Sarekat Islam was disastrous for the nationalist movement, destroying most of its peasant-based organization. The Communists within four years managed to get control of a probable majority of the branches, but in the course of the struggle most of the large peasant membership of these branches melted away. This probably was due principally to two reasons: (1) the government's increasingly effective barring of contact between the leaders (both non-Communist and Communist) and the peasantry, and (2) the fact that religion became a principal issue in the struggle, with the Communists alienating peasant members by violating their religious sensitivities, or at least those of their influential religious leaders. By 1926 the Communists had apparently realized the seriousness of this mistake and changed their tactics, but the damage had been done and they were unable to live down the charge of being anti-religious.

In order to win control of the Sarekat Islam branches the Communists, who had already heavily infiltrated many of them, at their congress of December 25, 1921 at Semarang decided to set up a Red Sarekat Islam headquarters to compete with the original central leadership of Tjokroaminoto, Salim, and Abdoel Moeis.[37] At the beginning of 1922, during Semaoen's and Darsono's absence in Moscow, Tan Malaka took the initiative in attempting to develop a strike of government pawnshop employees into a general strike embracing all Indonesian labor. The Revolutionary Trade Union Central called upon

[37] Blumberger, *De Nationalistische Beweging in Nederlandsch-Indie*, p. 35.

all workers to go on a sympathy strike but was not successful, and Tan Malaka, arrested by the government and given the choice of exile or leaving Indonesia, left for Russia. During the attempted general strike Semaoen had been in Moscow attending a Far Eastern labor conference. He returned after a visit of seven months on May 22, 1922, and devoted his attention to centralizing the leadership of all Indonesian labor organizations into the hands of his group. On September 3, 1922, at a general meeting of Indonesian labor organizations at Madiun he was successful in pulling the member unions of the Trade Union Central away from the control of its leaders into a new all-embracing union known as Persatoean Vakbonden Hindia (Union of Indian Labor Unions) in which the Communist party leaders were dominant.[38]

This coup and the continued growth of Communist influence in the local branches of Sarekat Islam brought its leaders in February, 1923, to attempt to extend party discipline to all the constituent parts of the organization. In retaliation the Communists at their March congress decided to establish sections of the Red Sarekat Islam wherever there was a branch of Sarekat Islam, recruiting their members from these branches. The name for these now Communist-controlled units was changed to Sarekat Rakjat (People's Association) and they were conceived of as "the foundation of the Communist Party in the masses." [39]

The Fifth Congress of the Comintern (June–July, 1924) emphasized that the top priority of Communist parties was to gain control of the trade union movement without which, it held, revolution could not be successful. This thesis was underscored by the Pan-Pacific Labor Conference held under Comintern auspices at Canton in June, 1924, and attended by two important Indonesian Communist leaders, Alimin and Boedisoetjitro. The response of the Indonesian Communist Party to this directive was so complete and so extreme as to very nearly demolish its base of peasant support. Despite the fact that at its previous meeting, the peasantry had been recognized as the party's indispensable mass base, Aliarcham, its secretary, at its meeting of December, 1924, introduced a resolution calling for the dissolution of the Sarekat Rakjats and their replacement by trade unions as the party's mass base. The Sarekat Rakjats, he argued, contained too many bourgeois nationalists who could not be counted upon in times of violent action. Aliarcham's proposition was strongly attacked and finally a compromise

[38] Blumberger in *Encyc. Nederlandsch-Indie*, p. 962; Sitorus, *op. cit.,* p. 27.

[39] Sitorus, *op. cit.,* pp. 38–42; See also P. Bergsma, "A Letter from the Dutch East Indies," *International Press Correspondence* (hereinafter cited as *Inprecor*), III, no. 62 (Sept. 27, 1923), 699.

solution emerged. The dissolution of the Sarekat Rakjats was accepted in principle, but the process of dissolution was to be carried out gradually so as to avoid enfeebling the PKI (Indonesian Communist Party). While neglecting the Sarekat Rakjats, the Communists were to concentrate their forces on the trade union movement. In addition it was agreed that the cadres of the PKI had to be disciplined and their quality improved so that they would be able to undertake effective revolutionary action.[40] Finally the program drawn up demanded the establishment of a Soviet Republic of Indonesia.[41]

During the course of 1925 the activity of the PKI among the trade unions increased greatly both in scope and aggressiveness. Control was gained over a greater number of unions, and frequent strikes were called.[42] Though Sarekat Islam leaders had tried to bring about nationalist solidarity early in 1924 at a joint meeting with the PKI and Boedi Oetomo,[43] the Communists appeared not to wish *rapprochement* with the "bourgeois nationalists." Substantial co-operation was effected by the PKI with Communists among the Chinese laboring community,[44] but in general the social base of the Communist movement shrank greatly during 1925. It forfeited a large proportion of its peasant associate-membership by turning its back on the Sarekat Rakjats and it lost all rapport with the "bourgeois national revolutionists" of Sarekat Islam, Boedi Oetomo, etc.

The leadership of the Comintern, particularly the leaders of Soviet Russia, had taken a particular interest in Indonesia [45] and were disturbed at the failure of Indonesian Communists to follow the orthodox interpretation of the 1924 Comintern directives. Stalin, speaking at the end of May, 1925, accused the Indonesian Communists of Leftist deviation consisting in:

overrating the revolutionary potentialities of the liberation movement and in underrating the importance of an alliance between the working class and the

[40] Blumberger, *op. cit.*, pp. 54–56; See also official report of Jan., 1927, of the N.E.I. government on the Communist disturbances to the Volksraad in *Annuaire de Documentation Coloniale Comparée* (Brussels, 1928), pp. 181–183.

[41] Semaoen, *op. cit.*, p. 1246.

[42] Sitorus, *op. cit.*, p. 30; Blumberger in *Encyc. Nederlandsch-Indie*, p. 963.

[43] Blumberger in *Encyc. Nederlandsch-Indie*, p. 945.

[44] See Semaoen, "International Imperialism and the Communist Party in Indonesia," *Communist International* (organ of the Executive Committee of the Comintern), (Leningrad and London), no. 17 (1926), p. 81.

[45] Bukharin at a meeting of the Executive Committee of the Comintern, Nov. 22, 1926, described Indonesia as "the bridge between Europe and Asia," *Inprecor*, VI, no. 63 (Dec. 1, 1926).

revolutionary bourgeoisie against imperialism. The Communists in Java, who recently erroneously put forward the slogan of a Soviet government for their country, suffer, it seems from this deviation. That is a deviation to the Left, which threatens to isolate the Communist Party from the masses and to transform it into a sect. A determined struggle against this deviation is an essential condition for the training of really revolutionary cadres for the colonies and dependent countries of the East.[46]

The Executive Committee of the Comintern in its plenary session of March, 1925, specifically called upon the Communists in Indonesia to form a united anti-imperialist front with the non-Communist Indonesian nationalist organizations and to utilize the Sarekat Rakjats as an independent national-revolutionary organization linked up with the wide masses.[47] A spokesman for the Comintern noted some six months later that despite growing pressure from the rank and file of non-Communist nationalist organizations for a united front against the Dutch and the efforts of Tjokroaminoto in the summer of 1925 to start negotiations with the PKI leaders for such a bloc, the negotiations had led to no results. He went on to say:

Our Java comrades have not sufficiently reacted to this process. The Communist press devotes too little attention to the idea of a united front and to a platform on which all the national-revolutionary elements could be united. Methods of approach to those masses still under the influence of the reformist leaders have not yet been worked out. . . . The Indonesian Communist Party despite all its activity has not yet got properly down to working among the peasantry and drawing the latter into the nationalist movement. The errors of the Indonesian comrades with respect to the national organizations are repeated with regard to the peasantry. The resolutions of the last Plenum of the ECCI [Executive Committee of the Communist International] . . . have not yet been put into force. If the Party does not adopt a correct policy towards the peasantry in time, the political movement of the latter will pass by the Party, as is to be observed to a certain extent in respect to the radical nationalist elements. Only a complete and unconditional enforcement of the resolution of the March Plenum of the ECCI can put an end to the isolated position of the Party and make it an indomitable mainstay around which all the active anti-imperialist forces of the Indonesian people will rally.[48]

Probably this advice from Moscow was received too late for the Indonesian Communists to reverse the line of action that they embarked

[46] Joseph Stalin, *Marxism and the National and Colonial Question* (Moscow, 1940), p. 192.
[47] "X," "The Revolutionary Movement in the East," *Communist International* (Leningrad and London), no. 18–19 (1926), pp. 113–115.
[48] *Ibid.*

on. Had these directives arrived in time, it is likely that they would have followed them, because their leaders were split over what course of action they should take.

During the course of 1925 the more extreme elements within the Indonesian Communist Party came under the control of Dahlan and Soekra, leaders who refused to take orders from the regular party leadership. They continually agitated for revolution and resorted to terroristic methods in order to dominate the party. In their efforts they were backed by two of the important established party leaders, Alimin and Musso. This group was able to dominate a decisive meeting of the Executive Committee of the party and the leaders of the principal Communist-controlled trade unions held at the temple of Prambanan (between Jogjakarta and Surakarta) in mid-October, 1925.[49] As a result revolution was decided upon. A strike by the railroad workers was to be the signal for a general strike which was in turn to develop into the revolution in which Dutch power was to be overthrown and replaced by that of the Communist Party.[50] For the revolution to be a success it was felt necessary to have the support of Moscow [51] and of the prominent Indonesian Communist leaders forced to remain outside of Indonesia. Of these the support of Tan Malaka—the Comintern's agent for Southeast Asia and Australia [52]—was felt to be particularly essential. To ask for Moscow's support without his backing would be awkward, it was realized. In order to have time to mobilize this support and to make the necessary preparations in Indonesia, the date for the revolution was set for June 18, 1926.[53]

The activities of the Communists during the interim period, how-

[49] This information is based primarily upon conversations of the author during 1948–49 with several prominent contemporary Indonesian nationalists.

[50] It is interesting to note that according to the government's report, Alimin had suggested approximately this same pattern of revolution at a secret meeting of the PKI held at Jogjakarta on June 27, 1925 (*Annuaire de Documentation Coloniale Comparée*, 1927, p. 190).

[51] It is unclear whether the support sought was financial as well as moral. Blumberger and the government report cited in the above-mentioned *Annuaire* assert that both were sought.

[52] According to Tan Malaka this position was given him at the 4th Congress of the Comintern in 1922, to take effect in 1923 (Tan Malaka, *Thesis*, in Indonesian [Jakarta, 1947], pp. 39–41, 59–60). Alimin in his bitter attack on Tan Malaka does not dispute this claim and by implication clearly substantiates it. He does, however, maintain that Tan Malaka did not possess a power of veto over decisions taken by the PKI (Alimin, *Analysis*, in Indonesian [Jogjakarta, 1947], pp. 3, 16–17, 28).

[53] See Tan Malaka, *op. cit.*, p. 38; see also Mauawar, "Report to 34th Session, 6th Congress of the Comintern, Moscow, Aug. 17, 1928," *Inprecor*, VIII, no. 72 (Oct. 17, 1928), 1325. Mauawar gives the date as July, 1926.

ever, did not develop as had been planned. On November 28, 1925, the government—possibly as a reaction to the mounting number of small strikes and increasing violence carried out by small armed bands and possibly because of knowledge of long-range Communist plans, or both—suspended the right of assembly throughout nearly all of Indonesia for the Communist Party, the Sarekat Rakjat, and most of the Communist-controlled labor organizations. As was undoubtedly intended, this action served to impede effective contact between the Communists and the labor unions. As a result, the strategic sequence of strikes that the Communists had planned at Prambanan did not go off as scheduled. The major strikes of workers in metallurgical concerns and dock workers broke out in Surabaya in the middle of December, 1925, six months ahead of schedule.[54] In the suppression of these strikes the government cracked down hard, arresting most of the important labor leaders concerned in addition to three of the few remaining top Communist leaders still in Indonesia, Darsono, Aliarcham and Mardjoha.[55]

The events that followed should be observed in some detail, for they help to explain not only the failure of the Communist revolutionary effort but also the development of the great schism in the ranks of Indonesian Communists that has existed ever since. Tan Malaka had been opposed to the drift of events in Indonesia beginning with the decision taken at the PKI Congress of December, 1924, calling for the dissolution of the Sarekat Rakjat.[56] Referring to the Prambanan decision, he stated:

I heard of this decision in Manila towards the end of March [1926]. I was invited to come to Singapore, but not for the purpose of discussing *whether or not the PKI was ready* to lead the revolution against the Dutch or *how* to lead that revolution. I was invited to come to Singapore in order to proceed to Moscow with Musso. There we were to ask for approval and moral assistance, since the decision made at Prambanan was against the regulations of the Comintern.[57]

Tan Malaka was strongly opposed to the Prambanan decision and refused to come to Singapore, probably because he knew that the peo-

[54] See *Annuaire de Documentation Coloniale Comparée*, 1927, p. 190; Mauawar, *op. cit.*, p. 1324. The Communists considered Surabaya to be the key industrial area for all Indonesia.

[55] Blumberger, *Le Communisme aux Indes Néerlandaises*, p. 61. Darsono was soon thereafter allowed to leave Indonesia. Alimin had escaped to Singapore before the others were arrested.

[56] Tan Malaka, *op. cit.*, p. 47.   [57] *Ibid.*, p. 38 (italics are Tan Malaka's).

ple assembled there would outvote him and his supporters and that according to the formula of "democratic centralism" he would be called upon to abide by their decision.[58] Alimin was then sent by the Communists assembled at Singapore to see him in Manila. Tan Malaka refused to sanction the plans for revolution and maintained that anyway the decision had to be made in Moscow in consultation with the Comintern. Finally he gave Alimin a document stating his reasons against the Prambanan decision to be communicated to the group in Singapore and the PKI leadership on Java and Sumatra. Alimin did not deliver this document to the group at Singapore and apparently led them to believe that Tan Malaka felt as he and Musso did. The group then voted to support the Prambanan decision, and Alimin and Musso were delegated to proceed to Moscow to ask its clearance and support for the revolution.[59]

Shortly after their departure Tan Malaka arrived in Singapore, where he persuaded at least two of the Communist leaders there, Subakat and Djamaludin Tamin, that conditions were not favorable for a revolution. Tamin was given a copy of the memorandum previously given to Alimin and immediately left for Indonesia. With this he traveled through Java and Sumatra contacting most of the local PKI leaders, many of whom he was able to dissuade from backing the projected revolution. Tamin's final efforts must have been considerably aided by the circulation of the booklet written by Tan Malaka in the middle of 1926, and printed in Singapore a few months before the revolution broke out in Java. This booklet, *Massa Actie,* incorporated the points made in his memorandum. In it he argued that a successful revolution demanded mass support. A *Putsch* by leaders divorced from the masses would never succeed, he warned. If indeed the Communist leaders possessed the necessary mass support, they had already let pass the psychological and practical moment for revolt, he said. That should have occurred, he maintained, immediately upon the Dutch arrests of PKI and labor leaders and the suspension of the right of assembly at the end of 1925.[60] He concluded by questioning whether the PKI had sufficient mass backing and "whether Marxist education had been correctly and sufficiently given so that our workers

[58] This interpretation is held by several prominent nationalist leaders and was communicated by them to the writer.

[59] See Tan Malaka, *op. cit.,* pp. 39–40; *Annuaire de Documentation Coloniale Comparée,* 1927, p. 195; Blumberger, *op. cit.,* p. 73.

[60] Tan Malaka, *Massa Actie* (Djakarta, 1947; reprint of 1926 Singapore ed.), esp. pp. 45–50, 56, 61.

have Marxist stability and Leninist elasticity." If this were not the case, as the preceding pages of his booklet had indicated, he foresaw:

. . . chaos in the whole revolutionary movement in Indonesia. Non-workers *will take the helm and lead the party to a Putsch or to anarchism, and ulti-mately it will be completely destroyed.* This danger becomes greater and greater as the great revolutionary leaders who have influence over the masses are exiled from Indonesia one after the other. . . .[61]

Alimin and Musso arrived in Malaya in the middle of December, 1926, having returned from Moscow via Canton. On December 18th they were arrested by the British at Johore; neither returned to Indo-nesia.[62] Whatever the reaction of Moscow to their proposals, they have never made it public. Not only does the published advice of Russian and Comintern leaders to Indonesian Communists in the months pre-ceding Alimin and Musso's arrival in Moscow suggest that the reaction was negative, but Alimin's silence as to their attitude when he is de-fending himself and attacking Tan Malaka also tends to support such a conclusion.[63]

The Communist Party was forced to operate more and more under-ground while deprived of its ablest leaders. Its activities became less and less co-ordinated, with the extremist leaders who had dominated the Prambanan conference managing to maintain their ascendancy in much of Java despite the anti-revolutionary proselytizing of Tamin.[64] During the first ten months of 1926 more and more of the Communist leaders were arrested. Intra-organizational contact was progressively disrupted as was attested by unco-ordinated sporadic outbreaks of violence at widely isolated places throughout Java. The accelerating disintegration of the Communist Party organization was accom-panied by a rapid loss of contact with former peasant supporters, many of whom were in any case being alienated by the policies of the inferior Communist leadership in Indonesia. The Communists post-poned the date of the revolution, and not until the night of November 12, 1926, did it break out. The disorganization then existing within

[61] *Ibid.,* p. 63 (italics are Tan Malaka's).

[62] See *Annuaire de Documentation Coloniale Comparée,* 1927, p. 191. They accuse Tan Malaka of having tipped off the British as to their arrival.

[63] See Alimin, *op. cit.* It bears the inscription: "This pamphlet is distributed after passing the Censor Department of the Agitation-Propaganda Branch of the Central Committee of the Indonesian Communist Party, Jakarta, April, 1947."

[64] In Sumatra Tamin was much more successful, managing to influence all but the Communist sections of the West Coast Residency against supporting a revolu-tion.

the party is demonstrated by the fact that though plans for the revolution called for its breaking out first in Padang on Sumatra's West Coast, actually it broke out first in Batavia, with the uprising in the Padang area coming a full two months later and after the insurrection in Java had been completely crushed.

At the end of December, 1924, there were 36 sections of the PKI with 1,140 members and 340 sections of Sarekat Rakjat totaling 31,124 members. The following year PKI membership was increased to 3,000 based on 65 sections.[65] Given the policy of gradual dissolution of the Sarekat Rakjats, it is reasonable to assume that their membership had not increased above the 1924 figure. Therefore, probably the most that the Communists could count on in their revolution were some 3,000 party members, and a mass base of no more than 31,000 peasants and a somewhat smaller number of urban laborers. As a result of the progressive weakening of the party and Communist-controlled organizations during the course of 1926, it might be expected that the actual numbers participating in the rebellion was much less, and that was certainly the case. It is unlikely that more than 5,000 persons were actively involved in either the Java uprising or the later one on the West Coast of Sumatra.[66] Only in Bantam (West Java) and in the West Coast Residency of Sumatra were the Communists able to rely on a measure of support from the local peasantry. There the fighting lasted for a few weeks, but elsewhere the undermanned Communist bid for power was suppressed within a day or two. As Semaoen himself admitted, "The masses of the workers in the cities, as well as on the plantations, adopted an attitude of indifference towards the rebel movement." [67]

To what extent the failure of the Communist rebellion is to be attributed to the efforts of Tan Malaka and Tamin, it is difficult to gauge. It seems likely that but for their work the Communist effort on Java might have been more widespread and somewhat more powerful and that on Sumatra it would not have been restricted to the West Coast district alone, but would have embraced a number of other

[65] See *Annuaire de Documentation Coloniale Comparée*, 1927, p. 200; Blumberger, *op. cit.*, p. 79.

[66] The figures given by Semaoen in his report before the Comintern of PKI and Sarekat Rakjat membership on the eve of the rebellion (9,000 and 100,000 respectively) are clearly exaggerated (Semaoen, "The Situation in Indonesia," Co-Report before 30th Session of the Comintern, Aug. 15, 1928, *Inprecor*, VIII, no. 68 [Oct. 4, 1928], 1246).

[67] *Ibid.*

areas on that island including the plantation district of the East Coast, a center of considerable Communist strength. Though their work undoubtedly did substantially weaken the revolutionary effort, it is probable that the above-mentioned government action against the Communists was at least of equal importance in undermining their strength, and on Java, at any rate, of considerably greater importance. Even had the whole of the Communist organization backed the rebellion the government would probably have had little trouble in suppressing it.

But it is Tan Malaka and his associates that the Communists who backed the rebellion blame as the chief cause of its failure, and it is he who has become their principal scapegoat. The charge by Musso, Alimin, and other members of the present-day PKI leadership that Tan Malaka is a Trotskyist has generally been represented by them to be based upon his refusal to accept the Prambanan decision, his efforts to stop the rebellion, and the fact that shortly after the end of the rebellion he established a new party, which they maintain was completely outside the Communist fold.[68] Probably, however, their attitude was also moulded by another event, one which they appear never to have made public. This was Tan Malaka's stand at the sixth meeting of the Comintern in August, 1928. In a speech there he made a vigorous attack against Bukharin and the program which the latter was attempting to pilot through. He maintained that this program ignored the experience of the Communist Party in China and that it called for an alliance between the native bourgeoisie and the Communists in the colonies which would result in the same victory of the bourgeoisie and destruction of the Communists as had just happened in China. In the course of what appeared to be a rather ineffective reply to Tan Malaka's attack, Bukharin called him a "Trotskyist." [69]

Tan Malaka's new organization, Pari (Partai Repoeblik Indonesia —Indonesian Republic Party), was established by him and his two lieutenants, Tamin and Subakat, in Bangkok in 1927. Pari's immediate objective was the training of Indonesian underground workers in Bangkok who were to return to Indonesia and there train additional members and build up underground cadres. Its long-term objective was the building up of a co-ordinated proletarian movement in "Aslia"

---

[68] For an account of the usual Trotskyist charge see Alimin, *op. cit.*, pp. 18–21; and Ir. Sakirman, *Menindjau Perdjoeangan PARI*, (Jakarta, 1946?) pp. 9–11, 29–30.

[69] Report on sessions 26, 28 and 29 of the 6th Comintern Conference, Aug. 13, 14, 1928, *Inprecor*, Oct. 4, 1928.

(Southeast Asia and Australia). Tan Malaka envisaged an eventual fusion of eight regional Communist federations: Aslia, West-Europe, Russia, India-Iran, Africa, China, North America, and South America. Possibly the fact that Tan Malaka had been appointed Comintern agent for Southeast Asia and Australia had something to do with this idea. There is no evidence to indicate that anything concrete was ever done towards the attainment of this objective. Tamin, however, did make some progress towards building up an underground in Indonesia. Though the membership of this underground was never large, its leadership in Java, eventually headed by Adam Malik and Sukarni, was a capable one and, while attaining influential positions in legal youth organizations, usually managed to keep clear of Dutch suspicion.

With the failure of the 1926–1927 rebellions, the Communists' organization was crushed, and the large majority of Communist leaders still in the Indies were arrested and deported to the concentration camp of Tanah Merah in New Guinea. Altogether some 13,000 people were arrested. Of these, 4,500 were given prison sentences and 1,308 were interned, 823 being sent to Tanah Merah. The remainder of the 13,000 were soon released.[70] Amongst those interned, the government is alleged to have included a number of nationalist political and labor leaders who were not Communists and who had nothing to do with the rebellion.[71] After these arrests the power of the Communists was broken for the remainder of the period of Dutch rule.

In 1928 a relatively weak comeback was developed by a group of Surabaya Communists who had lain low during the rebellion. In July, 1928, under the leadership of Soenarjo and Marsoeki, a close acquaintance of Musso, they established a small labor union federation, Sarekat Kaoem Boeroeh Indonesia. Its plan of operation was to infiltrate the various unions with its own cells which would eventually come to control them. After reaching a select and disciplined membership of some seven hundred and after a year's existence, the organization was dissolved by the government and its leaders arrested.[72] In April, 1935, Musso managed to re-enter Indonesia, remaining nearly a year in the

---

[70] J. Th. Petrus Blumberger, *De Communistische Beweging in Nederlandsch-Indie* (Haarlem, 1935), p. 111. This second and revised edition of Blumberger's work has new material not to be found in the earlier and previously cited French edition.

[71] This allegation has been made by several Dutch officials as well as by Indonesians.

[72] Blumberger in *Encyc. Nederlandsch-Indie;* p. 964; see also Musso, "The Independent Trade Union of Indonesia and its Suppression," *Inprecor,* IX, no. 61 (Oct. 25, 1929), 1322.

Surabaya area before leaving again for Russia. Here he built up what was to become the chief Stalinist-oriented Communist underground, the so-called "Illegal Indonesian Communist Party." Aspirant probationary members were organized into a closely associated organization, the Partai Komunis Moeda (Young Communist Party). It is probable that the unjailed membership of the Sarekat Kaoem Boeroeh Indonesia provided much of the nucleus of Musso's organization.[73] Both Musso's and Tan Malaka's undergrounds were, however, relatively weak, and the center of the stage in the nationalist struggle during the remainder of the period of Dutch rule was held by non-Communist leaders and their organizations.

The bitter struggle between Sarekat Islam and the Communists and later the sharp reaction by the government to the Communist rebellion convinced many strongly Moslem nationalists formerly associated with Sarekat Islam that work towards their socio-religious and national ideals could be better carried on through nonpolitical channels. Thus a large portion of the membership of Sarekat Islam that did not follow the Communists streamed into the Mohammadijah,[74] an organization founded in 1912 at Jogjakarta by Kiaji Hadji Ahmad Dahlan, a believer in Modernist Islamic ideas. Originally devoted largely to education, the organization broadened its activities to include a wide range of social services: free clinics, poor relief, orphanages, publishing of the Koran in Javanese and Malay, libraries, etc., as well as Moslem schools. It conceived itself essentially as a propagator of Moslem culture and the nonpolitical ideas of the Modernist movement. The organization, itself, undertook no political activity, leaving such activity to its members on an individual basis.[75] As Bousquet observed: "It would be very wrong, however, to suppose from this its members entertain no political bias. Indeed, it would not be wholly incorrect to say that they are quite as anti-Dutch as other nationalists, Moslem or otherwise." [76] Actually the progressive Moslem social concepts which it sought to advance could not be divested of political overtones. The Mohammadijah could not help but develop the political consciousness

[73] Musso's general whereabouts was known by the Dutch, but they were never able to catch him.

[74] Also spelled "Moehammedyah" and "Muhammadijah."

[75] Blumberger in *Encyc. Nederlandsch-Indie* (supp. 29: The Hague, 1931), pp. 914–915; G. H. Bousquet, *A French View of the Netherlands Indies*, pp. 2–5; Koch, *op. cit.*, pp. 96–97.

[76] Bousquet, *op. cit.*, p. 5.

of its members and of the pupils taught in its many schools. It was a still, but deep, tributary of the stream of political nationalism and quietly but sustainedly nourished and strengthened that stream.

Performing a roughly similar function was the Taman Siswa movement established in 1921 at Jogjakarta by R. M. Soewardi Soeryaningrat (Ki Hadjar Dewantoro) shortly after he returned from the exile consequent upon his earlier nationalist activities. His aim was to develop an educational system based upon a realistic synthesis of Indonesian and Western culture which would train Indonesian youth in self-reliance and develop in them a competence to meet the practical problems which they faced. Though the teaching of politics was expressly forbidden, teachers in the more than 200 Taman Siswa schools being forbidden to hold membership in a political party,[77] there is no doubt that these schools were extremely important in developing a nationalist mentality among the youth. It is no accident that so large a proportion of their graduates became active participants and leaders in the various political nationalist organizations.

Of greatest importance in determining the character of the Indonesian nationalist movement in the years following the Communist rebellion was the Perhimpoenan Indonesia (Indonesian Union). This essentially political organization of Indonesian students studying in Holland was formed there in 1922 from the ranks of a previous but less political organization. Its ideas and policies came to play a dominant role in the development of nationalism in Indonesia, and the majority of top nationalist leaders after 1927 were men who had been active in this organization in Holland. By 1923 its program stood for unequivocal independence for Indonesia to be attained by the unified efforts of all Indonesian groups and classes on the basis of noncooperation with the Dutch.[78] The Marxist orientation of most of its members was strong, but the large majority did not become doctrinaire Marxists. Support from and association with all anticolonial groups and organizations was sought, whether they were Communist or not.

Only a small proportion of the membership of the Perhimpoenan Indonesia finally emerged as members of the Communist Party. Among these were Setiadjit, Abdulmadjid, Suripno, and Maruto Darusman none of whom returned to Indonesia until 1946. After Hatta's de-

[77] See S. Mangoensarkoro, "De Taman Siswa Beweging," *Koloniale Studien*, June, 1937, pp. 287–296.

[78] See Sitorus, *op. cit.*, pp. 34–39; Blumberger in *Encyc. Nederlandsch-Indie*, supp. 29, pp. 898–899; Koch, *op. cit.*, pp. 100–101.

parture for Indonesia late in 1932, the organization came increasingly under the control of Setiadjit and Abdulmadjid. Though they never acknowledged their Communist affiliation until 1948, they succeeded after 1936 in changing the policy of the Perhimpoenan Indonesia, in line with Comintern policy, to one of co-operation with the Dutch. Symbolic of the dropping of the demand for full independence was their change of the name of the organization's official publication, *Indonesia Merdeka* (Free Indonesia) to *Indonesia*. Under Setiadjit and Abdulmadjid the organization strongly attacked the policies in Indonesia of Hatta and Sjahrir as well as those of Soekarno.

Semaoen and Tan Malaka established contact with the Perhimpoenan Indonesia and, though undoubtedly influencing some of its members, by no means dominated it. On December 5, 1926, Mohammad Hatta, leader of the Perhimpoenan Indonesia, signed a united front convention with Semaoen, as representative of the Indonesian Communist Party. According to this the Perhimpoenan Indonesia was to assume top leadership and full responsibility for the nationalist movement in Indonesia and the PKI and its subordinate organizations would refrain from any opposition to the Perhimpoenan Indonesia's leadership so long as it consistently continued to follow the policy of independence for Indonesia. A year later, however, on December 19, 1927, Semaoen felt obliged to repudiate the agreement and formally recant, saying that when he signed it he had not been in contact with either the Indonesian Communist Party or the Comintern. He had made a mistake, he stated, and after careful study of the agreement "in the light of Communist principles on the one hand and of events in Indonesia on the other" it was clear to him that to carry on with it would mean "the liquidation of the independence and leading role of the Communist Party." [79] This broke the bond between the socialistically inclined revolutionary nationalists of the Perhimpoenan Indonesia and the Communists. The bond between the organization and the League Against Imperialism (*Liga*) was dissolved in the summer of 1929, when the Perhimpoenan Indonesia delegates followed other socialists in resigning from that increasingly Comintern-dominated body.[80]

The ideas of the PI (Perhimpoenan Indonesia) affected the course of the Indonesian nationalist movement via the return of its members

[79] Blumberger, *De Communistische Beweging in Nederlandsch-Indie,* p. 142.

[80] *Ibid.,* pp. 142–143. The Liga apparently was established as a Comintern-front organization. At its height it attracted a large number of non-Communist anticolonialists.

to Indonesia and through its publications. In addition it maintained close contact with and exerted a strong influence on the thinking of the larger number of Indonesian students studying at Cairo and Mecca.[81] Almost all members of the PI upon finishing their studies in Holland returned to Indonesia to embark upon political careers. Between 1923 and 1927 these members helped establish a number of "study clubs" in some of the chief Indonesian cities and in them PI ideas were disseminated. In 1926 the PI in Holland decided that its returnees in Indonesia were strong enough to establish a political party. Because of the existing strength of the PKI, however, this plan had to be deferred.[82]

On June 4, 1927, such an organization, the Partai Nasional Indonesia [83] (Indonesian Nationalist Party), or PNI as it was usually referred to, was established by the members of the Bandung Study Club under the chairmanship of a young engineer, Soekarno, one of the few important members of the organization not a member of the PI. Soekarno had been a protégé of Tjokroaminoto and had earned his engineering degree and the title *Ir.* (*Ingénieur*) at the Bandung Technical College. Possessed of a considerable Moslem as well as Western education, he had the unique gift of being able to synthesize Western and Islamic concepts with those of the strongly surviving Hindu-Buddhist-tempered Javanese mysticism and translating this synthesis in terms which the peasant could understand. Other leading members of the new party were Mr.[84] Iskaq Tjokrohadisoerjo, as secretary, and Dr. Tjipto Mangoenkoesoemo, Ir. Anwari, Mr. Boediarto, Mr. Sartono, Mr. Ali Sastroamidjojo, Dr. Samsi Sastrowidagdo, and Mr. Sunarjo. The party's aim was complete independence for Indonesia, economic as well as political, with a government elected by and responsible to the whole Indonesian people. Such independence could be reached, it held, only on a basis of nonco-operation with the Dutch and would come only as the result of the united efforts of the Indonesians themselves. Unity among and self-reliance by Indonesians were held to be of primary importance. Soekarno frequently stressed that the party could not have an Islamic basis, for independence was as much the objective of Indonesian Christians as of Mohammedans. It

[81] Blumberger in *Encyc. Nederlandsch-Indie,* p. 900. It is here stated that there were (c. 1930) 125 members in the Indonesian student colony in Cairo and about 250 in Mecca.

[82] Sitorus, *op. cit.,* p. 39.

[83] Actually it was launched under the name of "Persarikatan Nasional Indonesia," but the name was changed 10 months later.

[84] The title "Mr." denotes that the person holds the degree of Master of Law.

was useless, he stated in his speeches, to wait for help from "an air-plane from Moscow or a caliph from Istanbul." Unity was also neces-sary, Soekarno warned, even in 1929, to defend Indonesia in the approaching Pacific war among the Great Powers. In its immediate program the party was active in building up the labor unions, in de-veloping co-operatives and in supporting national education, especially the Taman Siswa schools.

The PNI's program and able leadership, in particular Soekarno's oratorial skill, brought it rapid and large-scale growth. Within two years it had over 10,000 members. Undoubtedly some of this number was drawn from the former membership of the Sarekat Rakjats and formerly Communist-dominated trade unions. This rapid growth was also to no small extent made possible because of the relatively liberal policy towards the right of association allowed by De Graeff, the Dutch Governor-General whose five year term commenced just after the out-break of the Communist rebellion. He was far more tolerant of the nationalist movement than any of the Governor-Generals who pre-ceded or followed him.

The PNI became the most powerful nationalist organization in In-donesia, and, supported by the leaders of Sarekat Islam, it was able to establish a loose federation of all the important existing national-ist organizations. This federation, the PPPKI,[85] gave the nationalist movement a unity that it had never previously possessed. A result of this was to push the constituent co-operative nationalist organiza-tions more in the nonco-operative direction of PNI and Sarekat Islam.[86]

The rapidly gathering strength of the PNI and its outspoken anti-government tone combined with anticapitalist (though clearly non-Communist) overtones thoroughly alarmed the Dutch community in the Indies. It soon brought pressure to bear on the already uneasy government, and on December 24, 1929, Soekarno and seven other leaders of the organization were arrested. After more than seven months of detention, four of them—Soekarno, Gatot Mangoepradja, Maskoen, and Soepriadinata—were brought to trial and on September

[85] Permoefakatan Perhimpoenan Politiek Kebangsaan Indonesia (Union of Political Associations of the Indonesian People). This included: PNI, Partai Sarekat Islam, Boedi Oetomo, Pasoendan, Sumatra Bond, and the Surabaya Study Club.

[86] The foregoing account of the PNI is based upon Blumberger, *De National-istische Beweging in Nederlandsch-Indie*, pp. 206–244; Sitorus, *op. cit.*, pp. 41–47; "Communication du Gouverneur Général Au Volksraad (May, 1928); Aperçue de la Situation Politique Interieure," *Annuaire de Documentation Coloniale Comparée, 1928*, pp. 131–133; and Koch, *op. cit.*, pp. 101–104.

3, 1930, sentenced to from approximately one to three years imprisonment, Soekarno getting the maximum term. They were charged with "having participated in an organization which had as its aim the committing of crimes as well as . . . deliberately expressing themselves in words wherein the disturbance of public order and the overthrow of the established Netherlands Indies Authority were recommended." [87]

These arrests and the subsequent outlawing of the PNI served for some time to moderate the character of nationalist organizations and made their leaders more cautious. The PNI membership was absorbed by three new organizations, two of which adopted much more cautious policies and more moderate programs than had the PNI. The first of these, the Partai Rakjat Indonesia (Indonesian People's Party) was organized by Mohammad Tabrani, an outstanding Indonesian journalist, on September 14, 1930. Its program was based on co-operation with the Dutch and called for the eventual achievement of Indonesian self-government by parliamentary means; it attracted few members.[88] The majority of the PNI membership followed the lead of Sartono, who in conjunction with the remainder of the party's central board ordered its membership to cease activity. Sartono then established a new party, Partai Indonesia (usually referred to as Partindo) at the end of April, 1931. This aimed at complete independence on a basis of nonco-operation but was considerably more moderate in the methods it advocated than the PNI had been.[89]

There was an important minority of the old party, however, which violently opposed its dissolution and accused Sartono and his colleagues of lack of courage and character for their actions. Furthermore they maintained that he and the remaining party leadership had acted autocratically by forcing dissolution without first determining the wishes of the party membership. This group, the Golongan Merdeka (Independent Group) maintained substantially the same program as had the PNI. It was fortunate in obtaining two exceptionally able leaders, Soetan Sjahrir, a twenty-three-year-old law student at Leiden and prominent PI member who returned from Holland to head the or-

---

[87] Blumberger in *Encyc. Nederlandsche-Indie* (supp. 29: 1931), p. 907; Koch, *op. cit.,* p. 105. Soekarno's eloquent defense at this trial was later printed as a pamphlet, *Indonesia Klaagt aan!* ("Indonesia Accuses!") and was widely read in nationalist circles.

[88] Blumberger in *op. cit.,* pp. 911–912.

[89] Sitorus, *op. cit.,* pp. 48–49; Blumberger in *op. cit.,* p. 913.

ganization in early 1932, and Drs. Mohammad Hatta, the experienced leader of the PI who came back to Indonesia later in the year. Shortly after Sjahrir's arrival the name of the Golongan Merdeka was changed to Club Pendidikan Nasional Indonesia (Indonesian National Education Club). Hatta upon returning replaced Sjahrir as chairman, with the younger leader becoming his chief lieutenant.[90]

It is of long-term significance that Hatta and Sjahrir preferred not to work with Partindo, the mass political organization, but instead deliberately chose to associate themselves with the relatively small, and highly politically conscious, group of nationalists in the Golongan Merdeka. Both were convinced that such mass parties and the charismatic leadership upon which they depended were unsuited to the effective furtherance of the nationalist movement. The ability of the Dutch to jail at will any leader whose appeal to the masses became dangerous to their interests made reliance on such leadership useless, they felt. A national movement dependent upon a few key men at the top was doomed to failure since the Dutch could be relied upon to remove such leaders from the political scene. Such a movement, they believed, would have enduring strength only if a significant number of the Indonesian people were educated to political maturity and a thorough understanding of nationalist principles. This process of education they conceived of as a long-term, unspectacular operation. The building up of cadres of first- and second-echelon leaders was the necessary first step. These in turn could educate wider circles. Small cadres of self-reliant, strongly conscious nationalists would in the long run, they were convinced, achieve the independence that mass support of short-careered charismatic leaders could not.

The Dutch were not slow in understanding the threat to their ascendancy that the ideas of Hatta and Sjahrir posed. In February, 1934, both were arrested and without trial exiled to the Tanah Merah concentration camp at Boven Digul, New Guinea. There and afterwards on the tiny island of Banda they were confined until released just before the Japanese invasion in early 1942. The soundness of their ideas is attested to by the fact that after their exile four successive executive boards of their organization were arrested and yet it continued to carry on until their return to Java.[91]

Following his release from jail on December 31, 1931 (after a short-

[90] Sitorus, *op. cit.,* pp. 49–51.

[91] The two foregoing paragraphs are based on conversations with Sjahrir on Java in 1948–49 and Hatta on Bangka in 1949.

ening of his prison term), Soekarno worked hard to join the Partindo and the Pendidikan Nasional Indonesia into one party, but without success. Finally, in July, 1932, he decided to join Partindo, of which he was made chairman by unanimous acclaim. Under his leadership that party immediately adopted a firmer nationalist line, and its growth accelerated enormously. By mid-1933 it had 50 branches and 20,000 members as compared to about 1,000 members in the Pendidikan Nasional Indonesia.[92] With 20,000 registered members, the party undoubtedly had a mass following many times that great. Soekarno's exceptional ability to command the respect and loyalty of many intellectuals while establishing wide rapport with the masses was a dangerous combination; and with little hesitation the government intervened, summarily arresting him in August, 1933, and without trial exiled him to the island of Flores. Later he was transferred to Benculin, where he was confined until released by the Japanese in 1942.

With the arrest and exile of Soekarno, Hatta, Sajahrir, and other dynamic nationalist leaders, and with the continuance of a strongly repressive policy under Governor-General de Jonge, the Indonesian nationalist movement was forced in to much shallower political channels than it previously had reached. Those who had the courage to follow in the steps of the exiled leaders were promptly arrested, while the increased efficiency of the secret police made underground activity more difficult than ever. Though some of the most important parties refused to send representatives to the Volksraad and for the most part maintained a policy of nonco-operation, there was a general shift in the center of gravity of the movement towards limited co-operation, it being felt that such was the only practical way of winning political concessions.

This feeling provoked a schism within the Sarekat Islam, which in 1929 had changed its name to Partai Sarekat Islam Indonesia.[93] Its refusal to co-operate and its increasing emphasis on religion at the expense of social and economic questions were held by many to have been primarily responsible for its having withered to some 12,000 members. The split was finally precipitated in 1934 over the role of the *kiajis* (the local religious teachers and leaders). Dr. Sukiman and Abikusno Tjokrosujoso, two of the party's top leaders, wished to utilize these

[92] See Blumberger, *De Communistische Beweging in Nederlandsch-Indie*, p. 157.

[93] Indonesian Islamic Association Party. The incorporation of the word "Indonesian" into the organization's name reflected its abandonment of a Pan-Islamic outlook, an outlook which following the splitting off of the pro-Communist elements from the organization had become quite strong.

conservative local leaders to build up a nonco-operative mass party based primarily on religion. Opposed to this was the the group led by Hadji Agoes Salim who thought such a course would necessitate abandonment of the social and economic reform inherent in Modernist teaching, and furthermore that useful concessions from the government might be won through a policy of limited co-operation entailing participation in the Volksraad. Salim's group became known as the Penjedar Barisan PSII (Movement to Make the Partai Sarekat Islam Indonesia Conscious).[94]

Symbolic of the general trend towards evolutionary political organizations was the rise of the relatively moderate Parindra (Partai Indonesia Raja, Greater Indonesian Party). This became the chief Indonesian political organization and was co-operative or nonco-operative as it felt the occasion demanded. It was formed in 1935 out of a fusion of the federation of moderate study clubs known as the Persatoean Bangsa Indonesia, the Boedi Oetomo, and a number of smaller non-Javanese nationalist organizations. Under the leadership of Dr. Raden Soetomo,[95] Mohammad Hoesni Thamrin, Mr. Susanto Tirtoprodjo, Soekardjo Wirjopranoto, and Woerjaningrat, this became the most influential Indonesian group in the Volksraad. Though it was able to accomplish little in that body or in the political sphere in general, it did do considerable valuable work for Indonesian society in other fields. It established retail and peasant co-operatives, a bank granting reasonable credit terms to Indonesians, a hostel for impoverished laborers, a program to combat illiteracy, and a number of other socially valuable undertakings.[96]

The hopes for an evolutionary development toward self-government entertained by members of Parindra and other moderate nationalist groups soon experienced a rude shock. This resulted from the rejection by the Netherlands government of the Soetardjo Petition, a proposal passed by a majority (26–20) of the Volksraad in mid-1936. This asked that a conference be convened to discuss plans for the evolutionary development of Indonesia over a ten-year period toward self-government within the limits of the existing Dutch Constitution.[97] The rejection of

[94] This account is primarily based on talks of the writer with Hadji Agoes Salim and Abikusno Tjokrosujoso in Java, Sept. and Nov., 1948.

[95] Founder of the Surabaya Study Club and later of the Persatoean Bangsa Indonesia (Union of the Indonesian People).

[96] Mr. S. H. Tajibnapis, "De Laatste Tien Jaren voor de Japanese Bezetting," *De Brug-Djambatan*, April, 1946, pp. 12–13; Sitorus, *op. cit.*, p. 56. Such a social program had already been pioneered by Dr. Soetomo in his Surabaya Study Club.

[97] Koch, *op. cit.*, p. 128; and Th. de Booy and L. F. Jansen, "Indie's Staatkundige

this very moderate proposal was a sobering dash of cold water in the faces of those Indonesians who had believed that a policy of moderation and co-operation with the Dutch would be a sure, though perhaps slow, road toward self-government.

Partly as a result of the general reaction to the government's negative attitude towards the Soetardjo Petition and partly because of a growing consciousness among Indonesian intellectuals of the over-all world threat of Fascism, there was established at the end of April, 1937, a new party, the Gerindo (Gerakan Rakjat Indonesia, Indonesian People's Movement). Enrolled in it were the members of the dissolved Partindo as well as numerous individuals who had become dissatisfied with the more conservative parties. Under the leadership of Mr. Sartono, Mr. Amir Sjarifuddin, Dr. A. K. Gani, Sanusi Pane, Wikana and Mr. Mohammad Yamin, this party grew rapidly and soon became the powerful left wing of the nationalist movement. What might have emerged as a strongly militant nationalist force was tempered by the developing world situation and the keen sensitiveness of the nationalists enrolled in the Gerindo to the threat of Fascism. From the very beginning, the strongly socialistically inclined membership of this party displayed an international orientation. The struggle for national independence was seen as dependent upon the outcome of world-wide struggle between the forces of Fascism and anti-Fascism. Most of its members felt that the danger of world conquest by the Fascist powers was a problem which took immediate precedence over their struggle for national independence. They were convinced that the long-run attainment of Indonesian independence called for their short-run solidarity with the Dutch to defend Indonesia against the mounting threat of Japanese conquest. Thus the Gerindo, despite the inherently militant nationalism of its members, operated on a generally co-operative basis, supporting the government and participating in the Volksraad. But at the same time it exerted strong and constant pressure for the granting of self-government to Indonesia, and it made it clear that effective co-operation between Holland and Indonesia against the spread of Fascism called for co-operation on the basis of equality.[98]

In May, 1939, principally through the efforts of Mohammad Hoesni Thamrin of the Parindra, the principal Indonesian nationalist organ-

---

Ontwikkeling," *Rapport Visman,* I, 107–108. The Soetardjo petition was introduced in Sept., 1936. It was not formally rejected by the government until Nov. 16, 1938, but the government's adverse attitude was apparent early in 1937.

[98] See Tajibnapis, *op. cit.,* pp. 13–14; Koch, *op. cit.,* pp. 125–126.

izations were drawn together into one large federation,[99] the Gapi (Gaboengan Politiek Indonesia—Federation of Indonesian Political Parties). This united eight of the most important nationalist organizations[100] and was chairmaned by a triumvirate consisting of Amir Sjarifuddin, representing Gerindo; Abikusno, representing the Partai Sarekat Islam Indonesia; and Thamrin, representing Parindra. The principal points in the common program uniting the constituent groups of Gapi called for: (1) the right of self-determination for Indonesia, (2) national unity founded upon "political, economic and social democracy," (3) a democratically elected Indonesian parliament responsible to the people of Indonesia; and (4) solidarity between Indonesian political groups and the Netherlands in order to maintain a strong anti-Fascist front.

This program was given more definite form at the Indonesian People's Congress (Kongres Rakjat Indonesia) sponsored by the Gapi in December, 1939, and attended by representatives of ninety different nationalistic political, social, and economic organizations. Stressing the need for unity among the nationalist organizations, the Congress officially adopted the Indonesian language (Bahasa Indonesia) as the national language, the red and white flag as the national flag, and the song *Indonesia Raja* ("Greater Indonesia") as the national anthem.[101]

[99] The PPPKI had meantime become inactive following Government action against the non-cooperative parties that had chiefly energized it. Its 4th Congress, scheduled to meet in Surakarta in 1933, had to be cancelled because the government refused its permission.

[100] It included the Gerindo, Parindra, Pasoendan, Persatoean Minahassa, Partai Katholiek Indonesia, Partai Sarekat Islam Indonesia, Partai Islam Indonesia and Partai Arab Indonesia (see Koch, *op. cit.*, pp. 130–131). Because of the government's ban on its holding of meetings the Pendidikan Nasional Indonesia did not join (Sitorus, *op. cit.*, p. 58).

[101] Actually these nationalist symbols were already widely accepted. The oath to support one country and one language, the Bahasa Indonesia, went back to the 1926 conference of Pemuda Indonesia (Young Indonesia), the all-Indonesia youth organization. The following year this oath had been taken over by the chief political parties and religious social organizations. After that all official nationalist publications were in the Bahasa Indonesia. (The basic element in the Bahasa Indonesia was the "bazaar Malay" which had spread through most of the market places of Indonesia as a lingua franca from its source in central and south Sumatra, from whence it also spread to ·Malaya. However, this base was both refined and much expanded by reference back to the language as it had developed in Sumatra. Likewise a large number of Western words, Dutch in particular, were added to it along with a lesser number of previously unabsorbed Arabic expressions.)

Indonesia Raja was composed by W. R. Soepratman for a youth congress held in 1929. It was taken over by Soekarno's PNI and soon became the principal nationalist song.

It adopted a resolution stating that in view of the increased threat to the Netherlands Indies arising from recent international events, co-operation between the Dutch and Indonesian peoples was essential, and that the means for obtaining co-operation was through the grant-ing of more democratic rights to the Indonesian people. The principal demand was for the changing of the Volksraad into a democratic, broadly based representative body to which the government would be responsible. *Indonesia berparlemen* ("a parliament for Indonesia") became its chief slogan.[102]

A moderate version of this demand, calling for self-government within the framework of the Netherlands Constitution—which would entail an expansion of the number of members of the Volksraad, the responsibility of Netherlands Indies government department heads to this body, and revision of the powers of the Governor-General—was passed as the Wiwoho Resolution in the Volksraad in February, 1940. The reply of the Netherlands government to this did not come until August 23, 1940, three months after the German occupation of the Netherlands. Its general attitude was that until the postwar restoration of the mother country's political organs, no political reforms could be considered. It stated that it did not wish to consider the merits of the resolution and that furthermore it had no intention of drawing up any plans projecting the final constitutional development of Nether-lands India.[103] This rejection was very shortly followed by the govern-ment's reply to a question in the Volksraad concerning the signing by the Netherlands government of the Atlantic Charter, with its pledge of the right of self-determination for all people. The Atlantic Charter, the government emphasized, meant no change in the relationship be-tween the Netherlands and Indonesia. It stated:

As the principles of the Charter were already adopted long ago by the Nether-lands Government and . . . executed within the Kingdom, adherence to the Charter does not represent a special reason for new consideration regarding the aims of its policy, more especially as far as the Indonesian population is con-cerned.[104]

With respect to the flag a genuine difference of opinion existed. Many wished to incorporate the head of the *banteng* (Indonesian wild buffalo) into the flag. (This had been the principal symbol on the flag of Soekarno's PNI) . The flag finally adopted consisted of two equally wide horizontal stripes, the top one red and the bottom one white.

[102] See Koch, *op. cit.,* pp. 130–131.

[103] De Booy and Jansen, *op. cit.,* pp. 110–111.

[104] See Karl Pelzer, "Postwar Plans for Indonesia," *Far Eastern Survey,* June 11, 1943, p. 2.

The vague speech of Queen Wilhelmina from London on May 10, 1941, in which she promised that *after the war* there would be an indefinite reorganization of the relations between the Netherlands and Indonesia, hardly offset the disillusion that internationally oriented Indonesians had experienced because of the government's attitude toward the Wiwoho Resolution and the Atlantic Charter. This disillusion resulted in a rapid erosion of the Indonesian-Dutch solidarity which the threat of expansionist Fascism had induced. There occurred a wide-scale disaffection of Indonesians from the once considerable ranks of those who because of that threat had given first priority to Indonesian-Dutch solidarity. A decreasing handful of intellectuals still managed to see things in the same perspective. However, the majority of educated Indonesians who for a time had subordinated their nationalism to an international outlook now drifted back to the numerous ranks of those who had not done so. The gulf between the Dutch and the educated Indonesians grew wider, and the attitude of the latter and that of the Indonesian masses grew closer. Sjahrir observes that for the average Indonesian:

The fall of Holland evoked secret satisfaction, and it was expected that there would be still more radical happenings. . . . The consciousness of foreign domination coupled with an intense desire for freedom and independence became increasingly strong. As the war [in Europe] developed in those first years, the people derived a vicarious satisfaction from the misfortunes of their rulers. And this provided a stimulus for further estrangement from the Dutch and for the growth of a national self-consciousness.

For the average Indonesian, the war was not really a world conflict between two great world forces. It was simply a struggle in which the Dutch colonial rulers finally would be punished by Providence for the evil, the arrogance, and the oppression they had brought to Indonesia. Among the masses, anti-Dutch feeling grew stronger and stronger. This was naturally reflected in the nationalist movement and in its leadership, part of which expressed sympathy for the Axis openly.[105]

The small number of influential leaders of the nationalist movement who remained convinced that resistance to the threat of the Fascist powers to the freedom of the world as whole took precedence over the struggle for Indonesian independence were neither able to influence the masses in this direction nor to mitigate their mounting conviction that Japan's defeat of the Dutch would mean liberation. For as Sjahrir explains: "Essentially, the popularity of Japan increased as one

[105] Soetan Sjahrir, *Out of Exile,* tr. by Charles Wolf, Jr. (New York, 1949), pp. 218–219.

aspect of the growing anti-Dutch animus and as a projection of frustrated desire for freedom." [106] The mythical prophecy of Djojobojo, a Javanese king of the fourteenth century, reappeared and gained the widest currency. According to it the Indonesians after a long period of subjection (according to some versions of the prophecy, three centuries) by a white race would be freed after a yellow race from the north had driven out the whites. The yellow race would stay in Indonesia as long as the span covered by the growth of corn between planting and harvest. Long before their attack the Japanese were looked upon as the yellow liberators of the prophecy, so that as their aggressive designs became clearer those who believed in the prophecy felt their liberation that much nearer at hand.[107]

When finally the Japanese attack came, the overwhelming majority of the Indonesian people, including a large majority of educated nationalists, either welcomed it because of their anticipation that conditions under the Japanese would be better or remained apathetic because of the conviction that things would probably at least be no worse.

While during the last two years of Dutch rule the incipient *ad hoc* solidarity between the Indonesian intellectuals and the Dutch was disintegrating, the solidarity among Indonesian nationalists was increasing. A second Indonesian People's Congress was held September 13–14, 1941, at Jogjakarta with a representation even wider than the first. It decided to establish out of itself a permanent organization, the Madjelis Rakjat Indonesia (Indonesian People's Council), with an executive board made up of representatives of Gapi, the MIAI (a federation of nonpolitical Moslem organizations), and PVPN (a federation of trade unions of government employees). The Madjelis was regarded as a permanent representative body of the entire Indonesian national movement. Its chief objective was a representative parliament for Indonesia to which the Indies government would be responsible. It had just embarked upon a vigorous and widespread program dedicated to that aim when the Japanese reached Indonesia.

[106] *Ibid.*, p. 219.   [107] See *ibid.*, pp. 232–233.

❧ CHAPTER IV ❧

The Japanese Occupation

THE WEAK, half-hearted defense put up by most Dutch land forces against the invading Japanese made a tremendous impression on the Indonesians.[1] On February 14, 1942, the Japanese attacked and quickly overran South Sumatra. Early on March 1st they landed on Java and within eight days the Dutch Commander in Chief of Allied forces on Java, Lt. Gen. Ter Poorten, surrendered in the name of all Allied forces in Java. Though some 8,000 British and American troops on Java led by the British Major General Sitwell wished to continue fighting the Japanese and their intention was known to the Dutch, Ter Poorten surrendered on their behalf without consulting their commanders.[2] This fact became generally known and served to increase the conviction among Indonesians that the Dutch lacked courage.

[1] Dutch sea and air forces, on the other hand, made a courageous record against the Japanese.

[2] Air Vice-Marshall Sir Paul Maltby, "Report on the Air Operations During the Campaigns in Malaya and Netherlands East Indies from the 8th December, 1941 to the 12th March, 1942," *Third Supp. to the London Gazette,* Feb. 20, 1948, pp. 1401–2. In conclusion Air Vice-Marshall Maltby stated:

"Yet something might have been done but for the quandary in which the British had now been placed by reason of the Dutch C. in C's broadcast. This had been promulgated on behalf of the British forces, as well as on that of the Dutch, but without consultation with the A.O.C. or G.O.C. [the two British H.Q.'s] and although the British intention to continue resistance was well known to the Dutch C. in C. The broadcast contained the phrase 'All organized resistance having ceased.' This phrase had an important bearing. It was believed to have the effect in international law of placing those who continued to resist outside the protection of belligerent rights and subject to summary execution if captured. The Japanese were likely to exercise their rights in the matter" (*ibid.,* p. 1402).

101

To many educated Indonesians this eagerness of the Dutch to surrender and not to provoke Japanese hostility by the continuance of
warfare was positive proof of the strong rumors that they wished to
make a deal with the Japanese such as the Vichy French had done in
Indo-China, whereby they would continue to administer the country,
but under Japanese supervision.[3] Moreover most of the population received the impression that the Japanese troops were more poorly
equipped than the Dutch and, up until the Dutch capitulated, seemed
to be smaller in numbers. They had, of course, no means of knowing
that the jungle warfare and infiltration tactics of the attackers called
for small units and that actually the Japanese had a considerable
superiority in numbers, nor that the level of Japanese training was
far superior to that of most troops under Dutch command.

Regardless of one's analysis of the circumstances of the Dutch defeat,
it entailed two clear consequences. First, Dutch prestige in the eyes of
the Indonesians suffered a devastating blow. Second, many Indonesians
were convinced that, if given arms, they could have done as well as
the Japanese.

When the Japanese arrived, they were generally enthusiastically received. The popular feeling that they came as liberators was reinforced
by their immediately allowing the display of the red and white Indonesian national flag and the singing of *Indonesia Raja,* the national
anthem, both of which had been forbidden by the Dutch.

Of great importance in winning the initial acceptance by the majority of educated Indonesians of the Japanese occupation was the
tremendous upward rise in socio-economic status of such people which
expediency alone forced the new rulers to bring about. This was made
necessary because within six months of their arrival the Japanese interned in concentration camps practically the whole Dutch population plus a substantial proportion of the Eurasians, as well as a number
of Christian Indonesians whom they suspected of harboring pro-Dutch
sympathies. The Japanese had extremely few military government personnel and perforce had to rely on Indonesians to fill most of the middle
and upper-bracket administrative and technical positions vacated by

---

Under Maj. General Sitwell's command were: two squadrons of light tanks, two
underarmed Australian Infantry Battalions, a number of small administrative and
AA units, 5,100 RAF personnel of whom 2,200 were armed, one understrength
American artillery battalion.

[3] It is still widely believed among Indonesians that a considerable number of
Netherlanders did hold this view.

the Dutch and Eurasians.[4] Thus almost all such Indonesian personnel found themselves advanced at least one and frequently two or three ranks in the hierarchy in which they had been employed. Thereby the Japanese initially either won the support or neutralized the antipathy of a very large portion of educated Indonesians.

For this reason, and because of the welcome they received from the population, the Japanese do not seem to have anticipated any real opposition from the nationalist leaders.[5] They appeared to feel that they could exploit the resources of Indonesia for the benefit of their war effort without having to make concessions to Indonesian nationalism. On the basis of this conviction they launched the Triple A Movement (*Pergerakan Tiga A*) on April 29, 1942. The three A's stood for the slogans introduced and much propagandized by the Japanese: "Japan the Leader of Asia, Japan the Protector of Asia, and Japan the Light of Asia." The objective of the movement was to mobilize Indonesian support for Japan's war effort and the Greater East Asia Co-prosperity Sphere. The early belief of the Japanese that they did not need to work through Indonesian nationalism in order to attain their objectives is further borne out by the fact that the Indonesian whom they appointed to lead this movement, Mr. Raden Samsoedin, was clearly not a nationalist leader of the first rank.[6]

Speedily the Japanese were disabused of this idea. The Triple A Movement despite its high-powered propaganda was a complete fizzle. Asian solidarity against the West under the hegemony of Japan was an idea which in any case would have elicited small response from Indonesians. It was certainly not of sufficient attractiveness to outweigh the economic exploitation upon which the Japanese embarked. Very soon it was apparent that the country's economic welfare was being subordinated to the benefit of Japan with no *quid pro quo* for Indonesia.

[4] About six months before the Japanese invasion nearly all of the Japanese resident in Indonesia—mostly merchants, shopkeepers, barbers, and photographers—returned to Japan. Many of these returned with the Japanese army. For the most part, however, they were useful only as interpreters or Kempeitai agents. Only a small number were equipped with the necessary training to take over the jobs vacated by the Dutch and Eurasians. A former dealer in water pumps rather appropriately returned as chief engineer of the Tjepu oil fields.

[5] This feeling may have been strengthened because almost immediately upon their arrival Abikusno, one of the most important nonexiled nationalist leaders, presented himself to the Japanese with an offer to form an Indonesian government to work with them.

[6] Samsoedin had been a member of the governing board of Parindra and had represented that party in the Volksraad. In importance as a nationalist leader he ranked well below Soekarno, or Hatta, and below Abikusno as well.

The archipelago was being drained of foodstuffs, oil, and quinine, while badly needed consumer goods, such as cloth, and machine parts were not coming in. The harsh and heavy-handed control by the Japanese over school curriculum as well as their initial insistence that the Japanese language replace Dutch in the secondary and higher schools and as the language of governmental administration resulted in sharp negative reactions.

More important, and pervading almost the entire Indonesian population, was the strong antagonism created by the overbearing rudeness and frequent brutality on the part of many Japanese in their dealings with Indonesians. Within a few months the Japanese began to realize that they no longer enjoyed the support of either the masses or the large majority of educated Indonesians. A growing antipathy toward them among the population began to become noticeable and was punctuated by open small-scale insurrections against them even before the end of 1942. The Japanese were concerned about the obvious hostility and occasional defiance displayed by some of the college and secondary-school students, and they were particularly alarmed over the discovery that underground organizations enrolling some of these students as well as more seasoned political leaders were being established. They began to comprehend that the Indonesian nationalist movement was a real and powerful force with which some sort of *modus vivendi* would have to be reached if even the minimum aims of their occupation were to be attained. Realization of this brought the Japanese to embark on radically different policies. First of all they turned their attention to those nationalist leaders who they felt sure commanded real popular support.

Shortly after their arrival, the Japanese released Soekarno from his place of detention in Benculen and allowed him to proceed to Java. Here he quickly contacted Hatta and Sjahrir, both of whom had already been in touch with the underground being organized by Sjarifuddin and Darmawan Mangoenkoesoemo. It was mutually decided that the nationalist struggle could best be prosecuted at two levels—legally above ground and underground. Soekarno and Hatta were to work above ground through the Japanese, and Sjahrir, while maintaining contact with them, was to organize an underground resistance.

For several years it was repeatedly claimed by Dutch spokesmen that Soekarno was an unprincipled, pro-Japanese collaborator. In early 1949 substantially the same charge was made by Soviet spokesmen, it being applied by them to Hatta as well.[7] Gradually the Dutch have dropped their charge, Van Mook himself stating at the end of 1948: "From documents later discovered it is very clear that in all his objectionable activities he (Soekarno) was always governed by the objective of an independent Indonesia." [8] It is worthwhile noting what Sjahrir, one of the bitterest opponents of those who collaborated with the Japanese for their own personal ends, has to say of this early meeting with Soekarno and Hatta. Soekarno, Sjahrir says, regarded the Japanese "as pure fascists, and felt that we must use the most subtle countermethods to get around them, such as making an appearance of collaboration." Both Soekarno and Hatta, he continues, agreed to do "everything legally possible to give the nationalist struggle a broader legal scope, and at the same time secretly support the revolutionary resistance." It was expected, he says, that the Japanese would attempt to capitalize on Soekarno's popularity for propaganda purposes, and the three "agreed that political concessions from the Japanese must be pressed for in return." [9]

With regard to Hatta, the Dutch themselves were aware that, while he was still in exile on the island of Banda, and only a few weeks before the Japanese landed, he had the courage to write an article, widely circulated in the press throughout Indonesia, in which he declared his strong opposition to the Axis and his support for the Allies. Sjahrir states that Hatta "never made common cause with those Indonesians who went to work for the Japanese because of either material designs or political sympathies." Hatta accepted his position under the Japanese at the behest of Sjahrir's underground group. By them he was given the tasks of securing funds and facilitating the travel of its members. According to Sjahrir, he "acquitted himself of these tasks capably and faithfully. He also received our reports and warned us when he

[7] Soviet quarters have frequently embellished the charge with the terms "fascist" and "quisling." Since then Moscow has followed an alternating policy of pressing this charge and either allowing it to lie dormant or speaking in general terms which indirectly, at least, reflected favorably upon Soekarno and Hatta. This last variant occurred only once as far as the writer knows—during the weeks preceding and the weeks during which the Indonesian diplomatic mission (for formal exchange of recognition) was in Moscow in the summer of 1950. By early 1951 the press and radio of Communist China were referring to Soekarno and Hatta in the same critical vein as that initiated by Moscow in early 1949.

[8] H. J. van Mook, *Indonesia, Nederland en de Wereld* (Batavia and Amsterdam, 1949), pp. 104–105.

[9] Soetan Sjahrir, *Out of Exile*, tr. by Charles Wolf, Jr. (New York, 1949), p. 246. In this book Sjahrir refers to Soekarno as "Abdul Rachman" and Hatta as "Hafil."

heard something was brewing on the Japanese side. I heard from him everything that took place among the Japanese and among the collaborating Indonesians." [10] Through two exceptionally skillful underground workers, at first Djohan Sjaroezah and later Dr. Abdul Halim, Hatta was able throughout the Japanese occupation to keep in contact with the principal Indonesian underground organizations.

In order to enlist the support of Soekarno, Hatta, and some of the other influential nationalist leaders for their war effort, the Japanese promised that self-government would be granted in the near future and allowed the establishment on March 9, 1943, of an all-inclusive nationalist organization, the Poesat Tenaga Rakjat (Center of People's Power) or Poetera as it came to be known. This included all of the former Indonesian political and nonpolitical nationalist associations domiciled in Java and Madura. The new organization was limited to these islands [11] and was envisaged as a bridge to self-government. This idea was encouraged by Premier Tojo in a broadcast in June, 1943, and in his visit to Indonesia in the following month, when he announced that Indonesians should take part in their own government. A board of four members with Soekarno as chairman; Hatta as vice-chairman; and including Ki Hadjar Dewantoro and a prominent Mohammedan leader, Kiaji H. M. Mansoer, were appointed by the Japanese to head the Poetera.[12] The general conviction that Poetera was a genuinely nationalist organization headed toward self-government brought it widespread backing, even from many of the students who had been in contact with the underground organizations.

This belief was soon lent support in early September 1943, when ancillary to the Poetera, a Central Advisory Board, an appointed representative council for Indonesia, was established with Soekarno as president. This and similar local boards which were then set up were supposed to be consulted by the Japanese authorities before drawing up any important measure. On November 10, 1943, Soekarno and a leading member of the Central Advisory Board, Ki Bagoes

[10] *Ibid.*, p. 242.

[11] Java and Madura were administered by the Japanese 16th Army with H.Q. on Java. Sumatra was under the 7th Army with H.Q. at Singapore. The remainder of Indonesia was administered by the Japanese Navy with H.Q. at Makassar on Celebes.

[12] The Japanese were extremely anxious to insure support from important Islamic leaders, according to Hatta, and were under the illusion that he was such a leader. In late 1942, he had prevailed upon religious leaders heading an insurrection in Bantam to desist until a more propitious moment, thus convincing the Japanese that he was a powerful and influential religious leader.

Hadikoesoema, went to Tokyo in order to express the thanks of the people of Java for the step toward self-government considered implicit in the granting of this representative council.

There was an amusing twist to this. Hatta, because of his relationship with the underground, had come to be considered too dangerous by the Japanese authorities in Java. It was their plan that for safety's sake he be interned upon arriving in Japan and not allowed to return. Their intention was apparently misunderstood in Tokyo. For there he was assumed to be a member of the Commission of Thanks and along with Soekarno and Ki Bagoes was presented with a decoration making him immune from arrest by the Kempeitai [13] and then returned to Java with the others, much to the surprise of the authorities there.

For the Japanese the Poetera was primarily a means for rallying Indonesian support behind their war effort, wherein certain concessions to the nationalist leaders had to be made in order to keep them in line. To these nationalist leaders it was primarily a means for spreading and intensifying nationalist ideas among the masses and forcing concessions from the Japanese leading toward self-government. Secondarily and subordinately, they conceived of it as an organization dedicated to helping the Japanese war effort, but only to the minimum extent necessary in order to allow the furtherance of their own long-term nationalist aims. Active in the Poetera were a considerable number of purely self-seeking opportunists and a few Japanese sympathizers, but the majority of its leaders and active members conceived of it primarily as a means for supporting the long-term struggle for independence. For this end it was an imperfect and imprecise instrument. Certainly it did arouse Indonesian nationalism and advance the cause of Indonesian independence. But in the process it begot dangerous consequences. Not only did it strengthen the Japanese war effort, but also it helped establish organizations, particularly among the youth, among many of whose members the Japanese inculcated authoritarian mentalities with a positive respect for force and an emotional anti-Westernism. Particularly was this true among the youthful and slightly educated members of the military and para-military organizations which it sponsored. In the end the majority of their members emerged anti-Japanese and pro-Allied. However, the legacy of uncritical response to authoritarian command from above and the disposition to rely on violence and brutality with which the Japanese had so intensely indoctrinated them remained strong among many.

[13] The Kempeitai was somewhat similar to the German Gestapo or the Soviet NKVD.

Yet there is no doubt that the most important long-term result of the activities of the Poetera was the tremendous increase in political consciousness of the Indonesian masses, and in particular their will to independence. For the Poetera not only allowed but even encouraged the contact between nationalist leaders and the masses which the repressive apparatus of the Dutch regime had so severely limited. The objective of this contact from the standpoint of the Japanese was to indoctrinate the masses to support them and to hate, and if necessary fight, the Allies; to recruit labor battalions and rear-area troops for the Japanese army; and to mobilize raw-material resources. In a limited measure this was accomplished. But in much greater measure it resulted in the awakening of the national self-consciousness and desire for independence of the Indonesian peasant. In this respect the radio, and in particular Soekarno's speeches, were most important. The Japanese considerably built up the archipelago's radio network, making sure that many of the villages and every city square had receiving sets. Large public address systems linked to the radio network, "singing towers," were set up at important points throughout the cities. At prescribed hours the population was required to listen to their official broadcasts, including the frequent speeches of Soekarno. In these, according to his instructions from the Japanese, he attacked the Allies, extolled the Japanese and called upon the population to support their war effort. An examination of these speeches, however, will support Soekarno's contention that "75 per cent of their content was pure nationalism." Moreover, they were full of subtleties and double talk which generally passed over the heads of Japanese monitors but were meaningful to the population, especially those of Javanese culture. Such talk made it easy for the peasant to equate "anti-imperialism" with "anti-Japanese."

Under the aegis of the Poetera a number of organizations dedicated to prosecution of the Japanese war effort were set up. The first of these, the Hei Ho, consisted of conscripted Indonesian laborers, *romushas*, who were incorporated into the Japanese army as labor battalions and sent as far as Burma to work on roads, fortifications, etc. The casualty rate of these *romushas* was exceedingly high, and of the many thousands who left Java only a small proportion returned. Large numbers did not leave Java and were used by the Japanese to work plantations or on roads in the district from which they were drafted.[14]

[14] In order to mitigate the hardships suffered by the families of the *romushas*, the Poetera established a social-service organization headed by Otto Iskander Dinata to help them.

In September, 1943, was established the most important of the Poetera-sponsored organizations, the Soekarela Tentara Pembela Tanah Air (Volunteer Army of Defenders of the Fatherland) or Peta as it was commonly known. Its members were often referred to as *Soekarelas* (volunteers).

This was a Japanese trained, but Indonesian officered, military organization formed to help the Japanese defend Indonesia against Allied invasion. At its peak strength in the middle of 1945 it numbered about 120,000 armed men. It was the Peta which was to become the backbone of the Indonesian Republic's army. The continuous objective of Soekarno, Hatta, and other Poetera leaders was to indoctrinate the Peta's members with a pro-Indonesian point of view and only outwardly a pro-Japanese and anti-Allied orientation. Their success was not complete, but in conjunction with the efforts of several of the underground groups it was considerable. By 1944 the average Peta member was consciously strongly nationalist, anti-Japanese, anti-Dutch, but for the most part favorably disposed towards the other Allies, particularly the United States. Soekarno and Gatot Mangkoepradja, the Indonesian head of Peta, because of their influence on the Japanese officers making the selections, were able to insure the reliability according to nationalist considerations of most important Peta officers. They argued to the Japanese, and effectively, that in an army dedicated to the defense of the fatherland it was necessary to have strongly nationalist officers. In addition Soekarno convinced the Japanese that the Peta could be a good defensive organization only if its rank and file as well as its officers had an aroused national consciousness. Thus, they allowed him and others to speak to the various Peta units, inflaming them not against the Allies alone, but against imperialism in general. Many Peta members had no difficulty in equating Japan's activities with imperialism by themselves. To most of the less astute, this connection was soon made clear either by the educational work of the underground organizations or by the veiled innuendos dropped by Soekarno and Hatta in their speeches.

The Japanese were particularly conscious of the favorable political results that might be realized through organizing the uneducated Indonesian youth. These, having little knowledge of the West, could be most easily and effectively indoctrinated to hate and to fight the Allies. The training of these youth groups was not in the hands of the Poetera but was managed by the Japanese propaganda service, the Sendenbu, which established several youth organizations. These were given political indoctrination plus some military training. The first of them, the Seinendan, was established at the end of 1942 as a mass youth organization based particularly on the village. Its members were trained in simple military exercises, mass drill, and anti-Allied ideas by a member of their village who had attended a Japanese school for instructors. In 1943 was organized the Gakutotai, an organization of students from the seventh grade through high school (and thus found only in the cities). Its members were also given intensive indoctrination against the Allies (though with much less success) and some military training. Finally was established the Barisan Pelopor (Pioneer Column), the most heavily indoctrinated of all youth corps. The anti-Western orientation of the members of this unarmed, but militarily trained, mass youth organization was considerably stronger than that of any of the others.

By the end of 1943 it was clear to the Japanese that the Poetera was accomplishing considerably more for the Indonesian nationalist movement than it was for the Japanese war effort. In addition it was apparent that many of its supporters, in particular the educated youth, clearly evidenced attitudes that were more anti-Japanese than anti-Allied. Accordingly the Japanese military command dissolved the Poetera. In its place, on March 1, 1944, they set up a new organization which they felt they could control more effectively, the Perhimpoenan Kebaktian Rakjat (People's Loyalty Organization), more generally known by its Japanese name, Djawa Hokokai. To help neutralize and limit the force of the nationalists, the Japanese insisted that it represent the Chinese, Arab, and Eurasian community as well as the Indonesian and forced it to submit to a much closer supervision and control than had been the case with the Poetera. Though nominally chairmaned by Soekarno,[15] the new organization stood directly under the control of the Gunseikan, the Japanese commander in chief. The highly developed organization of the Hokokai, with a branch in every village, was maintained compulsorily. It did not win popular backing. By many Indonesians Soekarno and its other leaders were felt to be prisoners of the Japanese; and in fact they retained very little latitude for maneuvering the advancement of the nationalist movement.

Concurrently with their efforts to win Indonesian support through the Hokokai, the Japanese on Java and Madura attempted to win

[15] Hatta was vice-chairman, but only in an honorary capacity, having nothing to do with the movement's functioning.

support on another basis as well, that of religion. Special attention was paid to the *kiajis,* the local Islamic leaders—largely teachers and experts in Islamic law. They were given local positions of honor and importance. The attempt was made to enroll their support in a propaganda campaign aimed at arousing resistance to the Allies on the basis of defense of Islam against infidels bent upon again enslaving the Moslem population of Indonesia. To facilitate the organization of this effort the Japanese established towards the end of 1943 one large, all-inclusive Islamic organization subsuming all existing ones of a nonpolitical nature (including Mohammadijah, the more conservative Nahdatul Ulama, and also the MIAI (known as the Madjelis Sjuro Muslimin Indonesia [Council of Indonesian Moslem Associations] or Masjumi). Although through this organization the Japanese do appear to have increased the spirit of nationalism among the masses, they do not appear to have had much success in building anti-Allied, as distinguished from anti-Japanese, sentiment. Nearly all of the *kiajis* refused to lend themselves as instruments of Japanese aims. In fact the majority of them had already been outraged by the clumsy handling of the Mohammedan religion by the Japanese. The people being forced to bow towards Tokyo rather than Mecca and the exaltation of the Emperor on a religious plane were particularly important in this respect. This antagonism towards the Japanese brought them to emphasize Indonesian independence above all else, and this was more frequently accompanied by anti-Japanese than anti-Allied overtones. In enlisting Indonesian support the Japanese were no more successful with the Masjumi than they had been with the Hokokai.

Soekarno, Hatta, and a few other prominent leaders were able to an important, though much diminished, extent to utilize the organization and radio facilities of the Hokokai just as they had used those of the Poetera to maintain contact with and develop the national consciousness and will for independence among the Indonesian peasantry and other groups in Java and Madura. Other nationalists, the educated youth in particular, not being able to do this through the Hokokai, worked through underground channels to accomplish this end.

Initially the largest of all the anti-Japanese underground organizations was that headed by Amir Sjarifuddin. This was established in part under N.E.I. government auspices a few weeks before the Japanese landed. The government supplied 25,000 guilders for this purpose, it being given to Sjarifuddin by Dr. Charles van der Plas. This enrolled various people of strong anti-Fascist feelings, the most numerous among whom were the members of the underground Communist Party (the "Illegal PKI"), contact with them having been established by Sjarifuddin. But because of the early indiscretion of some of its members this group got off to an unfortunate start. During the first month of the Japanese occupation several of them were caught and under torture gave the names of many others in the organization. This considerably curtailed the ability of many of the remainder to operate. Early in 1943 Sjarifuddin and several other leaders were arrested, and on February 29, 1944, he and more recently apprehended leaders were sentenced to death. Soekarno's intervention was responsible for commuting Sjarifuddin's sentence to life imprisonment, but four of the other arrested leaders were executed.[16] Whether correctly or not, it was this predominantly Communist-led underground [17] of which the Japanese were most afraid and which they made the greatest effort to root out.

The underground which eventually developed the most strength was that headed by Soetan Sjahrir. It developed branches in Jakarta (Batavia), Cheribon, Garut, Semarang, and Surabaya, drawing its principal support from the educated youth of those cities. In the vicinity of Cheribon, under the leadership of Dr. Sudarsono, it established a wide network of efficiently functioning peasant co-operatives (sanctioned by the Japanese) and behind this façade gradually organized a loosely integrated, but extensive, revolutionary-oriented peasant base.

The third group, the Persatoean Mahasiswa (Student Union) was made up of university students in Jakarta, principally those from the medical faculty. This group in the middle of 1942 in protest against the order that all students crop their hair organized a wide protest strike among all university students. Though twenty of its members were roughly handled by the Japanese and jailed for a month, they were not intimidated. Their continued defiant attitude and open and public criticisms of the Japanese did much to spread anti-Japanese revolutionary sentiment. This group had some liaison with the Sendenbu group of Sukarni but maintained a particularly close relationship with Sjahrir.

[16] Executed were Pamudji, Sukajat, Abdul Aziz, and Abdurachim. Eight other leaders were jailed.

[17] It was loosely organized and contained many constituent semi-autonomous groups not all of which were Communist-dominated. It is doubtful whether more than a small minority of their rank and file were Communists.

A fourth and smaller nucleus of underground strength was headed by Sukarni and included among its leaders Adam Malik, Pandu Wiguna, Chairul Saleh, and Maruto Nitmihardjo. Through Maruto, it maintained fairly constant liaison with Sjahrir's group. However, since its leaders had intrenched themselves within the Japanese propaganda service, Sendenbu, it was not entirely trusted by the other organizations even though the core of the group soon gave up most of its ties with the Sendenbu.

There were also numerous small groups of young intellectuals and students who formed study clubs, such as that headed by Mohammad Natsir and Sjafruddin Prawiranegara, which operated partly underground and partly above and were important in disseminating anti-Japanese nationalist ideas and in collecting information which they passed on to the much larger organizations.

In addition mention should be made of an amazing individual, Djohan Sjaroezah, a well-educated Menangkabau of about thirty, who in 1942–1943 while serving as Hatta's secretary maintained contact with all four of the principal undergrounds and was for a time their chief means of liaison. He had particularly close relationships with the underground of Sjahrir and, according to Adam Malik, was for a time co-chairman with Sukarni of the latter's group.[18] Later in 1943 he went to East Java and with other leaders of the Sjahrir group organized an underground among the youth in Surabaya. Shortly thereafter he accomplished the same among the oil workers of Tjepu.

Infiltration of the Peta and the Japanese-sponsored youth organizations was the chief objective of all four undergrounds. The objective of this infiltration was two-fold: (1) to establish as much control as possible within the units of these organizations through reliable men holding key positions and (2) to influence their membership in an anti-Japanese and pro-Allied direction, specifically to prepare them to rise against the Japanese whenever the expected Allied invasion should come. Most of the underground leaders agreed with Sjahrir that Indonesia's bargaining position with the Allies for her independence would be strongest if there were a powerful Indonesian uprising against the Japanese coincident with the Allied landings. Having taken an important part in the defeat of the Japanese, the Indonesians would be in a much stronger position to demand independence. All

[18] Adam Malik, *Sedjara dan Perdjoeangan Berkenaan Dengan Proklamasi Indonesia Merdeka* ("History and Struggle Related to the Proclamation of Indonesian Independence"), (Djakarta, 1947?), p. 15.

of the groups met with considerable success in their efforts to infiltrate and indoctrinate the units of Peta. In this Sukarni's group was especially successful with units stationed in the general vicinity of Jakarta,[19] while Sjarifuddin's group was most successful in east Central Java. In some cases anti-Japanese indoctrination was not accompanied by sufficient infiltration to control a. unit's revolutionary impulses and several of them on their own initiative revolted prematurely and unsuccessfully against the Japanese. The most important of these uprisings was the Peta revolt in Blitar in 1944, probably a result of activity by Sjarifuddin's group. Infiltration and indoctrination of the Gakutotai and Seinendan was undertaken by all groups, with Sjahrir's taking the most active part, particularly in the Gakutotai where very great success was achieved.

To control the increasingly hostile educated youth and especially to keep them from effective participation in underground activity,[20] the Japanese had recourse to an ingenious device. In mid-1944, they established the Angkatan Muda (Youth Organization), an organization of educated young men from about twenty to thirty which they closely controlled. Many of those who were known or suspected by the Japanese to be active in the underground were forced to assume responsible positions of leadership in it. They were thus kept out in the open where the Japanese could more easily watch and control them. To help accomplish this, the Japanese had their own Indonesian spies within the organization. It was hoped that the anti-Japanese activity of these underground workers could be stopped and that by virtue of their leading position in the Angkatan Muda they would appear to its rank-and-file membership to be sanctioning its anti-Allied, pro-Japanese program. Thus Sukarni and Chairul Saleh were forced to take leading positions in the Jakarta branch of the Angkatan Muda; and Roeslan Abdulgani, the leader of Sjahrir's group in Surabaya, was forced to become chairman of the Angkatan Muda branch there. Made to serve on its Surabaya board of twenty were a number of other influential youth leaders, most of whom had also occupied leading roles in underground activity, including Sutomo (later "Bung Tomo"), Kaslan, and Krisubanu. The last two had been active in the PKI un-

---

[19] Sukarni had established a close relationship with Djokosujono, a high Peta officer. The latter was probably not then a member of the PKI.

[20] Since the primary objective of the Japanese at this point was to mobilize the population against the Allies, they could not afford summarily to kill or jail the widely popular youth leaders, many of whom were sons of influential members of the older generation.

derground; it is not certain, however, that they were then members of the Communist Party.

The Japanese strategem was only partly successful. They did manage to weaken the undergrounds by restricting the activity of many of the best leaders. However, the work of these men within the Angkatan Muda generally resulted in making its rank-and-file members more anti-Japanese and more pro-Allied (to the exclusion of the Dutch).

Beginning early in October, 1944, just after the announcement of Premier Koiso that Indonesia would be given independence "in the very near future," there developed marked changes in Japanese policy. Almost immediately the Japanese army administration in Java and Madura partially relaxed its controls over the Hokokai. Soekarno, Hatta, and other speakers were given greater opportunity to contact the masses, allowed much more freedom to talk unadulterated independence, and obliged to infuse less pro-Japanese content into their talks.

The most remarkable new departure was undertaken by Vice-Admiral Mayeda, Japanese naval chief in Java and in charge of naval intelligence for all Indonesia.[21] In October, he and his staff established a school for semi-educated youths of eighteen to twenty in Jakarta called the Asrama Indonesia Merdeka (Dormitory for Free Indonesia) and shortly thereafter set up a branch near Surabaya. The Japanese army was opposed to these schools but was unable to have them closed.

The Indonesian chosen to head the school, Wikana, was known by the Japanese to be closely connected with the "Illegal PKI" (Indonesian Communist Party underground). The behind-the-scenes organizer for the Japanese, Mr. Achmad Subardjo, was chief of the Consulting Office on Political Affairs of the Japanese naval headquarters in Java.[22] In the middle 1920's Subardjo had been generally regarded as a Communist. It was, however, rather widely believed that by the early 1930's he had divorced himself from the Communist movement, or at least from its Stalinist (PKI) branch.

[21] Japanese naval headquarters in Indonesia was at Makassar in Celebes. Mayeda was second in command and chief of intelligence for the Makassar H.Q. and at the same time was local commander of naval forces in Java and Madura.

[22] Subardjo had been known as "Abdoel Manap," during his early career in the nationalist movement, which he spent largely in Europe. Previous to Hatta's assumption of the chairmanship of the Perhimpoenan Indonesia (Student's Association) in Holland he had been its chief leader. After that, in the middle 1920's, Subardjo spent at least a year in Moscow.

Mayeda contacted many of the principal non-Communist nationalist leaders, requesting that they give lectures to the students on nationalism, economics, politics, sociology, and Marxism. The object, he told them, was to train the students as able nationalist leaders, fully conscious of the fact that the Indonesian independence to which they were to lead their people must have a social content meaningful to all of them, to those of the villages as well as of the towns. Among those nationalist leaders other than Wikana and Subardjo who lectured at the schools were Hatta, Sjahrir, Soediro, and Iwa Kusuma Sumantri.

Sjahrir and Hatta saw this as an opportunity to influence the students in accordance with their own ideas and for a while were able to exert considerable influence on them. They were given complete freedom to say whatever they wished, making open propaganda for Indonesian independence and, according to Sjahrir, even attacking the army-controlled Japanese administration.

Mayeda and the naval intelligence officers who helped him run the schools soon came to give principal emphasis to the study of communism. They stressed the necessity for nationalization of production, but the chief emphasis of their teaching was negative, anti-imperialism and anticapitalism being the dominant themes. The communism which they taught was strongly international. The students were taught to see Indonesia's fight for independence in terms of an international struggle against capitalist imperialism. Social justice for the world as a whole, not just Indonesia, was to be the objective. This international emphasis had little in common with the then current Soviet line. The subordination of anticolonialism to anti-Fascism and the temporizing policy towards the colonial powers and the United States demanded in the Dimitrov United Front policy found no place in these teachings. The enemy were the colonial powers and America, not the Axis.

Until the end of July, 1945, these schools ran two-month courses and turned out several hundred graduates. Beginning in May, 1945, those who had graduated were approached by Subardjo and asked to join an ostensibly underground anti-Japanese movement which he headed. Though subsidizing this organization, the Japanese did not interfere with it and let Indonesians believe that they knew of its existence only as an illegal underground movement. Besides a majority of the Communist-oriented graduates of these schools, a considerable number of other Indonesians were enrolled, including a number of those working in the central administration under the Japanese.

Soekarno and Hatta, it should be noted, had nothing to do with this movement. It is interesting to note that a great many of these non-student adherents were regarded as "Fascist" in outlook by Sjahrir and some other non-Communist left-wing leaders. According to several top Indonesian leaders, the principal common denominator of Subardjo's heterogeneous group, other than opposition to colonial rule and capitalism, was an outlook congenial to authoritarian political organization.

Subardjo's organization assumed increasingly impressive proportions. It carried over into the Republican period, and for a short time was a power to be reckoned with seriously. However, the strong opposition to it from most of those who had been connected with the chief anti-Japanese undergrounds, Sjahrir in particular, in conjunction with lack of support from Soekarno and Hatta caused it to fall apart less than three months after the revolution was launched.

Thereafter most of the organization's members who had entered it through one of the Japanese-sponsored schools joined one of three groups. A considerable number attached themselves to Tan Malaka, while a probably somewhat smaller number joined the PKI. It was Mohammad Jusuf, one of the older, nonstudent members who had been active in Subardjo's Japanese-sponsored political organization, who in late October, 1945, re-established the PKI. Though he had been a member of neither the prewar party nor its wartime anti-Japanese underground, he maintained himself as its head until March 1, 1946, when his fruitless terrorist activities were condemned by a party conference. Not until early May, 1946, was it clear that the orthodox, prewar leadership of the party had reasserted its control. However, probably the greatest number of the graduates of these Japanese-sponsored schools joined the Pesindo (Indonesian Socialist Youth), a large, armed organization in which some became third- and even second-echelon leaders. Though Wikana was from the outset one of its top leaders, the Pesindo did not come under effective control of the PKI until mid-1948.

Why did the Japanese establish these schools and sponsor Subardjo's organization? That question is still asked in Indonesia today, and there is no unanimity among those who believe they know the answer. Some are convinced, as is Sjahrir, that the primary purpose of the Japanese was to penetrate and eventually control the PKI underground through the youths trained in these schools. After having effectively infiltrated this underground, they would bring it into Subardjo's organization, where it could be controlled and turned against Britain and America, the powers most likely to invade Indonesia.

A leader of the Surabaya branch of Sjahrir's underground, also asked by Mayeda to lecture at the school, thinks differently. He agrees that the Japanese tactics called for penetration of the PKI underground by the school's graduates. However, he believes that their object was limited to splitting the PKI and detaching part of it. He believes that the Japanese felt that the strongly international emphasis of the communism they were teaching would be more attractive to the numerous marginal elements of the PKI underground than the line of its more orthodox Stalinist leadership with their greater emphasis upon the priority of Russian interests. Such a split would, of course, undermine the strength which the PKI underground could bring to the support of an Allied landing in Java.

But these explanations made it difficult to understand the use of such a bona fide leader of the PKI underground as Wikana by the Japanese. Moreover, he used the position in which they placed him to gather information about their activities and particularly about the organization they and Subardjo were building up, information which he promptly passed on to the PKI underground and the underground led by Sjahrir.

On the other hand, a number of intelligent nationalist leaders, including such a well-balanced person as Hatta, are convinced that Mayeda and many of the naval officers under him were genuinely sincere in their desire for Indonesian independence and that they approached domestic as well as world-wide social problems in an "extremely progressive manner." Several Indonesian intellectuals developed close acquaintance with them and were surprised at the depth of their knowledge of Marxism. Some of them were convinced that these officers were Communists with a strong international bias.

Some Indonesians speculate as to the possibility of a tie-up between these Japanese officers and Tan Malaka. They point to Tan Malaka's consistent attraction to the idea of anti-Western, pan-Asian solidarity, the fact that several years of his exile were spent in Japan, the further fact that two of his books dealing with communism were published there, and finally to the fact that somehow he managed to get back to Java early in 1944. In 1944 and 1945 he was working in a coal mine in West Java. A respected Indonesian newspaper editor swears that he saw him late in 1944 in the vicinity of this mine in the company of high-ranking Japanese naval officers. Also there are substantial grounds for believing that Subardjo, who soon after the declaration of Indonesian independence emerged as Tan Malaka's strong supporter, was in contact with him fairly early in 1945.[23]

It is perhaps arguable that the Japanese may have been willing to work with Tan Malaka to split the PKI underground and win more Indonesians to their side to fight an Allied invasion. They undoubtedly knew of the post-1926 schism among Indonesian Communists and they must have known of Tan Malaka's opposition to the line of the Stalin-dominated 1928 conference of the Comintern. Given the fact that the PKI underground was following the Russian line and was therefore disposed to fight beside an American invading force against the Japanese, it might be logical for the Japanese to back a Communist group not wedded to the Russian line in the belief it would join them in fighting the Americans if it could be assured that the Japanese would grant real independence to Indonesia.

Most relatively objective Indonesian leaders, even those bitterly opposed to Tan Malaka, are convinced that he would never have lent himself to a role where Indonesia's national interests would have been subordinated to those of any other nation, including Japan or Russia. To gain his co-operation they believe, Mayeda and his staff would have had to convince Tan Malaka absolutely of the genuineness of their interest in Indonesian independence. It is is this that leads a number of Indonesian leaders to speculate as to the possibility of an ideological affinity between him and these Japanese naval officers.

But there are additional facts which throw a somewhat different light on these puzzling Japanese activities. In their conversations with Indonesians, particularly with those whom they knew well, many Japanese officers, from the army as well as the navy, during late 1944

[23] With respect to the relationship of Subardjo and Tan Malaka and the question of their relationship to the Japanese it may be of significance that during 1935–36 Subardjo was in Tokyo as correspondent for the Indonesian newspaper *Matahari* ("The Sun"). It is widely believed that Tan Malaka was also in Tokyo during this period.

According to Adam Malik, he and Sukarni—the principle leaders of Tan Malaka's prewar Pari underground—did not know of Tan Malaka's return to Indonesia until after the declaration of Indonesian independence on Aug. 17, 1945. Adam Malik states that their first contact with him was on the night of Aug. 14, 1945, when an elderly man giving the name of "Husin" introduced himself to Sukarni as "a representative of the youth of southern Bantam," but that it was not realized then that "Husin" was Tan Malaka. On Aug. 18, he states, "Husin" visited Subardjo who recognized him as Tan Malaka. He affirms that this was the first time the two had seen each other since 1922 in Holland (Adam Malik, *op. cit.*, pp. 34, 37).

and through 1945 at least up until the Potsdam Agreement, appeared confident that Russia would eventually join with Japan against the United States. It is not clear whether they envisaged this Russo-Japanese alliance as arising before or after the end of World War II. However, officers of the political and psychological warfare detachment of the Japanese army in Java seemed convinced that a third world war would break out shortly after the end of the second and that in it Japan and Russia would be allied. According to Indonesians, it was in accordance with this conviction that they organized several suicide battalions of Indonesians, the Djibaku. Their mission was to maintain a constant and intensive guerrilla warfare against any Allied administration which sought to establish itself in Java. They were to keep Java in a state of chaos pending the outbreak of World War III and thereby make it impossible for the United States and/or Britain to consolidate themselves there and easier for Japan to dislodge them. Finally, Indonesians who had close personal acquaintance with Japanese naval and army officers were impressed at the apparent sincerity and conviction with which many of them, upon leaving, asserted that they would soon be back again.

It is possible that the puzzling attitudes and activities of these Japanese officers was a phenomenon not limited to Indonesia. Perhaps when more complete studies of Japanese occupation policies in other areas become available, it will be found that efforts at Communist indoctrination of their populations during the last year of Japanese control were not confined to Indonesia.[24]

For what to him seems to be one of the most plausible explanations of the above-described Japanese attitudes and activities in 1944–1945, the writer is indebted to Dr. Nobutaka Ike.[25] Dr. Ike notes that according to the United States Strategic Bombing Survey, the Japanese navy was prepared to fight a two-year war, and no more. By mid-1944, navy officers, particularly intelligence officers, stationed in Indonesia must have realized that Japan could not win the war. There appears to have been a rather widespread belief among both Japanese army and navy officers that, if Japan was defeated, it was probable that a Communist revolution would break out in Japan. Conceivably, Dr. Ike concludes, they reasoned that in case of such a revolution Russia would throw her support to Japan. Dr. Ike's conclusions help explain the

[24] There is some indication that Bose's Indian National Army trained by the Japanese in Malaya may have been given a Communist indoctrination.

[25] Of the Hoover Institute and Library at Stanford University.

apparent certainty of Japanese officers in Java that Japan and Russia would be allied. Anticipating the rise of a Communist regime in Japan and the possibility of an alignment of Japan and Russia against the United States, it might not seem illogical for them to endeavor to equip potential Indonesian leaders with pro-Communist leanings.

As Allied power drew near to Indonesia and anti-Japanese feeling mounted, the Japanese military authorities on Java began to take new steps towards the establishment of an independent Indonesian government. In late 1944, three Indonesians—Soetardjo, Soeiro, and Suroso—were appointed as residents (political head of a residency), and in the remaining residencies of Java and Madura, Indonesian sub-residents were appointed. These Indonesian sub-residents rather than their Japanese superiors, who were only nominally residents, actually ran their respective administrations. (Outside Java and Madura, the Japanese administrations did not allow Indonesians to occupy civil service posts higher than that of district head.) On March 1, 1945, the Investigating Committee for the Preparation of Independence (Badan Penjelidik Usaha Persiapan Kemerdekaan) was set up.[26] As chairman the Japanese appointed Dr. Radjiman Wediodiningrat. A Japanese, Ichibangase Yoshio, and an Indonesian, Suroso, were appointed vice-chairmen. The Committee's fifty-nine remaining members included representatives of all of the principal social and ethnic groups of Java and Madura, including Soekarno, Hatta, and other important nationalist leaders, plus seven additional Japanese.[27] In it were two co-secretaries, Abdul Gafar Pringgodigdo and a Japanese who did not know the Indonesian language, the language in which its deliberations were carried on. The committee had two plenary meetings, May 28–June 1, and July 10–17, and reached basic agreement concerning constitutional and economic questions. A committee endowed with a roughly similar function, but much more closely supervised, was established by the Japanese military administration on Sumatra on July 25, 1945, with Mohammad Sjafei, head of the previously established Sumatran Central Advisory Council, as chairman and Adinegoro as secretary.[28]

The Japanese naval command at Makassar set up no such organization for Celebes, Borneo, the Moluccas or Lesser Sundas. An almost

[26] A Preparatory Committee for Indonesian Independence had been established by the Japanese in Jan., 1944, and was made up of 80 representatives from Java. It began work on a draft constitution that was taken over by the new committee.

[27] See G. W. Overdijkink, *Het Indonesische Problem, de Feiten* (The Hague, 1946), p. 33.

[28] See Overdijkink, *op. cit.*, pp. 34–36.

functionless "National Party" was allowed by it to be established in June, 1945, with the Sultan of Bone (Arumpone) as chairman and Dr. Ratu Langie as vice-chairman, but in about six weeks it was suppressed.

Despite the concessions made by the Japanese administration to Indonesians on Java and Madura, their demand for increased self-government and an accelerated granting of independence mounted. Knowledge of Allied victories and the approach of American forces to Indonesia made them more self-confident, while the continuing brutality displayed by many Japanese troops strengthened antagonism towards the Japanese. The Peta revolt in Blitar was followed by an uprising against the Japanese at Indramaju in the middle of 1944. Thereafter there occurred a whole series of lesser but more frequent insurrectionary flare-ups, largely of peasant origin. Anti-Japanese activity by students became more daring. In June, 1945, at Surabaya the Japanese sponsored a mass meeting of more than 4,000 students organized around the theme that Indonesian independence was to be achieved by fighting alongside of Japan against the Allies. The meeting was broadcast by radio to all of Java. One of the Indonesian speakers, a member of the Angkatan Muda of Surabaya, agreed that Indonesians would have to fight for their independence, but very pointedly and firmly rejected the Japanese contention that the fighting was to be against the Allies. These remarks were greeted by thunderous applause, which was broadcast over the radio along with the speech. The meeting then turned into disorder, and the Japanese were able to break it up only by turning on the air raid sirens.

It was against this background of rising and increasingly articulate anti-Japanese feeling that Soekarno on June 1, 1945 delivered a speech before the Investigating Committee for the Preparation of Independence. In it he outlined the five basic principles, the *Pantja Sila,* that he felt should guide and serve as the philosophical foundation of an independent Indonesia. This speech clearly bordered on the revolutionary and, though it angered Japanese army authorities, they evidently did not feel it wise to take action against him. The ideas expressed by Soekarno in this speech are important in that they represented the matured social philosophy of the most influential of Indonesian nationalist leaders and of the man who was to become the most important political leader of the Republic of Indonesia. They are of great importance too because of their influence upon the social thinking of Indonesians during the revolutionary struggle that soon began, an influence which is still today of great importance. Much of this influence is because Soekarno formulated with clarity the ideas which were dominant but inchoate in the minds of many educated Indonesians and because he did so in a language and a symbolism much of which was and remains meaningful to the uneducated rank and file. Probably in no other exposition of principle can one find a better example of the synthesis of Western democratic, Modernist Islamic, Marxist, and indigenous-village democratic and communalistic ideas which forms the general basis of the social thought of so large a part of the postwar Indonesian political elite. Thus, a rather extensive examination of the principal points of Soekarno's speech will be useful.[29]

The first principle which must underlie the philosophical basis of a free Indonesia, stated Soekarno, is *nationalism*. He emphasized that he did not mean a nationalism in a narrow sense. The definition of Renan that the requirement of a nation is "le désir d'être ensemble" and that of Otto Bauer that it is "eine aus Schicksalgemeinschaft erwachsene Charaktergemeinschaft" were not adequate, he said, because they did not take into consideration the additional requisite of "unity between men and place." "According to geopolitics," he continued, "Indonesia is our country. Indonesia in its entirety. . . ." In this vein he went on to say:

Briefly speaking, the people of Indonesia, the Indonesian Nation is not only a group of individuals who, having "le désire d'être ensemble," live in a small area like Menangkabau or Madura, or Jogja, or Pasundan, or Makassar; but the Indonesian people are all the human beings who, according to geopolitics ordained by God Almighty live throughout the entire archipelago of Indonesia from the northern tip of Sumatra to Papua! . . . Only twice have we experienced a national state; that was in the time of Sriwijaja and in the time of Madjopahit.

However, Soekarno emphasized, "Undoubtedly there is a danger in this principle of nationalism. The danger is that men will reduce nationalism to chauvinism. . . . Gentlemen, do not let us say that the Indonesian nation is the noblest and most perfect, while belittling other peoples. We should aim at the unity and brotherhood of the whole world." With this thought he continued to expound his second principle, *internationalism* or *humanitarianism:*

[29] Soekarno's speech was not written out beforehand and was recorded stenographically at the meeting. The following quotations are from the English translation made by the Ministry of Information of the R.U.S.I. under the title of *The Birth of Pantjasila* (Jakarta, 1950). Italics are as given in the translation.

We should not only establish the state of Free Indonesia, but we should also aim at making one family of all nations. . . . This is the second principle of philosophy I propose to you, gentlemen, to which I give the name of *internationalism*. But when I say *internationalism,* I do not mean cosmopolitanism, which does not recognize nationalism, which says there is no Indonesia, no Japan, no Burma, no England, no America, and so on. Internationalism cannot flower if it is not rooted in the soil of nationalism. Nationalism cannot flower if it does not grow within the garden of internationalism. Thus these two, gentlemen, principle one and principle two, which I have first proposed to you, are dovetailed together.

As his third principle Soekarno postulated that of *representative government* or of *consent.* "I am convinced," he said, "that the chief condition for the strength of the Indonesian state is conferring, is representative government." Quite clearly answering the arguments of those who desired an independent Indonesia to be organized as an Islamic state, he went on to say:

This is the best condition for the Islamic religion to prosper. . . . By means of agreement we shall improve all matters; we shall promote the interests of religion. . . . The House of Representatives—this is the place for us to bring forward the demands of Islam. . . . If we really are an Islamic people, let us work hard so that most of the seats in the people's representative body we will create are occupied by Islamic delegates . . . We say that ninety per cent of us are Islam[ic] in religion, but look around you in this gathering and see what percentage give their votes to Islam? A thousand pardons that I should question that matter! To me it is proof that Islam does not yet flourish among the masses. Therefore, I ask you gentlemen, both those that are not Moslem, and in particular those who are, to accept this principle number three, that is the principle of conferring, of representative government. . . . Within the people's representative body, Moslems and Christians should work as if inspired. If, for instance, Christians wish every letter within the regulations of the state of Indonesia to accord with the Bible then let them work together to death in order that most of the delegates who enter the Indonesian representative body may be Christians. That is just—fair play! There is no state that can be called a living state if there is no internal struggle.

His fourth principle, stated Soekarno, was that of *social prosperity* or *social justice.* In explaining this he stated:

Do we want a free Indonesia where capitalists bear sway, or where the entire people prosper, where every man has enough to eat, enough to wear, lives in prosperity, feels cherished by the homeland that gives him sufficient keep? Do not imagine, gentlemen, that as soon as the People's Representative body . . . comes into being, we shall automatically achieve this prosperity. We have seen that in the states of Europe there are representative bodies, there is parliamentary democracy. But is it not in Europe that the capitalists are in control?

In America there is a people's representative body, and are not the capitalists throughout the Western Continent in control? There is no other reason but the fact that the people's representative bodies established there have merely followed the recipe of the French Revolution. What is called democracy there is merely a political democracy; there is no social justice and no economic democracy at all.

In explaining that political democracy does not insure economic democracy, Soekarno significantly quoted the Revisionist Socialist, Jean Jaurès rather than a doctrinaire Marxist. He then went on to say:

Gentlemen, if we are seeking democracy, the need is not for the democracy of the West, but for . . . politico-economic democracy, able to bring social prosperity! The people of Indonesia have long spoken of this matter. What is meant by 'Ratu Adil,' the God of Justice? It is *social justice*. The people wish for prosperity. The people, who recently have felt themselves what it is not to have enough to eat nor enough to wear, wish to create a new world in which there is justice, under the leadership of Ratu Adil. Therefore, if we truly understand, remember, and love the people of Indonesia, let us accept this *principle of social justice* which is not only political equality, gentlemen. In the field of economy, too, we must create equality, and the best common prosperity.

Gentlemen, the people's conference which we will establish should not be a body for the discussion of political democracy only, but a body which, together with the community, will be able to shape two principles: *political justice* and *social justice*.

Soekarno's fifth principle was that the organization of Free Indonesia should be in the light of a *belief in one God*. In elucidating this he stated:

Not only should the people of Indonesia have belief in God, but every Indonesian should believe in *his own* particular God. The Christian should worship God according to the teachings of Jesus Christ; Moslems according to the teachings of the Prophet Mohammad; Buddhists should discharge their religious rites according to their own books.

But let us all have belief in God. The Indonesian state shall be a state where every person can worship God in freedom . . . without 'religious egoism.' And the State of Indonesia should be a State incorporating the belief in God.

Let us observe, let us practice religion, whether Islam or Christianity, in a civilized way . . . the way of mutual respect.

In conclusion Soekarno went on to emphasize the mutual com-
patibility of these five principles and the similarity of their totality
with the spirit of indigenous Indonesian society. The first two principles, nationalism and internationalism or humanitarianism could, he
said, be reduced to a single principle—that of *socio-nationalism*. Likewise, he continued, the next two principles, those of democracy (or
consent) and social justice could be reduced to one principle, that of
socio-democracy. Thus three principles remained: socio-nationalism,
socio-democracy, and a belief in God. However, he said, that these three
could be reduced to a single principle: a principle for which there is
a "genuine Indonesian term, the term *'gotong rojong'* (mutual co-
operation). The State of Indonesia which we are to establish should be
a state of mutual co-operation. How fine that is! A *Gotong Rojong*
state!" In explanation of this term Soekarno continued:

'Mutual co-operation' is a dynamic conviction, more dynamic than 'brotherhood,' gentlemen. Brotherhood is a static conviction, but *Gotong Rojong*,
mutual co-operation, portrays one endeavor, one charity, one task. . . . *Gotong Rojong* means toiling hard together, sweating hard together, a struggle of
help-me-to-help-you together. The piety of all for the interests of all! That is
Gotong Rojong!

The principle of *Gotong Rojong* between the rich and the poor, between
the Moslem and the Christian, between those not originating from Indonesia
and their children who become Indonesians. This, gentlemen, is what I propose
to you.

Finally Soekarno stated that he thanked God that the Indonesian
state that they would establish would be set up "in the midst of war's
thunder" and that consequently it would emerge "a free Indonesia
tempered in the fury of war . . . a strong Indonesian state, not an
Indonesian state which would turn soft after some time." Attainment
of a free Indonesia based upon the five principles he had set forth
could only be realized, he emphasized, through *struggle*, struggle which
would continue, though in different form even after the attainment
of independence. He concluded his address in a militant tone, stating:

And particularly in this time of war have faith, cultivate in your hearts the
conviction that free Indonesia cannot come if the people of Indonesia do not
dare take a risk, do not dare dive for pearls into the depths of the ocean. If
the people of Indonesia are not united, and not determined to live or die for
freedom, the freedom of Indonesia will never be the possession of the Indonesian people, never until the end of time! Freedom can only be achieved and

owned by a people whose soul is aflame with the determination of *Merdeka* [freedom]—freedom or death!

On August 7, 1945, permission was granted by Lt. General Terauchi's headquarters at Saigon [30] for the establishment of an all-Indonesian committee, the announced function of which was to make preparations for transfer of governmental authority from the Japanese armed forces to it. Known as the Indonesian Independence Preparatory Committee (Panitia Persiapan Kermedekaan Indonesia), this enrolled an appointed membership of twenty-one drawn from all parts of Indonesia on a basis of representation roughly proportional to population. All of those Indonesians appointed were outstanding nationalists. Its members were: Ir. Soekarno, chairman; Drs. Mohammad Hatta, vice-chairman; K. R. T. Radjiman Wediodiningrat, R. Otto Iskander Dinata, Ki Abdoel Waschid Hasjim, Ki Bagoes Hadikoesoema, B. K. P. A. Soerjohamidjojo, B. P. H. Poerbojo, M. Soetardjo Kartohadikoesomo, R. P. Suroso, Prof. R. Soepomo, and R. Abdoel Kadir for Java; Dr. Mohammad Amir for Sumatra; Mr. Tenku Mohammad Hassan for Sumatra; Mr. Abdoel Abas for Sumatra; Dr. G. S. S. J. Ratu Langie for Celebes; Andi Pangeran for Celebes; A. A. Hamidhan for Borneo; Mr. I. Goesti Ketoet Poedja for the Lesser Sunda Islands; Mr. J. Latuharhary for the Moluccas; and Drs. Yap Tjuan Bing representing the Chinese community.

On August 8, 1945, Soekarno, Hatta, and Radjiman were called by General Terauchi to Dalat in Indochina. There on August 11 he promised them that independence would be granted to Indonesia on August 24. A constitutional assembly was to be called on August 19, and during the intervening week this was to round out and ratify the constitution which the previously established committees for the preparation of independence had been working on. The three returned on August 14 to find the Indonesian undergrounds opposed to any Indonesian independence that was a gift of the Japanese and absolutely determined to wrest unconditional independence from them by force. These underground movements in Java, and apparently those in Sumatra, were pledged to and organized for an uprising against the Japanese which was to coincide with the expected Allied attack against Java and Sumatra. Moreover, a few days after their return they found the Japanese military adminis-

[30] Under which were the Japanese commands in Indonesia and elsewhere in Southeast Asia.

tration obliged, because of Japan's capitulation to the Allies to maintain the political *status quo*. This was the situation which precipitated
the Indonesian revolution.

But to understand more clearly the revolutionary phase of the Indonesian nationalist movement and the character of that revolution we
should pause and assess the impact of the Japanese occupation upon
Indonesian society. The outstanding development during the Japanese occupation was the tremendous increase in national consciousness and the will to political independence which it fostered. The
harsh and arbitrary rule of the Japanese affected almost the entire
population. In comparison Dutch rule had been moderate and was
much less felt by most Indonesians. Japanese rule aroused a consciousness of common suffering and humiliation and a common resentment
against the Japanese that enormously strengthened the already existing national consciousness of Indonesians.

The indirectness that had characterized the relationship of the
Dutch administration with the peasantry was succeeded by a direct
and jarring intrusion by the Japanese military administration which
was only slightly cushioned by partially operating through the
Poetera and Djawa Hokokai. As Sjahrir has observed:

During the three and a half years of Japanese occupation, the foundations of
rural society were shaken and undermined by forced regulations, kidnapping
from homes for conscription as labourers abroad or as soldiers, compulsory
surrender of harvested crops, compulsory planting of designated crops—all
imposed with unlimited arbitrariness.[31]

In many areas village societies were severely wrenched and forced to
realign their structures because of the heavy demands on their labor
supply made by the Japanese. The conscription of hundreds of thousands of their most able workers into the Hei Ho, Peta, etc. meant
that traditional patterns of work and land apportionment had to be
altered. The cruelty of the Japanese, their exorbitant demands for
labor and crops, and their repayment in a worthless currency which
would buy almost none of the traditional needs, such as cloth, agricultural implements, etc. aroused in most peasants an intense bitterness against them. It is true that, because of the tremendous monetary
inflation that developed during the last two years of the Japanese occupation,[32] the widespread monetary indebtedness of the peasantry

[31] Soetan Sjahrir, *Onze Strijd* (Amsterdam, 1946), p. 11.
[32] See Mohammad Saubari, "Dua Tahun Uang Republik," *Sikap*, March 3, 1949.

was reduced in proportion to the value of its land. But this incidental result of Japanese rule could not long be capitalized upon by most peasants because the severity of Japanese exactions left them no recourse but to incur new debts from their traditional source of credit, the itinerant Chinese moneylenders. By 1944 these moneylenders had generally stopped advancing credit in kind (seed, cloth, and agricultural implements) for repayment in the increasingly inflated currency. Instead they agreed to make such advances only for a stipulated percentage of the peasant's crop. Thereby much of the benefit from the inflation by-passed the peasant.

As a reaction to and in order to resist the heavy demands of the Japanese, the peasantry became much more politically conscious than it had ever previously been. This and its feeling against the Japanese is attested to by the widespread and frequent local peasant revolts that occurred, particularly during the last year of the Japanese occupation. Indoctrination by the undergrounds plus the skill of the nationalist leaders in the Poetera and Hokokai, particularly Soekarno and Hatta, who by radio and personal appearance were given an almost unlimited contact with the peasantry by the Japanese, translated this political awakening and the grievances behind it into a national consciousness and will for national independence such as the peasantry had never previously possessed. In particular this was due to the speeches of Soekarno, broadcast as they were to almost every large village of Java and Madura. His ability to communicate with the peasantry in terms and concepts understandable to them allowed him to establish such rapport with them that when the revolution broke it was primarily to him that they looked for leadership.

The constant Japanese propaganda aimed at developing popular support for their war effort and castigating the Allies undoubtedly increased the political awakening that the material aspect of the Japanese occupation was provoking. Though Japanese propaganda and actions [33] were effective in increasing the population's feeling against the Dutch, the Japanese effort to make the people hostile toward the other Allies, particularly the United States, met with comparatively little success. The Japanese failed almost completely in their efforts to bring the Indonesians to identify their national interests with those of Japan. The efforts of the anti-Japanese Indonesian undergrounds to

[33] By "actions" is meant the military defeat of the Dutch and the subsequent increased loss in Dutch prestige resulting from the many humiliations heaped upon them in full view of the Indonesians, including being forced to sweep the streets, etc.

counter these Japanese aims was made easier and encouraged by American victories over the Japanese and the anticolonial attitude which America seemed to the Indonesians to have espoused. Reports of these victories and this attitude were received by the radios of the underground organizations and disseminated by them to the population, in particular to the Peta units and the youth organizations. The insistent proclamation of America's attachment to the terms of the Atlantic Charter and the Charter of the United Nations in overseas broadcasts from the United States picked up in Indonesia in conjunction with the definite American pledge of postwar independence for the Philippines convinced many Indonesians that America was in general opposed to colonialism and that this opposition extended to Indonesia.

Probably the deepest imprint of the Japanese occupation was left on the Indonesian youth, in particular those between fifteen and twenty-five years of age. Especially among those who had received little previous education, and that was the large majority, the sustained and intense Japanese propaganda left its mark. It narrowed and intensified their nationalist sentiments. Few developed a pro-Japanese orientation, but many developed an extremely militant nationalism with a strong, emotional anti-Western bias which frequently verged on sheer hatred and often extended itself to antipathy against Eurasians and Indies Chinese.[34] The number of those whose nationalism was so narrow should not be exaggerated. Though their number was large, they were probably not in the majority. Whatever the case, most of them proved willing to follow the counsel and example of the educated youth and older national leaders, whose nationalism was much less narrow. There did remain, however, a significant minority which early in the revolution was attracted to the support of less enlightened leaders.

Because of the dominant role they were to play in the first and most critical phases of the Indonesian revolution, it is particularly important to understand the effect of the Japanese occupation on the relatively educated youth, especially the secondary-school and college students. The Japanese policy of forcing their language on Indonesian students (most emphasized during the first year of the occupation) coupled with their harsh and autocratic administration of the schools very quickly antagonized the students. Many of the more spirited of them were either forced to leave school because of their open resistance

[34] Cf. Soetan Sjahrir, *op. cit.*, pp. 12–13.

to the Japanese school authorities or resigned in protest. A number remained in school only to hide better the anti-Japanese underground activities that absorbed most of their time.

A large portion of the student body came from homes outside the few large cities where the secondary schools and colleges were located. They were separated from their homes in most cases, and if they did not accept scholarship aid from the Japanese school administration, which soon became anathema to most, were forced to shift for themselves. Having to support themselves was a completely new experience for most of them. Because of the shortage of relatively educated government and commercial workers resulting from the incarceration of the European population, this was fairly easy. The ability to support themselves gave many of them a degree of self-confidence which they had not possessed before. Lacking it, many are convinced, they would have been much less able to play the revolutionary roles which they were soon to assume.

Moreover, those who left school and had homes to go to had to make the best of their free time. The same problem to a lesser extent was encountered by those who had got jobs and therefore did not have to devote their evenings to studying subjects of the school curriculum. From the beginning the extraordinary political events they had been witnessing and their hostility to the Japanese induced them to study the social sciences, subjects largely denied them by both the narrow curriculums of the Japanese and the Dutch-controlled school administrations. Many Indonesian students first encountered the writings of Western political writers during this enforced idleness, and many of those who had savored them before found their first opportunity to read them with any thoroughness. With the abolition of the Poetera at the end of 1943, most of the secondary and college students who had supported it established contact with one or more of the undergrounds, if they had not already done so. In these—in particular under the tutelage of Sjahrir and members of his group such as Djohan Sjaroezah, Roeslan Abdulgani, Subadio, Dr. Subandrio and Dr. Sudarsono—their political education was furthered while at the same time they engaged in the work of the undergrounds. Finally we must note the deep anti-imperialist, pro-Communist imprint left upon those students attending the Asrama schools.

Among literate Indonesians (between 6 and 8 per cent of the population) the development and spread of the Indonesian language during the Japanese occupation meant the strengthening of their national consciousness and the offsetting of parochial tendencies that might otherwise have been enhanced because of the division of Indonesia into three administrative spheres. Initially the long-run objective of the Japanese was to substitute their own language for Dutch as the administrative language and as the medium of instruction in the schools. Short-run expediency, however, forced them to rely on the only language other than Dutch which could be understood by significant numbers of Indonesians throughout the archipelago. This was the Malay language,[35] or *Bahasa Indonesia* (Indonesian language), as the dialect generally spoken throughout Indonesia had become known. Under the Japanese it became the official language for administration and for all education above the third grade. Indonesians who had held the top positions open to natives under the Dutch administration and who spoke flawless Dutch but little Indonesian were compelled to learn the latter in short order. The same was true of school teachers whose vehicle of instruction had been Dutch or perhaps Javanese, Sundanese, or Madurese. Takdir Alisjabana observes:

Because the Japanese were determined to enlist the energies of the entire Indonesian population in the war effort, they penetrated into the villages in the remotest backwaters of the islands, using the Indonesian language as they went.

Thus the language flourished and imbued the people with a feeling new to most of them. As more and more of them learned to speak it freely, they became aware of a common bond. The Indonesian language became a symbol of national unity in opposition to the efforts of the Japanese ultimately to implant their own language and culture. By the time, therefore, of the Japanese surrender, the position of the Indonesian language had improved enormously both in strength and in prestige vis-à-vis not only Dutch but also the various regional languages of the archipelago, which had no opportunity to develop during the occupation.[36]

Another consequence of the Japanese occupation, extremely important in developing nationalist sentiments amongst Indonesians and in particular their will to political independence, resulted from the tremendous increase in national self-confidence of Indonesians generally and in the individual self-confidence of most educated Indonesians. This arose, as we have seen, from the necessity for the Japanese to employ Indonesians in most of those administrative and technical positions from which they had removed Europeans. The railroad system

---

[35] See above, footnote 101 on page 97.

[36] Takdir Alisjabana, "The Indonesian Language—By-Product of Nationalism," *Pacific Affairs,* Dec. 1949, p. 390.

under the management of Indonesians may not have run as efficiently as it had under the Dutch, but it did run. It was suddenly apparent that the so-thought esoteric skills of the "superior Dutchman" not only could be but in many cases already had been mastered by Indonesians. This made a tremendous impression on the average man. By the individual Indonesian who performed these tasks, and with respect to a number of activities by the observing Indonesian public as a whole, it was noticed that frequently when a Japanese took over one of these administrative or technical jobs his level of performance was substantially below that attained by Indonesians. "Well," reasoned many Indonesians, "the Japanese easily thrashed the Dutch, and we can perform these jobs better than the Japanese. We certainly, therefore, are not an inferior people. Why should we be governed by anyone but ourselves?"

But quite apart from engendering this powerful self-confidence, the employment of Indonesians in positions formerly filled by Europeans strengthened the Indonesian will to independence in another important way. For the many Indonesians who had benefited from this revolutionary upward socio-economic movement had a strong vested interest in maintaining these changes. For them that meant resisting a return of Dutch rule. They were sure that its return would mean demotion to their old positions. On the other hand, independence was envisaged as promising even higher positions than they had already obtained. Attainment of their new positions did not satisfy them, but the enhanced self-confidence springing from their ability to handle these jobs merely whetted their appetite for the better positions retained by the Japanese or for the full occupancy of their new positions without the incubus of a Japanese "adviser" as their overseer.

The social revolution which expediency forced the Japanese to create benefited even many of those Indonesians who as members of the old indigenous aristocracy had been favored by the Dutch and had occupied relatively high administrative positions under them. In most cases these positions had been high enough to give them a strong interest in assisting in the maintenance of the Dutch colonial *status quo*. However, under the Japanese many such persons were pushed upward to positions which they had no hope of attaining under the old regime. In them, too, was born the conviction that they could handle positions higher than those they had been allowed by the Dutch, that they were entitled to such positions, and that in an independent Indonesia they would be assured of them. Thus were spoiled some of the most effective and reliable instruments of Dutch rule.

CHAPTER V

Outbreak of the Revolution

RUMORS that Japan had or was about to capitulate to the Allies spurred into action the several underground organizations that had been poised to rise against the Japanese when the Allies should land. As early as August 10, 1945, Sjahrir, who had received radio reports of Japanese peace feelers, urged Hatta that he and Soekarno should immediately proclaim Indonesian independence and assured him that he could count on the support of the undergrounds and many of the Peta units. When Soekarno and Hatta returned from Dalat on August 14, he informed them that the Japanese had requested an armistice and again urged their prompt proclamation of independence. Soekarno and Hatta were not yet convinced that Japan would surrender, felt that the undergrounds were not yet able to muster sufficient strength to overthrow the Japanese, and feared a useless blood bath might result.

Sjahrir, however, believing that Soekarno would soon proclaim independence in the strongly worded anti-Japanese terms of the declaration which Sjahrir and his co-workers had prepared, began at once to organize the undergrounds and the Jakarta students for mass demonstrations and military eventualities. Copies of their anti-Japanese independence declaration had been sent to all parts of Java to be published immediately upon the expected announcement of the fifteenth by Soekarno. After these preparations had been begun, it became clear Soekarno and Hatta would not make the proclamation on the fifteenth. Sjahrir was unable to contact all leaders of his organization in time to tell them of this. An isolated revolution which the Japanese suppressed was started in Cheribon on the fifteenth under Dr. Sudarsono.

Soekarno and Hatta still hoped to avoid bloodshed, while the underground groups joined Sjahrir in his demand for an immediate declaration of independence couched in terms so strongly anti-Japanese that the whole Indonesian population would rally behind it in one common surge to overthrow the Japanese. Meanwhile the underground led by Sukarni and supported by a considerable number of the Student Union group lost patience and at 4 A.M. on the sixteenth, kidnapped Soekarno and Hatta to the Peta garrison at Rengasdengklok. Here they convinced Soekarno and Hatta that the Japanese had really surrendered. They then tried to prevail upon them to make an immediate declaration of independence. Sukarni maintained that there were 15,000 armed youths on the outskirts of Jakarta ready to march against the city as soon as the proclamation was made. Soekarno and Hatta were sure that he exaggerated the armed strength he claimed and that the Japanese would easily suppress such an attempt. Apparently they felt it was possible that an understanding could be arrived at with the Japanese whereby they would not oppose the declaration with military force. In the interests of avoiding unnecessary bloodshed they wished at least to ascertain the attitude of the Japanese military authorities before calling upon the people to rise. Moreover, they both felt that any declaration must emphasize its all-Indonesian source and that therefore it should be done through the Independence Preparatory Committee with its all-Indonesian representation. Thereby, they felt, the whole of Indonesia would rise together to assert independence, and the chances of successful mobilization of the population against the Japanese would be greater. A meeting of the Committee was scheduled for 10 A.M. on the seventeenth, and it was then that they proposed to declare independence.

In the meantime the Japanese had learned of the kidnapping, and Subardjo, who was a close acquaintance of the Sukarni group,[1] went to Rengasdengklok, certainly with the knowledge of Admiral Mayeda, if not also of Japanese army officers, to persuade Sukarni and the student leaders to return with Soekarno and Hatta to Jakarta. This confirmed the suspicion of Soekarno and Hatta that the Japanese knew of the general plans for declaration of independence and reinforced their belief in the inadequacy of the armed Indonesians on the outskirts of

[1] Subardjo, it will be recalled, was chief of the consulting office of the Japanese navy's Java H.Q.

the capital, since now they could no longer attack with the advantage of surprise.

Upon returning to Jakarta late on the night of the sixteenth, Hatta immediately got in touch with the right-hand man of the commander in chief of the Japanese army on Java. This officer informed him that by the surrender terms the Japanese were "merely agents of the Allies" and that they could by no means countenance a declaration of independence by the Indonesians. It was thus clear to Hatta and Soekarno that a bloodless revolution was impossible and that the course advocated by Sjahrir, Sukarni, Wikana, and the other underground leaders was the only possible means of attaining independence. Sjahrir then visited Soekarno and elicited from him a promise to declare independence; however, he was unable to secure from him a commitment that it would be done in the strongly anti-Japanese terms that he and his group advocated.

The Japanese were now on the alert, and the movements of all Indonesian leaders were being closely watched. A place of meeting free from the Kempeitai was vital. At about midnight Hatta contacted Vice-Admiral Mayeda, who agreed to turn over his house to a meeting of the nationalists. Mayeda absented himself and at 2 A.M. on the seventeenth, Soekarno and Hatta met with the members of the Preparatory Committee and Subardjo, Wikana, and Sukarni to draw up a declaration of independence.[2] After much discussion the text was decided upon, and on the morning of August 17, 1945, Soekarno read the declaration to a small group outside of his own residence. Soon afterwards the declaration along with Hatta's personal message to his old nationalist friends was broadcast over the entire Domei Indonesian radio and telegraph network by Indonesian employees behind the locked doors of its Jakarta (Batavia)[3] office.

The Indonesian revolution had been launched, and the popular response throughout the archipelago, though not immediately known in Jakarta, was tremendous. The Japanese reaction was prompt. Upon orders of the commander in chief of the Japanese army in Java, Mayeda and his entire staff were quickly jailed, and independence announcements being posted around the city were torn down by the Kempeitai.

---

[2] Sjahrir and the leaders of his group refused to attend because convinced that Soekarno and Hatta would not agree to a proclamation that was militantly anti-Japanese in character.

[3] During the Japanese occupation Batavia was rechristened with its pre-Dutch Indonesian name, Jakarta (generally spelled "Djakarta" in Indonesia).

The following day the Japanese ordered the disbandonment of the Peta, Hei Ho, and all other armed Indonesian organizations.

Apparently, however, the Japanese authorities were at first not certain what action they should take towards Soekarno and Hatta. On the nineteenth these two leaders, urged on by the underground groups, undertook to address a mass meeting of enthusiastic Indonesians assembled at the great central park of Jakarta. This meeting was picketed by Japanese tanks and armored cars, and the original intention of the Japanese was to arrest Soekarno and Hatta. However, the swelling enthusiasm of the huge and increasing crowd evidently caused them to change their minds. Soekarno spoke to the crowd briefly in moderate terms, but sticking to the claim of independence. He then called upon the tens of thousands of Indonesians who listened to leave the park quietly and return peacefully to their homes. They did. The Japanese could not but be impressed with this demonstration of controlled power.

Where they were not too far outnumbered, Peta units throughout wide areas of Java resisted the Japanese orders to disarm, kept their arms, clashed with the Japanese, and in some places themselves disarmed Japanese units. The Japanese garrisons maintained military control in the larger cities and towns, but control over considerable areas began to pass to Indonesian armed groups, Peta, or units of youth organizations which had taken their arms from small Japanese formations either by force or in many instances because their commanders were demoralized and surrendered them, sometimes doing so willingly. The Indonesian flag was forbidden by the Japanese. But Soekarno, recognizing its revolutionary symbolism, ordered that it be flown from all public buildings. Indonesian youths began to risk their lives to put it up, inevitably provoking clashes with the Japanese, who immediately attempted to tear it down. Within six weeks the flag, the tangible symbol of independence, was flying from nearly every public building in Java. The students became the vanguard of the revolution, directing the demobilized youth from the Japanese-sponsored youth organizations and with them seizing arms from the Japanese, dragging Japanese officers from their cars, ousting Japanese functionaries from government buildings and in general providing the chief pushing force behind the new Republic that Soekarno was leading.

The Japanese military command was in a quandary. The orders it had received from the Allied Southeast Asia Command clearly called for its maintenance of the political *status quo* until Allied troops took over. Yet it was convinced, and Soekarno argued eloquently to increase its conviction, that any attempt to suppress the newly proclaimed Republic and the independence movement which backed it would result in a tremendous bloody struggle. The Japanese might possibly have emerged victorious in such a fight, but only at the cost of very heavy casualties. Their policy until the arrival of Allied troops at the end of September was uncertain, wavering, and compromising, and sought to avoid a head-on collision with the Indonesian revolution. In general, they were afraid to contest squarely the establishment of an Indonesian government, but with more vigor undertook to stop the growth of Indonesian military power.

The establishment of a government for the newly proclaimed Republic proceeded rapidly. At its first meeting on August 18, 1945, the Independence Preparatory Committee added six people to its membership, Subardjo, Kasman Singodimedjo (the commander of the Jakarta Peta garrison), Sukarni, Wikana, and Chairul Saleh. The expanded committee elected Soekarno and Hatta respectively President and Vice-President of the Republic of Indonesia. It appointed a commission of seven—Soekarno, Hatta, Professor Soepomo, Subardjo, Otto Iskander Dinata, Mr. Mohammad Yamin, and Mr. Wongosonegoro—to make the necessary and final changes in the national Constitution, already largely written during the last month before the Japanese capitulation.[4] Within a week the final draft of the Indonesian Constitution was completed and, though considered definitely provisional, was immediately promulgated. Providing latitude for wide-scale social and economic as well as political change, it soon became a revolutionary symbol of great power, a harbinger of the good life that would follow the overthrow of alien control.

A more widespread revolutionary symbol, symbolic of the revolution's egalitarian as well as fraternal content, was the mode of address introduced by Soekarno and soon in use throughout the Republic of Indonesia. This word *Bung* (pronounced būng) was best translated as "brother" and in a rough sense was comparable to the "citizen" of the French Revolution or the "comrade" of the Russian. It derived from the local Jakarta variant of the Indonesian word *abang*, elder brother. (This variant was also common to East Java.) However, the modifying "elder" was no part of the expression. The closest approximation of the idea it conveyed would probably be a synthesis of "brother revolutionary," "brother Indonesian nationalist," and

[4] It accepted that part of the Constitution that was already completed at this meeting on the 18th.

"brother Republican." Young and old, poor and rich, President and peasant could and usually did address each other with this word. A diner in a restaurant addressed the waiter as "Bung"; a cabinet minister or the humblest Indonesian peasant addressed President Soekarno as "Bung Karno."

The Indonesian department heads under the Japanese administration speedily declared for the new government. Along with several new appointees of Soekarno and Hatta—both men who had worked with the Japanese (such as Subardjo) and who had not (such as Amir Sjarifuddin and Ir. Soerachman)—they constituted the first cabinet of the new Republic, a cabinet which under the Constitution was responsible to the President, Soekarno. The following was the membership of the first cabinet of the Republic of Indonesia (August 31, 1945—November 14, 1945):

Minister of Foreign Affairs	Mr. Achmad Subardjo
" " Internal Affairs	R. A. A. Wiranata Koesoema
" " Justice	Professor Soepomo
" " Economic Affairs	Ir. Soerachman
" " Finance	Dr. Samsi
" " Education	Ki Hadjar Dewantara
" " Social Affairs	Mr. Iwa Kusuma Sumantri
" " Information	Mr. Amir Sjarifuddin
" " Health	Dr. Boentaran Martoatmodjo
" " Communications	Abikusno Tjokrosujuso
" " State (without portfolio)	Dr. Amir
" " " " "	Wachid Hasjim
" " " " "	Mr. Sartono
" " " " "	Mr. A. A. Maramis
" " " " "	Otto Iskandar Dinata
" " " " "	Soekardjo Wirjopranoto

After September 1, 1945, the Indonesian department heads who had served the Japanese, as well as the new men appointed by Soekarno and Hatta to head other departments, gave orders as ministers of the Republic. Soekarno decreed that all Indonesian civil servants were to ignore orders from the Japanese and follow those of the Republican government alone. The departments headed by his ministers at once received the backing of almost all Indonesian government personnel. Without that personnel, the Japanese administration could not function. Military control of the chief urban centers was for a time maintained by the Japanese, but they were powerless to check the rush of civilian functionaries to the service of the Republic.

On August 29, the Independence Preparatory Committee was dissolved by Soekarno and in its place was established the Komité Nasional Indonesia Pusat (Central Indonesian National Committee), or KNIP as it came to be known. This was to serve solely as an advisory body to the President and his cabinet, undertaking no legislative functions of its own.[5] To this new body Soekarno, assisted in his selections by Hatta, appointed 135 members (including those of the Independence Preparatory Committee), whom they deemed to be the outstanding Indonesian nationalists and the most important leaders of the chief ethnic, religious, social, and economic groups in Indonesia. They did not merely select amenable political stooges, but chose men and women nearly all of whom commanded wide popular support as outstanding leaders of Indonesian society.

By a decree of the Preparatory Committee on August 19, Indonesia had been divided into eight provinces: West Java, Middle Java, East Java, Sumatra, Kalimantan (Borneo), Sulawesi (Celebes), Maluku (the Moluccas), and Sunda-Ketjil (the Lesser Sundas). Soekarno appointed a governor for each province from among its own population, and the KNIP gave mandates to one of its own members from each of these areas to form provincial KNI's (Indonesian National Committees) to assist these governors in their administrations.[6] Speedily there developed a spontaneous eruption of local KNI's on the district and municipal level as well. For a considerable period these local revolutionary committees executed the real administrative power in their areas. Initially they were self-constituted by the recognized local leaders, but later, beginning in late November, according to a uniform pattern established by Government regulation. This was formalized in Java and Madura by a Governmental Act of November 23, 1945, which called for the establishment of such councils in all residencies, regencies, municipalities and such other territories as the Minister of Interior might designate. (On October 30, 1945 the Sultan of Jogjakarta had decreed the establishment of such a council in his own territory.) By 1946, where conditions allowed, many of these KNI's were created on the basis of local elections.

An August 29, the new government began to organize an army. Upon the base of armed and disarmed Peta units and from the ranks

[5] Sec. iv of the transitional regulations of the Constitution stated: "Before the People's Congress, the Council of Representatives and the Council of State [the regular representative organs of government] are elected . . . their competence shall be exercised by the President assisted by a National Committee."

[6] The governor of each province was to exercise his legislative duties in agreement with the provincial KNI (or Dewan Perwakilan Rakjat [Peoples Representative Council] as it was frequently called). *Peraturan Pemerintah* ("Government Decree") no. 8.

of the several youth organizations was established the BKR (Badan Keamanan Rakjat, People's Peace Preservation Corps), with head-quarters in Jakarta. This loosely organized army was composed of highly autonomous and virtually independent constituent units hav-ing a territorial basis and subject to varying degrees of control by the KNI's of their respective areas, which were charged with their main-tenance and supply. Beginning on October 5, 1945, the name of the national army was changed from BKR to TKR or Tentara Keamanan Rakjat (People's Peace Preservation Army),[7] its constituent units dur-ing the course of the next few months being brought under greater, but frequently ineffective, degrees of central control. The BKR units were quickly brought into the revolutionary struggle. They helped seize government buildings from the Japanese and arrested those who refused to leave them.

Fitful fighting between the Japanese and Indonesians continued with mounting frequency and scale throughout September. Indo-nesian attempts to secure Japanese weapons and Japanese contesta-tion of Indonesian civil authority brought more and more clashes. The first British troops began to land at Jakarta on September 29, just as Indonesian attempts to wrest arms and civil authority from the Japanese entered their most violent phase. During the first two weeks of October there was heavy fighting between Indonesian and Japanese troops for control of the cities of Bandung, Garut, Surakarta, Jogjakarta, Semarang, and Surabaya. In Bandung, Garut, and Surabaya the Indonesians won temporary control and retained control of Jogjakarta until December 19, 1948. Semarang was entered by the British on October 19 after the Indonesian forces had already sus-tained some 2,000 casualties fighting the hard-pressed Japanese gar-rison.

The task of the incoming British forces was formidable. The in-structions of the Allied chiefs of staff as interpreted by Lord Mount-batten, Allied commander in chief for Southeast Asia, called for ac-cepting the surrender of Japanese armed forces, release of Allied war prisoners and civilian internees, and disarmament and concentration of the Japanese in readiness for transport back to Japan. In addition they called for the establishment and maintenance of law and order

[7] Later as it became more integrated and its constituent units more responsive to central control, its name was changed to Tentara Republik Indonesia (Army of the Republic of Indonesia) or TRI and finally to Tentara Nasional Indonesia (In-donesian National Army) or TNI.

in Indonesia until the Netherlands administration in the Indies was able to function by itself. This last instruction, of course, antedated Allied knowledge of events within Indonesia. British officers in Java and Sumatra and Australian officers in parts of Celebes and the Lesser Sundas were bound by instructions based on premises that were no longer valid as to conditions in the Indies. British and Australian forces landing in Indonesia in October, 1945, encountered a situation for which they were totally unprepared.[8] Throughout most of the area, in Java and Sumatra in particular, civil administration was operating at a level of efficiency that quite amazed the Allied forces.

Soekarno and Hatta issued a general order against interfering with British troops, and groups of the students went out into the field to explain the situation to the Djibaku units and to see that they did not undertake irresponsible actions. However, not only the Djibaku, but all Indonesians soon came to have misgivings about British intentions. As early as September 29, Rear Admiral Patterson, commander of the British Fifth Cruiser Squadron, proclaimed that Allied troops had arrived to protect the people and "to maintain law and order until the time that the lawful government of the Netherlands East Indies is once again functioning." Netherlands law would be applied and enforced, he said, by Netherlands administrative officers in Java subject only to whatever commands Admiral Mountbatten might issue. The same day Lt. Gen. Sir Philip Christison, Allied commander in chief for the Netherlands Indies, announced that Japanese forces in Java would be used temporarily to maintain law and order.[9] These announcements were soon followed by the landing, under British cover, of small contingents of Dutch troops. Repeatedly Soekarno and other Republican leaders warned the British to stop these British-protected landings. They were convinced that the Indonesian population, already suspicious and antagonized by Patterson's and Christison's announcements, could not fail to interpret the influx of Dutch troops as positive indication of an intent to overthrow the Republic and return

---

[8] Dutch intelligence (NEFIS) based at Kandy in Ceylon was very poorly informed as to conditions in Java and Sumatra. A small Allied intelligence team did land at Jakarta airport on Sept. 8, 1945, and stayed in Java a week. However, its information was apparently based largely on contact with those relatively moderate nationalists who were willing to settle for considerably less than full and immediate independence. It can only be concluded that this team was unaware of the much stronger and more militant orientation of the Indonesian youth, the element which constituted the chief pushing power behind the revolution.

[9] N.Y. Times, Sept. 30, 1945.

Indonesia to colonial status. The Indonesian leaders feared that the popular reaction to this realization would lead to violence against the thousands of Dutch internees still quartered in the Japanese concentration camps.

Any remaining doubts on the part of the Indonesian population as to Dutch intentions were rapidly dispelled by the activities of Netherlands and Netherlands colonial troops.[10] The United States military observer attached to the staff of General Christison, Major F. E. Crockett noted:

Concurrent with General van Oyen's arrival there began to appear in the streets [of Jakarta] roving patrols of trigger-happy Dutch and Ambonese [of the KNIL—the Royal Netherlands Indies Army] soldiers. They shot at anything that looked suspicious, and when hunting was poor, they were not above forcing an Indonesian house and dragging off, without charges or warrants, some or all of the inhabitants. . . . The "incidents" increased. The Nationalists were instructed that any outbreaks on their part would be severely dealt with by the occupying authorities. In order to prevent trouble, Soekarno ordered all Indonesians off the streets of Batavia at dark. By eight o'clock the streets were empty except for the roving Dutch patrols. It was an impressive demonstration of Soekarno's control over his people.[11]

Such activity effectively undermined the possibility of carrying out the policy of non-intervention in Republican-Dutch political relations that Lt. Gen. Christison after his appraisal of local conditions had hoped to follow. Major Crockett's analysis of the situation and the apprehensions it raised within him were also felt by the Republic's leaders. According to Crockett:

It seemed clear to me from what I had seen that the Dutch, in view of Britain's political non-interference pronouncement, would try and were trying to involve the British inextricably by provoking unrest among the native population. I could see no other reasonable explanation for the brutal conduct of the Dutch patrols. What they would gain by such tactics was obvious: they would keep the British too busy to disarm the Japanese (which was their primary reason for being there) and they would force the British to commit more and more troops to the area, which would inevitably mean more and more involvement.[12]

[10] Both newly landed soldiers and ex-soldiers who had just been released from prison camp and forced back into uniform under orders of Lt. Gen. van Oyen, the top Dutch officer, who arrived with the British.

[11] Frederick E. Crockett, "How the Trouble Began in Java," *Harper's,* March, 1946, p. 281.

[12] *Ibid.,* p. 283.

Such activity by Dutch troops, their continued landing under British protection, and the equivocal announcements of the British combined to demonstrate to most Indonesians that their assertion of independence was being challenged and served to provoke their sharp response. No longer could the Djibaku be restrained. Its units subdivided into small combat groups and were soon followed by the various armed youth units in violent attacks against Dutch and British patrols. In several cases the objects of such attacks, usually where the Barisan Pelopor was involved, were not confined to foreign troops but extended to unarmed civilian Dutch internees, including women and children. Concurrently, all Indonesian armed units intensified their efforts to wrest arms and control from the Japanese.

The Allied command now placed the restoration of law and order under British control in the chief cities and ports of Java and Sumatra as the top priority, with the disarmament of the Japanese to come later. It ordered Japanese commanders to attack and recapture Indonesian-held cities such as Bandung. The Allied use of Japanese troops against the Republic further aroused the Indonesians against both the British and Dutch and reinforced their conviction that it was intented that Indonesia revert to colonial status. During November and December wide-scale and intense fighting raged throughout most of Java and much of Sumatra and Bali. The heaviest fighting occurred during the first half of November in Surabaya, where several of the large armed Indonesian youth organizations that had been loosely coordinated under the BKR resisted a division and a half of British and Indian troops for ten days, suffering extremely heavy casualties.

Though the British, backed by planes and the guns of their warships in the harbor, eventually after a long and bitter fight managed to gain control of the city, the battle was and still is looked upon by the Indonesians as a triumph. For the Battle of Surabaya was a turning point in their struggle for independence. It demonstrated to the British the fighting strength and the willingness to sacrifice life itself that were behind the popular movement they confronted. It awoke them to the fact that the Republic was backed by the Indonesian masses, not apathetically but positively and enthusiastically. The Battle of Surabaya shocked the British into the realization that, unless they were willing to bring to Indonesia and *expend* a greatly increased strength of soldiers and equipment, they would have to alter their policies and find some measure of common ground with the leaders of the Republic. As this became clear, the British commenced to stiffen against the refusal of the Dutch to deal with the Republic and put strong pressure on them to negotiate to the end that peaceful compromise might be effected. Thus the Battle of Surabaya, along with other examples of strong Indonesian resistance, made possible the diplomatic negotiations during 1946 and early 1947 between the Dutch and the Indonesians.

Fighting was by no means suspended during this later period, but its generality and intensity was considerably less than during the last ten weeks of 1945. In Java and Sumatra the British and later the Dutch for the most part restricted their operations to their enclaves around Jakarta, Bogor (Buitenzorg), Bandung, Semarang, Surabaya, Padang, Medan, and Palembang. In Borneo, Celebes, the Moluccas, and Lesser Sundas the Dutch encountered little difficulty in most areas and soon brought in enough troops to take over from the Australians, who had already disarmed the Japanese occupying forces.

Bali, the Minahassa area of north Celebes, and southwest Celebes were, however, important exceptions. Fighting between Dutch and Republican forces continued on Bali until mid-1948. Republican resistance in heavily populated southwest Celebes was so intense that the Dutch were obliged to resort to the most brutal tactics to gain conrol. Here in early 1946 they employed the notorious Captain Westerling to "pacify" the country, large numbers of Indonesians, civilians as well as guerrillas, being lined up and methodically executed by his firing squads. Republican authorities maintain that nearly 30,000 Indonesians were killed in this manner and in the course of fighting. Unofficial Dutch army sources affirm that only 4,000 were killed. The Netherlands government appointed a commission to investigate brutality on the part of Dutch forces, but no report was ever published. Most resistance leaders who were not killed were jailed. Over one-fourth of the Indonesian aristocratic rulers of southwest Celebes (including the most important of them) were removed by the Dutch and replaced by more amenable individuals. The remainder were thus convinced that retention of their positions depended upon their supporting Dutch policy.

In Minahassa in February, 1946 Indonesian soldiers of the KNIL (Royal Netherlands Indies Army) rebelled against the Dutch, proclaimed for the Republic, and with the assistance of local civilians maintained authority for a month.

Except for a few periods of truce, all but one of which were extremely short, the first four years of the Republic's existence were dominated by warfare against powerful adversaries—a warfare the outcome of which its leaders conceived as determining its very survival. Both the Republic's long negotiations with the Dutch and the internal politics of the Indonesian revolution as well must be seen against the background of that fact if they are to be understood.

There was a short period of relative peace during the last few months prior to the withdrawal of British occupation forces at the end of November, 1946 and for a month or two following the Linggadjati Agreement of March 25, 1947. The only considerable period of truce was that following the Renville Agreement of January 17, 1948. From then until the Dutch attack of December 19, 1948, fighting between Dutch and Republican troops was limited to clashes between patrols. However, even most of this period was rendered tense because of the continuing expectation of full-scale Dutch attack, particularly after June, 1948. In general, actual or threatened military pressure from the outside by a powerful foe was a constant conditioning factor of the Republic's internal as well as external political relations from its birth until late in 1949.

❧ CHAPTER VI ❧

The Internal Politics of the

Revolution until the First Dutch

Military Action

SJAHRIR and his group had refused to sponsor the declaration of independence of August 17 and had stayed away from the meeting held the previous night at Mayeda's house. The declaration of Soekarno and Hatta was too weak, they feared, to arouse the population to the revolutionary pitch against the Japanese that was necessary. Moreover, they felt that Allied support of Indonesia's claim to independence would be more likely if its leaders had gone on record as being more strongly and openly anti-Japanese. Thus, initially Sjahrir and most of the powerful group that backed him stood aside and refused to support Soekarno and Hatta and the new government they headed. For almost three weeks they maintained this stand, with Sjahrir turning down Soekarno's offer of an important cabinet post. Accompanied by several youth leaders, Sjahrir undertook a two-week trip through Java to ascertain the attitude of the population. He found that the newly proclaimed Republic had a tremendous and enthusiastic backing by the people everywhere. The whole population was fighting for its independence, and in that fight they looked for leadership principally to Soekarno. Seeing this, Sjahrir felt that he could not repudiate the revolution led by Soekarno and upon returning to Jakarta accepted the request by Soekarno and Hatta that he join in its leadership. From that moment on Sjahrir, though frequently opposing their programs, supported Soekarno and Hatta as leaders of the Republic. However, two other powerful leaders,

Subardjo and Tan Malaka were ambitious to assume the top positions in the Republic and at first separately and later jointly worked skillfully to attain them.

On August 22, 1945, at the same time that it had set up the KNIP (Komité Nasional Indonesia Pusat—Central Indonesian National Committee), the Preparatory Committee had established the Indonesian National Party (Partai Nasional Indonesia). Nine days later, however, on September 1, this monolithic national party was dissolved because it was felt to be redundant and competitive with the KNIP and therefore likely to foster disunity.[1]

Thereby, however, the party which Subardjo had been building up since the last months of the Japanese administration was left as the only large, well-developed political organization in the Republic. Among its leaders were several colleagues of his in the cabinet and a considerable number of local government officials outside of Jakarta who had given active support to the Japanese administration. After the dissolution of the government-sponsored Indonesian National Party Subardjo's organization commenced to expand rapidly. To many Indonesians, particularly Sjahrir's group, this created a dangerous situation. It appeared to them that the political vacuum thereby created was being filled by politically ambitious individuals distrusted by many because of their close collaboration with the Japanese and believed to have authoritarian political attitudes (according to Sjahrir's group "Fascistic"). Whatever the accuracy of these allegations, Soekarno and Hatta as well as a number of other top leaders felt it advisable by the end of October to endorse Sjahrir's proposal for the introduction of a multi-party system. Desirous as they all were for unity in the face of the struggle for independence, this was seen as the only way to undermine Subardjo's power and what many saw as an ominously authoritarian prospect inherent in the growth of his party. This maneuver resulted in the swift dissolution of Subardjo's organization. But it only partially undermined the political prospects of Subardjo. For, while building his party, he had at the same time been active in promoting Tan Malaka's bid for power, apparently on the basis that if Tan Malaka were successful he, Subardjo, would also benefit.

Noting Sjahrir's initial refusal to back Soekarno, Tan Malaka contacted Sjahrir immediately after his trip through the interior of Java. He proposed to him that the two of them join forces to overthrow

[1] See *Berita Badan Pekerdja* ("Report of the Working Committee" of the KNIP), no. 3 (Oct. 30, 1945).

Soekarno. Tan Malaka would then become President, and Sjahrir would emerge as cabinet head and holder of the portfolios of Defense, Economic Affairs, the Interior, and Foreign Affairs, while Subardjo would share some of the cabinet power. By this time Tan Malaka apparently believed he could rely on the support of the underground of Sukarni [2] and probably many of the armed units it now controlled or influenced. Presumably Tan Malaka reasoned that if Sjahrir and the powerful groups supporting him threw in their weight with the Sukarni group against Soekarno they would be strong enough to overthrow him.

Sjahrir bluntly refused to take any part in Tan Malaka's plan and suggested to him that if he had any illusions concerning his own popularity as contrasted with Soekarno's, he should take a trip through the interior such as he had just made. Tan Malaka soon left Bogor (Buitenzorg) on such a trip and came back convinced that Soekarno enjoyed immensely more popular backing than he.[3] Thereby he saw the necessity for changing his own strategy, for it was obvious that his own slender backing was insufficient to risk his head-on opposition to Soekarno.

To understand the strategy of Tan Malaka's second plan, which he carried out with the help of Subardjo, we must recall the condition of Jakarta in September, 1945. Soekarno and Hatta knew that the British were under great pressure from the Dutch to arrest them. They felt there was a strong chance that if they were not arrested by the British force occupying Jakarta, the Dutch would have them assassinated. Indeed, they were certain that the Dutch were already attempting this. Soekarno's car had been fired on (when he was not in it) and his chauffeur wounded. Dutch colonial troops had fired on the cars of both Sjahrir and Sjarifuddin.

Tan Malaka came to Soekarno [4] and emphasized to him the danger to him and Hatta in Jakarta and the disaster for the Republic if it should be deprived of able leadership at such a critical time. He proposed that there should be a standing arrangement for him to succeed them as head of the Republic should they be killed or jailed and sug-

[2] Though he did not agree with all of Tan Malaka's ideas, in particular his "Aslia" concept, Sukarni was widely considered to be a disciple of Tan Malaka and to wish him as President.

[3] The areas where Tan Malaka's influence was strongest were Bantam, the environs of Jakarta, Tegal, and parts of the East Coast and Menangkabau areas of Sumatra.

[4] Tan Malaka had contacted Subardjo on Aug. 25 and asked him to put him in touch with Soekarno.

gested that a secret but formal political testament be drawn up in anticipation of such an eventuality. Soekarno, while agreeing to the necessity
of providing for continuity of leadership, had no wish to make Tan
Malaka the sole political heir. Tan Malaka then got in touch with
Subardjo, who was party to his plans, and the latter invited Soekarno,
Hatta and Tan Malaka to his house. Here on October 1 he argued to
them the necessity for a political testament. Soekarno and Hatta agreed
to draw up such a testament, but they pointed out that Tan Malaka
represented only a minority of the backers of the revolution. Therefore
they decided to make their heir a quadrumvirate consisting of leaders
of what they conceived to be the four principal groups backing the revolution. These were: (1) Tan Malaka, representing the extreme Marxist
Left; (2) Sjahrir, representing the moderate Socialists; (3) Iwa Kusuma
Sumantri,[5] representing the Moslem organizations; and (4) Wongsonegoro, representing the aristocratic, old-line civil servants. Subardjo was
requested to inform the three designees of the testament not present of
the decision taken. A cabinet meeting was then held at which Soekarno
announced he was leaving a letter indicating whom the cabinet was to
follow should he and Hatta be killed or captured. Subardjo did not carry
out his mission of promptly informing Sjahrir, Iwa Kusuma Sumantri, and Wongsonegoro of their assignments under the political testament. Indeed he never informed Sjahrir and did not tell Wongsonegoro
until early February, 1946.

Tan Malaka then wrote out a document in which Soekarno and
Hatta transferred all power to him alone in case of their inability to
function as leaders and forged their signatures to it. Armed with this
he departed for the interior where it was known, as it was throughout
most of the Republic, that Soekarno and Hatta had made some sort
of a political testament. During most of October and November he
traveled through Java, showing his version of the testament to influential people and telling them that Soekarno and Hatta were prisoners of the British in Jakarta and unable to leave the city. Since they
were prisoners, he argued, it was his duty to assume the powers they

[5] Actually Dr. Sukiman was first designated for this place, but since he was out
of reach somewhere in Central Java his name was withdrawn in favor of Subardjo's
candidate, Iwa Kusuma Sumantri, who as a cabinet member was immediately available. The latter had been a strong Marxist, had (though not a Communist Party
member) taught Indonesian history in Moscow (1925–26), and on his return to
Medan as a lawyer had been accused by the Dutch of being a Communist. He was
then exiled to Banda, where he became a Mohammedan and appeared to Hatta,
Sjahrir, and Tjipto Mangunkusumo, who were in exile there for many years with
him, to be quite orthodox in his approach to Islam.

had asked him to take over in case they were incapacitated. There is no way of estimating how many influential people he was convincing and how much support he was actually building up. His success was apparently sufficient to induce Soekarno early in December to make a "whistle-stop" trip through much of the interior of Java in order to demonstrate to the population that he was a free agent. Tan Malaka's agitation also contributed to the decision a few months later for Soekarno and Hatta's permanent removal from British-occupied Jakarta to the inland city of Jogjakarta and the transfer there soon afterward of all ministries except that of Foreign Affairs. Sjahrir, in particular, strongly urged Soekarno and Hatta to go to Jogjakarta not only because of the danger of arrest by the British or assassination by the Dutch troops but also because he felt there was a danger of their being assassinated by Tan Malaka's group. Soekarno and Hatta left in great secrecy, their departure not being known in Jakarta until announced the following day in Jogjakarta.

Concurrent with Tan Malaka's and Subardjo's maneuvering for power, there occurred another political development of much greater long-term consequence. This was generated by the growing discontent of the most dynamic of the revolutionary groups, the students, with the authoritarian pattern of the emergency government headed by Soekarno and particularly with the composition of his cabinet. With only a few exceptions that cabinet was made up of men who had held high office under the Japanese and except for Sjarifuddin contained none of the underground leaders. Most of these men, they felt, had collaborated with the Japanese largely on an opportunistic basis for their own selfish benefit, more than for Indonesian independence. They felt that the presidential system, particularly under the emergency provisions governing its operation during the interim period before the anticipated elections, was far too authoritarian, particularly when it operated through such a cabinet. Their concern over the autocratic and totalitarian drift of government was considerably heightened by the growing success of Subardjo in creating a single authoritarian political party, organized from the top down. Their concern was shared by Sjahrir, Sjarifuddin, Supeno, Sukarni, Subadio, Mangunsarkoro and his wife, Ir. Sakirman, and a number of other leaders.

At the beginning of October, Supeno, Sukarni, Subadio, Ir. Sakirman, and the two Mangunsarkoros, all members of the KNIP, embarked upon a plan aimed at changing the form of government so that the presidential system would be replaced by a parliamentary system of government, with real legislative power in the hands of the KNIP, to which the cabinet would be directly responsible. Upon achieving this they planned to provoke a vote of no-confidence in the existing cabinet which would cause it to fall. They would then support Sjahrir as Prime Minister and *formateur* of a new cabinet.

Their first step was to convert the KNIP from a purely advisory body to one with real legislative power. To this end they secured the signatures of 50 of its 150 members to a petition demanding such a change and on October 7 handed this petition to Soekarno. Neither Soekarno nor Hatta opposed this change and both of them worked to expedite its consummation. On October 16, after a discussion and approval of the proposal in the KNIP, Hatta on behalf of Soekarno and himself issued a decree whereby the KNIP was vested with full legislative power jointly with the President.[6] This meant that all legislation had to be approved by the KNIP as well as by the President.[7] In the Presidential Decree, it was stipulated, as had been requested by the KNIP, that it would delegate its powers to a small permanently sitting representative body known as the Working Committee (Badan Pekerdja) which would be composed of members of the infrequently convoked parent body (the KNIP) and would remain responsible to it. The Working Committee was required to meet at least every ten days and the KNIP at least once a year.[8]

The KNIP thereupon elected Sjahrir and Sjarifuddin respectively as Chairman and Vice-Chairman of the Working Committee with the right jointly to select thirteen additional members of that body.[9] All the members whom they chose were their strong supporters, and most of them had been active in the anti-Japanese underground. The fifteen

[6] Presidential Decree no. 10 (1945), *Berita Repoeblik Indonesia* (official gazette of the Republic of Indonesia), I, no. 2 (Dec. 1, 1945); "Berita Badan Pekerdja" ("Report of the Working Committee"), Oct. 17, 1945–Nov. 25, 1945, app.

[7] Mr. Assaat, *Hukum Tata Negara Republik Indonesia Dalam Masa Peralihan* ("Constitutional Law of the Republic of Indonesia in the Transitional Period"), (Jogjakarta, 1948), p. 11. This is considered to be the definitive work on this subject. From mid-February, 1946, until he became acting president of the Republic of Indonesia at the end of December, 1949, Mr. Assaat was chairman both of the KNIP and of its Working Committee. Hereinafter this work will be referred to as *Hukum Tata Negara*.

[8] The idea of the Working Committee was in particular championed by Sjarifuddin, Sukarni, and Dr. Muwardi and was inspired by the example of the Indian National Congress, which between sessions was represented by a similar representative body.

[9] Sjahrir and Sjarifuddin refused to head the committee unless given the right to choose its members.

members of the Working Committee were Soetan Sjahrir, Mr. Amir Sjarifuddin, Mr. Suwandi, Mr. Sjafruddin Prawiranegara, Kiaji Wachid Hasjim, Mr. R. Hendromartono, Dr. R. M. Sunario Kolopaking, Dr. A. Halim, Subadio Sastrosatomo, Mr. Tan Ling Djie, Supeno, S. Mangunsarkoro, Adam Malik, Tadjaludin, and Dr. Sudarsono.

At the same time the KNIP called upon the President to enlarge its membership from 150 to 188 members, so that a number of influential leaders not yet included could be added. Soekarno immediately complied, several of the thirty-eight new members being appointed by virtue of the fact that Sjahrir desired them to serve with him as members of the Working Committee.

In order to avoid misunderstandings as to its status and functions, the · Working Committee on October 20 set forth a "Clarification" of its position. It interpreted the Presidential Decree of October 17 as giving it the duties and powers to:

a) Take part in shaping the outlines of the policy of the State. This implies that the Working Committee, with the President, sets out the *broad outlines* of State policy. The Working Committee does *not* have the power to interfere in the details involved in the pursuit of this policy. This is the sole right of the President.

b) Establish together with the President, the laws affecting all fields of administration. These laws are to be executed by the Government, i.e., the President, assisted by the ministers and their subordinate officers.[10]

During the first forty days of its existence, while led by Sjahrir, the Working Committee became the dynamic heart of the government and wrought great changes not only in the system of government but also in the balance of political power. Indeed the major consideration behind the changes in governmental structure and practice championed by Sjahrir and his followers was their desire to rescue the Republic from what they saw as an ominous drift towards authoritarian, totalitarian political forms and organization. Specifically they sought to destroy the formidable political machine being built up by Subardjo and some of his associates both in and outside of the cabinet. Principally these governmental changes were a means to that political end. An important, though distinctly secondary, consideration behind this policy was the desire to remove as much as possible of the collaborationist taint from

[10] "Pendjelasan Kedoedoekan Badan Perderdja Komité Nasional Poesat" ("A Clarification of the Position of the Working Committee of the Central National Committee"), *Berita Repoeblik Indonesia*, I, no. 1 (Nov. 17, 1945). Italics are as given in the document.

the government in the belief that this would give it a stronger position internationally from which to negotiate with the Dutch.

The first move of the Working Committee was to insure adequate supervision of the central government over the local KNI's and the harmonization of its activities with theirs. By its proposed legislation of October 30, 1945,[11] passed after presidential concurrence on November 23, the regional KNI's came under the chairmanship of local leaders appointed by the central government. These bodies were to have their own Working Committees consisting of a maximum of five members elected from the local KNI's and their chairmen were men who had been appointed by the central government as chairmen of the KNI as a whole.[12] Thereby the possibility of dissident elements utilizing the local KNI's as bases for building up their own antigovernment power was much reduced. The procedure for election of their representatives was left to the discretion of their respective communities and continued to vary widely. In some areas, particularly where fighting was frequent, conditions did not allow such local elections. But probably in about half of the KNI's in Java, Madura, and Sumatra, the representatives were elected. The general limits of legislative authority of these local KNI's remained the same. They could consider as their legitimate preserves the whole area of legislation not yet covered by the central government; subsequent legislation by it would always take precedence over any legislation passed by the local KNI's. Similarly, legislation by a provincial KNI took precedence over that of a district or municipal KNI.

The second important action of the Working Committee was by a subsequent legislative proposal on the same day, October 30, 1945. This called for the abandonment of the one-party system and its replacement by a multi-party system in which all important political currents would have representation. Presidential concurrence was speedily forthcoming with the appended request that these parties be formed before the elections for the Council of People's Representatives (which was to replace the temporary, non-elected KNIP) scheduled for January, 1946. During November and December there was a rapid formation of po-

[11] "Pengoemoeman (Announcement) Badan Pekerdja Komité Nasional No. 2," *Berita Repoeblik Indonesia,* I, no. 1 (Nov. 17, 1945).

[12] In practice the existing KNI chairmen were generally confirmed in their positions by the central government. Most local KNI's had taken over power themselves from the previous local Japanese authority rather than deriving it from the central government. Thus many of them felt considerable autonomy from Jakarta.

litical parties, with the result that Subardjo's party soon withered and died, many of its members joining the standard of Tan Malaka.

Of the many political parties launched, initially the most powerful was the Partai Nasional Indonesia (Indonesian National Party), or PNI as it was generally known. This new PNI was backed by a large percentage of the Republic's professional people and a probable majority of the civil servants who had worked in the prewar colonial administration. A large number of its intellectuals had been active in the prewar nationalist movement. For the most part it was an older-generation party, the majority of its leaders averaging well above those of any other in age.

The initial mass following of the PNI was attracted to a large extent because it bore the name of Soekarno's prewar mass party as well as that of the official government-sponsored party launched on August 22, 1945 with the backing of both Soekarno and Hatta. Thus a considerable amount of its original mass backing rested on the fiction that the PNI was "the party of Soekarno and Hatta." It took many Indonesians a year or more to become disabused of this fiction, and some foreign correspondents never were.

However, the PNI had an important long-term means of attracting mass support. This arose from the fact that it enrolled the backing of a probable majority of Republican local administrative officers, for the most part the same men who had made up the old aristocratic Indonesian civil service which had served the prewar Dutch administration. Likewise, it attracted considerable support from their nonaristocratic subordinates in the civil service, a large number of whom had also worked in the previous Dutch administration. Though the revolution was making a powerful impact upon the long-ingrained, authoritarian habits of Indonesian society, there still remained a strong tendency for the peasantry to look for political guidance and directives from its traditional governors, the experienced Indonesian administrative class.[13] This fact was the long-term political forte of the PNI.

It was widely believed that the peasantry's traditional and habitual response to authority gave the PNI a strong competitive advantage in the projected elections, an advantage surpassed only by that held by the Masjumi with its religious tie with the peasantry. In addition the PNI

---

[13] Though this was true in matters above the village level, generally within the village democratic political tendencies remained strong and were greatly invigorated by the revolution.

had the support of most of those members of the tiny Indonesian commercial and industrial middle class who were not attracted to the Masjumi. It was because of this and the fact that it incorporated a probable majority of the largest sector of the Indonesian middle class, the old regime Indonesian bureaucracy, that the PNI was often referred to as "the middle-class party" of Indonesia. Finally, the PNI developed a left wing, a small minority at first, but of increasingly substantial proportions. It was based principally upon the support of some non-Communist Marxist intellectuals, some small labor groups led principally by Wilopo and Mangunsarkoro (after his defection from Sjahrir), and a group of progressively inclined students.

However, it was neither the old-line aristocratic civil servant leaders of the party's right wing nor these increasingly influential leaders of its small left wing that dominated the party's leadership. That function was held by a small but powerful group of men who had distinguished themselves in the pre-war Indonesian nationalist movement, for the most part in the Partai Nasional Indonesia of the late 1920's and its successor the Partindo. Among the most important of these were Mr. Sartono, Mr. Ali Sastroamidjojo, Sidik Djojosukarto, Manai Sophian, Mr. Sujono Hadinoto, Mr. Susanto Tirtoprodjo, and Suwirjo. The socio-economic ideology of most of this group was considerably closer to that of the left wing of the party than to that of its right wing.

The heterogeneity of its constituent elements made the PNI an unwieldy political organization. Its basic tenet that national independence had to precede any basic social reform kept its constituent groups together and allowed the party to maintain a relatively consistent policy with respect to relations with the Dutch. However, the disparity in outlook of these groups in regard to domestic questions made it difficult for the party to follow a consistent and clear policy in that sphere.

On November 7, 1945, was founded the Masjumi (Madjelis Sjuro Muslimin Indonesia—Council of Indonesian Moslem Associations), which within a year was to surpass the PNI in size and become by far the largest political party in the Republic. Though it bore the name of the primarily social association established during the Japanese occupation, it was a new and distinct organization.[14] It enrolled all the

[14] It was only by a narrow margin, 52–50, that the congress of Moslem leaders which launched the party decided to call it Masjumi rather than Partai Rakjat Islam (Party of the Islamic People). There is no doubt but that it was able to gain something of a head start by utilizing some of the existing organization of the old Masjumi of the Japanese occupation.

nonpolitical Islamic organizations subsumed under the Masjumi of the Japanese period, including the Mohammadijah and Nahdatul Ulama as well as such prewar Islamic political organizations as the Partai Sarekat Islam Indonesia.

Because of support by the large, nonpolitical Moslem social organizations and particularly because of its support by village religious leaders, the Masjumi was able to build up a huge, if unintegrated and unorganized, mass backing. Almost all Moslem religious leaders of Java, Madura and Sumatra supported the Masjumi, which also attracted most of the vestigial Indonesian commercial and industrial middle class throughout that area. Likewise it attracted the majority of the larger Indonesian landowners.[15]

As was the case with all Republican political parties, national independence was the Masjumi's chief aim. Next to that, it was dedicated to the organization of the state according to Islamic principles. Only with a small minority of members did this dedication verge on religious intolerance and indeed the large majority of the party's leaders welcomed the idea of non-Moslems holding some cabinet and Working Committee posts. It was over the interpretation of what Islamic social principles were and how they should be applied in Indonesia that the two chief groups within the party—the "Religious Socialists" and the conservative, older-generation religious leaders—were generally at odds. The Religious Socialists drew much of their inspiration from the teachings of Mohammad Abduh. However, the views of this young and dynamic group were in large measure their own and new. They represented the impact of the Indonesian revolution upon sincere young Mohammedans possessed of enlightened minds and a strong sense of their duty to serve society. Their principal leaders—Mohammad Natsir, Mr. Sjafruddin Prawiranegara, Mr. Mohammad Roem, Mr. Jusuf Wibisono, and Dr. Abu Hanifah—found considerable common ground with the moderate socialists who followed Sjahrir and with such progressive leaders of the small but effective Christian Party as Dr. Leimena and Mr. Tambunan.[16] The differences between this left wing of the Masjumi and its right wing, based on the Nahdatul Ulama and the more con-

15 Frequently the religious leader was at the same time a member of this indigenous middle class or landlord group. This arose from the fact that only a man of some means could afford the costs of the pilgrimage to Mecca. Those who had made the pilgrimage, the *hadjis*, derived considerable prestige in the eyes of the Moslem community. However, many of the greatest religious leaders were not *hadjis*.

16 The Christian Party (Partai Kristen Indonesia or Parkindo as it became known) was established on Nov. 10, 1945. Other prominent leaders were Ir. Putuhena and Drs. Probowinoto.

servative elements of the Mohammadijah, was generally bridged, though frequently not effectively, by the more progressive members of the Mohammadijah, by the party's chairman, Dr. Sukiman, and later by another of its leaders, Prawoto Mangkusasmito.

. Also among the "big three" political parties that dominated the first two years of the Republic's existence was the Socialist Party (Partai Sosialis). This was established in early December, 1945, as a merger of the shortly previously established Partai Sosialis Indonesia of Amir Sjarifuddin and the Partai Rakjat Sosialis (Socialist People's Party) of Soetan Sjahrir. (Sjarifuddin's party had been established in early November and Sjahrir's on November 20, 1945.) The new, combined Socialist Party was headed by Sjahrir and commanded great strength among the younger intellectuals and a large proportion of the secondary and college students, including most of the members of Sjahrir's anti-Japanese underground and a large percentage of those from that of Sjarifuddin. It did not have the same large, loose and unorganized mass following as the PNI and the Masjumi. But the popular support it did have was more politically conscious, and more solidly and effectively organized behind it than the rank and file whose political allegiance was claimed by the other two major parties. Also it had the backing of most of the small group of actively pro-Republican Indonesian Chinese. For the first eighteen months of its existence no important splits occurred within the Socialist Party. Its membership was uniformly in favor of a relatively large measure of social reform but placed this, as did all the parties, after the struggle for independence and the national unity prerequisite thereto. However, like the Masjumi, it did not believe that all social reform had to wait upon full independence for all Indonesia.

During the last months of 1945 there also occurred a rapid burgeoning of small parties. In addition to the Christian Party there emerged a small but articulate Catholic Party (Partai Katholik Republik Indonesia) under Kasimo.[17] On October 21, 1945, re-emerged the Indonesian Communist Party (Partai Komunis Indonesia—PKI) under the leadership of Mr. Mohammad Jusuf. (The party actually emerged into the open on November 7, but Jusuf claimed it had been re-established on

[17] There were under 50,000 Indonesian Catholics on Java and Sumatra, but their average level of education and social position was high. Most of the Indonesian Catholic population was in areas early reoccupied by the Dutch, such as Flores, Timor, and Ambon. For a good account of the Catholic Party see Grondho Pratomo, "De P.K.R.I.—Partai Katholik Repoeblik Indonesia," *Indonesia*, July 27, 1946.

October 21.) He and a number of his followers had been associated with the Japanese-sponsored "Communist Movement" which Subardjo had helped organize. He had no connection with the actual PKI underground or either the "Illegal PKI" established by Musso in 1935 or the earlier PKI which launched the rebellion of 1926–27. His group was responsible for antigovernmental activities in Pekalongen at the end of October and in Cheribon in mid-February 1946. In the latter its armed adherents attacked a Republican police barracks, killing several police before being disarmed, after which Jusuf was arrested. The party developed little following or prestige until May, 1946, after the arrival from Australia of the old-time Communist leader Sardjono,[18] who replaced Jusuf as chairman. On August 12, 1946, Alimin returned to Indonesia after twenty years abroad, the last year or more of which had been spent in Yenan. Though with Sardjono, who remained chairman, he added prestige and able leadership to the party, it never until 1948 attained a stature approaching that of the PNI, Masjumi, or Socialist Party.

It is of importance to note that a large number of the Indonesian Stalinists, including some of the most important of them, did not enter the PKI. Instead they entered one or the other of the three chief noncommunist Marxist parties, the Socialist Party, Labor Party, and Pesindo. Probably as many members of the "Illegal PKI," the group originally organized by Musso in 1935 and which later became one of the two chief anti-Japanese undergrounds, entered these groups as entered the post-Jusuf PKI. They may well have initially been deterred from entering Jusuf's organization because of the low caliber of his leadership as well as because of its obvious deviation from the Moscow line. There are also grounds to believe that some stayed out of the PKI after Sardjono and Alimin had captured its leadership because of differences in outlook with these leaders.[19] It may well be that because of this initial

18 At its Jogjakarta meeting of March 1–3, 1946, the PKI condemned the activities of Jusuf. At its Surakarta conference of April 29–30, 1946, it delegated the party leadership to Sardjono. He had been chairman of the PKI in 1926, had been arrested before the rebellion of 1926–27 and exiled to Boven Digul concentration camp. He remained there until removed to Australia by the Dutch in 1942. There he worked for the Dutch information service until March, 1946, when the Dutch sent him along with all Indonesians (including all others whom they had removed from Digul) in Australia back to Indonesia at the request of the Australian government.

19 It is reported that in setting up his underground party in 1935, Musso refused to have anything to do with "Alimin's failures of 1926." Musso's regard for both Alimin and Sardjono was indicated when in returning in mid-1948 he managed to have them demoted to party positions of nonentity; it would be hard to argue,

character of the PKI, that some of the Indonesian Communist leaders upon returning to Indonesia from the Netherlands in late 1945 and early 1946, felt their political prospects would be better if they were associated with the much more powerful Socialist Party. Certainly their interpretation of the Dimitrov Doctrine did not bar such a course. Their Communist affiliations were not then known to the leaders of the Socialist Party and their record during the war in the Socialist-led underground in the Netherlands made them highly acceptable as members and subordinate leaders.

The Communists who joined the Socialist Party, the Labor Party, and the Pesindo ultimately emerged in control of these organizations and in August 1948, undertook to fuse them with the PKI. This has led some Indonesians to conclude that there was a long-term conscious design on the part of these Communists to infiltrate and wrest control of these parties to the end of subverting them to Stalinist objectives. Though this in fact did happen, the proof is lacking to demonstrate conclusively that this was their conscious long-term plan. It does seem clear that when they first arrived in Indonesia late in 1945 and early in 1946, they were adhering closely to Moscow's line, at least as it was interpreted by the Netherlands Communist Party. Their initial orientation was, paralleling that of the Netherlands Communist Party, anti-Republic. They conceived of the Republic as Japanese-made and Fascistic and their objective was to reunite the Netherlands and Indonesia. Thus the Netherlands government was happy to fly them out free of charge to Indonesia. At first they sought to bring the Republican leaders to accept the proposals of the Netherlands government. In this they met no success, but in attempting to do so they saw the Republic from the inside. They soon concluded that it was neither a Japanese product nor a Fascist dictatorship. It was clear to them that the Republic had the enthusiastic support of the population and that the future of the nationalist movement in Indonesia lay with it. Wishing to be realistic about their own political future they made an adjustment which constituted a sort of synthesis between their own nationalist views, personal political ambitions and the Communist line. The Lt. Governor-General of the Netherlands East Indies, Dr. Hubertus J. van Mook,

---

however, that Musso was not fully as much to blame for the failure of the 1926–27 revolution as was Alimin. Possibly consideration should be given to the fact that Alimin and Sardjono were generally considered (in mid-1948) to have more content of nationalism in their Communism than Musso. It also may be significant that Alimin spent some time just before the end of the war with Mao Tse-tung in Yenan.

gave them permission to enter the Republic, where they associated themselves with those political forces within it that were willing to try negotiating with the Dutch for independence before resorting to force. They apparently felt able to rationalize this conduct in terms of the still-prevailing Dimitrov Doctrine or at least in terms of how their own wishful thinking prompted them to interpret it. Thus, though of this group Maruto Darusman joined the Sardjono-and-Alimin-led PKI, Abdulmadjid joined the Socialist Party and Setiadjit the Labor Party.

On November 9, 1945, the leaders of the recently established and short-lived General Indonesian Trade Union (Barisan Buruh Indonesia) formed the Indonesian Labor Party (Partai Buruh Indonesia). For several months this party was largely under the control of Indonesians who had worked in the Labor Department of the Japanese occupation administration and helped it recruit forced labor.[20] However, in early 1946 with the arrival of Setiadjit [21] from Holland control of the party was wrested from this collaborationist group; he emerged as its chairman, and it became more representative of the interests of labor. For the next eighteen months of its existence the party closely followed the lead of the much larger Socialist Party and consistently supported it.

Some of those who looked to Tan Malaka for leadership formed in November, 1945, the Partai Rakjat Djelata (Common People's Party) headed by Soetan Dewanis. The majority, however, waited for more than six months before establishing political parties. However, as we will see, they were energetically engaged in politics, particularly in building Tan Malaka's national front organization, designed to subsume all political parties and bring him to political ascendancy.

During the first year of the Republic's existence, but to a rapidly diminishing extent thereafter, an importance in the internal politics of the revolution almost equal to that of the formal political parties

[20] See Soemyoto, "De Arbeidersbeweging in de Indonesische Republiek," *Indonesia,* June 29, 1946, p. 7.

[21] Setiadjit along with Abdulmadjid came to control the Perhimpoenan Indonesia in Holland shortly after Hatta's departure for Indonesia. Its publication began to pattern to the Communist line shortly thereafter. He is reported to have studied at the Lenin Institute in Moscow in 1934 or 1935 along with Abdulmadjid and to have been a member of the Communist Party, though both these facts were known to very few people and not public knowledge in Indonesia when he returned. During the war he was active in the anti-Nazi underground in Holland as a member of the resistance group led by the Socialist leader Schermerhorn. He did not announce himself a Communist until Aug., 1948.

was held by the principal factions within the TRI (the national army) [22] and the several powerful semi-autonomous [23] irregular military organizations.

Politically the most potent and in a military sense probably the strongest of these irregular armed organizations was the Pesindo (Pemuda Sosialis Indonesia—Indonesian Socialist Youth). This was established from the amalgamation of seven youth organizations [24] at a conference held on November 10, 1945, at Jogjakarta. The objective of the conference had been to merge all twenty-two Republican youth organizations. Merger into one integrated body was agreed upon only by the seven organizations that fused to become Pesindo. The remaining fifteen organizations in conjunction with Pesindo did form a loose federation, the Badan Kongres Pemuda Republik Indonesia (Congress of the Organization of Youth of the Republic of Indonesia). Differences in views of its constituent groups handicapped the effectiveness of this federation, however, and on only a few occasions was opinion within it sufficiently uniform to allow it to take concerted action.

The Pesindo, on the other hand, because of the relatively homogeneous outlook of its members and the ability of many of its leaders, became by far the most dynamic and powerful of all youth organizations in the Republic. A considerable number of the young men making up its membership were organized into well-armed, disciplined fighting units of battalion strength. The total armed strength of the Pesindo

[22] Until Jan. 25, 1945, the national army was known as the TKR—Tentara Keamanan Rakjat. It was then changed to TRI (Tentara Republik Indonesia—Army of the Republic of Indonesia). On June 3, 1947, its name was again changed and it became known as the TNI (Tentara Nasional Indonesia—Indonesian National Army).

[23] Their autonomy from the high command of the TKR was very great during the first months of independence; but thereafter more and more of these organizations were absorbed into the TRI and the latter's authority over those still separate was considerably increased. Complete integration of all military organizations into the national army under a single command was not effected until the end of Oct., 1948.

[24] These were (1) Pemuda Republik Indonesia (PRI—Youth of the Indonesian Republic), largest of the armed youth organizations, and the one which had just established a brilliant record in the Surabaya fighting and was represented in the KNIP; (2) Angkatan Pemuda Indonesia (Indonesian Young Generation), also large and well armed, but less well organized and disciplined than the PRI; (3) Angkatan Muda Republik Indonesia (Young Generation of the Republic of Indonesia); (4) Gerakan Pemuda Republik Indonesia (Youth Movement of the Republic of Indonesia); (5) Angkatan Muda Kereta Api (Young Railroad Workers); (6) Angkatan Muda PTT (Young Postal Telegraph, and Telephone Workers); and (7) Angkatan Muda Gas-Listrik (Young Gas and Electric Plant Workers).

during the first year of the Republic probably totaled about 25,000. It won great prestige because of the effective part it played in fighting the British troops. Both its general membership and its armed units identified their interests with those of the Socialist Party and by consistently backing it contributed greatly to its political strength.

Military strength backing the Masjumi was provided by the Hizbullah, an armed organization of strongly Moslem young men between eighteen and twenty-five-years-old.[25] Organized into battalion units, it probably mustered between 20,000 and 25,000 armed men during most of the first year of the Republic. It was organized under the leadership of the Masjumi and was considered as its armed auxiliary. In practice, however, liaison between Masjumi leaders and many of the Hizbullah commanders was frequently very loose. Largely on paper there also existed the Sabillilah, a sort of territorially based home guard in which all Masjumi members were liable for service. In some areas, however, its units were armed and of importance.

The Japanese-sponsored Barisan Pelopor (Pioneer Legion) continued its existence after August 17, and in mid-December, 1945, changed its name into Barisan Banteng (Buffalo Legion). Next to the Pesindo it was the strongest of the armed youth organizations. In number of armed adherents it may have initially surpassed the Pesindo; but it was much less well disciplined, had fewer able officers, and the educational level of its rank and file was below that of the Pesindo. As a result, its fighting power and political strength were considerably less. Occasionally during 1945 and early 1946 it gave support to the PNI (particularly in Surakarta, chief headquarters of the Barisan Banteng) as well as to Tan Malaka. Later it became more exclusively attached to Tan Malaka.

An irregular armed organization of considerable size during the first six months of the Republic's existence, but of diminishing strength both absolutely and relative to other irregular armed organizations, thereafter, was the Barisan Pemberontakan Rakjat Indonesia (Revolutionary Legion of the Indonesian People) headed by Sutomo (Bung Tomo). This was a loosely organized youth organization which took an important part in the Surabaya fighting. It had no formal political affiliations but, possessed of several radio stations, managed to exert some political influence. It consistently and strongly opposed any negotiations with the British or Dutch and attempted to rally the

25 The Hizbullah had actually been set up as a youth organization of the Japanese-sponsored Masjumi in 1944. It had been given some military training, but no arms.

population to an all-out resistance of the most militant character.

Smallest of the more important irregular armed organizations was the Kebaktian Rakjat Indonesia Sulawesi (Loyalty of the Indonesian People from Sulawesi) [26] or KRIS as it was usually known. This was made up of men from Celebes, mostly Christians from the Minahassa resident in Java at the end of 1945. Initially it was formed for mutual protection of its members against those Indonesians who assumed that Christians were pro-Dutch, as well as for the purpose of fighting the Dutch. Its combat record against the Dutch was so good that it soon won the high regard of all Republicans. Probably no other group did so much to convince Mohammedan Indonesians that Christians could be just as reliable Republicans as they. Though having only about 6,000 armed soldiers, the high average level of education among them gave its battalions a higher discipline and more able leaders than were possessed by most of the other irregular armed organizations.

The largest of the irregular armed organizations was the Laskar Rakjat (People's Army). This was made up of loosely integrated, frequently almost autonomous, territorially based and raised units—a sort of home guard. Set up in October and September, 1945, largely on the initiative of the Sultan of Jogjakarta, it was considered as the auxiliary of the regular army (the TKR, later TRI) and its units were in varying degrees amenable to army leadership.[27] Progressively the control of the TRI over its units grew—but it was not until mid-1947 that this process was largely complete. For the most part the Laskar Rakjats remained outside of politics, but occasionally local units associated themselves with and supported one or another political group.[28]

At the end of October, Sjahrir published a small booklet, *Perdjuangan Kita* ("Our Struggle"), which during the first days of November was widely circulated. Its impact upon political thinking in Indonesia

---

[26] "Sulawesi" is the Indonesian name for Celebes.

[27] Mohammad Saleh and later Ir. Sakirman were chairmen of the Central Committee for the Laskar Rakjats.

[28] Thus after the withdrawal of the Republic's regular troops from West Java following the Renville Agreement of Jan., 1948, several Laskar Rakjats in West Java which had previously been partly under the influence of Tan Malaka's group became—because of their isolation from the TNI command—even more so. They were then fused into one organization, the Laskar Rakjat Djawa Barat (People's Army of West Java, previously known as the Laskar Rakjat Jakarta Raja—People's Army of Greater Jakarta) headed by Chairul Saleh and Sutan Akbar and based after Aug., 1947, chiefly on the Krawang delta area.

was tremendous, particularly among the former underground workers and the educated youth. In this he called upon the youth to act with a responsibility commensurate with their revolutionary importance; specifically to refrain from antiforeign and anti-Eurasian violence, and to bend their energies towards formation of a democratic, nonfascist, nonfeudalistic government. He warned that Indonesia must adjust to the reality that she lay in the American-British power sphere and that she would have to live under the influence of American and British capitalism and imperialism. Even upon attainment of full political independence from the Dutch, he asserted, the limits of the political and economic independence attainable by Indonesia and the scope for internal social change would be circumscribed by that condition. Indonesians must distinguish between the outward aspects of their revolution—nationalism—and its internal social aspect. There was great danger, he said, that in concentrating on the nationalistic aspect of the revolution, the democratically based, internal social aspect would be neglected. Given the strongly surviving feudalistic heritage in the country, this absorption with the nationalistic aspect to the exclusion of the internal democratic aspect would lead to fascism; for the requisite ingredients of fascism are "feudalism and supernationalism." Democracy and not nationalism, he emphasized, should be the primary objective of the Indonesian revolution.

Finally, Sjahrir called on the Indonesian people to reject the leadership of all those who had actively collaborated with the Japanese or the Dutch and to entrust leadership in the revolution only to those untainted by such a relationship and whose goal was democracy. He stated:

Our revolution must be led by revolutionary, democratic groups and not by nationalist groups, which have let themselves be used as servants of the Fascists, whether Dutch-colonial Fascists, or Japanese military Fascists.

The revolutionary-democratic struggle must begin by purifying itself of all Japanese fascist stain and opposing all those whose spirit is still under the influence of Japanese propaganda and education. Those who have sold themselves and their honor to Japanese fascism, must be thrown out of the leadership of our revolution—that is those who have ever worked for the Japanese propaganda organizations, the secret police, in general, everyone who has worked for the Japanese fifth column. All these persons must be considered as traitors to our struggle and be distinguished from the common laborers, who have had to work for the enemy in order to support themselves. Thus all the above-mentioned collaborators must be considered as our own fascists, as accomplices [29] and tools of Japanese Fascism, who bear a heavy guilt and have committed treason to our struggle and our people's revolution.[30]

It has often been asserted by foreign writers that Sjahrir's demand for this purge was due to his conviction that the Allies would be more disposed to negotiate with and ultimately to recognize an Indonesian government untainted by collaboration with the Japanese than one which was. Though this was from Sjahrir's standpoint an important consideration, it was distinctly secondary to his fear of the fascist potential of the existing government. Sjahrir opposed its dominantly collaborationist cabinet [31] for the same reason that he opposed the one-party system [32] and urged replacement of the monolithic presidential system of government by a parliamentary-presidential system where power would be widely diffused. He feared the development of a totalitarian government in Indonesia because of the legacy of feudalistic authoritarianism which had been kept alive and reinforced by the long period of colonial government. The members of Subardjo's clique within the cabinet and sprinkled widely throughout the Republican administration were, he felt, collaborationists with fascist outlooks close to the Japanese whom they had served. In the positions of power which they controlled, he felt, they might be able to lead the nation towards a fascist form of government.

Whatever the justification of Sjahrir's fears concerning the political orientation of those who worked with the Japanese administration,

[29] In his original Indonesian edition Sjahrir used the term "running dogs" (andjing kaki tangan) rather than "accomplices" of Japanese Fascism. To be referred to as a "dog" is anathema for a Mohammedan, and anti-Sjahrir bitterness among those who had worked for the Japanese administration was made even greater by his use of this epithet. In later editions, the word "accomplice" was substituted for "running dogs."

[30] Soetan Sjahrir, Onze Strijd (Dutch transl. of Perdjuangan Kita), (Amsterdam, 1946), p. 23.

[31] He did not consider all such members of the cabinet to be fascist in mentality, nor all to have been willing servants of the Japanese.

[32] Sjahrir had originally been advocate of a one-party system to last until achievement of independence so that national solidarity might be maintained during the period of struggle. At the end of October, however, it appeared to him that Subardjo and his group were emerging at the head of the one major national party and that because of their dominant position in its leadership the party would be authoritarian and fascist. Because of this fear he took a leading role in promoting a multi-party system calculated to win over the potential mass support of Subardjo's following.

they were immediately echoed by many members of the underground and a large portion of the students, most of whom were soon to become members of the Socialist Party. They rallied behind Sjahrir in his campaign to oust these people from the government.

Though Sjahrir had not meant to suggest that Soekarno and Hatta were collaborationists to be ousted from the government, for a time there was confusion among many as to his stand on this. In any case the positions of Soekarno and Hatta had been weakened by Tan Malaka's continuing propaganda that they were under the control of British and Dutch occupation forces in Jakarta.

The first move of Tan Malaka's group was an attempt to detach Hatta from Soekarno. Apparently on October 31, Sukarni approached Hatta, suggesting that Tan Malaka replace Soekarno as President, urging that he was better fit to lead the revolution. This proposal was abruptly turned down by Hatta.

Within a few days thereafter the effects of Sjahrir's anticollaborationist brochure began to be noticeable. It was undoubtedly the heavy rallying of much of the most dynamic revolutionary element—the youth—to Sjahrir's standard that convinced Tan Malaka of the desirability of uniting his own considerable backing from the same element with Sjahrir's. He personally contacted Sjahrir and told him of the Political Testament of Soekarno and Hatta. The evidence is considerable that Tan Malaka then suggested that means be found for removing Soekarno and Hatta from their positions so that the Political Testament might "legally" take effect. Many people feel that Tan Malaka had in mind nothing less than assassination. In the new government envisaged by Tan Malaka, Sjahrir and he would be dominant. Sjahrir would be President and Tan Malaka asked only the key ministries of Interior and Labor, with one other ministry going to Subardjo. Sjahrir refused to have anything to do with Tan Malaka's proposal.

A split between the two had already begun because of their differences over the course which the revolution should take. Among other things, Tan Malaka advocated immediate seizure by the masses of all foreign properties without compensation, feeling that stronger mass support for the revolutionary struggle would thereby be gained. Sjahrir opposed this, arguing that if this occurred America and Britain would certainly rally to the support of the Dutch and crush the Republic.

Sjahrir's categorical rejection of Tan Malaka's proposal decisively widened the split between them.

Almost immediately Tan Malaka shifted to a new tactic, hoping to profit by the strong opposition of Sjahrir's group to the government. Capitalizing on the strong antigovernment sentiment aroused among the vanguard elements of the revolution, Tan Malaka, Subardjo, and the other leaders of their group on or about November 9, 1945, pressed Soekarno and Hatta to resign. The situation was extremely critical. As between Tan Malaka's group and Soekarno and Hatta, the group led by Sjahrir clearly held the balance of power. But the latitude of maneuver of Sjahrir and the leaders around him was, as Tan Malaka must have realized, extremely limited. Sjahrir himself had led the anticollaborationist crusade, and his supporters expected him to carry it out. Adherence to the political *status quo* was impossible. Change was demanded, and if Sjahrir opposed it, he would probably lose much of his following, which might then swing over to follow the leadership of Tan Malaka. The weakness of Sjahrir's position was that in launching his anticollaborationist movement he had not sufficiently distinguished between Soekarno and Hatta and other leaders who had collaborated chiefly to advance the cause of Indonesian independence as against those Indonesians who collaborated principally out of self-interest. Because of this Tan Malaka was in a position to utilize the movement to oust both groups, including Soekarno and Hatta. Probably feeling that Sjahrir would be forced to follow Tan Malaka's lead, Subardjo approached him and asked him in his capacity as Chairman of the Working Committee to back Tan Malaka's demand that Soekarno and Hatta resign.

The problem of Sjahrir and the leaders around him was a difficult one. How were they to maintain their support of Soekarno and Hatta while meeting the demands of the swelling anticollaborationist movement sufficiently to keep Tan Malaka out of power? The formula devised to accomplish this was announced by the Working Committee on November 11 and was in fact completely in harmony with the previously launched objectives of the Supeno-Subadio-Mangunsarkoro-Sukarni group of the previous month. It called for a basic change in the system of the Republic's government, namely, the introduction of cabinet responsibility to parliament (the KNIP). Between meetings of the KNIP, the Working Committee would serve as its deputy, with the cabinet accountable to it. Should a difference arise between the President or cabinet and the Working Committee, it was anticipated that the matter would be referred to a meeting of the KNIP for settlement.[33] Thus a *modus vivendi* was reached which sufficiently satisfied the anti-collaborationist backing of Sjahrir and kept it from drifting from him to Tan Malaka. For now the collaborationists in the cabinet were responsible to the KNIP and therefore, it was felt, under its control.

Soekarno quickly grasped the realities of the political situation. He promptly approved the Working Committee's proposal for cabinet responsibility to the KNIP, contacted Sjahrir, who it was clear backed him rather than Tan Malaka, and asked him to become Prime Minister. Sjahrir accepted the post on the condition he be given complete freedom to select the members of his cabinet. Soekarno agreed and abruptly dismissed his own cabinet, thereby taking from Tan Malaka practically all of his political capital.

For about two months the bitterness of most of the dismissed cabinet members against Soekarno was intense. Thereafter they directed their animosity against Sjahrir—feeling his anticollaborationist attack was the real basis of their fall from office and that their reputations had been unjustly sullied by that attack. In Sjahrir's estimation the enmity which he and his followers aroused through their bitter anticollaborationist campaign among most members of the ousted cabinet and among other politically prominent persons who had worked for the Japanese was the basic factor in internal Republican politics until his replacement as Prime Minister in June, 1947. Since a number of those against whom his attack was launched were prominent within the PNI and the Masjumi, particularly the former, there was a tendency for these persons to urge their parties to oppose Sjahrir and the policies of his cabinets. Also of extreme importance was the fact that this antagonism to Sjahrir generated by his attack against collaborationists spread to a major portion of the armed forces. Since their training had largely been received under the Japanese, there was a tendency for them, their officers in particular, to feel that they, too, were the butt of Sjahrir's attack.

On November 14, Sjahrir, as Prime Minister, announced the membership of his first cabinet. It was composed of either his own followers or competent nonpolitical administrators, all of whom had a record

[33] Mr. Assaat, *Hukum Tata Negara*. The writer has made certain of these points in an interview with Mr. Assaat (Jogjakarta, Sept. 17, 1948). These principles were not actually put to the test until the KNIP session of Feb., 1947, at which time they were vindicated. What powers remained with the President was for a time uncertain, but were disclosed during the events of the next year and a half, as we shall see, to be considerable.

of nonco-operation with the Japanese. Only two members from Soe-
karno's cabinet were retained—Amir Sjarifuddin, who held the posts
of Minister of Defense and Minister of Information, and Ir. R. P.
Soerachman, who was placed in charge of the Ministry of Finance.
Sjahrir, himself, assumed responsibility for the Ministries of Foreign
Affairs and Internal Affairs.[34]

Immediately Sjahrir's cabinet was bitterly attacked by both the ousted
cabinet members and the Tan Malaka group. Both the cabinet and the
Working Committee, they claimed, were unrepresentative and should
become coalition bodies embracing all political currents and composed
only of representatives of parties. To some extent these demands were
generated by desire for national solidarity, but certainly they were also
activated by personal ambition for political position and the wish to
oust Sjahrir and his group. The opposition to his cabinet became so
great that Sjahrir could not ignore it, and on November 19, Sjarifuddin
announced that the cabinet had decided to call a meeting of the Central National Committee (KNIP) "in view of internal criticism of our
cabinet." The cabinet would ask for a vote of confidence from the
Committee, he stated, and "if the Committee endorses our policy, we
will continue our work. Otherwise, I expect that the cabinet will have
to resign. . . ."[35] From November 25 to 27 the KNIP met in Jakarta.
It overwhelmingly endorsed the introduction of cabinet responsibility
to the KNIP and its agent, the Working Committee (which idea the
latter had already approved). Then by a vote of eighty-four to eight
with fifteen abstentions it voted confidence in Sjahrir and his cabinet.[36]

Since Sjahrir, Sjarifuddin, and several others of those forming the
new cabinet had been members of the Working Committee, the rump
of that body resigned so that a full new Committee could be elected by
the KNIP. That body decided that the Working Committee should be
enlarged from fifteen to twenty-five members so that the various political currents within the KNIP could be more completely represented
by its smaller agent-body. Seventeen of the members were to represent

[34] Initially Mr. Amir Sjarifuddin was both Minister of Defense and Minister of
Information. On January 1, 1946, Mohammad Natsir assumed Sjarifuddin's duties
as Minister of Information. The other Ministers were Dr. T. G. S. Mulia, Education;
Mr. Suwandi, Justice; Dr. Sudarsono, Social Affairs; Dr. Darmasetiawan, Health; Ir.
Darmawan Mangunkusumo, Economic Affairs; Ir. Putuhena, Public Works; Ir. Abdul
Karim, Communications; and Hadji Rasjidi, Religion.

[35] Aneta, Nov. 19, 1945. (Aneta is the principal Netherlands news service and had
a large branch in Indonesia.)

[36] The remaining members of the KNIP (mostly from outlying areas) were unable to attend because of fighting and disrupted transportation.

the chief social groups and were to be directly elected by the KNIP, and they in turn were to elect eight other members—one from each province—on the basis of nominees submitted by the governors and representative bodies (KNI's) of those provinces and/or their residencies.[37] There was a general demand within the KNIP that the "fighting youth, peasants, and urban workers" be given a wide representation in the Working Committee, and this idea carried. As a result of the voting Sjahrir and Sjarifuddin were able to count on at least seven of the seventeen members elected by the KNIP as being their consistent backers, five of these being members of their own party.[38] At least two others could be counted on to back them in most cases.[39] The PNI's strong position in local government administration [40] was reflected by the fact that the majority of nominations submitted by provincial representatives were for individuals from its membership. Thus six out of the eight provincial representatives elected by the seventeen members of the Working Committee already chosen by the KNIP were from the PNI.

The political affiliation of the twenty-five members of the Working Committee following the election of the provincial nominees was as follows: [41] PNI, ten members; Socialist Party,[42] five; Masjumi, four; Christian Party, one; PPI (Young Women's Party), one; nonparty, four. Two of those designated as nonparty, Adam Malik and Sukarni, were strong supporters of Tan Malaka.[43] Supeno of the Socialist Party was elected by the KNIP as its and the Working Committee's chairman.

[37] See "Pengoemoeman Badan Pekerdja Komité Nasional Poesat," Berita Repoeblik Indonesia, I, no. 1 (November 17, 1945).

[38] The two non-Socialist Party members in this category were Dr. Halim (nonparty) and Miss Susilowati (Pemuda Putri Indonesia—Indonesian Young Womens' Assn.).

[39] Mohammad Natsir of Masjumi and Mr. Tambunan of the Christian Party.

[40] In most of the regional KNI's the old-line Indonesian administrative civil servants held at this time dominant positions. Since most of them were adherents of the PNI, it was natural that their influence was used to nominate provincial candidates who were members of their party. Most of the local KNI's had just been formed. As time went on, particularly as the members in many of them came to be elected, the PNI's dominance frequently gave way to that of other parties, particularly the Masjumi, and secondarily the Socialist Party.

[41] Berita Badan Pekerdja Komité Nasional Poesat, March 4, 1946–Feb. 17, 1947, pp. 3, 5, 6.

[42] One of the five representatives of the Socialist Party was Tan Ling-djie, an Indonesian-born Chinese. He was considered by his Working Committee colleagues, though by only a small minority of Indonesian-born Chinese, as representing the interests of the Indonesian-born Chinese (Peranakan) community.

[43] Both had been among the 17 elected by the KNIP.

With the cabinet dominated by Sjahrir's group, and the majority of the Working Committee and the KNIP itself along with Soekarno and Hatta backing it, the position of Tan Malaka and the dissident ex-cabinet members who joined his opposition was difficult. The interim, pre-election, government was firmly in the hands of the Sjahrir group, Soekarno, and Hatta. It was probable that the holding of national elections, scheduled for the end of January, 1946, would confirm their claim to power and almost certain that it would demonstrate the overwhelming mass-support commanded by Soekarno. Thus Tan Malaka and his group were forced to work rapidly in order to seize power before the strength of the political incumbents could be consolidated, whether through elections or other means.

To build up his opposition organization Tan Malaka relied upon three sources of support:

(1) his own prestige and the attraction of the political and social program he advocated, this bringing him the hard core of his organization, a number of militant youth led by young leaders such as Sukarni, Adam Malik, Chairul Saleh, Pandu Wiguna, and Maruto Nitimihardjo;

(2) the strong anti-Sjahrir feeling among the many influential political and military leaders who had worked with or under the Japanese administration, including (a) cabinet members who had been ousted by Soekarno and who felt that by joining the most powerful nucleus of opposition, that of Tan Malaka, they stood the best chance of regaining power; (b) many others who had worked under the Japanese—military (ex-Peta) leaders and holders of high administrative posts—who felt insecure in their positions in the light of Sjahrir's anticollaborationist campaign, particularly after the dismissal of Soekarno's cabinet, and were anxious for the overthrow of Sjahrir's group so that their positions would be more secure;

(3)the surging tide of nationalism which made it difficult for many people to countenance any negotiations whatsoever with the Dutch so long as their troops were on Indonesian soil, and in particular when the number of their troops kept steadily increasing.

Drawing upon these strengths and potential strengths, Tan Malaka and his lieutenants undertook to build a mighty political organization which would compete with and ultimately supplant the existing government as the leader of the Indonesian revolution. In the form of a mass movement—the Persatuan Perdjuangan (the Fighting Front), supposedly oriented towards mobilization of the widest possible national support *behind* the government rather than *opposed* to it, they launched their bid for power. In the interests of national solidarity a meeting of 300 delegates from most of the political and military organizations of the Republic was called at Purwokerto on January 4 and 5, 1946. Here Tan Malaka made an address which set the course for the Persatuan Perdjuangan established ten days later at Surakarta by an even larger number of delegates. He called for monolithic political solidarity during the struggle for freedom, the abolishment of the recently established political parties, and an end to all political division. In addition, he demanded repudiation of the negotiations recently begun with the Dutch and the confiscation of all foreign properties. Tan Malaka stated:

The seed which can spread trouble, which can cause dissensions in our case, must be avoided by not bringing forward proposals which can lead to disagreements, and for this purpose we must make a minimum program, the most concise program which can be accepted by all parties, and solely in connection with our struggle. . . .

While we are facing the enemy, we must watch that no trouble arises among us as a result of the bringing forward of various "isms" which in reality should not be brought into discussion at this time before we obtain our freedom completely. The existence of trouble among ourselves will cause weakness in our struggle, as it will tend to weaken the zeal of the entire population.

Twenty-three years ago we also experienced a conflict between the PKI (Indonesian Communist Party) and the Sarekat Islam. We became weak. That was our weakness, our plight which was also known by the enemy. . . .

We are not willing to negotiate with any one else before we obtain our 100 per cent freedom and before our enemy has left our shores and our seas in good order. We are not willing to negotiate with a thief in our house. Let us not have the idea that the public does not understand diplomacy. We are not willing to negotiate as long as the enemy is still in our country.

If we are willing to hold negotiations, we are doing it against the will of the general public.

Therefore, as long as one single enemy remains in the country, as long as there is an enemy ship on our shore, we must continue to fight. . . .

We wish the government to act in accordance with the desires of the public, in agreement with the ideology of the public.

If we base our fate on diplomacy alone, we will certainly be entangled in poor diplomacy. . . .

At this moment, the speedy formation of a Fighting Front (Persatuan Perdjuangan) is badly needed, along with the centralization of all fighting forces, to demand a mimimum program:

To negotiate upon the basis of 100 per cent recognition after foreign troops have left the shores and the seas of Indonesia.

A well-organized body to carry out the desires of the public in the struggle for freedom. . . .

Leadership is badly needed by the general public in the midst of its revolution; a leadership that is strong and visible is the kind of leadership that is needed and suitable to the fighting spirit of the public aflame with patriotic fire. . . .

The Persatuan Perdjuangan ought to become a central fighting organization which is able to settle all dissensions between organizations and the central government and between individuals and the central government. The lack of unity will cause the defeat of our people in the struggle. . . .

We acknowledge our weaknesses, and the biggest is organization. Therefore, we ought to establish a strong and powerful organization. Parties have arisen everywhere, parties that are difficult to control. This causes separation. It is of the utmost importance that unity be restored.

The most practical way to restore this unity is the formation of a Persatuan Perdjuangan with a minimum program. Why should the factories and the agricultural estates be confiscated before freedom is obtained 100 per cent? Why should they be distributed among the masses? Because if they have become the properties of the masses, they will be able to fight as lions if the enemy ever comes back.[44]

These proposals immediately attracted wide support, not only from those opposed to Soekarno and/or Sjahrir but also from a great many other political and military leaders who agreed with Tan Malaka's emphasis upon national solidarity and the refusal to negotiate with the Dutch until after they had left Indonesian soil. The Persatuan Perdjuangan grew rapidly and within a month embraced 141 organizations, including all important political parties and military organizations. It had the outspoken backing of General Sudirman, the commander in chief of the national army (the TRI), and for a brief time even enjoyed the support of the Socialist Party and the Pesindo. The Working Committee itself initially endorsed the Persatuan Perdjuangan's stand and urged the whole population to join it; [45] for the over-all objectives of Tan Malaka and his associates were not immediately discernible.

Not until early in February did these objectives begin to be revealed. To the more astute these began to be comprehended when at that time the PP (Persatuan Perdjuangan) leadership directed that no constituent party could be represented in the cabinet so long as the entire

[44] For the full text of his speech in English see *The Voice of Free Indonesia*, no. 4 (Jan., 1946), pp. 7–9.
[45] "Pengoeman Badan Pekerdja Komité Nasional Poesat, no. 21—Jan 25, 1946," *Berita Repoeblik Indonesia*, II, no. 7 (Feb. 15, 1946), 56–57.

PP minimum program had not been carried out. It then became apparent to many that the overthrow of Sjahrir's cabinet was the immediate objective of the PP high command. Thereupon the Socialist Party and the Pesindo pulled out of the PP coalition. While the Masjumi did not join them in this move, it did not call upon its two members represented in the cabinet, Natsir and Rasjidi, to resign. However, the remainder of the important constituent organizations of the Persatuan Perdjuangan stood fast, and its leaders, with wide support, claimed that it was more representative of the national will than was the KNIP.

Beginning with the resolution of the Congress of the PNI on January 29–31, 1946, several political organizations commenced to urge that the composition of the KNIP and the cabinet be altered in accordance with what they maintained was an actual balance of political forces different from what was represented in either of them. On February 16 the Working Committee formally backed these demands.[46] The facts that important areas were under military control of British and Dutch troops, that in others fighting was taking place between them and Indonesian troops, and that in some other areas the Republican government exercised only a partial control over occasionally insubordinate leaders of irregular Indonesian troops ruled out the possibility of the previously contemplated early national elections. The challenge of the PP as a whole and of many of its various constituent groups individually as to the validity of the popular mandate claimed by the government forced the government, in the face of the impossibility of holding elections, to go part way in meeting their demands. On February 26, the Working Committee handed in its resignation to the KNIP. However, after several days of debate the KNIP found itself unable to accept the resignation, since it could find no formula agreeable to a majority of its members for either increasing its own total membership or altering the composition of its existing membership.[47]

Unable to change the power structure of the KNIP and its agent, the Working Committee, the PP leaders then pressed home their chief demand, the dismissal of the Sjahrir cabinet and its replacement by a coalition cabinet, "national" in character, which they would dominate. Here their argument for "national unity" had such wide popular backing that their pressure could not be ignored by either the KNIP or

[46] "Pengoeman Badan Pekerdja Komité Nasional Poesat, no. 23," *Berita Repoeblik Indonesia*, II, no. 8, 65–66 (March 1, 1946).

[47] *Berita Badan Pekerdja Komité Nasional Poesat*, March 4, 1946–Feb. 17, 1947, pp. 1–3.

Soekarno. Realizing this, Sjahrir suddenly, and to the surprise of the
PP leaders, on February 28, 1946 handed in his resignation to Soekarno.

For a time it appeared as if Tan Malaka and the other PP leaders
had triumphed and had succeeded in overthrowing and supplanting
the Sjahrir group. Soekarno gave them the mandate to form a new
cabinet. Immediately the weakness of the dissident coalition manifested
itself. Its leaders were divided as to the allocation of the positions of
power which lay within their grasp. Their diverse social interests—
those of anti-Marxist Moslems, conservative bureaucrats, and nationalist Communists—and in particular their competing personal ambitions
could not be reconciled. The facility of creating an opposition front
was not matched by that of building a workable governing coalition.[48]
Many in the PP coalition, including General Sudirman and several
other army leaders, while desirous for Sjahrir's overthrow, did not want
a cabinet dominated by Tan Malaka and his group. They feared, with
some justification, that once having reached that rung in the ladder of
power, Tan Malaka, would attempt to supplant Soekarno. The majority of the PP coalition wanted Soekarno to remain as president.
Most of the military and political figures of this group were primarily
interested in weakening the position of Sjahrir while maintaining that
of Soekarno. They had no wish to strengthen Tan Malaka. They were
willing to go along with his group only as far as its first objective,
the overthrow of Sjahrir.

After having offered the PP leaders a mandate for forming a cabinet
which they had been unable to carry out, Soekarno was free to ask
Sjahrir to form a new cabinet. The KNIP, still in session, immediately
approved this action by a strong vote of confidence in Sjahrir, but at
the same time voted that his cabinet be broadened so as to be more
widely representative of the chief political currents in the nation. This
was agreeable to Sjahrir so long as the choice of members would be
principally his. After a week of consultation with Soekarno and
Hatta, Sjahrir announced the membership of his new cabinet. The
selection of its new members had been principally Sjahrir's and only

[48] According to Tan Malaka, his group did not carry out the mandate for forming a cabinet because it could not get the necessary backing (presumably from
Soekarno and Hatta and/or the KNIP) for the program it wished to carry out.
Moreover, he states, "We never knew the exact extent of power of the President
in relation to that of the Prime Minister, with the former in Djogja [karta] and the
latter in Dutch-occupied Batavia" (Tan Malaka, *Thesis* [Jakarta, 1947], p. 28).

secondarily that of Soekarno and Hatta, there being, however, mutual agreement among the three on the choices made. Ten of the eleven ministers of Sjahrir's first cabinet stayed on in his second. One, Dr. Mulia, gave up his post of Minister of Education to a newcomer, Mohammad Sjafei of the PNI, but remained in the cabinet as Vice-Minister of Education. Two additional ministerial posts were added; one—Agriculture—went to a PNI member, Mr. Rasat, and the other—without portfolio—went to Wikana of the Pesindo. Of the eleven relatively powerless vice-Ministers added to the new cabinet, three were nonparty, three were from the Masjumi, two from the PNI, two from the Christian Party, and one was from the Socialist Party. None of the new cabinet members, ministers or vice-ministers had been leaders of the Persatuan Perdjuangan.

Thus the new cabinet, despite the strong agitation of the PP, was clearly dominated by Sjahrir's group. Moreover, the powers of the cabinet were increased and clarified. They now derived from the KNIP as well as from the President. A clear mandate of legislative power had been delegated to the cabinet by the KNIP in its session of February 28–March 2. Thereby the KNIP was by-passing the Working Committee and was in effect giving the cabinet roughly equal stature with it as a legislative body. All cabinet measures still had to secure concurrence of the Working Committee, but certainly much legislative initiative had been thus transferred from the Working Committee to the cabinet.

The mandate included: (1) conduct of discussion with the Netherlands authorities based on recognition of the Indonesian Republic; (2) preparation of the defense of the Indonesian Republic; (3) establishment of a democratic basis for central and provincial governments; (4) provision for maximum production and fair distribution of goods; (5) the running of essential estates and industries under government supervision.

The disappointment of the Persatuan Perdjuangan leaders and their opposition to Sjahrir's new cabinet were strong. Almost immediately they called a large meeting of their organization at Madiun, where they made plain the unacceptability of the new cabinet and its program and their intention to take matters into their own hands. The government met this challenge immediately; its troops in Madiun on March 17 arrested and jailed Tan Malaka and six other important leaders of the Persatuan Perdjuangan—Abikusno Tjokrosujoso, Chairul Saleh,

Sukarni, Suprapto, Mohammad Yamin, and Wondoamiseno.[49] Thereby the PP sustained an important setback in Java. In Sumatra, however, it continued to grow.

To understand the rapid burgeoning of the Persatuan Perdjuangan in Sumatra it is first necessary to know something of the situation there following the outbreak of the revolution. News of Soekarno and Hatta's declaration of Indonesian independence was received in Sumatra on August 17, just as it was elsewhere in Indonesia. There soon developed in Sumatra the same rising against Japanese authority as there did in Java. There, too, some Japanese officers offered no resistance. The situation was less difficult for the revolutionists in Sumatra than in Java because of the very limited operations of the British on the larger island. Sumatra never became the major battlefield between the Indonesians and British that Java did, the British being content to limit their occupation there to three tiny enclaves—the port cities of Palembang and Padang and half the port city of Medan.

The revolutionary leaders on Sumatra acknowledged the Republic as their government and Soekarno, Hatta, and Sjahrir as its top leaders. However, in practice until the spring of 1946 the revolutionary movement in most areas of this great island was largely autonomous. There were Republican government officers in Sumatra appointed by the central government in Java. But their authority was limited. Only in limited areas, such as Atjeh (of which he was native) and in Medan, his capital (where he had the able assistance of the Republican mayor, Mohammad Jusuf), was the Republic's governor of Sumatra, Tengku Hasan, able to exercise even a small amount of authority. Actually until the beginning of April, 1946, the only contact between the Republican government in Java and Sumatra was by radio.

There had grown up in Sumatra political organizations with the same names as those on Java. However, they were quite autonomous; many of them even after 1946 did not come under the discipline of the Java headquarters of their party.

The East Coast Residency of Sumatra (before the war by far the

---

[49] Tan Malaka was the operative head of the Persatuan Perdjuangan and Sukarni its secretary. Suprapto was a PKI leader whose inclinations in domestic politics apparently differed considerably from those of Alimin and Sardjono, who were strongly anti-Tan Malaka. Abikusno and Wondoamiseno were members of the Masjumi, but did not actually represent it at the meeting, being sent there in the capacity of observers. The arrests were probably made by the Pesindo troops stationed in Madiun.

most important center in Indonesia of plantation-based export agriculture) was an area which the Dutch had ruled indirectly through local aristocrats. The strength of this nobility vis-à-vis the local peasantry had been much strengthened because of the backing given them by the Dutch. Most of them had badly abused their augmented strength to the serious detriment of the local peasantry. With little regard for the rights of the peasantry, they had leased wide tracts of land, the disposal rights over which frequently had lain traditionally with the village, to foreign companies needing land for plantations devoted to export agriculture. Generally a disproportionate amount of the rental paid by the Western enterprises went directly into the hands of these aristocratic rulers, many of whom became very wealthy, and generally benefited the peasantry little or not at all.

Not only did few of the aristocratic rulers govern in the interests of the local population, but also most of them took pains to emphasize their Malay peninsula ancestry and cultural orientation, rather than identifying themselves with the local population. Moreover, they served the Japanese as well as they had the Dutch.

Thus, when after the launching of the Republican revolution most of these rulers held back from joining the movement,[50] the long-smoldering popular hatred of them markedly increased. When in late February reports circulated that these rulers were contacting the Dutch in the hope of reinstating themselves in their old positions, a spontaneous movement to oust them quickly developed.

This movement, later known as the "Sumatra Social Revolution,"[51] soon gathered momentum and became wantonly brutal. The local

[50] The Sultan of Siak, one of the most important of them, was an exception and from the outset supported the Republic. (He was not molested in the course of the Social Revolution.)

[51] The Sumatra Social Revolution should not be confused with the earlier (mid-December, 1945 until mid-January, 1946) revolutionary developments in Atjeh (the northern end of Sumatra adjacent to the East Coast Residency) which were quite distinct. In Atjeh the local religious leaders (most of whom were affiliated with the Masjumi) led a popular movement to oust the 102 local aristocratic rulers which was successful and during which about half of these rulers (most of whom put up a strong armed resistance) were killed. Atjeh had not been an area of Western plantations (estates) as the East Coast Residency had been. However, most of the local rulers were strongly disliked by the population. Until 1904 there had been one over-all Indonesian ruler for all Atjeh, the Sultan of Atjeh. However, following the successful completion of their long and costly war against him, the Dutch replaced him by 102 petty aristocratic rulers, each with his own domain. There were too many rulers for the taxes of the area to support, and thus the burden on the peasantry was greatly increased. Backed as they were by Dutch power, many of

Republican authorities possessed too little power to restrain it. Several irresponsible, opportunistic political leaders—of whom two PKI Communists, Karim Marah Sutan and Luat Siregar, were the most important—apparently saw the movement as a means to political power. In order to reach their end they stimulated it through the wildest sort of agitation. As a result the mobs and armed gangs they exhorted killed many of the local aristocratic leaders and their families. In addition they looted almost any imposing-looking house, sometimes killing its occupants without bothering to find out who they were. However, this was not always simply indiscriminate action against the wealthy. Often it was a result of the long dose of anti-Western propaganda the Japanese had fed Indonesians during their occupation. There was a frequent tendency for members of these mobs to turn upon Western-educated Indonesian professional people, particularly those living in a conspicuously Western manner. Thus, a number of pro-Republican nationalists or members of their families [52] were killed at the same time as were the pro-Dutch aristocrats and their families.

It should be noted that the major result of the "Social Revolution" in the East Coast Residency was the killing of aristocratic rulers whose authority, however, was already disregarded. Their palaces were looted, but generally there was little interest shown in seizing their private lands. At that time, as a result of Japanese policy, there was an actual glut of arable land in the Residency. The Japanese, being able to export very little, simply turned over most of the plantations (estates) in the area to the labor force of some 350,000 which had formerly worked them and to anyone else who wished to grow his own food on them. There was plenty of land available before the "Social Revolution."

The social ferment generated by the "Social Revolution" in the East

---

these petty rulers acted in an extremely harsh and arbitrary manner towards their subjects, squeezing as much from them by taxation as possible and sometimes taking their land from them. Some of this numerous aristocracy had administered their areas before in a semi-autonomous manner vis-à-vis the paramount power of the Sultan. However, the majority of them were simply the local military officers of the Sultan—the *Ulu Balangs*—whom the Dutch transformed into petty rulers.

[52] An example was Dr. Nainggolan. During the prewar period his courage as a nationalist had lost him several jobs—many doctors were in government service—because of the antagonism his action incurred among the Dutch authorities. He had immediately declared for the Republic, and his two sons were serving in the Republican army. During the course of the "Social Revolution" his wife and daughter both of whom dressed in the Western manner were killed. Because of his embitterment at this and because he felt the Republic was not strong enough to maintain order, he crossed over to the Netherlands side to work for their administration. Several other previous supporters of the Republic did likewise for similar reasons.

Coast Residency spilled over into parts of Tapanuli and the Menang-kabau area on the west coast of Sumatra. However, partly because social cleavages were relatively slight in these areas, its manifestation there was much more moderate. The principal result in these areas was the replacement of a number of village heads.

Taking note of what was going on in Java the same leaders who had ridden to positions of power on the crest of the "Social Revolution"—Luat Siregar, Karim Marah Sutan, and Sarwono (of the Sumatra Pesindo), and several others—organized themselves and the armed gangs associated with them into the nucleus of an East Sumatran branch of the Persatuan Perdjuangan, seeking to attract as wide a political following as possible. So constituted, they continued to defy the local Republican authorities, issuing their own orders over their heads. Apparently taking example from this action as well as from events in Java, a large number of political leaders in the West Coast Residency of Sumatra set up their own branch of the PP a few days later. It was reported, that a meeting there on March 23, 1946, of representatives from thirty-four political and military organizations, including the TRI, had set up a new branch, the announced purpose of which was to "defend the integrity of the country against corrupt strategems from within and without." [53] Undoubtedly in Sumatra as in Java the PP was receiving the support not merely of political leaders who sought to gain political advantage but also of those who were critical of Sjahrir's willingness to negotiate with the British and the Dutch and feared that Indonesian independence might be compromised in the process.

Clearly the criticalness of the situation in Sumatra required prompt action by the central government in Java. Late in March a mission was dispatched by it to Sumatra headed by the Minister of Defense, Amir Sjarifuddin, and including the Minister of Information, Mohammad Natsir; Mr. Abdulmadjid, and Mr. Ismael Thajeb, all but Abdulmajid being Sumatrans. First the mission went to Medan, capital of the East Coast Residency and headquarters of the Republican governor of Sumatra, Tengku Hasan. With the prestige of the Republican government and its leaders behind it, and by dint of its own able efforts in winning the support of many local military and political organizations, the mission succeeded in re-establishing the authority of the Republican Government in this area, not in any absolute sense, but

[53] Antara as reported by Aneta, March 23, 1946. Antara was the chief Republican news agency. It was privately owned and managed.

making it at least somewhat stronger than it had been before the "Social Revolution" and the rise of the local PP branch. The leaders of the latter found it expedient to acknowledge their submission to the authority of the central government.

Next the mission went to Bukit Tinggi (formerly Fort De Kock), capital of the West Coast Residency. Here the Persatuan Perdjuangan's autonomous branch was stronger than the one in the East Coast Residency had been and even more defiant of the Republican Government's authority. Not only had it begun issuing its own orders over the head of the latter; it had announced that the hundred-rupiah bills of the Republic's paper currency were no longer valid and had begun calling them in, paying seven ten-rupiah bills in return. In a speech before a mass meeting in Bukit Tinggi Mohammad Natsir made clear that since the Republican government had issued the money, it alone could declare it invalid and left the distinct impression with the audience that the local PP leaders had nothing less in mind than using the hundred-rupiah bills they had acquired so cheaply for purchases in some other area where they expected to get the full value of these notes.

In order to strengthen the Republic's authority in the West Coast Residency as well as throughout Sumatra as a whole, Sjarifuddin's mission organized a Sumatra KNI (Indonesian National Committee). The first meeting of this was held under the mission's auspices at Bukit Tinggi on April 15, where over 100 delegates from all parts of Sumatra were represented. At this meeting Sjarifuddin issued directives for the establishment of a network of Sumatran KNI's such as had been established on Java. The top KNI for the Republic remained the Central KNI (the KNI Pusat—KNIP), meeting on Java and in which sat representatives from Sumatra. However, interposed between it and the local Sumatran KNI's was the all-Sumatra KNI established on April 15. In theory the same general division of competencies between the national, regional, and local KNI's existed on Sumatra as on Java, the subordinate bodies being competent to legislate on whatever subject had not already been fixed by legislation of the higher body, with legislation of the latter taking precedence in case of conflict. In practice the regional KNI's in Sumatra and the regional administrations there in general were much more autonomous than those in Java.

As a result of Sjarifuddin's mission, Sumatra, though still highly autonomous, was more effectively incorporated into the Republican administration than previously. Within Sumatra the local administration under Tengku Hassan was strengthened, but its control over most local districts in Sumatra was still infinitely weaker than that of the Republican government in Java over most districts there. In general, however, the power of the Persatuan Perdjuangan in Sumatra had been seriously weakened. When in mid-May it attempted to stage a comeback in the East Coast Residency, again defying government authority, the local KNI was successful in having its leaders arrested.

Meanwhile on Java, the PP, though deprived of its top leaders, remained strong. The demands for Dutch acknowledgement of Indonesian independence prior to negotiations,[54] and to a lesser extent for national unity as expressed by a coalition cabinet, and for nationalization of important industrial and plantation enterprises, though championed by Tan Malaka and other leaders of the PP, were by no means restricted to them. They were popular and widespread. If not met by the government, at least partially, they would continue to provide important political capital for any group seeking its overthrow. Moreover, since even a partial meeting of these demands necessitated considerable time, it was felt essential that in the interim period they be given a channel of flow alternative to that already provided by the PP. Such a new channel, it was hoped, would divert a major portion of the PP's source of strength, leaving with it only those political elements which, though undoubtedly genuinely convinced of the value of these demands for Indonesia's welfare, were also interested in utilizing them as a means of overthrowing and replacing the existing government.

Thus the government encouraged the formation of a new political coalition, the Konsentrasi Nasional (National Concentration), which provided just such an alternative channel. Considerable success attended this effort. Many groups switched their allegiance from the PP to the new organization because they were uncomfortable at what they believed to be the ultimate aim of many of the PP leaders, overthrow of the existing government. This process was undoubtedly expedited when the government let it be known that it was contemplating the formation of a widely-based coalition cabinet, the composition of which would be determined by consultation among Soekarno and Sjahrir and the Konsentrasi Nasional. When it was launched on May

[54] These negotiations had progressed to a point where on April 4, 1946, it was felt justified to send a Republican delegation including A. K. Pringgodigdo, Dr. Sudarsono, and Dr. Suwandi to the Netherlands armed with a draft agreement drawn up by Sjahrir. After several weeks of discussions (the Hooge Veluwe Conference) no agreement could be reached, and the delegation returned to Indonesia on April 29.

11, 1946, the Konsentrasi Nasional included not only the Socialist Party and the Pesindo, but also a major part of the backing of the PP as well, including the Masjumi, the Labor Party, the PKI, and the principal peasant and labor organizations, i.e., the Barisan Tani Indonesia (Indonesian Peasant Front) and the Barisan Buruh Indonesia (Indonesian Labor Front). Conspicuously absent, however, were two powerful political groups, that of Tan Malaka and the PNI.

Though greatly weakened, the PP still remained dangerously strong because of the continued backing of most of the PNI, Tan Malaka's following, and a considerable number of leaders of the TRI, as well as of several of the irregular armed organizations. Its strength relative to that of the government was considerably enhanced because of the equivocal attitude taken by General Sudirman and several other high TRI officers. With Sjahrir as Prime Minister these officers felt their positions insecure and were disposed to back the PP's campaign to overthrow him. Continuously leaders of the PP whispered into Sudirman's ear that Sjahrir was maneuvering to replace him as commander in chief of the army. The same technique was applied, often with success, to other high officers who, having received their military training under the Japanese, had been antagonized by Sjahrir's denouncements in his pamphlet, *Perdjuangan Kita*. As a result, the PP, despite its extensive loss of civilian support to the Konsentrasi Nasional, was able to maintain most of its military backing. If it should openly challenge Sjahrir, it could count on the support of a number of important military leaders and the helpful neutrality of an even larger number.

There was undoubtedly some basis to the whispering campaign which alleged that Sjahrir sought to replace the top Japanese-trained officers. Certainly both he and Sjarifuddin felt that some of the officers, both in the TRI and in the irregular armies, might prove unreliable in face of a *coup d'état* directed against their government. To combat this threat they embarked on a two-fold program. First they made sure of the loyalty of a number of the irregular armies by incorporating them into the regular army and giving their leaders high rank within it. Secondly, they undertook to build up a new and elite army division out of some of these irregular armies, including a number of Hizbullah units and other TRI troops, under officers who had not been trained by the Japanese, but rather by the Dutch before the war. This, the Siliwangi Division, was composed of Indonesians most of whom had some education and a large proportion of whom were literate.[55] Under Colonel Didi Kartasasmita, Colonel Hidayat, Colonel Nasution, and Colonel Simatupang, it came to be the strongest division in the Republican army. To the same end and with similarly trained officers, Sjahrir built up the Mobile Police Brigade. The educational level of the men in it was generally even higher than those in the Siliwangi Division and it was to prove itself one of the most effective and dependable fighting units in the Republic. The control of General Sudirman over both of these units was largely nominal; they looked chiefly to the Minister of Defense and the Minister of Interior for their orders.

In certain areas where the PP or its constituent organizations remained strong, it continued to operate in defiance of government directives, notably in Surakarta, Salatiga and the Krawang area. Surakarta was the great stronghold of the PP. Here were the headquarters of Tan Malaka's organization as well as that of the Barisan Banteng.[56] Here the PNI was particularly strong and here also were centered most of those Masjumi leaders who were opposed to Sjahrir.

The city of Surakarta was also capital of the largest and the third-largest of the four remaining principalities of Java, Surakarta and Mangkunegaran. The *Sunan,* prince of Surakarta, was a weak ruler possessed of little positive popular backing.[57] By the spring of 1946 there was certainly considerable popular feeling in Surakarta for stripping the *Sunan* of his governmental powers and all of his wealth outside of his palace. Certain PNI and Barisan Banteng leaders and Rono Marsono, a powerful but corrupt local labor union leader,[58] had worked hard to increase this sentiment. Sjahrir and his cabinet

[55] Siliwangi was a well-known Sundanese king. The unit included a considerable number of Javanese as well as Sundanese.

[56] The Barisan Banteng closely supported the PNI. Though strongly hostile to Sjahrir, it was a staunch supporter of Soekarno. The fact that its membership was largely drawn from the Japanese-sponsored Barisan Polopor undoubtedly colored its attitude towards Sjahrir.

[57] He had succeeded his predecessor during the period of Japanese occupation, had ruled through a grand vizier and had had almost no contact with his people, in whose behalf he had never exerted himself. Most of the prestige which he had possessed was lost during the first months of the revolution when, panic-stricken, he toured his realm telling the people: "I am one of you. Just call me 'bung' [brother]; there is no more royalty; we are all just the same now."

[58] He had already disposed of much of the contents of the government warehouse of which he was in charge in Surakarta for his own benefit, making gifts to local Barisan Banteng officers and to powerful political figures, and thereby building himself a very strong political position.

did not oppose this trend, but insisted that determination of the popular will as to the *Sunan's* and *Mangkunegara's* (ruler of Mangkunegaran) futures be decided by ballot. Elections were scheduled, but both rulers began to campaign so vigorously and effectively that their prospects as against the political parties opposing them began to appear better and better. To Rono Marsono and some of the other local leaders this was an unwelcome prospect, particularly since they were probably at least as interested in obtaining control of the well-stocked warehouses of the *Sunan* as they were in the social issues involved. They put pressure on those leaders primarily interested in these social issues to act immediately.

On April 28, the PNI in Surakarta demanded the abolition of the *Sunan's* rule and the incorporation of his province into the Republic on the same administrative level as its directly administered territory.[59] On the twenty-seventh the Working Committee of the KNI of the Sragen District of the *Sunan's* province broke off relations with him. On the twenty-ninth, the parallel body in the Klaten District, in concert with local military organizations and civil servants called for the abolishment of the royal government and its replacement by a popular, democratic administration. On April 30, the *Sunan,* in response to these demands, announced that he would transfer his authority to the government of the Republic if such was indeed the wish of his people.

A few days later the troops of the Barisan Banteng undertook to back the PNI leaders in their demands on the *Sunan*. Its troops surrounded the *Kepatihan* (administrative office) and the warehouse of the *Sunan,* forced out a number of his officials, and replaced them with its own men. The *Sunan* was shorn of his powers and left only his *kraton* (large palace). A detachment of Barisan Banteng was concurrently sent to the palace of the *Mangkunegara* to parallel this performance. However, the resistance of his troops turned them back.

Upon receiving orders from Jogjakarta from Dr. Sudarsono, Minister of Interior, the state police intervened and deterred the Barisan Banteng from further activity. Sjahrir and Sudarsono soon arrived and ordered the arrest of the twelve top leaders of the outbreak, including Dr. Muwardi, head of the Barisan Banteng, and his chief lieutenants,

[59] Since September, 1945, the Republic had supervised the *Sunan's* rule through a directorate of 5 men appointed by the KNIP. Somewhat later the President had appointed a commissioner to Surakarta, Suroso, who shared power with the directorate. Between them, there had developed considerable friction, and Sjahrir was seeking to replace Suroso by Surjo, Governor of East Java, who was regarded as a stronger man. Suroso would then take the latter's place in East Java.

Rono Marsono, several other trade union leaders, and a number of important local leaders of the PNI. Shortly after the middle of May, the police had rounded up and jailed all twelve of the leaders.

The Barisan Banteng then held large protest demonstrations and appealed to General Sudirman to release those arrested. Sudirman responded promptly and ordered a unit of TRI troops stationed in Surakarta to effect their release immediately.[60] On May 31, the twelve leaders were released from jail and never recommitted. Sudirman was summoned to and appeared before a plenary cabinet session to explain his actions. He stated that with strong Dutch forces based on Semarang and poised to strike at Surakarta he felt it essential to restore order and unity there and that this consideration had prompted his action. Though his explanation was hardly satisfactory from the standpoint of the cabinet, the general situation was evidently too precarious for it to attempt his chastisement. Thus the position of two of the strongest constituent elements of the PP, the PNI and the Barisan Banteng, was not only maintained but even enhanced. The coup they had engineered in Surakarta remained a *fait accompli* and was not undone.

In the meantime, however, the majority opposition to the PP was becoming better organized and more effectively marshaled in support of Sjahrir and his group. On May 28 and 29 meetings were held in Jogjakarta among Soekarno, Sjahrir, and leaders of the constituent organizations of the Konsentrasi Nasional with a view toward establishing agreement upon the composition of the expected coalition cabinet. Many competing claims had to be resolved before a workable balance could be achieved among these leaders and the groups they represented. But during early June, as this work progressed and the new cabinet's emergence became more and more imminent, the prospects of those who hoped to otherthrow Sjahrir through political maneuvers steadily decreased. For the smaller group, which had hoped to overthrow Soekarno as well, and which had looked particularly to Tan Malaka for leadership, the prospects for success through such methods were even less. Increasingly it must have become apparent to these PP leaders that to gain power they would have to resort to force, and increasingly the government came to sense this prospect.

In anticipation of such a move, Soekarno and the cabinet with the approval of the Working Committee on June 6 proclaimed a state of

---

[60] Sudirman dispatched a note to Dr. Sudarsono asking that the 12 be released. The latter did not receive it, however, until the TRI soldiers had already secured their release.

siege for the principality of Surakarta, and the next day extended this to the whole of Java and Madura.[61] The following day, June 8, these three organs of the government jointly established a National Defense Council, responsible to the cabinet and through it to the Working Committee, but able to take immediate decisions when the situation demanded, subject only to later reversal by the cabinet or the Working Committee. The law providing for this emergency organ of government stipulated that its membership consist of the Prime Minister; the Ministers of Defense, Interior, Finance, Economic Affairs, and Communications; the Commander in Chief of the Army; and representatives from three popular organizations to be chosen by the President.[62] As Commander in Chief of the TRI, General Sudirman assumed membership. The three presidential appointees were Masjur, representing the Sabillilah; Sumarsono, representing Pesindo; and Sardjono, representing the PKI.

The Defense Council was, of course, no stronger than the support which its members and member organizations were willing to give it. In the face of the continuing equivocal position of General Sudirman, its effectiveness was seriously weakened. Though a vital member of the council he maintained his opposition to Sjahrir, the council's chairman, and his base of power was sufficient so that neither Sjahrir nor Soekarno could dictate to him. On the other hand, he apparently had no desire to see real power in the hands of Tan Malaka.

On June 27, a government spokesman stated that it was expected that the long-awaited cabinet reorganization would be announced the following day. This was apparently the sign for the revolutionaries to strike. Most high government officials were aware by the twenty-seventh that the expected coup was imminent, but none was sure how extensive the backing of the revolutionaries would be. Indeed, there is considerable evidence that a number of very important political leaders had tentatively thrust one foot into the camp of the revolutionaries, while maintaining one in that of the government, in order to be certain of being on the winning side.

It was probably during the day of June 27 that Tan Malaka and the other jailed PP leaders were released from the Surakarta jail by the troops under the command of Major General Sudarsono, commander

---

[61] Act No. 16, 1946, *Berita Repoeblik Indonesia*, II, no. 24 (Nov., 1946).

[62] "Peratoeran Pemerintah" ("Government Regulation") no. 6, 1946, *Berita Repoeblik Indonesia*, August 1 and 15, 1946. This final draft law of about a month earlier had been amended by the Working Committee. See *Berita Badan Pekerdja Komité Nasional Pusat*, March 4, 1946–Feb. 17, 1946, pp. 15, 16.

in chief of the TRI Third Division. That evening Sjahrir, as had been expected, arrived in Surakarta on his way back from a trip to East Java. With him in Surakarta were Darmawan Mangukusumo, the Minister of Commerce and Industry, and Major General Sudibjo, in charge of evacuation of Allied POW's captured by the Japanese.[63] Late that night these three and several lesser figures were kidnapped [64] and taken to the mountain town of Paras by a small unit of the TRI soldiers of General Sudarsono's command. These soldiers had no idea who the men were, having been informed by the officer in charge only that they were Dutch agents.

Immediately after having heard the news of the kidnapping,[65] the remaining members of the cabinet under the leadership of Amir Sjarifuddin, Minister of Defense, met together and proposed that for the duration of the emergency all powers be transferred to President Soekarno, with the cabinet becoming responsible to him. The Working Committee quickly approved this decision and likewise made explicit that ministerial responsibility to it and the KNIP was to be re-established as soon as conditions had returned to normal.[66] This decision was then announced by radio to the nation by Soekarno at midnight on the twenty-eighth shortly after he had proclaimed a state of war and siege throughout Indonesia.

Though a number of the PP's leaders and much of its backing were concerned largely with the overthrow of Sjahrir's cabinet, the plans of those who seized the initiative and launched the coup went much further. The conspiratorial leaders—Tan Malaka, Subardjo, Yamin, Sukarni, Pandu Wiguna, Iwa Koesoema Soemantri, Sajuti, Sumantoro, Dr. Buntaran, and several high army officers, including General Sudarsono—sought the overthrow of the entire government, including Soekarno and Hatta. However, since for the successful achievement of their plans they felt it necessary to secure the neutrality, if not the support, of General Sudirman, the unfolding of their plans called for two phases. First Sjahrir and his cabinet were to be removed from power and sup-

[63] Some leaders of the PP opposed their evacuation to the Allied-held ports.

[64] Sjahrir states that they were not surprised at being kidnapped, since the Dutch army radio had already announced it the evening previous to the event. He feels that General Spoor, commander in chief of Dutch forces, and Van der Plas (then political advisor to NEFIS—Dutch Army Intelligence) must have had their agents planted within the PP.

[65] At his public trial 18 months later General Sudarsono was also charged with having ordered the kidnapping of Vice Pres. Hatta and Defense Min. Sjarifuddin.

[66] These decisions were codified in a law of July 6, 1946, "Regulation No. 6, 1946, Concerning State of Emergency," Berita Repoeblik Indonesia, Aug. 1–15, 1946.

planted by a "Supreme Political Council" of ten men headed by Tan Malaka and including Subardjo, Sukarni, and Yamin. Soekarno would be forced to transfer his military powers to General Sudirman, but would for a time, until the revolutionary government was consolidated, remain as nominal head of the government. The second phase called for Tan Malaka's replacement of Soekarno as president, and possibly— though this is not clear—his assumption of the presidential military powers taken over by General Sudirman as well.[67] It is difficult to ascertain whether or not the leaders of the Barisan Banteng were a party to the second phase of the plans as well as to the first. It is equally difficult to establish how far General Sudirman was actually backing General Sudarsono, in particular whether he wished to take over powers from Soekarno.

On July 2 General Sudarsono, accompanied by Mohammad Yamin, called on President Soekarno. Acting as the spokesman for Tan Malaka and the other recently freed conspiratorial leaders, he allegedly [68] stated to Soekarno that he had received instructions from General Sudirman to request that he sign four decrees. These provided for disbanding the Sjahrir cabinet and its replacement by a "Supreme Political Council" headed by Tan Malaka as well as the transfer of Soekarno's military powers to General Sudirman. Soekarno bluntly refused and ordered his bodyguard to arrest General Sudarsono and Yamin.

On July 2 while Sudarsono and Yamin were seeing Soekarno in Jogjakarta, the Republican capital, events elsewhere were moving rapidly and confusedly. A loyal army unit released Sjahrir and those who had been kidnapped with him; in Surakarta Barisan Banteng troops attempted to kidnap the Minister of Defense, Amir Sjarifuddin, but though killing his two bodyguards, were unsuccessful.

In the meantime General Sudirman remained noncommittal and out of contact with the government. He and many of the other top army leaders appeared to be remaining neutral and on the fence. Sudirman and they took no action against the rebellious Third Division and the Barisan Banteng. However, immediately upon hearing of Sjahrir's kidnapping, strong units of heavily-armed Pesindo troops struck westward from their base near Surabaya, announcing by radio that if Sjahrir were not freed they would occupy Surakarta, the Persatuan Perd-

---

[67] The president under the Republican Constitution was commander in chief of the armed forces.

[68] Such was the allegation levelled against him by the attorney general in his public trial in Feb., 1948. See Antara, Feb. 19, 1948.

juangan's stronghold. Within a few days they had occupied both Madiun and most of Surakarta. In the meantime the pro-Sjahrir Siliwangi Division stationed in West Java began to march eastward, threatening to occupy Jogjakarta. It dispatched its Special Troops Battalion, completely motorized and equipped with tanks, ahead of the main force, and this arrived in the environs of Jogjakarta the following day, June 29. Here it and additional Siliwangi units which arrived later remained poised until the trouble subsided.

The actions of the Pesindo and the Siliwangi Division made it clear that any further attempt to carry out the *coup d'état* would be contested with vigor and could only lead to a serious civil war. It appeared that the population in general and most of the army was against such a development, if for no other reason than that the Republic would be dangerously weakened in the face of mounting Dutch military strength. Probably Sudirman was impressed by this prospect; along with other thus far "neutral" military leaders, he abandoned his previously ambiguous attitude and finally made it clear that he would not back the coup. That ended the prospects of the revolutionaries. Even with the benevolent neutrality of Sudirman and other high military leaders, they could not alone, supported only by the Barisan Banteng and the Third TRI Division have stood up to both the Pesindo and Siliwangi. Moreover, it is unlikely that most officers and troops of the Third Division would have followed General Sudarsono in actual fighting against their own countrymen.

The PP leaders had counted on a sudden, successful coup which would then be accepted by Sudirman and other army commanders. There are indications that Sudirman and some of these officers may have expected such an eventuality and been prepared to support them (on certain terms) once the coup had been successfully carried off. But none of these military leaders was willing to weaken the Republic against their common enemy, the Dutch, in order to back the PP leaders. Furthermore the probability is that had a civil war actually broken out a majority of military units would have fought alongside the Siliwangi and Pesindo in support of Sjahrir. Moreover, once it had become evident that the Persatuan Perdjuangan leaders were seeking to force concessions of power from Soekarno, the opposition to them would have been even greater.

Sudirman was finally prevailed upon by Soekarno to back Sjahrir, and agreed to support the arrest of the PP leaders who had planned for the second phase of the rebellion—Tan Malaka, Subardjo, Sukarni,

Iwa Koesoema Soemantri, Mohammad Yamin. But in return for his support he insisted upon and obtained terms calculated to maintain intact his own powerful position. None of the PP leaders concerned only with the first phase of the rebellion were to be arrested, and, except for General Sudarsono and a few officers under him, no other TRI or Barisan Banteng leaders were to be either demoted or arrested. And finally, the Pesindo was obliged to evacuate Surakarta, with the military *status quo ante* to prevail there.

Thus, though the attempted coup was frustrated, and the prospects of future coups much diminished, though the PP was dissolved, and though many of its important leaders were jailed, the balance of power within the Republic was only partially altered. The organization of the anti-Sjahrir forces was disintegrated, but many of the elements that had made up the PP were about as strong as they had been previously. The important exception was the amorphous Tan Malaka group, which, deprived of its top leaders, lost its effectiveness for a considerable time to come and never regained the power and following which it possessed during the first months of 1946.

Though the attempted coup of the Persatuan Perdjuangan only partially altered the actual pattern and balance of power within the Republic, it made clear as never before their outline and character. It became apparent as it had not been previously that the division and dispersion of forces within the country was so considerable that no faction or probable combination of factions was likely to muster overwhelming power, except as the consequence of a bitterly contested civil war. The actions of the Pesindo and Siliwangi Division demonstrated that attempts at *coup d'état* would not be met by apathy, but would certainly entail strong resistance. Given the powerful nationalist spirit gripping almost all Indonesians, it was clear that the prospects of future *coups d'état* was much diminished. So long as civil war was likely to result therefrom, few patriotic Republicans would be likely to countenance them; for the internal division and the weakness consequent upon such a war would be an open invitation to a probably successful Dutch attack. This strong desire for national solidarity in conjunction with the realization that existing power was diffused and unlikely to be consolidated short of civil war combined not only to increase internal stability but also militated toward the practice of mutual compromise and adjustment of competing interests that is essential to the development of democratic government.

Following the suppression of the *coup d'état,* Soekarno undertook to make the government more widely representative. He proposed that the pattern of representation of the KNIP be reformed so that, pending the holding of general elections, that body would in the meantime be as representative as possible. His proposal of July 10 [69] called for a revision of the composition of its membership of 200 [70] that would leave much of the initiative of choice for 110 of the members to regional election committees and for sixty of the other members to the political parties. Only thirty members would be directly chosen by the President. (All 200 members of the existing KNIP, with the exception of those still remaining from the twenty-one-man Independence Preparatory Committee, had been appointed directly by Soekarno after consultation with Hatta and other important political leaders.)

Implementation of the law, however, required agreement among the parties as to the composition of regional election committees. (The terms of the law provided that regional representatives could be members of political parties.) Since they could neither agree on this nor upon the apportionment of the sixty seats among the parties, the law lapsed. Thus until February, 1947, the composition of the KNIP remained the same. Out of its membership of 200 there were 129 who were members of political parties. Of these, forty-five were from the PNI, thirty-five from the Masjumi, thirty-five from the Socialist Party, six from the Labor Party, four from the Christian Party, two from the Catholic Party and two from the Communist Party (PKI). Of the remaining seventy-one nonparty members, five represented the Chinese community; two, the Arab community; and one, the Dutch.[71]

By mid-August, 1946, the KNIP at its session in Jogjakarta was able to announce that the extraordinary internal situation had ended and that the reinstatement of a parliamentary cabinet responsible to it was now fully justified. It called for the "revision of the composition and the strengthening of the government through the establishment of a coalition cabinet." [72] To effect the compromises necessary for the building of such a coalition took more than six weeks of negotiation between

[69] *Oendang Oendang* ("Law") no. 12, 1946 (promulgated July 10, 1946), "On the Revision of the Formation of the KNIP." This was a revision of an earlier presidential proposal of April 18, 1946, which had not yet been approved by the Working Committee. See *Berita Badan Pekerdjan KNIP,* March 4, 1946–Feb. 17, 1946, pp. 14–15.

[70] Twelve additional members had been appointed during the previous six months.

[71] *Presidential Regulation No. 6, 1946,* Dec. 29, 1946, app.

[72] Soemyoto, "Het Nieuwe Kabinet Sjahrir," *Indonesia,* Oct. 12, 1946, p. 1.

Sjahrir, whom Soekarno with concurrence of the KNIP had designated as Prime Minister and cabinet *formateur,* and Soekarno and Hatta and the leaders of the powerful PNI and Masjumi.

Sjahrir no longer had the freedom of choice in selecting his cabinet colleagues that he had enjoyed in forming his first two cabinets. His position in his third cabinet was much weaker. He felt, however, that he had to accept the post of Prime Minister if a settlement with the Dutch was to be reached. When finally announced on October 2, it was apparent that the new cabinet was the most widely representative that the Republic had yet known. Members of every important political party and the Chinese and Arab communities as well were represented in it.[73] One ministry was headed by a woman, Maria Ulfah Santoso, and another cabinet post was held by the Sultan of Jogjakarta.[74] The coalition nature and wide basis of the new cabinet can best be grasped by listing its members with their party affiliations:

Third Sjahrir Cabinet (October 2, 1946–June 27, 1947) [75]

Post	Name	Party
Prime Minister	Soetan Sjahrir	Socialist
Minister of Foreign Affairs	Soetan Sjahrir	
Vice-Min. of Foreign Affairs	Hadji Agoes Salim	nonparty [76]
Minister of Interior	Mr. Mohammad Roem	Masjumi
Vice-Min. of Interior	Wijono	Socialist
Minister of Justice	Mr. Susanto Tirtoprodjo	PNI
Vice-Min. of Justice	Mr. Hadi	nonparty

[73] The Masjumi as a party was not represented in the cabinet. Those Masjumi members who participated in it did so as individuals, not as representatives of the Masjumi party, and were not responsible to it. Apparently the same was true in the case of the PNI members of the cabinet. Thus only in a limited sense could the cabinet be designated as a "coalition cabinet."

[74] At the outset of the revolution, the Sultan of Jogjakarta had supported the Republic and the social change it represented. On his own initiative he introduced important and far-sighted political and economic reforms in his territory—before they had been adopted in the Republic as a whole. His territory came to constitute a sort of "pilot area" for political and economic change and the reforms that he introduced frequently were later introduced into other areas of the Republic. He was the principle founder of the Laskar Rakjat and a colonel in the TRI.

[75] The order of posts as listed is not necessarily in order of importance, but conforms to that in the official cabinet list as supplied the writer by Ratmoko, the Assistant Secretary of State.

[76] Hadji Agoes Salim has often been referred to as belonging either to Masjumi or (after July 3, 1947) to the Partai Sarekat Islam Indonesia. He was actually a member of neither, though he was an influential unofficial advisor of the Masjumi's progressive wing.

Minister of Finance	Mr. Sjafruddin Prawiranegara	Masjumi
Vice-Min. of Finance	Mr. Lukman Hakim	PNI
Minister of Economic Affairs	Dr. A. K. Gani	PNI
Vice-Min. of Economic Affairs	Mr. Jusuf Wibisono	Masjumi
Minister of Health	Dr. Darmasetiawan	nonparty
Vice-Min. of Health	Dr. J. Leimena	Christian
Minister of Education and Culture	Mr. Suwandi	nonparty
Vice-Min. of Education and Culture	Ir. Gunarso	nonparty
Minister of Social Affairs	Mr. Maria Ulfah Santoso	nonparty
Vice-Min. of Social Affairs	Mr. Abdulmadjid	Socialist
Minister of Religion	Faturrachman	Masjumi
Minister of Defense	Mr. Amir Sjarifuddin	Socialist
Vice-Min. of Defense	Harsono Tjodroaminoto	Masjumi
Minister of Information	Mohammad Natsir	Masjumi
Vice-Min. of Information	A. R. Baswedan	Arab Community
Minister of Communications	Ir. Djuanda	nonparty
Vice-Min. of Communications	Setiadjit	Labor
Minister of Public Works	Ir. Putuhena	Christian
Vice-Min. of Public Works	Ir. Laoh	PNI
Minister of State	S. P. Hamengku Buwono IX	Sultan of Jogjakarta
Minister of State	Wachid Hasjim	Masjumi
Minister of State	Wikana	PKI (Communist Party)
Minister of State	Dr. Sudarsono	Socialist
Minister of State	Mr. Tan Po Gwan	Chinese Community
Minister of State	Dr. Setiabuddhi [77]	Eurasian Community

Though Sjahrir's party occupied only a few of the posts, it should be noted that most of the numerous Masjumi ministers were from the progressive wing of the party and fairly close to Sjahrir with respect to most basic questions of policy. The same can be said of the majority of the nonparty representatives and of those from parties other than the PNI. The PNI and the center- and right-wing of the Masjumi remained adamant in their opposition to negotiation with the Dutch until after their troops had left Indonesian soil. Furthermore most PNI leaders felt strongly that their party was entitled to more cabinet positions than it had been given, including the post of Prime Minister.

[77] Formerly known as Douwes Dekker.

THE LINGGADJATI AGREEMENT

The British were extremely anxious to leave Indonesia and the uncomfortable role they had assumed there. They served notice to the
Dutch that they would commence withdrawing their troops by the
end of November, 1946, and put great pressure on them to come to an
agreement with the Republic. This pressure combined with the willingness of progressive Dutch elements to make realistic concessions to the
Republican point of view enabled the Dutch Commission-General in
Indonesia, headed by Willem Schermerhorn, leader of the Netherlands
Labor Party, to initial on November 15 what was envisaged as a final
settlement between the Netherlands and the Republic. Known as the
"Linggadjati Agreement" this settlement established broad principles
of agreement, according to which the specific implementing details were
to be gradually worked out.

Charles Wolf, Jr. has ably and succinctly summarized the principal
provisions of the Linggadjati Agreement stating that it called for:

(1) That the Netherlands Government recognize the Republic as the *de facto*
authority in Java and Sumatra;

(2) That the Netherlands and Republican Governments co-operate toward
the setting up of a sovereign democratic federal state, the United States
of Indonesia, to consist of three states, the Republic of Indonesia, embracing Java and Sumatra, the state of Borneo, and the Great Eastern State
[all the rest of Indonesia—i.e. the areas of the former Netherlands East
Indies lying to the east of Java and to the east and south-east of Bor-
neo];

(3) That the Netherlands and Republican Governments co-operate toward the
formation of the Netherlands-Indonesian Union, to consist of the Kingdom of the Netherlands—including the Netherlands, Surinam, and Curacao
—and the U.S.I. [United States of Indonesia], which Union would have
as its head the Queen of the Netherlands;

(4) That the Netherlands-Indonesian Union and the U.S.I. be formed no
later than January 1, 1949, and that the Union set up its own agencies for
the regulation of matters of common interest to the member states, specifically, the matters of foreign affairs, defense and certain financial and
economic policies;

(5) Finally the Agreement provided for a mutual reduction in troop strength
and a gradual evacuation of Dutch troops from the Republican areas as
quickly as possible consistent with the maintenance of law and order, and
for the recognition by the Republic of all claims by foreign nationals for

the restitution and maintenance of their rights and properties within the areas controlled by the Republic.[78]

Wolf notes that "according to the Agreement the U.S.I. would be a sovereign democratic state and an *equal partner of the Kingdom,* rather than a partner of the Netherlands within the Kingdom as the Dutch had proposed." [79] "From a purely political point of view," Wolf observes, "the Netherlands seemed to have made the greater concessions." [80] However, the Agreement protected the great Netherlands economic investments in the Indies and incorporated several political provisions which seemed important to the Dutch: e.g., maintaining Indonesia symbolically at least under the Dutch Crown (only as an equal partner in the Netherlands-Indonesian Union did it come under the Crown); and organization of Indonesia on a federal basis, with the Republic one of at least three constituent states, with any territory having the right if it so wished to "decide by democratic process" to establish "a special relationship" with the Netherlands rather than joining the United States of Indonesia.[81]

As Wolf concluded, the Agreement had two vital weaknesses. It called for *"cooperation* between the Netherlands and the Republic toward the construction of the United States of Indonesia and the Netherlands-Indonesian Union; cooperation in the reduction of military forces and in the regulation of economic matters." [82] Its keystone was co-operation between the two parties, and if that did not develop, most of the clauses in the Agreement could not be implemented. Unfortunately, as Wolf notes, "there were still many strong elements on both sides which were not yet ready for such cooperation, largely because they lacked the conviction that the other party was sincere and trustworthy." [83] In the second place, as Wolf observes, the Agreement stipulated "a *federal* United States of Indonesia to consist of three semi-autonomous states, the Great East and Borneo as well as the Republic. It implied a paper equality of areas which are not, cannot and will not be equal—economically, politically, or culturally." The area of the Republic (Java and Sumatra), Wolf noted, contained "about 85% of the total Indonesian population . . . and before the war . . . accounted for be-

---

[78] Charles Wolf, Jr., *The Indonesian Story* (New York, 1948), pp. 43–44. An excellent analysis of the Linggadjati Agreement and of the events leading up to it is found in this book.

[79] *Ibid.,* p. 44 (italics are those of the present writer).

[80] *Ibid.*   [81] Linggadjati Agreement, arts. iii and iv.

[82] Wolf, *op. cit.,* p. 45.   [83] *Ibid.*

tween four-fifths and nine-tenths of the total export and import trade of the whole Indonesian archipelago." [84]

Though it soon became apparent that the clauses contained in the Agreement were open to conflicting interpretations, it was felt by many that they might be resolved peacefully because of its arbitration clause. This stipulated that the two governments would "settle by arbitration any dispute which might arise from this agreement" which could not be solved between themselves. In such a case it was provided that "a chairman of another nationality with a deciding vote shall be appointed by agreement between the delegations or, if such agreement cannot be reached, by the President of the International Court of Justice." [85]

It is important to note that this extremely important clause as well as the first article of the Agreement, in which the Netherlands government recognized the *de facto* authority of the government of the Republic of Indonesia over Java, Madura, and Sumatra, were agreed to by the Netherlands Commission General in the absence of its fourth member—Dr. Hubertus van Mook, Lt. Governor General of the Netherlands East Indies. Whether or not the report is true that he refused to subscribe to these clauses when he learned of them, his policy as head of the Dutch administration in Indonesia certainly does not appear to have been based upon their acceptance.

Though the establishment of a federal system was called for in the Linggadjati Agreement, it was expressly stipulated that this was to be the product of Dutch and Republican co-operation.[86] Van Mook unilaterally undertook to create a federal system along the lines he saw fit. The system which he began to establish was seen by Republicans as a superficially disguised policy of divide-and-rule calculated to establish eventual Dutch hegemony over all Indonesia. Shortly after the agreement was initiated, he called a conference for December 18, 1946 at Den Pasar in Bali to begin the establishment of his federal system by formation of a major constituent state, East Indonesia. The Republic had agreed to the establishment of such a state in the Linggadjati Agreement, but only on the basis of co-operative effort between it and the Netherlands. The unilateral character of Van Mook's action was emphasized by the constitution which the Den Pasar Conference produced. By its terms the new "state" of East Indonesia was effectively controlled from Batavia by the government of Van Mook, and people

[84] *Ibid.*   [85] Art. xvii, sec. b.   [86] Art. ii.

in the Republic were largely justified in their feeling that it was his puppet.

Many Indonesians, particularly supporters of the Masjumi, PNI, and Tan Malaka, had been critical of a number of articles in the Linggadjati Agreement, especially articles vi–viii and xiv, providing for a Netherlands-Indonesia Union under the Queen of the Netherlands and the restoration to all non-Indonesians of their previous rights and goods. Van Mook's actions confirmed their doubts as to Dutch sincerity in implementing the Agreement and increased their already considerable opposition to it. His action also brought other lesser, but important, groups such as the KRIS (the armed organization of Celebes men living in Java) to join them in opposing ratification of the Agreement. This opposition to Linggadjati formed itself into a powerful political coalition, the Benteng Republik (Republican Fortress).

It is impossible to disentangle and to assess the relative weight of the two chief *raisons d'être* of this opposition, (1) genuine opposition to the Republican government's Linggadjati policy, and (2) the desire to achieve higher political positions at the expense of Sjahrir and his group. Many individuals of all constituent groups of the Benteng Republik, and undoubtedly the KRIS as a whole, joined it and its antigovernment stand exclusively out of genuine opposition to Linggadjati. But certainly there were some political leaders whose opposition to that agreement derived at least in part from their conviction that this might be a means of mobilizing a popular support sufficient to induce the KNIP to refuse to back Sjahrir. Thereupon, they anticipated, his cabinet would fall and they might supplant him.

Lined up in opposition to the Benteng Republik and behind the Government's Linggadjati policy, was the Sajap Kiri (Left Wing), a coalition of the Socialist Party, Pesindo, Labor Party, and the PKI. Supporting it were several small political groups, including the Christian and Catholic parties. By mid-December it had become a matter of some conjecture as to whether or not the Sajap Kiri and these smaller parties would be able to command sufficient support in the KNIP to insure its ratification of the Linggadjati Agreement.

Thus Soekarno's Presidential Decree of December 29, 1946, to increase the membership of the KNIP by 250 per cent was interpreted by the leaders of the Benteng Republik as a means of guaranteeing ratification of Linggadjati. Whatever the truth of their allegation, which was vigorously denied by Soekarno, it is true that he had long been attempting to present a plan for reformation of the KNIP acceptable to the Working Committee. The latter body had debated and worked at amendments to his previous proposals of July 10, but had never arrived at a final conclusion. It was widely felt that there had emerged in the country a pattern of political forces which found little congruence with the pattern of representation in the KNIP, nearly all whose members had been appointed over a year previously at the very outset of the revolution. Certainly this general sentiment was shared by Soekarno and constituted a major reason for his plan of expansion of the membership of the KNIP. The desire to assure adequate support for the Linggadjati Agreement may well have been an extremely important consideration, but it was by no means the sole important reason for the expansion.

Soekarno's decree of December 29, 1946 called for increasing KNIP membership from 200 to 514. Of the 314 new members, ninety-three were to represent political parties; forty were to represent the peasantry; forty, labor; seventy-eight, the regions outside of Java and Madura; and five, ethnic minorities; the remaining 121 members were to be appointed on the basis of general social prominence or as representatives of minor parties and irregular armed organizations. Whereas in the old KNIP, the PNI held forty-five seats out of 200, or 22.5 per cent, in the new KNIP projected in Soekarno's decree it was to have the same number of seats, forty-five out of 514, or only 8.8 per cent. The leaders of the PNI were understandably dissatisfied with this. Dissatisfaction was also felt by Masjumi leaders. Although their party's representation was to be increased from thirty-five to sixty seats, there is no doubt that they were correct in their claim that Masjumi's strength in relation to the other parties entitled it to a considerably greater increase. Furthermore, though the Benteng Republik held eighty out of 129 party seats in the old KNIP, as against the forty-three of the Sajap Kiri, it was to hold only 105 out of 222 in the new KNIP as against 105 for the Sajap Kiri.

Table 9 contains a breakdown of membership in the old KNIP and the one proposed by Soekarno.

On January 6, 1947, at the first meeting of the Working Committee following announcement of Soekarno's decree of December 29 strong objections of PNI and Masjumi members were raised against the decree. The cabinet on January 17 announced its belief that issuance of such a decree was the prerogative of the President. However, the feeling was strong among many members of the Working Committee that though

Table 9. COMPARISON OF PARTY REPRESENTATION.*

Parties	Old KNIP	Soekarno's Proposal
PNI	45	45
Masjumi	35	60
Socialist	35	35
Labor	6	35
PKI (Communist)	2	35
Christian	4	8
Catholic	2	4
	129	222
Occupational:		
Workers	0	40
Peasants	0	40
	0	80
Regions: †		
Sumatra	1	50
Borneo	4	8
Celebes	5	10
Moluccas	2	5
Lesser Sundas	2	5
	14	78
Minorities:		
Chinese	5	7
Arab	2	3
Dutch	1	3
	8	13
Individuals, minor parties and armed organizations	49	121
TOTAL	200	514

* Figures derived from Presidential Regulation No. 6, 1946 (Dec. 29, 1946), app.
† No regional representation was given Java and Madura, because it was felt that they were adequately represented through the fact that the political parties were most strongly developed there and that a majority of their representatives were from Java and Madura. In general, however, the representation of the areas outside of Java and Madura as compared to that of the latter was, under Soekarno's proposal, greater than their population warranted.

the President might assume initiative in issuing such a decree, it could not come into force, any more than could ordinary legislation, until approved by the Working Committee.

On the seventeenth, following the cabinet's statement of position, the Working Committee held another meeting attended by only eleven of its twenty-three members.[87] Ten of those present, including eight out of the ten PNI and two out of the four Masjumi representatives voted to draft a bill repealing the President's decree. Of the eleven present, only Mr. Assaat, the chairman, opposed the measure. Apparently there were enough other members on the Committee to have given the sponsors of the bill a majority if the whole active membership of twenty-three had been present.[88] Presumably, though agreeing with the ten sponsors, some of those members who stayed away did not wish to place themselves publicly in open conflict with the President. Apparently they were not opposed to his unilateral exercise of the prerogative of appointment to the KNIP per se, but opposed the decree primarily because of what they envisaged as its certain consequence, ratification of the Linggadjati Agreement.

The Working Committee's decision raised the critical question of whether or not the President retained any power at all of which the exercise was not subject to approval by the ad interim House of Representatives, the KNIP, and its agent, the Working Committee. The only body competent to answer this question was the KNIP itself. Between February 25 and March 5, 1947, at Malang, this body held its first session since that held in Surakarta a year previously.[89] In his speech opening the session, Soekarno made clear his belief that solution of the problem lay with the KNIP, but went on to state his personal position, saying:

In my opinion until we are able to leave the composition of the representative bodies to the electorate, it is the task of the President himself to nominate and appoint members because of the fact that the President himself is regarded as the representative of the whole people.

A vigorous debate within the KNIP ensued between the members of the existing 200-member body, it being unanimously agreed that the new appointees were not competent to pass judgment on a question concerning their own status. After two days of debate, its membership was about evenly divided as to whether or not it should support or reject the decision of the Working Committee.[90]

At this juncture Vice-President Hatta in an impassioned speech pointed out that if the KNIP backed its Working Committee's decision

[87] Two members, Sukarni and Adam Malik had been jailed in June, charged with plotting the overthrow of the government in connection with Tan Malaka's attempted *coup d'état*.

[88] *Berita Badan Perkerdja*, March 4, 1946–Feb. 17, 1947, pp. 5–6, 42–43.

[89] This session was already scheduled. But if it had not been it would have been necessary to call it in order to decide this issue.

[90] Mr. Assaat, *Hukum Tata Negara*, p. 7.

to reject the President's decree, then Soekarno and he would be forced to resign. The only alternative would be, he said, for the KNIP to dissolve. The response of the KNIP to Hatta's speech left no doubt but that its overwhelming majority was ready to back him and Soekarno. Faced with this situation, the Working Committee withdrew the bill it had sponsored opposing Soekarno's decree. Tacit approval had thus been given by the KNIP to Soekarno's decree, and this brought the Working Committee to withdraw its opposition. Thereby this specific decree of Soekarno was considered to have the force of law.

However, there had been no formal and positive resolution by the KNIP of the principle at issue.[91] To the extent that the issue was resolved and precedent established, this was accomplished by Hatta's speech. Mr. Assaat, Chairman of the KNIP, has stated to the writer that Hatta's threat of resignation tended to fix the principle that if on a matter of prerogative [92] the President was opposed by the KNIP, he and the Vice-President would have to resign. A new President and Vice-President would then be elected by the KNIP. Assaat states, however, that the general consensus was that unless the point of difference between the President and the KNIP was vital to the Republic and the President irrevocably committed to his action (e.g., his signing of a treaty with the Dutch which the KNIP rejected) the President would merely yield to the KNIP and remain in office.

However, as Mr. Assaat makes clear, with respect to matters of ordinary legislation (outside the sphere of presidential prerogative) if "a serious conflict arises between the cabinet and the KNIP where the President is convinced that the KNIP no longer represents the people," he may dissolve the KNIP and provide for the establishment of a KNIP which is "more representative." Thereafter should the conflict between the cabinet and the new KNIP continue, "the President may not dissolve the KNIP again. In this case the President is obliged to dissolve the cabinet." [93]

On March 2, 1947 Soekarno's new appointees were sworn in as members of the greatly expanded KNIP. The old Working Committee was

[91] *Ibid.*, pp. 34–35.

[92] In addition to the power to appoint members to the KNIP, the sphere of prerogative was generally considered to include (1) the declaration of a state of emergency; (2) the sole right of initiative to enact emergency ordinances during a state of emergency (such ordinances, however, being later revocable by the KNIP); and (3) the sole right of initiative in declaring war, making peace, and concluding treaties (all, however, requiring ratification by the KNIP).

[93] *Hukum Tata Negara*, p. 33.

dismissed, and the next day, March 3, elections for a new one were begun by the new KNIP. The object again was to make the smaller agent-body mirror as precisely as possible the basic political pattern represented in the larger parent-body. The new Working Committee had forty-seven members of whom forty were elected from the KNIP on the basis of each getting the votes of at least twelve of that body's membership. Seven of the seats were reserved seats, the occupants being elected by a majority of the KNIP, and being filled by representatives from Borneo, Celebes, the Moluccas, the Lesser Sundas, and the Chinese, Arab, and Indies-born Dutch communities. The pattern that emerged within the new Working Committee was one that lasted until the Communist rebellion of late September, 1948. A member might resign because of the necessity to assume other duties (particularly cabinet office), but his successor had to be from the same party or area or community.

Table 10. COMPOSITION OF THE WORKING COMMITTEE ELECTED BY THE KNIP AT MALANG (MARCH 3, 1947).

	Name	Party
1	Mr. Assaat (Chairman)	Socialist Party
2	Subadio Sastrosatomo	"
3	Sugondo Djojopuspito	"
4	Supeno	"
5	Tan Ling Djie	"
6	Dr. A. Halim	nonparty
7	Nona Susilowati *	PPI (Pemuda Putri Indonesia—·Indonesian Young Women's Organization)
8	Krissubanu	Pesindo
9	Mr. M. Tambunan	Christian Party
10	Abu Umar	Sarekat Tani Islam Indonesia
11	S. M. Kartosuwirjo	Masjumi
12	Mahmud L. Latjuba	"
13	Prawoto Mangkusasmito	"
14	Mr. Samsuddin	"
15	Moh. Sardjan	"
16	S. Mangunsarkoro	PNI
17	Mr. Sartono	"
18	Sidik Djojosukarto	"
19	Sjamsuddin St. Makmur	"

* The word "Nona" signifies "Miss" while "Nonja" signifies "Mrs." Three of the 47 members were women.

Name	Party
20 Mr. Sujono Hadinoto	PNI
21 Njoto	PKI (Communist Party)
22 Dr. Rustam	"
23 Hutomo Supardan	"
24 Sundjoto	Barisan Tani Indonesia (Indonesian Peasant Front)
25 S. Sardjono	"
26 Maruto Nitimihardjo	Partai Rakjat (People's Party)
27 Pumidjo	"
28 S. M. Abidin	Labor Party
29 Nona Suwarti	"
30 Tjugito	"
31 Asarudin	Labor (as an occupational group)
32 Kusnan	"
33 K. Werdojo	"
34 Sadjarwo	Peasant
35 Sundjoto	"
36 Mr. Luat Siregar	Sumatra
37 I. Tedjasukmana	"
38 Nonja Sasuna Said	"
39 Zainal Abidin Achman	"
40 Zainal Baharudin	"
41 Gusti Djohan	Borneo
42 Manai Sophiaan	Celebes
43 J. D. Syaranamual	Moluccas
44 I. R. Lobo	Lesser Sundas
45 Mr. Tan Po Gwan	Chinese community
46 Hamid Algadrie	Arab community
47 A. De Roock	Dutch community

It should be noted that a number of the nonparty representatives were actually closely associated with parties. Thus numbers 6, 37, 40, 44 and 46 almost always supported the Socialist Party. Number 42 supported the PNI; number 36, the PKI. Several representatives of the smaller parties were generally to be counted on as supporting the Socialist Party up until the split between the Sjahrir and Sjarifuddin factions of that party in January 1948. These included numbers 7, 8, and 9. Number 10 was a supporter of Masjumi. Numbers 26 and 27 looked to Tan Malaka and Sukarni as their leaders. The Socialist Party, Labor Party, PKI, Labor representatives, Barisan Tani and the Pesindo, Christian Party, and PPI representatives were able to agree on most policies until the beginning of 1948. Thus the Sajap Kiri coalition (all of these last-named groups except the Christian Party), held a strong edge in the Working Committee over the Benteng Republik coalition (Masjumi, PNI, and Partai Rakjat).

The last act of the Malang session of the KNIP before its adjournment on March 5, 1947 was to adopt a vote of confidence in Sjahrir's cabinet, in particular its handling of negotiations with the Dutch. Despite the opposition to the motion and abstention from voting by the Masjumi and PNI members, the motion was carried by a substantial majority of the KNIP's membership. Thereby it ratified the Linggadjati Agreement, which was formally signed by the governments of the Netherlands and the Republic of Indonesia on March 25. This ushered in a brief period of relative inter-party solidarity with the Benteng Republik, the Masjumi in particular evincing willingness to back the Sjahrir cabinet until its fears regarding the Dutch interpretation of the Agreement were borne out.

These fears were soon substantiated. As Wolf notes, even at the signing of the Agreement on March 25, 1947 both parties "bound themselves to different interpretations of the key terms 'cooperation' and 'federal.'" On the one hand, "The Netherlands Government assumed that cooperation with the Republic nevertheless implied a continuation of Dutch leadership and sole responsibility pending the formation of the U.S.I. [United States of Indonesia]." On the other hand, "The Republic interpreted the term to mean joint responsibility and mutual consultation in the setting up of the projected federation." Also, Wolf observes, "The Dutch interpreted the term 'federal' to mean equal states with equal voices tuned in key with that of the Netherlands; while the Republic interpreted it to mean that a federal U.S.I. did not deny either the Republic's own primacy among the component parts by virtue of its greater political and economic wealth and maturity, nor its equal position as co-sponsor of the U.S.I. along with the Netherlands Government." [94]

This area of disagreement between the Dutch and Indonesians not only remained but rapidly grew. Charges and countercharges of violation of the Agreement increased.[95] On May 27, 1947, the agent of the Netherlands government in Indonesia, the Commission-General, presented an ultimatum to Sjahrir which was interpreted by the Republican government as posing the alternatives of capitulation to the

[94] Wolf, *op. cit.*, p. 46.
[95] For a balanced account of these charges see Wolf, *op. cit.*, pp. 106–118.

Netherlands or all-out war. This called for *de jure* Netherlands sovereignty over Indonesia until January 1, 1949. Pending that date, Indonesia was to be governed by an interim government in which the representative of the Dutch crown was to have final power of decision. This Dutch-dominated interim government was to set up the general political structure and constituent government organs of the envisaged sovereign United States of Indonesia which was to come into power on January 1, 1949. It was to control all matters relating to exports, imports, and foreign exchange for all Indonesia until that date. In addition, during the period of interim government a joint Indonesian-Dutch gendarmery was to be established. It would be composed of an equal number of Indonesian and Dutch troops with the duty of maintaining law and order throughout Indonesia, including the territory governed by the Republic.[96] The Dutch categorically refused to abide by the arbitration clause of the Linggadjati Agreement, and Van Mook made it clear that noncompliance with the ultimatum would mean war.

Realizing that the Dutch were prepared to go to war, Sjahrir undertook to go as far as he could in meeting their demands. In a series of counterproposals to the Dutch, he accepted on June 8 the principle of an interim government and on June 20 agreed to the *de jure* "special position" of the Dutch Crown's representatives in such a government and to what amounted to Netherlands control of Indonesia's foreign relations during the period of the interim government.[97]

The magnitude of Sjahrir's concessions seriously undermined his political support in the Republic. Before making his counterproposals of June 20, 1947, he had secured the concurrence of those members of his cabinet then in Jakarta, namely Gani, Natsir, and Abdulmadjid. The following day Sjarifuddin arrived in Jakarta and likewise supported the concessions.

In the meantime Abdulmadjid had been sent to Jogjakarta to explain to the rest of the cabinet why the concessions had been made. However, upon arriving there, both before the cabinet and before a meeting of the Sajap Kiri, he strongly opposed the concessions and attacked Sjahrir for having made them. When Sjarifuddin arrived the next day, he found that several of the top leaders of the Sajap

[96] The Dutch contention was that such a gendarmery was necessary for the protection of Dutch properties located within the Republic. For more details of this ultimatum see Wolf, *op. cit.*, pp. 118–120; see also *N.Y. Times*, June 22, 1947, p. 39.
[97] Wolf, *op. cit.*, p. 122.

Kiri, including Tan Ling Djie and Wikana, had lined up with Abdul-madjid and finally agreed to follow them in condemnation of Sjahrir's concessions.

All of the major parties except the Masjumi now began to abandon support of Sjahrir.[98] The five Masjumi members of his cabinet continued to support him and successfully urged their party to do likewise. In an attempt to reconsolidate his crumbling support, Sjahrir journeyed to Jogjakarta, where on June 26 he addressed a meeting of the leaders of the Sajap Kiri, except for Setiadjit, head of the Labor Party, who was then abroad. There he was strongly attacked by Tan Ling Djie, Abdulmadjid, and by Sjarifuddin for the concessions he had made. Here was the first symptom of the impending schism in the Socialist Party that was only fully to emerge six months later. The Sajap Kiri representatives voted their disapproval of his concessions and thereby joined the already considerable opposition led by the PNI. With Sjahrir's own party opposing him, the Masjumi felt it had no recourse but to join the opposition. On June 27 Sjahrir handed his resignation to Soekarno.

The gravity of the situation which Sjahrir had sensed in Jakarta was soon felt by the Sajap Kiri leaders in Jogjakarta. Within nineteen hours of Sjahrir's resignation they reversed their position, agreed to his concessions, and expressed their wish that he resume his post as Prime Minister. Soekarno likewise urged him to do so. However, Sjahrir refused to accept the post. Undoubtedly he was convinced that with the Dutch attitude of "either, or" further negotiations would be impossible.

Upon Sjahrir's resignation, Soekarno, in view of the dangerous situation, announced the existence of a state of emergency and, as he had done the year previously during Tan Malaka's attempted *coup d'état*, assumed full powers of government. On the following day, June 28, the Working Committee ratified his decree and it became law.[99] He requested the members of Sjahrir's cabinet to remain in office until a new cabinet was formed and undertook himself the task of negotiations with the Dutch. Pressure from the United States probably removed any doubts he may have entertained as to whether or not Sjahrir's concessions should be maintained.

A United States *aide-mémoire* of June 28 called upon the Republic

[98] The Masjumi as a party was not in Sjahrir's cabinet. Those Masjumi members who participated in his cabinet did so as individuals and were not responsible to the Masjumi Party.

[99] Aneta, June 27, 28, 29, 1947.

to "co-operate without delay" with the Dutch in the immediate formation of an interim federal government for the whole of Indonesia, a
demand that had just been accepted by Sjahrir. However, the note
went on to state, "The Linggadjati Agreement specifies an interim
period from now until January 1, 1949, during which the Netherlands
is to retain sovereignty and ultimate authority in Indonesia." [100] Since
actually this concept appears nowhere in the Linggadjati Agreement,
and since this constituted one of the chief demands in the Dutch
ultimatum, the Republican leaders could only conclude that the United
States, while anxious to avoid the outbreak of full-scale war in Indonesia, was backing the Dutch as against the Republic. Thus, they felt
the strength of their political position vis-à-vis the Dutch weakened
because of this obvious American backing of some of the most important
of the Dutch demands.[101]

On June 30, Soekarno called upon the leaders of the four largest
parties—the Masjumi, PNI, Socialist, and Labor—to form a coalition
cabinet. The Masjumi demanded the post of Prime Minister and the
ministries of Defense, Foreign Affairs and Internal Affairs. The other
parties refused to enter a coalition cabinet so dominated by Masjumi.
Eventually, on July 3, Sjarifuddin was able to form a cabinet based
on support by the three other large parties and a small, newly emerged
party which had split off from the Masjumi, the Partai Sarekat Islam
Indonesia (PSII).

The leaders of this new party had been leaders in the prewar party
of the same name.[102] Initially they commanded little popular following but hoped to be able to attract the many ex-members of the
prewar party that had become members of the Masjumi.[103] For the

---

[100] *N.Y. Times*, June 29, 1947, p. 12. A somewhat different wording is given in
Wolf's book; this points to a possible later revision of the initial statement as released by the State Dept. Here the text reads: "From the reading of the Linggadjati
Agreement, it is clear that a transitory period is envisaged (between now and Jan. 1,
1949), during which the Netherlands is to retain sovereignty and ultimate authority
in Indonesia" (Wolf, *op. cit.*, p. 181). However, the actual wording of the Agreement
countenances no such interpretation.

[101] An AP dispatch from The Hague on June 28 reported that "an authoritative
source" there stated that this American *aide-mémoire* was "much appreciated" by
the Netherlands government (*N.Y. Times*, June 29, 1947, p. 12).

[102] However, at least as many of the prewar leaders of the party remained within
Masjumi as left it to resurrect the old party. The other two chief constituent groups
of Masjumi, the Mohammadijah and Nahdatul Ulama, remained.

[103] When the Masjumi was established as a political party in the fall of 1945, the
prewar Partai Sarekat Islam Indonesia, which had been outlawed by the Japanese,
fused itself into the new party without, however, liquidating itself as an organization.

most part they were older-generation nationalists who felt that the positions they held within the Masjumi were not as high as they merited on the basis of the positions they had held in the prewar Islamic nationalist movement. They resented the capturing of party leadership by Dr. Sukiman and the Religious Socialists of the party's younger-generation left wing (Abu Hanifah, Mohammad Natsir, Mohammad Roem, Sjafruddin Prawiranegara, and Jusuf Wibisono). Since many of them had been the butt of Sjahrir's anticollaborationist drive, they bitterly opposed him. Because of this they were all the more antagonistic towards the left wing of the Masjumi, which in general had been Sjahrir's strong supporter. Some of them undoubtedly entered the new party largely to gain a position in Amir Sjarifuddin's cabinet, an action which he strongly encouraged.

The feeling among Masjumi and other political circles was overwhelming that political opportunism was the chief impulse toward formation of the new PSII. Indeed, Abikusno Tjokrosujoso, who later became chairman of the party,[104] states that it was re-established in July, 1947, against his express wishes, by Wondoamiseno and Arudji Kartawinata as a result of a deal between them and Sjarifuddin, who needed Islamic political backing for the cabinet he was attempting to form, the Masjumi having refused to support him. As *quid pro quo* for re-establishment of a PSII pledged to support him, these two men were given respectively the posts of Minister of Interior and Vice-Minister of Defense in his cabinet.[105] Six others of the new party were offered cabinet posts, all of whom except S. M. Kartosuwirjo and Surowijono [106] accepted.

The initial membership of Sjarifuddin's cabinet was as follows:

Post	Name	Party
Prime Minister	Mr. Amir Sjarifuddin	Socialist
Deputy Prime Minister	Dr. A. K. Gani	PNI
Deputy Prime Minister	Setiadjit	Labor
Minister of Internal Affairs	Wondoamiseno	PSII
Vice-Min. of Internal Affairs	Mr. Abdulmadjid	Socialist
Minister of Foreign Affairs	Hadji Agoes Salim	nonparty

[104] Abikusno, who was later to replace Wondoamiseno as chairman, was at this time still under arrest on the charge of complicity in the attempted *coup d'état* of June, 1946.

[105] Abikusno's interpretation is generally agreed with by disinterested political observers. See also *Guntur* (chief Masjumi newspaper), Oct. 21, and Sept. 1, 1948, and *Sikap* (independent progressive weekly), Oct. 23, 1948, "Abikusno dan PSII."

[106] Kartusuwirjo was offered the post of 2d Vice-Minister of Defense and Surowijono was offered that of Vice-Minister of Education.

Post	Name	Party
Vice-Min. of Foreign Affairs	Mr. Tamzil	Socialist
Minister of Economic Affairs	Dr. A. K. Gani	PNI
Vice-Min. of Economic Affairs	Kasimo	Catholic
2nd Vice-Min. of Economic Affairs	Dr. A. Tjokronegoro	Socialist
Minister of Defense	Mr. Amir Sjarifuddin	Socialist
Vice-Min. of Defense	Arudji Kartawinata	PSII
Minister of Education	Mr. Ali Sastroadmidjojo	PNI
Minister of Finance	Mr. A. A. Maramis	PNI
Vice-Min. of Finance	Dr. Ong Eng Die	Socialist
Minister of Information	Sjahbudin Latif	PSII
Vice-Min. of Information	Setiadi	nonparty
Minister of Communications	Ir. Djuanda	nonparty
Minister of Public Works	Ir. Moh. Enoch	nonparty
Vice-Min. of Public Works	Ir. Laoh	PNI
Minister of Health	Dr. J. Leimena	Christian
Vice-Min. of Health	Dr. Satrio	Labor
Minister of Social Affairs	Suprodjo	Labor
Vice-Min. of Social Affairs	Sukoso Wirjosaputro	PSII
Minister of Justice	Mr. Susanto Tirtoprodjo	PNI
Minister of Religion	Kiaji Achmad Asj'ari	PSII
Vice-Min. of Religion	H. Anwarudin	PSII
Minister of Labor	Nona S. K. Trimurty	Labor
Vice-Min. of Labor	Mr. Wilopo	PNI
Minister of State	Sultan Hamengku Buwono	nonparty
Minister of State	Wikana	Youth Congress [107]
Minister of State	Sojas	▸Peasant Legion [108]
Minister of State	Siauw Giok Tjhan	Chinese Community
Minister of State	Maruto Darusman	PKI

Although the concessions to Dutch demands advanced by Sjarifuddin's government went further than those of Sjahrir and Soekarno, the Dutch were not satisfied.[109] They continued to demand joint control over and joint manning of an Indonesian gendarmery operating inside the Republic. Against this demand Sjarifuddin and all the Republic's leaders remained adamant. With the Republic's continued

[107] Badan Kongres Pemuda Republik Indonesia.

[108] Barisan Tani Indonesia

[109] The maximum Republican concessions to the Dutch demands were contained in a note from Setiadjit of July 8, which stated: (1) The Republic accepts the *de jure* authority of the Netherlands crown representative in the interim government during the transition period and agrees to an interim government composed of representatives of the crown and representatives of the future states of Indonesia. (2) The Republic withdraws its request for separate Republican representation in foreign capitals during the interim period. (3) Rights of foreigners to estates [plantations] will be recognized by the Republican Government. (4) The Republic accepts Netherlands proposals for federal organs such as customs and economic agencies (*N.Y. Times*, July 9, 1947, p. 13).

refusal to yield on this and a few less important points, the Dutch Prime Minister, Beel, on July 20 upon the recommendation of Van Mook,[110] ordered the Dutch army to launch an all-out attack designed to crush the Republic. The next morning Dutch armored columns with powerful air support fanned out inland from their seaport bases in Java and Sumatra.

Generally the Dutch rationalized their decision to resort to military force by maintaining that the Republican government did not exercise sufficient control over dissident extremist elements within its territory to implement agreements which it entered into. Though it is true that its control over all areas and over all its armed elements was not complete, this control had been steadily increasing. At the time the Dutch launched their attack the Republic's control over its territory was greater both as to extent and effectiveness than it had ever been before; likewise its control over and the discipline and integration of its armed units were greater than they had even been. It was ironic that in order to meet the Dutch attack most effectively it was necessary to decentralize the Republican military organization and give back to unit commanders the autonomy which the Indonesian leaders had been engaged in diminishing during the previous eighteen months.

[110] Wolf, *op. cit.*, p. 128.

❧ CHAPTER VII ❧

War and United Nations

Intervention

TANK-TIPPED Dutch mechanized columns aided by strong aerial support soon cut deep into Republican territory. Within two weeks the Dutch had secured control of most of the chief cities and major towns of West and East Java, had obtained a partial control (though none too securely) over the major communication links between them, and had occupied all remaining Republican deep-water ports in Java. In Sumatra Dutch forces spread out from Medan to occupy key points within the rich estate area of the East Coast Residency, gained control of the valuable oil-producing areas surrounding Palembang, and occupied the chief west Sumatran coast ports. Finally, they had secured a bridgehead on the western end of Madura.

Though in this short time the Dutch were able to reach many of their geographical goals, they were unable to attain their other chief objective, destruction of the major body of the Republic's armed forces. Except at a few points, the Republic's lightly armed forces refused to engage in frontal combat with the heavily armed Dutch forces. Instead, and according to plan, they withdrew from the flat tank country and the principal communication arteries to the mountains and hills that flanked them. Within these pocket areas, some of which held large populations and towns, they settled down for a protracted hit-and-run guerrilla warfare.

In the undefendable plains of Java, as much as possible of the accumulated export crops, transportation equipment and machinery

213

was moved by the Republicans ahead of the advancing Dutch columns in towards the heartland of the Republic—the Magelang, Jogjakarta, Madiun, and Kediri areas. Plans called for a scorched-earth policy's being applied to such of these assets as could not be moved. The rapidity of the Dutch advance and the disorganization of Republican efforts were such, however, that only a small amount of produce and equipment was evacuated. The scorched-earth tactics, though widespread, often emphasized buildings and equipment rather than stocks of export produce. As a result the Dutch were able to attain one of their chief secondary aims, capture of large quantities of the export products which their blockade of Java had kept bottled up there since shortly after the Japanese capitulation.

Both the United States and Great Britain were undoubtedly opposed to the Dutch attempt to settle their dispute with the Indonesians by force and made efforts to restrain them. What was most noticed in Indonesia and throughout most of Asia as well, however, was the fact that though both the United States and Great Britain had recognized the Republic of Indonesia *de facto* and had both been vociferous in their denunciation of the Dutch aggression, neither showed willingness to take effective measures to stop it. The British almost immediately made a relatively positive move by offering to mediate the dispute but were rebuffed by the Dutch.[1] The United States government made a weaker effort, offering not mediation but only its "good offices"[2] to both parties. Moreover, this limited American offer of July 31 came the day *after* India and Australia had laid the Indonesian conflict before the Security Council. The Dutch, already having attained most of their geographical objectives and undoubtedly in the hopes of removing the dispute from the U.N. arena, agreed on August 3 to accept the American proposal. The Republic, however, rejected it, believing its interests would be better protected by the United Nations. This rejection of American good offices[3] was symptomatic of the fact

[1] The British also took the initiative (July 30) in prohibiting the selling of war material to the Dutch for use in Indonesia. Shortly thereafter the U.S. followed suit. Several months before the American government had refused to sell the Dutch its vast stocks of military supplies still stored at bases on New Guinea.

[2] "Good offices," as Wolf notes, "implies simply that a third party stands ready to be of service in bringing two disputants together for discussions. It does not necessarily imply mediation, since the latter term connotes active participation in the discussions by the third party" (Wolf, *op. cit.*, p. 138 ft. n.). See also statement of Michael McDermott of State Dept. Press Relations *N.Y. Times,* Aug. 1, 1947, p. 4.

[3] The rejection was at first not explicit and was not made so until Aug. 17, when Sjahrir formally rejected the offer to which the U.S. had requested an immediate answer the previous day.

that even at this early date the formerly overwhelming pro-American sentiment among Republicans had become strongly overlaid with the suspicion that covertly the United States was partial to the Dutch and that, if it had strongly desired to, it could have stopped them from resorting to force.

India's response to the Dutch aggression was prompt. Prime Minister Nehru on July 24 stated: "What has become of the United Nations Charter? The spirit of new Asia will not tolerate such things. No European country, whatever it may be, has any business to set its army in Asia against the peoples of Asia. When it does so, Asia will not tolerate it." [4] On July 28, Nehru announced that India would refer the Indonesian situation to the United Nations.[5] Two days later both India and Australia brought the dispute before that body, the Australian request for U.N. intervention taking precedence over that of India inasmuch as it was based upon the contention that there had been a breach of the peace (Article 39 of the United Nations Charter), while that of India was based upon the contention that maintenance of international peace and security was endangered (Article 34). In invoking Article 39 of the Charter, Australia proposed a resolution calling upon the Dutch and Indonesians to cease hostilities immediately and submit their dispute to arbitration by a third party as provided in the Linggadjati Agreement.[6]

The debates that then ensued were closely followed and long remembered in Indonesia and were influential in developing the attitudes of many Indonesians towards Russia and the United States. Whether or not American action proceded from a desire to avoid a Council deadlock or a French veto, the refusal of the United States to back the Australian proposal except in a drastically amended form was profoundly disillusioning to Indonesians. In breaking the deadlock produced by the differences of opinion concerning the Australian proposal, the United States did not appear to Indonesians to throw its weight against the colonial powers on the Council: Britain, France and Belgium. The compromise solution which it sponsored appeared to them to be much closer to the stand of the colonial powers than to the Russian-backed Australian proposal. It was a compromise which in Indonesian eyes drew the teeth of the Australian proposal. The American compromise proposal accepted on August 1 by a vote of eight to three (with Britain, France, and Belgium abstaining) called upon the Netherlands and the Republic: "(a) to cease hostilities forthwith, and

[4] *N.Y. Times*, July 25., 1947, p. 3.   [5] *Ibid.*, July 29, p. 7.
[6] *Ibid.*, July 31, p. 1.

(b) to settle their disputes by arbitration or other peaceful means, and to keep the Council informed about the progress of the settlement."[7]

Russia and Poland, on the other hand, consistently called for the withdrawal of Dutch troops to the points from which they had launched their attack. Gromyko insisted that "any negotiation, whether by arbitration or some other method, conducted while the troops of one party are on the territory of another cannot conduce to creating equality for both parties."[8] A Russian proposal calling upon both sides to withdraw to the positions held prior to the Dutch attacks was decisively defeated, all other council members except Poland abstaining.[9]

On August 3 the Netherlands government instructed Van Mook to carry out the cease fire order at midnight on August 4-5, and the Republican government issued like instructions to its forces. As Emerson observes: "The location of opposing forces when the cease fire orders were issued was no more stable and no more suited to become the basis of even a temporary settlement than that which existed after the first few days of the Nazi invasion of Poland in 1939."[10] The Dutch halted their drive on the Republican capital of Jogjakarta, but they did not cease forward operations. Their spearheads advanced laterally to encircle large islands of by-passed Republican forces and then converge inwards on them to obliterate them, an activity euphemistically referred to by the Dutch as "mopping up operations." In addition, in a number of critical areas Dutch forces continued to advance further forward into what remained of Republican-controlled territory.

Thus when Soetan Sjahrir, appointed by the Republic to represent it at Lake Success, was finally allowed to appear before the Council on August 14, he emphasized that the only way to end the fighting was for the Council to dispatch a commission to supervise obedience to its cease fire order. In addition he called upon the Council to hold to the original Australian proposal and itself arbitrate the dispute and insisted upon the withdrawal of Dutch troops to the positions they had held before their attack. Strong support was given this position only by Russia and Poland. A Russian proposal for the setting up of a commission of the Council to superintend the cease fire order then received the backing of the United States, Australia, Brazil, Colombia,

---

[7] Security Council, *Official Records*, 2d. yr., no. 68, 1702-3.
[8] *Ibid.*, p. 1691.   [9] *Ibid.*, p. 1710.
[10] Rupert Emerson, "Reflections on the Indonesian Case," *World Politics*, I, no. 1 (Oct. 1948), 75.

Poland and Syria, a sufficient number for its adoption. France, however, vetoed the proposal.[11] The maximum that France would allow was a consular commission made up of representatives of those governments having career consuls at Batavia to *report* back to the Security Council as to the observance of the cease fire order.[12] Thus rather than establishing its own agency to superintend the cease fire, the Council on August 25 agreed to rely upon a commission to *report* to it on how the cease fire was being observed, a commission over which it had only indirect control and which had a more pro-Dutch composition [13] than the Security Council.

An impasse was also reached in the attempt to provide for an effective procedure for attaining a political settlement between the parties. A Polish proposal providing for arbitration of the dispute by a commission made up of representatives from the eleven nations sitting on the Security Council received the support of only Russia and Syria. An Australian proposal calling for arbitration by a committee composed of three members of the Council, each party to the dispute selecting one member and they selecting the third, received the support of only Colombia and Syria.

This impasse was later on August 25 broken by an American proposal which was supported by all members but Russia, Poland and Syria, who abstained.[14] The plan provided that the Security Council "tender its good offices to the two parties in order to assist in the pacific settlement of their dispute in accordance with" the second part of its resolution of August 1. This expressed the Council's readiness, *"if the parties so request,* to assist in the settlement through a committee of the Council consisting of three members of the Council, each party selecting one, and the third to be designated by the two so selected." [15] By September 18, the Netherlands had selected Belgium; the Republic had chosen Australia; and the two so chosen had selected the United States as the third representative on the committee. However, the committee, generally known as the "Committee of Good Offices," did not hold its first

[11] Security Council, *Official Records,* 2d. yr., no. 83, 2199–2200.

[12] U.N., S/513, Aug. 22, 1947.

[13] Nations having career consuls at Batavia and thereby represented on the Consular Commission were: Australia, Belgium, China, France, Great Britain, and the United States. Thus four of the members of the Security Council favorable to the Republic—Russia, Syria, Colombia, and Poland—were not represented, while all those whose positions on the Security Council clearly favored the Dutch—Belgium, France, and Great Britain—were represented.

[14] Security Council, *Official Records,* no. 83, p. 2209.

[15] U.N., S/514 (italics are the writer's).

official meeting until October 20, 1947, and did not arrive in Indonesia until a week later.

In the meantime the Dutch were having things very much their own way in Indonesia. On August 29 they unilaterally proclaimed the "Van Mook line," supposedly defining the positions they held at the time of the cease fire. In general, this line connected up the isolated Dutch spearheads thrust far into Republican territory and enclosed extensive tracts of territory between their spearheads that were still under the effective control of the Republic's troops and civil administration. Thus, long after the cease fire order Dutch troops captured such important by-passed towns as Garut and Tasikmalaja. Moreover, as Van Mook himself admitted, in a number of critical areas the demarcation line was drawn to include tracts of Republican territory into which the Dutch armored columns had not even penetrated.[16] According to his line, the Republic was limited to a little over one-third the area of Java—the east central area (minus all deep water seaports) and the extreme western tip of the island, half of Madura, and the largest but poorest part of Sumatra. (See Map 2, p. 233.)

Such actions and the refusal of the Security Council to contest them demonstrated to Indonesians how little in awe of the Security Council the Netherlands stood. This feeling was increased by Van Mook's public advocacy on August 30, the eve of his departure to the Netherlands for consultation, that the Dutch put an end to the authority of the Republic.[17]

The Council's cease-fire order was not observed. Continuing Dutch advances forward and their wide scale efforts to eradicate Republican military and civil control in the extensive areas originally by-passed by their spearheads provoked resistance and bitter fighting. Such actions continued to be justified by the Dutch as "mopping up operations" and were held to be quite consistent with their interpretation of the cease fire. The viewpoint of the Republicans was not unnaturally different and was thus described in a telegram of Dr. A. K. Gani, the Vice-Prime Minister, to the Council dated September 29, 1947:

Dutch army occupied big towns and main communication lines between those towns. Areas surrounding big towns and adjacent to main communication lines still fully under Republican control. In those areas complete units of Republican army still in continuous contact with general headquarters and Republi-

16 Statement of Van Mook before a press conference, Batavia, Oct. 25, 1947, as reported by U.P.

17 For a report of his statement see *N.Y. Times*, Aug. 30, 1947, p. 9.

can civil administration still is functioning as usual. As soon as Dutch have succeeded in occupying few towns and main roads they start claiming that entire area covered by imaginary demarcation lines they draw on map becomes *terra nederlandica*. Subsequently follow inevitable mopping up operations. Not astonishing at all that in such a way fierce fighting continues unabated. Penetration is not occupation. Nor does it confer right to penetrators to regard areas between converging lines of penetration as occupied territory or even patrol the same.[18]

The Republic's continuing demand that Dutch troops retire to the positions from which they launched their attack, though still receiving support from the Russian bloc and Australia, as well as from India outside the Council, was consistently opposed by the United States. Throughout October, this issue dominated the Council debates on Indonesia. On October 9, the United States delegate to the Council, Mr. Austin, justified American support of the Dutch refusal to withdraw their troops on the grounds that this would contravene the U.N. Charter by possibly prejudicing the rights of the parties to the dispute.[19] A Soviet resolution of October 31, calling for withdrawal to positions held before the Dutch attack, received the support of Australia, Colombia, and Poland, but was opposed by the United States, Britain, France, and Belgium, with the other Council members abstaining.[20]

Reports of the Consular Commission of October 14 and 22 [21] stating that the cease-fire order was not being carried out made it clear that further action was demanded of the Council if its intervention was not to prove a complete fiasco. Attempts in the Council to meet this situation effectively were unable to secure majority backing, and finally a weak United States compromise was accepted on November 1.[22] This resolution called upon the two parties "forthwith to consult with each other, either directly or through the Committee of Good Offices, as to the means to be employed to give effect to the cease-fire resolution." Also it advised the parties that its resolution of August 1 was to be interpreted as meaning "that the use of the armed forces of either party by hostile action to extend its control over territory not occupied by it on August 4, 1947, is inconsistent with the Council resolution of August 1." [23]

18 U.N. S/568.   19 See *N.Y. Times*, Oct. 10, 1947, p. 7.
20 Security Council, *Official Records*, 2d. yr., no. 102, 2698.   21 U.N. S/586.
22 Poland voting against and Russia, Colombia and Syria abstaining (Security Council, *Official Records*, 2d. yr., no. 103, 2750).
23 *Ibid.*, pp. 2723-4.

The Council's feeble caveat appears to have made little impression on the Dutch. They did not withdraw from the territory they had seized after August 4, and just ten days after the resolution was made, their troops crossed their own Van Mook line and overran the remaining half of Madura.[24]

The refusal of the majority of the Security Council to order the Dutch to withdraw from the territory they had seized or to compel them to submit to peaceful arbitration, or even to abide by the weak resolutions it had been willing to agree on, made a powerful impression on Indonesians. In general, their assessment of the attitudes of the Security Council members was based exclusively upon their knowledge of the debates and the votes taken there. A few guessed that Secretary of State Marshall had made it clear to Van Mook when he visited Washington in early September that the United States was firmly against his plan for wiping out what remained of the Republic. But even they believed that the United States was consciously following a policy which in most respects backed the Dutch. Their following of events in the Security Council convinced them of this and in addition that Russia was the Council member who most strongly supported the Republic. Moreover, the feeling was widespread among Indonesians that the Dutch military campaign against the Republic could not have been undertaken without American and British military equipment.[25] Among educated elements it was widely believed that Dutch dependency upon American credit for reconstruction of the Netherlands home economy put the United States in a position where it could force the Dutch to suspend military operations in Indonesia any time it wished. These sentiments were shared by representatives from both the extreme left and extreme right of the political spectrum.

An official statement of the principal Republican trade union federation, the SOBSI (not then under Communist domination), broadcast over the Jogjakarta radio on October 17, 1947, declared that Dutch

[24] A group of foreign correspondents toured Madura on Nov. 27–28 and found this to have occurred. The dispatch of U.P. correspondent Arnold Brackman stated on Nov. 27, 1947:

"Sumenep, Madura—I am leaning against Dutch sandbag post in center this town situated 31 miles over Madura demarcation line. Dutch flag flying up main street. Sumenep as well as a dozen other towns and villages in east Madura militarily occupied by Dutch forces November 11 when Dutch troops and American-trained Dutch marines crossed Pamekasan demarcation line in open violation Security Council's August 4th and November 1st cease-fire resolutions."

[25] Following the Dutch attack both the U.S. and Great Britain refused to sell the Dutch any more arms for use in Indonesia.

defiance of the Security Council's cease-fire order was explained by the
fact that "certain Western powers" were "secretly providing the Dutch
with war materials to carry out their colonial war in Indonesia." It went
on to say: "Our hopes for a peaceful settlement in Indonesia have been
smashed to atoms because three months after United Nations intervention there is still no solution to end the bloodshed on Indonesian
soil. It has become unmistakably clear that the so-called civilized
Western nations justify Dutch aggression and have no intention of
ending the bad conditions in Indonesia caused by the presence of Dutch
troops." In conclusion the statement accused the United States of
granting credits to the Netherlands which were used by it "to suppress
the national upsurge in Indonesia." [26]

On November 12, in a speech before the Republican Parliament, Mr.
Kasimo, Vice-Minister of Economic Affairs and chairman of the Indonesian Catholic Party spoke of the "obvious partiality of the United
States" in favor of the Dutch and stated that the Indonesian people
were unable to understand why "certain powerful nations so obviously
side with the Dutch" and "refuse to acknowledge the same rights of
freedom and self-determination for Indonesians that they subscribe to
in the Atlantic and U.N. Charters." [27]

Meanwhile time was working against the Republic and in favor of
the Netherlands. The Van Mook line cut the Republic off from the
richest agricultural areas of both Java and Sumatra. But particularly
in Java the situation was serious. The area remaining under the Republic's control was a deficit food area with a per-capita rice production
calculated by its government as being only 62.6 quintals as compared
with a production of 85.9 in the area cut off by the Dutch.[28] In addition this area left to the Republic in Java had its normal population
of about 23,000,000 swelled by an influx of more than 700,000 refugees
from the areas overrun by the Dutch. This figure was later considerably
increased.

The blockade which the Dutch threw around the area left the Republic cut off not only from outside sources of arms, but from sources
of food and clothing as well. The Republic's need for swift action by

[26] Antara (chief Republican news agency), Jogjakarta, Oct. 17, 1950.
[27] Ibid., Nov. 12, 1947.
[28] See U.N. S/649, "Memorandum Received by the Committee on 27 November
1947 From the Government of the Republic of Indonesia Concerning the Economic
Situation in the Republic," p. 37. The Dutch, it should be noted, received the benefit of only part of the rice crop in the remainder of Java, much of this still being
under the control of by-passed Republican units.

the United Nations toward effective implementation of the cease fire and arrival at a political settlement is shown in Prime Minister Sjarifuddin's memorandum to the Security Council of November 26, 1947:

Any delay in reaching an overall political settlement, and the implementation of the cease-fire, will enable the Netherlands Government to consolidate its economic gains, and must therefore inevitably weaken the position of the Republic. We feel that the economic blockade which the Netherlands is now imposing will not only create dire distress within the areas under the control of the Republic, but will also prejudice a proper appreciation of the political situation in the islands and seriously hamper a proper impartial judgement of the situation.

Even before July 21st, the Netherlands Government was seeking by naval blockade to impose an economic stranglehold on the Republic. The Republic was cut off from supplies by sea and unable to repair and maintain essential transport which had seriously deteriorated during the Japanese occupation and which was needed for internal distribution. In occupying some areas the Dutch have consequently been able to distribute supplies to alleviate shortages for which they themselves were responsible. Thus they have sought to cloak aggression in the guise of liberation, to appear to the people and the world as benefactors instead of aggressors.[29]

The Committee of Good Offices set up by the Security Council was faced with an impossible task. It had been delegated a problem of the greatest difficulty but had not been given the power with which to solve the problem. It had become a symbol of the great aspiration of the United Nations, the resolving of conflict by peaceful means. Yet it was possessed neither of power of its own nor of backing by the Security Council sufficient to live up to this expectation. Initially there was a belief that the Security Council would not let its agent down and could be relied upon when the time came to give it the minimum support necessary for its effectiveness should the two parties to the dispute prove intransigent; but this was not the case. The Committee of Good Offices soon found itself in the position of an unwanted child, for the most part spurned by its parent, the Security Council. Despite its entreaties to that body, it was unable to get the support necessary for carrying out its task.

What was surprising was that the Committee was able to achieve even transient success. That achievement was in a very large measure due to the determination of the Committee's American member, Dr. Frank Graham. This fleeting success was made possible by the concessions the

[29] U.N. S/649, pp. 34–35.

Republic was willing to make on the basis of its trust in him and its belief that his proposals would, as he honestly expected, be backed up by the American government. The transitory nature of this success was principally a result of the subsequent refusal of the State Department to back him and the belief of the Dutch that it would not. More specifically it was because of the opposition to Graham's views by certain personnel of the State Department interposed in its chain of command between him and Secretary of State Marshall. In the words of Dr. Graham:

The Committee at all times was up against such realities as: (1) not only the lack of power to act as arbitrators but also the lack of power even to mediate the dispute; and therefore, (2) the lack of power to make public its suggestions to the parties; (3) the necessity for the committee to be unanimous in order for its confidential suggestions to the parties to have some moral power; (4) the power of either one of the parties to continue to veto any suggestion of the committee even when unanimous; (5) the possibility of the political overthrow of either cabinet or the realignment of the political parties on the basis of the negotiations in the Indonesian dispute; (6) the possibility of negative action on recommendations of the committee in the Security Council by one veto or a combination of negative votes or abstentions from voting; (7) the lack of instant public consideration by the Assembly. . . .[30]

In addition the Committee was continually handicapped by the deep-seated suspicion between the two parties regarding each other's desire or ability to live up to any agreement that might be made. Moreover, as Graham observes:

A strong obstructing Dutch factor was the underlying and not always submerged determination of some powerful economic and political interests in the Netherlands not really to use the Committee of Good Offices and to eliminate the Republic from any real part in the preparation for an organization of the promised United States of Indonesia.[31]

There was a feeling among important Dutch civil and army leaders in Indonesia that time was on their side. The political and economic pressures they could apply against the rump Republican area would be sufficient, they believed, either to insure such a further deterioration of the Republic's economy as to cause its government to collapse or at least thereby to create political conditions of so disorderly and unstable a nature as to allow a Dutch-sponsored and controlled Indonesian fed-

[30] "Statement of Senator Graham on the Indonesian Situation," *Congressional Record—United States Senate*, April 5, 1949, p. 3921.
[31] *Ibid.*, p. 3922.

eral government to request the assistance of Dutch armed forces in eliminating the Republic. Such action could be undertaken in self-protection against Republican "aggression" or to clean out a source of "Communist infection."

If, however, the Republic (reduced in size as it now was) were to become a member of such a Dutch-sponsored federal Indonesian government, particularly if it entered it under some sort of U.N. guarantee whereby it had fair representation in the new government, it would be very much more difficult, if not impossible, for the Dutch to carry out such plans. Thus the major effort of Graham and his Australian counterpart [32] on the Committee was to keep the Republic in the projected independent United States of Indonesia.

On December 8, 1947, the Good Offices Committee finally opened its first formal session with the Republican and Dutch delegations in the neutral territory provided aboard the U.S.S. "Renville" anchored in Batavia harbor. Its first proposals were accepted in full by the Republican delegation but only in part by that of the Netherlands. Its second plan was likewise agreeable to the Republic but acceptable only as a working paper by the Netherlands.[33]

In the face of this Dutch intransigence, the Committee on December 26 submitted its "Christmas Message," an over-all proposal much closer to the Dutch position. This called for a truce, with the "Van Mook line" to be accepted as the military boundary between the two disputants but providing among other things that within a period of not less than three months the Netherlands would withdraw its troops to the positions held prior to their attack of July 21, 1947, and that the Republican civil administration would return to the areas so evacuated. The proposals were accepted by the Republic.

The Netherlands agreed to accept the Committee's proposals only in part, countering them with its own set of twelve political principles in which those parts of the proposals acceptable to it were incorporated.[34] These Dutch counterproposals did provide that within "not less than six months and not more than one year after the signing of the agreement during which time uncoerced and free discussion and consideration of vital issues will proceed" free elections would be held for self-determination by the people of their political relationship to the United States of Indonesia, and further that each party would

---

[32] Justice Richard C. Kirby. (Mr. Thomas K. Critchley served as his deputy and after signing of the Renville Agreement replaced him.)

[33] Graham, *op. cit.,* p. 3922.   [34] *Ibid.*

"guarantee the freedom of assembly, speech and publication at all times, provided that this guarantee is not construed so as to include the advocacy of violence or reprisals." [35] However, they eliminated any mention of the withdrawal of Dutch troops or the restoration of the Republic's civil administration in the territory they had occupied. There was no provision for representation of the Republic in the interim government pending the transfer of sovereignty, and indeed there was no mention of the Republic by name and in any of the twelve principles. More alarming from the Republic's point of view was the lack of any guarantee of international observation between the signing of the agreement and the transfer of sovereignty.[36] In submitting this proposal the Netherlands indicated that "if not accepted unconditionally by the Republic, it would not be bound by the 12 principles and liberty of action would be resumed." [37]

The Netherlands position was made yet clearer on December 29 when Van Mook announced the unilateral establishment of the "state" of East Sumatra, the richest of the areas seized by the Dutch from the Republic.[38] Thus, without reference either to the Republic or the Committee, the Dutch were proceding independently to set up a federal Indonesia of their own design in territory annexed from the Republic.

On January 4 the Dutch convoked a conference of representatives from ten areas in Indonesia, three of whom came from areas detached from the Republic (West Java, Madura, and East Sumatra). The Dutch-selected delegates from these ten areas attended the meeting as representatives of future components of a federal Indonesia. This conference meeting with the Dutch Prime Minister, Dr. Beel, resolved that an interim federal government preparatory to the establishment of a sovereign United States of Indonesia be formed immediately.[39] The Republic was invited to enter this government, but only as a minority partner, with the several Dutch-sponsored states to have at least twice its voice therein.[40]

With respect to negotiations with the Republic, Dr. Beel stated: "Holland reserves the right to resume her freedom if satisfactory results are not soon achieved." [41] On January 9 this warning was made

[35] The full text of these Dutch counterproposals can be found in Wolf, *op. cit.*, p. 187.

[36] Graham, *op. cit.*, p. 3923.   [37] *Ibid.*, p. 3922.

[38] See *N.Y. Times*, Dec. 30, 1947, p. 12.   [39] See *N.Y. Times*, Jan. 5, 1948, p. 8.

[40] See *Het Dagblad* (Batavia), Jan. 5, 1948.

[41] B.W.J., "Nationalism in Indonesia," *The World Today* (pub. by Royal Institute of International Affairs, Feb. 1948), p. 60.

by the Netherlands delegation directly to the Committee in a letter stating that unless it received an unqualified acceptance by the Republic of its counterproposals within three days, it would ask its government for further instruction, "indicating that there was reason to believe that its Government would decide to resume their freedom of action." [42]

Knowing that the Republican government could not accept this ultimatum, the Committee attempted to resolve the impasse by itself suggesting six additional principles, supplementing the twelve proposed by the Netherlands. Implementation of these promised to insure that the people of Indonesia themselves would determine the fate of their own country. It was envisaged, according to Dr. Graham, that these six additional principles "would transfer the struggle from a provisional military demarcation line, which would disappear, to a democratic political line which would endure." [43]

These principles provided for Netherlands sovereignty over Indonesia until "after a stated interval" sovereignty was to be transferred to an independent United States of Indonesia, of which the Republic was to be a constituent state. In any provisional federal government created prior thereto each constituent state would be offered "fair representation." Either party was to have the right of requesting the assistance of the Committee of Good Offices "in adjusting differences between the parties which relate to the political agreement and which may arise during the interim period." "Within a period of not less than 6 months and not more than one year from the signing of the agreement" a plebiscite was to be held "to determine whether the populations of the various territories of Java, Madura, and Sumatra wish their territory to form part of the Republic of Indonesia or of another state within the United States of Indonesia," with the Committee of Good Offices observing it if so requested by either party. Following this delineation of states a constitutional convention convened "through democratic procedures" would draft the constitution for the new federal state. Any state would be free to remain out of the federal United States of Indonesia and negotiate "a special relationship" with either it or the Netherlands.[44]

The Netherlands indicated it would accept the six proposals of the

[42] First Interim Report of the Committee of the Security Council S/649 (Feb. 10, 1948), p. 22.

[43] Graham, *op. cit.*, p. 3923.

[44] *Ibid.* The full text of these principles may also be found in Wolf, *op. cit.*, pp. 188–189.

Committee if the Republic would accept them and the twelve proposed by the Netherlands within the time set in its ultimatum of January 9. This limit was later extended forty-eight hours.

The twelve principles proposed by the Dutch were vague and ambiguous, and the Republic asked for their clarification. With the time limit set by the Dutch approaching an end, there was not time for regular negotiations. Members of the Committee therefore flew to Jogjakarta and on January 13 at the nearby hill station of Kaliurang undertook to answer the questions of the Republican leaders concerning them. In part they accomplished this through a draft statement of their own views, not binding on either party, which contained most of the consensus of the Committee's three members.

This interpretation of the Committee, though unacceptable to the Dutch, was important in inducing the Republic to agree to the military truce and the twelve Dutch counterproposals, "for they tended to quiet the Republic's concern over certain matters such as the link between the Truce Agreement and the political principles, and the future status of the parties, particularly in relationship to the Security Council." [45] Dr. Graham in particular calmed the fears of the Republican leaders over possible diminishment of the Republic's internal powers during the transitional period pending the transfer of Netherlands sovereignty to a federated Indonesia. "You are what you are," he assured them, and left them with the impression that the Committee would countenance no such diminishment until the Republic had secured "fair representation" in the independent all-Indonesian federal government that was to be formed.

Nonacceptance of the truce and the twelve Dutch counterproposals

[45] J. Foster Collins, "The United States and Indonesia," *International Conciliation*, March, 1950, p. 148. (Collins served as the Committee's Assistant Secretary.) The first of the five paragraphs of the Committee's statement read "Referring to the relation between the Netherlands truce proposals (S/AC.10/Conf. 2/2) and statement of political principles (S./AC.10/Conf. 2/3), the Committee of Good Offices understands that the parties, while reserving fully their legal interpretations of the stipulations of the resolution of the Security Council, shall be committed to the twelve political principles, at the very moment the truce agreement is signed, so that in fact the very signature of the truce agreement will have created *de facto* an integrating link between the truce agreement and these political principles."

The second paragraph reads: "It is the understanding of the Committee of Good Offices that the eventual acceptance by the parties of the six political principles . . . can in no way change or modify the status of the parties, particularly in relation to the Security Council" (U.N. S/649, 10 Feb. 1948, "Committee of Good Offices on the Indonesian Question: First Interim Report of the Committee to the Security Council," pp. 23, 98).

would, the Committee emphasized, bring its functioning to an end and return the dispute to the Security Council. There, it pointed out, a French veto could be relied upon to halt any attempt to impose arbitration of the dispute. Dr. Graham made it clear that unless the terms demanded by the Dutch were accepted by the Republic, the American government would probably not be inclined to oppose further Dutch attempts to impose a settlement by force. He convinced the Republic's leaders that if they did accept these terms they would be able to count upon the American government's exerting its influence to assure that the Dutch carried out their part of the bargain, in particular the promised U.N.-supervised plebiscites. It was this assurance that finally brought the reluctant leaders of the Republican government to agree to a truce based upon the Van Mook line and the vague and unpalatable demands contained in the Dutch counterproposals. They felt sure that these plebiscites could only result in overwhelming pro-Republican majorities. With the battle transferred "from bullets to ballots," as Dr. Graham expressed it, they were certain that the vast areas overrun by the Dutch army would come back to the Republican fold. Thereby they felt certain that the Republic, and not the Dutch, would dominate the envisaged federal Indonesian government.

It was only by a very narrow margin and with the greatest reluctance that the Republican government finally decided to yield to the Committee's—and particularly Dr. Graham's—urgings [46] and sign the agreement demanded by the Dutch in their ultimatum. To the very end Sjahrir, the leaders of the Masjumi, and most of the leaders of the PNI opposed such a course. At first, Prime Minister Sjarifuddin, President Soekarno, and Vice-President Hatta opposed it as well. However, reports from some of the most important Republican army commanders to Soekarno of their critical shortage of ammunition, the certain conviction that the Dutch would launch another all-out campaign if the Republic refused to accept their demands, and the Committee's blunt warning that nothing effective could be expected from the Security Council in that case combined to convince them how desperate the situation was. The Republic, they realized, could refuse to accept the Dutch ultimatum and fight alone. After several years of grueling guerrilla warfare it might force out the Dutch, but the casualties among

---

[46] In the words of one of the most dispassionate members of the Republican delegation, Dr. Johannes Leimena, the Republican government accepted the Dutch demands "under perceptible American pressure" (Dr. J. Leimena, *The Dutch Indonesian Conflict* [Jakarta, 1949], p. 7).

Indonesians and the suffering of the whole population would be tremendous. Could they be responsible for such a decision? No, they decided; not so long as in accepting the ultimatum they were offered some reasonable hope of attainment of independence via peaceful means. For them such hope did exist in their belief that the American government could be relied upon to insist that fair, U.N.-supervised plebiscites be carried out in the areas overrun by the Dutch army.

Thus on January 17 and 19, 1948, the Republican government joined the Netherlands in signing the Renville Agreement incorporating a military truce based on the Van Mook line, the twelve political principles of the Dutch, and the six additional principles proposed by the Committee of Good Offices.

⚸ CHAPTER VIII ⚸

Aftermath of the Renville Agreement

SIGNING of the Renville Agreement provoked a cabinet crisis in the Republic. Anticipating its signature, the Masjumi, the largest of the political parties, on January 16 withdrew from the cabinet.[1] Though opposed to the agreement, it agreed to abide by it, since it had been signed by the Republic's government.[2] Following the signature of the agreement both the Masjumi and the powerful Indonesian Nationalist Party (PNI) made clear that they would no longer support Sjarifuddin as Prime Minister and that their support of any future government would be conditional on their dominant position therein.[3] Their attitude was that they could not be expected to support the implementation of an agreement to which they had been opposed [4] unless they, rather

[1] Antara, Jan. 16, 1948. On Nov. 13, 1947, the Masjumi had agreed to support and join Sjarifuddin's cabinet. Thereupon Samsuddin of the Masjumi replaced A. K. Gani (PNI) as first Vice-Prime Minister, Gani becoming third Vice-Prime Minister and Setiadjit (Labor Party) becoming fourth Vice-Prime Minister. Wondoamiseno (Partai Sarekat Islam Indonesia—PSII) gave up the post of Minister of Interior to Dr. Mohammad Roem of the Masjumi and became second Vice-Prime Minister. Hadji Maskoer of the Masjumi became Minister of Religion, replacing Kiaji Achmad Asjari of the PSII, and Kasman Singodimenjo of the Masjumi became Vice-Minister of Justice.

[2] *Merdeka* (influential Republican newspaper printed in Jakarta), Jan. 19, 1948.

[3] Cf. *Soember* (Republican newspaper printed in Batavia), Jan. 30, 1948.

[4] Their opposition to the agreement was rather dramatically vindicated only three days after its signature when on January 22 "reliable Dutch circles" stated to the U.P. bureau chief in Indonesia: "Under no conditions will the Dutch accept the Kaliurang conditions (the interpretation of the Agreement's principles by Graham and other members of the Good Offices Committee which had induced the Republican govern-

230

than the group primarily responsible of the agreement, were in power.

In the face of their withdrawal, Amir Sjarifuddin, now supported only by the Sajap Kiri, on January 23, 1948, resigned as Prime Minister.[5] Because of the need for strong leadership to begin prompt implementation of the Renville Agreement and because of the delicateness of the situation both with respect to the Dutch and elements within the Republican army (many of which were bitterly critical of the terms of the agreement), it was imperative to form a new cabinet immediately. However, neither the Masjumi nor the PNI appeared anxious to assume primary responsibility for carrying out the distasteful terms of the agreement. In addition, they could not quickly agree upon a mutually acceptable division of the major cabinet posts, and the urgency of the situation did not allow sufficient time to work out these differences.

Formation of a presidential cabinet [6] with a national, all-party character seemed to be the only means of creating quickly the strong leadership needed. Accordingly, immediately following Sjarifuddin's resignation, President Soekarno appointed Drs. Mohammad Hatta, who as Vice-President stood above party, to form a presidential cabinet. Hatta sought to form a "National Government," enrolling all the chief parties. He was, however, unable to reconcile the conflicting demands of the Masjumi and the PNI as against the Sajap Kiri. The

---

ment to sign). There will be no further meetings between the Indonesian and Dutch Delegations for political talks until this situation is cleared up. We know the Republicans thought our acceptance was also based upon the Kaliurang decisions, but the Republic was duped and cheated into acceptance of the Six Political Principles by the Committee of Good Offices" (U.P. Dispatch, Jan. 22, 1948). Dutch rejection of the Committee's Kaliurang interpretations was made official on the following day (U.P. Dispatch, Jan. 23, 1948).

[5] Antara, Jan. 24, 1948. Sjarifuddin's only remaining support was a small minority within the Working Committee of the KNIP made up exclusively of representatives belonging to the Sajap Kiri (coalition of Socialist and Labor parties, PKI, and Pesindo) representatives minus those members belonging to Sjahrir's faction of the Socialist Party.

[6] A "presidential cabinet" was immediately responsible only to the President. However, by the very nature of the relationship that had developed between the President and the KNIP (see ch. vi) it was also in an indirect sense responsible to the KNIP and its agent, the Working Committee, though not in the immediate and direct sense that a parliamentary cabinet was. The President had the legal right to maintain a presidential cabinet even though it no longer commanded the support of a majority of the Working Committee or the KNIP itself. Such action would, however, bring the President himself into conflict with the KNIP in case a major dispute between them arose. In practice, Soekarno never asserted this legal right and preferred working with a cabinet whose actions conformed with the sentiment of the parliamentary majority.

latter demanded a minimum of four cabinet posts, with Sjarifuddin as Minister of Defense. (In the previous cabinet he had been concurrently Prime Minister and Minister of Defense.) In particular, the Masjumi was opposed to Sjarifuddin's appointment to the defense post, believing, with justification as events were to show, that in controlling this ministry in the previous cabinet he had been using its funds to build up a personal following among military circles. In the cabinet finally formed on January 29, 1948,[7] the Masjumi and PNI were dominant. Also included were members from the Catholic and Christian parties and, significantly, from Sjahrir's wing of the Socialist Party.

Though initially conceived as a temporary expedient pending the formation of a new parliamentary cabinet responsible directly to the KNIP and its Working Committee, Hatta's cabinet was to last until the transfer of Dutch sovereignty on December 27, 1949. Though as a presidential cabinet it was officially responsible only to the President, in practice it held itself accountable to the Working Committee of the KNIP as well. Its membership was the following:

Ministry	Name	Party
Prime Minister	Drs. Mohammad Hatta	nonparty
Defense	Drs. Mohammad Hatta	nonparty
Interior	Dr. Sukiman Wirjo-sandjojo	Masjumi
Foreign Affairs	Hadji Agoes Salim	nonparty
Justice	Mr. Susanto Tirtoprodjo	PNI
Finance	Mr. A. A. Maramis	PNI
Economic Affairs	Mr. Sjafruddin Prawiranegara	Masjumi
Food	Kasimo	Catholic Party
Education and Culture	Mr. Ali Sastroamidjojo	PNI
Health	Dr. Johannes Leimena	Christian Party (PKRI)
Religion	Kiaji Hadji Maskoer	Masjumi
Social Affairs	Koesnan	PGRI (Teachers Union)
Reconstruction and Youth	Supeno [8]	Indonesian Socialist Party
Communications	Ir. Djuanda	nonparty
Public Works	Ir. Laoh [9]	PNI
Information	Mohammad Natsir	Masjumi
Without Portfolio	Hamengku Buwono IX (Sultan of Jogjakarta)	nonparty

[7] Officially announced two days later. See Antara, Jan. 31, 1948.

[8] On Feb. 13, 1948, Supeno left the Socialist Party and joined the newly-formed Indonesian Socialist Party headed by Sjahrir. In entering the Hatta cabinet he had acted as a private individual and not as a member of the Socialist Party.

[9] Until April 13, 1948, this post was held by Ir. Djuanda along with that of Communications.

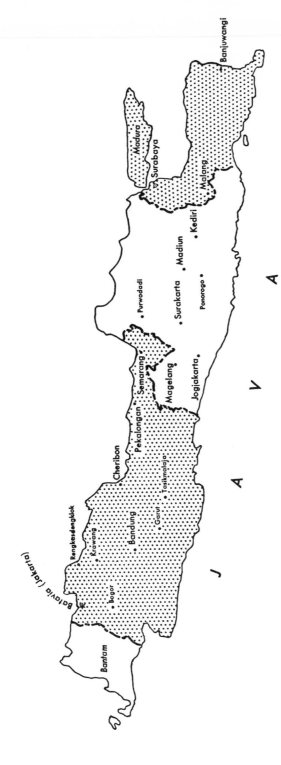

Map. 2. Division of Java under the Renville Agreement (January 19, 1949). White (unshaded) areas remained under Republican control. Shaded areas were to be under Netherlands occupation. Heavy dotted lines show the Renville truce line; they approximate the previous Van Mook line as last proclaimed by the Dutch.

The four-point program announced by Hatta for his cabinet in-cluded: (1) implementation of the Renville truce agreement and politi-cal principles and continuation of negotiations with the Dutch through the Security Council's Committee of Good Offices; (2) acceleration of the formation of a sovereign, democratic United States of Indonesia; (3) rationalization of the Republic's army and economy; (4) reconstruc-tion of damage caused by the war and the Japanese occupation.

Almost immediately Hatta's cabinet began to carry out the most dis-agreeable terms of the Renville Agreement, recognition of the Van Mook line. This necessitated withdrawal of some of the Republic's best troops from the considerable pockets that they occupied behind the Dutch side of the Van Mook line and their removal into the trun-cated area that was left to the Republic. By February 26, 1948, all regular Republican army units (TNI)—35,000 in number—had with-drawn from their pockets and crossed over the Van Mook line into Republican-held territory. It was not easy for the Republican govern-ment to persuade them to abandon the easily defended guerrilla bases from which they withdrew. Only its assurance that U.N.-observed plebiscites would soon be held in these areas induced them to leave. There remained only about 4,000 irregular troops who refused to be evacuated, for the most part troops of the Hizbullah. (Originally militia of the Masjumi, the Hizbullah had been incorporated into the TNI. Most Hizbullah units did withdraw.)

In the meantime U.N.-sponsored political discussions between the Dutch and the Republic had not begun and did not begin until the middle of March, largely because of the Netherlands' delay in appoint-ing representatives.[10] This apparently calculated delay, the unilateral Dutch sponsorship of new states in the areas seized from the Republic, the suppression of freedom of speech and assembly in these areas, and the inauguration of a Dutch-sponsored Interim Federal Government— all combined to make Indonesians progressively more convinced of the unwillingness of the Dutch to abide by the Renville Agreement. The fact that these developments elicited no protest from the Security Council made them increasingly skeptical of its intention to see that the Dutch honor the agreement.

The Netherlands claimed that no violation of the Renville Agree-ment was involved in the establishment of these states and the Interim

[10] Cf. J. Foster Collins, "The United States and Indonesia," *International Recon-ciliation*, March, 1950, pp. 152–153.

Federal Government since they were merely "provisional." Regardless of the merits of this position, which the American and Australian members of the committee viewed privately as pure sophistry,[11] these states were not, as the Dutch maintained, the spontaneous creations of their Indonesian populations. In the formation of every one of them the actual initiative came from the Dutch. Moreover, in none of these areas did the Dutch allow the "freedom of assembly, speech, and publication" and the "uncoerced and free discussion and consideration of vital issues" that they had agreed to insure under the Renville Agreement.

MADURA

Less than a week after signing the Renville Agreement the Dutch unilaterally conducted a plebiscite on the island of Madura which determined its status between the Republic and the newly-created Interim Federal Government sponsored by the Dutch. This plebiscite was contrary to the provisions of the Agreement in that it was not "conducted under observation by the Committee of Good Offices" and was not carried out at least six months after the signing of the Agreement nor under conditions which had allowed "uncoerced and free discussion and consideration of vital issues," and "freedom of assembly, speech, and publication." The Committee witnessed neither the plebiscite nor the subsequent elections for a popular assembly of Madura. In its report to the Security Council concerning them the Committee merely forwarded to it the conflicting versions concerning them supplied it by the Netherlands and the Republic.[12]

During the Dutch occupation of half of Madura in early August, 1947, its Republican Resident,[13] Tjakraningrat, did not evacuate to the western half of the island along with the other officers of the Republican civil administration. He remained behind in the area then overrun by the Dutch and, giving sickness as his reason, resigned his post as Republican Resident.[14] During the first week of September, a month before the Dutch overran the remaining half of the island, Tjakraningrat entered into an agreement with the Dutch.[15] In return

11 This view was communicated by several of them to the writer.

12 See U.N., S/786, "Report to the Security Council on Political Developments in Madura."   13 Chief administrative official.

14 Statement to the writer by Roeslan, secretary of Tjakraningrat, Pamekasan, Madura, April 12, 1949.

15 See U.N., S/786, pp. 4–6, for an account of this agreement as reported by the Netherlands delegation to the Committee of Good Offices.

for being installed as chief of the administration of Madura with no other administration competing with his, he agreed to co-operate with the Dutch, recognizing their *Recomba* (Government Commissioner for Administrative Affairs) as co-ordinator and representative of the central authority." [16]

In an interview with seven foreign correspondents in mid-November, 1947, Tjakraningrat stated:

As soon as I was cut off from the Republic when the Dutch landed in Madura in early August, I was forced to act on my own initiative for the sake and welfare of the people of Madura. I requested the Dutch Governor of East Java, Mr. van der Plas, to help the distress of the people by supplying food and clothing. I was cut off from the Republic and received no orders or directions from the Republican authorities in Jogjakarta. I am still a nationalist, but I am no longer in sympathy with the Republic because of its actions. The Republic never observes the rules of democracy. It has always been the wish of the people of Madura to be governed by themselves, and therefore this step which I have taken is in conformity with the wishes of the people. We will form a special area for this country and co-operate with the other states of Java which ultimately will be included in the United States of Indonesia under the terms of the Linggadjati Agreement. I was isolated from the Republic. My sympathy and opinion of the Republic changed when the Dutch landed on Madura, August 3.[17]

In his capacity as Dutch-appointed Resident, Tjakraningrat helped the Dutch *Recomba* of East Java, Charles van der Plas, organize a plebiscite, the purpose of which was to make Madura a separate "state" in the envisaged federal government. This plebiscite was announced on January 16, 1948 and was conducted just seven days later under a "state of war and siege," wherein the exercise of basic civil liberties was not permitted. Public gatherings were not allowed; private meetings of more than four persons required permission from the Dutch authorities five days in advance and the police had the right to attend.[18] All radio sets were collected by the Dutch,[19] thus ruling out

[16] *Ibid.,* p. 5.

[17] Verbatim notes of this interview were preserved by an American correspondent in this group and given to the writer.

[18] Stated to the writer in interviews with the principle Madurese political leaders (Pamekasan, Madura, April 11–12, 1948).

[19] Statement of Roeslan, secretary of Tjakraningrat, and others to the writer (Pamekasan, April 12, 1948). It is interesting to note that in replying to the Republican contention that no announcement was made of the plebiscite over the radio, the Netherlands representative replied that no radio facilities existed in Madura (U.N., S/786, p. 10). Radio sets in Madura could easily have picked up broadcasts from nearby Surabaya, headquarters of Van der Plas.

any contact with the Republic and any presentation of the Republican government's views to the population. The population had no means of knowing that Tjakraningrat was no longer recognized by the Republic as its representative on the island.

To the Committee of Good Offices and via it to the Security Council the Netherlands represented the question asked at the plebiscite as having six points, the first of which was "to declare the relations between Madura and the Republic of Indonesia severed." [20] The writer in visiting Madura a little over a year later found no Indonesian among those whom he questioned who recalled the plebiscite question having been posed in this manner. Both Dr. Suparmo, one of the most widely respected of pro-Republican leaders on the island, and Roeslan, secretary of Tjakraningrat, stated that the plebiscite choice was limited to the double question: (1) in these difficult times is it not desirable that we create a state of our own which can look after the interests of all of us? and (2) do you wish Tjakraningrat as Wali Negara (Chief of State) of this state? [21]

Much of the population had no inkling of Tjakraningrat's defection from the Republic, and, therefore, the linking of his name to a state of Madura meant for them a retention of an association with the Republic. For those who had some idea of the real situation there was no opportunity to express their view on the plebiscite by private ballot. The plebiscite was public. In each village all in favor of the double question were asked to stand on one side and those opposed on the other.[22] It was not altogether surprising under these circumstances and in view of the fact that the island was under garrison of Dutch troops that less than 5 per cent of those participating voted in the negative on the question.[23] On January 21 Van Mook recognized the "State of Madura" and Tjakraningrat as its president (Wali Negara).

A better measure of the real sentiments of the population of Madura was expressed in the ensuing election for a Madura parliament held by ballot between March 15 and April 15, 1948. Even though this, too,

[20] U.N., S/786, p. 9.

[21] Statements of Dr. Suparmo and Roeslan to the writer (Pamekasan, April 12, 1948).

[22] Statements to the writer by the various Madurese political leaders whom he interviewed (Pamekasan, April 11–12, 1948).

[23] Of Madura's population of 2,075,000 a total of 315,566 (all males) were eligible to vote. Of these 216,663 voted with 199,510 in favor, 9,923 opposed and 10,230 abstaining (U.N., S/786, p. 11).

was held under the condition of "war and siege" with its attendant lack of civil liberties, though a number of the Republican leaders were in jail, and though the election was highly indirect, it returned a pro-Republican majority of thirty-one out of the forty members elected.[24] However, this victory at the polls did little to strengthen the Republican position on Madura. This parliament had no powers,[25] but many of its members did at first dare to express their political views. As a result within a month of their elections twenty of the forty members of parliament were arrested and jailed by the Dutch military intelligence.[26]

WEST JAVA

The fears of the Republican leaders raised by the Netherlands' actions in Madura were soon increased by activities in that part of western Java (the major part) which Dutch troops had overrun. The Netherlands' actions here in particular convinced them that the Dutch would not honor the Renville Agreement and that the Security Council could not be relied upon to enforce their adherence to it.

Previous to the signing of the Renville Agreement the Dutch had made a number of moves which had appeared calculated to establish a non-Republican regime in the area. The initial attempt, the "Pasundan Movement," launched early in March, 1947, had been, as Wolf states, "a misguided plan engineered by overzealous units of the (Dutch) Army and the Civil Administration," [27] within the small enclaves of West Java then under Dutch control. The Indonesian who had been "President" of this movement, Kartelagawa, stated to the writer that the idea for it was that of Colonel Santoso, political adviser to Van Mook, and that it was carried out with help from the Dutch army intelligence (NEFIS). He said he knew nothing of the movement himself until two days after it had been started.[28] Apparently the movement was a sort of trial balloon launched in order to determine the prospects for weaning the dominantly Sundanese

[24] *Ibid.*, p. 18.   [25] A year later it still had been granted no powers.

[26] Stated to the writer by the top non-jailed political leaders in Madura and by Roeslan, secretary of Tjakraningrat, Pamekasan, Madura, April 11–12, 1949. In an interview with the writer, Lt. van der Kaj, chief of Dutch military intelligence (Inlichtings Veligsheid Groep) on Madura, stated that 20 was an exaggeration and that actually "about 10" had been jailed and that all but 2 had been released within 3 months. These 2, he said, were still in jail (Pamekasan, April 12, 1949).

[27] Wolf, *op. cit.*, p. 109.

[28] Statement of Soeria Kartalegawa to the writer (Bandung, Feb. 9, 1949).

population of West Java away from the Republic by holding out to them the prospect of forming their own separate state. As Wolf observes, "the whole 'movement' was a farce from start to finish." [29] For the Sundanese it was an object of derision and did not weaken their support of the Republic.

Following their military occupation of most of West Java, the Dutch had embarked upon a new course of action also interpreted by Republicans as calculated to establish a Sundanese regime amenable to Netherlands control. Between October 12 and 19, 1947 the First West Java Conference was convened by the Dutch *Recomba* (Government Commissioner for Administrative Affairs) of West Java at Bandung. It was attended by forty-five Indonesians, all of whom had been appointed by the Dutch authorities. The *Recomba* called upon them to discuss an agenda containing, among others, the following points: "the quickest way for the population of West Java to participate in government" and "the way in which West Java could participate now in the central administration and in the establishment of the United States of Indonesia." [30] The conference obliged by resolving to "establish a contact commission to request the authorities to call a Second West Java Conference of representatives of groups of the population and all parts of West Java in order to bring about the establishment of a provisional governing organization of West Java on a democratic basis." [31]

A Second West Java Conference was called by the *Recomba* to implement this resolution and met from December 15 to 20, 1947. The Dutch appointed all of the 154 delegates (112 Indonesians, 18 Chinese, 16 Netherlanders, 8 Arabs).[32] One of the bolder delegates appointed by the Dutch voiced during the meeting the feelings of many of his Indonesian colleagues, stating that the conference "did not represent the majority of the people," that it was "not democratic," and that the majority of representatives were "government officials" of the Netherlands Indies administration.[33] However, the majority of the appointees obliged the Dutch by passing a resolution calling for the convocation of a Third West Java Conference which was to establish a

---

[29] Wolf, *op. cit.*, p. 109.

[30] U.N., S/729 (May 1, 1948), Committee of Good Offices on the Indonesian Question: "Report on Political Developments in Western Java," p. 4.

[31] *Ibid.*, p. 5.

[32] *Ibid.*

[33] Statement of Male Wiranata Koesoema (son of R.A.A.M. Wiranata Koesoema) at the Second West Java Conference as reported by *Sin Po* (largest Chinese newspaper in Indonesia), Dec. 19, 1947.

provisional government and representative assembly for a state of West Java.[34]

Though Republican leaders had assumed that the terms of the Renville Agreement precluded the calling of such a conference, it soon became clear that the Dutch were making preparations for its convocation on February 24, 1948. In vain, the Republican government protested to the Dutch and the Good Offices Committee that such action was a violation of those terms of the Agreement concerning the promised U.N.-supervised plebiscite.[35] The minimum of six months of "uncoerced and free discussion" and "freedom of assembly, speech, and publication" was, as they pointed out, hardly compatible with a one-month period under Dutch martial law wherein such conditions were not allowed.

The refusal of the Dutch to live up to these terms of the agreement was highlighted by their prompt suppression of the Republican-sponsored Plebiscite Movement. This movement had been organized by Republicans on February 1, 1948, to express the Republican point of view in accordance with the above-mentioned terms of the Renville Agreement in the areas the Dutch had overrun. The Constitution of the Plebiscite Movement was as follows:

Article i—A Working Committee has been formed called the Plebiscite Movement of the Republic of Indonesia and having its seat and head office at Jakarta.

Article ii—This movement has as its objective: (a) To impress upon the population of the occupied areas the significance and purpose of the plebiscite; (b) To impress upon the people the importance of choosing and defending the Republic of Indonesia in a plebiscite. This objective shall be reached by all legal means.

Article iii—The organization of this movement is as follows: (a) Board of Management, (b) members.

Article iv—The Board of Management of this Movement consists of: (a) The Board, (b) Council of Representatives of the Board, (c) Cadre of the Board.

Article v—Membership of this movement is open to all adult men and women.

Article vi—The finances of this movement are derived from (a) Contributions, (b) Donations and funds obtained legally.

Article vii—This movement shall be dissolved immediately upon the completion of the plebiscite.

[34] U.N., S/729, p. 5.
[35] Cf. U.P. dispatch from Batavia Feb. 14, 1948.

On February 13, Mr. Ali Budiardjo, Chairman of the Plebiscite Movement was summoned by the Attorney General for the Dutch Indies administration, Dr. Felderhof, and told that the movement was "premature." Felderhof's reasoning was in terms of what had now become the Dutch interpretation of the Renville Agreement, an interpretation diametrically opposed to that held by the Republic when it signed the Agreement and likewise opposed to that held by the Good Offices Committee and communicated by it to the Republican leaders in the Kaliurang conversations that immediately preceded their signature. This Dutch interpretation was that the envisaged plebiscite was to be held not six months to a year after the Renville Agreement, but six months after a final political agreement between the Dutch and the Republic, reached according to the terms of the Renville Agreement. Before this hypothetical future date, Felderhof insisted, neither the Dutch nor the Republicans were empowered to take any steps toward preparing for a plebiscite. The Republican government protested this interpretation and the suppression of the Plebiscite Movement to both the Dutch and the Committee,[36] but without effect.

Dutch officials and the Dutch-controlled press and radio, however, waged a powerful and unrestricted campaign to bring the population of West Java to support the Third West Java Conference and form a separate state of West Java. The conference was to convene on February 23, 1948 and consist of 100 delegates. Forty-seven of this number were appointed by the Dutch—twenty-two Indonesians, twelve Dutch, nine Chinese and four Arabs.[37] Fifty-three were to be elected, all of whom were to be Indonesians, in elections starting on January 25. In reporting on these elections at the request of the Committee of Good Offices, the Dutch stated that announcements of the elections were made between January 10 and 15. However, the Republican delegation claimed to have heard about them only two days before, on January 23.[38] Moreover, the importance of these elections was not made clear; there was no indication that these one hundred delegates would serve as the provisional government of a state of West Java.

[36] Cf. U.P. dispatch from Batavia Feb. 19, 1948.

[37] U.N., S/729, "Report on Political Developments in Western Java", pp. 5–6. It is significant that the leading Arab social organizations framed a joint resolution which they sent to the West Java Conference in which they refused to recognize these Arabs as their representatives. Of the 12 Dutch appointed, none was a member of the Progressive Concentration, a group critical of Netherlands policy in Indonesia.

[38] Ibid., pp. 5, 7.

Not only were these elections rushed through with short notice but also they were held under conditions which ruled out the basic civil liberties generally associated with democratic electoral processes. Freedom of the press did not exist, and most publications and all radio facilities in the area were in Dutch hands. The state of war and siege ("staat van oorlog en beleg") still imposed by the Netherlands administration prohibited public meetings and allowed private political meetings only after five days' notice of such a meeting had been given. Approval for such private meetings had then to be given by the Dutch Assistant Resident, and the police had the right, which they frequently exercised, to attend. Not only were meetings of the Republican Plebiscite Movement forbidden, but meetings of Republican political parties were also forbidden.[39]

The fifty-three elected representatives to the conference were to represent the fifteen regencies of West Java over which the Dutch claimed control, each regency having three or five delegates depending upon its population.[40] The Netherlands Delegation stated to the Committee of Good Offices that no attempt had been made to carry out elections in Jakarta, a regency which was allotted five delegates.[41] Also they informed the Committee that they were unable to obtain election statistics from four other regencies.[42] This plus the fact that the Netherlands Delegation presented to the Committee letters from the heads of several regencies stating that "owing to the disruptions of administration and communication, it had proved impossible to hold elections in many areas," [43] gives support to the Republican assertion that the delegates of these four other regencies were actually appointed and not elected. Thus at least five and very possibly from seventeen to twenty-one of those delegates officially designated as "elected" were actually appointed. Moreover, two of the delegates elected "were excluded from taking part in the conference by the Netherlands authorities." [44] This would mean that possibly as few as thirty of the ninety-eight delegates to the conference had any claim to an "elected" status.

However, even in those areas where an attempt actually was made to carry out the electoral process, its character frequently took on authoritarian overtones. Elections were held in three stages. First an oral vote in the village selected a delegate to the second stage, that of the

[39] Cf. U.N., S/729, pp. 7, 8.   [40] See U.N., S/729, pp. 6, 7.
[41] *Ibid.*, p. 8.   [42] *Ibid.*, p. 9.   [43] *Ibid.*, p. 8.
[44] *Ibid.*, p. 9. One had been imprisoned for embezzlement (a disqualification under the election rules) and the other was excluded because of suspicion that he had committed misdemeanors. However, charges against him were later dismissed.

district. In each district the delegates from the villages were to choose three of their numbers to go on to the third stage of the election, that of the regency. There the district delegates chose by secret ballot from three to five of their members to represent the regency in the West Java Conference.[45] However, as the Committee of Good Offices noted: "For a variety of reasons, including the absence from their homes of numbers of the population who had removed to the mountains at the time of the action by Netherlands forces six months before, it was necessary in a number of cases for the elector to be . . . elected by a reduced electorate or appointed by the *Lurah* (village chief)." [46]

The Third West Java Conference met in Bandung from February 23 to March 5, 1948, without representatives or observers from either the Republic or the Good Offices Committee. Mr. Ali Budiardjo, chairman of the Plebiscite Movement, attempted to attend but was forced by the Dutch police to leave Bandung. Giving as its reason "lack of staff," the Committee sent no observer to the conference,[47] and its response to the Security Council's request of February 28 for a report on political developments in western Java consisted of merely transmitting to the Security Council a report based only on secondhand information submitted to it by the two interested parties, the Republic and the Netherlands. The factor of time, it stated, made it impossible to address questions to the West Java Conference itself.[48]

Despite the semi-controlled manner of the elections and the police-ridden atmosphere of Bandung, most of that minority of the delegates who had won their places through the electoral process set up by the Dutch, as well as several of those Indonesian delegates who had been appointed directly, made clear from the outset their pro-Republican feelings. Twenty-seven of them did so unequivocally, and thirty-five had courage enough to oppose the formation of a West Java state. However, the steam-roller methods by which the Dutch ran the conference gave them little chance to be heard. Soejoso, leader of the pro-Republican

---

[45] *Ibid.*, pp. 6–7.

[46] *Ibid.*, p. 8. *Lurahs* held their positions either through direct appointment by the Dutch authorities or through local elections. However, when elected they generally had to be confirmed in their authority by the Netherlands administration.

According to most leading Indonesian officials in the Dutch-sponsored state of Pasundan which emerged from the West Java Conference, most of the Indonesian intelligentsia for whom the electors would ordinarily have voted were at the time of these elections either still in the mountains, within the Republican-controlled area of Java, or jailed by the Dutch (consensus of leading Pasundan officials in interviews with the writer [Bandung, Feb. 4–11, 1949]).

[47] U.P. dispatch, March 5, 1948.   [48] U.N., S/729, p. 1.

faction, introduced a motion that the conference, and not the chairman (Dutch-appointed), alone had the right to determine its agenda. The motion was passed, but when on the next day (February 24) Soejoso moved to change the agenda so that the pros and cons of establishing a state of West Java could be discussed, the chairman adjourned the conference, and an informal meeting was held between him and several other appointed members and the leaders of the pro-Republican faction. As a result a compromise was effected whereby it was agreed that the conference would vote on a resolution calling upon the Netherlands Indies government to transform the conference into a "Provisional Representative Body" of a "Provisional Government" but that "the status of West Java" was "to be determined by a plebiscite as referred to in the Renville Agreement." [49]

However, the following day, the chairman read to the conference a letter from the Netherlands Indies governmental agent in West Java (the *Recomba*) stating that the State of West Java was already in the process of being created. He went on to say that West Java had already been recognized as a state by the Netherlands Indies government and in consequence withdrew his agreement to the compromise motion he had signed the previous day. Soejoso promptly sought to protest the chairman's ruling, but was given no opportunity. He then urged that the conference undertake a general discussion of the future status of West Java and also urged adoption of the previously agreed compromise proposal. The chairman allowed neither general discussion nor consideration of the compromise proposal.[50]

Finally on the same day, with a vote of sixty-two in favor and thirty-five against, a resolution was passed expressing the delegates' desire that the conference be transformed into "a provisional representative assembly of West Java" and that as such they draw up a constitution for such a state and in accordance with it "establish a provisional government of West Java." [51] The final phrase of the originally agreed compromise solution that "the status of West Java is to be determined by a plebiscite as referred to in the Renville Agreement" was conspicuously missing. Promptly on the following day, February 26, the Netherlands Indies government approved the resolution.[52] Thus was born the State of West Java, or "Pasundan" as it came to be called.

---

[49] *Ibid.*, p. 11.

[50] *Ibid.*, p. 12. This version coincides with that given the writer by Indonesian leaders of the West Java (Pasundan) regime (Bandung, Feb. 4–11, 1949).

[51] *Ibid.*, p. 12.   [52] *Ibid.*, p. 13.

Increasing indications that the Dutch were undertaking unilaterally and without reference to the Good Offices Committee to create a central federal government for the envisaged United States of Indonesia added to the alarm that Republicans felt over the rapid establishment of Dutch-sponsored states in areas which previous to the military action had been administered by the Republic.[53] Such a move was seen as the logical corollary to the formation of Dutch-controlled member states of the federation. The combined maneuver spelled for Republicans a thinly disguised, centralized Dutch control behind a façade of decentralized papier-mâché puppet regimes.

In his first policy statement before the Working Committee of the Republican parliament on February 14, Hatta made it clear that the Republic not only was prepared to join an interim federal government of the projected United States of Indonesia, but also that it was prepared to relinquish a number of its powers to such a government.[54] However, the Republic's proposal was immediately turned down by the Dutch. A letter from Van Mook to Hatta stated that the Republic could not be admitted into any such government until after a final political agreement had been negotiated between it and the Netherlands.[55]

The Dutch then proceeded with their plans to organize such a government unilaterally and without the Republic as a constituent element. On March 9 Van Mook announced the establishment of such an interim federal government which was to function until the establishment of a United States of Indonesia.[56] This new government represented no real change in the power structure of Dutch-controlled Indonesia. It was merely the old Netherlands Indies regime in new dress and was run by the personnel of the colonial regime with a few anti-Republican Indonesians included to present a better façade.[57] Cer-

[53] In those areas of Sumatra taken from the Republic the Dutch likewise embarked on the organization of states amenable to their control. East Sumatra, where they had laid the groundwork for a separate state before the signing of Renville, was established as such on Feb. 16, 1948. A South Sumatra Council was formed April 16, 1948, and this area was accorded the status of "state" on Aug. 30, 1948.

[54] U.P. dispatch, Feb. 14, 1948; see also A.P. dispatch, N.Y. Times, Feb. 16, 1948, p. 14.

[55] U.P. dispatch, Feb. 14, 1948.

[56] N.Y. Times (A.P.) March 10, 1948, p. 17.

[57] Its President was Van Mook, and the key secretariats of Interior and Commerce and Industry were headed respectively by H. van der Wal and Dr. J. E. van Hoogstraten. In addition the commanders in chief of the Dutch army and naval forces were Secretaries of State. See N.Y. Times, March 10, 1948, p. 17, for a complete list of the members of Van Mook's cabinet.

tainly there was little basis for claiming that it was a step towards Indonesian self-government.

Though formally the Republic was invited to join in this government, the Dutch still attached the same prior condition, negotiation of a final political agreement between the Dutch and the Republic. The Republican leaders immediately challenged this cart-before-the-horse procedure and lodged a formal protest with the Good Offices Committee, charging the Dutch with acting "contrary to the letter and spirit of the Renville Agreement," and pointing out that according to the Agreement, "The two governments undertook to cooperate in the political settlement including the formation of a provisional federal government." [58]

Equally disquieting to the many Republicans who had placed their faith in the Renville Agreement was the federal conference called by the Dutch at Bandung for May 27 and lasting nearly two months. Several members of the Good Offices Committee as well as the Republicans found it difficult to reconcile the Dutch contention that this conference was merely "consultative" with Van Mook's opening address to its Dutch-selected delegates at Bandung: "But it did not seem possible to continue waiting for the moment when the Republic would join us: the problems we have to deal with are too urgent and of too great importance to all of us to postpone this conference any longer." [59] For Republicans this seemed to underline and give top-level sanction to the statement made ten days previously by the chairman of the Netherlands Delegation:

The further expansion of the federation goes on. Even if the Republic contends that a federation without its participation is an impossibility, the federalists are of exactly the opposite opinion. They consider a federation without the Republic in no way an impossibility. [60]

The Republican government protested the holding of this conference and called upon the Good Offices Committee to submit a report on it to the Security Council. This was done; but again the report had as its basis nothing more than the formal documents relating to the

[58] U.P. dispatch, March 16, 1948.

[59] U.N. S/842 (16 June 1948), Committee of Good Offices on the Indonesian Question: "Report to the Security Council on the Federal Conference Opened in Bandung on 27 May 1948," pp. 22–23. J. Foster Collins notes that such statements heightened the impression that "The Netherlands was proceeding unilaterally with the territory outside of the Republic as a counter-balance to its influence" (op. cit., p. 155).

[60] Nieuwsgier (Dutch language Batavia newspaper), May 18, 1948, quoted in U.N. S/842, p. 12.

conference and the conflicting interpretations of the two delegations.[61] The report elicited no response from the Security Council.

BREAKDOWN OF NEGOTIATIONS

At the same time that the Dutch were unilaterally attempting to shape the future of Indonesia along their own lines, and while they were maintaining the impossibility of allowing the Republic to partake in this process until after a final agreement between it and the Netherlands had been reached, they appeared to the American and Australian members of the Good Offices Committee as well as to the Republicans to be committed to a policy of making any such agreement impossible unless based on their own terms.

The Dutch, within the limits of their own approach and their own interpretation of the Renville Agreement, had their grievances also. The Republic's continued expansion of its foreign relations was, they insisted, in violation of the terms agreed. (The Republic's interpretation of them, as buttressed by Dr. Graham's "you are what you are" clarification of the Renville principles at Kaliurang, was that there was nothing in the agreement contrary to such action.) More generally the Dutch insisted that political negotiations could not be held unless the Renville truce was strictly observed. Both the Dutch and the Republic continually accused each other of responsibility for the frequent localized, small-scale clashes that occurred along the Van Mook line, or *status quo* line as it came generally to be called. Responsibility for these incidents lay with both parties; it is difficult to say who was to blame for most of them. However, there is no doubt that Republican officers were responsible for a considerable number of them, particularly in the area to the west of Surakarta.

The negotiations between the two parties under the auspices of the Good Offices Committee soon bogged down with conflicting accusations as to responsibility for truce violations and particularly with conflicting interpretations of the Renville Agreement which made the prospect for reaching any settlement hopeless. In general the American and Australian members of the committee were impressed with the co-operative spirit and willingness to compromise evidenced by the Republican Delegation, as contrasted with what seemed to them to be a nonco-operative and uncompromising attitude on the part of the Dutch. Likewise they felt that the Republican interpretation of the Renville principles was much more closely congruent to both their

[61] U.N., S/842.

letter and spirit than that given by the Dutch. Repeated cables by the
Committee to the Security Council emphasizing that the impasse could
only be resolved by the Council's intervention brought no response.

In order to break the deadlock the American and Australian members of the Committee themselves then took the initiative and drafted
a careful and realistic set of compromise proposals for the settlement
of the dispute. These principles, known as the DuBois-Critchley Plan
were submitted privately to both the Dutch and Indonesian Delegations on June 10, 1948. Graham gives a good summary of the plan:

One or more electors in proportion to the population were to be elected from
all the smallest administrative units throughout Indonesia. These chosen
electors would then get together on the next highest administrative level and
elect delegates to the Constituent Assembly which would be both the provisional legislative assembly and the constitutional convention.

This provisional parliament (1) would, on the basis of geography, ethnogra-
phy, history, tradition, and sentiment of peoples, delineate the states of the
new United States of Indonesia; (2) would elect the President who would appoint the Prime Minister who would, in turn, form a Cabinet responsible
to the provisional parliament; (3) and would have full powers of self-government including the command of all Indonesian armed forces. The Netherlands High Commissioner would retain certain veto rights and have power
to declare an emergency in a situation beyond the control of the provisional
government, in which case he would have the power to command the armed
forces.

The Constituent Assembly, as the provisional parliament, would, with the
Netherlands, frame a statute of the Netherlands-Indonesian Union which
would safeguard legitimate economic, cultural, and military interests of each
country in the other and provide the framework for cooperation of the two
governments in all fields of common interest. As the constitutional convention, the Constituent Assembly would write the Constitution of the United
States of Indonesia. When the constitution and the statutes of the union be
ratified, the Netherlands would transfer sovereignty to the United States of
Indonesia.[62]

Although the Republic agreed to accept the principles of the plan for
negotiations, the Dutch flatly rejected it, refusing even to discuss it and
charging the American and Australian members of the committee with
overstepping their authority.[63] However, the reasonableness of the
proposals was of such a nature that dismissal of them on their merits
alone would have been extremely awkward for the Dutch. Presumably

[62] Graham, op. cit., p. 3925.   [63] Ibid.

to escape the accusation of having done so, the Dutch resorted to a remarkable expedient. On June 16, with self-righteous indignation they broke off the U.N.-sponsored negotiations with the Republic because of leakage of the confidential contents of the DuBois-Critchley plan to Daniel Schorr, correspondent of *Time* magazine.[64] The Dutch in Batavia unofficially intimated that Coert DuBois, chief American delegate of the Committee of Good Offices, had deliberately leaked the contents. DuBois categorically denied that either he or any member of the American delegation had done so, and the body of foreign correspondents in Batavia stood ready to back him up in this assertion.[65] *Time* did not print Schorr's story covering the contents of the plan. The fact that it had not yet printed Schorr's story when the Dutch broke off negotiations "in view of the *publication* of the strictly confidential document . . ." [66] aroused the suspicions of many. However, most persons dismissed this incongruity, as did *Time*, as meaning only that Dutch authorities were "snooping into correspondents' outgoing cablegrams." [67] Though it was kept secret for a long time, the actual fact of the matter as known to the top foreign correspondents in Batavia,[68] was that the Dutch authorities in Batavia had confidentially leaked this story to Schorr themselves.

On June 22 the Dutch agreed to resume negotiations. However, when at the first meeting of the parties on the following day the Republican Delegation called for discussion of the DuBois-Critchley proposals, the Dutch categorically refused and returned all their copies of the plan to the Good Offices Committee.[69] An impasse again resulted. Because of this and because of a series of cablegrams dispatched by the Committee to the Security Council emphasizing clearly its impotence to halt the deterioration of the situation, it was the expectation of both the American and Australian members of the Committee and of the Republican Delegation that the Security Council would take the positive action necessary to resolve the impasse. This expectation was disappointed. On July 1 the Security Council again debated the Indonesian question, and a Chinese motion was made that the Council study the DuBois-Critchley proposals. However, the United States re-

---

[64] The writer is uncertain whether or not Schorr was a regular correspondent of *Time*. At any rate he did cable it a story incorporating the contents of the DuBois-Critchley proposals.

[65] U.P. dispatch, June 16, 1948.   [66] *Time*, June 28, 1948, p. 17.   [67] *Ibid.*

[68] Stated by them to the writer in the spring of 1949.

[69] U.P. dispatch, June 23, 1948.

fused to support this motion and it was defeated.[70] The departure home of DuBois the following day was interpreted by Indonesians as meaning his recall and seen as further proof of the United States' repudiation of the DuBois-Critchley proposals.[71] To the Republican leaders this all spelled the definite withdrawal of the United States from any positive association with the Renville Agreement. They were now completely disillusioned with the expectation that had prompted them to sign the Agreement, namely, that fulfillment of its basic provisions would be underwritten by the United States.

THE DUTCH BLOCKADE

In the words of one member of the Good Offices Committee, "This failure of the Security Council to act at a decisive moment gave the Netherlands special opportunities. They maintained their pressure on the Republic and made every effort to sow seeds of dissension and create difficulties for it." [72] The political pressure applied by the Dutch against the Republic was matched by their economic pressure. As another member of the Committee, Dr. Graham, noted:

Time worked heavily against the weaker government. In the summary record of negotiations with the Republic, or lack of negotiations . . . is revealed a Dutch policy pattern of delay and attrition. . . . The Netherlands Government used the policy of delay to carry on what the Republic considered a program of economic strangulation instead of the opening of trade as provided for in the agreement. . . .[73]

The "export-import controls" established by the Dutch were a mere euphemism for what in effect was a blockade of the Republican area which almost completely closed off trade with areas outside. As the Committee of Good Offices noted, the several agreements "in principle" entered into by the Dutch to open up this trade were in general never implemented.[74]

[70] U.N., Security Council, *Official Records*, 3rd. yr., no. 91 (July 1, 1948), pp. 14, 34. Those in favor included Canada, China, Colombia, Syria, Ukraine, and U.S.S.R. Those abstaining were: Argentina, Belgium, France, United Kingdom, and the United States.

[71] Actually DuBois was not recalled, but returned home because of critical illness. It should be noted that his immediate successor, Charlton Ogburn, had been his deputy and was a strong proponent of the DuBois-Critchley proposals.

[72] Stated in a conversation with the writer.

[73] Graham, *op. cit.*, p. 3926.

[74] The Committee stated in its cablegram of June 21, 1948, to the Security Council: "Although important agreements for the resumption of normal trade and commerce between territories under the control of the Republic and those outside have

To understand the significance of this Dutch blockade it must be realized that the truncated area of Java left to the Republic under the terms of the Renville Agreement was a deficit food area which in normal times imported considerable food from the surplus rice and maize areas now shut off by the Dutch. Into it had streamed nearly a million refugees from the areas overrun by the Dutch army. Whereas per-capita production of rice for the whole of Java and Madura in 1940 had been 84 kilograms and that of maize 41 kilos, the corresponding figures for the area of Java controlled by the Republic in 1948 were estimated at 60 and 35 kilos respectively.[75]

The supply of textiles became even more critically short. Upon arrival in the Republican area in August, 1948, the writer was struck by the large proportion of both the rural and urban population literally dressed in rags or in gunny sacks.[76] The average yearly consumption of textiles for the area of Java controlled by the Republic was computed as being about 350,000,000 meters in the years just previous to the Japanese invasion, of which over 330,000,000 had been imported. From the end of July until the end of December, 1947, the total of such imports was computed as being only slightly over 15,000,000 meters.[77]

The acute shortage of these basic necessities generated an inflationary problem of the most serious proportions which the government, handicapped even by shortage of the proper facilities for printing money, found impossible to keep within manageable proportions.[78]

---

been reached in principle, no significant increase in the volume of trade in and out of Republican controlled territory can yet be reported. Such an increase will take place only if agreements are implemented satisfactorily" (U.N., S/848, p. 2).

[75] These figures are drawn from data compiled for the writer by the personnel of the Republican Ministry of Food under the direction of Mr. A. Sofjan, Jogjakarta, Nov. 11–18, 1948. As a consequence of the Republic's intensive campaign to raise food output, the over-all situation was somewhat mitigated because of cassava and sweet potato production which was raised from a per-capita output of 151 kilos to one of 175 kilos. However, the over-all food production of all kinds in terms of *rice-equivalent* was computed at 177 kilos per person in 1940 (for all Java and Madura) as compared to 153 kilos per person in 1948 for the Republican-controlled area of Java.

[76] The writer arrived in Republican-controlled territory on Aug. 24, 1948, and stayed there until forced to leave following the Dutch attack on Jogjakarta on Dec. 19, 1948.

[77] These figures were computed from data supplied the writer by personnel of the Ministry of Economic Affairs under the direction of Kaslan A. Tahir. Jogjakarta, Nov., 1948. Figures for the period after Dec. 31, 1947 were not available.

[78] Statement to the writer by Mr. Saubari, Secretary-General, Department of Finance, Jakarta, Feb. 11, 1949.

The potential impact of this inflation upon political attitudes within the Republic can be judged from Table 11, showing market prices of the key Indonesian foods.

Table 11. AVERAGE PRICE IN RUPIAHS PER KILO IN CHIEF MARKET-CENTERS OF REPUBLICAN-CONTROLLED JAVA.*

Product	Aug., 1947	April, 1948	June, 1948	Aug., 1948
Rice	1.66	6.76	7.44	17.50
Sugar	1.58			7.30
Salt	3.48			14.30
Meat	4.50–13.60			76–187.50
Soybeans	2.00			12.00
Coconut oil (per 600 cu. cm.)	5.09			38.20

* Figures for the months of Aug., 1947, and Aug., 1948, were supplied the writer by Kaslan A. Tahir and his staff at the Ministry of Economic Affairs, Jogjakarta, Nov., 1948. The figures for April and June, 1948, are computed from figures appearing in Berita Perekonomian (official publication of the Ministry of Economic Affairs), June, 1948, p. 67, and Aug., 1948, p. 158.

These figures take on added significance when it is realized that the average daily wage of a nonagrarian laborer in the Republic in August, 1948, was from 15 to 25 rupiahs per day. Though beginning in March, 1948, civil servants and army personnel were given rice allotments of 10 kilos each plus 5 for each dependent, which they could purchase from the government at somewhat below the market level, they frequently suffered more than nonagrarian labor. The government-fixed monthly salary for lower class civil servants ranged only from 70 to 160 rupiahs per month; for middle-rank civil servants the range was from 92 to 380 rupiahs, and for the upper-rank bracket from 175 to 700 rupiahs.[79]

Civil servants who no longer had possessions which they could sell to supplement these incomes very frequently had to accept the fact that their families would remain undernourished. A large proportion of them, particularly in the capital of Jogjakarta, were in this category. Thousands, particularly those from West Java, had fled ahead of advancing Dutch troops with only those possessions they could carry with them. Their lot was particularly hard and the suffering they

[79] Figures here cited were also supplied by the Department of Economic Affairs. With respect to rice allotments see also Saubari, "Dua Tahun Oeang Republic, V," Sikap, April 25, 1949.

endured often heroic. Very quickly they had sold all but the barest necessities in order to buy food supplementing that purchasable with their salaries. Though the President of the Supreme Court, Koesoemah Atmadja, earned the top civil service salary of 700 rupiahs per month, one of his children began to go blind because of the dietary deficiency arising from the father's inability to buy enough proper food for his family. He was one of those many unfortunate Sundanese from West Java who had been forced to flee precipitously, leaving almost all his possessions behind.

The Dutch blockade impinged sharply on other sensitive points. It was almost impossible to get medicine and surgical equipment through to hospitals and clinics in the Republican area. Many illnesses could not be treated,[80] and even such basic things as bandages were virtually unobtainable.[81] The blockade extended even to ideas. Mail service with the outside was cut off. There was no regular means for bringing in books or periodicals and as a result the strongly subsidized Communist news organs in such cities as Jogjakarta and Madiun were able to propagate their ideas without the necessity of overcoming the antidote of more objective material from outside Indonesia. The seriousness of this blockade of ideas is expressed in the following excerpt from a letter from Bishop Soegiopranoto, leader of the Catholic community in the Republic, to the editors of *Commonweal* magazine. Though written shortly after the suppression of the Communist rebellion, it describes very well the similar conditions that preceded it.

The appeal of Communist ideas remains strong so long as the Dutch blockade us—as they intensively now do—letting no food, no cloth, no mail, no books, no magazines, no ideas in to us from the outside. Your magazine has begun to let ideas in to us—not just about what is really happening outside, like news. More importantly it gives us to know that it is not just the Communists

---

[80] As of Oct. 7, 1948, there were on hand for the 22,000,000 people of Republican-controlled central and east Java exactly 810 sulfathiazine, 407 sulfathiozole, 90 codein, and 14 novocain-adrenelin tablets (figures from the Indonesian Red Cross at Jogjakarta, Oct. 7, 1948; through its headquarters were dispensed all medical supplies to all hospitals and army medical units). Dr. Yap, Java's famous Chinese eye specialist, had his eye clinic across the street from where the writer lived in Jogjakarta. The writer recalls vividly numerous conversations with this venerable man wherein he pathetically bemoaned the fact that for the lack of a few ounces of a certain vitamin concentrate which he could not import because of the Dutch blockade scores of his patients were needlessly going blind.

[81] The writer can testify personally to the ineffectiveness of the sterilized banana leaves which the Republican medical authorities attempted to use as substitutes for cotton bandages.

who like social justice. It gives us to know that Americans also want this and that they want protection of the individual and to allow for his development too. We hope, too, to find that they want these things and freedom for colonial people too. Please continue to send us *The Commonweal* so we are not closed off from the outside.[82]

Thus throughout the spring and summer of 1948 the character of Indonesian nationalism was subjected to a powerful political and economic conditioning. The violation of the Renville Agreement by the Dutch, the refusal of the Security Council even to note these violations, and in particular the failure of the American government (which most Indonesians saw as dominating Security Council decisions) to honor what Indonesians considered to be its promise to oversee the implementation of the Renville principles, were extremely disillusioning and embittering to Indonesians. To what end had they agreed to Dutch occupation of the richest areas of the Republic, to the arbitrary Van Mook line, and the withdrawal of their own troops from behind Dutch lines? The great *quid pro quo* which they had counted on for having made these concessions—freedom of expression and political association in the territories overrun by the Dutch, followed by U.N.-supervised plebiscites—had failed to materialize. Instead they saw the Dutch cavalierly proceeding with the unilateral erection of their own puppet states in these contested areas, quite obviously with the intention of creating a federal Indonesian structure amenable to their own control.

The refusal of the United States, the power which had induced the Indonesians to sign the Renville Agreement and which they had counted upon to insure its implementation, to contest these actions of the Dutch generated a mounting disillusionment with America among Indonesians, who increasingly tended to view the United States as the covert ally of the Dutch. America, they felt, was also giving direct aid to the Dutch through its powerful backing of the Netherlands' economy. The $506,000,000 in Marshall Plan aid granted the Dutch in the spring of 1948, with the provision that $84,000,000 of this amount could be used by the Netherlands administration in Indonesia, was for many Indonesians added proof of their conviction that the United States stood aligned with the Dutch and against the Republic of Indonesia.

[82] Printed in *Commonweal*, Dec. 31, 1948, p. 303. The writer found means for having this magazine and limited numbers of other American and British publications sent through the blockade.

These conditions were not alone in aggravating the frustration of Indonesian hopes for national independence. It was likewise increased by the progressively harsh material conditions experienced by the urban elements, the principal leaders and organizers of the revolutionary effort. Indeed, for many of them there was a tendency to link their sufferings in the material sphere and the psychological sphere with what they conceived to be the pro-Dutch policies of the United States and the Western European members of the United Nations.

Thus it is perhaps understandable why some of the officials of the Netherlands Indies administration confidently expected that these factors would soon bring about the collapse of the Republic without the necessity for any further Dutch military effort. It is also understandable how many Indonesian Communist leaders, evaluating the same factors, concluded that conditions were becoming increasingly propitious for an attempt to overthrow the Republican government and seize power in its place. They could not help but develop hopes for popular backing in a situation where the Republican government appeared to many to have sacrificed the interests of the nation by an apparently unwarranted and disastrous faith in the United States, and in which Soviet Russia consistently appeared to champion the cause of the Republic against the Dutch.

❧ CHAPTER IX ❧

The Internal Struggle for Power from Renville through the Communist Rebellion

THROUGHOUT 1947 the leaders of the PKI (Indonesian Communist Party) and those unproclaimed Communists who had joined the Socialist and Labor parties and the Pesindo appeared to follow policies determined chiefly by what best served their own political advancement rather than what a conscientious Stalinist might have considered would have best served the Kremlin. Beginning only at the end of 1947 did their attitudes commence to show any significant increase towards conformity with Moscow policy, and not until early March, 1948, did this increase become substantial. No approximation of real congruity was reached until August, 1948.

There were two principal reasons for this increasingly orthodox Stalinist orientation. In the first place, the actions of the United States in the Netherlands-Indonesian dispute were more and more interpreted by Indonesians to be definitely partisan and in favor, of the Dutch. Particularly did this sentiment grow following the U.N.-sponsored Renville Agreement of January 17, 1948. This mounting conviction brought many Indonesians, non-Communists as well as Communists, to the conclusion that the force of Indonesian nationalism alone was not sufficiently strong to win independence for their country. Believing that one of the two great powers was backing the Dutch, many felt they had no alternative but to tie themselves more closely to the other great power. Though not usually joining it, more and more Indonesians began to look to the PKI for leadership. The tendency grew, both among the membership of the PKI [1] and among its larger and rapidly growing fringe element, to take seriously the Kremlin's claim that genuine independence for colonial areas could never be won until the United States and its Western allies were dominated by Russia. Increasingly the followers of the PKI and the minority of Communists within the Socialist and Labor parties and the Pesindo were ready to believe that the "narrow course of nationalism" had to be abandoned in favor of a long-term struggle between the Communist and non-Communist worlds, a struggle in which the role of the Indonesian Communist Party was to conform to the dictates of Moscow's world-wide policy rather than to what might be deemed the immediate interests of Indonesian nationalists.

The second principal reason for this change in orientation dovetailed snugly with the first. Within the PKI itself it may well have been the more potent of the two. This was the revolt of the second echelon of the party leadership against the policies formulated by and being pursued by their top leaders. For actually the policies of the PKI during the last quarter of 1947 and the first two months of 1948 deviated very far from the orthodox Stalinist line then being laid down in Moscow and by the Cominform. It is impossible to tell whether the top PKI leadership knew the content of the Zhdanov report to the first meeting of the Cominform. But certainly it was many months before the PKI showed any signs of reacting to and changing its policies in conformity with the new international line for Communists which was laid down at the end of September, 1947.[2] Despite the general strikes launched on November 12 in Italy and November 18 in France—the clearest indication of a major change in international Communist policy—there was no indication during the next three months of any change in PKI policy.

In February, 1948, however, the young, second-echelon Indonesian

[1] According to Mohammad Hatta, Prime Minister and Vice-President of the Republic, actual membership of the PKI in mid-1948 did not exceed 2,000 (statement to the writer, Jogjakarta, Oct. 9, 1948). According to Suripno, a member of the Politbureau of the PKI, its membership amounted to only 2,500 in Java and 500 in Sumatra. He stated it was a matter of policy to restrict actual membership to an elite of convinced and reliable Stalinists (statement to the writer, Jogjakarta, Sept. 1, 1948).

[2] The new program emphasized the division of the world into two blocs—the "aggressive capitalist" bloc led by the U.S. and the "democratic" bloc led by Russia —and called upon all Communist Parties to wreck the Marshall Plan.

Communist leaders attending the Calcutta conferences met delegates from the Soviet Asian republics.[3] They learned the new Communist line with its divided-world basis and its anti-Marshall-Plan emphasis, a line which their leaders in Indonesia had not been following. They returned to Indonesia as bearers of the true gospel and as ideological experts, and they demanded conformity with the new line. Their demand was reinforced by Indonesian delegates returning to Indonesia early in the summer from the Conference of the World Federation of Trade Unions and the International Youth Conference at Prague. The older top leadership of the party had no alternative but to adopt the policies communicated to its subordinates at Calcutta. Refusal would undoubtedly have led to a serious challenge to its position of ascendancy within the party. Even so, many of its members lost prestige and influence to the younger, second-echelon leaders.

During the latter half of 1947, there had been developing a growing split within the Socialist Party between the faction led by Sjarifuddin and the smaller group led by Sjahrir. Sjahrir's group was becoming increasingly antagonized by the growing emphasis of the larger group upon class warfare and alignment with Russia. In December, 1947, Sjahrir wrote that Sjarifuddin would have to decide whether he was first a nationalist or first a Communist. Sjahrir and most of his group felt then as they do now that application of the Marxist doctrine of class warfare was absurd in the Indonesian community since there was practically no Indonesian bourgeoisie, that class in Indonesia being almost exclusively made up of Dutch and Chinese. Secondly, they were strongly opposed to a policy of alignment with either Russia or the United States. As between the great world powers and in the context of the cold war in particular, Indonesia must, they were and remain convinced, maintain a "positive neutrality." This meant no advance commitment to either side by Indonesia and the following of an independent course best suited to her interests as governed by the international situation at any given moment. In addition "positive neutrality" was seen as the course whereby Indonesia could offer its maximum contribution to the cause of world peace.

The split between the two groups became dangerously wide in January, 1948, when Sjahrir's group opposed the Renville Agreement

[3] The first of these conferences, the Southeast Asia Youth Conference, met from Feb. 17–21 and was attended by two Indonesian delegates, Francisca and Supeno (not to be confused with the Supeno of the Indonesian Socialist Party). Delegates from the Asian Republics of the U.S.S.R. also attended.

sponsored and approved by Sjarifuddin as Prime Minister, most of his cabinet, and the majority section of the Socialist Party, as well as by the Labor Party and Indonesian Communist Party. The split became decisive soon after the establishment of Hatta's presidential cabinet. Sjarifuddin's group within the Socialist Party along with the other Sajap Kiri parties (PKI, Labor Party, and Pesindo) demanded as a price of their support of Hatta as Prime Minister four of the key ministries with the express stipulation that Sjarifuddin continue on as Minister of Defense.[4] The Masjumi and PNI refused to participate in the cabinet if this happened and ultimately Hatta formed his cabinet without the Sajap Kiri.[5]

Thereupon the Sajap Kiri went into opposition against the Hatta government. This action was strongly opposed by the Sjahrir faction, which, because of this and its other differences with the group led by Sjarifuddin, split off from the Socialist Party (Partai Sosialis) and the Sajap Kiri coalition on February 13, 1948, and formed its own party, the Indonesian Socialist Party (Partai Sosialis Indonesia). This new party[6] immediately pledged its support to Hatta's government. Thereupon control of the rump Socialist Party passed to Sjarifuddin and his associates, Tan Ling Djie and Abdulmadjid.[7]

Initially the only basis of the Sajap Kiri opposition was its demand that Hatta's presidential cabinet be replaced by one whose character was parliamentary. In such a cabinet it hoped to acquire a strong position. In its conference of February 21, Sjarifuddin's Socialist Party, still the central party of the Sajap Kiri, maintained this position, making explicit that it continued to approve the Renville principles and urged their implementation.[8]

At a mass meeting at Surakarta on February 26 the Sajap Kiri underwent a reorganization and emerged as the Front Demokrasi Rakjat (People's Democratic Front) or "FDR" as it was popularly known. The

[4] It will be recalled that in the outgoing cabinet Sjarifuddin was both Prime Minister and Minister of Defense.

[5] Except for Supeno, a member of Sjahrir's faction who joined the cabinet on his own responsibility.

[6] Other than Sjahrir, its chief leaders were Subadio Sastrosatomo, Sitorus, Djohan Sjaroezah, Supeno, and Sugondo Djojopuspito.

[7] As a result of the split, 4 of the 5 Socialist Party members of the Working Committee joined Sjahrir and only one, Tan Ling Djie, remained with Sjarifuddin. Within the KNIP, 19 members joined Sjahrir's party, 13 stayed with Sjarifuddin, and 2 quit both parties. However, the most of the rank-and-file organization of the party remained with the Socialist Party under Sjarifuddin.

[8] See Antara, Feb. 23, 1948.

program then announced by Sjarifuddin, chairman of the new coalition, put more emphasis upon the interests of labor and the peasantry,
but otherwise was almost identical with the Sajap Kiri program of
February 21.[9] During the course of the next two weeks, however, the
program of the FDR underwent a basic change. No longer could the
members of its constituent groups—the Socialist Party, Labor Party,
PKI, Pesindo—and the closely associated Indonesian Federation of
Trade Unions (SOBSI) be reckoned amongst the political moderates.
Their individual programs and that of the FDR as a whole now called
for repudiation of the Renville Agreement, cessation of all negotiations with the Dutch until they withdrew from Indonesia, nationalization of Dutch and other foreign properties without compensation, and
in general a program almost identical to that supported from the inception of the revolution by the more strongly nationalist group of
Communists led by Tan Malaka and Sukarni. Yet the breach between
the two groups remained, and there was no co-operation between them.

The relations between the FDR and the Hatta cabinet became progressively less friendly. A second attempt by Hatta to include it in his
cabinet failed, the FDR leaders insisting as they had just previously
as members of the Sajap Kiri that they be given the dominant positions
within it, chiefly at the expense of the Masjumi.

During the next six months a struggle of mounting intensity developed between the FDR and the Hatta government. The long-term
aim of the FDR was domination of governmental power. If possible it
hoped to attain this through forcing the liquidation of Hatta's presidential cabinet and substituting a cabinet of parliamentary character
(responsible directly to the KNIP and its agent the Working Committee) wherein it would control the key ministry of Defense and if
possible that of Interior as well. However, during the course of this
struggle there developed a growing disposition upon the part of Sjarifuddin and other top leaders of the FDR to be prepared for all
eventualities and if need be to prosecute the struggle along revolutionary lines.

The FDR had two principal bases of strength: within the army, and
among the ranks of labor. In his capacity of Minister of Defense from
July 3, 1947 to January 28, 1948, Sjarifuddin had managed to build up
a strong personal position within the army. His power over appointments and the disposition of funds had secured him the loyalty of a
substantial number of officers in the regular army, the TNI. He and a

[9] Antara, Feb. 26, 1948.

handful of his more trusted followers were often the only ones who knew the location of the numerous arms and munitions caches being set up in mountainous areas in anticipation of further Dutch military action.

Even more important was the strong position Sjarifuddin had built himself within the army's principal auxiliary organization, the TNI Masjarakat (People's TNI).[10] This had been established in early August, 1947, shortly after the beginning of the Dutch military action, for the purpose of organizing popular defense on a local basis to supplement the regular army. It absorbed the old Biro Perdjoeangan (Struggle Bureau) which had been dedicated to integrating the many semi-autonomous militias into the regular army. The process of integration was stopped and actually reversed in order to meet the needs of dispersed guerrilla tactics necessary to fight the Dutch effectively. Top appointments to many of the reconstituted Laskjars (semi-autonomous militias) and all of those in the rapidly burgeoning TNI Masjarakat were made by Sjarifuddin, and were largely men of his choice and upon whom he had reason to believe he could depend. The many small nuclei sent out from the headquarters of the TNI Masjarakat undertook to organize and train militarily the communities to which they were assigned. In addition they attempted to inculcate political ideas, ideas particularly hostile to the Masjumi and which during the first months of 1948 became closer and closer to the increasingly Communist line emerging in the FDR.

In addition, the FDR held a clearly dominant position within SOBSI,[11] by far the largest labor organization in the Republic. This was based upon both urban and plantation labor within the Republic, and its membership probably stood between 200,000 and 300,000.[12] However, a considerable proportion of this membership was relatively passive with respect to the opposition of the FDR to the government, and some of its constituent unions were far from enthusiastic about this course.

A large number of the nearly 1,000,000 refugees who fled into the

[10] Literally Society's TNI.

[11] Sentral Organisasi Buruh Seluru Indonesia—Central Organization of all Indonesian Labor. The second largest group of trade unions (much smaller in membership than SOBSI), looked to Tan Malaka and his associates for leadership and operated politically through the Partai Indonesia Buruh Merdeka headed by Samsu Harja Udaya. It claimed 17,000 dues-paying members in mid-1948. See Sukrisno, "Gerakan Revolusi Rakjat," *Siasat*, Sept. 5, 1948, for an account of this party.

[12] Prior to the Dutch military action of mid-1947 SOBSI claimed a membership of 1,307,000.

shrunken area left to the Republic from the areas overrun by the Dutch consisted of skilled and semi-skilled labor which from the standpoint of the Republic's economy was redundant to the labor supply already existing within its shrunken borders. Thus in the Republic's oil field and refinery at Tjepu there were available more than twice as many qualified workers as there were jobs. At the Republic's principal railroad shops in Madiun the proportion of skilled workers to jobs was even higher. No matter how inefficient the ratio of workers to jobs, all these workers had to be fed. In addition there were at least 200,000 excess troops in the Republic, men for whom the supply of arms and ammunitions was inadequate.[13]

To meet the critical problems—economic, military, and political—arising from this situation Hatta and his cabinet immediately embarked upon a "Rationalization Program." With respect to this Hatta stated in his address to the Working Committee of Parliament on February 16, 1948:

That the revenues of the state do not cover expenditures should be no reason for wonder. But the difference can be narrowed by judicious rationalization, by transferring labor from unproductive work to productive fields of activity. This transfer of labor will not at once show a decrease in the state's expenditures; the contrary may even be the case in the beginning, because the creation of productive enterprises requires previous preparation and investment to work on. But once the preparations are completed, the productive labor will begin to yield its profits and the income of the State will increase. . . . Especially in regard to our armed forces the rationalization project must be carried out along a determined and clear-cut line, for in the armed forces there is an unwarranted use of manpower which cannot be productive in the future. If we do not begin rationalization soon the country will find itself in the grip of an inflation of such calamitous proportions as to be paralyzing. . . . For every worker who has to be dismissed as surplus personnel a new occupation has to be provided that assures him of a fair living.

Reorganization of the army called for an initial demobilization leaving 160,000 men. Eventually it was hoped that this could be reduced to a final figure of 57,000 regular troops. This well-armed and well-trained regular army, it was planned, would be prepared to operate at battalion strength in a mobile, hard-hitting guerrilla war against

[13] Prior to the Dutch military action in mid-1947 the total number of men in the Republic's armed forces (regular and irregular) in Java, Madura, and Sumatra was 463,000. Even then a great many had no rifles.

the Dutch, should they again attack. The old "static defense" would be changed into a "mobile offensive system" of shifting pockets that could not be mopped up.[14] Supplementing this force of highly trained regulars would be a wide network of territorial militias made up of the local peasantry, who would be called upon to devote part of their time to military training.

Demobilized soldiers were to be employed in creative activities. In the initial stage of mobilization about 100,000 of those demobilized were to return to rural communities to practice agriculture. The rest were to receive training in new jobs or rehabilitation to old skills under a program run by the newly instituted Ministry of Youth and Reconstruction [15] headed by the former youth leader, Supeno, a member of Sjahrir's new party. In addition, this Ministry was to transfer surplus industrial workers from the jobs where they were not needed to jobs where their skills would be productive and if necessary to new and different kinds of work.

Finally the rationalization program was to extend to the sphere of governmental administration. Surplus personnel was to be dropped, and there was to be a general organizational integration. This was particularly necessary in Sumatra, where the decentralized units of the Republican administration were almost completely autonomous. Hatta's program called for organizing the residencies in Sumatra into three provinces. Each province was to have a high degree of autonomy from the central Republican government at Jogjakarta and real authority over its constituent residencies. This program was carried out with partial success in the summer of 1948.[16]

For the FDR the Rationalization Program had two principal consequences. Once its implementation had got under way in early March, 1948, it resulted in a gradual erosion of the base of the FDR's strength within the army. Though this was slight during the first few months, it became considerable once the program had begun to gain momentum. As the peasant-based territorial defense was organized, the TNI

---

14 Col. A. H. Nasution, "Rasionalisasi dan Pembangunan," *Merah Putih,* April 13, 23, 1948.

15 See Saubari, "Dua Tahun Oeang Republik, VI," *Sikap,* May 7, 1949.

16 It proved impossible, however, to unify the island's several different currencies with each other, much less with the Republican currency of central and east Java. In mid-1948 the values of the several Republican currencies in Sumatra in terms of the Straits $ varied from 7:1 (Atjeh) to 40:1. Republican-controlled Bantam (extreme West Java) also had a separate currency system.

Masjarakat was liquidated. Also, as the regular army was reorganized, there was no certainty that key positions would go to the officers who had formerly been sponsored by Sjarifuddin.

On the other hand, the discontent of many of the troops being demobilized was most frequently projected against the government, and often their tendency was to look for leadership to the FDR, which announced its vigorous opposition to any demobilization of the army. Similarly, in the frequent cases where surplus laborers could not find jobs employing their particular skills and where the government was tardy, as it frequently was, in finding new jobs for them or where it found them jobs with less pay or prestige value than they had held before, the FDR often benefited. Such persons, too, tended to hold the government responsible for their plight and naturally gravitated towards its principal organized opposition. Because of the widespread dissatisfaction amongst labor with the government's rationalization program, the hold of the FDR on SOBSI became stronger.

Implementation of the government's rationalization program within the army not unnaturally met with resistance. For many officers this spelled a loss of prestige and power to which they could ill adjust. Some sincerely believed that, quite apart from their personal interests, the program was a mistaken one and that, no matter how under-equipped, military units should not be disbanded. Likewise it was difficult to persuade soldiers of one unit that they were less well-trained than those of another, and that consequently they should disband and yield their arms to them. Moreover, many soldiers as well as officers slated for demobilization were unconvinced that the government would provide them with alternate occupations of a desirable character.

Certainly the FDR could not claim that the early stages of the rationalization program discriminated against it. Except for the over-all long-range program of transforming the TNI Masjarakat into a locally-based peasant minuteman militia, the principal bases of FDR power within the army were not touched. The first regular army division slated for demobilization, the Fifth, was one in which the FDR's influence was weakest. By mid-summer this entire division [17] had been successfully demobilized and reasonable progress achieved in rehabilitating its personnel for civilian occupations. In addition, the first of the large *laskjars* (semi-autonomous militias) ordered to demobilize, the Pem-

[17] Strength of a full Republican division before the rationalization program was between 20,000 and 30,000 men.

berontakan [18] Republik Indonesia, led by Bung Tomo,[19] was strongly anti-FDR.

The Pemberontakan refused to comply with the government's demobilization order and sat behind its guns in its barracks in Surakarta. If it made its refusal stick, other *laskjars* slated for eventual demobilization would take example and the government's whole program would collapse. Into this breach leaped one of the elite organizations of the army, the highly disciplined Tentara Peladjar (Students' Army). Composed almost entirely of young men who had been attending middle and secondary schools just prior to the Japanese invasion, it was one of the most effective of the army's units and could always be relied upon to back the government in times of crisis. Wearing white cloths over their clothes as symbols of purity, they volunteered to force the Pemberontakan to turn in its arms. On March 27, supported by the local detachment of state police (Polisi Negara) they marched against the dissidents' barracks. After two days of fighting the Pemberontakan had had enough and agreed to disarm. Under pressure of the Tentara Peladjar several smaller armed groups in the city quickly followed suit. During the course of the next month another powerful *laskjar* based in Surakarta, that headed by Mardjuki, was forced to disband by troops of the regular army, and after short fights *laskjars* based near Magelang and Wonosobo were likewise disarmed. Similar successes were being encountered by the government's regular troops in Sumatra, and by early May it seemed probable that no further disobedience would be encountered among the *laskjars*.

Thereupon the government turned its chief attention to rationalization of the regular army. Again the unruly Surakarta area commanded its chief attention. Here the rump Fourth, or Senopati Division, only some 5,000 strong, was slated for demobilization. Half its number being Republican marines (ALRI),[20] it was particularly appropriate that this organization have a high priority in the rationalization program. However, within the Fourth Division the influence of the FDR was par-

---

[18] A reasonably close translation of this would be "Revolutionaries."

[19] Bung Tomo (Sutomo) had risen to fame as a leader of militant youth during the battle of Surabaya in Nov., 1945. The orientation of his organization was somewhat pro-Tan Malaka. Members of this organization had a rather wild appearance, since they had vowed to let their hair grow until full Indonesian independence was achieved.

[20] Angkatan Laut Republik Indonesia. The bulk of the remainder consisted of Pesindo troops.

ticularly strong, many of its troops being armed formations of the Pesindo. Although the larger Fifth Division had already begun carrying out the government's demobilization orders, the Fourth Division's commander temporized and refused to begin the mobilization process within his own command. As will be seen, this was to have extremely important consequences.

In the meantime the FDR did not abandon its efforts to force the resignation of Hatta's cabinet, with the objective of having it supplanted by a parliamentary cabinet wherein it would control key positions. Beginning in May it launched a two-fold program [21] to attain this end. Firstly, this sought to weaken and discredit the government through widespread strikes among urban and agricultural labor. It succeeded in launching one serious strike involving some 20,000 agricultural workers in the extremely important Delanggu cotton-growing area which lasted from the middle of May until the middle of June. This strike was of critical importance because these cotton fields were the chief source of raw material for the Republic's limited textile industry. Under conditions of the Dutch blockade domestic production of textiles was, of course, particularly important. (A government arbitration board set up by the Working Committee of Parliament investigated and settled the strike. There was no doubt but that the agricultural laborers involved had some legitimate grievances.)

In general, however, the FDR's success was limited. With the Republic standing with its back to the wall and blockaded by the Dutch, it was difficult to convince most laborers that this was the proper time to carry out strikes. Soekarno in several radio addresses was effective in demonstrating the unpatriotic nature of strikes at such a time, pointing out that strike organizers could serve their country best by operating in Dutch-occupied territory.

The pro-Tan Malaka Independent Labor Party (Partai Indonesia Buruh Merdeka) strongly opposed strikes at such a time of national emergency. In addition, it, in conjunction with other Tan Malaka-oriented groups, in early June formed a strong political federation, the Gerakan Revolusi Rakjat (People's Revolutionary Movement), or GRR [22] which, though close in its program to that of the FDR and

[21] Drafted at a meeting of its leadership in Bodjonegoro in mid-April.

[22] The other groups which joined the GRR were the Partai Rakjat (People's Party), the Partai Rakjat Djelata (Poor People's Party), the Angkatan Komunis Muda (Young Generation of Communists), the Partai Wanita Rakjat (People's Women's Party), the Persatuan Invaliden Indonesia (Union of Disabled Men of Indonesia), the Laskjar Rakjat Djakarta Raja (People's Militia of Greater Djakarta)

opposed to many aspects of Hatta's program, made clear its support of Hatta's government.[23]

The second aspect of the FDR program centered about the idea of promoting national unity, an idea thoroughly acceptable to all political parties. The first step in this strategy was to be achieved by drafting a "National Program" which was to be the highest common denominator of agreement between all the major political parties including the FDR. Upon achieving this, the FDR leaders felt that they would be in a strong position to demand an all-party "National Government" to implement such a National Program. They not implausibly felt it would be difficult for anyone to advocate their exclusion from such a government, since such advocacy could be easily attacked as being against the interests of national solidarity.

This strategy of the FDR was, however, very soon perceived by the other principal parties. They all co-operated in working out a mutually agreeable general program, accomplished by mid-June, and then sat down to work out its details. This served a useful purpose in delineating in fairly precise language the opinions of the parties with respect to all aspects of governmental policy, thereby serving as a guide to the government. Though it contained a vague clause to the effect that "the government should be democratized," the most the major parties outside of the FDR were prepared to do by way of a change was to reshuffle the cabinet under the leadership of Hatta.[24]

---

and the Barisan Banteng (Buffalo Legion). The last of these was based in Surakarta, had some 3,000 armed men and had been incorporated into the regular army as a semi-autonomous unit. The Laskjar Rakjat Djakarta Raja was in territory in West Java nominally under Dutch control and was waging a guerrilla warfare against Dutch troops particularly in the Krawang area where it had strong backing from the local population. Of the actual political parties making up the federation, the Partai Rakjat, led by Maruto Nitimihardjo, was the largest. It was the only one with representation on the Working Committee of the KNIP (however, it ranked in size well after the larger Republican parties). For an account of the GRR see Sukrisno, "Gerakan Revolusi Rakjat," *Siasat*, Sept. 5, 1948.

[23] Like the FDR, the GRR called for cutting off negotiations with the Dutch. However, it insisted upon a policy of neutrality in the Cold War at least until after Indonesian independence had been attained. It urged the Government to "take strong action against destructive elements," i.e., the FDR and "exclude the heroes of Linggadjati and Renville [the parties making up the FDR were considered chiefly responsible for both agreements] from the leadership of parties, revolutionary organizations, the government, army, police, and labor, peasant, and youth organizations." Decision of the Central Committee of the GRR, Jogakarta, Sept. 1, 1948, as reported by *Murba* (official newspaper of the GRR) Sept. 6, 1948.

[24] On July 5, 1948, both the Masjumi and PNI made it clear that though they might consent to a slight reshuffle of the cabinet, it would have to remain under the leadership of Hatta. See Antara, July 5, 1948.

On July 27, 1948, Hatta announced that his cabinet officially accepted the National Program, which in most respects actually differed very little from the program he was already committed to,[25] and thereby pulled the rug out from under the FDR's strategy and dimmed its hopes of ousting him. The major parties other than the FDR then concluded that it was not even necessary to reshuffle Hatta's cabinet.

Despite the failure of these tactics, the FDR continued to attack Hatta's government and call for its replacement by a new parliamentary cabinet. It derived new ammunition for this attack because of the government's refusal to ratify a consular treaty with Soviet Russia which that country had itself ratified. Suripno, who it later developed was a Stalinist Communist, had been sent by the Republican government as its envoy to Eastern Europe shortly before the Dutch launched their attack of July, 1947. His mission was to line up whatever diplomatic support in the area he could for the Republic. In January, 1948, Suripno had approached the Soviet Ambassador to Prague, who appeared receptive to the idea of negotiating a consular treaty with the Republic. An agreement was initialed later in January and Suripno asked the Republican government for instructions. However, Sjarifuddin was then in the midst of negotiating the Renville Agreement and did not wish the treaty with Russia consummated. The succeeding Hatta government likewise refused to take any more action with respect to the treaty.[26] However, the Soviet government itself finally took the initiative, and on May 22, its ambassador to Prague informed Suripno that the Russian government had ratified the consular treaty.[27]

Whether or not this Russian move constituted formal recognition of the Republic, it was so interpreted by the FDR.[28] In fact, the Russian ambassador refused to make any commitment to Suripno as to whether Russia would send any material aid to the Republic once consuls had been exchanged.[29] However, the FDR made the most extrav-

[25] At least it was possible so to interpret its provisions.

[26] Such a step would have been contrary to the Dutch interpretation of the Renville Agreement. Probably of more importance was the fact that some Republican leaders were convinced that such an action would unreservedly align the United States with the Dutch.

[27] Stated to the writer by Suripno (Jogjakarta, Sept. 6 and 7, 1948).

[28] India and Nationalist China had consular representatives in Jogjakarta, but neither had formally recognized the Republic.

[29] Suripno stated to the writer that the Russian ambassador had promised nothing specific as to Russia sending the Republic any help. All the ambassador would commit himself to, Suripno acknowledged, was that, with a Russian consul in the Republic, trade relations would be possible (Jogjakarta, Sept. 7, 1948).

agant claims as to the material aid Russia had pledged to send to the Republic once the establishment of a Soviet consulate in the Republic had opened up the channels of trade. Some in propagandizing this idea went so far as to paint a picture of Russian planes and ships running the Dutch naval blockade in order to bring arms and munitions to the Republic.

For many Indonesians the fact that the Republican government made no move to match Russia's ratification of the treaty, but instead called Suripno home for consultations, lent considerable weight to the FDR's assertion that Hatta's government was truckling to the United States. Against the background of mounting feeling that the United States backed the Dutch, this allegation was a powerful weapon for the FDR.

Increasingly the government became suspicious of the aims of the FDR. These suspicions appear to have been well justified. Apparently by early July Sjarifuddin and the other leaders of the FDR had come to entertain little hope of winning governmental power by purely political means. Though by no means abandoning that approach, they began to think more and more in terms of attaining their objective through military force should political means fail. The outlook and plans that were developing among them are demonstrated in a report drafted by them in mid-July [30] combining an analysis of the situation and long-term plans of strategy. (The document here cited did not come into the government's hands until after the outbreak of the rebellion two and a half months later.)

In its initial analysis of the contemporary situation this report noted that attempts of pro-FDR officers in the army to influence the course of the rationalization program in favor of the FDR had not been successful. Only two out of twenty key positions in the central leadership of the army were in their hands, the Deputy Commandership of the Java Territorial Command and the post of Head of Public Relations. The report noted that the TNI Masjarakat had been divided into six small units under the control of the staff of the Territorial Army. The Political Information Division of the TNI Masjarakat, which had been controlled by FDR officers, had in the process been entirely dissolved.

However, the report went on to make clear that despite this the military position of the FDR was still strong. "The government's efforts

[30] This seven-page document, *Mingindjak tingkatan perdjuangan militer baru* ("Stepping to the New Stage of Military Struggle"), is not to be confused with the 11-point document made public by the Republican government just after the beginning of the Communist rebellion and considered to be in part (point 11) a fabrication by some persons hostile to the FDR as well as in part (points 1–10) genuine.

to divide our units have been for the greatest part prevented, so that practically speaking our real strength is still intact and still under the command of our men or those influenced by us." It estimated that about thirty-five per cent of the armed forces were under FDR control.[31] Considerable percentages of certain other army units were considered to be under FDR influence, and it was believed that if the cards were played correctly some of these might well support the FDR when the time came, or that at least they could be counted upon to adopt a neutral position.

The strategy outlined in the document was divided into two phases, the first calling for the use of "parliamentary means" and the second, to be invoked if the first failed, calling for the adoption of "non-parliamentary means." It was apparent that the FDR, despite its initial setbacks, had not yet given up hope for attainment of power through its National Program strategy. The first or "parliamentary phase" of this program of mid-July was still dedicated to this strategy and was formulated in the following terms:

(a) To influence the Working Committee [of the parliament—KNIP] for passing a motion in which it is stated that the National Program be made the program of the government and therefore the present government should be dissolved and a new responsible [i.e., parliamentary] cabinet be formed; (b) to accelerate the formation of the National Front [organization], especially regional National Fronts; (c) the National Front will stage a large-scale campaign for dissolving the present cabinet; (d) if the above-mentioned plan fails, large-scale demonstrations will be staged by those workers, peasants, army men, and other groups which can be persuaded to join us. . . . Large-scale demonstrations must be directly followed by a general strike and if necessary by forcible measures.

(1) In this mass-action the workers, peasants and soldiers participate who will execute our discipline fully; (2) Army cadres which lead the mass-action must be those which have had political and ideological education in accordance with the responsibility we give them; (3) This mass-action should only be staged in areas where we have sufficient military strength to balance the strength of the enemy.

If the government then continued to refuse liquidation and the formation of a new national cabinet wherein the FDR would hold key posts, a switch would be made to the second phase of the strategy,

---

[31] Listed in this category were the Pesindo units, the Laskjar Rakjat, Laskjar Buruh, Laskjar Merah, ALRI (Marines), PTL (Naval Police), and that part of the TNI (regular army) stationed in the Purwodadi area.

where the drafters of the program stated: "We will cut off all relations with the government and continue our struggle under our own leadership either as rebellion or as separate government." Preparation for this called for the following:

(1) Withdrawal of a part of our troops from the front lines [i.e., the "status quo line" dividing Republican and Dutch-occupied territories].

(a) The brigades of Martono and Jadau will be ordered to strengthen our internal operations;

(b) If we are forced to send troops to the front lines, then troops which we do not yet completely trust will be sent there.

(2) Removal of our troops to areas which we consider as being strategic and abandonment of those areas which can no longer be defended.

(a) The Madiun area will be made the strongest guerrilla stronghold for the long-term struggle.

(b) We must station at least five battalions in Madiun, which should already be there this month or in August.

(c) We will make Solo [Surakarta] a "Wild West" in order to attract attention there; but we must have the strongest troops in Solo, so that the de facto authority is always in our hands.

(d) Kedu, Jogjakarta, Pati, Semarang, Bodjonegoro, Surabaya, and Kediri [residencies—that is those portions of them under Republican control] will be made neutral territories, which means that as circumstances permit we will fortify these areas or abandon them. The forces in each of these areas must not exceed two battalions.

(e) We can completely evacuate Malang, Banjumas, and Pekalongan territories. [These were the residencies most peripheral to the central core of Republican-controlled territory, which was the Madiun area.]

(3) Alongside the official armed forces we must now begin to establish a People's Army in the widest sense of the term. In a general sense we will form these forces illegally.

(a) In every subdistrict which we consider strategically situated and in which our influence is implanted, a group of sixty armed soldiers led by a commander will be stationed.

(b) These sixty persons will be divided into smaller groups of six or ten and sent to the villages.

(c) The general leadership in a subdistrict is in the hands of a committee representing the workers, peasants, and the commander of the sixty armed soldiers.

(4) Our program for the second phase can be determined further according to the circumstances. We can state in advance that we must realize the National Program, especially in regard to agrarian reform, people's defense, and the struggle of the workers. . . .

These were the long-term plans of the FDR. The government never learned of them in this detail until after the Madiun rebellion had been launched. However, it did learn of their general nature in mid-July, about the time that these detailed plans were being drafted. Accordingly it then began to take steps to remove FDR officers from their commands or shift them to less strategic commands at the rate and to the extent possible short of provoking the FDR to revolt. Given the fact that concentrations of heavily armed Dutch troops were drawn up along the borders of the Republic this was a difficult and delicate operation and had to be carried out slowly and with extreme caution.

The plans of Sjarifuddin and the other leaders of the FDR ran into an unexpected development. On August 3, 1948, there arrived at Bukit Tinggi, the Republican capital on Sumatra, an airplane bearing Suripno and an older Indonesian who he stated was his secretary and who had accompanied him from Prague. The older man sent a note to a friend which was intercepted by Republican governmental authorities and which stated that he hoped to form a cabinet soon. On August 11, Suripno and his "secretary" flew on to Jogjakarta. Here a few days later at a meeting of the PKI leadership Suripno dramatically revealed the real identity of his companion, introducing him as Musso. Here was returned after an absence of more than twelve years a revolutionary leader who had been a member of the Politbureau of the PKI in the early twenties, a leading figure in the 1926 rebellion, founder in 1935 of the underground organization, the "Illegal PKI," and in addition fresh from Moscow. Musso's reception among the PKI members was enthusiastic, and by acclamation they voted him in as secretary of the party in place of Sardjono.

From the standpoint of the PKI, Musso's return could not have been better timed. His arrival coincided with the full tide of general Indonesian disillusionment with the United States when the belief that it backed the Dutch was strongest. His return to Indonesia after more than a decade of residence in the U.S.S.R. could not but be interpreted as tangible evidence of Moscow's immediate interest in Indonesia. Among members of the FDR this accelerated the tendency, already increased by Russia's willingness to establish consular relations, to look to Moscow for fulfillment of their long-frustrated desire for full national independence.

On August 29, 1948, Sjarifuddin publicly announced that he had been a Communist since 1935 when, he claimed, he had joined Musso's

"Illegal Communist Party" in Surabaya.[32] On the same day Setiadjit, chairman of the Labor Party, and soon afterwards Abdulmadjid and Tan Ling Djie of the Socialist Party announced that they too had long been Communists. There is little doubt that the claims of the last three were correct. Beginning in 1936 in Holland Setiadjit and Abdulmadjid appeared to follow the Communist line, and the following year they went to Moscow to study at the Lenin Institute. Tan Ling Djie spent five years in Moscow and was later affiliated with the underground "Illegal Communist Party."

However, the legitimacy of Sjarifuddin's claim has been the subject of wide dispute among Indonesian leaders. Stalinist leaders backed his claim, while the followers of Tan Malaka accused him of being a secret agent of the Dutch, commissioned by them to disrupt and weaken the Republic, an accusation which they likewise leveled at Setiadjit and Abdulmadjid. As related by them to the writer, however, the opinion of most responsible non-Communist leaders, including Soekarno, Hatta, and Sjahrir, was that Sjarifuddin had not previously been a member of the PKI, though he did have connections with the "Illegal PKI" underground beginning in 1939.

In 1939 Sjarifuddin was arrested by the Dutch because of his activities as a nationalist leader and was given the choice of working with them or being exiled. He chose the former and was given an important post in the Department of Economic Affairs. Shortly before the arrival of the Japanese, Dr. Charles van der Plas, one of the top officials in the Dutch regime, gave Sjarifuddin 25,000 guilders to be disbursed by him to the "Illegal PKI" underground for operations against the Japanese. He joined their underground with the knowledge and approval of the Dutch. This undoubtedly is the only real basis of the charge by Tan Malaka's group that he was a Dutch agent. The point is, of course, that at this time Stalinist Communists in all colonial countries were expected to subordinate immediate nationalist aims to helping the colonial power in its struggle against Fascism. In Indonesia this

[32] See *Kedaulatan Rakjat* (one of the two chief nonparty papers in Jogjakarta), Aug. 30, 1948. In a public elucidation of this statement on Sept. 9, Sjarifuddin stated: "As a Communist I recognize my mistake, and I promise not to make errors again." Acknowledging that he had received 25,000 guilders from Dutch authorities prior to the Japanese occupation for the purpose of carrying on underground activities, he stated: "However, I accepted the offer because the Comintern had proposed to us to co-operate with the colonial powers in a joint front against Fascism." He went on to say that now that World War II had ended, "Communists have dispensed with this policy of collaboration" (Antara, Sept. 11, 1948).

subordination was also followed by a number of non-Communist anti-Fascists as well, and a considerable portion of those joining the "Illegal PKI" underground to fight the Japanese were actually not Communists.

Even if Sjarifuddin actually did become a nominal member of the "Illegal PKI," the consensus among non-Communist Indonesian leaders is that he was certainly never an orthodox Stalinist Communist and to the end was more of a nationalist than a Communist. They attribute his final public espousal of a Stalinist position to two principle factors, disillusionment with the United States and political opportunism.

Many of those who were close to Sjarifuddin feel that his disillusionment with the United States was of central importance in his development of a more Stalinist orientation. His feelings were particularly bitter, they say, because he felt himself more responsible than any other person for the Republic's signing of the Renville Agreement; for in signing this he believed that the United States would insure its implementation. His belief that the United States backed the Dutch must be seen against the background of his conviction that war between the United States and Russia would break out during the course of 1949.

Even so it took Sjarifuddin some time to make up his mind. As late as August 27, one influential non-Communist leader felt that his decision was still in the balance and urged the writer to see him on that day in order to try and disabuse him of his belief that the anticolonial forces in the United States and the ideas of Franklin Roosevelt towards colonial peoples were now too weak to influence American policy. In the course of a long talk with the writer, Sjarifuddin expressed keen interest in the probable outcome of the impending American presidential elections and was in particular anxious for an estimate as to when progressive forces of the character of Roosevelt's New Deal could be expected to regain power. In response to the writer's estimate that probably this would not develop within less than four years, he indicated that this was already his conviction, too, and stated: "That will be too long."

Instability of character and political ambition were certainly of great importance in Sjarifuddin's decision to cast his lot with the Stalinists. Those who knew him well testify to the instability of his philosophical and religious moorings.[33] None of his convictions seemed

[33] At 24 he was converted from Mohammedanism to Christianity while serving a jail sentence which he was not taking easily. He was converted largely through the

very solidly based to them, and they remark that when depressed he was especially amenable to the persuasion of others. Though there is general agreement among top noncommunist leaders who knew Sjari-fuddin well that he was too religious to become a Communist at heart, they all agree that his character did not stand in the way of his working with Stalinists to attain his own political ends. Few Indonesians who knew him are prepared to say that Amir Sjarifuddin was not an ex-tremely ambitious man, and the belief is widespread that Musso's dramatic arrival must have somewhat panicked Sjarifuddin. They believe that he felt it necessary to co-operate with Musso or else be-come politically isolated and lose control over many of the FDR ele-ments. On the other hand, he probably believed that Musso's arrival strengthened the public appeal of the FDR. Undoubtedly both Musso and Sjarifuddin felt that they could use each other to wrest govern-mental power from the incumbent regime. Had they succeeded in doing so, it would seem almost inevitable that a struggle for power between the two of them would have ensued.

Musso arrived with plans of his own, but in most respects they were very close to those already laid out by the leaders of the FDR. He referred to his plan as his "Gottwald Plan," making it clear that he hoped to duplicate in Indonesia what Gottwald had just accomplished in Czechoslovakia. If possible power was to be acquired without a major resort to force; only if this proved impossible, was there to be reliance upon actual insurrection. Fresh impetus was to be given to the FDR's demand for the formation of a new and parliamentary cabinet within which key positions would go to its men. Efforts in this direction were, however, coldly received by Soekarno, Hatta, and other Republi-can leaders outside the FDR.

Apparently it was becoming clear to the FDR leaders that their organization was too loosely knit to force the government to make concessions. Likewise, because of the strong popular conviction that the FDR was chiefly responsible for the Linggadjati and Renville "debacles," it was not capitalizing effectively on the growing anti-American, pro-Russian sentiment developing outside as well as within the FDR. This prompted the FDR leadership, now strongly under Musso's influence,[34] to embark upon a two-fold campaign designed to

efforts of his Dutch teacher, Schepper, who came to see him with a Bible almost every day while he was in jail.

[34] Aside from the general prestige arising from his revolutionary record and having come fresh from Moscow, Musso also had the advantage of being looked

remedy these deficiencies. First, the FDR was to be reorganized and so integrated as to be more effective in exerting political pressure both legally and illegally, and second, a new psychological foundation was to be laid to attract more people to its leadership.

During the last ten days of August the leaders of the FDR took the initial steps towards integrating and strengthening their organization. Musso insisted that all its constituent organizations merge with the PKI, so that there would be only one integrated organization, this enlarged PKI. The Politbureau of the PKI was reported to have approved this policy on August 21, and its recommendation was approved by an extraordinary conference of the party held between August 25 and 27 and attended by its section committees and residency committees as well as members of the Politbureau.[35] On August 27, the Labor Party leaders decided to fuse their party with the PKI,[36] and two days later a similar decision was taken by the Socialist Party Council, with the understanding that its decision was subject to confirmation in a party congress scheduled for October.[37]

A first step in the fusion was the establishment of a new Politbureau for the expanded PKI which would include most of the chief leaders of the FDR. As announced on September 1, its composition was as follows:

General Secretariat: [38] Musso, Maruto Darusman, Tan Ling Djie, Ngadiman;
Labor Secretariat: A. Tjokronegoro, Aidit, Sutrisno;
Youth Secretariat: Wikana, Suripno
Women's Secretariat: (Temporarily managed by General Secretariat);
Defense Secretariat: Amir Sjarifuddin;
Propaganda-Agitation Secretariat: Lukman, Alimin, Sardjono;
Organization Secretariat: Sudisman;
Occupied Territories Secretariat: Managed by the General Secretariat;
Secretariat of Foreign Affairs: Suripno;
Representation Secretariat: Njoto [a member of the Working Committee];
Cadre Secretariat: Managed by the General Secretariat;
Financial Secretariat: Ruskak.[39]

---

upon by the powerful group of PKI and Socialist and Labor Party members who had been members of the "Illegal PKI" (founded by Musso in 1935) as their special leader.

[35] *Suara Ibu Kota* ("Voice of the Capital," official newspaper of the PKI), Sept. 1, 1948.

[36] *Ibid.*, Aug. 30, 1948.   [37] *Kedaulatan Rakjat*, Aug. 30, 1948.

[38] *Suara Ibu Kota,* Sept. 1, 1948. "While the Politbureau is not in session the day to day work will be executed by the General Secretariat."

[39] *Ibid.*

In the contemplated fusion of the constituent elements of the FDR into one integrated, disciplined party, the new PKI, it was planned to incorporate only the "select part" of their membership. To the 3,000 members of the original PKI there would be added only 30,000 out of the approximately 60,000 members of the Socialist Party [40] and a roughly similar proportion of the much smaller Labor Party. This apparent selection of members may well have been in large part a rationalization of the fact that considerable portions of the membership of both the Socialist and Labor parties in Java were opposed to such a fusion with the PKI. In Sumatra and Bantam, as it developed, the Socialist Party opposed the fusion. There seems little doubt but that the period envisaged for working out this fusion was calculated at no less than six weeks, and very likely was expected to last somewhat longer.

Roughly concurrent with the early stage of this process of fusion there developed a well-publicized campaign of self-criticism of the mistakes made by the FDR parties in the past, in particular their prominent part in supporting the Linggadjati and Renville negotiations and their failure to stress the socialist as well as the nationalist aspect of the Republican revolution. Characteristic of the sort of self-criticism and correction embarked upon by all the constituent elements of the FDR (Socialist Party, PKI, Labor Party, Pesindo, and SOBSI) was the following resolution adopted on August 22, 1948, by the Presidium of the SOBSI.

Considering: that on account of the exaggeration of the imperialist power and the minimization of the anti-imperialist power, the SOBSI has made basic errors by pursuing a compromise policy with the imperialists, which has had as its results that (a) the national revolution is not led by a consistent anti-imperialist and revolutionary Labor Class in alliance with the peasants and in co-operation with all progressive people; (b) the colonial government apparatus has not been changed and the remains of feudalism are not eliminated; (c) no real efforts have been made for improving the living conditions of the workers and the peasants; (d) no consistent anti-imperialist National Front has existed; (e) agreements, colonialistic in nature, have been approved;

Whereas the SOBSI deems it necessary to take positive actions in order to correct the above-mentioned principle errors, it therefore decides:

(1) to acknowledge the mistakes of pursuing a compromise policy with the imperialist powers and afterwards to follow a consistent anti-imperialist policy;

(2) to call upon the government:

[40] Statement to the writer by Suripno, member of the Politbureau of the PKI (Jogjakarta, Sept. 1, 1948).

(a) to withdraw the Political Manifesto of November 1, 1945,[41]

(b) to repudiate both the Linggadjati and the Renville Agreements,

(c) to reject the American-Australian [DuBois-Critchley] compromise proposals,

(d) to negotiate on the basis of the recognition of the full sovereignty of the Republic of Indonesia,

(e) to realize immediately the exchange of consuls with the Soviet Union and to endeavour to obtain the recognition of the People's Democratic States such as Czechoslovakia, Poland, Hungary, Jugoslavia, Albania, Romania, and Bulgaria,

(f) to nationalize the properties of all those who are hostile to the national revolution, without giving any compensation,

(g) to stop all negotiations with the Dutch as protest against the fascist Dutch shooting of children and boy scouts who were celebrating the third anniversary of the Republic of Indonesia in Jakarta; negotiations can only be resumed on the fulfillment of clause 2 d.,

(h) to cleanse the composition of the entire State's apparatus of the remains of colonialism and to appoint officials with a consistent anti-imperialist spirit;

(3) to approve and be prepared to implement the National Program;

(4) to pioneer the establishment of a democratic National Front, the membership of which body enters as individuals;

(5) to urge the Head of the State to dissolve the present Cabinet and change it into a responsible National Front Cabinet on the conditions:

a. that it be based on the National Program,

b. that the Ministers are persons who agree with the establishment of and are members of the National Front;

(6) to participate in forming the National Front Cabinet;

(7) to intensify the preparation of the scorched earth policy and the people's defense by arming the whole people;

(8) to support the claim of the peasants for ownership of the lands they cultivate;

(9) to fight actively for the realization of this resolution and make preparations for all consequences.[42]

Elaborate rationales of the past mistakes of the FDR parties and leaders were then developed and publicized. On August 31, the Socialist Party in its official newspaper, *Buruh,* stated:

[41] Undoubtedly this has particular reference to the clause in that document guaranteeing the return of foreign investments and the honoring of all prewar debts of the Dutch East Indies government once the independence of the Republic had been recognized.

[42] *Buruh* ("Labor," chief newspaper of the Socialist Party), Aug. 23, 1948.

Admission of mistakes made in the past by the Socialist Party:
I. In the field of organization:

     (1) In October, 1945, the Illegal Communists established the Indonesian Socialist Party (Parsi). This was a mistake because Communists should not establish a Socialist Party, but should have established a Communist Party.

     (2) After the Indonesian Socialist Party (Parsi) fused with the Socialist People's Party (Paras). Paras was the right wing of the Socialist Party and was led by Soetan Sjahrir. This was a mistake because a party based upon Marxist-Leninism should not fuse with reformists.

     (3) The leadership of this fused Socialist Party was seized by the right-wing Socialists.

Self-correction in the field of organization began to succeed when the Sjahrir cabinet was repudiated in June, 1947, followed by the expulsion of the right-wing Socialists from the party in February, 1948.
II. In the political field:

     (1) It was a mistake to co-operate with imperialist nations on the assumption that this could be done because they and anti-Imperialist nations were fighting a common enemy [i.e. the Axis Powers]. Because of this attitude in Europe, the Communists here agreed to fuse with the reformist Socialists.

The new position of the FDR and the rationalization of its former mistakes took on clearer form in articles appearing during the next few days in its several leading newspapers.[43] Characteristic of this was an article entitled "Politik SOBSI" submitted by the Central Bureau of SOBSI in the September 3 issue of *Buruh:*

The world is divided into two fronts, the Anti-Imperialist Front and the Imperialist Front. Who rally behind the Imperialist Front? All countries with colonies. . . . Imperialist America is the leader of the Imperialist Front. We cannot remain neutral; we must choose one of the two fronts. The talk about a 'Third Force' is nonsense. Nehru who says he is going to form a third force is pursuing a pro-Imperialist policy. The Communist Party which was allowed to function in British India can now function only illegally; the same is true with Burma.

The Republic of Indonesia faces not only a Dutch imperialism; it faces an international imperialism . . . We must find our friends among the New Democratic States of Eastern Europe and the Balkans, and we must immediately exchange consuls with Soviet Russia. We must not only make friends with Russia, but we must have a strong relationship with Russia.

Why did we pursue a compromise policy with the enemy?

43 *Buruh* (Socialist Party), *Suara Ibu Kota* (PKI), and *Revolusioner* (Pesindo).

(1) The labor movement was infected with the disease of reformism. After the Second World War the Communist Parties in France, Great Britain, and the Netherlands calculated that next to the unsolvable controversies between the Soviet Union and the United States there were also controversies between the small imperialist countries and the United States. The small imperialist countries were opposing imperialist America. Consequently the Communist Party in France suggested to Ho Chi Minh that he accept a pact of union with France. And the Communist Party in the Netherlands suggested a pact of union between the Netherlands and Indonesia. And the Communist Party in Great Britain suggested a Commonwealth for India. This reformist and compromise policy is wrong as there is now no controversy between the small and big imperialists.

(2) We exaggerated the strength of the imperialists so that we were afraid to oppose them. Because of these two mistakes we pursued a compromise policy although we have the strength to oppose the imperialists.

Historically speaking only the labor class can lead a national revolution, as is evident in the Soviet Union. A national revolution led by the bourgeoisie will fail, cf. India under Nehru, and also Burma and China. Because of its weakness this group is uncertain as to what to do both externally and internally. We are therefore convinced that only the labor class, supported by the peasants and the progressive group, can finish the revolution.[44]

A few leaders of the fringe elements of the pro-Tan Malaka Gerakan Revolusi Rakjat (GRR) at first attempted to distinguish between Musso and the leaders of the FDR and in a few instances indicated a desire to join with Musso. However, the overwhelming majority of the organization demonstrated the same strong hostility towards Musso that they had already been showing towards the FDR leaders. This may well have had something to do with the government's decision to release the still-jailed leaders of the Persatuan Perdjuangan, who had been the chief instigators of the attempted *coup d'état* of June–July, 1946. On August 17, Soekarno in a speech commemorating the third anniversary of the Republic's declaration of independence, the keynote of which was national unity, announced that all those who had been jailed in connection with this occurrence were being released from jail. Almost immediately Mr. Subardjo, Mr. Iwa Koesoema Soemantri, Pandu Wiguna, and Dr. Buntaran were released. On September 16, Tan Malaka, Sukarni, and Abikusno were freed.

As a result of the counterpropaganda of the GRR as well as of the government and the parties associated with it, the effectiveness of the

[44] There then followed a recapitulation of the principle points in the above-quoted SOBSI resolution of Aug. 22.

propaganda of the revamped FDR, or PKI-Musso as it came to be known, was somewhat diminished. It was unable to take full advantage of the atmosphere of nationalist frustration and disillusionment with the West that had developed. Except for the plank in its program calling for alignment with Russia, the program of the PKI-Musso was in its essentials no different from the program which the groups within the GRR had been advocating ever since the first days of the revolution. The publications of the GRR lost no opportunity in pointing this out. and likewise emphasized their contention that those parties most responsible for the "Renville debacle" could not excuse themselves from having so seriously prejudiced the nation's welfare by mere admission that they had been wrong.[45]

Mohammad Hatta, the Prime Minister, though no Communist, was possessed of a Marxist training and an acquaintance with Soviet interpretations of Marxist principles fully as great as the most knowledgeable of the PKI leaders. In his address to the Working Committee on September 2, 1948, where he answered the blistering criticisms of its PKI-Musso members, he employed this skill with great effectiveness. This meeting was attended by the writer. Some excerpts from Hatta's speech will serve to demonstrate the principal basis of the government's "nationalism versus communism" argument.

If our struggle were to be regarded merely from the Communist point of view, then indeed there would be much to say for identifying ourselves with Soviet Russian policy. To the Communist, Russia represents the foundation on which to work for the realization of his ideals; for the Communist, struggle rises or falls with the Soviet Union . . . and therefore the interests of the Soviet Union take precedence over all other matters in international political controversies. If necessary in the interest of strengthening Soviet Russia's position any other interests except those of the Soviet Union will be sacrificed, including the interests of the subjugated countries, as happened in 1935 and in the subsequent years. For so the Communist line of thinking goes: once Soviet Russia has won the victory over imperialism, freedom will automatically come.

Not so, however, the standpoint of the nationalist, even though he may have a socialist outlook. From the nationalist point of view, independence of the country takes all-out precedence, so that all efforts are concentrated on the struggle for the attainment of that independence. He is primarily occupied with the question of how the independence of the people can be achieved in the shortest possible time. And for this reason the methods he follows in his struggle differ widely from the methods to which the Communist resorts.

45 *Murba* (principal newspaper of the GRR), Aug. 29, 1948

National independence stands in the first place; the tactics of the struggle are adapted to the circumstances. And therefore the nationalist does not blindly choose the side of either of the two conflicting ideologies. However great may be his sympathy towards that one of the two currents which attracts him most, he takes his own steps in dealing with the problems of independence.

No matter how weak we appear to be as a nation that has only recently won its independence when compared to the two giants in the conflict—the United States and the Soviet Union—it is the view of the government that we must continue to base our struggle on the principle that we must have confidence in ourselves and that we must struggle on our own strength and abilities.

Mr. Chairman! The difficulties which confront us within the country are still further magnified on account of a certain trend which has been a constant feature of our struggle. I refer to the trend that fails to see the distinction between a national revolution and a social revolution. The fact has often been overlooked that in the present stage of our struggle we are engaged in our *national* revolution. Our national revolution is certain to break down midway if we allow elements of social revolution to creep into it. Even those who formerly quoted Marx's and Mao Tse Tung's maxims to remind us of the fact that we have not yet passed the stage of national revolution and that therefore the time had not yet come for a social revolution, these people have forgotten their own theories and are ardently advocating a social revolution.

Hatta then went on to show that the government had done the best it could towards bettering social conditions, given the severe limitations imposed by the Dutch blockade and the overpopulation of the Republican-controlled area.[46]

However, the effectiveness of the government, the parties associated with it, and the GRR in replying to the new PKI's propaganda was only partial. The keen disillusionment with the course of political events in Dutch-occupied territories following the Renville Agreement, the Dutch blockade, increasingly harsh economic conditions within the Republic, and the unrest of soldiers and laborers already rationalized or slated for rationalization soon combined to lay a real and substantial basis for the widespread popular discontent upon which the PKI-Musso sought to capitalize.

It was natural that this discontent would flow into whatever channel of protest lay at hand. The PKI-Musso was the largest and best or-

[46] In particular he cited the facts that during the previous six months 75,000 hectares of newly cultivated land, derived from forests, plantations, and formerly foreign-occupied small holdings, were now planted with rice or other food crops, and that bills had been prepared for the organization of co-operatives (principally among the peasantry) and for the control of prices and the elimination of hoarding.

ganized of the existing channels. The GRR had long criticized the government in almost the same terms that the PKI-Musso and its predecessor the FDR had so recently adopted. However, its organization was smaller and less effectively integrated. In addition, many of those persons whose nationalist frustration was keenest, and who had developed the most embittered disillusionment with America and Western Europe during the course of the previous year, could not find satisfaction in the policy of self-reliance and alignment with neither the United States nor Russia pending attainment of full Indonesian independence,[47] advocated by most of the nationalist Communist leaders in the GRR. For such people the conviction that America supported the Dutch seemed to dictate the necessity of Indonesia's reliance on and alignment with the opposite international pole, Soviet Russia.

Undoubtedly aware of this feeling, Musso and other leaders of the new PKI put great emphasis on the theme that, within a world divided between the two great blocs, Indonesia could not possibly stay neutral, but had to choose between the United States and Russia.[48] With respect to this proposition Musso stated in his address of September 5 to the Indonesian Student Federation: "Obviously a nation such as Indonesia, which is fighting imperialism, cannot side with an imperialistic power; it must align itself with the forces fighting against imperialism, and that means Russia." [49]

Particular attention was paid by the PKI-Musso leaders to winning increased support among demobilized soldiers and among the peasantry. They persisted in the unrealistic demand that the government maintain the whole ill-equipped army. Their propaganda aimed at soldiers who had been demobilized or were designated for demobilization— "You've done your duty; you've protected the government, and now

[47] The feeling of most GRR leaders, in line with the ideas of Tan Malaka, was that Indonesia should not commit itself to either side until after independence had been achieved. Thereafter, *insofar as consistent with its own national interests*, they expected that eventually Indonesia would align itself with Soviet Russia vis-à-vis the U.S.

[48] Cf. Musso's speech before the Congress of the Barisan Tani Indonesia (Indonesian Peasants' Corps) (Jogjakarta, Sept. 3, 1948), as reported by *Buruh*, Sept. 4, 1948.

[49] The writer attended this meeting as a guest of the Indonesian Student Federation (Jogjakarta, Sept. 5, 1948). It was obvious that Musso did not "go over" well with the large majority of the college students who attended the meeting. In the question period folowing his talk they gave him a difficult time, pointing out the inconsistency of his speech to them with speeches given by him elsewhere and asking embarrassing questions concerning the status of religion in Russia and the question of Tito vs. the Cominform.

they're through with you"—found a sympathetic response among a considerable number. Despite the particular efforts of Musso and other
top leaders of the PKI, the principal peasants' organization, the
Barisan Tani Indonesia, though considerably influenced by them refused to follow their lead.[50] The program adopted by its congress between September 4 and 6, demonstrated that in some important
respects its program differed from that of the PKI.[51] In the residency
of Madiun the PKI sponsored and controlled a peasant organization
known as the Sarekat Rakjat (People's Association), but in comparison
with the Barisan Tani and the somewhat lesser Masjumi peasant organization, Sarakat Tani Islam Indonesia (Indonesian Islamic Peasants'
Association), it was small.

In general by mid-September, 1948, the leaders of the new PKI had
only begun to reorganize and strengthen their organization. They did
not expect to be able to act with anything approaching their full
effectiveness for at least another six weeks. They still had not given up
the idea of winning power through legal or quasi-legal political pressure. There is no doubt that concurrent with these plans for winning
power short of force they were also making preparations to seize power
by violence if that should prove necessary.[52]

[50] Prior to the Feb., 1948, split within the Socialist Party this organization looked
primarily to Sjahrir and his group within the party for leadership. Thereafter the
FDR acquired increasing influence. Suripno stated to the writer on Sept. 1, 1948:
"The PKI has great influence in the Barisan Tani, but that organization still has
discussions before deciding on policy and retains freedom of action even though
it is strongly influenced by the PKI" (Jogjakarta, Sept. 1, 1948).

[51] E.g., "The citizen should be given a hereditary right to private ownership."
The PKI, though agreeable to the idea of individual peasant ownership would hardly
have gone along with so broad a statement of social principle. And, "Capital may be
accepted as foreign investment from 'Progressive Democratic States' *and for the
time being also from other countries* if the investment is not monopolistic in nature
with the provision that the latter source of capital is as small as possible." Italics
are the writer's; this qualification was, of course, not parallel to the PKI line.

[52] There were indications that the PKI leaders would have welcomed a Dutch
attack on the Republic and had laid plans for this eventuality, believing that as a
consequence of the resulting chaos and guerrilla warfare they would in the long
run benefit, emerging at the head of the guerrilla resistance. Though there is reason
to doubt the certainty of their being able to accomplish this, there is no doubt
that in such a situation some important advantages would have been on their
side. In the first place, several of the constituent elements of the new PKI were
among the most highly organized political groups in the country. In the second
place, most of the munitions dumps and arms caches prepared in anticipation of
possible Dutch attack were established during the long period that Sjarifuddin was
Minister of Defense, and the whereabouts of many of them were known only to
him or his close associates.

However, the available evidence points toward the conclusion that the top leadership of the new PKI did not intend to resort to revolutionary tactics until it had made further efforts for capturing power through nonrevolutionary means, and certainly not before it had completed reorganizing the constituent FDR organizations into one integrated and well-disciplined political organization such as it envisaged the projected "PKI-Musso" to be.[53] Whatever the case, it is the consensus among most non-Communist Republican leaders that the top FDR leaders and Musso were not prepared to resort to revolutionary methods before early November, 1948. Some of them do not believe that the Communists would have been ready to resort to revolutionary methods before January 1, 1949.

On September 9, the Central Committee of the new PKI gave its first formal invitation to the Masjumi and PNI party councils for a joint conference for the purpose of "building national unity."[54] The leaders of these parties interpreted this bid as indicating that the new party was adopting the tactic of its predecessor, the FDR, of establishing a national political front calculated to form the basis of a new "national cabinet." The Masjumi leaders formally declined the invitation[55] the

---

The writer in his talks with Suripno gained the strong impression that PKI leaders would welcome a Dutch attack. Suripno stated that in the event of a Dutch attack, the top government leaders planned to evacuate to Sumatra, where the area for guerrilla warfare was larger than in Java, and that thereby they would be abdicating to the PKI as well as to the Dutch in Java. He seemed confident that in this eventuality the Communists, by virtue of superior organization and training, would soon dominate the guerrilla organizations on Java and would finally emerge on top politically in Java (conversation with the writer, Jogjakarta, Sept. 7, 1948).

[53] With respect to this subject, a newspaper interview with Sjarifuddin following his arrest and the collapse of the Communist rebellion is of interest. In response to the question, "What made you start this rebellion which has brought so much havoc to the country?" Sjarifuddin answered: "I never started a rebellion." A little later in the interview he went on to explain: "Even if it is assumed that there were preparations made for a coup, the time for such an action was still premature, because it would not be possible to start the action with any chance of success if there were as yet no political unity, and our policy was to bring about this political unity first" (Tjekampa, "Interview dengan Bung Amir," *Hidup* [Republican Catholic newspaper printed in Jogjakarta], Dec. 18, 1948).

[54] Antara, Sept. 9, 1948.

[55] *Ibid.*, Sept. 10. A long explanation of the Masjumi's rejection of the bid appeared on Sept. 16 and stated in part: "The PKI (FDR) has pursued a capitulation policy by signing the Linggadjati and the Renville Agreements, which have caused the loss of territory and properties of the Republic. The FDR has staged an unsound opposition by organizing strikes, insulting the Hatta Government and organizing antitax campaigns. Musso stated that the Masjumi and PNI are pursuing a capitulation policy; he requested the co-operation of the PNI and Masjumi while at the

following day, and on September 13, the PNI leaders followed suit.[56]

Concurrent with this maneuver, the top PKI leaders appear to have planned a series of speaking engagements designed to step up their attacks on the government and to secure backing for their continued demand that the Hatta cabinet step down and allow the formation of a new parliamentary cabinet wherein the PKI-Musso would control key positions. Beginning on September 7, the party's top public speakers, Musso, Sjarifuddin, Wikana, and Harjono, embarked upon what was undoubtedly planned as a junket lasting well over two weeks. The evening of September 7 they spoke in Surakarta, on the eighth in Madiun; on the tenth and eleventh in Kediri, where they were joined by Setiadjit; on the thirteenth in Djombang; on the fourteenth in Bodjonegoro; on the sixteenth in Tjepu; and on the seventeenth in Purwodadi. Plans called for visiting many other towns. Wonosobo, near the opposite extremity of Republican-held territory was, for instance, to have been the locus of a mass meeting addressed by Musso on September 24.[57]

But Purwodadi was the last town that Musso and Sjarifuddin visited in accordance with the plan of their itinerary. There they learned that the initiative had been taken from their hands and that the decision as to what tactics would be followed had been assumed by the subordinate leaders of their organization's peripheral elements, the Pesindo and the pro-PKI Fourth TNI Division. Purwodadi on the morning of September 18 was a mass of red flags, and Musso and his party left for Madiun, escorted by a heavily armed truck.[58] They arrived at Redjoagung, near Madiun, on the night of the eighteenth to find that the local PKI organization, led by the Pesindo, had already launched a coup and seized control of the city and the surrounding residency. They were presented with a *fait accompli*. The Communist revolution had begun.

While Musso, Sjarifuddin, Setiadjit, Wikana, and Harjono were on

---

same time making a public statement that he will kick the PNI and Masjumi from the government. . . . The Masjumi is always ready to co-operate with any other party which can be trusted" (*Guntur* [unofficial newspaper of the Masjumi], Sept. 16, 1948).

[56] Antara, Sept. 13, 1948.

[57] This fact is noted in an official report to the central government by the Wonosobo Information Office.

[58] Eyewitness account of an Antara photographer who had been assigned to cover the speaking tour.

their speaking tour, and while other top leaders such as Tan Ling Djie, Abdulmadjid, and Suripno were in Jogjakarta, developments began to take place in Surakarta and Madiun [59] very much out of line with the strategy and tactics which they had planned. Initiative was taken from their hands by pro-PKI military groups, particularly the leaders of those groups, who felt that their own personal interests dictated immediate action. These groups were able to stampede most of the PKI organization on Java into an ill co-ordinated and poorly executed revolt against the Republican government. For the most part their action appears to have been dictated by their realization that the government had come to learn of the long-term plans of the FDR and its successor, the PKI-Musso, in particular their preparations for ultimate revolutionary action should that prove necessary to win power.

During early September the government had been stepping up considerably its removal of pro-PKI officers in the regular army from key positions either through transfer or outright retirement. As a result the military support which the PKI might count on within the TNI was being increasingly diminished. Of more importance was the fact that the government was now beginning to put real pressure on both the Pesindo and the ALRI (Republican Marines) to submit to its demobilization orders in connection with the general army rationalization program. Particular pressure was being applied by the government on the Fourth ("*Senopati*") TNI Division, stationed in Surakarta. Its commander, Lt. Col. Suadi, had for well over a month defied the government's order that his unit be demobilized. His undermanned division of some 5,000 men was for the most part made up of ALRI and Pesindo troops and probably contained about one-third and one-quarter respectively of the armed men of these two organizations. The Fourth Division was the principal military force in Surakarta and PKI (FDR) plans called for its maintaining PKI military ascendancy there if and when the revolutionary phase of its strategy was entered upon.

The situation in Surakarta was rendered complicated and tense because the other chief military force in the city (probably between 2,000 and 2,500 armed men) was composed of partisans of Tan Malaka, most of these troops being members of the Barisan Banteng. The only other important military force inside the city was one battalion of the

---

[59] Surakarta and Madiun were the second and third-largest cities in Republican-controlled territory with populations of about 400,000 and 150,000 respectively. Jogjakarta, the Republican capital, had a population of about 500,000.

highly disciplined and reliable Siliwangi Division, under Lt. Col. Sadikin. At least one other Siliwangi unit stationed a short distance outside Surakarta was also under his command.

Early in August, Lt. Col. Sutarto, Suadi's predecessor as commander of the Fourth Division, like him a member of the PKI and unwilling to carry out the government's demobilization order, had been murdered. It was not certain who was responsible, but members of the PKI suspected the Barisan Banteng. On September 7, five army officers who were members of the PKI disappeared in Surakarta. Two days later, two other high pro-PKI officers disappeared.[60] It is possible that actually these men had been arrested by government order and removed to Jogjakarta. The PKI press did claim that two members of the Pesindo, one of the PKI, and one of the Socialist Party were arrested by the government in Blitar on September 13.[61] In addition the news agency Antara reported that State Police and army troops had been carrying out "cleanup operations against armed elements" beginning on September 12 in Blitar and on September 13 in the Njandjuk area, another PKI stronghold.[62]

It is possible that these isolated events may have been symptomatic of a general and widespread government drive aimed at cutting down the military strength of the PKI. Given the fact that the government was now acquainted with the long-term plans of the PKI, such action would seem very plausible. However, it is also possible that some of these actions, in Surakarta at least, may actually have been undertaken by the bitterly anti-PKI, pro-Tan Malaka, nationalist-oriented Communists within the GRR. Whatever the case, the reaction of the PKI was not only to accuse Sadikin's Siliwangi battalion, but also the GRR, particularly its constituent organization, the Barisan Banteng, of responsibility for the disappearance of PKI members and pro-PKI officers in Surakarta and for a night raid on the local Pesindo office.

On September 11, Lt. Col. Suadi accused the Siliwangi battalion of Sadikin of responsibility for kidnapping the missing PKI officers and demanded that it return them by 2 P.M. on the thirteenth. When that time arrived and the men had not returned, Suadi ordered the men of his ALRI unit to storm the barracks of the Siliwangi. The latter fought back and repulsed the attack. On the same day a unit of the Pesindo kidnapped Dr. Muwardi, head of the Barisan Banteng and

---

[60] The new PKI's publication *Buruh* (Sept. 13, 1948) stated that these two men were lieutenant colonels.

[61] *Buruh*, Sept. 18, 1949.   [62] Antara, Sept. 14, 1948.

chairman of the GRR, along with three other members of the GRR. On the fourteenth a Siliwangi unit which had been stationed a short distance outside of Surakarta arrived in the city to reinforce the battalion already stationed there. Together they attacked the barracks of the ALRI and forced that unit to flee the city.

On September 15, Soekarno proclaimed a state of martial law for Surakarta and the surrounding residency with Col. Gatot Subroto as Military Governor. On the same day General Sudirman, Commander in Chief of the TNI, sent 3,000 reinforcements from the Siliwangi Division to Surakarta. These took up positions on the outskirts of the city, it apparently being expected that pro-PKI reinforcements might arrive from the northern front, i.e., from their positions along the Van Mook line facing the Dutch.

In the meantime the Barisan Banteng had demanded that the Pesindo surrender Dr. Muwardi and the three others captured with him by the sixteenth.[63] When this time had expired and the ultimatum not been met, the Barisan Banteng together with the two small Siliwangi units within the city launched an attack against Pesindo headquarters and succeeded in driving the Pesindo troops to the south of the city.

On September 15, a powerful ALRI unit stationed facing the Dutch along the Van Mook line to the north of Surakarta had left the lines and marched off to Surakarta hoping to arrive in time to help the ALRI stationed there, not realizing that they had already been ejected to the south of the city. On the outskirts of the city it ran into the Siliwangi troops recently dispatched from Jogjakarta by General Sudirman. Sharp fighting ensued and on the night of the sixteenth the ALRI were finally driven off. Thus they were unable to form a juncture with the troops under Suadi's command to the south of the city.

The following morning, September 17, Lt. Col. Suadi, having regrouped the ALRI and Pesindo troops under his command, launched an all-out attack to capture Surakarta. Apparently he did so without knowledge of the potential source of reinforcement of the strong ALRI force to the north of the city and without knowing that reinforcements of Pesindo troops were on their way from Madiun to help him. His forces pushed through the Barisan Banteng forces defending the southern edge of the city and penetrated to its center. Here heavy fighting ensued; the Siliwangi, including at least part of those sent by Sudirman, and the Barisan Banteng forced Suadi's troops out of the

[63] It later developed that they had been killed.

city, this time for good. Thereby the PKI lost a battle of critical importance.

Events in Surakarta were undoubtedly making the Pesindo leaders at that organization's central headquarters in Madiun increasingly uneasy. With the Pesindo and ALRI units in Surakarta fighting troops of the regular army there in open violation of the government's orders, they must have felt their own position and that of the new PKI in general becoming increasingly compromised. Certainly they must have reasoned it would be natural for the government to assume their defection too. Government arrests of Pesindo members in Blitar on the thirteenth probably removed any doubts they may have had on this score. Also it is extremely likely that the government's "cleanup operations against armed units" in the near-by Njandjuk area referred to Pesindo units. For the top Pesindo leaders, who had already defied the government's demobilization orders, it must have appeared that the die had been cast and that they now had only two alternatives, (1) to submit to the government's demobilization order and thereby give up their own personal positions of power as well as a major source of the revolutionary military potential of the new PKI, or (2) to take the initiative themselves and embark upon the revolutionary phase of the PKI's strategy, hoping thereby to preserve their own immediate positions and the prospects of the PKI revolution, the outcome of which they must have believed held the key to their long-term futures.

It was the latter course which Sumarsono and the other top Pesindo leaders in the Madiun area chose. The local pro-PKI officers of the regular TNI units stationed in the eastern part of the Republican-controlled area apparently decided likewise and such officers as Colonel Djokosujono, Lt. Col. Dahlan, and Lt. Col. Sumantri joined with the Pesindo leaders. On their own, without the consent or knowledge of the top leadership of the PKI, they formally launched a revolution against the government of the Republic. One might say that the revolution had already been informally begun by the Fourth Division in Surakarta. It is possible that its leaders reasoned that their resort to fighting would force the other military units of the PKI as well as its top political leadership into the revolutionary phase of strategy. Whether or not they did so calculate, it seems almost certain that the Pesindo and other PKI military leaders in the Madiun area must have believed that their actions would have such a result.

Beginning on September 13, just after the Fourth Division had been ejected from Surakarta, the Pesindo units in East Java and the Twenty-ninth Brigade [64] from the eastern front embarked upon the military phase of the FDR plan drawn up in June. They and some smaller detachments of the pro-PKI troops converged on the Madiun area, where some Pesindo troops were already stationed. Of this force, one battalion was stationed in the city of Madiun, one each in the adjoining regencies of Magetan and Ponorogo, and two in Ngawi regency. During the first four days these troops left the administrations of the cities and towns in this area alone and concentrated their efforts in the villages, where without having to fight they secured control. A delayed report from a *Murba* correspondent in Madiun (probably dispatched late on the thirteenth) who witnessed the first phase of this take-over stated:

In an active and aggressive way the FDR movement to seize power has been started especially in the villages. . . . This movement is protected by four territorial and one mobile battalion which are taken from nearly the entire force in East Java. . . . These battalions have been divided up among the various villages. . . . The civil administrators feel uneasy, while the police cannot take any action because of helplessness. They agitate that the Soekarno-Hatta government has abdicated and that Tan Malaka and his colleagues and the Masjumi and its colleagues are traitors. . . .[65]

After consolidating its control over the villages, the Pesindo and other PKI troops seized control of the towns and the city of Madiun, thereby bringing to a head the incipient clash with the local Republican administration. This militant phase began at 3 A.M. on September 18 in Madiun with Sumarsono and Djokosujono leading the operation. Armed men quickly seized the local government offices, telephone exchange, and army headquarters. There were almost no loyal troops on the spot, and the fighting was brief, two loyal officers being killed and four wounded. "From Madiun victory begins," announced Sumarsono over the local radio, reportedly exhorting the PKI as a whole to follow the example set in Madiun.[66]

At about midnight of the eighteenth, some twenty hours after the coup in Madiun and the surrounding residency had been launched, Musso, Sjarifuddin, Setiadjit, and Wikana arrived at the house of Sumarsono in the town of Redjoagung, near the outskirts of Madiun.

[64] Many of its troops had originally been of the Pesindo.

[65] *Murba* (official newspaper of the GRR), Sept. 14, 1948. Though *Murba's* violent hatred of the FDR (PKI) frequently led to highly tendentious reporting, the report here quoted was closely in accord with fact.

[66] The writer has been able to obtain only secondhand accounts of Sumarsono's pronunciamento.

Here they talked to Sumarsono and Djokosujono and learned how far events had gone. They were presented with a *fait accompli*. Whether they liked it or not, they found themselves catapulted from the Gottwald-Plan phase of their campaign into the revolutionary phase that the Fourth Division and the Madiun Pesindo headquarters had prematurely stampeded. It is possible that once they had learned the full facts concerning the developments in Surakarta, they would have themselves made the same decision as Sumarsono and Djokosujono and switched PKI strategy over to the revolutionary phase. Very possibly they would have felt that they could not afford to repudiate such a major source of armed strength as the now-committed Fourth Division. Even had they decided to remain passive and accept such a loss, however, it must have seemed probable to them that the government, now understandably alarmed over general PKI intentions, would have begun to remove all pro-PKI officers from their commands and would attempt to disarm pro-PKI military units. In any case once the Madiun coup had taken place, Musso, Sjarifuddin, Setiadjit, and Wikana undoubtedly reasoned that they had no choice but to associate themselves with this new revolutionary phase and make the best of it.

Any reservations they may have had were eliminated by Soekarno's radio address at ten o'clock on the night of September 19. He brought the issue clearly to a head, calling upon the population to make a choice between "Musso and his Communist Party" and himself and Hatta. In the core of his speech Soekarno stated:

Yesterday morning the Communist Party of Musso staged a coup in Madiun and formed a Soviet government there under the leadership of Musso. They consider this seizure of power by force as a preliminary step in the seizure of the entire government of the Republic of Indonesia. From this fact it is obvious that the Solo [Surakarta] and Madiun incidents are not isolated events but are constituent parts of an over-all pattern of action designed to overthrow the government of the Republic of Indonesia. To achieve this end, the rebels have used units of the Twenty-Ninth Brigade, the former irregular force commanded by Lt. Col. Dahlan. By so doing Dahlan has betrayed the country and has violated the oath of the army. Therefore I hereby dismiss Dahlan from the army.

Brothers, consider carefully the meaning of this: Musso's Communist Party is attempting to seize our beloved Republic of Indonesia.

My beloved people, in the name of the struggle for independent Indonesia I call on you at this extremely critical moment when you and I are experiencing the greatest test to make a choice between following Musso and his Communist Party, who will obstruct the attainment of an independent Indonesia, or following Soekarno-Hatta, who, with the Almighty's help, will lead our Republic of Indonesia to become an independent Indonesia which is not subjected to any other country whatsoever. . . .

Support the government; exert yourselves to the utmost in supporting the organs of government in combating the insurgents; and restore the lawful administration in the region concerned. Madiun must be returned to our hands as soon as possible.

An hour and a half later, at 11:30 P.M., Musso replied. Calling on the population to overthrow Soekarno and Hatta and seize the power of the state in its own hands, he stated:

On September 18, 1948, the citizens of Madiun seized the authority of state in their own hands. With that the citizens of Madiun have done their duty in our national revolution, which as a matter of fact must be led by the people and not by any other class!

Our revolution has continued for three years under the leadership of the national bourgeois class, which has always been uncertain and vague in its stand in facing the Imperialists in general and America in particular. This is one of the reasons why economic and political conditions within the Republic are continually getting worse. That is why the people in general and the workers in particular have not been able to find any difference between present conditions and those existing under Dutch and Japanese regimes. Actually those in the Government have used our revolution for enriching themselves. During the Japanese occupation these persons acted as Quislings, Romusha [forced-labour]-dealers and Heiho [Work-Corps]-propagandists. More than two million women became widows, because their husbands were Romushas. And now, the same persons are going to sell Indonesia and her people once more, to the American Imperialists.

Soekarno, using false accusations and proofs, accused the People's Democratic Front (FDR) and Musso's Communist Party (PKI) as obstructionists. Has Soekarno forgotten that in Solo [Surakarta] he made use of Trotskyite traitors to terrorize and kidnap all Communists? Has Soekarno forgotten that he promoted and sanctified the crimes of the Siliwangi Division and these terrorists? What is the objective of Soekarno, the ex-Romusha-dealer, in releasing Tan Malaka, a criminal who endeavored to overthrow his Presidency? It is clear that during the past three years Soekarno-Hatta, the ex-Romusha-dealers, the sworn Quislings, have executed a capitulation policy to the Dutch and the British, and at this very moment they are going to sell out Indonesia and her people to the American Imperialists. Can people of this kind claim that they have the just right to govern our Republic? The people of Indonesia are not blind! They understand that these Romusha-dealers are not fit to rule the country. The citizens of Madiun and some other places are breaking off connections with these imperialist satellites. . . .

It was neither Soekarno nor Hatta who have opposed the Dutch, the British, and now the Americans; but rather the Indonesian people themselves. Therefore the happenings in Madiun and elsewhere are a signal to the whole people to wrest the powers of the state into their own hands. This is the only guarantee that the Republic will be truly sovereign, and capable of facing all attacks from within and of liberating itself from these imperialist satellites.

The people of Indonesia were asked by Soekarno to choose Soekarno or Musso!

The people should answer back: "Soekarno-Hatta, the slaves of the Japanese and America! Traitors must die!"

We are certain that the people will say: "Musso always serves the people of Indonesia!" [67]

According to one report, a few hours later the Moscow radio geared in with Musso's announcement, and backed the Madiun regime, stating:

There has been a People's Government set up in Madiun and People's Committees are being established in other leading towns. This was a popular uprising against the Government of the Fascist Japanese Quislings, Soekarno and Hatta.[68]

The government of the Republic moved swiftly. Early on September 19 its police had begun rounding up PKI leaders in Jogjakarta and other cities. The unscheduled nature of the Madiun coup and the general unpreparedness of the top PKI leaders for the change-over to revolutionary tactics was attested by the fact that several of the most important of them knew nothing of what had happened in Madiun when, much surprised, they were arrested in Jogjakarta on the morning

[67] This is the official PKI version of the broadcast as printed the following day in the official newspaper of the revolutionary government, *Front Nasional*, Sept. 20, 1948. This paper was printed in Madiun and ran 8 consecutive daily issues, from Sept. 20 through Sept. 27, 1948.

[68] Moscow Home Service Radio broadcasting in Russian, Sept. 19, 1948, as reported by a member of the Secretariat of the U.N. Committee of Good Offices. The writer is unaware whether similar broadcasts were beamed to Indonesia in Indonesian or any other language. However, the report of this broadcast was almost immediately made known to the top Republican leaders. Neither this broadcast nor their knowledge of it was ever given publicity in Indonesia. Possibly, if they gave credence to this report, as they seemed to, they did not wish to antagonize what they evidently still considered to be a potential source of diplomatic support in the difficult times they saw lying ahead. Probably once it became known in Moscow, as it soon must have been, that the rebellion was not likely to succeed, considerations of political expediency brought the Soviet propaganda apparatus to desist from further broadcasts of this character. But four months later Soviet news organs were again describing the Madiun rebellion and Soekarno and Hatta in these terms.

of the nineteenth. Among them were such top men as Tan Ling Djie, Abdulmadjid, Djokosudjono,[69] and Ir. Sakirman.

The following day before an emergency session of the Working Committee, Prime Minister Hatta declared that proclamation of a national emergency was not sufficient and asked that "absolute authority" be vested in the President for a period of three months so that the emergency could be dealt with adequately. The Working Committee [70] quickly consented to this request,[71] and martial law was then proclaimed by Soekarno for the whole area of the Republic.

Though less than 25,000 troops fought on the side of the Communists, the government was severely handicapped in dealing with them because the bulk of its loyal troops were immobilized along the Van Mook line facing the Dutch. It had no assurance that the Dutch would not attack while it was engaged in putting down the Communists, and it was mortally afraid they would attempt to intervene, ostensibly to help put down the insurrection. Such action would have played directly into the hands of the Communists, lending support to their constantly repeated assertion that the government had capitulated to the Dutch and that its troops were operating under Dutch command against the Madiun regime. Likewise, the Republican leaders were certain that once the Dutch had intervened they would not leave. At this juncture the United States government wisely put strong pressure on the Dutch not to intervene, and they were restrained from doing so. Nevertheless, throughout the course of the Communist rebellion the Republican government was never certain enough of Dutch intentions to risk pulling more than a small part of its troops back from the Van Mook line to fight the rebels. It relied almost exclusively on its crack Siliwangi Division, its Police Mobile Brigade, and a part of the Sungkono Division, stationed on the eastern border, to put down the rebels. Altogether this force was only slightly larger than that available to the Communists. However, it was better trained, better armed, and better officered.

[69] Not to be confused with Djokosujono, one of the principal leaders of the Madiun coup. Djokosudjono had been active in the PKI at the time of the 1926 rebellion and was considered a close friend of Musso.

[70] The PKI (FDR) members of the committee were, of course, not present.

[71] The law embodying the request read: "For three months beginning on 15 September, 1948, the President is empowered with full authority (*plein pouvoir*) to take measures and to adopt regulations which may deviate from all existing Laws and Regulations in order to preserve the welfare of the State in the mounting state of emergency."

During the first few days following Musso's proclamation of revolution the Communists expanded their control over most of the residency of Madiun and some towns and small areas peripheral to it, the most important of these being Purwodadi. There were a few small and isolated uprisings in relatively unimportant areas in the north and west of Republican central Java (such as at Parakan), but they quickly collapsed. Thereafter, the core of the revolutionary regime, the residency of Madiun, progressively shrank under pressure from the simultaneous advance of the Siliwangi Division and Police Mobile Brigade from the west and elements of the Sungkono Division from the east. In those instances (such as at Wonogiri, Blora, and Tjepu) where a new town outside of this area passed under Communist control, it was primarily because of the arrival of Communist armed forces which had been ejected by loyal troops from some other area.

The program promulgated by the revolutionary regime, or "National Front Government" as it called itself was announced on September 20. It read:

Owing to the state of affairs in Madiun, we, the people of Indonesia, must now undertake to execute the duties of our National Revolution, not only in Madiun, but also in the whole of Indonesia. . . . Only when the people have the leadership of the revolution and consequently of the Government, will the Republic pay attention to the whole need of the people, and it will then certainly be stronger and better able to resume further struggles against the Dutch Imperialists. All other classes have proved incapable of rendering such leadership in this anti-Imperialist struggle.

To achieve all this, the people, in taking all government powers into their hands, must also execute the following:

I. The old Government apparatus, which for the most part consists of hesitating elements and which created a feudal-bourgeois Government, must be thoroughly annihilated with all speed and replaced by a new apparatus, which from the lowest to the highest is chosen by the people. Those elements which are conscious of the needs of the people must be elected to the central government apparatus as well as into the governments of regions and villages.

II. The military power must be thoroughly in the hands of the people, so that it can be truly a weapon in the defense of the country and the people against our enemies' agents internally. The structure and order of the People's Army from the lowest to the highest must be radically reshuffled so that it can receive real democratic tendencies. The army must have closer association with the peasants and workers. . . . Our army must be based upon proletarianism. . . .

III. After the people have taken power, all departments, factories, banks, and other things must be handed to the State, and the workers granted wide democratic rights by placing them in positions of leadership in production and distribution.

IV. According to the laws of a National Revolution, this revolution must be led by the workers united with the peasants. A revolution can gain victory only when supported by the peasants, especially the poor peasants. Therefore these poor peasants must be given lands. Our motto is "Lands for those who work them." All lands that can be divided must be given to the peasants.

V. In the economic field, the People's Government must seize all factories, plantations, banks, transport, and all means of communications and other things which were owned by our enemy, the Dutch. In the towns and villages all foodstuffs must be controlled so that prices can be fixed so as to simplify distribution when necessary.

VI. The whole people, workers, peasants, men, and women, must be reorganized so that they effectively stand behind the new Government. All efforts of the People's Government must be done with the people and for the people. Only with this can the people be a mighty revolutionary factor which can easily defeat the attacks of the enemy within or without.

VII. Internal security must be guaranteed by the people themselves. A Security Department must be established, made up of all socially conscious elements . . . This sort of Security Department will be able to arrest the agents and spies of the enemy. The same Security Department can work more effectively, if in all public enterprises, factories, and in the offices, there are action committees formed, having as their duties the guarding of the safety of the enterprises from all antinational elements.

Further, for the strengthening of internal security, the workers and farmers are given arms. This will not only simplify the means of guaranteeing internal security, but will also lighten the burden of the State in defense as a whole.

That is the only way to discharge our national revolution for the needs of the working people and for the strengthening and defending of our Proletarian Republic.

Freedom! Victory!

Long Live our Proletarian Republic!

The National Front Committee, Indonesia [72]

By the evening of September 20, it must have been clear to the PKI leaders in Madiun that the widespread popular uprisings that they had counted upon were not taking place elsewhere in the Republic. Perhaps they felt that this lack of popular support resulted in part from the extreme and uncompromising tones of their initial pronouncements and that they had alienated potential supporters by going too

[72] Printed in *Front Nasional*, Sept. 20, 1948.

far. Whatever the case, beginning on the evening of the twentieth, the tenor of their pronouncements altered sharply and became much milder.

In the revolutionary government's official news organ of September 21, Musso in the lead article (undoubtedly written the day before) took pains to point out that the Madiun coup was not directed toward the establishment of a Soviet government. The National Front government that the PKI had established was, he explained, dedicated to the national revolution. Only at a later date, after completion of the national revolution and the commencement of a socialist revolution, would a Soviet government be established. Soekarno and Hatta and the "nationalist bourgeois groups" in Indonesia, he stated, had sided with the "Imperialists" and betrayed the Indonesian revolution. There were, however, "progressive" bourgeois elements such as those backing the Madiun regime, he said, and they were still needed in the nationalist or "democratic-bourgeois" phase of the revolution.[73]

On the evening of September 20, Col. Djokosujono, Military Commandant in Madiun, broadcast over the local radio:

Many people, including the President, think that we wanted to overthrow the Republic and establish another Republic with its own armed forces. This, however, is not true. The Madiun affair is not a coup; it is not an attempt to overthrow the Republic. The Madiun affair is only a correction of the policy of those elements which wished to lead the revolution in another direction. . . . It is, therefore, clear that the Madiun affair is not an attempt to overthrow the Republic, but is merely an attempt to eliminate colonial and feudal elements.

An equally mild speech was broadcast by Suripno the same night. On the night of September 23, Amir Sjarifuddin in the last recorded broadcast by a member of the top PKI leadership stated in his opening paragraph:

The struggle we are now carrying on here is no more and no less than a movement to correct the evolution of our revolution. Therefore the basis remains the same and never changing. The revolution according to our considerations remains one which is national in character, which can be called a revolution of bourgeois democrats. Our constitution remains the same one; our flag is the same red and white; while our national anthem is none other than the *Indonesia Raja*.[74]

[73] *Ibid.*, Sept. 21, 1948.   [74] *Ibid.*, Sept. 24, 1948.

On the following day when Siliwangi troops were getting uncomfortably close to Madiun, Sumarsono, the original leader of the Madiun coup, himself came out with a pronouncement, the mildness of which contrasted sharply with his original revolutionary statements. In an official announcement signed by himself as Military Governor of Madiun he stated:

We herewith officially announce that our government has never harbored any intention of creating a Soviet or a Communist government, as has often been stated by our Enemy. The government in Madiun is a regional popular administration, and was established as a part of the democratic Republic of Indonesia.

The accusation that the objective of our movement begun in Madiun is to abolish the Republic is hereby rendered false. This movement is only an endeavor to make a proper correction of the political aims of the Hatta government and of other leaders who intended to bow to the Dutch.

The whole people of Indonesia and the soldiers must support this movement if they really do not wish to be the slaves of the imperialists again.[75]

However, the new tone of the PKI leaders brought no discernible increase in their popular support. Government troops drove their armed forces from the key towns of Magetan and Ngawi, and finally on September 30 Lt. Col. Sadikin's brigade of the Siliwangi Division entered and secured control over Madiun itself.

Thereafter the strategy of the PKI leaders was to avoid battle with the government forces and retire to mountainous areas suitable for long-term guerrilla warfare. They hoped to maintain themselves and most of their remaining troops intact until the Dutch launched an attack against the Republic. They were confident that such an attack would develop by the first of January, 1949. They apparently believed that once it was launched, the pressure against them would be eased and they would be able to rehabilitate their political position on the basis of an appeal for national solidarity against the Dutch.

In their retreat from Madiun the destination of the PKI leaders, now significantly under the command of Sjarifuddin rather than Musso, was the guerrilla base of Kandangan. This was a well-prepared and easily defended area where large supplies of munitions and arms had been built up in anticipation of an eventual Dutch attack. However, before Sjarifuddin could get there, the place was occupied by the battalion of the Sungkono Division led by Major Sabarudin. De-

[75] *Ibid.*, Sept. 25, 1948.

prived of this base, Sjarifuddin was forced to move to weaker, less-defendable bases in the Mount Willis area.

There followed a month of shifting, hit-and-run warfare with the government's troops closing in tighter and tighter around the principal Communist units. As Communist forces became harder pressed, many of them, particularly some of the smaller units, became increasingly brutal. Several hundred civil servants and school teachers were executed by them, fifty-one out of fifty-six policemen in Magetan alone. In particular, members of the Masjumi appeared to be singled out for cruel treatment, sometimes this being limited to robbery, but frequently extending to torture and execution. At Ponorogo on October 4, the armed peasant auxiliary of the PKI, the Sarekat Rakjat, in attempting to recapture the town from a Siliwangi unit forced about 2,000 civilians to march in front of it to screen its advance. As a result almost 500 civilians were killed.

On October 28, the last large rebel military unit, numbering about 1,500 men, was captured, and the back of the rebellion was considered definitely broken.[76] Three days later Musso was shot and killed in a skirmish. On November 29, Djokosujono and Maruto Darusman were captured, and two days later the same fate befell Sjarifuddin and Suripno. In the meantime all the other top PKI leaders [77] except Setiadjit, Sumarsono, and Wikana had been captured. These last three never were. On December 7, 1948, TNI headquarters announced the final "extermination" of the rebellion and stated that approximately 35,000 persons, mostly troops (particularly of the irregular military organizations), had been arrested.[78] On December 15, the mandate of emergency powers granted to Soekarno to meet the situation came to an end and was not renewed.

A major reason for the failure of the PKI rebellion was undoubtedly the fact that its leaders had been prematurely stampeded into action for which they were not yet prepared. The process of fusion of the constituent FDR parties into one monolithic PKI had only just begun when the rebellion started. The new successor political organization could hardly have been in a more amorphous and disorganized state. Large portions of the memberships of the Socialist Party, the Labor Party, the SOBSI, and the Pesindo were actually strongly opposed to the fusion. They were even more strongly opposed to the idea of revo-

---

[76] Communiqué of the H.Q. of the Java Command (TNI), Dec. 6, 1948.
[77] Including Alimin, Sardjono, and Harjono.   [78] Antara, Dec. 7, 1948.

lutionary action against the government. The FDR parties in Sumatra and Bantam opposed the idea of fusion. All of them, including the Sumatra branch of the PKI, almost immediately following the Madiun coup announced their loyalty to the government of Soekarno and Hatta. Even in Republican central Java, several local branches of the FDR parties, including the Bodjonegoro branch of the PKI,[79] refused to back the rebellion and promptly announced their support of Soekarno and Hatta.

Had the Communists had time to organize their revolutionary effort effectively, and had it been co-ordinated, it would undoubtedly have been a far more serious affair. The psychological and economic conditions described in the preceding chapter would then have undoubtedly been much more effectively exploited. However, even had the organization and co-ordination of the Communist effort been optimum, it is probable that they still would not have succeeded. There were other basic factors which probably would have militated decisively against their success.

In the first place, the Communists were attacking leaders who had become the very symbol of the Republic and of Indonesian independence. Soekarno, in particular, had for an undoubted majority of the Indonesian rank and file come to symbolize the Republic. For them an attack on Soekarno was an attack on their Republic.

Also of great importance was the fact that the majority of the peasantry within the Republic was reasonably well off. Though they suffered from an acute shortage of textiles, most of them had more to eat than they had had during the period of Dutch colonial rule, and all or a large part of their indebtedness had been wiped out. For the most part this arose from the fact that they were required to pay the same monetary land tax that they had been obliged to pay during the period of Dutch rule. With the tremendous inflation that had occurred since then, this meant that they were required to pay well under one-tenth of the land tax in terms of crop percentage that they had formerly paid. The fractional amount of land tax which they now paid meant that more of their crop could be kept to themselves, thereby giving them a surplus which they could either eat or sell at the high

[79] At its meeting of Sept. 21, the Bodjonegoro branch of the PKI was reported to have expressed its loyalty to the Soekarno-Hatta government, condemned the Madiun coup, and accused its leaders of being Trotskyists. (See *Kedaulatan Rakjat*, Sept. 23, 1948. This newspaper was the largest in circulation in the Republic. It was non-party, but occasionally its reporting and editorials showed a partiality to the GRR.)

prevailing market prices to pay off their standing debts. Thus the appeal of Communists to peasants who owned the land they worked was negligible.

In addition, the appeal of the Communists to landless peasants was limited except in a few places, notably where there were foreign estates. It was realized by most of those who worked the land that except for these foreign-owned plantations there was little land available for distribution. The incidence of indigenous landlordism in Indonesia was very slight, particularly in central and east Java, where very few landowners had more than enough land to work themselves. In addition, the forced-labor programs of the Japanese had resulted in the death of many farm laborers, and a great many more were serving in the Republican armed forces. These two factors had decreased the number of farm laborers sufficiently to relieve significantly, though certainly only temporarily, the excess of landless peasants in relation to the land available.[80] Also most of the land which the Communists slated for division amongst landless peasants was village communal land, used for paying the cost of the village administration. It was generally realized that loss of this land to the village would mean that the local peasants would have to provide cash funds to pay for the services of the village officers, irrigation, schools, etc. This was, of course, particularly opposed by the landowning elements since it would mean very considerable taxes for them.

Actually one can in general say that the bourgeois group that the Communists so vehemently maligned had suffered on the average a good deal more than the peasantry. Certainly most of its members, struggling as they did on the meager pay of civil servants, ate less than the average peasant. Though they lived in buildings of masonry and brick, they probably averaged less floor space per family than the typical peasant house. In visiting villages the writer was struck by the fact that often the houses of wealthy peasants were much better furnished with such items as china tableware than those of many middle-rank civil servants. Upon inquiry he found that generally such items had been acquired at the market from civil servants who had come to trade their possessions for rice in order to supplement what was purchasable with their inadequate salaries.

Also the Communists overestimated the support they could get from

---

[80] This mitigation of the condition of agrarian labor appears to have been only partially counteracted by the influx of refugees from Dutch-occupied areas. A large proportion of such refugees, probably a substantial majority, were not peasants.

organized labor. In certain areas, such as Madiun and Tjepu, where labor discontent was particularly great, they did get considerable backing. In general, however, except where their troops led the way, organized labor was apathetic to their exhortations for militant action and a general strike.

Finally, they miscalculated seriously the support they could count on within the armed forces. Here as well as among the ranks of labor there frequently was resentment against the government's rationalization program. Here, too, there was dissatisfaction because of economic conditions and thwarted nationalist hopes, for which the government was in varying degrees held to blame. Frequently this dissatisfaction was strong enough to induce elements of these groups to back the Communists in their demands on the government for rectification of these conditions, particularly since they were the principal organized channel of protest. However, in most such cases they were not willing to back them in an attempt to overthrow the government, a government which, despite its limitations, for most of them as well as for the peasantry had come to symbolize their own nationalism.

✣ CHAPTER X ✣

Ideological Orientations and the Development of Internal Politics, October-December 19, 1948

ONLY a small number of the members of most Republican political parties were fully acquainted with the ideology and platform advocated by the leaders of their party. However, it is of importance to realize that *some knowledge* of their party's program and ideology (beyond the mere fact that it was anticolonial and pro-independence) was possessed by a probable majority of the adherents of all parties. This did not mean that the majority of backers of most parties were not usually supporters of them primarily because of their support of their particular leaders as individuals. Nor did it mean that most of the supporters of the Islamic parties did not back them primarily because they were identified with Islam. But with probably a majority of the backers of every party there was some significant degree of understanding of part of its program and ideology and a disposition to support it partly because of that.

There was an active and dynamic minority in almost every party's membership which did attach great importance to its ideology and platform. Because of their own active political leadership, or simply because as individuals they were held in respect in their community, members of these minorities generally influenced large numbers of more apathetic and untutored members of their party, translating for them in simplified terms and familiar symbols its program and relatively more esoteric ideology. They served as a sort of bridge between the top leaders of the party, its ideology, and platform and a large part of its mass following.

Thus, the relationship between the party's ideology and platform and its mass backing, though in general less substantial in revolutionary Indonesia than in most countries of the West, was of real importance.

An interesting aspect of the Communist uprising was the fact that except in a few places the Chinese population fared extremely well. This was a matter of surprise to many Indonesians because in most previous instances where fighting occurred the Chinese population generally suffered the most. There was a tendency for most Indonesians to look upon the Chinese as collaborators of the Dutch or at least as desirous of maintaining Dutch ascendancy. Certainly it was true that the majority of wealthy and middle-class Chinese were unsympathetic to the nationalist hopes of Indonesians and would have preferred the continuance of Dutch hegemony.

Thus when fighting broke out there had frequently been a tendency for Indonesians to loot Chinese shops and occasionally to kill Chinese. However, no Chinese were reported killed during the course of the PKI rebellion, while a great many noncombatant Indonesian civilians were. Except in marginal areas where the central leadership of the revolutionists was weakest, the Chinese sustained almost no property losses. The tendency of many Indonesians was to infer that this unusual development was a consequence of conscious, strongly-enforced policy on the part of the PKI leadership and to ascribe this policy to the desire of these leaders to develop the basis for friendly relations with the new Communist regime in China. These Indonesians note that in cases where armed adherents of Tan Malaka's variant of communism have been involved the situation has been quite the reverse, and the Chinese population has suffered more, rather than less, than usual.

MASJUMI

It was the members of the Masjumi Party who were the special victims of the revolutionists' violence. This cannot be satisfactorily explained by the fact that a majority of the larger Indonesian landowners were from the Masjumi and that the incidence of members of that party among Indonesian moneylenders was high. Probably a majority of the incidents of violence where Masjumi members were victims befell civil servants and teachers who had nothing to do with agriculture or moneylending. Whether this apparently general anti-Masjumi policy arose principally in a spontaneous way from the rank and file of the revolutionists, partly as a consequence of an undoubted anti-Masjumi indoctrination given them by leaders of the FDR,[1] or whether it actually arose largely as a result of conscious direction on the part of some of those leaders, the tendency among most Masjumi members was to believe the latter.

As a result, the anti-Communist orientation of many Masjumi members became even stronger than it had previously been. For a great many the reinforcement of this attitude covered not only the Stalinist Communists who led the PKI, but extended to the nationalist Communists of the pro-Tan Malaka camp who had furnished some of the most militant opposition to the rebels. A lesser but important number for a short time projected this attitude to cover noncommunist socialists as well, such as Sjahrir's anti-PKI Indonesian Socialist Party.

For a time, too, as a result of this general anti-leftist sentiment the influence of the Religious Socialists within the Masjumi suffered a setback. However, they soon recovered the strong position which they had been steadily building up during the course of the previous three years and continued to strengthen it. Just before the outbreak of the Madiun rebellion the number of Religious Socialists on the Masjumi Party Council had grown to six out of a total of seventeen. (Twelve of the seventeen members were persons of Western education, one of the twelve being a woman.) With several other members of the council, including its chairman, Dr. Sukiman, holding views reasonably close to theirs, the Religious Socalists had by December, 1948, come to exercise more influence over Masjumi policy than the remainder of the Council's members combined. Their growing influence was reflected by a gradual shift in the outlook of most of the other leaders of the party to positions closer to their own.

The character of the Masjumi that had been developing since its formation in November, 1945, cannot be understood by mere reference to the constitution under which it was then established. Only a little more than six months later the broad and cautious phrasing of that document was eclipsed by the more vigorous and socially dynamic language of the party's "Urgency Program," of which the Religious Socialists and those closest to them were the principal architects. Among other things this called for: (1) Realization of the Islamic ideology in matters concerning the state in order to be able to establish

---

[1] Undoubtedly in some rural areas economic grievances against landlords and moneylenders were a factor.

a state based on popular sovereignty and justice in harmony with teachings of Islam; (2) Enactment of laws which guarantee to workers minimum wages, maximum working hours, accident and old age allowances, protection as to security, health, and housing; and (3) Enactment of laws which guarantee for the peasant private ownership of land sufficient to support him and his family, protection in the sale of his products, and the general enhancement of his status.

Finally with regard to the general organization of the economy, the program stated: (1) The principal duty of the state must be to open the possibility to work and to have a job to all citizens; (2) The economy should be based upon collectivism in which individual initiative may not be detrimental to the general interest and should be directed towards the general prosperity; (3) The right of private ownership is recognized, limited by the provisions laid down in religion (taxes, charity, etc.); and (4) Capitalism which obviously consists of individual interest alone must be opposed [i.e., socially harmful capitalism is to be opposed].

Not only did the party press the government to adopt this program, but it also undertook to implement much of it directly. Via the Islamic system of zakat,[2] a form of charity incumbent upon all who can afford payment, it financed the measures which it introduced. In Western parlance zakat would be recognized as akin to the tithe that formerly was paid to the Church. In Islam, however, there is no organized church to undertake tithe collection, and if it is to be taxation distinct from that of the state, the community itself must organize it. Without such community organization, the individual is not apt to pay. Masjumi leaders maintain that the Koran stresses that zakat does not mean merely giving the funds collected to beggars, it must be an organized system to expand the economic wealth of the community as a whole and must not be sterile investment.

Late in 1946, in the residency of Kediri, the Masjumi undertook the collection of zakat in order to apply it to the social reforms to which it was committed. For this purpose it established the Sarekat Tani Islam Indonesia (Indonesian Association of Islamic Peasants). The governing board of each local branch of the Sarekat Tani was elected by all the landowners of a village or village complex. Each board assessed the zakat that the landowners of the area should pay. Those assessed then

---

[2] In Indonesia zakat calls for the following yearly payments: 5% of the crop from irrigated land; 10% of the crop from unirrigated land; 2½% of a merchant's trade capital.

had the option of giving their assessment either to the Sarekat Tani or for the support of schools or mosques. Whereas previously the relatively small amount of *zakat* collected by local religious leaders had gone almost exclusively to the support of Islamic schools and mosques, a major portion of the much larger amount now collected went to the Sarekat Tani.

Under the guidance of Masjumi leaders the Sarekat Tani utilized its *zakat* funds for helping poor and landless peasants. In each community waiting lists of the most diligent landless peasants were drawn up by the local boards, and land was bought each year for those whose diligence put them at the top of the list, no repayment being demanded of them. In addition consumer and producer co-operatives were organized among the peasantry to free them from dependency on the itinerant Chinese moneylender, previously their principal source of credit. These co-operatives marketed the crop and bought at wholesale tools and fertilizers for the peasant, while advancing him sufficient credit to tide him over until the crop was harvested and sold. Loans were at the extremely low rate (for Indonesia) of 10 per cent per annum, did not require the usual extensive collateral, and could be repaid either in money or in kind. So successful were these co-operatives sponsored by the local Sarekat Tanis that within two years the large majority of the peasants in the areas served by them had turned to them and away from the Chinese moneylenders. Many of these Chinese were forced to emigrate to Dutch-occupied areas (in particular the residency of Pekalongan) in order to make a living. By mid-1948, there were over 30,000 members of the Sarekat Tani in Kediri and Madiun residencies and more than 10,000 in the Magelang-Wonosobo area. Branches were being set up throughout most of Republican-controlled Java in what was envisaged as a tremendous program of expansion. (Masjumi leaders stated to the writer that it had not been deemed necessary, as yet at least, to introduce the program into Sumatra since the communal organization of agriculture generally remains stronger there and there is also plenty of land.)

In early 1947, the Sarekat Dagang Islam Indonesia (Indonesian Islamic Commerce Association), an organization of merchants roughly paralleling the Sarekat Tani Islam Indonesia, was established under the auspices of the Masjumi. This undertook to organize the merchants for the collection of the *zakat* along the same lines as the collection from landowners. *Zakat* funds collected by the local Sarekat Dagang Islam branches were utilized to establish a Bank Pembanguman Umat (Bank for the Reconstruction of Society). Its function was to advance credit at low rates with minimum security requirements to small merchants and to worthy poor persons needing capital to start businesses. By mid-1948, the success of the Sarekat Dagang Islam had been established, and its number of branches was beginning a rapid expansion.

The feeling of Masjumi leaders in mid-1949 was that with the attainment of independence the government should co-ordinate the activities of the local units of the Sarekat Tani Islam and the Sarekat Dagang Islam, but should not interfere in their local administration. For they felt that the population must not lean on the government, but must be made conscious of its own responsibility and ability to take action on its own initiative.

During the years following the Masjumi's Urgency Program of early 1946, the ideology of the Religious Socialists took on outlines that became more and more distinct, and they became increasingly articulate in expressing it. One of the clearest expositions of their ideas is to be found in the pamphlet, *Politiek dan Revolusi Kita* ("Politics and Our Revolution"), published in the middle of 1948 by one of their most influential leaders, Mr. Sjafruddin Prawiranegara. The following excerpts from it may help to illustrate the viewpoint of that increasingly influential left wing of the Masjumi:

What is the aim of our national revolution? The aim is the unity of the Indonesian people and the realization of social justice and prosperity for our people. Therefore the abolition of the colonial system alone is not enough. We need an economic and political structure which can guarantee the realization of social justice, and this could not be realized in the Dutch time which was colonialistic and capitalistic in nature.

Our constitution is also influenced by socialism, as is proved by article 33. However socialism in the constitution has no spiritual connection with Marxian Socialism, because article 29, clause one, stipulates that our state is based on Religion. The followers of the constitution who are now following Marxian Socialism unconsciously pursue a wrong path.

Collectivism without individualism is like a flock of sheep which can be dispersed easily. It is Fascism if a certain ideology will impose collectivism upon the people by forcibly eliminating a class of people.

Islam forbids the forcible imposition of a certain ideology. Individualism is properly respected by Islam; each individual is responsible for himself to God. Islam calls for the reaching of agreement by means of discussion among the people. In our revolution many Moslems are forgetting the principles of Islam; they support Marxian Socialism and participate in actions which merely create troubles and hamper the revolution.

Our national revolution needs an ideology which can guarantee the realization of social justice. However, I believe that Marxism can not fulfill the need; in addition, Marxism is contrary to the Constitution. The ideology which is suitable to our society is Religious Socialism, an ideology which is in harmony with the Constitution. Religious Socialism does not abolish individualism, individual initiative, and individual responsibility. Thus, not only the freedom of the whole nation is guaranteed but also the freedom of the individual, without closing the door for possible nationalization or socialization of certain vital enterprises. This is the ideal of our national revolution.

Therefore it is not correct to state that it is not yet the time to begin socialist revolution. On the contrary, our national revolution obviously indicates elements of socialism, which are similar to Marxian Socialism. If the elements of socialism do not exist, the national revolution means nothing to us, as it does not give new hope. However, the basis of socialism in our revolution is not the historical materialism of Marx, but its basis is the duty of man towards man and the duty of man towards God.

Therefore the means of realizing socialism must be different from the means used by Marxian Socialism with its class struggle. According to Religious Socialism, socialization is only a means to realize social justice and the people's prosperity. Therefore to achieve socialization it is not necessary to eliminate a certain class or groups, and it is also not necessary to introduce an over-all socialization; it is enough if socialization is introduced when necessary. . . .

Competition arising out of private initiative as such is not bad, but the contrary, because competition increases production and improves the quality of goods. We must not forget that the progress of production and economy in Europe and America was possible because of competition. Only at a certain stage does this liberal economy not increase production and is there a tendency to limit production. At that stage the government must intervene by nationalizing certain private enterprises or establishing enterprises itself.

Generally speaking the limitation of competition and/or socialization should not be introduced merely because of a desire to realize a certain theory; the time and circumstances must also be taken into consideration. If the government organs are not yet well enough organized to carry out and supervise the regulations made by the state because of the lack of capable personnel, and if home production is not yet sufficient to supply the needs of the people, we must think twice before we introduce socialization or limit competition. Otherwise merely for the sake of realizing a certain theory, we will cause our own people to die.[3]

The success of the Religious Socialists in bringing the Masjumi as a whole towards their point of view is attested by the extent of agree-

[3] S. Prawiranegara, *Politiek dan Revolusi Kita* (Jogjakarta, 1948).

ment reached by a substantial majority of the seventeen members of the Masjumi Party Council by the end of 1948. The following is a paraphrase of the principles espoused by the council's majority at that time, principles which as far as the writer knows are still held:

(1) Complete independence of Indonesia.

(2) Following of and emphasis upon the principles of social justice and democracy found in Islam.

(3) The state must be governed according to the will of the majority, with its principal officers being chosen through elections.

(4) Opposition to capitalism in principle, but acknowledgment of the necessity of its continuance for some time in certain spheres.

(5) A mixed economy should be followed—co-operative, socialistic, and capitalistic.

(6) Emphasis should be on the co-operative sector, with the state advancing credit to develop this.

(7) As the government acquires sufficient capital and administrative personnel, it should gradually nationalize transportation, communications, mining, oil production, large plantations, and any large-scale industry so long as such nationalization is to the country's best interests. Nationalization should be accompanied by payment of reasonable compensation to those whose property is expropriated.

(8) Small-scale economic enterprise on an individual basis, so long as it is not uncontrolled, is socially healthy, in particular because it develops individual initiative and responsibility.

(9) Small-scale economic enterprise should remain in the hands of the individual. But only where it cannot be integrated into co-operatives should it remain on a purely capitalistic basis.

(10) Foreign capital is welcomed so long as it is non-political and so controlled that the Indonesian worker is protected and excessive profits are not taken out of the country.

(11) Wages must be equivalent to the social value of the work performed.

(12) In non-nationalized economic enterprises the government should insure that owners of the capital do not take excessive profits and that the workers share in the profits.

(13) Absolute neutrality in the Cold War; alignment with neither U.S.S.R. nor U.S.A.[4]

[4] This paraphrase is based on conversations of the writer with 5 of the 17 members of the Party Council: Dr. Abu Hanifah, Mohammad Natsir, Mohammad Roem, Sjafruddin Prawiranegara, and Dr. Sukiman, as well as several non-Masjumi political leaders. The principles here listed are, of course, not uniformly interpreted by the 17 members of the Council. Moreover, the conservative minority of the Council would put more emphasis upon Moslem education and formal religious practice than upon the socio-economic aspect of the Masjumi program. A few of that

PARTAI SAREKAT ISLAM INDONESIA (PSII)

Within the Partai Sarekat Islam Indonesia (PSII) a shake-up of leadership and a change in orientation followed the suppression of the Madiun rebellion. On July 5, 1948, a conference of the party at Kediri had called for Wondoamiseno's replacement as chairman by Abikusno. However, Abikusno was then under house arrest [5] and could not effectively fight to enforce the decision, while at the same time Wondoamiseno's position was strong because his political sponsor, Sjarifuddin, was still in a position of power. Following the rebellion, however, Wondoamiseno found himself without a powerful sponsor and confronted by Abikusno, who was now no longer in jail. On October 15, he consented to yield place as chairman to Abikusno.

Though after Abikusno's assumption of leadership the orientation of the PSII became more definite, its program with respect to domestic policy, at least, remained far from clear. Its leaders, unlike those of the Masjumi and like those of the PNI, stressed that domestic social reform would have to await the attainment of full independence. It was probably in part because of this that their socio-economic platform remained vague. According to Abikusno, the PSII opposed socialism and considered Indonesian socialists to be no different from Communists. "We respect individual rights and private property," he stated in November, 1948, to the writer. Defending economic individualism, he continued: "The activities of the individual are more intensive than those of the government, and the individual can be better relied upon." But he qualified his defense of economic individualism. "As long as private enterprise is able to meet the needs of the people, it is all right," he said. "Otherwise the government must regulate economic enterprise." Should it be found to be in the country's interests, his party would, he stated, countenance the nationalization of transport and large-scale industries. "The prescriptions of Islam are not narrow," he concluded, "and to a large extent can be interpreted to meet the needs of the situation."

The PSII was strongly opposed to negotiations with the Dutch,

---

minority are much less hostile than the majority toward capitalistic economic enterprise.

[5] On March 15, 1948, Abikusno had escaped from Madiun jail where he had been confined on the grounds of having participated in the *coup d'état* of July 3, 1946. He was not rearrested until June 21, after which he was placed under house arrest until Sept. 17, 1948.

which it feared would never end in real independence for Indonesia. In working to keep the government from entering into further negotiations it was willing even to co-operate closely in this sphere with the Murba Party.

With respect to foreign policy the stand of the PSII was approximately the same as that of the Masjumi—strict neutrality between the United States and Russia and refusal to be drawn into either the Cold War or a fighting war.

PARTAI MURBA

The demise of the FDR parties in Java (except in Bantam, where they had not backed the rebellion) left a vacuum in political leadership which several of the other parties, particularly the GRR, the PNI, and Sjahrir's Indonesian Socialist Party sought to exploit. Obviously any party which could attract a considerable proportion of that majority of the memberships of the Socialist and Labor parties and SOBSI which did not back the rebellion would find its strength substantially enhanced.

To capitalize on this opportunity the principal loosely federated parties which made up the pro-Tan Malaka GRR decided to join together in one solid, monolithic party. Therefore on October 3, the Partai Rakjat (People's Party), the Partai Rakjat Djelata (Poor People's Party), and the Partai Indonesia Buruh Merdeka (Independent Indonesian Labor Party) announced their merger into a single political party, the Partai Murba (Proletarian Party), to take effect on November 7, the anniversary of the Russian Revolution. Meanwhile the GRR continued to exist as a federation of political organizations, and its three principal constituent parties which had merged into the Murba collectively maintained their membership in the federation.

Neutral estimates credited the new party with having about 80,000 members.[6] Its leadership was drawn from the ablest supporters of Tan Malaka, for the most part young men possessed of a militant idealism. They included Sukarni as chairman; Maruto Nitimihardjo, vice-chairman; Sutan Dewanis, second vice-chairman; Sjamsu Harja Udaja, secretary-general; and Pandu Karta Wiguna, secretary. Actually the party's behind-the-scenes mastermind was Tan Malaka himself. In an article in the October 20 issue of the party's newspaper he laid down the official definition of the word "Murba." He stated:

[6] See *Rakjat,* Nov. 12, 1948. *Rakjat* was a PNI newspaper started shortly after the Madiun rebellion.

By the word "Murba" we mean the group of people who have nothing except brain and body. The word is approximately covered by the term "proletariat." However, the historical development and the characteristics of the Indonesian Murba are different from the Western proletariat. The Indonesian Murba is not yet completely separated from the family, as in the West. Moreover, the struggle and the enemy of the Indonesian Murba are different from the struggle and the enemy of the Western proletariat, especially in matters concerning detail.[7]

Among the various working groups constituting the Murba, Tan Malaka included the *Murba Intellek* (intellectual Murba). He went on to say:

The Murba is the result of the exploitation of the capitalist-imperialist Dutch and other foreigners who have succeeded in reducing the peasants, the artisans, and even the Indonesian landowners and middle class that existed at the time the Dutch landed in Indonesia. The Indonesian Murba results from the transformation of the Indonesian "have" into the Indonesian "have-not" during the course of the past 350 years.

The Indonesian Murba class has suffered most under the yoke of foreign exploitation and, therefore, according to the theory of Dialectical Materialism, the Murba class must have the truest desire for freedom and the strongest desire for freedom.

In the struggle for independence and against fascism, imperialism, and capitalism, it is natural that the Murba class forms the moving force, since the Murba class is the largest and has suffered most.

By forming an Indonesian Murba organization with steel discipline, and by executing a tactic and strategy which are best fitted to the Indonesian Murba, the Indonesian Murba will play the Historic Role which is imposed upon it, namely:

TO ORGANIZE AND MOBILIZE ALL REVOLUTIONARY POWERS OF THE INDONESIAN PEOPLE WITH THE PURPOSE OF DESTROYING THE AGGRESSION OF THE CAPITALISTS AND IMPERIALISTS AND LAYING DOWN THE FOUNDATION OF A SOCIALIST SOCIETY IN INDONESIA.[8]

The constitution of the Murba as announced on November 12, 1948, contained among its provisions the following central points: (1) The basis of the party is antifascism, anti-imperialism, and anticapitalism, and it bases its struggle on the orderly action of the proletariat; (2) to negotiate with the Dutch on the basis of full recognition after foreign troops have left Indonesia; (3) confiscation and exploitation of enemy properties; (4) nationalization and collectivization of vital economic

---

[7] "Tafsiran Istilah Murba," *Murba,* Oct. 20, 1948.

[8] Capitalization is Tan Malaka's.

enterprises (including plantations, mining, industry, and transport); (5) nationalization of banking and of exports and imports; (6) to strive for Indonesia's becoming a member of the United Nations and other international organizations on the basis of equal status and democracy, and with the purpose of establishing a proletarian world government; and (7) organization of the Murba Party according to the principle of "Democratic Centralism." [9]

The concepts and phraseology of the constitution in general appeared calculated to attract not only ex-FDR members who had become disillusioned with its actions,[10] but a much broader group as well. The mass party that was envisaged was to be somewhat in the nature of the old Persatuan Perdjuangan of early 1946, and certainly its program closely approximated it.[11] In endeavoring to attract a large mass following particular pains were taken not to alienate prospective members on religious grounds or because of doctrinaire ideological attitudes. Thus at the first public meeting of the Murba Party on November 7, 1948, its secretary-general, Sjamsu Harja Udaja, stated that the party was "based upon religion, nationalism, and socialism, with the purpose of strengthening the independence of the Republic . . ." and that "prior to the attainment of full Indonesian independence the party would not lay too much stress on ideology." [12]

In attracting new adherents the Murba Party already possessed the very real advantage of having followed a consistently nationalist policy, a quality which, in the minds of many, its chief Communist competitor, the PKI, had not possessed. Though pro-Soviet, its leaders were reservedly so. They had consistently adhered to the position that Indonesia's immediate interests took precedence over those of Russia. Emphasis upon this was one of the most vital elements in the particular variant of Communism espoused by its leaders, and this factor put the party in a strong position to attract many ex-FDR members. The international orientation for Indonesia advocated by Tan Malaka was

[9] *Murba,* Nov. 12, 1948. The full text of the constitution of the party is given in this issue.

[10] The lead article in *Massa* (a newly established GRR newspaper) for Nov. 6, 1948, stated: "The Murba Party will make big progress because the socialists from the FDR will not be able to revive their parties; so if the Murba Party follows a wise policy these socialists will join the Murba Party."

[11] See statement of Samsu Harja Udaja, secretary-general of the Murba Party, Nov. 7, 1948, as reported in *Nasional,* Nov. 8, 1948. *Nasional* was nonparty and printed in Jogjakarta. It was generally considered to be the most objective newspaper in the Republic.

[12] *Ibid.*

well adapted to attracting those Indonesians who, though qualifiedly pro-Communist and disillusioned with American policy towards Indonesia, had had some of their illusions about Soviet Russia strained by their belief that it had backed the Madiun rebellion.[13]

However, in attracting the former political backing of the FDR parties it was not the policy of the Murba Party to play up Soviet Russia's moral support of the rebellion. Despite their actual deviation from the Kremlin's line, the Murba Party leaders still professed themselves to be the true exponents of orthodox Soviet communism. They felt convinced that the wave of the future was communism and that Soviet Russia would ultimately become ascendant over the United States and Western Europe. If they attempted to advertise and exploit Soviet Russia's moral backing of the Madiun rebellion, they would probably have lost the support of a large number of the many Indonesians (both those already in the Murba and those ex-FDR supporters whom they hoped to attract) who identified communism with Soviet Russia. Thus they would have cut off much of their immediate existing and potential source of strength, while at the same time seriously undermining the long-run prospects for communism in general in Indonesia.

Therefore, in order to exploit the situation fully and attract support both on the basis of nationalism and communism the Murba Party waged a propaganda campaign to convince the Indonesian public that the Madiun rebellion had no connection with Soviet communism, that it had never been endorsed by Soviet Russia, and that Musso and the FDR leaders were actually secret agents of the Dutch. This propaganda encountered a fair measure of success because of the fact that such top Stalinist leaders of the FDR as Setiadjit, Abdulmadjid and Maruto Darusman during the early period of the revolution actually had opposed the Republic and had worked as agents of the Dutch. (See Chapter VI.)

Some Murba leaders even insisted that the whole "Illegal PKI" established in 1935 by Musso was a Dutch-sponsored operation. They intimated that the United States backed the Dutch in promoting the Madiun rebellion and that an American army officer had been involved. Finally, they suggested that the Communist parties in Holland and the United States followed an imperialist line, inasmuch as they

[13] Though few Indonesians knew of the report of the Moscow radio broadcast of Sept. 19, backing the Madiun rebellion, the tendency was for some to interpret Musso's arrival from Moscow as indicating Soviet sponsorship of his actions in Indonesia.

had voiced their support of the rebellion. Meanwhile, they alleged, no indication of support had come from Russia. The length to which they went is illustrated by the lead article in the Murba Party's official newspaper for October 15, 1948. It was entitled "Sudjadi, alias Musso, a product of the Dutch" and read:

Who is Musso? After the acceptance of the Linggadjati Agreement following the July 3 affair [the *coup d'état* led by Tan Malaka and other elements of the Persatuan Perdjuangan in July, 1946] Alimin came to the fore. People who know tell us that Alimin came to Indonesia in a Dutch submarine and landed at Tegal. His name at that time was Hassan. Together with him came a well-built man [Musso was well built] by the name of Suleiman. The third man of the company fled, while Hassan and Suleiman were arrested by the Republican Army. . . . When Musso arrived in Jogjakarta, no one was permitted to see him. However, the attitude of this Musso was different from the Musso whom we knew before. There is nothing new in his theory. He copies most of the theories of the Persatuan Perdjuangan. When this Musso began to accuse Tan Malaka as being a Trotskyist, people began to doubt his identity.

If this Musso is the same Musso who established the Young Communist Party [a branch of the "Illegal PKI"] of 1935–36, then this Musso, according to the followers of the Young Communist Party, was a product of the Dutch, and the Young Communist Party was the party of Van der Plas [one of the top officials of the Dutch colonial regime and considered by Indonesians to have been in charge of its division of political intelligence]. And the actual name of this Dutch Musso was Sudjadi. Is not this Musso the same person who came to Indonesia together with Hassan, or Alimin, in 1946?

Now another important fact. On the night of August 30 at 22:30 hours a plane arrived at Maguwo airfield [outside of Jogjakarta] and left the airfield at 3:30 hours. According to the report we received, the plane brought the American officer, Colonel Frank, who at that time talked with Musso alone.

After the outbreak of the Madiun uprising no comment came from Russia. But the Communist Party in America voiced its approval.

When the Madiun rebels were suppressed by the government, it was the Dutch who actively circulated false news. The Dutch reported that Musso and Amir [Sjarifuddin] had fled to Bangkok. This false news aimed at suggesting to people that they did not need to pursue Musso and Amir because they had gone away.

When Madiun was recaptured, Amir sent a message to the Dutch for help, and a Dutch vessel was waiting on the south coast of Java.

Conclusion: The Madiun coup was not staged by Communists according to instructions from Moscow, but the coup was sponsored by the Dutch. Amir himself has acknowledged that he himself established the Van der Plas-PKI;

and when Van der Plas fled to Australia during the Japanese invasion, Amir received money from Van der Plas. Amir himself acknowledged this fact. When the Japanese interrogated Amir, he openly declared that Indonesia could not be free without the support of the Dutch.[14]

The official synthesis of the Murba Party's nationalist and pro-Soviet positions was presented in a serialized article by Tan Malaka printed in the newest of the party's two official newspapers, *Massa* (Masses), between November 9 and 19, 1948.[15] Into a series of relatively orthodox Stalinist statements, including a long attack on the Marshall Plan, he wove the following dominant theme.

The international controversy is a struggle between two systems, capitalism and socialism. . . . The core of the controversy lies in the fact that the capitalistic system is prevented from having a free hand in the socialist countries, in the capitalistic countries themselves, and in the colonies and semi-colonies.

To state that the result of the struggle will be so or that the course of the struggle will be so without knowing the facts is not Marxist. We need time in order to take a definite attitude, although we know that victory will be ours and the proletariat will win. This is as certain as that if we sail from west to east we will come to the American continent.

When will the war come? Who will win? We cannot give the answer to these questions because an uncalculated answer will have consequences for the 70,000,000 people here. . . .

We cannot yet state which powers will win the war. Because it might be that the present ally of the Soviet Union would later become its enemy, and the same is true with the United States. . . .

The old capitalism will still survive for a certain period because of the injections it receives. However, in the long run because of too many injections this old capitalism will die. . . .

The part of the globe in which our country lies cannot be excluded from the world controversy. However, this does not necessarily mean that we must participate in the dispute, i.e., join one of the parties in order to attack the other. The primary conditions for an alliance are: (1) to increase one's own strength and weaken that of the enemy; and (2) to take care that you are not eaten up by your ally.

Geographically and strategically speaking it is not yet time to choose one of the parties. Land, air, and sea distances are not yet favorable for increasing our power if we make an alliance with the Federation of the Socialist Countries.

Tan Malaka's exegesis helped make clearer the party's orientation. Actually, however, his statements and such documents as the Murba

14 *Murba,* Oct. 15, 1948.

15 Tan Malaka, "Pertentangan Internasional" ("International Controversy"), *Massa,* Nov. 9, 12, 13, 15, 16, 17, 18, and 19, 1948.

Party's constitution described only the basic points of agreement shared by the majority of the party's more active membership. Among most party members there existed considerable confusion and division of opinion over the attitude to be taken towards Soviet Russia, Yugoslavia,[16] the Cold War, and some of Tan Malaka's geopolitical ideas with respect to the regional organization of Southeast Asia. It was perhaps because the Murba Party did not establish rigidly dogmatic attitudes towards these questions that it was able to attract a fairly large fringe of sympathizers. Such persons were often not enrolled as party members, but they gave it a strong potential should events move in certain directions. It was the party's apparently successful synthesis of nationalism and communism that brought it most of this support. For even a considerable minority of the party's high leaders were critical of Soviet Russia's international policies and some others were at least suspicious of them. It was undoubtedly this feeling that brought some of the party's members to consider themselves as socialists and not communists, stating that "communists base their struggle on world revolution, while socialists base theirs on national revolution."

PARTAI SOSIALIS INDONESIA

Though some members of the Indonesian Socialist Party were anxious to compete with the Murba Party for the support of that majority of ex-FDR members who had not backed the Madiun rebellion, most of its leadership felt otherwise. At a meeting of the party's leaders on November 21, 1948, Sjahrir argued that the party should continue with its emphasis upon developing cadres of convinced socialists, who understood the meaning of socialism and its application to Indonesia, rather than seek to build up an amorphous mass party of nominal socialists who would blindly follow the orders of their leaders. He felt that elimination of the PKI only partially eliminated the threat of totalitarianism and that the best antidote to this threat was to train politically self-sufficient individuals who could discriminate and act politically on the basis of their own training and judgment without having to rely on the directives of a few leaders at the top. Some of the more enlightened antitotalitarian FDR members who had not supported the Madiun rebellion were welcomed into the fold of the Indonesian Socialist Party, but the process was a highly selective one.

16 When the writer talked to a residency head of the Murba Party in early December, 1948, he found that the Tito-Stalin split was already a cause of considerable anxiety to this person and that he was reluctantly prepared to admit that he thought Tito was right.

It was and still is incorrect to say, as some opponents of the party do, that "Sjahrir is the Indonesian Socialist Party." Actually the party has always enrolled a particularly high percentage of independent thinkers some of whom—Hamid Algadrie, Subadio Sastrosatomo, Djohan Sjaroezah, and Sitorus, for instance—have exercised considerable influence on social thought outside as well as inside the party. But there is no doubt that the ideas of Sjahrir have been and continue to be of paramount importance in the development of the ideology and program of the Indonesian Socialist Party. The ideas of some of the party's leaders have in certain respects varied somewhat from his. In general, however, and certainly since late 1948, it can be said that the warp and woof of their social ideologies and their political platforms have been generally congruent with his. Thus knowledge of his ideas provides a general understanding of the basic orientation of the party as a whole. Likewise it helps one gain a better appreciation of the ideas of many nonparty intellectuals as well as those of some other political groups in Indonesia, including the Religious Socialists within the Masjumi, the Christian Party (Parkindo), and even a section of the left wing of the generally strongly anti-Sjahrir PNI. For Sjahrir's influence has not been restricted to his own party.

Though several leaders of the party maintain that their socialism stems directly from Marx, Sjahrir and most other leaders have been definitely "revisionist" [17] and consciously eclectic in their approach to Marxism. It is not merely fortuitous that their party is called the *Indonesian* Socialist Party. Their socialism is adapted to Indonesian conditions, and bears a distinctly Indonesian character. As was mentioned before, they have, for instance, felt that the Marxian doctrine of class war is inapplicable to the pattern of social conditions existing in Indonesia.

Sjahrir is a young man, only forty-three, but he does not feel that a socialist society can be established in Indonesia within his lifetime. The society that he advocates and does envisage as possible of development during the next two or three decades is based upon a mixed economy with a substantial sector of economic life left to private enterprise. For a long time it will be physically impossible, he feels, for the state to direct more than a limited share of economic life, for there is not sufficient administrative personnel available to carry out any widespread management of economic life by the state. There is no

[17] In the sense that the term is associated with Eduard Bernstein.

capitalistic Indonesian middle class from which such personnel with the requisite managerial skills can be recruited, and it will be impossible for a considerable period to train more than a small fraction of those necessary. Sjahrir believes it unlikely that Indonesian capitalism will develop very greatly and has little fear of any significant dangers arising from it. Indeed he would welcome a considerable measure of capitalist development, because this would demonstrate that Indonesians had rid themselves of much of the encumbrance of their "feudal" heritage and would show that they had developed initiative and individualist élan. Moreover, to the extent that capitalist enterprise does develop, he feels that it will have two considerable advantages, (1) it will help fill in those gaps in the economic life of Indonesia that a socialistically inclined government will not have the necessary administrative personnel to manage itself, at least not efficiently nor well enough to serve the national interests; and (2) it will develop people endowed with sufficient administrative experience to provide the government with the personnel necessary to operate the growing government-managed sectors of the economy.

It will be much better for Indonesia, Sjahrir believes, if the socialism that is introduced is decentralized and administered locally as much as possible. He feels very strongly on this point; for his greatest fears are totalitarianism and authoritarianism. Given the strongly surviving heritage of a "feudalistic," authoritarian mentality among many Indonesians, he believes that his grounds for these fears are very real. The Communists, he states, were able to exploit this heritage by building a powerful party organized along authoritarian lines. The Communist leaders themselves, he says, exemplify the effect of this heritage; most of them come from the old aristocratic families, and ingrained in them is a paternalistic authoritarianism.

Because of this danger and because of a strong belief in the democratic potential of the Indonesian people, Sjahrir and the other leaders of the Indonesian Socialist Party insist that the efforts of their party be devoted to political education of the people in order to make them politically mature, critical, and endowed with the capacity for independent analysis and judgment of political issues. Their endeavor has not been to build up a mass party of blind, uncritical followers. Rather they have sought to build up cadres of convinced and enlightened Indonesian socialists accustomed to act, not merely on the basis of orders from above or in terms of dogmatic doctrine, but in accordance with what they as individuals conceive to be best suited to their own country under the particular circumstances obtaining there at any given time.

With respect to Indonesia's foreign policy Sjahrir and the other party leaders have vigorously opposed their country's alignment with either Russia or the United States. Between the two great power blocs, Indonesia must, they have held, remain neutral. But this neutrality must not be passive. It must be a "positive neutrality" and contribute to a "third factor" in international relations. Maintaining and developing this factor is of crucial importance, they feel, if the dangerous threat of a growing and increasingly brittle polarization of the world between the Russian and American blocs is to be mitigated. They do not envisage this "third factor" as a closely organized, monolithic, commonly oriented group of states constituting a "third force" of roughly the same power-character as the two great existing power blocs. But they do see the possibility for states such as Indonesia and India to maintain that minimum of political and economic independence from the two Great Powers that can assure them a fair measure of freedom of action. Through exercise of that freedom, Indonesia can, these men believe, best protect its own interests and at the same time make its maximum contribution towards assuaging international friction, particularly in Asia. The fact that most Indonesians are ideologically protagonists of neither communism nor capitalism is held by many members of the party to be a factor both calling for and making more possible a foreign policy of "positive neutrality" whereby Indonesia's weight is added to that of those few other states capable of generating "third factor" influence on the course of international affairs.

PARTAI NASIONAL INDONESIA (PNI)

During the course of 1948 there appeared to be developing an increasing unity of orientation and action between the center and left wing of the Indonesian Nationalist Party (Partai Nasional Indonesia). This tended to develop a polarization within the party between its right wing and the center-left coalition which was reducing the right wing to a position of increasing impotence in the formulation of party policy. The party principles expounded at this third annual congress on June 24, 1948, by Sujono Hadinoto, its chairman, undoubtedly put more emphasis upon a post-independence socialist goal than a number of the more conservative members of the right wing liked. Some of the more relevant passages of Sujono Hadinoto's address were:

The social revolution which is to establish the new society we are striving for must be carried out through the national revolution. . . . Our goal, the establishment of a socialistic society, will never be achieved as long as national freedom and a sovereign national State have not been attained. . . . From the beginning the PNI has declared that nationalism (socio-nationalism, but not jingoistic nationalism) is the road to a national State; the latter will provide the bridge which will bring us to the realization of a socialistic society. . . . Socio-nationalism is a kind of nationalism which is based on broad principles and differs entirely from narrow-minded or jingoistic nationalism, because socio-nationalism in its relationship to the international world recognizes the duty of the nations to constitute a community of nations, free from domination and oppression, not only in a political, but in an economic and cultural sense as well. . . . National freedom is the gateway to prosperity. The social structure and the way of life we seek can only be realized after the achievement of independence.[18]

The PNI's efforts to bid for the support of some of the ex-members of the FDR, particularly its competition with the Murba Party and the Indonesian Socialist Party for influence within the labor unions, appeared to push the orientation of the party somewhat further to the left. This was probably a factor in the split within the PNI that developed during November, 1948, wherein elements of its right wing became disgruntled and split off to help form a new party. Though this may have been a factor of importance, another development was the chief cause of the split. This arose from a series of meetings between Prime · Minister Hatta and the Dutch Foreign Minister, Dirk Stikker, at Kaliurang between November 4 and 9.

These informal and tentative negotiations were held without the intermediary of the Good Offices Committee and concerned the possibility of a mutually agreeable basis for the establishment pending the transfer of sovereignty of an interim federal government for all Indonesia in which the Republic would participate. It appeared to some members of the PNI that it was possible to interpret an *aide-mémoire* written by Hatta on November 10 as a willingness to surrender key powers to the Dutch during such an interim period.[19] Though when

---

18 Mr. Sujono Hadinoto, *Riwajat dan Dasar-Dasar Perdjoangan Partai* ("History and Principles of the Party Struggle"), speech delivered at the 3rd Annual Congress of the PNI and later printed as a pamphlet (Jogjakarta, 1948).

19 Specifically they, as well as a number of people from other parties, believed it might be possible to interpret this document as meaning that ultimate power to send Netherlands troops anywhere in Indonesia (including within the Republican area) would be lodged with the Dutch High Representative of the Crown during the interim period. This was also the interpretation given the document by Stikker. A reading of this document makes it clear that it could easily be so interpreted.

Stikker returned to Jogjakarta on December 2, Hatta made it clear that his *aide-mémoire* was not to be so interpreted,[20] the belief remained with many of the PNI leaders that he was disposed to make concessions to the Dutch that might result in their virtual domination of the envisaged federal interim government.

Because of this, the PNI made clear its opposition to Hatta's policy of negotiation and began to organize a political front together with the other parties most violently opposed, namely the Murba Party and the Partai Sarekat Islam Indonesia. This political federation, known as the Indonesian People's Congress, had as its principal objective opposition to Hatta's policy of negotiation. With the object of widening its membership, the leaders of its constituent parties scheduled a national congress in Surakarta for December 24–26 to which all major Republican parties were invited.[21]

PERSATUAN INDONESIA RAJA (PIR)

Some leaders and members of the PNI's right wing, however, were strongly opposed to this decision and wished to support Hatta's policy. It was thus natural that they should be attracted to the new party being organized by a number of prominent nonparty individuals who felt that support of Hatta's policy of negotiation was essential. On December 10, 1948, these dissident PNI members followed the lead of a larger number of prominent persons who previously had belonged to no political party and joined with them in launching the Persatuan Indonesia Raja (Greater Indonesian Union) or PIR as it came to be generally known. For the most part the party's founders were older-generation civil servants having aristocratic backgrounds. Though the initial membership of the PIR was only a fraction of that of the PNI, it was generally considered to have a substantial political potential. For most of its members, those previously unconnected with any party as well as those from the PNI, were administrative civil servants whose positions would give them an excellent opportunity to organize the peasant vote. The principal officers of the new party were: chairman, Mr. Wongsonegoro (Governor of Middle Java); vice-chairman, Mr. Tadjuddin Noor; secretary, Kadarman Reksonotoprodjo; [22]   and

[20] He stated that his *aide-mémoire* was meant to express the idea that the High Commissioner of the Crown could dispatch Netherlands troops only to deal with an internal situation where the federal Indonesian government concurred with his judgment that a "state of insecurity" existed.

[21] Officially announced on Dec. 14; see Antara, Dec. 14, 1948.

[22] Following the Dutch military action beginning Dec. 19, 1948, Kadarman de-

treasurer, Pangeran Purbojo. Other prominent members of the party were Dr. Sunario Kolpaking, Sewaka Suwardi, Professor Johannes, Mr. Latuharhary, T. Pello, and Mr. Wahab.

The point of view of the majority of the PIR's founders in December, 1948 can be paraphrased as follows:

The PIR is to be a mass-backed party without the religious orientation of Masjumi and without being based upon the Western political concepts of the PNI. It is to be based upon traditional Indonesian political and socio-economic concepts partially modified and adapted to those of the West. The present is seen as a transitional period between the old authoritarian society and the more Western-oriented Indonesian society that is yet to come. The ballot cannot alone serve to insure that the interests of the common people will be looked after. Not only will many of the common people not vote, but when they do they may well vote in a way that does not serve their interests. They are not individualistic enough to look after their own interests directly and are accustomed to and expect authority from above.

The great danger is that the peasant vote will go to irresponsible demagogues who do not understand the people and are not in a position to represent their interests. The people need and expect guidance from above; this has been ingrained in them for centuries. The people themselves are not accustomed to pushing their own interests in a politically articulate manner and cannot over night be expected to become politically responsible individualists of the character of people living in the Western democracies.

Some means must be found for giving real representation to the agrarian population. Such representation was given them in the past by the civil servants because of the fact that they went out to and among the people and learned what their interests and desires were. Somehow this virtue must be incorporated into the structure of Indonesian government. The leaders of the government must be able to know the interests of the people and must to a very large extent depend upon themselves, rather than upon the people, to ascertain what their interests are. The character of the Indonesian government that is to be developed must allow for "fatherly authority" from above to look after the needs of the peasantry.

It is significant that these ideas frightened away the important younger sector of the nonparty group led by Mr. Ali Budiardjo, which had been prepared to support the PIR on the basis of its backing of Hatta. Within this sector were two large organizations of older students, one of which was the Tentara Peladjar (Student Army). These withdrew their initial support from the PIR when it became clear to

---

cided to work for the Netherlands Indies regime and was expelled from the party, his post being filled by Mr. Hermani.

them that the older-generation civil servants and their ideas would dominate the party. They were uneasy at what they termed an "over-paternalistic" attitude evinced by the PIR leaders toward the peasantry, fearing it might eventuate in an authoritarian political pattern with "fascist" characteristics. They foresaw a party led by aristocratic older-generation civil servants, endowed with what they felt were reactionary socio-economic ideas and nondemocratic political ideas, in control of a large and uncritical mass-following steeped in the ideas of authoritarian rule and willing to respond without question to directives from above. They felt that implantation of the ideas of the PIR leaders would lead to a hardening of the authoritarian political mentality of the peasantry instead of weakening it. On the other hand, they felt that the revolution had already considerably undermined the characteristic of docile acceptance of paternalistic authority, and they felt that the PIR leaders greatly exaggerated it. The renewed vigor of peasant democracy at the village level, they insisted, augured well for peasant participation in politics on higher levels in a manner consistent with the real interests of the peasantry.

DARUL ISLAM

Finally in West Java, outside the area left to the Republic under the Renville Agreement, was a newly formed but powerful political organization also dedicated to Indonesian independence but independent of the Republic. It did not recognize the Renville Agreement and had become locked in combat with the Dutch. Known as Darul Islam (the Islamic State), it did not manifest itself as mere concept, as the usual ideological formulation of the character and qualities which the Islamic state *should* possess. Darul Islam in West Java purported to be the actual physical implementation of that concept. It was a political organization having an independent government, controlling its own army and territory and seeking to expand its area of control. It constituted an aggressive, growing political force with what appeared to be a powerful potential.

The Darul Islam movement arose in an area of central and east-central West Java (chiefly in the Preanger areas of Tasikmalaja, Garut, and Tjiamis and around Madjalenka and Kuningan), where the influence of Modernist Islamic thought had never become strong and where that of more old-fashioned Mohammedan leaders, strongly opposed to Western learning and ideas, had long been extremely powerful. In this area there had occurred during the previous two years a rapid alteration in the pattern of landholding, with a large number of peasants who had owned small plots of land losing all or part of their land to landowners most of whom had only moderate holdings of land prior to the revolution. It is the writer's belief that this arose chiefly through dislocation of the traditional system of agrarian credit during the Japanese occupation and the subsequent revolution.

Before and during the Japanese occupation the chief source of credit for the peasant was the itinerant Chinese moneylender. During the course of the Japanese occupation of Indonesia there occurred a tremendous monetary inflation which often resulted in the easy liquidation of long-standing peasant debts to these Chinese. Having been dealt a severe economic blow thereby and correctly anticipating further inflation, the Chinese moneylender during the last year of Japanese occupation refused to advance credit for a monetary return, but demanded instead a specific percentage of the crop in return for the credit—now usually in the form of cloth, agricultural implements, etc.—which he advanced to the peasant. Still desperately needing credit, most peasants acquiesced in this arrangement, but having already tasted the benefits brought to the debtor by inflation, accepted the usually severe terms of the Chinese moneylender with a good deal more resentment than in the past. Apparently because of this resentment and their awakened feelings of individual dignity and strength, as well as because of increased animosity toward those associated with the old colonial regime—as the Chinese were—stimulated among much of the peasantry by the declaration of independence and the stirring events of the revolution that followed, there was a tendency among many of them to repudiate the debts which they owed to the Chinese.

This was in itself a revolutionary phenomenon. In the Preanger and some adjacent areas of West Java the degree of land concentration, though negligible in relation to most areas of the Far East, was greater than in any other part of Java. These concentrations of land had given to their owners, frequently absentee landlords living in nearby towns and cities, a small—but in Javanese terms large—amount of liquid capital. Some of these West-Java-Indonesian landlords had previously engaged in moneylending activities to poorer peasants. But their operations had been restricted because of Chinese competition which few were competent to meet. Now suddenly Chinese competition was removed, and although the revolution might sanction repudiation of debts to the Chinese, it did not do so to the Indonesian creditor. Thus there was opened up to the Indonesian landlord-moneylender a virtually uncontested monopoly in the lucrative field of agrarian credit. But the Indonesian landlord-creditor did more than merely replace the Chinese. For the Netherlands East Indies agrarian laws, which the Republic inherited, had prohibited the sale of agricultural land to any non-Indonesian. Thus the Chinese creditor, no matter how much he was owed, could not obtain legal title to his debtor's land. (Often the Chinese creditor did manage to obtain a fairly complete functional control, but at least the prestige and social perquisites of landownership remained with the legal owner.) But there was no such impediment barring the Indonesian landlord creditor. He could and did assume legal title to the land of his debtor. This had occurred on an unprecedented scale during the previous few years, and it is the writer's belief that the widespread discontent arising from this among the peasantry throughout much of West Java was utilized by the leaders of Darul Islam, providing them with a major portion of their political capital.

The idea of establishing a Darul Islam, a purely Islamic state governed exclusively by Mohammedan law, had been held by a number of West Java Islamic leaders for some time. But not until the United Nations-sponsored Renville Agreement of January, 1948, did circumstances lend themselves to the practical implementation of their idea. That agreement called for the withdrawal of the numerous units of the army of the Indonesian Republic from the extensive pockets over which they continued to maintain control in West Java following the attack of Netherlands forces. Though within two months some 35,000 Republican troops were withdrawn into the shrunken area left to the Republic, about 4,000 irregular troops—for the most part Hizbullah battalions of the Masjumi—remained behind. There was a tendency for the troops left behind and for much of the population of West Java in general to feel that they had been abandoned by the Republic. Particularly did this feeling grow when the Dutch refused to allow preparations for the plebiscite which the Renville Agreement called for in the territories they had overrun. The regular Republican troops upon retiring had made it clear to the population that the only reason they were leaving was in order to get the soon-expected and supposedly U.N.-backed plebiscite. Therefore the frustrated nationalist aspirations of the strongly Moslem peoples of the central mountainous areas of West Java from which the TNI troops had withdrawn, the recent and increasing agarian discontent widespread among much of the peasantry of the area, and the fortuitous circumstance that most of the irregular Republican troops left behind were the strongly Mohammedan Hizbullah units of the Masjumi combined to create especially favorable conditions for those local Mohammedan leaders who had long been advocates of the theocratic state, Darul Islam.

A conference was convened in an area of Preanger Residency controlled by Hizbullah troops in March, 1948, by Kartosuwirjo and a number of other prominent Islamic leaders of West Java. Kartosuwirjo had been an ardent, sincere, and somewhat mystical religious leader of great influence in south Preanger. Before the war he had been a prominent leader in the old Sarekat Islam and had set up his own Islamic school at Tjiamis. After the revolution he had joined the Masjumi and headed one of its local branches in West Java. Among leaders of the Masjumi his relationship and outlook had been closest to the group which broke away and re-established the Partai Sarekat Islam Indonesia. This must partly at least account for his having been offered in July, 1947, the post of second Vice-Minister of Defense in the cabinet of Sjarifuddin, a post he did not accept. The initial March conference in Preanger was not called to establish a separate state, but merely to organize the population of the area in co-ordination with the Hizbullah for defense against the Dutch. This defense organization took the name of Darul Islam and was considered as an organization loyal to the Republic and, as specifically stated by Kartosuwirjo, with no connection with the Masjumi.

At a second conference, probably around the end of March, 1948, it was decided to convert the defense organization of Darul Islam into an autonomous state, the Negara Darul Islam (State of Darul Islam). This new organization, with Kartosuwirjo as president, undertook to govern, as well as to defend, the population of West Java over which its military power extended. For some time it still did not oppose the Republic, and the leadership stipulated that it would later join the Republic, so long as its own internal autonomy was respected.

The new Negara Darul Islam was organized along theocratic lines. Not only were its chief civil officers kiajis, Moslem religious teachers, but also its laws were exclusively those of Islam. In addition to advocating complete conformance with the prescripts of Islam, its emphasis was on "anticolonialism" and "anticapitalism." Its army, the Tentara Islam Indonesia (Indonesian Islamic Army), successfully campaigned against the Dutch and wrested territory from them. Its civil service collected taxes and ran schools. For a time, apparently, a sincere attempt was really made to run the Negara Darul Islam in rough conformance with the lofty principles of the Islamic concept of what Darul Islam should be. But this state of affairs did not last long. The pressure of continual warfare against the Dutch created circumstances that made it difficult for the actual operation of the government to conform to the theory to which it was dedicated. Even more important was the inability of Darul Islam's original leadership to maintain effective control over the organization.

As Darul Islam became the chief core of resistance to the Dutch in West Java,[23] to its standard flocked most of the religious leaders of Preanger and adjacent areas as well as the peasantry that looked to them for guidance. In addition, many ambitious political and guerrilla leaders whose concern with Islam was very much secondary to their concern for their own fortunes joined the movement. Likewise many of the old-time professional bandit gangs of the area felt their fortunes might improve if they were connected with the military power and friendly peasant base of Darul Islam. Kartosuwirjo and other religious leaders were gradually jockeyed out of their positions of dominance by the more powerful of the unscrupulous, and sometimes fanatical, religious and nonreligious adherents attracted to the organization. Within a year of the Preanger conference of March, 1948, Kartosuwirjo and others of the original leadership had lost much of their power. Though still maintaining most of the top positions in the central leadership, they frequently and increasingly were unable to control the activities of many of their military and civil subordinates. Whether or not Kartosuwirjo and the original top leadership concurred, by late December, 1948, Darul Islam had become openly anti-Republican.

As the organization of the Negara Darul Islam disintegrated, its local military and civil leaders became more and more independent. The duties which were imposed upon the peasantry increasingly took the form of forced exactions. Noncompliance with their regulations and demands for food and services frequently met with sanguinary brutality. Co-operation of the peasantry with Darul Islam was increasingly on the basis of terrorization rather than of freely given support deriving from feelings of nationalism or religion. Even so, the population had little inclination to turn to the Dutch, and those that had the inclination were too fearful of retribution by Darul Islam soldiers to do so. When a Dutch patrol entered a Darul Islam area, it was rarely

[23] Except for Bantam (the extreme west) which, in accordance with the terms of the Renville Agreement, remained a Republican territory and the Krawang Delta area, largely controlled by the pro-Tan Malaka Laskjar Rakjat Djawa Barat (People's Army of West Java), formerly called Laskjar Rakjat Djakarta Raja (People's Army of Greater Jakarta).

able to encounter the population of the villages. The villagers were afraid to remain. If they did, upon the withdrawal of the patrol Darul Islam troops would return and accuse them of collaboration with the Dutch and might kill some of the village leaders "as an example."

The Dutch were unable to suppress or even contain the growth of Darul Islam. In fact in late 1948 and early 1949 almost as much of their West Java puppet state of Pasundan was controlled by Darul Islam as by their own troops. Pasundan officials, including the *Wali Negara* (chief of state), Wiranata Koesoema, were convinced that only Republican troops would be able to suppress the Darul Islam.[24]

[24] This was the unanimous opinion of Wiranata Koesoema and the numerous other Pasundan officials interviewed by the writer in Feb., 1949.

CHAPTER XI

The Second Dutch Military Action and the United Nations' Reaction

FOLLOWING the breakdown in negotiations between the Netherlands and the Republic a new attempt was made early in September, 1948, by the Committee of Good Offices to have them resumed under its auspices. The Committee's new American representative, Merle Cochran, a former foreign service inspector, put forward a draft agreement for over-all political settlement in the form of a confidential oral note submitted simultaneously to both parties.[1] His proposal, which became known as the Cochran Plan, was similar in its general outlines to the Du Bois-Critchley Proposals of three months before. However, it was considerably more favorable to the Netherlands, making, as Foster Collins notes, "several important concessions to the Netherlands' point of view." [2] Despite these concessions, neither the Netherlands nor the Republic would commit themselves to accepting the substance of his proposals and both insisted upon such preliminary conditions as to make the resumption of negotiations under the Committee's auspices impossible.[3]

[1] U.N., Security Council: Committee of Good Offices on the Indonesian Question, *Fourth Interim Report of the Committee to the Security Council* (S/1085), Nov. 15, 1948, p. 10.

[2] J. Foster Collins, "The United States and Indonesia," *International Conciliation*, March, 1950, p. 162. As Collins points out, the Netherlands High Commissioner was given a veto power over legislation. Also of great importance was the provision whereby constituent states of the envisaged federation could maintain their own militias immediately subject to their own orders. As will be seen this concession was of key importance to the Dutch.

[3] See U.N., S/1085, pp. 11–14. (In a purely formal sense the Republic on Sept. 20

Following Cochran's failure and the arrival in Indonesia on November 1, 1948, of the Netherlands Foreign Minister, Dr. D. U. Stikker, direct talks (by-passing the Committee) were begun between the Netherlands and the Republic. It was believed in Republican circles that Stikker represented a more liberal point of view than most members of the Dutch cabinet, and for a time there was hope that positive results might result from the talks between him and Hatta. The *aide-mémoire* of Hatta given Stikker just before his departure for the Netherlands on November 11 (as was noted in the previous chapter) did not clearly represent the Republican point of view. However, despite the informal nature of this document, it gave Stikker grounds for believing that the Republicans, at least insofar as Hatta spoke for them, had come significantly closer to the Dutch point of view. But when Stikker returned to Jogjakarta on December 2, Hatta made it clear that the interpretation Stikker had given his *aide-mémoire* was not correct. On the other hand, the briefing given Stikker in the interim at the Hague appeared to have changed his position to one much less easily reconciled with that of the Republic. Moreover, the cabinet minister who accompanied him on his return visit, Dr. Sassen, the Minister of Overseas Territories, appeared to take a more irreconcilable position than Stikker and to insist on Stikker's yielding ground in his direction.[4]

These direct talks between the Netherlands and the Republic soon broke down over the vital question of the powers of the Netherlands High Representative of the Crown during the envisaged period of an interim federal government preceding the transfer of Dutch sovereignty. The Dutch demanded that their High Representative have the right to dispatch Netherlands troops on his own authority into areas where he himself found a case of internal disturbance to exist. The Republicans, who had gone far in acceding to the other Dutch demands,[5] re-

---

and the Netherlands on Oct. 14, accepted Cochran's proposals as "a basis upon which to resume negotiations," but the preliminary conditions demanded, which were particularly heavy from the Netherlands side, were such as to make negotiations out of the question.)

[4] Sassen represented the Catholic Party, largest in the government coalition, which was much less disposed to compromise with the Republican point of view than either the Labor Party (slightly smaller and the other principal partner in the government) or the much smaller Party of Freedom and Democracy of which Stikker was chairman.

[5] The Republic was willing to agree to the recognition of formal Netherlands sovereignty during the period of interim government and to incorporate both its

mained adamant in their refusal to submit to this. Their position was that internal disturbances should be dealt with by the Indonesian forces of the interim federal government, and that only in case that government requested assistance from the Netherlands High Representative of the Crown should Netherlands troops assist Indonesian troops in such matters. It seemed to the Republicans that submission to the Dutch on this point would mean abdication of the power they had built at so much sacrifice during the course of the revolution, with the result that the independence that they had achieved in the territory controlled by the Republic would be subject to the mercy of the Netherlands government. The record of their dealings with the Dutch did not, they were convinced, warrant their taking this chance. Moreover, in the event this Dutch formula was accepted by the Republican government, it is not at all certain that the latter could have induced the Indonesian army to carry out its terms.

On December 11, 1948, the Netherlands authorities informed the Committee of Good Offices that it had been absolutely impossible to reach agreement with the Republican leaders and that "negotiations under the auspices of the Committee at this stage are futile." [6] They stated that they planned to go ahead and establish an interim federal government without the Republic, though a place would be left open for its possible later inclusion. Two days later Prime Minister Hatta asked Mr. Cochran to assist in reopening negotiations, sending him a note for transmittal to the Dutch Delegation. In this he stated that "the Republic" recognized Netherlands sovereignty during the interim period, but that it asked that the Netherlands "impose upon itself certain limitations on the exercise of its power." He then went a long distance towards meeting the principal and most insistent Dutch demands stating:

We are fully prepared to recognize [that] the High Representative has the right of veto over acts of the various organs of the Federal Interim Government. We ask only that definite standards be set forth or perhaps definite categories of acts giving precise formulation to guide the High Representative in the exercise of his power of veto.

We are prepared further to concede that the High Representative be given emergency powers to act in a state of war, a state of siege or a state of insecurity. As part of an over-all agreement we should be ready to stipulate that the High

---

armed forces and its diplomatic relations into the projected federal organization under control of the interim federal Indonesian government.

[6] U.N., S/1117, p. 4.

Representative himself be the ultimate judge of the necessity for the exercise of extraordinary powers under these circumstances. Again we ask only that definite standards be laid down to govern the High Representative's decision.[7]

Four days after receiving Hatta's note, the Netherlands Delegation made its reply. This was in effect an ultimatum demanding that the Republic agree to complete compliance with the Netherlands point of view within eighteen hours. It stated that Hatta's letter was not in itself sufficient to induce the Netherlands government to revise the conclusions set forth in its note of December 11. It made clear that the Netherlands would countenance no change in its stand concerning the powers of its High Representative of the Crown and that the Republic could be incorporated into the projected federal organization only "on the same footing as the other federal areas." [8] Thus the Republic with 40 per cent of the Indonesian population still within its administrative boundaries was to enter the federation on the same footing as the fifteen Dutch-sponsored, Dutch-controlled states. That it would be swallowed thereby and that Indonesia as a whole would take on the characteristics of the fifteen individual puppet states set up by the Dutch seemed certain to most members of the Good Offices Committee as well as to the leaders of the Republic.

Though this message was dispatched to Jogjakarta as soon as possible, there was obviously not time enough before the expiration of the eighteen-hour deadline to allow the Republican government to assemble and express formal assent to the capitulation demanded even had its members been disposed to do so.[9] Although the Committee had in the meantime in a cable of December 12 informed the Security Council of the minatory situation developing,[10] the Council, then meeting in Paris, had made arrangements to end its meetings on December 16, and not to reconvene before the end of Christmas recess.

[7] U.N., S/1129 (Dec. 19, 1948), p. 3.   [8] *Ibid.*, pp. 5–6.

[9] In his reply to the Dutch Cochran stated: "I cannot, consistently with my obligations as a member of the Committee, press Dr. Hatta to reply summarily on the conditions imposed by your telegram because it calls for a non-negotiated blanket assent which would preclude the possibility of *bona fide* negotiations, rather than effect their resumption" (*ibid.*, p. 10).

[10] In its cable on Dec. 12, the Committee stated: "In light of the statements made by the Netherlands delegation that 'Negotiations under the auspices of the Committee at this stage are futile,' and that there are '*irreconcilable*' positions of the parties on certain issues, the Committee does not foresee the possibility of bringing the parties together in *bona fide* negotiations. The Committee has no confidence that even the presently unsatisfactory level of truce enforcement can be maintained as the possibility of political agreement becomes more remote" (U.N., S/1117, p. 4).

Very likely this fact played a part in determining the Dutch timing.

At 23:30 hours on December 18, Cochran, who was then in Batavia, was handed a letter addressed to the "Chairman of the Security Council's Good Offices Committee at Kaliurang." (All but the American member of the Committee were then assembled at Kaliurang in Republican territory near Jogjakarta.) [11] The note stated that the Netherlands was terminating the Renville Truce Agreement. However, when Cochran attempted to transmit the note by telegraph to the Committee's chairman at Kaliurang the Dutch refused to allow him to do so. At 23:45, the secretary-general of the Republican delegation in Batavia was given a similar note but likewise not allowed the telegraphic facilities to communicate it to his government. An hour later he was summarily arrested. Four days later, four days after the Dutch had launched their all-out attack against the Republic, the chairman of the Committee of Good Offices finally received the message that Cochran had attempted to transmit on the night of December 18.[12]

Though the Republican government had realized that relations with the Dutch were seriously deteriorating, it had not expected the attack. Particularly with the Committee of Good Offices ensconced at Kaliurang in Republican territory and only fifteen miles from Jogjakarta it was felt that the Dutch would not dare attack. (The Committee had arrived at Kaliurang only a few days before the attack, planning to stay there two or three weeks before returning to Batavia.) Moreover, Cochran's statements to Indonesian leaders indicating his conviction that the Netherlands would not resort to force—in conjunction with their belief that he spoke for the American State Department—tended to be interpreted by them as meaning that the United States would not countenance such a move by the Dutch. Republican leaders believed that the Dutch would dare attack only after they had established the projected federal interim government made up of the Indonesian states which they had set up and which they controlled. It was anticipated that such a puppet federation would obligingly call upon the Dutch for armed assistance to help it against alleged Republican frontier violations or instigation of uprisings within one or more of the puppet states adjacent to the Republic. Only by masking their action

[11] Chairmanship of the Committee alternated every week between its American, Australian, and Belgian representatives.

[12] U.N., Security Council, *Report Dated 26 December 1948, from the Committee of Good Offices on the Indonesian Question* (S/1156), pp. 1, 5, 6.

as assistance at the behest of one Indonesian party against another did Republican leaders believe that the Dutch would dare fly in the face of the United Nations and repudiate the Renville Truce. Thus on the morning of December 19, President Soekarno was anticipating the arrival of the private plane of the Indian Prime Minister, Pandit Nehru, which was to take him to India on a good-will trip intended to establish closer relations between India and the Republic of Indonesia.[13] The Republican army was scheduled to begin manuevers that morning, and Prime Minister Hatta was in Kaliurang.

The first news of the Netherland's abrogation of the Renville Truce was received in Jogjakarta at 5:30 A.M. in the form of an attack of Dutch bombers (American Mitchels) on the nearby airport. After the small Indonesian force defending the airport had been eliminated by an hour of heavy bombing and rocket fire, some 900 Dutch parachutists were dropped. They quickly secured the area, and soon a steady stream of Dutch transports began funneling troops and supplies from the Dutch airbase at Semarang, some eighty miles away. Thereupon, Dutch bombers and rocket-firing P-51's and Spitfires began softening up Jogjakarta for an assault by the Dutch Marine Brigade,[14] whose strength was being built up at the airport. Bombs and rockets were loosed at various objectives, mostly of military value, within the city, and planes strafed the streets both lengthwise and crosswise.[15] According to plan, the Indonesian army units stationed in the capital, commenced to evacuate the city to rendezvous points outside in preparation for the guerrilla tactics which they had planned to embark upon in such an eventuality. By mid-afternoon, after having surrounded the city, the Dutch Marine Brigade, augmented by a large number of Ambonese troops of the Dutch Colonial Army (KNIL), had fought its way to the center of the city to the Presidential Palace. The President's small bodyguard resisted, but was soon ordered by Soekarno to lay down its arms in face of the overwhelming odds. By virtue of their unannounced abrogation of the truce and their blitz tactics, the Dutch had captured

[13] Nehru's plane got as far as Singapore, but the Dutch refused to give it landing permission at Batavia or transit permission to Jogjakarta. It is possible that the timing of the Dutch attack was in part a result of their desire to keep Soekarno from reaching India. (Soekarno very nearly left Jogjakarta in a Pacific Overseas Airways plane that had flown in through the Dutch blockade and left Jogjakarta airfield the night before the Dutch attack. Though many persons urged him to do so, he declined, believing that Nehru's plane would arrive the next day.)

[14] This was the crack unit of the Netherlands forces. Before the end of the war with Japan it had been trained at a U.S. Marine base in Virginia.

[15] The Dutch attack was witnessed by the writer who was then in Jogjakarta.

Soekarno, Hatta, Sjahrir, and half of the Republic's cabinet, including the Foreign Minister, Hadji Agoes Salim.

Of great importance to the Dutch was the fact that they were able to knock out the Jogjakarta radio station before Soekarno, Hatta, and Natsir were able to deliver the speeches of exhortation and guidance to the population that they had begun to prepare shortly after the cabinet meeting held at Soekarno's Palace at 10 A.M. on December 19. The content of these speeches was not known to Indonesians outside the vicinity of the Jogjakarta area nor to the Good Offices Committee until almost mid-January, 1949, after an American secured copies of them from the Republican underground in Dutch-occupied Jogjakarta through the help of two courageous Indonesian girls, Jo Abdurachman and Jo Kurianingrat.

On the morning of the twentieth, the Dutch commander in Central Java, Major General Meyer, requested Soekarno to order the Republican army to cease resistance. Soekarno firmly declined and on December 22, he, Hatta, Sjahrir, Mr. Assaat (chairman of the Working Committee and Parliament), Mr. Abdul Gafar Pringgodigo (chief secretary to the President), Hadji Agoes Salim, Mr. Ali Sastroamidjojo (Minister of Education), and Air Commodore Suriadarma were flown by the Dutch to the island of Bangka (off the east coast of central Sumatra). There Soekarno, Sjahrir, and Salim were separated from the others and flown to Brastagi and later to Prapat on Lake Toba, both in north-central Sumatra.[16]

During the next week, Dutch armored columns with heavy air support had reached and seized control of the principal remaining Republican-held cities in both Java and Sumatra. To the world outside, the Dutch were reporting that only slight Republican resistance was being encountered and that the population was welcoming their troops as liberators.[17] To insure the success of this policy they enforced a strict censorship on news going out of Indonesia so that the true facts

[16] Soekarno and Salim were brought to Bangka from Sumatra about a month later. At that time, Sjahrir was allowed to return to Batavia, since he was not a government official. (His position had been as adviser to Soekarno.)

[17] Because of the indoctrination they had been given, many Dutch soldiers started out on this campaign honestly believing that they were relieving an oppressed population from unpopular rulers. The slogan of those marching on Jogjakarta was "On to Jogja to free the Sultan!" It was widely believed by officers and men alike that they were freeing him from 3 years of captivity by the Republican authorities, when actually from the beginning of the revolution he had been one of the foremost Republican leaders.

would not be known.[18] This was not lifted until January 1, 1949. In addition, the Dutch refused to allow the Committee of Good Offices to use its plane for observation purposes and ordered all of its military observers in from the field to Batavia where they were detained until January 7. It seemed that the Dutch wished to present the world with a *fait accompli* and that they believed that if the sordid details involved in their accomplishing this could be suppressed until after their effort had been consummated, the world would be more likely to countenance it.[19] However, to some extent, suppression of news from Indonesia was compensated for by the exceptionally able and tireless work in the Republic's behalf performed by its representatives abroad, in particular its brilliant observation mission to the United Nations headed by L. N. Palar and his deputy, Soedjatmoko Mangoendiningrat, and two particularly dynamic individuals who exerted their efforts chiefly in Washington and New York, Dr. Sumitro Djojohadikusumo (Minister Plenipotentiary for Economic Affairs) and Soedarpo Sastrosatomo (Press Officer with the U.N. Observer Mission).

Despite the meagerness of details available to it, much of the world outside was outraged at the very fact of Dutch aggression, particularly since it was in violation of a United Nations-sponsored truce. On December 20, the American representative on the Security Council, Dr. Philip Jessup, requested an emergency meeting of the Security Council. The Council met on the twenty-second, and a draft resolution was presented jointly by the United States, Colombia, and Syria. This called upon the parties "to cease hostilities forthwith; and immediately to withdraw their armed forces to their respective sides of the demilitarized zones established under the Truce Agreement of January 17, 1948." [20] However, enough support could not be mustered in the Council to pass this. Belgium, France, the Ukraine, and Soviet Russia abstained throughout the voting on its provisions; and with respect to

[18] Thus the writer in telephoning to the U.S. after his evacuation from Jogjakarta following the Dutch occupation was not even allowed to mention that the city had been bombed.

[19] In late December, during the period of censorship, a high official of the Information Service of the Netherlands Indies administration who was jubilant at the course being taken by his government stated to the writer as justification for the existing censorship on outgoing news: "You Americans are a sentimental people; you don't like what we're doing now. So it's best you don't hear more about it. In a week or two you'll have cooled off and have forgotten all about this thing." (It is only fair to state that this official was slightly intoxicated when he said this.)

[20] U.N., S/1142.

that part concerning withdrawal of troops they were joined by Argentina and Canada. With only the United States, the United Kingdom, China, Colombia and Syria in favor of the resolution, only five of the necessary seven votes were received. France and Belgium abstained on the grounds that the Council was not competent to intervene in the dispute, while Soviet Russia and the Ukraine stated that they were abstaining because the resolution did not go far enough and because it did not label the Netherlands as the aggressor.

Two days later the U.S.S.R. introduced its own draft resolution. This condemned the aggression of the Netherlands government and listed the following points:

(1) Requires the immediate cessation of military operations;

(2) Requires, as the first step towards the settlement of the conflict, the withdrawal of the Netherlands troops to the positions they occupied before the renewal of military operations;

(3) Requires that the Netherlands Government shall set free immediately the President of the Indonesian Republic and other Republican political leaders arrested by the Netherlands authorities;

(4) Resolves to set up a commission of the Security Council composed of representatives of all states members of the Security Council;

(5) Instructs the Commission to supervise the fulfillment of the resolution on the cessation of military operations and the withdrawal of troops, and to assist in settling the conflict as a whole between the Netherlands and the Indonesian Republic.[21]

Though China, Colombia, and Syria were prepared to support parts of the U.S.S.R. resolution, only the Ukraine gave full support. Both the United States and the United Kingdom abstained.

Finally on the same day a compromise resolution was introduced jointly by the United States, Colombia, and Syria. Because of its omission of any demand for the troops of the disputants to withdraw to their previous positions this resolution obtained the support of Argentina and Canada, and hence the required majority, the United Kingdom and China likewise supporting it. The four abstaining powers were France, Belgium, the U.S.S.R., and the Ukraine. The resolution adopted stated:

The Security Council, noting with concern the resumption of hostilities in Indonesia, and; having taken note of the reports of the Committee of Good Offices; calls upon the parties (a) to cease hostilities forthwith; and (b) im-

[21] U.N., S/1148.

mediately to release the President and other political prisoners arrested since 18 December. Instructs the Committee of Good Offices to report to the Security Council fully and urgently by telegraph on the events which have transpired in Indonesia since 12 December 1948; and to observe and report to the Security Council on the compliance with subparagraphs (a) and (b) above.[22]

When the Security Council reconvened three days later the Netherlands had done nothing to carry out this resolution and was continuing its forward military action at full pace. In addressing the Council on December 27, the Netherlands representative stated that his government had "immediately given the resolution of the Security Council its serious attention" and had "communicated with the Government of Indonesia [i.e., its own administration there] in order to obtain additional information and advice to enable it to determine its position with regard to the resolution. . . . The operational phase of the action in Java has now practically reached its end except for possible clashes with irregular armed bands." [23] Quite obviously the Netherlands government was not carrying out the Council's resolution. This unsatisfactory reply, in conjunction with a report received the same day from the Good Offices Committee in Batavia indicating the continued wide scope of Dutch army advance into Republican territory, made clear that unless the Council was willing to accept this Dutch rebuff, it would have to take further action.

Resolutions then introduced by the Ukraine calling for the withdrawal of Netherlands troops "immediately to the positions which they occupied before military operations against the Indonesian Republic were renewed" [24] and by the U.S.S.R. ordering "military operations to cease within twenty-four hours" [25] were both defeated. The Ukrainian resolution was supported by China, Colombia, Syria, and the U.S.S.R.; with Argentina, Belgium, Canada, France, the United Kingdom, and the United States abstaining. That of the Soviet received the support of only Colombia, Syria, and the Ukraine, with all the other members abstaining.[26]

Finally on December 28 a compromise resolution introduced by China was accepted by the required majority of the Council, receiving the support of Argentina, Canada, Colombia, Syria, the Ukraine, the

[22] U.N., S/1150.
[23] U.N. Security Council, *Official Records, 3rd Yr.,* no. 135, p. 2, quoted in J. Foster Collins, *op. cit.,* p. 171.
[24] U.N., S/1158.   [25] U.N., S/1159.
[26] U.N. Security Council, *Official Records, 3rd Yr.* (393rd Meeting), no. 135, Dec. 27, 1948.

United States and the U.S.S.R. Abstaining were Belgium, France, and the United Kingdom.[27] The Chinese resolution noted "that the Netherlands government has not so far released the President of the Republic of Indonesia and other political prisoners as required by the resolution of December 24, 1948," and called upon the Netherlands "to set free those political prisoners forthwith and to report to the Security Council within 24 hours of the adoption of the present resolution." [28]

To many Indonesians the original "cease hostilities" resolution, unaccompanied as it remained by a demand that the Dutch retire to the positions they had held before attacking, spelled a tacit confirmation of the latest Dutch conquests. It seemed to indicate to them that the Dutch were being allowed to retain their conquests while the still-intact Indonesian army was called upon not to counterattack in order to oust the invader. It, and the subsequent Chinese resolution, seemed to them to skirt the realities of the situation. The pertinent observations made by the Committee of Good Offices in its report of December 26 to the Council appeared to them to have been ignored. Among other things this report noted:

Negotiations presuppose two parties, each uncoerced by the armed force of the other and each prepared to move toward the reasonable viewpoint of the other.

Politically, the people of one party [i.e., the Republic] without whose support any agreement, even if achieved, may well be unenforceable, will be reluctant to accept as bona fide any negotiations in which again they start with an area under their control diminished as a result of the resort to armed force by the other.[29]

The Netherlands' rebuff to the Security Council following its second resolution, along with the disinclination of the Council to take measures to counter it, was a chilling cold shower for those Indonesians who had staked their hope on the Council's aid. In answer to the Council's two resolutions, the Netherlands U.N. representative, Dr. J. H. van Royen, stated on behalf of his government, not that it had terminated hostilities, but that Netherlands forces in Java would cease hostilities by January 1, and on Sumatra "two or three days later." He then broadly qualified even this by stating: "It will of course remain necessary to act against disturbing elements who, either individually or collectively, endanger public security or interfere with or prevent the supply of food and other essential commodities to the needy popula-

---

[27] *Ibid.* (394th Meeting), no. 136, Dec. 28, 1948.
[28] U.N., S/1162.   [29] U.N., S/1156, p. 9.

tion." [30] Obviously, this qualification could be so interpreted as to give blanket authorization for undertaking military action against all Republican forces which did not submit to Dutch authority.

In response, Col. William R. Hodgson and Faris el-Khouri, the representatives respectively of Australia and Syria on the Council, charged that the Dutch were delaying their compliance with the cease-fire order so as to have time to eliminate all effective Indonesian resistance. Gromyko, the Soviet delegate, accused the "Anglo-American majority" of having encouraged the Dutch to reject the Council's authority and asked whether the United States and Britain intended, like Pontius Pilate, to wash their hands of the question.[31] Though the American delegate, Dr. Philip Jessup, had termed the Dutch reply "unsatisfactory," both he and the British delegate opposed further action by the Council until after it had reconvened at Lake Success eight days later.[32] In fact, no further action was taken by the Council for a full month.

In the meantime, the Dutch continued to flout the U.N.'s resolution. They maintained their aggressive military actions, and they refused to free the top Republican leaders. In fact, on January 10, 1949, the imprisoned Republican leaders on Bangka [33] were officially informed by the Netherlands authorities that the Dutch government no longer recognized the Republic as a political organization with a territory of its own and therefore no longer recognized the internees as having any governmental position. They were informed that the Dutch government would agree to set them free *within the limits of the island of Bangka* and permit their families to join them there *provided they were prepared to give a written statement that they would refrain from all political activity.*[34]

Thus it was that Indonesian Republicans entered the new year with a feeling of lonely abandonment. As far as they could discern, the United Nations, despite its verbal admonishment of the Dutch, was doing absolutely nothing effective to restrain the Netherlands. They felt that they were now on their own and that they could count on their own efforts alone to save their independence. Many began to give serious thought to the last-minute radio broadcast of Tan Malaka from Kediri on December 21. The purport of his speech was that the Indo-

[30] *N.Y. Times*, Dec. 30, 1948, p. 2.   [31] *N.Y. Times*, Dec. 30, 1948, pp. 1, 2.
[32] *Ibid.*, p. 1.

[33] The entire group was confined to one room and a half, the entrance to which was closed off by barbed wire.

[34] This was made known to the Good Offices Committee on Jan. 15, 1949.

nesian people should repudiate the policy of fruitless negotiations with the West and repudiate the Indonesian leaders who had followed this policy in the belief that just treatment could be expected from the West. Indonesians could only achieve their independence through their own efforts, he insisted. They should countenance no more negotiations until after full independence had been won. They must fight until the Dutch were ejected from Indonesia and root out all Dutch puppet states. As 1949 opened, much of Tan Malaka's speech began to ring with a more convincing tone for many Indonesians.

Indonesian representatives abroad near the nerve centers of the West were equally disheartened as to the prospects of effective Western action against Dutch aggression. In general, they felt that Indonesia's future was being sacrificed to what American and Soviet leaders believed to be their own interests in the world struggle that divided them. The Soviet's action appeared to some of them to be more dictated by the desire to embarrass the United States and Great Britain and to acquire a strong propaganda base against them than to help Indonesia win its independence. However, practically all of them saw the United States as so obsessed with the desire not to antagonize its continental Western European allies (France and Belgium as well as Holland), with their strong colonial interests, as to pay no more than lip service to the principle of colonial self-determination. Though these Indonesians could not themselves see that these countries, certainly Holland, had any alternative but to follow America's lead, they encountered the argument that too much pressure by the United Nations on the Netherlands might dangerously weaken the relationship between the Netherlands and the United States and thereby the whole system of Western security. The mood which they found in Washington was reflected by an article of Arthur Krock in the *New York Times*. Krock stated: [35]

The fact remains that the Dutch are the very keystone of the military and economic security system in Western Europe that is vital to the United States. And, as was shown by the debates and votes in the Security Council of the United Nations on the American proposals for a *status quo ante* in Indonesia, our most important European allies will not go along with a drastic program against the Netherlands on the basis of its action in Java.

The delicate fabric of Western security against Russian communism woven with such difficulty and still far from complete, could readily be shattered by an American attempt to isolate Holland unless it completely recedes from

[35] *N.Y. Times,* Dec. 25, 1948, p. E-3.

its present position. Of this, the Government of the United States is uneasily aware, as it is also aware of the stubbornness of the Dutch character, the provocations of Indonesian conduct and the intention of Soviet Russia to make all the capital it can out of the episode. Thus our Government is caught in another dilemma of foreign policy which it hopes can soon be resolved but does not yet know how.

The lack of hope for American support derived by Indonesians encountering this point of view was reinforced by an experience they had in Washington a few days before the Dutch launched their attack. At that time, Indonesian representatives expressed to the State Department official primarily concerned with Southeast Asian affairs their apprehension that the Dutch would soon launch an attack. They asked him whether in this case the United States would recognize new territorial gains made by the Dutch at the expense of the Republic. According to these Indonesians, the State Department official answered, "It depends on the situation." His answer and the context of general conversation within which he gave it convinced them that the United States would give real support to the Indonesian position only if and when Indonesian arms had demonstrated their ability to prevent the Dutch from achieving their objectives. This incident, it is important to note, was later widely reported among Republican leaders in Indonesia.

There were enlightened and liberal elements in the Netherlands, principally within the Labor Party, and a small circle of Netherlanders in the Indies as well who genuinely desired a real untrammeled transfer of Dutch sovereignty to Indonesians. Many of them believed that Indonesians, particularly the dominant Republican group, were capable of doing a reasonably good job of governing themselves. All were convinced that the only way peace would return to Indonesia was for Indonesians to be governed by people of their own selection unimpeded by any strings of outside political control. However, this group of Netherlanders was smaller and less influential, at least until mid-1949, than those representing other currents of opinion.

Of these other groups, the largest, but the least organized and cohesive, was that whose chief characteristic was one of strong paternalism. The character of the paternalism of its various constituent elements had a broad range. On the one hand was the considerable number of those sincerely devoted to what they believed was in the best interests of the Indonesian people and who definitely subordinated Dutch material interests to those of the Indonesians. This group genuinely desired to transfer the basic attributes of sovereignty to the Indonesian people, but it wished them to exercise that sovereignty in the manner it thought best for them. Consequently it wished "independence" to be granted to Indonesia in such a way as to insure this, and it wished it to be transferred to "reasonable" Indonesians who would understand the necessity of continuing dependency upon Dutch administrative officials for at least a decade to come. The majority of Republican officials, it realized, would not enter into such a relationship. The "extremists" and "demagogues" who controlled Republican policy were, therefore, to be forced out of their positions of power and replaced by "moderates" willing to rely on the Dutch for guidance. To insure that amenable Indonesian elements remained in power following the transfer of Dutch sovereignty, a decentralized, federal system of government was to be established wherein ultimate authority would be indirectly, but effectively, under Netherlands control for some time to come.

In general, members of this group felt that liquidation of the Republic was necessary before a federal system could be established. Some believed it might be possible to include it and secure its impotence through a federal system, the political mechanics of which would smother it among a congeries of Dutch-dependent states. However, the preferable course was deemed to be its destruction and replacement by several new political units—headed by "reasonable" Indonesians— which would join the fifteen-to-twenty-member Indonesian federation separately. It was realized that at least indirect Dutch force would be necessary to maintain this system for some time, including the lodgment of military and police powers in Dutch hands. However, it was believed that "reasonable" Indonesians would see the necessity of this and welcome it for the general welfare of Indonesian society, or at least in order to guarantee the security of their own enhanced positions.

Among the members of this relatively progressive wing of the large group of paternalists were such men as the recently dismissed Lt. Governor General van Mook and his chief lieutenant, Dr. P. J. Koets. Such men were socio-economic progressives, anxious to protect the Indonesian people from exploitation by Western and Chinese economic enterprise. They knew a great deal about Indonesia. But one vital thing they did not understand, the dynamics of colonial nationalism. Most of them had apparently lived too long in the distorted, artificial colonial social environment. Whatever the reason, they did not seem to comprehend that colonial nationalism and even their own altruistic brand of paternalism could not mix. In addition, perhaps because of their own wishful thinking, they underestimated the extent of popular backing which the leaders of the Republic enjoyed.

However, among the paternalists there was another powerful wing, larger than the first and made up of those whose paternalism was in varying degrees much less colored by the quality of altruism. To a large extent, their paternalism was a rationalization of their economic interests or, more accurately, what they believed were the conditions for maintaining and promoting Dutch economic interests in Indonesia. For some, the desire for Indonesian dependence upon the Netherlands was a matter, not only of Dutch prestige and the desire to compensate for the smallness of Holland in a world of giants, but derived from other less-easily-described characteristics of Dutch nationalism as well. The outlook of many of them was strongly conditioned by feelings of racial superiority toward Indonesians. This conservative wing of the paternalists envisaged a much longer period of Dutch supervision of Indonesian affairs and a much more direct system of control than did the progressive wing. In general, they had much less confidence in the ability of Indonesians to govern themselves and were more certain that Dutch economic interests would suffer in proportion. They were willing to accept some internal Indonesian self-government but insisted that it be sufficiently contained by ultimate Dutch power to safeguard and promote their economic interests. Thus they were willing to grant no more than a nominal independence to Indonesia.

Finally there was another important group, not so large as the others, but better organized and highly potent. There were two chief elements in this group. The first was represented by a probable majority of those Dutch interests having large investments in Indonesia and an undoubted majority of their managerial representatives in Indonesia. They felt that any substantial relaxing of Dutch control would seriously threaten both their existing investments and the possibility of any future investments' garnering equally high returns on capital. The second element in this group was made up of army officers, from the KNIL (Netherlands Colonial Army) [36] and of probably a majority of those Dutch and Eurasian middle- and upper-rank civil servants whose employment began before World War II. (It should be noted that most civil servants from the Netherlands who joined the service for the first

[36] It is of probable significance that a large portion of the officers of the KNIL had before the war been ardent members of the NSB, the Dutch counterpart of the Nazi party.

time after the war were much more progressive in their approach to the question of Indonesia's political future.)

Here was, in short, the group having the principal vested interest in the positions provided by the colonial military and administrative apparatus. Maintenance of its position was clearly incompatible with any substantial amount of Indonesian independence. This Indonesian-domiciled element, both its Dutch and Eurasian components, was generally strong in its feeling of racial superiority toward Indonesians. It opposed any significant amount of internal self-government, even if contained by ultimate Dutch power and was adamantly opposed to granting any real independence. With regard to all these questions it found itself in close agreement with most managerial agents of Dutch economic interests in Indonesia; with respect to the issue of independence it was in close agreement with most of the Netherlands-domiciled persons controlling or holding responsible positions with the conservatively oriented majority of these concerns.

With the Dutch elections of the summer of 1948, there had been a slight shift to the right, with the Labor Party as well as the small Communist Party losing strength to the Protestant parties of the right, to the Catholic Party, and to the newly-formed Party for Freedom and Democracy. There also appears to have been a shift to the right within the Catholic Party, the largest in Parliament, holding thirty-two out of one hundred seats.[37] Policy towards Indonesia had been a major issue in these elections, and the results of the voting appeared to indicate a slight increase in the relative strength of those advocating a less progressive Indonesian policy. The kind of limited independence aimed at by the *de facto* Governor General [38] in the Indies, Dr. Hubertus van Mook, appeared to be considered by the majority of Dutch voters as going too far in the direction of real independence. It was probably

[37] Seats held by other parties following these elections were: Labor, 27, Antirevolutionary, 13; Christian Historical, 9; Communist, 8; Freedom and Democracy, 8; Political Reformed, 2; and Catholic Action, 1. The Catholic Party was more progressive with respect to the Indonesian question than either of the two largest Protestant parties, Antirevolutionary and Christian Historical, but less so than the Labor Party. (Catholic-Labor coalitions characterized postwar Netherlands government.) The Party for Freedom and Democracy (of which Dr. Dirk Stikker was Chairman) was formed in mid-1948 and made up primarily of members of the former Freedom Party and secessionists from the Labor Party; its approach to the Indonesian question was more progressive than that of the Catholic Party.

[38] His title was Lt. Governor General, but since following the war no Governor General was appointed, he assumed the duties of that office and was the highest Netherlands official stationed in the Indies.

because of this that following the formation of a new cabinet [39] headed by Dr. William Drees of the Labor Party, Van Mook was relieved of the position he had held since 1945. (Because of the outbreak of the Madiun Rebellion, Van Mook was requested to stay on until after it was over and did not actually leave his office until November, 1948.) The man replacing him and holding the new title of High Commissioner of the Crown was Dr. L. J. M. Beel, the outgoing Prime Minister and one of the top leaders of the Catholic Party. Beel was generally believed to be more conservative in his approach to the Indonesian question than Van Mook. The general result appeared to be a weakening of the position of the progressive paternalists relative to that of the other principal groups.

The Netherlands policy towards Indonesia that began to jell during the last months of 1948, and which with slight modifications was to continue until mid-1949, was a rough synthesis of the four basic points of view described above. It was not a completely smooth synthesis; nor was it very clearly defined; and it did not result in fully consistent actions.[40] In its basic characteristics it approximated a position roughly midway between that of the progressive paternalists and that held by the majority of conservative paternalists.

Implementation of this policy involved a three-fold strategy. First, it called for the application of sufficient military force to destroy the Republic and administer a decisive defeat to its armed forces. Second, it called for an over-all program of divide-and-rule, maintained through a skillfully operated form of indirect rule of the fifteen to twenty states into which Indonesia was to be divided and which together were to be known as the United States of Indonesia. Third, it called for obtaining international sanction of this program through the granting of sovereignty to this indirectly Dutch-controlled federal Indonesia.

During the first half of 1949, the Dutch endeavored to bring to consummation the first two phases of this strategy and made formal plans for the third. Though the military phase was beginning to encounter

---

[39] Within the new cabinet, 6 seats were held by the Catholic Party (including the post of Minister of Overseas Teritories, Sasse͏n); 5 by the Labor Party, 1 by the Party of Freedom and Democracy (the Ministry of Foreign Affairs under Dr. Stikker); and 1 by the Christian Historical Union. Two seats were held by nonparty men.

[40] Inconsistency derived not only from changing objective conditions but also from the fact that certain people, particularly those on the scene in Indonesia and mostly those who were members of the most conservative of the four groups, sometimes strayed rather far from the mean position relating to these four outlooks that approximated government policy and followed paths closer to the outlook of their own particular groups.

more resistance than had been expected, there was widespread optimism among Dutch officials in Indonesia at the beginning of January, 1949, that the successful completion of this phase could be expected within a month at most. The aspect of Dutch policy which was most complicated and confusing and whose analysis and interpretation have occasioned most controversy is the second phase. An understanding of it is vitally necessary for an understanding of the projected third phase and also for an understanding of the history of Indonesia following the transfer of sovereignty that finally did take place.

❦ CHAPTER XII ❧

The Strategy and Tactics

of Indirect Rule

THE FEDERAL political system begun by Van Mook and continued by his successors was essentially Dutch-created and Dutch-maintained. Its constituent states, the most important of which were set up in territory wrested from Republican control by force, were of the same general character and were by no means the spontaneous creations of Indonesians. Undoubtedly genuinely altruistic Dutch paternalism was one important factor behind this policy. But it was not the only important factor. Whatever one accepts as the mean of the divergent ultimate objectives of the diversely oriented groups of Netherlanders who sponsored the federal system, their immediate objective was *control*. Certainly that was clearly the objective of Dutch government policy as it operated in Indonesia from mid-1948 to mid-1949.

The characteristics that chiefly distinguished this federal system from prewar colonial Indonesia were: (1) a new and elaborate formula of indirect rule wherein ultimate Dutch control was much more skillfully camouflaged than previously; (2) more Indonesians holding middle and upper governmental administrative posts and having in a few of the constituent states a small measure of governmental initiative subject to supervision and control from Batavia; (3) more Dutch military and police power standing in back of this structure; and (4) more Indonesian nationalists in jail. The small minority of Indonesians whose positive support the Dutch were able to enlist in the fifteen "states" (*negaras*)

351

and "autonomous areas" (*daerah istimewas*) [1] which they established consisted largely of elements of the local aristocracies who feared loss of their political and economic positions under Republican rule, [2] and political opportunists dissatisfied with their positions under the Republic.

The only important exception to this general pattern was in the state of East Sumatra. There, in addition to these two elements, there was a third made up of certain professional and civil service elements possessing undoubted integrity who were clearly not political opportunists. This circumstance arose as a consequence of the so-called "social revolution" which took place in the residency of East Sumatra in January, 1946, prior to the establishment of firm Republican authority there. In the Communist-led disturbances that broke out, the families and houses of a number of pro-Republican middle-class elements, including those of several leaders of the local Republican administration, suffered from the same brutal violence as did most of the much-hated, pro-Dutch local nobility.

Because of their bitterness at this, and because of the fact that it was several months before Republican authority was well established in the area, a number of these persons cast their lot with the Netherlands authorities then ensconced behind British bayonets in the sector of the residency capital and port of Medan then occupied by the British. Though after the re-establishment of Republican authority in the area some of them came to regret their decision, they had already attached to themselves the record of collaboration with the Dutch and had thereby forfeited the positions of leadership in East Sumatran society which they had formerly held.

Once these Dutch-backed states and autonomous areas had been set

---

[1] Literally "special areas."

[2] Sometimes, however, such elements refused to work with the Dutch, particularly in central Java and south Celebes. In central Java the Sultan of Jogjakarta and the Paku Alam (ruler of the small adjoining state of the same name) positively supported the Republic from its inception, the Sultan becoming one of the foremost and ablest leaders of the Republic and pioneering in his realm many of the political and social reforms later adopted by the Republican government. The rulers of the two other central Java states, the Susuhunan of Surakarta and the Mankunegara of Mankunegaran, from the beginning apparently found it expedient to give the Republic their unenthusiastic support. Initially the majority of aristocratic rulers in South Celebes gave strong support to the Republic. Only after the application of a great deal of Dutch military force did the situation there change. One of the most important rulers in Sumatra, the Sultan of Siak, was from the outset a strong supporter of the Republic.

up, other Indonesian elements came to participate in them. In some cases sincere Republicans freely participated in their parliaments out of the conviction that by doing so they could to some extent offset the anti-Republican attitudes of the aristocrats and self-seeking opportunists who were generally the dominant element in their "governments." However, a more widespread reason for what passive Indonesian support these regimes were able to command was economic. "Co-operate, or no job" was the formula employed by the Dutch. Most members of the tiny Indonesian middle, white-collar, and skilled labor classes held out as long as they could by selling the family silver and furniture, their tools, and most of their clothes for food. But after three and a half years of Japanese occupation and a year or two of fighting the Dutch most of them had little of such "resistance capital" left. Moreover, nonco-operation was sometimes interpreted by the Dutch as resistance and in such cases resulted in a person's being sent to jail for an indefinite period. A man with a family dependent upon him usually thought twice before embarking upon such action. The large majority of the tiny Indonesian middle-class and white-collar element had been civil servants. With the Dutch-controlled regimes in the federal areas monopolizing such jobs, the bargaining position of the Indonesian nationalist was practically nil. If he was a merchant or sought to enter trade, he found that the licenses or foreign exchange necessary for such activity were closely controlled by the Dutch. Nonco-operators were generally unable to obtain them.

In most of the federal states and autonomous areas which they established, the Dutch, after jailing many of the most able and active pro-Republicans who had not already left for Republican-controlled areas, carried out elections and set up local Indonesian "governments." The controlled character of these elections was such that the Dutch were able to insure that the majority of those elected were men of their own choice. The amenableness of these governments was further increased by the fact that a substantial minority of the members of their parliaments were appointed by the Dutch. Even so, with surprising frequency appointed as well as elected members who had been thought by the Dutch to be "reliable" and "reasonable" in their nationalism turned out to be ardent Republicans and a source of great embarrassment. In fact the majority of members of these federalist governments with whom the writer spoke, and all of them who did not have a special stake in the artificial regimes, were frank in stating that what limited degree of self-government they enjoyed was a result of the Republic's fight against the Dutch. "Had there been no Republic," they stated, "the Dutch would not have felt compelled to give it to us."

Actually each of these federal states and autonomous areas rested on Dutch bayonets, in particular troops of the KNIL (Royal Netherlands Indies Army) and large Dutch-officered police forces. In several of them, KNIL soldiers were being formed into "state Security Battalions" so that the supporting bayonets would look less Dutch; but Dutch military and police control remained unquestioned. They were police states.

To appreciate clearly the nature of these states and the over-all Dutch strategy of which they were such a vital part, it will be helpful to explore in some detail the political organization and relationships that existed in the most important of them. Of the fifteen federal units created by the Dutch, six were states (*negaras*), while nine had the status of autonomous territories (*daerah istimewas*). Those in the second category were usually much smaller in population than those in the first or else had been more recently created. The theory upon which this distinction was based was that the less populous of these territories (and usually the most backward with respect to cultural level and economic development) were fit to receive a lesser degree of self-government than the larger, and were to be more dependent upon the central government of the federation. Until the actual transfer of sovereignty at the end of 1949, the central government remained the Dutch-controlled regime at Batavia, subject as it was to directives from The Hague. The six states with the approximate populations they claimed to administer (considerable areas often being in fact under Republican control) [3] were: East Indonesia (comprising Celebes, the Moluccas and Lesser Sundas), 11,000,000; Pasundan (West Java), 10,000,000; East Java, 8,000,000; Madura, 1,800,000; East Sumatra, 1,700,000; and South Sumatra, 1,500,000. Except for Central Java, with a population of 7,500,000, the autonomous areas ranged in population from about 100,000 (Riouw) to about 1,000,000 (West Borneo); the other six autonomous areas being Bandjar (in south Borneo), Great Dayak (central and south Borneo), Southeast Borneo, East Borneo, Bangka, and Billiton. (Bangka and Billiton are the two largest islands between

[3] Within 6 weeks of the Dutch attack of Dec. 19, 1948, more than half of Pasundan was controlled by Republican troops or the anti-Dutch Darul Islam movement; about a third of East Java and Central Java and much of South Sumatra also came under Republican control. Effective Dutch control was exercised over no more than 25% of Pasundan or East Java.

Borneo and Sumatra; Riouw is the name of the archipelago of small islands to the north and northwest of Bangka. See Map 3.)

EAST INDONESIA

Established December 24, 1946, the State of East Indonesia was the largest and by far the oldest of the federal units established by the Dutch. According to them it possessed considerably more self-government than any other of the units [4] and was frequently held up as a model to which it was hoped the newer federal units would eventually conform. Because of this it is of particular value to make a somewhat extensive analysis of the political pattern developed there by the Dutch. An understanding of it, in conjunction with the knowledge that more self-government had been granted East Indonesia than any other Dutch-sponsored state, gives a substantial insight into the plans for developing the other constituent units as well as into the over-all nature of Dutch political strategy in Indonesia.

The nationalist movement in East Indonesia had for several years been operating under conditions much different from those obtaining in Java and Sumatra. In the first place, during the three and a half years of Japanese occupation, East Indonesia was administered by the Japanese navy, which sought to suppress the nationalist movement rather than to allow it to develop within limited bounds, as was the policy of the Japanese army in Java and to a lesser extent in Sumatra. Thus the Japanese collapse and the proclamation of the Republic in the middle of August, 1945, found the nationalist movement in Celebes and other parts of East Indonesia poorly organized. Its leaders immediately declared for the Republic and established contact with the Republican leaders in Java. But lacking adequate arms and organization, they were in a weak position to resist the force that the Dutch, supported by Australian troops, were able to bring against them. The Republican administration on Celebes endured until April 5, 1946, when the Dutch arrested and jailed the Republican Governor, Dr. Ratu Langie, and his staff. Since almost all the rajahs and other aristocratic leaders of Celebes had also supported the Republic,[5] the Dutch at the same time arrested their most prominent members, either jailing them or sending them into exile. However, despite the removal

---

[4] The writer fully agrees with this estimate.

[5] In November, 1945, they addressed a petition to the U.N. requesting that Celebes be considered an integral part of the Republic of Indonesia. This was given to the Australian military authorities in Makassar but apparently never reached the U.N.

of these leaders, the Dutch, in attempting to re-establish their control, encountered an extremely tenacious resistance, particularly in populous southwestern Celebes, led by those remaining intellectuals and aristocratic leaders who had not been intimidated.

Not until the beginning of 1947 were the Dutch able to muster the overwhelming force necessary to crush this resistance,[6] and in the "pacification campaign" which they conducted from mid-December, 1946, until March, 1947, they were forced to employ extremely brutal methods in order to succeed. In the areas where Indonesian resistance was most stubborn, authority was given to the savage Captain "Turk" Westerling to do what was necessary to break it. His most effective method was to have his troops round up village populations in the areas of principal resistance and arbitrarily pull men out of the crowd and shoot them, continuing this process until he was satisfied that the assembled villagers had yielded sufficient information concerning which of their members had been active in the resistance and the whereabouts of resistance forces. Probably between 500 and 1,000 Indonesians were killed in this manner, while probably at least 10,000 others were killed in the course of the whole campaign.[7] Most of those associated with the resistance who were not killed were jailed and for the most part remained in jail until after the transfer of Dutch sovereignty at the end of 1949. By mid-1947, the Dutch had replaced more than 25 per cent of the rajahs, karaengs, village heads, and other Indonesian rulers in South Celebes with more amenable persons. Among those replaced were the most important of the aristocratic leaders. These included the Rajahs of Bone and Luwu and the Karaengs of Gantarang, Bonthain and Pangkadjene. The remaining aristocratic leaders, after witnessing this, were easily convinced that the security of their positions was dependent upon their backing Dutch policy.

By contrast, in Java and Sumatra, the Dutch were not able to dispose of force so overwhelming as to enable them to deal in a similar fashion with the nationalist movement there (though the attack of December 19, 1948, was undertaken with the conviction that they did have such force at their command). The fact that East Indonesia was the only one of the major federal political units where the Dutch had

---

[6] Not until the middle of 1948 did the resistance on Bali end.

[7] The character of this pacification campaign provoked a wave of popular indignation in the Netherlands and a special commission was appointed by the government to make an investigation. However, no result of the commission's investigation was made public. Republican authorities maintained approximately 29,500 Indonesian civilians were killed during this campaign.

enough force available to control nearly the whole area is one which must not be lost sight of in understanding and evaluating political developments there. (The only important area of Republican guerrilla strength remaining in East Indonesia at the beginning of 1949 was in the hills and mountains of south Celebes.)

The extent of this force and the scope of its application were observed by the writer during his visit to East Indonesia from March 15 to April 8, 1949. At that time the following conditions obtained. Dutch army units still occupied East Indonesia and were scattered around the islands in units of battalion strength. Dutch army officers were making civilian arrests. All the top officers and well over 90 per cent of the minor officers of the police force were Dutch. The Prosecutor General made arrests on orders of Batavia. Dutch Residents overruled Indonesian officers of the Department of Justice. The jails were crowded with political prisoners living under conditions so bad that the Dutch prison doctor at Rappang, one of the principal prisons, stated that he could no longer be responsible for their health. Most of these political prisoners had been in jail for more than two years and had not yet been brought to trial. Nearly all of them had been imprisoned by order of Dutch military or civil officers. The arresting of people on political grounds was still continuing. On December 16, 1948, over one hundred members of the Badan Pimpinin Pemuda, East Indonesia's largest youth organization, were jailed and had not been released. Members of the East Indonesian Parliament had asked information as to the number and names of political prisoners but had been given no answer. The Minister of Justice, Mr. Soumokil, stated to the writer that he had no idea how many political prisoners were in jail.[8]

Makassar, the capital, along with several other areas of South Celebes and the entire island of Bali were still under a state of "war and siege" (*staat van oorlog en beleg*). This directly or indirectly ruled out the basic civil liberties in those areas. Private political meetings, Soumokil confirmed, could not be held without five days' notice and permission from the police; and when permission was granted, a police officer was required to be present at the meeting; public meetings could be held only if permission were given by the Dutch Resident. Indonesians

[8] Stated to the writer by Mr. Soumokil (Makassar, March 23, 1949). Soumokil, it should be noted, worked very closely with the Dutch and was more of an apologist for their regime than any other high Indonesian official of the East Indonesian government encountered by the writer.

were not allowed to travel from Makassar to any other town without a pass.[9] People were reluctant to speak frankly if they feared they were being overheard. There was no freedom of the press. Editors who were too outspoken were jailed and their papers closed down. Over 90 per cent of the newspapers were being put out by the Government Information Service, headed by and largely staffed by Dutch civil servants.

In those areas where the state of war and emergency had officially been terminated, conditions were little better. In the Minahassa area of northern Celebes, for instance, soldiers of the Royal Netherlands Indies Army (KNIL) had through intimidation kept the largest pro-Republican party there, the Barisan Nasional Indonesia (Indonesian National Legion), from holding public meetings.[10] In addition, the Dutch Resident allowed Dutch soldiers from both the KNIL and the Royal Netherlands Army (KL) stationed in the Minahassa to vote in the local elections there, held on March 6, 1948.[11] The leaders of every major political party in the Minahassa except that made up primarily of KNIL and ex-KNIL soldiers and their families, the Singa Minahassa (Lion of Minahassa), expressed to the writer the hope that the United Nations Commission for Indonesia would supervise the coming elections (July, 1949) for the East Indonesian Parliament; they feared that otherwise they would not be conducted fairly.

The economic control of the Netherlands Indies government over East Indonesia was as effective as its military and police control and helped maintain them. Export and import licenses and foreign-exchange allocations were issued exclusively by the Netherlands Indies government in Batavia and constituted important instruments of political control over the commercial elements of the population. Dutch control of credit sources was equally important. Moreover, since the government of East Indonesia was sharply limited in its means of securing revenue,[12] it incurred a large budgetary deficit which it could

---

[9] *Ibid.*

[10] This information was supplied the writer by leaders of rival political parties in the Minahassa.

[11] This was testified to by leaders of three political parties including Jan Maweikere, chairman of the Singa Minahassa, the anti-Republican party for which the soldiers voted. Interview with Jan Maweikere, Tomohon, March 27, 1949.

The local Dutch military commander was reported to be chief adviser to the Singa Minahassa. This party was largely made up of Minahassan soldiers and ex-soldiers of the Royal Netherlands Indies Army and their families. One of their chief fears was that under the Republic their pensions would cease.

[12] Revenues derived from all export, import, property, and corporation taxes were reserved for the Batavia government.

meet only with funds provided by Batavia. Estimated income of the government of East Indonesia in 1949 was 59,000,000 guilders as against an anticipated expenditure of 95,000,000 and an additional capital outlay of 14,500,000; the deficit was to be met by Batavia. The secretary-general of the Department of Finance in Makassar told the writer that, although he believed that East Indonesia would have to repay the 14,500,000 guilders for capital expenditure, his department did not know whether or not it would be required to refund the remaining 36,000,000 supplied by the Netherlands Indies government.[13] Indonesian officials asserted that it was generally considered impolitic in their departments to exhibit attitudes different from those of Batavia when they were dependent on the latter for so much of their operating funds.

Firm in the possession of these means of control, the Dutch relinquished governmental functions to Indonesians more widely in East Indonesia than in any other federal area. While the transfer of powers looked impressive on paper (though not sensationally so), the disparity between what appeared there and what in fact obtained was on the whole very great. The powers transferred to the state of East Indonesia by Lieutenant-Governor-General van Mook on December 31, 1946,[14] were almost identical with those assigned to the Indonesian aristocratic rulers in that area and in Borneo by the Governor-General in 1938.[15] Indeed, the only important difference was that the powers transferred to East Indonesia were to be enforced with respect to non-Indonesians as well as Indonesians. Moreover, whereas the 1938 regulations applied only to those areas under indirect Dutch rule—about 70 per cent of the area of East Indonesia and a somewhat larger percentage of its population—the new regulations governed both these areas and those formerly ruled directly by Dutch civil servants.

At the end of 1947, the powers transferred on paper by the Netherlands Indies government to the state of East Indonesia included responsibility for finance, justice, general economic affairs, police, education, information, health, social affairs, industry, shipping, forestry, and irrigation; in 1948, agrarian affairs was added.[16] The East Indo-

13 Statement by Mr. Van Ness, Secretary-General, Department of Finance (Makassar, March 22, 1949).

14 "Ordonnantie houdende een voorloopige staatkundige organisatie van den Staat Oost Indonesie. Tekst van de regaling tot vorming van den Staat Oost Indonesie." *Staatsblad van Nederlandsch-Indie* (1946), no. 143.

15 "Vastelling van de 'Zelfbestuursregelen, 1938,' " *Staatsblad*, 1938, no. 529.

16 *Staatsblad*, 1947, nos. 62, 63, 86, 87, 129, 130, 131, 182, 185, 188, 190, 192; and 1948, no. 22.

nesian government actually did exercise a limited initiative in the fields of education, social affairs, health, irrigation and, to a much lesser extent, industry. However, the exercise of most of the powers theoretically transferred to it was vitiated by the numerous general and particular powers specifically reserved to the Netherlands Indies government at Batavia.[17]

Even where it appeared that no reserved powers interfered with the exercise of a delegated power, the East Indonesian government was in some instances virtually powerless. For example, the paper transfer of authority over shipping meant very little as long as the Dutch protected the inter-island monopoly of the Koninklijke Paketvaart Maatschappij, a large Dutch steamship company. The East Indonesian government's ostensible power over economic affairs was limited, not only by Batavia's control over exports and imports, but also by the fact that the purchase and sale of the area's major crop, copra (on which almost half the population was either primarily or to a significant extent dependent for a livelihood), was a strict monopoly of the Dutch administration at Batavia. The latter's agency, the Copra Fund, fixed the price at which the Indonesian producer could sell his copra to the Fund, the only legal purchaser. The price averaged far less than the price obtainable at the nearest world market outlet in the Philippines.[18]

Though the ostensible reason for the Copra Fund's existence was to stabilize the price of copra for the benefit of the Indonesian producer by building up an insurance fund from the margin between purchase price and sale price, this rationale appeared to have little in common

[17] These included powers over the following functions, among others: foreign relations and anything having "a close connection" with foreign relations; defense, including the proclamation and regulation of states of war and siege; pardons and amnesties; the highest court; the police insofar as federal interests are concerned; internal travel passes, immigration, and emigration; regulations concerning nationality, citizenship, and residence; banking and foreign-exchange regulation; foreign trade; import and export duties; monopolies; corporation and property taxes; directives concerning information, radio broadcasting, and supervision over the import and exhibition of films; social regulations of a general nature; and trade, industry, agriculture, forestry, etc. insofar as they concerned foreign countries or other areas of Indonesia ("Regeling tot Vorming van den Staat Oost Indonesíe," ch. i., art. 2, par. 3, *Staatsblad*, 1946, no. 143).

[18] Indonesians and Chinese in Makassar and Manado informed the writer that approximately twice as much could have been gotten for their copra at world market prices as was paid to them by the Copra Fund. This tempted many Indonesians to try smuggling copra to Davao despite the severe prison penalty for those who were caught by the Dutch authorities.

with the actual operation of the Fund. Even despite the low level being paid Indonesian producers the price of copra had not been stabilized but had been in the long term significantly reduced.[19] Several of the more candid Dutch officials of the Ministry of Interior with whom the writer spoke in Makassar in confidence gave credence to the widespread and bitter allegation of Indonesian officials of the East Indonesian government that the Copra Fund was selling copra to Dutch processors [20] at far below the world market price and that most of the still substantial margin between this price and that paid the Indonesian producer was not used to stabilize the price of copra but rather went directly into the coffers of the Netherlands Indies government. This amount, Indonesian officials in Makassar alleged, was considerably greater than the deficit in the East Indonesian budget for which their government was dependent upon annual subventions from Batavia. The East Indonesian government was powerless to remedy this situation, and it and its Parliament were unable to learn from the Copra Fund what the latter's income was or what price it was selling the copra for.[21]

Apart from all this, however, the lack of Indonesian personnel available to the East Indonesian government hindered its exercise of the functions allowed it and facilitated control by Batavia. Since so many of its own people were either in the service of the Republic or in jail, East Indonesia relied heavily on Dutch personnel to execute even the limited duties assigned to it. Although all cabinet posts except that of Finance (a critically important one) were filled by Indonesians,[22] the majority of the remaining high government positions were filled by Dutch civil servants put "at the disposal" of the government of East Indonesia by the Netherlands Indies government at Batavia. Certainly some of these Dutch officials, particularly those without prewar experience in Indonesia, did try to serve primarily East Indonesia rather than Batavia; but they quite naturally tended to regard themselves as Netherlanders first of all, and their actions were often likely to be

[19] In March, 1949, the price was reduced by an additional 10% (Netherlands Indies government information service, A.E. 1087, Batavia, March 17, 1949).

[20] *Ibid.* It is of significance that out of a total East Indonesian copra export of 20,662 tons for February, 1949, the latest figure available to the writer, 18,122 tons was shipped to the Netherlands; 2,032 tons to Belgium (which had a customs union with the Netherlands); and the rest, 508 tons, to Switzerland.

[21] When the writer in an interview with Mr. A. F. Jeronimus, assistant to the director of the Copra Fund at Makassar, asked why this was, the latter stated that this information could not be divulged (Makassar, March 24, 1949).

[22] The Minister of Economic Affairs was an Indies-born Chinese, and the Minister of Health was a Eurasian.

influenced by what they deemed to be in the best interests of Holland as well as of East Indonesia. Although Batavia on occasion supported the Prime Minister of East Indonesia against high Dutch officials in the employ of his government,[23] most Indonesians in the government appeared to be convinced that Dutch officials of East Indonesia commonly acted as agents of Batavia and that, in the unlikely event of their decisions' being contested by Indonesians, the Dutch could generally count on backing from Batavia.

In administrative affairs a more complete transfer of authority was in train. Dutch civil servants were being replaced by local councils administering the regulations stemming from both the powers reserved to Batavia and those delegated to the government of East Indonesia. These local councils were, in addition, receiving certain subordinate legislative powers. At the level of the *daerah* (territory), of which there were thirteen in East Indonesia,[24] the authority transferred to the councils was, in theory, to correspond to that formerly exercised by a Dutch Resident; at the next lower level, that of a district, it was to correspond to that of an Assistant Resident. On the *daerah* level (except in Minahassa and South Moluccas, where elected people's councils existed) such powers were entrusted to councils of aristocratic rulers possessing both executive and legislative powers. In theory, this legislative power was shared with indirectly elected people's councils, but in fact at least as late as April, 1949, the latter remained merely advisory bodies. At the district level, all legislative authority was reserved to councils of aristocratic leaders; the role of the people's council there was, even in theory, wholly consultative. Despite the widespread establishment of such councils, Dutch and Indonesian members of the East Indonesian government told the writer that, with the exception of Bali, and to a lesser extent, the Minahassa and South Moluccas, Dutch Residents, Assistant Residents, and *Controleurs* who remained as advisers to these councils continued to exert decisive influence on local affairs.

The limited experience of the writer lent substance to this assertion. For instance, when he interviewed the *Arumpone* (Rajah of Bone), chairman of the *Hadat Tinggi* (High Council) of the *Daerah* of South Celebes, the Dutch secretary of the Rajah, an Assistant Resident, in-

---

[23] One Dutch resident was transferred elsewhere from East Indonesia at the insistence of the Prime Minister.

[24] South Celebes, North Celebes, Middle Celebes, Minahassa, Sanghe and Talaud Islands, Bali, Lombok, Sumbawa, Flores, Sumba, Timur and Islands, South Moluccas, and North Moluccas.

structed him as to how to answer the writer, his instructions being given in Indonesian. In answer to one of the writer's questions the Rajah's initial reply was that the United Nations should intervene in the dispute between the Netherlands and the Republic. Upon being politely admonished by the Assistant Resident, he gave the answer which the latter suggested as being most appropriate, namely that he was in complete agreement with the position taken by the Batavia government on this question.

At a meeting of the District Council of Pangkadjene in southwest Celebes (established in May, 1947) attended by the writer, he was told beforehand by the local Assistant Resident that the latter was there merely as a guest. However, the Assistant Resident dominated the meeting; he offered most of the proposals, and all those made by him were adopted.

In Bali, where the few remaining Dutch officials actually had come to limit themselves to advisory functions, the Rajah Council had exhibited authoritarian tendencies. In April, 1947, prior to the transfer of administrative authority by the Dutch to this body, it had been able to control elections to the Bali People's Council to such an extent that few nonamenable elements were elected to it. (Well over half of that body's thirty-four members were civil employees of the Bali government whose jobs were dependent upon maintaining good relations with the executive organ of that government, the Rajah Council). During the course of these elections in two rajahdoms, a sizeable number of pro-Republicans were elected to the People's Council, whereupon the Rajah Council annulled the results of the elections in these areas and ordered new ones held. This second time the rajahs were more successful. (It should be noted that the Dutch army still occupied the island and a state of war and siege still prevailed there, conditions which continued to exist when the writer visited Bali in April, 1949.)

In the spring of 1949, most Indonesian intellectuals in East Indonesia felt that the Dutch were imposing a political system which would dam or force into Dutch-controlled channels their nationalistic impulses. They believed that this system reserved positions of political power to those Indonesians most ready to compromise Indonesian in favor of Dutch interests, and that it developed for such men a vested interest in maintaining East Indonesia in a state of pseudo-independence in which their retention of political power was contingent upon Dutch support. They feared that they were being saddled with a political system which would be controlled by and operated for the benefit of the Dutch and a small reactionary minority of indigenous aristocrats and political opportunists, and that under it the social change which they identified with nationalism would be unobtainable. They believed that it was not through mere physical force that the Dutch were establishing control over East Indonesia. In varying degrees they perceived them to be coupling this application of force with a pattern of shrewd political maneuvers and a subtle system of political mechanics which dovetailed with their basic policy of force, making it both more effective in function and more respectable in appearance.

The process of supplementing physical and economic force with political means started with the Den Pasar Conference, which set up the state of East Indonesia. It was called by Lt. Governor-General van Mook and held December 18–24, 1946. According to official Dutch publications fifty-five of the seventy delegates to the conference were elected and fifteen appointed. It is perhaps hard to understand why at least forty of those elected were either employees of the Netherlands East Indies government or aristocratic rulers and members of their staffs [25] unless one notes that those members referred to as "elected" were chosen by councils appointed by, or largely appointed by, the Dutch Residents. These seventy delegates together elected a Balinese nobleman, Tjokorde Gde Rake Sukawati, as President of East Indonesia. These seventy plus a later addition of seven appointees of the President [26] became the Provisional Parliament of East Indonesia.

When the Parliament began to meet, it soon became apparent that a considerable number of these Indonesians employed by the Netherlands Indies government were talking in terms of undiluted Indonesian nationalism and unabashed support of the Republic rather than in terms of a nationalism tempered to suit the minimum objectives of the Dutch, a line which might have seemed to be more compatible with their immediate economic security and pensions to come.

For their part, most of the aristocratic element [27] became alarmed

[25] *Staatsblad,* 1946, no. 144.

[26] As of Feb. 19, 1949. The President had the right to appoint a total of 10 members. Of these 7, 4 were civil servants (one being a Eurasian); one was a pastor; one was Dutch; and one was Chinese. *Daftar Nama Anggota 2 Badan Perwakilan Sementara Negara Indonesia* (Makassar, Feb. 10, 1949).

[27] It should be noted that the majority of aristocratic rulers had very little education. This was particularly true in South Celebes, an area containing over one-third of East Indonesia's population. One of the best educated of the rulers of this area estimated that following the Dutch purge of 1946–1947 more than 80% of these rulers had only three years of schooling or less and that only 3% had more than 7 years of schooling.

over the tendency toward social reform displayed by many of these same members. With only twenty representatives in the Parliament, and even a few of these inclined to advocate progressive social legislation, most aristocrats felt their positions and their prerogatives insecure. Moreover their Dutch advisers and other Dutch civil servants had implanted in the minds of most of them the firm conviction that the Republic stood for the immediate abolishment of their powers and wealth. Most of them, particularly those who had replaced the actively pro-Republican rajahs and karaengs in 1946, felt that the security of their positions demanded the retention of ultimate Dutch authority in East Indonesia. Thus they were easily convinced of the necessity of building up a state as completely divorced from the Republican areas of Indonesia as possible and possessed of a constitutional structure that would insure them an unassailably dominant position therein.

The chief political weapon of the Dutch in bending this situation to their purpose was their relationship with the aristocratic Indonesian rulers. These rulers were in most cases dependent upon the military and police power with which the Dutch buttressed them. In addition, they all were legally bound to the Dutch by a political contract known as the Short Declaration (*Korte Verklaring*). Under these contracts each ruler recognized the sovereignty of the Netherlands, swore loyalty (on the Koran if he was a Mohammedan) to the Queen and the Governor General, and agreed to obey all regulations applicable to his area made by the appropriate Dutch authorities. The importance of this relationship can be appreciated when it is recalled that approximately 70 per cent of the area and 75 per cent of the population of East Indonesia were governed through these aristocratic rulers. A major objective of nationalist elements in the East Indonesian Parliament was to remove this manifestation of colonial status. In their desire to have the government of East Indonesia replace that of the Netherlands as the chief partner in the contract with the aristocratic leaders, many strong nationalists overlooked the possibility that in the process they might lose much of what power they already had within the government of East Indonesia. During the late spring and early summer of 1949 they did in fact suffer just such a loss.

In order to maintain their position, the aristocratic elements followed a course enabling the Netherlands to secure a more effective political control over East Indonesia unembarrassed by outward signs of such control. The Short Declaration contracts were renegotiated, with the state of East Indonesia replacing the Netherlands as sovereign.

However, in return for accepting this change, these aristocratic rulers obtained a position in the government of East Indonesia, their new sovereign, which assured them not only of being able to defend the positions and privileges which they enjoyed under the old Dutch regime, but also substantially increased their power relative to that of the pro-Republican element in that government. In accordance with their demands, a Senate was established on May 28, 1949.[28] This body had thirteen members, one from each *daerah* government. Since the aristocratic elements controlled ten of these,[29] they were assured of absolute control of the Senate, and, in fact ten members of the new Senate were from their group. The new and final constitution that was being prepared for East Indonesia jointly by the Dutch and the existing Provisional Parliament could not be introduced until ratified by this Senate.[30] This being the case, it was generally expected that the constitution finally ratified would protect the interests of the aristocratic rulers and guarantee them a strong position in the new government. This was exactly what did happen. Its provisions specifically protected "uncurtailed" the rights of their private domains as outlined in the political contracts inherited from the Dutch; [31] In addition, all such contracts had to be approved by the Senate.[32] Moreover the method of election of the President, whose office commanded very considerable powers (including dissolution of Parliament and calling of new elections as well as appointment of the Prime Minister) [33] was such as to make it virtually certain that no one other than a representative of the aristocratic rulers could be elected to that office.[34] Sukawati,

[28] The ultimate provision for a senate had been adumbrated in the Den Pasar regulations, but the exact powers it would exercise upon its establishment had not been fixed ("Regeling tot Vorming van den Staat Oost-Indonesia," ch. 1, art. 4, *Staatsblad*, 1946, no. 143).

[29] All but Minahassa, South Moluccas and Lombok. These three areas had formerly been directly governed by the Dutch rather than indirectly through a local nobility. In the other 10 *daerahs* Rajah Councils chose their senators.

[30] Those sections of the Constitution relating to the establishment of the Senate and the maintenance of the position of the aristocratic rulers were drafted provisionally at a joint conference of representatives of the Provisional Parliament, the aristocratic leaders, and the Dutch Crown at Malino in May, 1948. The character of the decisions arrived at in the conference indicated that the aristocratic rulers and the Dutch dominated the proceedings.

[31] *Constitution of the State of East Indonesia* (Advance Dutch language edition, mimeo., Makassar, 1949), art. 93, (1).

[32] *Ibid.*, art. 93 (2).

[33] *Ibid.*, art. 15 (2); art. 72 (1) and (2).

[34] The Constitution provided that the President be elected by a college of electors composed of: "(a) the members of the Parliament, (b) the members of the Senate,

the Balinese nobleman, remained as President, and it seemed certain that under the new constitution any successor of his would be from the same class.

In addition to a full right of veto with respect to legislation concerning the areas administered by the indigenous nobility, the Senate was provided by the Constitution with considerable powers over the whole range of legislation. Any legislation with which it disagreed it could hold up for as long as a year unless it was overridden by a two-thirds majority of the House of Representatives.[35] Thus it held a virtual power of veto with respect to budgetary matters. Moreover, since approximately one-third of the members of the lower house had outlooks similar to or easily harmonizable with those of the majority of the Senate, the possibility of overriding its year-long deferment of a bill was slight. Though there was some danger of such a majority being mustered by the old Provisional Parliament, this danger was removed by the introduction of a new election law so designed as to make almost certain that more than one-third of the membership of Parliament would have points of view in general similar to those of the Senate majority.[36] By the elections held under this law in the summer of

---

(c) two electors from each *daerah* to be chosen by an absolute majority of votes by the legally named governing organs of each *daerah*" (art. 17 [2]). Since 10 of the 13 daerahs had Rajah Councils as their dominant governing organ this meant that 20 out of the 26 electors from category "c" would be certain to have the same general outlook as the 10 senators elected by the same Rajah Councils. These combined with the one-third of the members of the new Parliament of 73 members who could be expected to support the aristocratic rulers added up to a block of more than 50 out of an electoral college of 112. This was much bigger than the pro-Republican bloc in Parliament and moreover it could count upon the support of not only a probable majority of the Dutch and Chinese members of Parliament but almost certainly upon that of a few of the more opportunistic of the Indonesian members who did not themselves represent the aristocratic element. Quite apart from this, the fact that the Constitution stipulated that the President be elected by "an absolute majority" of the electors [art. 17 (1)] made it almost certain that any group which controlled 50 votes would get its way. Those representatives of the aristocratic rulers who might desert their group were few. Also 10 of the 73 members of the new Parliament were appointed by the incumbent President Sukawati, this being stipulated in the new election law.

35 *Ibid.*, art. 80–87.

36 In large measure this was accomplished by drawing the boundaries of election districts to coincide as much as possible with boundaries of the major aristocratically governed domains. For instance, Bali, rather than constituting a single election district with candidates chosen on a basis of proportional representation (as desired by pro-Republican elements), was divided into 8 election districts (each of which could elect just one candidate), each approximately the area governed by one of the rajahs.

1949, the representation of the aristocratic rulers in Parliament increased substantially and was well over one-third.

In general, the changes in the system and composition of the East Indonesia government between December, 1948 (when its cabinet resigned in protest against the Dutch attack on the Republic), and July, 1949, were such as to make it significantly less pro-Republican in character and more amenable to the interests of anti-Republican aristocratic elements and their Dutch sponsors.

PASUNDAN

The second largest of the states established by the Dutch, Pasundan, was much younger than East Indonesia, dating only from the spring of 1948. Like the latter, it had been formed on the initiative of the Dutch and was brought into existence only through very considerable pressure on their part.[37] In Pasundan, there were no autonomous Indonesian aristocratic rulers, persons who felt that the retention of their powers and lands was dependent upon Dutch rule, as in East Indonesia. Thus Pasundan was without the aristocratic underpinnings that characterized such federal units as East Indonesia, East Sumatra, West Borneo and East Borneo. In Pasundan, the only positive Indonesian support upon which the Dutch could rely was from political opportunists, particularly persons who had felt that their positions under the Republic had been inadequate, and a few Sundanese[38] who felt that the Republic's cause was doomed and wished to insure that Sundanese interests (or at least what they conceived them to be) would be protected by a semi-autonomous Sundanese state (Pasundan) within the projected Dutch-sponsored federal order.

From the beginning the outspokenness of pro-Republican sentiment

[37] See Ch. VIII for an account of its origins.

[38] The principal local language of West Java is Sundanese. Though the basic culture of the area is the same as that of central Java and east Java there are some differences and in general in pre-Dutch times the cultural level of the area was not as high as that in central Java. During most of the pre-Dutch period the Sundanese area was ruled by locally rooted aristocracies independent of political control by the states of central Java. During the later years of their rule the Dutch divided Java into three provinces, one of which, West Java, was (minus Bantam) roughly congruent with the administrative areas claimed for Pasundan and somewhat more roughly with the area where the Sundanese language was dominant. Certainly the large majority of the area's population was more conscious of being Indonesian than Sundanese. It should be noted that a substantial minority of the population of the area designated as Pasundan, particularly in its northeastern sector, spoke Javanese as its local language.

among the Indonesians forming the Parliament and cabinets of Pasundan was greater than among the Indonesians heading any other federal regime with the possible exception of Madura. Because of this and basically because of the lack of enough amenable Indonesian elements the Dutch were obliged to apply much more direct and undisguised force against those Indonesians heading the Pasundan regime than against those heading that of East Indonesia. Undoubtedly this was also a reason for their granting less autonomy to Pasundan than to East Indonesia.

From its inception on April 24, 1948,[39] Pasundan never measured to the boundaries claimed for it by the Dutch. At the outset aproximately one quarter of its area was controlled by such anti-Dutch Indonesian organizations as Darul Islam and the Laskjar Rakjat Djawa Barat.[40] Dutch troops were in general more on the defensive than the offensive against these organizations, particularly by the fall of 1948. With the Dutch attack against the Republic of December 19, 1948, the latter's crack Siliwangi Division fought its way to West Java and soon thereafter no more than one-third of the area claimed by the Dutch to constitute the state of Pasundan was under effective Dutch control.

Within the area of west Java which the Dutch actually did control, the Dutch army played a very important political role, much more direct and evident than was the case in East Indonesia. In all essential matters Pasundan was governed by it and the central Netherlands Indies administration at Batavia. A state of war and siege existed throughout Pasundan whereby, as in East Indonesia, the basic civil liberties could not be exercised. Political parties could not be formed without their being approved by the Dutch authorities, and the limitations on public and private meetings were quite as severe as in East Indonesia. In general the Dutch held a considerably tighter control over political activities in Pasundan than in East Indonesia. At least as late as May, 1949 (when the writer was last in Indonesia), the radio, newspapers, and even the local (regency) information offices in Pasundan were all directly managed by the N.E.I. Government Information Service in Batavia or controlled by Netherlands citizens.

Even the powers transferred to the "state" of Pasundan on paper were

[39] Actually its first cabinet was not sworn in until May 8, 1948, and its Parliament did not sit until May 13, 1948. The first provision for a transfer of power was on June 11, 1948.

[40] These two armed organizations—particularly the Darul Islam—soon greatly expanded in size from their original small memberships.

pitifully meager. Not only did the charter of power transfer to Pasundan [41] stipulate the same extensive list of express reservations of
authority and competencies to the Batavia government as limited the
autonomy of East Indonesia and all other federal units,[42] but there were
numerous additional limitations of a broad character. Between August
25, and September 23, 1948, powers in the fields of agrarian affairs,
internal affairs, police, social affairs, economic affairs, education, justice,
and industry were transferred; however, the extent of these transfers
was miniscule. Though article one of the instrument transferring power
over internal affairs called for a transfer of power over internal administration, article two stipulated that "provisions concerning the rehabilitation of municipalities and regencies" (territorial administrative
subdivisions) would continue to be taken care of by the Batavia government until such time as the latter made other arrangements.[43] This
in conjunction with the fact that Pasundan's principal territorial administrative officers (Residents and Regents) continued to be appointed
by the Dutch government in Batavia, three of the state's Residents'
being Netherlanders, meant that the ostensible grant of power in article
one had little real substance.[44]

The ostensible transfer of the exercise of police authority was in fact
farcical. In the first place the instrument of transfer specifically stipulated the exercise of such authority did not apply where federal interests were concerned,[45] and in practice the scope of federal interests
was very widely conceived. Likewise the Attorney General of the
Netherlands Indies government was empowered to issue such instructions to the head of the Pasundan police as he thought desirable with
respect to all cases where the wide range of powers reserved to the
Batavia government were concerned.[46] Since these residual powers
could be easily interpreted to cover the whole range of important
governmental activity, this article in effect meant that the police power
delegated to Pasundan was under the direct control of the Attorney
General in Batavia. Any doubts as to the complete subordination of
such power to Netherlands authority were removed on January 14

[41] "Bevoegdheidsregeling Pasundan," *Staatsblad* no. 116 (June 11, 1948).
[42] See n. 17.
[43] "Overdrachtsbesluit Binnenlands Zaken Pasundan," no. 192 (Aug. 25, 1948).
[44] That what appeared to be the case from a reading of these documents was
indeed so was attested to the writer by the various officers of the Pasundan Department of Interior that he spoke to in Bandung, Feb. 7–13, 1949, and in late April in
Batavia.
[45] *Staatsblad,* no. 194 (Aug. 25, 1948), art. 2.   [46] *Ibid.,* art. 3.

when Ating, Police Commissioner for Pasundan, was summarily arrested by the Dutch army commander in Pasundan, Major General Engels.

Limiting the transfer of powers in the field of justice were several subjects reserved to the Batavia government which insured that it would maintain intact its exceptional powers in this field over political life in Pasundan. The most important among these were registration of prison sentences of more than one year, prison statistics, the organization and administration of the Soekamiskin prison for intellectuals at Bandoeng, the prison of Cheribon, and the house of detention at Koeningan.[47] Considering the large number of "political prisoners" in Pasundan jails (generally estimated at somewhat over 2,000),[48] the importance of these residual Dutch powers is apparent. The Pasundan government was powerless to hinder the wide-scale political arrests of members of its Indonesian population by the Dutch: it could no nothing to succor them once they were arrested.

Though restrictions on the transfer of powers in the field of education were not so severe as in other fields, it should be noted that there was an over-all limitation for all federal areas, namely that secondary and higher education were under the direct control of the Batavia government.[49] Moreover, in the Pasundan instrument of transfer the supply of textbooks and other educational equipment remained in the hands of Batavia.[50]

The transfer of authority over the rather amorphous field of social affairs was considerably limited by the reservation to the Batavia government of "regulations of a general character (i.e. having a relevancy according to Batavia for the whole of Indonesia) in matters of labor relations and those related to the circumstances of war and the consequences therefrom in the social field as well as, insofar as necessary, the supervision of their execution."[51] Also specifically reserved to Batavia were all subjects concerned with the work of foreigners within Pasundan.[52]

The transfer of powers over economic life as stipulated in the instru-

---

[47] *Staatsblad,* no. 232 (Sept. 23, 1948), art. 4.

[48] The Pasundan Minister of Justice stated before Parliament on March 28, 1949, that the number of political prisoners in Pasundan totalled approximately 2,000, including 1,700 inmates of the Soekamiskin jail in Bandung held in detention by the Dutch military authorities (see *Merdeka,* April 1, 1949).

[49] *Staatsblad,* no. 116 (June 11, 1948), art. 3 (u).

[50] *Ibid.,* no. 231 (Sept. 23, 1948), art. 3.

[51] *Ibid.,* no. 220 (Sept. 16, 1948), art. 2 (d).   [52] *Ibid.,* art. 2(a).

ments concerned with agrarian affairs, industry, and economic affairs
were particularly disappointing to Pasundan officials. The wide powers
reserved to the Batavia government in these fields made it impossible
for the Pasundan government to undertake any measures which could
significantly alter the colonial economic pattern existing within its
area. Directives concerning "general agrarian policy" were reserved to
Batavia as were all regulations concerning the rights of foreigners or
Netherlands subjects outside Indonesia over lands within Pasundan.[53]
An equally blanket reservation of control by Batavia over Dutch and
other non-Pasundan-owned agrarian interests was stipulated in a clause
providing for such reservation with respect to "subjects of an agrarian
nature lying within the field of civil and commercial law" which were
either "of general commercial interest" or of "particular significance
for important elements of the population which as such did not belong
to a particular state." [54] Control over foreign-owned industry located
in Pasundan was ruled out, as was that over all industrial enterprise
whose regulation Batavia might deem to be in the interests of all Indonesia.[55]

Pasundan was granted a reasonably unfettered power to regulate its
economic life *outside the sphere of colonial economic relations,* in
particular with respect to the development of intra-Pasundan trade
and native agriculture and handicrafts. However, effective prosecution
of such activities required funds of a magnitude not possessed by the
Pasundan government. The Indonesian officials of Pasundan felt that
the long list of centrally important powers in the economic field reserved to the Netherlands Indies government was hardly balanced by
the list of specific, unqualified [56] powers in the economic field that
were granted to the government of Pasundan. The list of these powers
as conveyed in the instrument for transfer of economic affairs was the
following: "internal [intra-Pasundan] trade, sea and coast fishing;
stimulation of local proa-shipping, pearl, mother-of-pearl, and sponge
fishing; the hire of birdsnest cliffs and caves, bats' caves and the collection of turtle eggs." [57]

Even the limited powers transferred to Pasundan on paper were
largely vitiated by the inadequacy of the funds available to it and the
fact that almost all of such funds were grants at the discretion of the

[53] *Ibid.,* no. 193, Aug. 25, 1948, art. 2 (a and b).
[54] *Ibid.,* art. 2 (c).   [55] *Ibid.,* no. 237 (Sept. 23, 1948), art. 2.
[56] Except as qualified by the over-all list of reservations as set forth in the Bevoegdheidsregeling Pasundan. See n. 17.
[57] *Staatsblad,* no. 236 (Sept. 23, 1948), art. 1.

Batavia government. This almost complete dependency upon Batavia, of course, increased Netherlands control over the Pasundan administration. As the chairman of the Pasundan Financial Committee stated in an interview on April 29, 1949, Pasundan had actually had no budget during 1948 and "only disposed of funds supplied as an advance by the central government." [58] With respect to the year 1949, he estimated expenditures at 147,000,000 guilders of which Pasundan had the means for raising only 17,000,000. Of the balance the Batavia government was expected to advance 97,000,000 guilders, leaving a deficit of 33,000,000.[59] Actually the funds being made available for expenditure per month in 1949 were approximately 25 per cent less than had been available per month during 1948.[60]

Thus the scanty funds for the departments of the Pasundan government were sharply cut, and even less of its meager powers could be carried out than previously. In view of the fact that the budget of his department (computed on a yearly basis) was being cut from 16,000,000 to 5,000,000 guilders the Pasundan Minister of Social Affairs announced on April 27, 1949 that his department was being forced to abandon its emergency social program in a way which he could not justify. He went on to say that, though Pasundan had requested an integral transfer of social affairs to it from the Batavia government, this request had remained unanswered. So far, he affirmed, his department was actually nothing more than an affiliate of the Department of Social Affairs of the central government at Batavia, with the latter determining the regulations and his department merely implementing them.[61] All departments of the Pasundan government were being forced to curtail their activities in the face of the diminishment of the already inadequate funds made available by Batavia.

Netherlands control over Pasundan was, as in the case of all the federal units, further insured as a result of the fact that most upper-

[58] *Merdeka,* April 29, 1949. It should be noted that pro-Republican papers printed in Batavia, such as *Merdeka,* were under close control by the Dutch with respect to the news that they printed, and anti-Dutch tendentiousness on their part was usually curbed. The content of this *Merdeka* dispatch and the following *Keng Po* dispatch was checked by the writer with Pasundan officials and found to be correct.

[59] *Ibid.*

[60] Two-thirds of the 1949 budget for Pasundan equalled approximately 40,000,000 guilders less than the total funds available to it for the period April–December, 1948; the fiscal inception of the state was in April, 1948 (stated to the writer by several Pasundan officials, April 3, 1949, Batavia).

[61] *Keng Po* (independent, relatively progressive Chinese-owned and managed Indonesian-language newspaper printed in Batavia), April 28, 1949.

rank civil service positions were filled by Netherlanders. This condition was rationalized by the Dutch through maintaining in force in Pasundan the prewar salary regulations of the Netherlands East Indies civil service. According to these, rank was determined by education, with many of the top positions requiring the possession of a law degree. There were, however, only five Indonesians in Pasundan with such a degree (out of slightly under 300 among Indonesians in all Indonesia). Moreover, nearly 90 per cent of the civil servants in Pasundan were directly employed and paid by the Netherlands East Indies administration. Indonesian members of this group were generally cautious not to indulge in activities which would alienate those upon whom they felt dependent for employment and pensions. (Indonesians eligible for pensions within a few years felt particularly constrained.)

Following the second Dutch military action against the Republic, launched December 19, 1948, the majority of the Pasundan Parliament evinced a pro-Republican attitude which was distinctly embarrassing to Netherlands officials in Batavia and at the Hague. In order to counteract this, Dutch interference in what political life Pasundan was allowed became increasingly persistent and heavy handed. Shortly after the Dutch launched their second action, the Pasundan cabinet, headed by Adil Puradiredja, not only resigned, as did the cabinet of East Indonesia (headed by Anak Agung), but also openly condemned the Netherlands' aggression.

The Dutch Prime Minister, Dr. William Drees, who had come to Indonesia with much world publicity for the announced purpose of consulting with the representatives of the federal units on the establishment of an interim Indonesian federal government, was obviously in an embarrassing position. The two principal federal states had no governments and therefore could not send representatives to the federal conference he was to meet. The Dutch had no great difficulty in getting a majority of the East Indonesian Parliament to back a new cabinet headed by Anak Agung. However, Adil Puradiredja and the majority of the Pasundan Parliament refused to form a new government for Pasundan. Thereupon, both Lt. Gen. Simon Spoor, commander in chief of the Netherlands armies in Indonesia, and Dr. R. W. van Diffelen, the Dutch Crown Commissioner for Pasundan, visited Wiranata Koesoema, the *Wali Negara* [62] of Pasundan and demanded

[62] Literally, "State Guardian." Wiranata Koesoema had formerly been an important member of the Republican government, having been chairman of the presidential advisory body known as the Council of State. He had left the Republic to

that he appoint a new cabinet *formateur* and see that a new government was promptly formed.[63]

Finally, Wiranata Koesoema was able to get Djumhana, a nonparty member of the Pasundan Parliament, to attempt formation of a new cabinet. The program upon the basis of which he attempted to form it called for: (1) rehabilitation of the Republic as of December 18, 1948, under Soekarno and Hatta; (2) immediate formation of an interim government in which the Republic was included; (3) continuance of negotiations between the Republic and the Dutch under United Nations auspices; and (4) representation of each constituent state of the projected federal Indonesia (including a reconstituted Republic) in proportion to its population. On this basis, Djumhana was able to obtain majority parliamentary backing for his cabinet; [64] but because of its defiantly anti-Dutch nature he was able to enlist only six other persons in his cabinet.

Promptly, Djumhana went to Batavia for the federal conference with Drees. Here he was told by the Dutch that the program of his cabinet was absolutely unacceptable. He refused to yield to their demand for change, but consented to proceed to Bangka along with four other representatives of the Dutch-sponsored states to talk with the interned Republican leaders there. This raised strong protests from some of the members of the Pasundan Parliament who had backed him on the basis of his pro-Republican program,[65] such an action being considered

---

take up his post in Pasundan after having been elected Wali Negara by a majority of the members of the 3rd West Java Council.

[63] Because of disabilities suffered by Wiranata Koesoema (presumably deriving from a recent stroke), the Dutch were frequently able to deal with him in a way which would probably have been impossible had he been in possession of his full faculties. This knowledge was communicated to the writer by a number of Indonesians including two sons of Wiranata Koesoema. The writer's own limited personal contact with this man lent substance to what they told him.

[64] Republican parties had been outlawed by the Dutch authorities. Out of a membership of Parliament totaling 93, the following groups backed Djumhana: Fractie Kesatuan (Unity Faction), 14 seats; Fractie Nasional (National Faction), 12 seats; Fractie Tengah (Middle Faction), 8 seats; and Eurasian group, 8 seats. The largest parliamentary group, and the most Republican in sentiment, the Fractie Indonesia, with 30 seats, refused to support him. The fact that the Chinese and Eurasian groups did not join the small rightist opposition to Djumhana may possibly be explained in part by the strong unitarian, antifederalist sentiment of many of them. In a unitarian Indonesia possessing a strong central government, they felt that their minority interests would be better protected. The majority of members of the Fractie Kesatuan and Fractie Nasional were civil servants who received their salaries from Batavia.

[65] The Fractie Indonesia had endorsed Djumhana's program but refused to par-

as geared to Dutch plans and at variance with that program. There quickly developed plans for introducing a no-confidence motion in Parliament. Aware of this and angered by the announced basis of the program of Djumhana's cabinet, the Dutch acted with force and dispatch.

Beel, the Dutch High Commissioner of the Crown for Indonesia, wrote to Wiranata Koesoema that if the program of Djumhana's cabinet were not promptly dropped the Pasundan government would be scrapped in favor of a strictly military government. Major General Engels, territorial and troop commandant of West Java, speaking for the Dutch Commander in chief, General Spoor, and Dr. van Diffelen, speaking for the N.E.I. civil authorities, called on the unhappy *Wali Negara* in person and bluntly told him that, unless the program of the cabinet were changed, a number of the leading members of the Pasundan government would be arrested. Engels made the seriousness of this threat abundantly clear by presenting him with a black list of persons who would be jailed if his demand were not fulfilled. The names on this list included Male Wiranata Koesoema, eldest son of the *Wali Negara* and regent of Bandung; Adil Puradiredja, member of Parliament and former Prime Minister; Mr. Hasan, member of Parliament and a leader of the pro-Republican Fractie Indonesia; Mr. Kosasih, State Secretary of Pasundan; Makmun Sumadipradja, Secretary-General of the Department of Internal Affairs of Pasundan; and Wirasupena. It was made clear that this was a partial list and that "other prominent people who sympathize with the Republic" could also expect to be jailed in case of non compliance.[66]

Wiranata Koesoema's reply was that if these persons were arrested he would resign. Possibly it was because of this that, in the face of continued noncompliance with their demands, the Dutch arrested five others instead. On January 14, 1949, while Wiranata Koesoema was out of Bandung on an inspection trip and Djumhana was still on Bangka, Dutch army authorities in Bandung summarily arrested Soejoso, a member of Parliament and chairman of its strongly pro-Republican Fractie Indonesia; Mohammad Enoch, another strongly pro-Republican member of Parliament; Ating, High Commissioner

---

ticipate in his Cabinet, its tactic being to delay the formation of a Cabinet as long as possible.

[66] This information was made available to the writer during his visit to Bandung in Feb., 1949, by a large number of high Pasundan officials including persons extremely close to the Wali Negara. It was corroborated by both pro-Federalist and pro-Republican elements.

of Pasundan police; and two other prominent pro-Republican Sundanese, Dr. Suratman Erwin and Gondokusumo. This action thoroughly intimidated most members of Djumhana's cabinet and many members of Parliament. It was generally believed that continued noncompliance with the Dutch demand for a change in cabinet program would mean further arrests.

On the night of the fifteenth the four members of the cabinet then in Bandung held a meeting and resolved to resign as individuals. Wiranata Koesoema refused to accept their resignations. The following day Djumhana returned and was able to delay their resignations for a week. However, his arguments against their resigning were demolished when Major General Engels again intruded himself into the political situation by way of a public announcement which most of the ministers felt was pointed directly at them. The pertinent part of Engels' proclamation read:

Influences are active again, especially during the last days, which have endangered the order, peace, and security in Pasundan to such an extent that I, as Territorial and Troop Commandant of West Java charged with the military power have been obliged to my regret to order some arrests to be made.

To the population peace, order and security must be guaranteed and *I will not hesitate to take even more stringent measures against whosoever obstructs the execution of my task.*[67]

Immediately the four wavering members of his cabinet turned in their resignations. Left with only two ministers,[68] Djumhana tried vainly for another week to reconstruct his cabinet and on January 28 resigned his post.[69]

The Netherlands policy of intimidation had been successful. The only way in which Djumhana could form a new cabinet was by dropping his former program and substituting an extremely mild one. The program of the new government which he formed at the beginning of February called for establishment of a sovereign and free federal Indonesia as soon as possible and formation of an interim government

[67] Made available by the Netherlands Army Information Service, Batavia, Jan. 22, 1948. Italics are the writer's and indicate that part of Engels' proclamation interpreted as a threat to Pasundan government and parliament members.

[68] Judawinata, the outspoken Minister of Social Affairs, and Prawiradinata, Minister of Education.

[69] The Fractie Indonesia, which had refused to support his cabinet previously, now came forward and offered to support him. However, the number of his previous supporters in Parliament willing to remain behind him was not sufficient, even with the support of the Fractie Indonesia, to give him a majority.

in which the Republic would take part. The Dutch were probably cognizant of the parallel *sub rosa* program which the parties backing the cabinet had given Djumhana the directive of attaining: namely, implementation of the program of the previous cabinet. However, they probably felt that they could keep enough pressure on Djumhana and his cabinet to make such an endeavor relatively ineffectual.[70] More important, they had eliminated most of the sheen from the example which Pasundan had begun to set for weaker or timider pro-Republican elements in other federal units as well as the embarrassment it was causing the Netherlands with respect to the world outside. Such was the political autonomy of the "state" of Pasundan.

EAST JAVA

East Java had been advertised as a "state" to the outside world and so represented in the Dutch-sponsored Federal Consultative Assembly [71] for more than four months prior to the writer's visit to Surabaya, its capital, in April, 1949. However, upon arriving there he found that no powers, even on paper, had yet been granted this "state." Members of its Indonesian "government" with whom he spoke somewhat apologetically explained that no power transfer could take place yet because the constitution of the state had been written in Dutch and had not yet been translated into the Indonesian language. However, they stated that this document, drawn up by some of them under the supervision of the Dutch Government Commissioner (*Recomba*) for East Java, was expected to be approved soon by Batavia. It had been sent to Batavia for translation into Indonesian, and as soon as this was completed it would be submitted to the East Java Representative Assembly for ratification. Then the "government" of East Java would be able to function within the framework of whatever powers the Dutch had been willing to grant it.

Dutch officials with whom the writer spoke talked enthusiastically of the "reasonableness" of most of the members of the East Java government and appeared to have high hopes for their performance. Dr. Charles van der Plas, the Government Commissioner for East Java (as such he was also in charge of the N.E.I.'s administration of Madura, where he undertook to establish a separate *negara*), reiterated

[70] Djumhana stated to the writer that despite a continuation of pressure from the Dutch army he felt he would be able to carry on with his program (Bandung, Feb. 8, 1949).

[71] Bijeenkomst voor Federaal Overleg, generally referred to by its initials "BFO."

this sentiment and assured the writer that the members of its Representative Assembly had been selected by democratic elections giving real representation to the people of East Java.

However, the whole range of Indonesian opinion encountered by the writer contested this assertion. Because of this and the qualities of Machiavellian political cunning, shrewd intelligence, and keen understanding of Indonesian society attributed by so many Indonesians to Dr. van der Plas [72] the writer felt that it would be not only important but interesting to probe further into the electoral process in East Java. The common denominator of the accounts from the various Indonesians of East Java whom the writer questioned concerning this is contained in the following paragraph.[73]

At the end of August, 1948, Dr. van der Plas ordered elections held for the regency councils of East Java. Before the war these bodies had been virtually powerless and largely advisory in nature. Consequently much of the populace was apathetic towards these elections, having no inkling that Van der Plas would soon be giving those elected a very important political role. Among Indonesian intellectuals there was concern over the seriousness with which the Netherlands officials seemed to view these elections, but they could not fathom their reasons. The Dutch went to very great lengths to insure that pro-Republican membership of these councils was kept at a minimum. Dutch civil servants told the population in several regencies prior to the elections that those who voted for Republican candidates would automatically be forced to leave their homes and go to the Republican-controlled area of Java. There were wide-scale arrests of those pro-Republican leaders not already in jail, so that few pro-Republican candidates remained.

[72] Dr. van der Plas had become a semi-legendary figure in Indonesia with nearly as much fantasy as fact attaching his name. Certainly he was an exceptional person. Many top Indonesian leaders, though considering him the devil incarnate, believed he knew more about the Indonesian people than any other Netherlander alive or dead and had a very considerable respect for his ability. Whenever the Netherlands Indies government managed to do something displaying shrewd intelligence, there was a tendency among Indonesian intellectuals to say: "Ah, that is the work of Van der Plas!" (The appellation "Machiavellian" is not quite correct, but it is the closest English equivalent to "pintir busuk," the attribute generally used in describing Van der Plas and literally translated as "rotten-intelligent.")

[73] The writer believes that his sampling of opinion was wide enough to insure that this account is reasonably accurate. The mean of the accounts given was much more extreme than the common denominator here given. The writer did not have an opportunity to interview the two delegates of East Java to the BFO, one of whom was the Wali Negara. They might well have expressed opinions more closely in line with Dr. Van der Plas. At the time they were not in Surabaya, however.

Elections were held, and the twelve regency councils constituted as they had been before the war. Thus the elected members of the councils were outnumbered by these appointed by the Dutch. (The composition of each council was made up of one elected and one appointed member from each district plus several other appointees—Dutch, Chinese, Arab—to represent these three minorities.) Even so the results were apparently not entirely pleasing to the Dutch, a considerable number of pro-Republicans being elected to the councils. In Djember, one of the most militantly pro-Republican of the twelve regencies, the Dutch Assistant Resident refused to accept the results of the election (approximately three-fourths of those elected being pro-Republican) and ordered a second election held. In the interval several of those elected the first time were jailed, thereby convincing a number of others that it would be unwise to run for office again. Six to eight weeks after the election had been completed throughout East Java between 5 and 10 per cent of the total membership of the regency councils were jailed. Since nearly all those jailed were elected members of the councils, this meant that at least 10 per cent of the elected membership of the councils was jailed. For instance, in the case of the fifty-three-member council of Lumadjang Regency, twenty-four members were elected and of these eight were jailed.

After having carried out these actions, the Netherlands authorities apparently felt that they could rely on the large majority of the members of the regency councils. They announced that these members had requested that East Java be given the status of *negara*. Accordingly the Government Commissioner, Dr. van der Plas, obliged by calling a conference of representatives of the regency councils at the town of Bondowoso in mid-November, 1948. It is to be observed that Van der Plas did not call a conference of all the members of the regency councils, only three to twelve representatives from each being sent.[74] Thereby the representation of pro-Republican elements was further minimized; for with so few representatives being sent, minority groups had little chance of being selected, particularly from the nine to twelve regencies having only three or four delegates.

Dr. van der Plas appeared to have little difficulty in steering the Bondowoso Conference in the direction he wished. The conference formally called for the establishment of a state of East Java and asked

[74] Of the 75 delegates to the conference, 65 were listed as being elected and 10 appointed. Of the total number 57 were Indonesians, the rest being Chinese, Netherlanders or Arabs (N.E.I. Government Information Service, Batavia, Nov. 16, 1948).

that it (the conference) become the provisional representative body of this state. The Batavia government promptly complied with this request and one week later, November 26, 1948, formally approved the formation of the "constitutional unit of Djawa Timur (East Java) with the status of *negara* and recognition of the Djawa Timur Conference as the provisional representation of the people of that territory." [75] The success of Van der Plas was complete when on December 1 the conference elected a man agreeable to the Dutch authorities, Achmad Kusumonegoro, Regent of Banjuwangi, as *Wali Negara* of the new state and agreed upon a pattern of government favored by them. The system agreed upon by the delegates was much more easily controlled by the Dutch than the parliamentary systems of Pasundan and East Indonesia. It was similar to that introduced in the *negara* of East Sumatra, the *Wali Negara* having a five-year term with the cabinet responsible directly to him rather than to the representative assembly, and he and his cabinet having co-legislative power with the assembly.

During the next four and a half months, the "government" of the "state" of East Java had no powers to exercise, and insofar as it was able to keep occupied did so principally by drawing up its constitution in conjunction with Dr. van der Plas and his staff. Seven of the members of its Provisional Representative Assembly [76] had courage enough to sign a petition on March 10, 1949, asking that the Dutch clarify the status of the considerable, and recently much augmented, number of Indonesians in East Java jailed as political prisoners.[77] However, the large majority of its seventy-five members continued to behave themselves.

MADURA

Dr. van der Plas' establishment of the state of Madura was described in Chapter VIII. When the writer visited its capital of Pamekasan in mid-April, 1949, more than fourteen months after Van Mook had recognized Madura as a "state" and Tjakraningrat as its *Wali Negara,* he found that no transfer of powers had yet been made. Tjakraningrat explained to the writer that Batavia had not yet granted his state a constitution, and that because of this no governmental departments

---

[75] N.E.I. Government Information Service, A.E. 1003, Batavia, Nov. 26, 1948.

[76] Djaswadi Suprapto, Indrakusuma, Dr. Anwar, Alwi Isa, R. Sudarsono, Djarosugondo, and Tjoa Sie Hwie.

[77] A month later the Dutch authorities had still made no reply to this petition. The text of this petition was printed in the intermittently suppressed Surabaya newspaper *Trompet Masjarakat,* March 11, 1949.

had been set up. He claimed that he, himself, was administering most of the authority in behalf of the N.E.I. government, but admitted that finance and judicial affairs were still under the direct control of the office of Dr. van der Plas in Surabaya, with Dutch civil servants representing that office stationed in Madura.

Zainal Alim, top Indonesian police officer for Madura, was frank in stating to the writer the limitations of his position. According to him there were still over one hundred persons from Madura in jail under political arrest by the Dutch authorities; he and other Madura authorities had no power to intervene in such matters. "At present," he stated, "one can't speak of the popular will in Madura, for the people are not yet freq of fear." "If one makes a nationalist speech," he continued, "he is considered by the Dutch to be anti-Dutch; therefore, it is difficult to get the real opinion of a person." Most Madurese, he explained, were afraid of contravening the law of "disturbance of peace and order" whereby it was merely a matter of interpretation as to whether what a person said constituted an offense. The state of war and siege still existed throughout Madura, and its application was strictly interpreted, he said. The Dutch did not allow the holding of public meetings, regardless of whether permission was applied for in advance. No political parties existed in Madura, he stated, not because of any express regulation forbidding them, but simply because people feared arrest if they undertook to form them.

Among Indonesians in general with whom the writer spoke in Madura, the single incident that had done most to stifle political activity was the example set by the Dutch in the spring of the previous year (1948), when they summarily arrested twenty of the forty elected members of the Madura Parliament. Two of those arrested were still in jail, the chief Netherlands army intelligence officer on Madura informed the writer. This officer declined to say on what grounds these two men had been arrested and told the writer that he would have to take up a request for this information with Netherlands army authorities in Surabaya, or with Dr. van der Plas. He did state that regular Netherlands army units on the island had been largely replaced by the Madura Security Battalion numbering some 1,200 men, but that the officers of this organization were from the KNIL. Finally this intelligence officer stated categorically to the writer: "It is not possible to maintain law and order here without the Netherlands army intelligence service." [78]

[78] Interview of the writer with Lt. Van der Kaj, chief of the Madura branch of

SOUTH SUMATRA

In early May, 1949, the writer visited Palembang, capital of the "state" of South Sumatra. Though South Sumatra had enjoyed its status of "state" for some eight months already, the following conditions obtained. The actual area of the state covered only the residency of Palembang, approximately one-quarter the area of South Sumatra.[79] The state of war and siege with all its limitations on civil liberties and democratic political processes was still in force. No political parties existed. Beginning on February 1, 1949, powers over some branches of government had been transferred to the "government" of the state of South Sumatra. These included internal affairs (transferred February 1); traffic, reconstruction and irrigation; health; social affairs; information; and education. In effect, this transfer of powers meant only that Dutch and Indonesian officials formerly listed as working for the Netherlands Indies administration in the residency of Palembang were now listed as working for the state of South Sumatra. However, the latter could not dismiss such personnel and their salaries continued to be paid by Batavia. In the regional administration of the area those under the rank of *Wedana* (District Officer) were paid by the *Recomba* of South Sumatra.

Though the Interior Department was headed by an Indonesian, that individual, Alwi, spent most of his time in Batavia as a representative of South Sumatra to the BFO. The department was actually run by a Netherlander, Mr. van der Griend. The head of the police department was Dutch, as were all the police inspectors (generally Eurasians). The head of the Land Service Division ("Agraria") of the Department of Internal Affairs, W. V. Doop, was a Eurasian. His office had the important function of leasing land to non-Indonesians and was in charge of urban property rights. This person was also mayor of Palembang. The former head of the Department of Social Affairs and the current acting head were both Dutch. The head of the Department of Education was an Indonesian, but the Department was actually run by Mr. Boekhove, a Netherlander who was Director of Schools. Very likely the

---

the Inlichtings Veligheid Groep of the Netherlands army (Pamekasan, April 12, 1949).

[79] This had been admitted at the outset by the *Wali Negara*, Abdul Malik, in a press conference on Aug. 20, 1948 (Aneta, Aug. 20, 1948), and the condition still existed in May, 1949. Most of the remainder of South Sumatra was even then Republican-controlled; even parts of the residency of Palembang were under Republican control.

Recomba for South Sumatra would have preferred to have more Indonesians in these offices; however, he was limited by the fact that the majority of well-educated Indonesians from Palembang Residency either refused to co-operate, were in jail, or were serving in the civil administrations and army of the adjacent Republican-controlled areas of Sumatra.

The means whereby the Dutch obtained political control over the state which they sponsored in South Sumatra were relatively simple and employed in general approximately the same formula which they used in other federal areas. In early May, 1948, they announced the establishment of an "Advisory Council for South Sumatra" of thirty-six members, twenty-two of whom they stated had been elected by the Indonesian population of that area in democratic elections. Of the fourteen appointed members, two were Dutch, two Chinese, one representative of the Indian and Arabian popoulation groups, and eight Indonesians, of whom five were to represent the city of Palembang,[80] the Dutch being reluctant to hold elections there.

As usual, the principal key to understanding why a majority of this representative body was amenable to Dutch wishes is to be found in the nature of the elections that were held. Even if one discounts the widespread and insistent Indonesian claims that in several districts these elections were characterized by coercion and other irregularities, it is simple to understand how the Dutch obtained their majority control of the Advisory Council. The gaining of nine of these twenty-two elected seats could be accomplished without any coercion since the electors of these nine were mostly appointed by the Dutch authorities. The ordinance providing for the elections stipulated that nine of those elected were to be *marga* heads (chiefs of village complexes). [81] The electors for these nine representatives had to be *marga* heads themselves.[82]

Thus the nine representatives in question were limited to administrative officials of the Netherlands Indies regime elected by their own colleagues. Futhermore the majority of the electors had been appointed to their positions by the Netherlands East Indies government. They had replaced the previously elected *marga* heads of the Republican

---

[80] "Instellingsbeluit Adviesraad Recomba Zuid Sumatra," *Register der Besluiten van den Regeeringscommissaris voor Bestuursaangelegenheden voor Zuid-Sumatra te Palembang*, no. 153/Rec., April 6, 1948.

[81] *Ibid.* The local Indonesian term for *marga* head is *pasirah*.

[82] *Ibid.*, no. 154.

regime after it had been driven out of this area following the first Dutch military action against the Republic in 1947. Thus most the electors were persons who from the Dutch point of view were considered "reliable" and who were certain to lose their positions if a Republican regime were re-established, and probably would if subject to election by the populations of the *margas*.

In all, a total of twenty-three, not merely fourteen, of the thirty-six members of the council were persons upon whom the Dutch had substantial reason to believe they could rely. As far as the amenability of the council as a whole was concerned, it was not of vital importance what the political attitudes were of the remaining thirteen elected representatives (that group whose election was characterized according to a number of Indonesians as sometimes marked by undemocratic procedures). [83]

Assured of their control of the Advisory Council, the Netherlands authorities proceeded to establish (with the council as the foundation) the new state of South Sumatra. On August 17, 1948, the council petitioned the Netherlands Indies government to grant South Sumatra the status of "state" and asked that it (the Advisory Council) be recognized "as the provisional parliament of the Dutch-controlled territory of South Sumatra." The Batavia government granted both these requests on August 30 and authorized the council to draw up a constitution for the new state to be completed by the end of November. This was achieved, and a form of government similiar to that being established in East Java was set up, with the cabinet responsible to a president and the latter sharing legislative power with a representative assembly. The council transformed itself into such an assembly and elected for a four-year term as *Wali Negara*, Abdul Malik, a man long regarded by Republicans as one of the most unprincipled of opportunists, ambitious for position, and willing to serve the Dutch in order to achieve it.

Such were the *negaras* or states which were to be the elite, most

[83] It was stipulated that these 13 be other than *marga* heads and that they be selected by electors chosen by the *marga* councils and the councils of the autonomous market towns (*passers*). In each of the 9 districts these electors met and chose one or two representatives according to the size of the districts. Indonesians whom the writer spoke with in Palembang were critical of these elections because of the narrow franchise which, they alleged, operated under the Dutch administration. They stated that whereas under the Republican administration all male and female inhabitants over 18 voted for members of the *marga* councils, that the Dutch had reintroduced their prewar system of according this right to only those members of the *marga* who paid a certain minimum tax.

autonomous, members of the federal political order the Dutch were bent upon establishing.[84]

PLANS FOR AN INTERIM FEDERAL GOVERNMENT

Simultaneously with its attack on the Republic, the Netherlands government announced its plans for establishing the central governmental organization that was to subsume and incorporate these *negaras* and the other less important federal units, and ultimately the Republican areas of Indonesia as well. This was to function as the "Interim Federal Government" of Indonesia until the transfer of sovereignty to it by the Dutch. In conjunction with the Dutch, it was to create the final federal Indonesia to receive that sovereignty. The blueprint of the structure and political articulation of this interim government and the way in which the envisaged ultimate Indonesian state was to be established were set forth in a decree of the Netherlands government of December 14, 1948, generally referred to as the "BIO Decree." This was drawn up by the Netherlands government after consultations in Holland in September and October with the delegation of the Federal Consultative Assembly (BFO), a committee sponsored by the Dutch and made up of representatives of the various federal units they had established, each unit regardless of its size having one vote in BFO decisions.[85] Ostensibly the "BIO Decree" was a joint product of the

[84] It will be recalled that of the 15 federal units established by the Dutch those with the status of *negara*, or "state," were distinguished from the less populous and generally more economically and culturally backward *daerah istimewas*, or "autonomous territories" (literally "special territories") by virtue of being granted (supposedly, at least) more self-government and more autonomy from the central Government at Batavia. The writer visited 5 of the 6 *negaras*, all but East Sumatra. Dutch officials in Batavia were unanimous and explicit in their judgment that the *negara* of East Indonesia enjoyed considerably more self-government and autonomy from Batavia than did East Sumatra. The general pattern of government existing in East Sumatra was reported to be approximately the same as that in South Sumatra and roughly similar to that in East Java, with a transfer of power approximating that in Pasundan. The Dutch army there was being replaced by a Security Battalion made up largely of soldiers from the KNIL, along the lines of that being established in Madura. The writer also visited the *daerah istimewa* of Bangka and the "special area" of Middle Java which was then (April, 1949) being groomed for the status of *daerah istimewa*, but where no administrative, much less substantive, powers had yet been transferred.

[85] Thereby Riouw with a population of approximately 100,000 had a voice equal to East Indonesia or Pasundan with populations over 10,000,000. Thus the five *daerah istimewas* of Borneo in conjunction with Riouw, Bangka and Billiton could form a majority of 8 within the BFO even though their total population was only about 3,000,000. Four of the five Borneo territories, plus Riouw, Billiton, East Sumatra, and South Sumatra did in fact, form the right-wing majority group within

Netherlands government and the BFO. Actually, however, the members of the latter body were chagrined to find that the decree bore little trace of their suggestions.

The "BIO Decree" was classified as "confidential," and as far as the writer knows its full text was for several months at least not made public.[86] The official public pronouncements made by the Netherlands government concerning the decree gave a grossly distorted picture of its content. Thus a statement of December 18 said that the establishment of the interim government provided by the decree was expected "to come as close as possible to the ultimate aim of a completely free and sovereign federation, united to this country in a Netherlands-Indonesian union," with the provision that "entire control of internal affairs is placed in the hands of Indonesians trusted by their fellow-countrymen . . . although Netherlands sovereignty will remain in effect in the interim period." [87] Actually the terms of the decree put the "entire control of internal affairs" solidly in Dutch hands. Nothing could be done by the Indonesian governmental administration provided for by the decree with which the Netherlands government did not agree, and the latter or its agent, the High Representative of the Crown, could undertake whatever positive action in Indonesia they desired, whether the Indonesian authorities established by the decree concurred or not.[88]

---

the BFO, the group within it most inclined to work closely with the Dutch. Furthest to the left (most strongly pro-Republican) were Pasundan and Madura. This position of Madura reflected the sentiment of its functionless parliament and not of its *Wali Negara*.

[86] The writer possesses a copy of the text. Paraphrases of it which were obviously carefully sifted from the original were seen by the writer in the press while he was in Indonesia (which he left May 18, 1949), but he never saw its most pertinent phrases in literal form made public while he was there.

[87] *N.Y. Times*, Dec. 19, 1948, p. 1.

[88] The BIO Decree read: "The Representative of the Crown shall suspend the enforcement of a decree and the taking effect or the further effect of a federal law or federal order [i.e., of the federal interim Indonesian government], in the event that in his opinion this decree, federal law, or federal order is at variance with the Netherlands Constitution, the present Decree, or Our [i.e., the Netherlands Crown] directions or decisions" (BIO Decree, sec. 57, par. 2). In case the federal government did not agree with such a decision of the High Representative of the Crown, the Netherlands government was to decide the issue (sec. 57, par. 4).

The positive powers of the Representative of the Crown were equally widely conceived. Thus the decree provided: "The Representative of the Crown may submit to the federal government proposals for the adoption of the following measures: . . . (b) for the fulfillment of safeguarding of a legal obligation of Indonesia, the requirements of legal security, the fundamental human rights and freedoms and sound administration; (c) for making provision for interests which have to be protected in

Likewise the decree gave the Netherlands government or its representative in Indonesia absolute and unrestricted power to do as they pleased in the establishment of the final constitutional order in Indonesia to which the Netherlands had pledged to transfer sovereignty. This power was such that if it so desired the Netherlands could completely disregard the wishes in this matter of the interim federal Indonesian government that it was establishing under the BIO Decree.[89]

Thus, though the decree provided that power could be exercised by the interim federal government with respect to its own operation and its preparation of the constitutional order that was to succeed it, such power was exercised on sufferance of the Netherlands government and its agent in Indonesia, the High Representative of the Crown, strictly in accordance with their wishes. Failure to do so was unlikely because any action contrary to their desires could be summarily halted and negated by the Netherlands government or its High Representative of the Crown, with the latter able to take whatever positive action in these two spheres they deemed appropriate.

At the same time, however, as the decree provided for these absolute powers of the Netherlands government and its representative in Indonesia, it also provided for a means of indirect control. Given the ex-

---

mutual co-operation between the Netherlands and Indonesia." In the case of measures taken with respect to these broad subjects (which could obviously be interpreted so as to cover almost any subject) the Representative of the Crown was bound only to *consult* with the interim federal government, he did not have to refer the matter to the Netherlands government if there was disagreement; in the event he should feel it necessary, he could take action on his own authority without any previous consultation with the interim federal government (sec. 58, pars. 1–4). There were also a host of more specific delineations of power to the Representative of the Crown and the Netherlands government which could not be abridged by the interim federal government. Most important were control over appointment and discharge of the top executive leadership of the federal government (sec. 14, par. 4); "supreme authority over all armed forces present in Indonesia" (sec. 28, par. 4); and control over regulations concerning the state of war and siege (sec. 29, pars. 1, 2).

[89] Sec. 58 of the decree also stipulated that "The Representative of the Crown may submit to the federal government proposals for the adoption of the following measures: (a) for the transition to and the creation of the new legal structure in pursuance of Chapter Fourteen of the Netherlands Constitution;" (sec. 58, par. 1, a.). If the federal government opposed his action under this power it could "consult" him on the matter, but that was the limit of its power. In case of disagreement he was not bound to confer with the Netherlands government, and if he felt delay inadvisable did not even have to wait for consultation with the federal government (sec. 58, pars. 1–4). In addition, with respect to the projected constitutional order, the Netherlands government reserved to itself the exclusive right to make provisions concerning territories which as of Dec. 14, 1948, were under the control of the Republic of Indonesia (sec. 67, par. 1).

istence of certain conditions, this would obviate the necessity of employing the above-mentioned absolute powers, allowing them to be kept in reserve and making the operation of the Indonesian interim federal government appear outwardly to be genuinely autonomous and its role in constructing a new and definitive Indonesian constitutional order genuinely independent. The two prerequisites necessary for effective employment of this indirect means of control were: (1) amenability to Dutch control of the constituent units of the projected federal state and (2) possession by the Dutch of the same preponderance of physical force throughout Indonesia as they already commanded in the states and special territories which they had established outside the residual Republican area. The first of these conditions, as we have already seen, was being achieved. There remained only the second. This required the destruction of the Republic of Indonesia and its military forces, and to this end the Dutch had committed themselves at the same time that they announced the BIO Decree.

The key to the system of indirect control provided by the BIO Decree was to be found in its provisions for the establishment of the organs of the federal interim government. The essence of the formula employed was to vest control over the most important of these organs in the collectivity of constituent units of the federation whose individual amenability the Dutch had already secured. In other words, it was a means for linking together the individual amenabilities of the "states" and "autonomous territories" into one tractable unity.

Thus the most powerful of the two legislative bodies of this government was to be the Federal Council, composed of just one delegate from each constituent state or autonomous territory (regardless of its size) appointed by and responsible to their "governments or administrations." [90] In addition, the minority groups of Indonesia— Dutch, Chinese, and probably the Arab group as well—were to have representation on this council and a vote in it with respect to certain cases to be fixed later and presumably concerning their own interests.[91] Thereby additional support for Dutch interests by the Federal Council would be insured. Practically all, if not all, action of importance undertaken by the interim federal government required the approval of the Federal Council.[92] In addition, the Federal Council and the

[90] BIO Decree, sec. 20, par. 1.   [91] *Ibid.*, sec. 20, par. 2.

[92] Sec. 48 of the BIO Decree stipulated that consent of the Federal Council was required for federal laws "concerning important financial and economic matters," "concerning the status of the autonomous principalities [the areas under the administration of the aristocratic Indonesian rulers] in the new constitutional structure,

"Federal Government" (the executive organ, the appointment and discharge of whose members required the consent of the Representative of the Crown) were empowered to regulate "the composition, the chairmanship, the term of session, and the procedure to be followed by the Federal Representative Body." [93] Finally, the predominance of the Federal Council and the executive arm, the "Federal Government," over the Federal Representative Body (or one might say the predominance of the organs of the interim federal government which were most susceptible of indirect control by the Netherlands over that organ which, potentially at least, was most representative of the Indonesian people) was unequivocally assured. They could enact over its objections whatever legislation they felt to be required.[94]

The Dutch appeared confident that before the end of January, 1949, they would have attained the only unrealized prerequisite barring their effective indirect control of Indonesia: namely, clear preponderance of physical power throughout the whole of its area. If able to achieve this, there was substantial reason to believe that they would be able to establish an Indonesian regime sufficiently under their control to make safe the transfer to it of the formal attributes of "sovereignty" and possessing a convincing-enough façade of "autonomy" and "self-government" to satisfy at least a majority of Security Council members.

Between them and this objective stood the army and the citizens of the Republic of Indonesia.

---

insofar as falling under the jurisdiction of the federal legislature" [the contracts of these rulers with the Netherlands Crown were being taken over or were to be taken over by the constituent states of the federation themselves, not by the federal government], "regulating the transition to and the creation of the new legal structure pursuant to Chapter Fourteen of the Netherlands Constitution, except insofar as the regulation thereof comes under the jurisdiction of the participating territory."

[93] *Ibid.*, sec. 22, par. 1.

[94] Sec. 54 of the BIO Decree read: "The Federal Government may in concurrence with the Federal Council enact on its own authority and responsibility a federal bill or law, which is submitted to the Federal Representative Body if: (a) the Federal Representative Body has failed to notify approval or rejection within the terms prescribed for this purpose; (b) no agreement has been reached with the Federal Representative Body, and immediate provision should be made to meet urgent requirements."

❧ CHAPTER XIII ❧

The Final Struggle and
the Republic's Victory

THE DUTCH were not able to present the world with the *fait accompli* they had counted on. They had gone into the month of January with the confident expectation that well before the month was ended Republican resistance would have collapsed and the way be left open for their creating the kind of political order for the whole of Indonesia that they wished. However, both Republican military resistance and civilian nonco-operation developed a magnitude and intensity which was of stunning surprise to them. By late January the 145,000 Netherlands troops in Indonesia were actually more on the defensive than on the offensive. Their initial control of the chief Republican cities and towns was soon strongly contested by powerful night attacks of large Republican units. By day Dutch armored columns knifed out from their bases in these towns into areas where they believed Republican forces to be concentrated. But at dusk they returned to their bases, where sometimes they had to fight for sheer survival through much of the night. They held strong points between these towns and cities but exercised only a limited control over the roads between them, being able to negotiate many of them only by heavily armed convoys. The major city of Madiun was through much of January completely isolated and had to be supplied by air. Plantations were being abandoned, the Dutch having no troops to spare for their protection, even having to pull their garrisons from some of the smaller towns.

Outside the towns and just back from the main roads Republican civil servants, though frequently on the move to escape Dutch patrols, maintained the Republican civil administration as best they could. In central and east Java this administration was headed by five cabinet ministers who had escaped the Dutch—Dr. Sukiman, Susanto, Kasimo, Maskur, and Supeno—and Dr. Murdjani, Republican governor of East Java. In the cities and towns that they had "liberated" from the Republican regime the Dutch encountered a sullen and hostile citizenry. The co-operation they could obtain from it even during the first ten days of their attack, after Republican troops had evacuated the towns and before they had indicated the power to undertake effective counteroffensives, was practically nil. With the development of Republican counterattacks from their bases outside of the towns, the resistance morale of the urban dwellers became even higher.

Certainly the outlook of the Republic's leaders showed no spirit of defeatism. The attitudes which they evinced in the face of the Dutch attack indicated their conviction that a final and decisive phase of all-out struggle had begun and their expectation that the Indonesian people could be relied upon themselves to see it through to the bitter end.

A few weeks before the Dutch attack Sjafruddin Prawiranegara, Minister of Finance in the Republican government, had gone to Bukit Tinggi, the Republican capital of Sumatra on a mission connected with the affairs of his ministry. Before his departure Prime Minister Hatta, so as to be prepared for all eventualities, gave him a mandate to take over the leadership of the government in case he and Soekarno might be captured by the Dutch while he was away. The fighting spirit of Sjafruddin's Emergency Government was indicated by the instructions which he broadcast from his central Sumatra headquarters to the Indonesian delegation to the United Nations on December 23. The full text read:

The Government of the Republic of Indonesia is prepared to order a cease fire and enter into negotiations with the Netherlands government on the basis of:

(1) the immediate release of the members of the Republican government now detained by the Dutch;

(2) the withdrawal of Dutch troops to their original positions of December 18, 1948;

(3) the de facto and de jure recognition of the Republic's sovereignty over the islands of Java, Sumatra, and Madura;

(4) the formation of an all-Indonesian government on a democratic basis—

and which is independent and sovereign—by the Indonesian nation itself and without Dutch interference;

(5) the withdrawal of the whole Dutch army from Indonesia as soon as possible after the formation of an all-Indonesian government. The economic interests of the Netherlands will be properly observed.[1]

In the Jogjakarta area typewritten copies of the speeches to the Indonesian people prepared by Soekarno, Hatta, and Natsir on the morning of December 19 (but undelivered by them because of the bombing of the Jogjakarta radio station) were circulated from hand to hand and their contents passed on by word of mouth. These speeches were of importance in bolstering Indonesian morale and in making the interned leaders of the Republic seem more alive to the people. In spirit, at least, they were still leading the struggle for independence. In addition, Natsir's set forth the government's specific instructions to the population, showing the way to be followed in the struggle by those who were indecisive or confused as to what the most effective course was. Within two or three weeks of the Dutch attack copies of these speeches had circulated as far as Surakarta and Magelang. It was not until the evening of January 10 that copies of them finally found their way to Batavia and then into the hands of the Good Offices Committee and Republicans there. Shortly thereafter, however, their contents were made known throughout Java and to the Republican Emergency government on Sumatra, exerting an influence such as they had in central Java.

The closing words of Soekarno's address read:

We know that with their arms the Dutch will possibly capture and occupy several important places, but they will not be able to smash our fighting spirit, to erase, or to decrease the independence of the people of Indonesia, the independence which we have learned to love and defend during these last three years. The independence which we proclaimed on August 17, 1945 and which has saturated our souls will never be crushed by force.

My people, let us stand together now in the defense of our country and our freedom with every strength available. Continue our struggle and believe that the ultimate victory is ours.

In the core of his speech Hatta stated:

[1] Radiogram through All-India Radio, Singapore and Bangkok, Dec. 24, 1948. An approximately similar version was broadcast on the 24th over the Republican radio in Madiun shortly before that city fell to the Dutch. The version given over the Madiun radio stated, "The economic interests of the Dutch will be properly cared for."

The enemy desires to capture the government, but the Republic of Indonesia does not depend upon the fate of the persons who are at the head of the State or who are members of the government.

The people must fight and I am convinced that the entire population of Indonesia is prepared to take over the struggle from us.

Mohammad Natsir, Minister of Information and one of the most influential leaders of the nation's largest political party, the Masjumi, included the specific instructions of the government in his address, the most important part of which was the following:

The fall of Jogjakarta, which the Dutch assume will be the end of all their troubles, is—essentially—the beginning of every conceivable struggle and trouble for the Dutch, the end of which lies far in the future.

The fall of the capital, Jogjakarta, under the Dutch attack does not mean the end of our struggle, but from there on will the Indonesian people begin its tenacious and fierce struggle, wherein quarter shall be neither asked nor given. . . .

The Republic will continue to exist even though the leaders of the state are captured by the enemy. The essential principle is that *the people shall continue its struggle.* The big cities can be occupied by the Dutch forces, but the rural countryside cannot be captured. The Dutch lack the power to dominate the whole Republican territory, and they lack the money to maintain thousands of soldiers. So the Republican government must and will continue to function outside the big cities. For this purpose each territory must organize its battle strategy without too much dependence upon the central administration. The first aim of the struggle in Republican territory is:

(*a*) Continuous obstruction, leaving the Dutch no opportunity to organize a regular administration. We must *obstruct and sabotage* every effort to consolidate the Dutch government. This means that the civil-servants must be 100 per cent nonco-operative. It means that rich men and socially minded men must establish a relief fund for the most important civil servants to prevent their forced co-operation with the Dutch because of a hungry stomach. They must undertake as soon as possible these social efforts, especially for the political victims and the unemployed civil servants. The women's organizations must pave the way.

(*b*) *Economic consolidation* of the Dutch can be prevented by obstructing the production of goods they need for foreign exchange. The means thereof are known to our fighters, and the merchants must understand what is to be done.

(*c*) *Political consolidation* of the Dutch, namely, the constitution of a puppet regime made up of men of their own choice, must be prevented. This is the duty of every political leader from every political party. The way is clear: better to be jailed than to be a puppet and a traitor.

Our struggle against the Dutch in the territories outside of the Republic and in foreign countries shall be continued. The results of this fight depend largely upon our own struggle within the Republic.

From January 6 to 10, 1949, the writer visited Jogjakarta and was able to witness how closely the situation there conformed to that which the Republican leaders had relied upon the people to create, and how different it was from what the Dutch were telling the world existed in the areas which their troops had "liberated." [2] He found that it had become for the most part a city of women, children, and old men. A majority of the young men had gone to the countryside to fight the Dutch from there. Few people ventured out of their houses. The city was not under complete Dutch control. Its central area and part of its suburbs were occupied by a Dutch garrison of about 1,000 men possessing ten Stewart tanks and large numbers of armored cars and Bren-carriers. But much of the periphery of the city was either no man's land or actually occupied by Republican guerrillas. The Dutch military authorities informed the writer that several areas of the city to which he wished to go were "not safe." Both Dutch and Indonesian sources affirmed that in a major attack on December 29 Republican troops had penetrated to within four blocks of the city's center. On the night of January 9, while the writer was still in the city, a heavy battalion of the Republic's crack Police Mobile Brigade supported by a KRIS [3] company of the Republican army launched a four-hour attack which penetrated to the very center of Jogjakarta, where they fought for two hours before Dutch tanks and armored cars finally ejected them.[4]

[2] After having left Jogjakarta on Dec. 19, 1948, following its bombing and invasion by the Dutch the writer revisited the city in early January as a correspondent for Overseas News Agency. Only by becoming a correspondent was he able to visit the city at that time.

[3] Made up of men from Sulawesi (Celebes), a large number of whom were from the Minahassa area.

[4] The objective of the Republican attack was the Hotel Merdeka (Freedom Hotel). It was rather fatuously renamed Grand Hotel by the Dutch after their occupation of the city. The writer was staying there at the time of the attack. Though he was aware of fighting within the block in which the hotel was situated, he did not realize until afterwards how nearly successful the Republican attack had been. He later learned that a Republican squad had penetrated the back entrance of the hotel and was laying dynamite charges there when driven off by Dutch soldiers. One month later in Dutch-occupied Bandung the Republican lieutenant who had been in charge of the dynamite squad was kind enough to express to the writer his regrets that he had been placed in such an unhealthy predicament and assured him that there had been no desire to dynamite him personally.

The nonco-operation of the Indonesian civilian inhabitants of Jogjakarta was almost absolute. The head of the Dutch economic administration in Jogjakarta, Mr. B. J. Muller, informed the writer that out of the city's population of approximately 400,000 only 6,000 people were working for the Dutch. Out of about 10,000 civil servants in the Jogjakrata area no more than 150, he stated, were working for the Dutch administration. With regard to even these he was frank to state that it was his belief that they were working only because expressly ordered to by the Sultan of Jogjakarta so that the civilian population would not suffer unduly. These few civil servants were from the city's water works, sanitary department, power station, and hospitals. This condition persisted, Mr. Muller stated, even though there was an acute food shortage in the city, the supplies coming in being at the most only 50 per cent of what they had been before the Dutch attack. About half of the approximately forty tons of food coming into the city per day was being brought in by the Dutch via convoy from Semarang, but this, he stated, went exclusively to the Dutch occupation forces and those 6,000 Indonesians willing to work for them. Noncollaborators (except for persons in the hospital) were given none of this food.[5]

Thus at least 350,000 of the city's preattack population of some 500,000 were dependent upon a daily incoming supply of food approximately equal to one-third that which was being supplied the city before the attack.[6] This plus whatever meager store these people had been able to accumulate previously was their source of food. Fortunately for them the slim supplies of food which peasants from nearby areas were bringing in could be purchased for Republican currency and only Republican currency, the peasants refusing to accept the N.E.I. currency brought in by the Dutch.

One significant effect of this, a factor which helped buoy Republican morale, was that the rate between the N.E.I. guilder and the Republican rupiah prevailing among Chinese shopkeepers in Jogjakarta, which had fallen from 1:50 before the Dutch attack to 1:500 a

[5] Interview of the writer with Mr. B. J. Muller, chief representative of the N.E.I. government's Department of Economic Affairs, Jogjakarta, Jan. 7, 1949. Mr. Muller was undoubtedly one of the most completely candid Dutch officials whom the writer met during his stay in Indonesia.

[6] Relatively few peasants were bringing food into the city compared with normal times. Only those living fairly close were doing so. Not one ox cart was seen in the city by the writer during this visit. Rice from outlying districts had previously been brought to the city primarily in ox carts.

few days thereafter, had climbed back to 1:130. Some Chinese shopkeepers with whom the writer spoke in Jogjakarta at this time stated
a preference for Republican currency over N.E.I. currency, explaining
that they had to have the former in order to buy rice. Ten days after
the writer left the ratio was back to 1:110 and by the end of January it
reached 1:90. The faith of the Indonesian peasant in the Republican
regime and its dog-eared paper notes with the picture of Soekarno on
them appeared to be exerting a greater power over the relative values
of the currencies than Dutch military might.

Gradually the acuteness of the food situation was somewhat relieved
after more peasants from outlying areas lost some of their fear of
bringing food into a Dutch-occupied city, with the Dutch encouraging
their coming and the high prices obtained for rice undoubtedly serving as an additional inducement. However, at the time the writer was
in Jogjakarta and for some weeks thereafter the situation remained
extremely critical. Considerable credit for meeting this situation must
go to Indonesian women such as Mrs. Suriadarma, Dr. Sulianti
Suleiman, Miss Budiardjo, and Miss Kurianingrat who set up clandes-
tine "rice kitchens." Here Indonesian civil servants who did not wish
to collaborate with the Dutch, but who had no food in reserve,
could obtain the minimum to keep themselves and their families
alive.

The treatment of the civilian population by the Dutch served to increase its resolve not to co-operate with them. The majority of wounded
civilians in the hospital had sustained their wounds after, rather than
during, the Dutch attack on Jogjakarta. Almost every night a few
civilians were killed and wounded in the fighting between Republican
patrols and the Dutch garrison, and the Dutch were held ultimately
responsible for this. Moreover, several well-known Republican leaders
had been summarily shot by Dutch troops. Among these were Dr.
Santoso, secretary-general of the Department of Education, who on
the day of the Dutch attack was lined up with eight other civilians and
shot by a Dutch major.[7] Three other prominent persons were shot in
their homes: Masdoelhak Nasution, adviser to Prime Minister Hatta;
Mr. Hendromartono, a former cabinet minister; and Sumarsono, a
high Ministry of Interior official. Two sons of Abikusno, chairman of
the Sarekat Islam Indonesia party, were dragged from his home on

---

[7] There were two eye witnesses to this shooting both of whom were interviewed
by the writer. The bodies were recovered by the Indonesian Red Cross, whose
autopsy found that these 9 had been shot at close range by a pistol.

December 25 by Dutch soldiers and found shot to death the next morn-ing,[8] the official Dutch explanation being that they were shot because they were out after curfew.[9]

The Dutch authorities understood clearly that, even if they could maintain military supremacy in the Jogjakarta area, their situation was hopeless unless they could bring a substantial number of Indo-nesians, particularly civil servants, to co-operate with them. They knew how strong was the popular support in central Java, particularly in the Jogjakarta area, for Hamengku Buwono IX, the Sultan, and they hoped that he would provide them the key for solving this vital problem. If they could secure his support, they believed that a substantial part of the population might give up its attitude of nonco-operation. To do so they were prepared to make him *Wali Negara* of a state to be included in the federation they were sponsoring. His state would include all or most of the area administered by the Republic in central and east Java prior to their attack. However, the Sultan shut himself up in his *kraton* (walled complex of the buildings of his court) and refused to treat with the Dutch military or civilian authorities. Finally after Gen-eral Spoor, the Netherlands commander in chief, threatened to enter the *kraton* doors in a tank, the Sultan agreed to grant him a ten-minute interview. However, the only subject the Sultan wished to discuss was the departure of Dutch troops from Jogjakarta, and at the end of the ten minutes indicated coldly that the interview was over and left the room.

Approximately the same conditions found by the writer in Jogja-karta were encountered during the same week in Surakarta and Madiun by Quentin Pope, the able staff correspondent for the Far East of the *Chicago Tribune*. Indeed, as later reports demonstrated, bitter armed resistance and stubborn civilian nonco-operation was be-ing encountered by the Dutch throughout the Republican areas of Java and Sumatra. However, the conditions which actually existed in

[8] Interview of the writer with Abikusno (Jogjakarta, Jan. 8, 1949).

[9] Stated to the writer by Capt. Vosveld, chief of Dutch army intelligence in Jog-jakarta. The poor quality of Dutch army intelligence is indicated by the fact that Vosveld did not realize who Abikusno was. Apparently the writer's inquiry con-cerning this stirred him to telegraph Batavia regarding the matter. The following morning (Jan. 9) the writer was placed under house arrest in the Merdeka Hotel by Vosveld on orders from Batavia, and shortly thereafter Abikusno was arrested. On Jan. 10 the writer was flown with a military police escort back to Batavia, where he was released. He was never given a satisfactory explanation of this action by the Dutch authorities despite requests on his part and that of several other foreign correspondents.

these areas were not being reported to the outside world by the Dutch. Though they had ended censorship of outgoing news at the beginning of January, most news flowing out of Indonesia for the next two weeks was based upon the Dutch version of events.[10] Most foreign correspondents in Indonesia were agency men without assistants and forced to spend most of their time in Batavia. To visit the fighting areas involved three or four days away from the telegraph office in Batavia and whatever important news might break there. Not until the second week in January did a second staff correspondent, Robert Trumbull of the *New York Times,* arrive on the scene. The Committee of Good Offices and its military observers had been confined to Batavia until January 7 and were unable to collect sufficient data to draw up a report even partially covering the situation until January 24.

During the latter half of January reports from foreign correspondents in Indonesia made it increasingly clear to the world outside that the course of events there was hardly what the Dutch had been representing them to be. The report of the Committee of Good Offices cabled to the Security Council on January 24 indicated in the most temperate terms, but very clearly, the complete failure of the Dutch to live up to the Security Council's resolutions and their misrepresentation of conditions in Indonesia. Noting that its military observers were "able to observe only the localities taken by the Netherlands Army in its occupation of large towns and the main roads connecting them" and that being attached to the Netherlands forces they could not employ Republican military sources in their reports, the Committee even so was forced to conclude:

As a result of the Netherlands Army occupation and the consequent guerrilla activities, law and order within the former Republican controlled territories have, in general, not been established. Until now, in fact, serious disorders have been created . . . Since the Republican Government has been prevented from functioning, there is no authority on the Republican side to implement the Security Council's resolution directing both parties to "cease hostilities." Despite the Netherlands order to its troops to "cease hostilities," such cessation has not been, and cannot be, attained in the present situation.[11]

[10] Thus Robert Trumbull cabled the *N.Y. Times* on January 10 with respect to the writer's account of the heavy Republican attack on Jogjakarta: "Mr. Kahin's story is the first outside account of the current guerrilla warfare in the interior since the Dutch 'cease-fire' order of Dec. 31. . . . There have been no Dutch communiqués on major actions since the cease-fire" (*N.Y. Times,* Jan. 11, 1949, p. 3). Quentin Pope returned from the interior two days after the writer. U.N. military observers did not begin their investigations in the field until Jan. 9.

[11] U.N., S/1223, pp. 1–3.

Clearly this report coupled with that of a week before stating that the Republic's leaders were still imprisoned [12] called for further action from the Security Council.

The inclination of the Council to take new action was undoubtedly increased by the decisions taken at the conference on Indonesia convoked by Pandit Nehru, the Indian Prime Minister, at New Delhi from January 20–23. Recommendations to the Security Council were made jointly by the participants—Afghanistan, Australia, Burma, Ceylon, Egypt, Ethiopia, India, Iran, Iraq, Lebanon, Pakistan, Philippines, Saudi Arabia, Syria, and Yemen.[13] These resolutions went farther than most members of the Security Council were prepared to go and probably resulted in that body's taking a firmer stand than it was preparing to.[14] Even so the resolution finally adopted by the Security Council [15] was not strong. Again Soviet Russia went on record as opposing a resolution which Indonesians felt to be strongly favorable to the Netherlands. Again Indonesians noted that the Soviet insistence that Dutch troops withdraw promptly to the positions from which they had launched their attack was opposed by the United States and the United Kingdom.[16]

[12] U.N., S/AC. 10/250 (Jan. 16, 1949). The Committee was finally given permission by the Dutch to visit Bangka on Jan. 15. Regarding the condition of the 6 Republican leaders interned there it stated in its report: "They have one doorless bedroom 6m x 6m in which are located 6 beds. In addition, they were originally allowed an area of 4m x 10m wired off from a large reception room. Since 12 January this wire has been removed and the entire reception room 19m x 16m is open to their use. They are permitted limited access to the roof under guard. All windows are enclosed by wire netting as is the area around the door. Guards are on duty in sentry boxes immediately outside. They are not allowed to leave the wired area."

[13] Prior to the conference India, Pakistan, Burma, Ceylon, and Saudi Arabia had withdrawn all transit facilities, both sea and air, from the Netherlands.

[14] See U.N., S/1222, pp. 3–5.

[15] Beginning with the new year the membership of the nonpermanent members of the Council had partially changed, with Cuba, Egypt, and Norway replacing Syria, Belgium and Colombia. From the standpoint of the Netherlands, replacement of Belgium was considered a distinct loss.

[16] A Soviet proposal calling for the withdrawal of Dutch troops to areas occupied by them before the attack of Dec. 19 received the support of only the Ukraine, Cuba, and Egypt (N.Y. Herald Tribune, Jan. 29, 1949). It is to be noted that Cuba followed in the footsteps of its predecessor on the Council, Colombia, in refuting the frequently made Communist assertion that the Latin American states in the United Nations voted as puppets of the United States.

Few Indonesians were aware of the fact that in mid-January the United States had taken the initiative in proposing that the United Nations Commission for Indonesia be established with powers to recommend to the Council what areas of Java, Sumatra and Madura overrun by the Dutch "consistent with reasonable requirements of public security" should gradually be evacuated by Dutch troops and returned to

On January 28 the Security Council finally passed a resolution submitted jointly by the United States, China, Cuba, and Norway a week previously.[17] This noted that the Council's resolutions of December 24 and 28, 1948 had not been carried out and (1) called upon "the Government of the Netherlands to insure the immediate discontinuance of all military operations" and upon "the Government of the Republic simultaneously to order its armed adherents to cease guerrilla warfare;" (2) called upon the Netherlands "to release immediately and unconditionally all political prisoners arrested by them since 17 December 1948 in the Republic of Indonesia; and to facilitate the immediate return of officials of the Government of the Republic of Indonesia to Jogjakarta in order that they may discharge their responsibilities under paragraph 1 above, i.e., ordering cessation of guerrilla warfare and in order to exercise their appropriate functions in full freedom, including administration of the Jogjakarta area, which shall include the city of Jogjakarta and its immediate environs;" (3) recommended that the Netherlands and the Republic again undertake negotiations on the basis of the Linggadjati and Renville Agreements and the proposals submitted by Cochran on September 10, 1948, with these negotiations being based on the establishment by March 15, 1949 of an interim federal government "granted the powers of internal government in Indonesia," elections for an Indonesian Constitutent Assembly completed by October 1, 1949, and a "transfer of sovereignty over Indonesia by the government of the Netherlands" to a "United States of Indonesia" by July 1, 1950. In addition, the Council reconstituted its Committee of Good Offices as the "United Nations Commission for Indonesia," endowing it with more competencies than it possessed previously and allowing it to make decisions on the basis of the agreement of two of its three members (still the United States, Australia and Belgium). It was given the power to make recommendations to the Council and to the two parties to the dispute, assisting the latter in their negotiations and in implementing the resolutions of the Council.[18]

---

the administration of the Republic (see *N.Y. Times,* Jan. 14, 1949, p. 1). Most of them knew only of the American opposition to the Soviet resolution on outright withdrawal of Dutch troops from the areas of the Republic that they had overrun since Dec. 18.

[17] Abstaining (i.e., opposed) were France, Russia, and the Ukraine on the most important sections, and Argentina on those sections dealing with the U.N. Commission (*N.Y. Herald Tribune,* Jan. 29, 1949).

[18] U.N. Security Council, S/1234, pp. 2–3. Also the commission was specifically re-

Two facts were in particular noted by Indonesians: (1) the Council did not call upon the Dutch to evacuate anything more than the Jogjakarta area; and (2) the Council made no provision for the enforcement of its resolutions. In the light of the refusal of the Netherlands to live up to the previous resolutions of the Council this omission was obviously extremely serious. The lack of teeth in the Council's resolution convinced Indonesians all the more that no effective help could be expected from the United Nations. The defiant response of the Netherlands government to the Council's resolution certainly did not encourage them to think otherwise. The Netherlands representative in the United Nations stated on January 28 in reference to the Council's resolution that his government would carry it out "to the extent to which it is compatible with the responsibility of the Netherlands for the maintenance of real freedom and order in Indonesia, a responsibility which at this moment no one else can take from us." [19]

In Indonesia the reaction of much of the Dutch population to the Council's resolution was reflected in a cartoon covering the front page of the Sunday supplement of one of the principal Dutch language newspapers. This cartoon was entitled "The UNO Desires Free Elections for Indonesia" and depicted a long queue of individuals each bearing the name of one of the Soviet satellite countries and dressed in prison garb standing before a booth marked "UNO," the first person in the queue inquiring "Is this where we get free elections, Excellency?" An obvious intent of the cartoon was to suggest the anomaly of expecting free elections in Indonesia when so much of the world was without them. But that was not the only idea which the cartoon got across. Also depicted was a small dog identified as "NICA" (Netherlands Indies Civil Administration) with one hind leg raised and in the process of urinating on the booth marked "UNO." [20]

Among educated Indonesians with whom the writer spoke at this

---

quested to help in achieving "the earliest possible restoration of the civil administration of the Republic," recommending (after consultation with the parties) the extent to which the areas controlled by the Republic under the terms of the Renville Agreement "should be progressively returned to the administration of the Republic of Indonesia," and supervising such transfers. Also it was to recommend "which if any Netherlands forces" were to be retained temporarily in any area outside of the Jogjakarta area to assist in the maintenance of law and order (*ibid.*, p. 4).

[19] U.N. *Bulletin* (1949), VI, 159.

[20] *De Ronde Tafel* (weekly supplement of the *Bataviaasch Nieuwsblad*), Jan. 29, 1949.

time the position taken by the United States towards the Indonesian-Netherlands dispute was not measured by the speeches of American representatives before the Security Council. In part the position of the United States was indicated to them by its voting record in the United Nations. However, their chief index of its attitude was provided by its economic relationship with the Netherlands. They were absolutely convinced that the Netherlands would never have been able to undertake its military measures against the Republic had it not been able to rely on very great economic help from the United States under the ECA program. The more knowledgeable of them did not insist that the United States was providing the Netherlands directly with the financial means for mounting this effort. But they did insist most adamantly that the subsidizing of the Netherlands home economy under the Marshall Plan allowed the Dutch to divert a major portion of the wealth of that economy to the reconquest of Indonesia. This was a financial outlay, they insisted, which could not possibly have been made had not Marshall funds replaced this drain on the home economy. They noted that maintenance of the Netherlands armed forces in Indonesia during the single year 1948 was estimated to total well over $400,000,000 [21] and that ECA aid allotted the Netherlands during the year April, 1948, through March, 1949, was reported to total $402,800,000.[22]

There had been an additional ECA grant of $68,000,000 to the Netherlands regime in Indonesia of which $54,000,000 had been expended at the time of the Dutch December attack. On December 22, 1948, the Economic Co-operation Administration, with State Department concurrence, suspended allocation of the $14,000,000 balance pending "clarification" of the situation growing out of the Netherlands attack.[23] To Indonesians this stoppage was in general seen as nothing more than a publicity gesture of little real effect. If the United States had genuinely wished to restrain Dutch military aggression, they held, it could have done so by threatening to cut off Marshall Plan aid to the Netherlands. If it now really desired to make the Dutch abide by

[21] Cf. dispatch from Batavia by Robert Trumbull, *N.Y. Times*, Jan. 12, 1949, p. 6. The exact figure given by Trumbull is $436,297,874 and included only the cost of maintenance of the Dutch army and air force in Indonesia, the navy not being included.

[22] *Ibid.* A dispatch of Felix Belair from Washington to the *N.Y. Times*, Dec. 22, 1948, p. 1, indicated that three-quarters ($298,500,000) of this ECA aid was a grant allocation.

[23] Felix Belair, *ibid.* According to Belair: "The ECA acted on information supplied by the State Department and only after those responsible for foreign policy had been fully consulted on the implication of the move."

the Security Council's resolutions, it could do so, they insisted, if it threatened to stop further ECA allocations to the Netherlands.

However, the American State Department appeared to remain committed to a policy of absolute priority to development of the military and economic strength of Western Europe. Despite their strong disapproval of Dutch actions and genuine anger at the Netherlands' refusal to abide by the Security Council's recommendations there was a general reluctance among most top State Department personnel to apply sanctions against the Dutch that would weaken the Netherlands economy and thereby perhaps undermine the over-all strength of the Western European economy which they were trying to build up.[24]

But, as the Dutch were aware, there was in the United States an increasingly powerful criticism of this policy of the State Department from outside the government, a criticism that soon came to be echoed by a growing number of Congressmen. The CIO made known its views as early as December 23 in a letter of its President Philip Murray to Secretary of State Marshall. Speaking in behalf of the 6,000,000 members of his labor federation, Murray stated:

We feel that insofar as American aid is now available to the Netherlands government, it is being used for purposes inconsistent with the original intent and objectives of the European Recovery Program.

I voice the hope, on behalf of the members of the CIO, that the government of the United States will continue to take every feasible step in the realm of diplomacy *and economics* to help terminate the Dutch aggression in Indonesia, and to assure a speedy settlement recognizing the rightful interests of the Indonesian people in their quest for democratic self-rule. You may rest assured that the State Department will enjoy the full support of American workers in whatever steps it may take in this direction.[25]

Opposition to the State Department's subordination of the interests of a sound Indonesian policy to what it conceived to be those of a strong Western Europe became increasingly manifest in nongovernmental circles. Reflecting this was a column of Walter Lippmann published on January 10 in which he stated:

Our friends in Western Europe should try to understand why we cannot and must not be maneuvered, why we dare not drift, into general opposition to

[24] In a press conference on Feb. 2, 1949, Dr. Alan J. Valentine, chief of the ECA Mission to the Netherlands stated: "To cut off aid to the Netherlands would certainly impair recovery of all Western Europe" (*N.Y. Herald Tribune,* Feb. 3, 1949).
[25] *N.Y. Times,* Dec. 23, 1948 (italics the writer's).

the independence movements in Asia. They should tell their propagandists to stop smearing these movements. They should try to realize how disastrous it would be to them, and to the cause of Western civilization, if ever it could be said that the Western Union for the defense of freedom in Europe was in Asia a syndicate for the preservation of decadent empires.[26]

This point of view also became increasingly strong in Congress.[27] A number of Democratic Congressmen shared this mounting sentiment but restrained themselves from undertaking any overt action because of the position taken by the State Department. Many Republican members, however, felt no such limitation and soon made clear their position. On February 7 a resolution was presented in the Senate by Owen Brewster and signed by nine other Republican Senators. This called for the stopping of all ECA and any other financial aid to the Netherlands until it ceased hostilities against the Indonesian Republic, withdrew its armed forces to its side of the Renville truce line, released all Republican government leaders arrested since December 18, and opened "bonafide negotiations with the Indonesian Republic under the terms of the Renville Agreement." [28]

As Quentin Pope reported from Batavia to the *Chicago Tribune* at the end of February this move greatly disturbed Hollanders in Indonesia and was very seriously viewed by them. Dutch representatives in Washington were undoubtedly aware that a considerable number of Democratic Senators shared the sentiments of the ten Republicans who signed the Brewster Resolution and would have been more outspoken except for their desire not to embarrass the Administration. However, there was no certainty that they would maintain this restraint or that more Republican Senators might not soon associate themselves with the Brewster Resolution. It must have become obvious to the Dutch that their initial stubborn stand against the Security Council's resolution of January 28 was too extreme and too likely to beget a dangerously hostile reaction, not only in the United States, but in other countries as well.

During the first two weeks of February a cabinet crisis developed

[26] *N.Y. Herald Tribune,* Jan. 10, 1949.

[27] To an important extent this was due to the unflagging efforts of the Indonesian Republic's representatives in the United States, who brought to the attention of a number of Congressmen facts concerning the Indonesian situation which otherwise they would not have known.

[28] U.S. Senate, 81st Congress, *S. Res. 56* Feb. 7, 1949. This resolution was signed by Senators Brewster, Bridges, Butler, Wherry, Malone, Smith (Maine), Baldwin, Langer, Morse, and McCarthy.

in the Netherlands over what policy was to be followed in Indonesia. The Catholic Party itself was torn by the dispute, the chief protagonists being two of its important leaders—Sassen, Minister of Overseas Territories and Beel, High Commissioner of the Crown in Indonesia. Official Dutch sources in Batavia stated that, whereas three months previously these two men had seen eye to eye with respect to policy in Indonesia, they were now far apart.[29] Both men were committed to the "federalist solution" of the Indonesian problem as outlined in the BIO Decree. However, it appeared that Sassen was absolutely intransigent towards the Security Council's resolutions while Beel felt that a formula existed whereby a sufficient gesture could be made towards compliance with those resolutions while adhering to the plans of the BIO Decree.[30] On February 11 Dr. Sassen resigned and Beel, his policy accepted, soon departed for Indonesia.

Upon his return to Indonesia on February 26, Beel's plan was officially announced by the Netherlands government, a fuller explanation being given by him in a press conference in Batavia held on March 1.[31] In introducing his explanation of the plan Beel stated that "there was full agreement between the Netherlands government and the Security Council with respect to the *aims* of both parties." The only difference, he asserted, was with respect to "the *means* for reaching this goal." The Netherlands was willing not only to accept the Security Council's timetable for the transfer of sovereignty to Indonesia but planned to accelerate that timetable.

Though it would be unable to form an interim Indonesian federal government by March 15 as the Security Council had requested, the Netherlands government planned to convoke a round-table conference at the Hague on March 12 to which all Indonesian elements, including the Republicans, were invited and which it hoped would be attended by the U.N. Indonesian Commission. The announced purpose of this conference was "to discuss the conditions for and the ways along which the earliest possible transfer of sovereignty" could be effectuated.

[29] Cf. U.P. dispatch from Batavia, Feb. 12, 1949.

[30] A *N.Y. Times* dispatch from the Hague reported Sassen as having "uncompromisingly opposed the Security Council resolution." It reported that he had been replaced by Dr. J. H. van Maarseveen, "also from the Catholic Party but not so extreme as Dr. Sassen." *N.Y. Times*, Feb. 11, 1949, p. 1.

[31] Attended by the writer. The text of the statement of the Netherlands government on the Beel Plan released at the Hague on Feb. 26 was reported in the *N.Y. Times*, Feb. 27, 1949, p. 1. The following account of the Beel Plan is based upon the original text released at the Hague and Beel's elucidation on March 1.

"The simultaneous establishment of the Netherlands Indonesian Union and the arrangement for the intermediary period, including the creation of a federal interim government" were to be considered in relation to such an accelerated transfer. The endeavor would be made to conclude the work of this conference by May 1, 1949, to have an interim federal government established by that date, and to complete the transfer of sovereignty to it on July 1, 1949—a full year ahead of the final date suggested by the Security Council. In addition, the Netherlands government anounced that it had "decided to lift the re-maining restriction on the liberty of movement of the Republican lead-ers and to consult with them concerning their wishes as to their future residence and the arrangements which will have to be made in this re-spect." However, "conditions," it was later explained, would not allow them to be returned to Jogjakarta, nor was the Security Council's re-quest for a return of Jogjakarta to Republican authority to be ful-filled.[32] Beel made clear that if the Republican leaders refused to ac-cept the invitation to attend the conference at the Hague, it would be held without them.

As the United Nations Commission on Indonesia noted in its report of March 1, 1949, the Beel Plan did not constitute a compliance with the Security Council's resolution of January 28. In fact, the Com-mission regarded it as "comprising a counterproposal, or substitute, for the provisions of the 28 January resolution." [33] The Dutch had not abandoned the essence of their original plans. The only change in their position, other than agreeing to impose fewer restrictions on the freedom of movement of the interned Republican leaders,[34] had been

[32] This was not made clear until after Beel's press conference of March 1. There he refused to answer the questions of correspondents on this question, saying only: "It is better not to go into the question of the return of the Republican leaders to Jogja [karta]." However, this had been made clear to the Republican leaders on Bangka on Feb. 28 when they were visited by Dr. Koets, chief assistant of Beel (see U.N., S/1270, add. 1, p. 4).

[33] U.N., S/1270, p. 15.

[34] At his March 1 press conference Beel explained that the Republican leaders would "later" be granted the "same rights and duties as any ordinary citizen in this country." He stated that their rights were to be governed by the conditions of the state of war and siege that existed throughout Indonesia. Manifestly this meant that they could not engage in ordinary political activity, much less return to Republican-controlled parts of Java or Sumatra. The interned leaders elected to remain on Bangka rather than go to Batavia or some other Dutch-controlled area. By late January Soekarno and Hadji Agoes Salim had been brought to Bangka from Sumatra to join the other Republican leaders there. Shortly thereafter Sjahrir, be-cause he was not technically a member of the Republican government, was allowed to go to Batavia.

to set specific target dates for the formation of an interim federal Indonesian government and for the transfer of sovereignty to it.

Furthermore, that "transfer of sovereignty," however complete or incomplete it might turn out to be, was still to be to a federal government which the Dutch had created and which was to be indirectly controlled by them. As Beel made clear in his press conference, the Netherlands army would be maintained in Indonesia until after this transfer of sovereignty; thereafter, but only "on the request of the federal government," it would stay on until the Indonesian government had built an army of its own capable of maintaining law and order. There was little doubt but that such a federal government would make this request. Should it not do so, it was obvious that Republican troops would quickly take over.

As had been expected by the Dutch, the interned Republican leaders refused to accept their invitation. On February 28 after the Dutch proposals had been brought to Bangka, Mr. Roem, chairman of the Indonesian delegation, after consulting with the Republican leaders there, announced the refusal and stated that the Republican government "will never take part in any action evading implementation of the Security Council's resolution." [35] However, the next day the BFO (Federal Consultative Assembly), following its consultations with Beel, formally and unanimously (i.e., all the fifteen states and special territories represented in it) accepted the invitation to attend the conference at the Hague and accepted it on the basis of the Netherlands government statement of February 26.[36] Thus it was that at his press conference on the night of March 1 Beel's obvious pleasure at the course of events was generally remarked.

However, Beel's pleasure did not last long. Five days later the BFO announced that its position had changed. A majority of its members now demanded that the Netherlands carry out the Security Council's resolution that the Republican government be restored to Jogjakarta. This, they insisted, would have to precede the projected conference at the Hague. There was no longer unanimity in the BFO, and the division among its constituent delegations between pro-Republican and anti-Republican blocs became increasingly sharp with those daring to be openly pro-Republican, for the time at least, in the majority.

Many Republican leaders were convinced that this defection of so

[35] *N.Y. Times,* March 1, 1949, p. 1.

[36] The letter stating this is reproduced in the report of the U.N. Commission of March 1, S/1270, p. 10.

many "Federalists" was to a large extent a consequence of conditions in the interior of Java and Sumatra. Republican resistance to the Dutch had through January and February significantly increased, in some areas spectacularly so. Moreover, this resistance had come to extend over an increasingly wider area. Following the Dutch attack of December 19 the entire body of the Republic's crack Siliwangi Division had spilled over the old Renville truce line and marched for West Java, the area where it had operated before evacuating under the terms of the Renville Agreement. Marching in units of one or two battalions and often with the wives and children of the men in the rear the Siliwangi Division fought its way some 200 miles through central and part of West Java, its various battalions finally halting, according to plan, in the vicinities of Bandung, Kuningan, Cheribon and Garut.

Their way was bitterly contested not only by the Dutch but by the troops of Darul Islam as well, with as many casualties being lost to the latter as to the former. (This was totally unexpected, many Siliwangi units being caught completely off guard, for at the time they set out they had believed Darul Islam still backed the Republic.) Wherever the units of the Siliwangi went, they were enthusiastically received by the local inhabitants as deliverers not only from the Dutch, but from Darul Islam as well. Wiranata Koesoema and other top officials of the Dutch-sponsored West Java state of Pasundan unanimously agreed that the Dutch could not liquidate Darul Islam; only the troops of the Indonesian Republic, they declared to the writer, would be able to do that.

Were it not for the fact that many of the Siliwangi units were tied down in combat with the troops of Darul Islam, the situation for the Dutch in West Java would have been dangerously critical. As it was, their position there was very difficult. By the end of February only about one-third of the area supposedly comprising their state of Pasundan was controlled by Dutch troops. Another third was controlled by the Siliwangi Division and other Republican troops, and the remainder by the forces of Darul Islam. Roughly the same situation existed in East Java. There, following the Dutch attack, the entire Sungkono Division crossed over the Renville truce line into areas from which Republican troops had withdrawn nearly a year previously. By the beginning of March less than half of East Java was under Dutch control.

Though the delegation from Pasundan to the BFO was well aware of the military situation in Java,[37] it was known to be strongly pro-Republican, and apparently because of this its counsel was discounted by other representatives of the BFO. The only other delegation to the BFO coming from an area where Republican resistance was obvious and widespread was that from East Java, whose Indonesian Government, as we have seen, was of a kind considered "reliable" by the Dutch.[38] Most Federalist representatives in the BFO, particularly that large majority of them coming from outside Java and Sumatra, had been given little opportunity to learn the real facts concerning the Republican resistance in these areas. For the most part they had been forced to rely upon the Dutch version of events in the interior of Java and Sumatra as relayed to them by the press and radio of the Dutch-controlled information services of their state or autonomous territory. The writer was surprised in traveling through the Dutch-sponsored federal states outside Java by how little Indonesians there knew even as late as March and April, 1949, about the real nature of military developments in Java and Sumatra. Likewise they generally had no knowledge of the extent and intensity of civilian nonco-operation with the Dutch in the newly overrun territories. Indeed, the news they received from the Dutch had given them the impression that there had been widespread co-operation with the Netherlands authorities on the part of Republican elements.

Even in Batavia news of the real situation was not easily available to Indonesians, newspapers there being suspended if they published too much news of the strength and aggressiveness of Republican military activity. For the newspaper reader it was actually much easier to learn what was going on in the interior of Java in New York than it was in Batavia. The Indonesian press could not freely print all dispatches from Batavia by United Press and Associated Press correspondents, even though its papers subscribed to these agencies. Moreover, Federalists were usually under the chaperonage of Dutch officials when they were in Batavia and when alone believed themselves to be

37 The writer interviewed both its delegates.

38 The territory of Central Java (comprising that part of Central Java occupied by the Dutch prior to their attack of Dec., 1948) did not have a vote in the BFO until April 14, 1949. At that time (when it was visited by the writer) it had a functionless "representative council" composed of persons elected by a restricted list of Indonesian, Chinese, Arab, and Dutch organizations approved by the Netherlands authorities. The vice-chairman of this body, Mr. Zainal Abidien informed the writer that at least 80 per cent of its Indonesian members (72 out of its 82 members being Indonesians) were civil servants employed by the N.E.I. Government. "So far," he said, "our representative council has absolutely no power."

under close watch by intelligence agents of the Dutch. Thus they were generally reluctant to have contact with members of Indonesian underground organizations who were in a position to tell them facts they could not learn from Dutch officials or the newspaper or radio. In short, most delegates to the BFO and most Federalist leaders in general, particularly those from outside Java and Sumatra, were aware that Republican resistance was continuing, but thought it to be weak, futile, and doomed to suppression by what they believed was the irresistible weight of Dutch arms.

On March 3, 1949, two events coincided to shake these convictions of the BFO leaders. On that day they had sent a delegation to Bangka which found the Republican leaders interned there more confident than ever of the ability of the Republic's forces to resist the Dutch successfully [39] and clearly determined not to consider proposals of the Dutch which were not in accord with the Security Council's resolution, particularly not until they and Republican authority had been returned to Jogjakarta. On their return to Batavia these BFO delegates learned some startling news, news which probably gave a fresh perspective to the experience they had just had on Bangka. What had been dismissed as rumor the day before now turned out to be fact. The Republican army had very nearly captured Jogjakarta. The situation there was so serious that the Dutch authorities had felt obliged to admit that there had been heavy fighting lasting two days and involving some 2,000 Republican troops, and that those troops had "gained temporary successes."

For many Indonesians such an admission meant that at least twice as many Indonesian troops had been involved and that, had the Dutch not been able to fly in heavy reinforcements from Semarang, Jogjakarta would have fallen to the Republican army. Of more importance, this report meant to them that the host of reports of guerrilla successes during January and February—which the Dutch had so consistently dismissed as Republican propaganda—were probably mostly true. Undoubtedly this same reaction was shared by many Federalists. Presumably this and the attitude of the Republican leaders on Bangka stiffened the spines of many BFO leaders. Certainly it was a factor in the sudden disaffection of a majority of BFO delegates encountered

[39] Despite their isolation on the island of Bangka Republican leaders there were able to get considerable news concerning events outside over and above what the Dutch conveyed to them. This they received from members of the U.N. Commission for Indonesia and those few correspondents who visited Bangka.

by the enraged High Commissioner of the Netherlands Crown, Dr. Beel, on March 5.

This attitude of the majority of BFO leaders continued and indeed appeared to increase through most of March. More and more reports of powerful guerrilla attacks against the Dutch and the increasingly defensive posture of the Dutch army in Java and Sumatra convinced most of them that the Dutch plan for a federal Indonesia could be realized only if the Republic were included. Fighting would never cease, they believed, unless a reconstituted Republican government sitting in Jogjakarta and led by Soekarno and Hatta ordered Republican soldiers to stop. This did not mean that most of these Federalist representatives were not still wedded to the creation of a federal order in which they, backed by Dutch power, would be dominant. But they felt that this could not be achieved unless the Republic was included as a minor partner.

Moreover, the feelings of some of these Federalists were being turned against the Dutch because of the brutal tactics to which their army was resorting, tactics which were alienating the Indonesian population as a whole even more widely from the Netherlands than before. Almost every correspondent who traveled with Dutch army convoys in February related at least one instance of the increasingly frequent machine-gunning and cannonading of villages near the roads to be sure no guerrillas were lurking there, with no apparent regard for the killing of unarmed civilians. This was by no means general practice; it was the exception; but enough Dutch officers resorted to this tactic to create a popular impression that it was widespread. Undoubtedly many of the increasing accounts of atrocities were exaggerated; but many, it was clear, were not, for instance, the forthright report of the East Java Mission of the Dutch Reformed Church concerning the brutal killing of Indonesian civilians in Peniwen by Dutch troops on February 20.[40]

40 In Report no. 299 of the East Java Mission of the Dutch Reformed Church to the H.Q. of its mission board in Oestgeest, the Netherlands, was included the following report from the Peniwen church to the executive board of the Malang Synod dated Feb. 25, 1949, and signed by the parson of Peniwen and a member of the synodal board. "In Peniwen there is a polyclinic and maternity clinic which has been operating four years and is supported by the parsonage, the former mission vicarage. . . . When the Dutch army unit entered the building, everybody, patients as well as nurses, was ordered to go outside. Then on the front grounds three men of the establishment and two patients were shot down, and a third patient was heavily injured. Eight members of the establishment were taken away, along with nearly all medicines; and the furniture was destroyed. . . . Among the parish members three women were raped, while the husband of one and the fiancée of another

Letters smuggled out of such Dutch-occupied cities as Jogjakarta and Surakarta and the corroborating reports of foreign correspondents visiting those cities gradually made clear the absence of law and order that existed there. The struggle of Republican civil servants and laborers there to resist the pressures exerted upon them to co-operate with the Dutch was an example which began to afford inspiration to many in other areas.[41]

Proof of the veracity of these reports and the general character of the Dutch regime in the newly occupied areas was lent by the public letter of January 21 of the Sultan of Jogjakarta which was widely circulated in Java and found its way to Batavia by early March. In this the Sultan stated that the report in the Dutch-controlled press that he was co-operating with them was "a lie." He said that he had resigned his office as head of the Jogjakarta area and that his resignation extended to "all officials and workers" of the Jogjakarta local government. He had done so, he stated, because:

(1) I cannot approve of the Dutch action towards our Republic.

(2) I cannot work to safeguard the peace and welfare of the people of Jogjakarta, because of brutal actions of the Dutch toward the people —male, female, youth, and the people in general. They have been arrested without any due process; houses and villages have been burned down until nothing remains. This was done not only against the Indonesian people, but against Chinese as well. Their protests have been answered with: "Yes, we are at war. The people have to suffer. . . ."

Although we have met with a great many difficulties, we will fight on from here. I am prepared to face any action the Dutch will employ toward me, but it is for the Dutch to understand that my attitude is the result of their actions.

However, an outside event administered a rather sharp check to this growing defection among the Federalists. In answer to the deteriorating situation the Security Council on March 23 passed a new resolution, known as the "Canadian Proposal," by an eight-vote majority

---

were shot dead. Another member of the board, a peasant, and a 62-year-old man were shot although they had taken cover and held their hands up. . . ."

[41] Arbitrary arrests of the members of the families of nonco-operators was one means of pressure. More widespread were the raids on houses of noncollaborators. At night in Jogjakarta and Surakarta Dutch army trucks manned by masked soldiers would drive up in front of these houses, the soldiers force their way inside, loot whatever was of value, and drive off. Netherlands M.P.'s were generally indifferent to these occurrences. As far as the writer knows all these raids were carried out by Eurasian and Ambonese personnel of the KNIL.

(including the United States).[42] The Canadian Proposal was clearly a substantial concession to the Netherlands' point of view. The *New York Times* correspondent at Lake Success reported that "delegations of the Republic of Indonesia, India, and other Far Eastern countries looked upon this latest resolution as giving away to Dutch demands and a face-saving gesture to make it appear that the council was not backing down on its earlier resolution." [43] Republicans in Indonesia were bitter and discouraged about the Council's actions. They believed that the resolution, despite its name, was American instigated, and they noted that the Soviet Union opposed it. Republican sympathizers in the federal states were deeply disheartened,[44] and the revolt of Federalist representatives within the BFO against Dutch dictation was markedly curbed.

The Council did not again direct the two parties to cease fighting, nor did it direct the Netherlands to restore the Republican leaders and their government to Jogjakarta. It merely requested that its agent, the United Nations Commission for Indonesia, "in accordance with the Council's resolution of 28 January, 1949, and without prejudicing the rights, claims, and positions of the parties" should assist them in reaching agreement as to implementation of the resolution of January 28, in particular that part of it dealing with the cessation of hostilities and the restoration of the Republican government and of its leaders to Jogjakarta. It also called upon the Commission to assist the parties in reaching agreement as to "the time and conditions for holding the proposed [by the Netherlands] conference at the Hague, to the end that negotiations contemplated by the resolution of 28 January may be held as soon as possible." If these agreements were reached, the Council stated, the holding of such a conference and the participation therein of the U.N.'s Commission for Indonesia, "in accordance with its terms of reference," would be considered by the Council as "consistent with the purposes and objectives" of its January 28 resolution.[45]

Responding to this ambiguous directive,[46] the U.N. Commission for

---

[42] All but the Soviet Union, Ukraine, and France.

[43] Report by George Barrett to *N.Y. Times,* March 23, 1949, p. 3.

[44] This was clearly apparent to the writer in traveling through these areas.

[45] *First Interim Report of the United Nations Commission for Indonesia,* S/1373, Aug. 4, 1949, p. 7.

[46] The writer is not responsible for the ambiguity in this abbreviated rendering of the Security Council directive. The full text is equally ambiguous and was so remarked to be at the time. The *N.Y. Times* correspondent covering this meeting of the Security Council, wrote: "After the meeting ended delegations sympathetic to the Indonesian Republic's cause complained that three different interpretations had been

Indonesia on March 26 called upon the Netherlands and the Republic to resume under its auspices their long suspended negotiations. Both parties agreed to this, and Dr. J. H. van Royen, leader of the Netherlands delegation arrived in Batavia on April 12. In the meantime the American Secretary of State, Dean Acheson, stressed to the Netherlands Foreign Minister, Dr. Stikker, on the latter's visit to Washington on March 31, the desire of the United States for a prompt and amicable settlement of the dispute. It is probable that in their discussions Acheson emphasized to Stikker the necessity for this if the State Department were not to be under a perhaps irresistible pressure from Congress to suspend ECA help to the Netherlands.

In its reporting of Acheson's talks with Stikker the *New York Times'* dispatch from Washington stated: "The State Department has been opposing efforts on Capitol Hill to eliminate European Recovery Plan allocations to the Dutch pending a settlement of the Indonesian questions. Thus far these efforts have not succeeded." [47] However, there was increasing and soundly based fear in the State Department that the Senate's mounting and progressively articulate opposition to Netherlands actions in Indonesia might delay passage of the entire $5,580,-000,000 European Recovery bill and that ultimate agreement to its passage might not be won until the $350,000,000 earmarked for the Netherlands was stricken out of the bill.[48]

At the same time Senate opposition to the refusal of the Netherlands to live up to the Security Council's January 28 resolution threatened to delay and possibly defeat the Administration's proposed military equipment program for Western Europe, or at least to restrict it from extending to the Netherlands. As the *New York Times* reported from

---

given in the Council for the Canadian resolution" (dispatch of George Barrett, (*N.Y. Times,* March 26, 1949, p. 4).
As a spokesman for the Indian Foreign Office stated two days later:

The suggestion that the United Nations Commission should assist the parties to reach an agreement on implementation in particular of the Council's resolution of Jan. 28 without prejudice to the rights, claims and positions of the parties is regarded as contradiction in terms. Par. 2 of the resolution of Jan. 28 made the return of the Republican government to Jogjakarta unconditional. It is difficult to make this conditional upon agreement of the parties, of whom the Dutch are one, without prejudice to the Republic" (*N.Y. Times,* March 26, 1949, p. 9).

[47] *N.Y. Times,* March 31, 1949, p. 14.
[48] Thus a Herald Tribune dispatch from Washington by Robert J. Donovan on April 2 reported that "The Indonesian question was about the last formidable issue confronting the measure [i.e., the ERP bill]. . . ." (*N.Y. Herald Tribune,* April 3, 1949). The present writer discussed this situation with two of the Senators involved in these debates.

Washington: "There is strong opposition to the arms program in general, so strong in fact, that the State Department is now seriously concerned about it. The opposition contains more than a few influential legislators who argue that the United States should not give arms to the Netherlands to replace or supplement military equipment being used in the Netherlands Indies." [49]

However, passage of the ERP program was of the most immediate and critical concern to the State Department and the Administration in general. There was before the Senate an amendment to the European Recovery Bill introduced by Senator Owen Brewster which enjoyed the support of a large number of Republican Senators and the possibility of backing from enough Democratic Senators to make its adoption a very real possibility. This amendment was of a general character, but specifically aimed against the Netherlands. It read:

No funds authorized for the purposes of this act shall be allocated to or expended for any foreign government which fails to comply with the orders or requests of the Security Council of the United Nations until such times as the Administrator is advised, in writing, by the president of the Security Council that such compliance has been effected.[50]

This was the situation which the Netherlands Foreign Minister, Dr. Stikker, found when he arrived in Washington, and there is little doubt that Mr. Acheson emphasized to him its seriousness. It is probable that it was made clear to the Dutch at this point that only if they

[49] *N.Y. Times,* March 31, 1949, p. 14. According to this dispatch Dr. Stikker upon arriving in Washington had said in regard to the projected negotiations in Batavia: "The whole problem is that somebody has got to trust somebody." Referring to this remark, the dispatch continued: "The problem of getting the trust and understanding of Congress, however, is complicated by the colonial tradition of the Netherlands and the anti-colonial tradition of the United States. These clashing traditions have brought relations between the Hague and Washington to a much more serious position than is generally known on Capitol Hill. Dr. Stikker's reference to 'trust' is only a polite allusion to the feeling among the Dutch that they have a right to expect equal treatment under the Economic Cooperation Administration and the North Atlantic treaty without being penalized for an Indonesian policy that they believe to be honorable. At the State Department and especially on Capitol Hill, however, less noble adjectives are used in describing the use of force by the Dutch Government against the Indonesians. Mr. Acheson and Dr. Stikker, therefore, will probably have to talk again before these differences can be cleared away. Meanwhile," the dispatch concluded, "the arms program for Western Europe is likely to get under debate on Capitol Hill long before the Batavia conference on Indonesia is completed. That is one of the reasons why Mr. Acheson was said to have expressed the hope that a compromise would be reached soon."

[50] *Congressional Record,* XCV, no. 58 (April 6, 1949), 4073.

agreed to go at least a substantial distance in carrying out the January 28 resolution of the Security Council would the State Department be able to convince the necessary number of senators not to cut off ECA allocations to the Netherlands.

Because of its importance in determining later Indonesian attitudes towards the United States, it is relevant to note in some detail how Indonesian leaders have regarded these talks between the Netherlands Foreign Minister and Mr. Acheson. They believe that by this time the United States government was concerned about the damage being done to the prestige of the United Nations by the Netherlands' defiance of its resolutions. They feel that of even more importance from the standpoint of the United States was the dangerous potential that developments in Indonesia held for Indonesia itself. It is their belief that the State Department was now fully aware of the sustained effectiveness of Indonesian military resistance to the Dutch and the tenacious nonco-operation of Indonesian civilians, and that it had finally become convinced that the Netherlands would never be able to marshal sufficient force in Indonesia to maintain law and order, much less to enforce a viable political decision. The State Department was now believed to fear that continued separation of the anti-Communist leaders of the government of the Republic from the leadership of the irrepressible independence movement in Java and Sumatra might result in the repudiation of their leadership, with a majority of the population coming to acknowledge that of Communist leaders instead.

The leaders of the Republic's government were seen by many of the Indonesian people as having risked the prospects of independence by a willingness to negotiate with the Dutch and make concessions to them (e.g., the Renville Agreement) at the behest of the United States and because of a belief that by so doing they could rely on America to make the Dutch live up to their end of the agreement. This policy of reliance upon the United States with which the Republic's interned leaders were identified was now widely believed to have been unjustified and ruinous for the cause of Indonesian independence.

Aware of this situation, the State Department, so Indonesians believe, felt that to keep Communist leadership from becoming ascendant in what appeared to be an unsuppressible Indonesian resistance movement, it was necessary to bring the interned leaders on Bangka back to Jogjakarta and to the active command of the Republic's forces. Likewise the State Department is believed by them to have concluded that the projected federal Indonesian state to which the Dutch had promised to transfer sovereignty would not be viable in an environment of Communist pressure unless the Republic of Indonesia was included as a constituent unit.

With these considerations in mind, the State Department, Indonesian leaders believe, put strong pressure on the Netherlands government, principally in the form of a threat of ECA aid suspension, to enter into an agreement whereby the Netherlands would live up to the Security Council's resolution of January 28, 1949—or at least that part of it calling for the cessation of hostilities, the unconditional release of the interned Republican leaders, and the return of them and their government to Jogjakarta. Also they believe the Dutch were asked to guarantee a transfer of sovereignty by the end of 1950 to a federal Indonesian state in which the Republic was to be a constituent unit.

As *quid pro quo* these Indonesians believe that the State Department agreed: (1) to use its influence with the Senate to keep ECA funds flowing to Holland; (2) to use American influence to insure that in any transfer of sovereignty to Indonesia Dutch investments and Dutch trade with Indonesia would be protected; (3) that the transfer of sovereignty would be via a conference to be held at the Hague; and (4) that sovereignty would be transferred to a federal Indonesian state which, though including the Republic as one of its constituent states, would also be based on the fifteen-odd states and territories already set up or in the process of being set up by the Dutch, with the latter group having preponderant representation in the government of the federal state.

It is the belief of these Indonesian leaders that the Dutch interpretation of this agreement was that the Republic to be included in the projected federal Indonesian state could be a small and weak one and that in this federal state the Netherlands would be able to exercise paramount control along the general lines envisaged in its BIO Decree.

It was on the basis of such an agreement, these Indonesian leaders feel, that the State Department was able to bring most Senators who had been prepared to support the Brewster Amendment to the European Recovery Program Bill (including Brewster himself) to hold off on any move cutting off ECA assistance to the Netherlands until the Dutch had been given a reasonable opportunity to carry out their end of the bargain.

On April 2 it was reported from Washington that a compromise amendment in the place of Brewster's had been prepared by Senator

Arthur Vandenberg which was said to have been worked out with State Department approval.[51] The essence of this compromise was that ECA aid for the Netherlands would be halted only if the Security Council ordered sanctions to be taken against the Dutch for their refusal to abide by its resolutions.[52] Manifestly the "if" involved was a purely hypothetical one. The composition of the Security Council was such that even in the unlikely event of mustering the necessary majority of seven members in support of such action, some member of the Council would have been certain to veto it. France had already vetoed much milder action by the Security Council with respect to Indonesia and, given the situation in Indo-China, could hardly be expected to concur in establishing such a precedent.[53]

It is logical to assume that this sharp reversal in position of the many Senators whose sympathies lay with the Brewster Amendment was only made because of assurance from the State Department that the Netherlands had made commitments that it would go at least a substantial distance towards meeting the Security Council's resolution. Such a warm friend of the cause of the Indonesian Republic as Senator Frank Graham would hardly have supported this move otherwise. He certainly spoke for other Democratic Senators as well as many of the Republicans who had supported the Brewster Ammendment when on April 5 he made it clear that, if the Dutch should continue to evade the Security Council's resolution and the Council itself be unable to secure compliance, the United States should then cut off ECA aid to the Netherlands.[54]

The widely respected independent Republican, Senator Morse, refused to accept the Vandenberg compromise and made the defense offered by its backers appear shabby indeed. The soundness of his arguments was admitted by many of those who supported the compromise, and it seems safe to assume that they would be remembered if Dutch intransigence continued. In the heart of his address to the Senate, Senator Morse said:

I do not see how we can escape the conclusion that to whatever extent we have been helpful to the Dutch economy under the Marshall plan, we neces-

[51] *N.Y. Herald Tribune*, April 3, 1949.

[52] *Congressional Record*, XCV, no. 58 (April 6, 1949), 4073.

[53] Moreover, as Senator Wayne Morse indicated, it would not be beyond the realm of possibility for Soviet Russia to veto such action (*ibid.*, p. 4079).

[54] See *N.Y. Times*, April 6, 1949, p. 18. Though Senator Graham was not quite as explicit as this in his statement quoted in the *N.Y. Times* dispatch, he at a later date stated to the present writer that this was indeed the attitude that he held.

sarily thereby have been helpful to the Dutch Government in carrying out its violations of what I consider to be one of the most basic principles of our pledges under the United Nations Charter, the pledge that we would seek at least to protect the interests of people in the world who sought to make a fight for freedom as we believe in freedom. . . . We should not adopt the compromise amendment. We are dealing with great moral and ethical issues, and I do not think it is right to sanction here . . . approval for the expenditure of American dollars in the Netherlands under ECA, while the Netherlands stands in open defiance on the record of its obligations under the United Nations Charter. I say it has been found guilty of trampling freedom in Indonesia . . . I hold to the view, Mr. President, that so long as we permit the Dutch to get by with the course of defiant action which has been theirs since the violation of the Renville Agreement, we are going to be misunderstood in Indonesia; we are going to be misunderstood elsewhere in the world where weak people are looking to us to take a dominant role in protecting freedom.[55]

It was therefore made clear to the Dutch that the American Senate was closely watching their actions in Indonesia and prepared to apply severe economic sanctions against them if they did not abandon their defiance of the Security Council's resolutions.[56] In addition, in the General Assembly of the United Nations there had developed strong dissatisfaction with the manner in which the Security Council was handling the Indonesian question. On April 12 by a vote of forty-one to three this body agreed that it would look into and debate the question.[57] With the large majority of its members supporting the Republic, it seemed certain what the tenor of these debates would be. They would mobilize world opinion, including that of the United States Congress, even more powerfully behind the Republic's position. These debates were scheduled for early May, and this fact was certainly an added goal to the Netherlands to arrive at some agreement with the Republic before then.

[55] *Congressional Record*, XCV, no. 58 (April 6, 1949), 4877–78.

[56] An example of the continuing surveillance under which developments in Indonesia were kept was a letter to President Truman drafted by Senator Brewster and signed by 23 Republican Senators requesting the President to instruct the Secretary of State and the American delegation to the U.N. to take immediately those steps necessary to assure enforcement of the U.N. resolution. A report of this, via Aneta, reached Batavia on April 22.

[57] The motion for this debate was sponsored by Australia and India. The 3 opposition votes were from the Netherlands, Belgium, and the Union of South Africa. A motion to postpone this debate was defeated, 40 to 10, with 6 abstentions, including the U.S. Among those urging postponement were Britain, France, and the Scandinavian group (*N.Y. Times*, April 13, 1949).

On April 14 negotiations were finally resumed between the Netherlands and the Republic at Batavia under the auspices of the UN Commission for Indonesia. A week later the negotiations reached an impasse with the insistence of J. H. van Royen, chief of the Netherlands Delegation, that his government would restore the Republic to Jogjakarta only *after* the Republican government ordered "its armed adherents to cease guerrilla warfare and co-operate in the restoration of peace and the maintenance of law and order" and agreed to attend the proposed Round Table Conference at the Hague.[58] The position of the Republican delegation, led by Mohammad Roem, was that the opposite sequence should obtain and that it was unreasonable to expect such undertakings to be pledged by a Republican "government," when in fact the members of that government were widely dispersed, out of contact with one another, and unable to meet in their capital. This impasse continued until May 7, during which Indonesians affirm that the Republican delegation was under very strong pressure from the American representative on the U.N. Commission, H. Merle Cochran, to give ground in the direction of the Dutch position.[59]

Because this episode has had an important bearing upon subsequent Indonesian attitude towards the United States, it is of importance to understand the Indonesian version of it. Among Indonesian leaders it is generally believed that Mr. Cochran was attempting to bring about the implementation of agreements arrived at in the talks between Acheson and Stikker five weeks before. But they affirm that the concessions being asked of the Republic were much greater than those being requested of the Netherlands. They believe that the respective positions of the two parties on April 21 at the time of the deadlock as compared to those obtaining when they were prevailed upon to accept the terms of the Roem-Van Royen Agreement of May 7 clearly demonstrates that the Republic yielded by far the most and that actually the Dutch were going no further than Stikker had already agreed the previous month in Washington.

The tactics of Cochran were such as to arouse keen resentment among members of the Republic's delegation, particularly among those who later became convinced that he had deliberately misrepresented to them the temper of American Congressional sentiment.[60] Members of

---

[58] For the text of the Dutch demands see "First Interim Report of the Commission to the Security Council," U.N., S/1373 (Aug. 10, 1949), p. 14.

[59] So stated to the writer by several key members of the Republican delegation.

[60] It may be that they all became so convinced, but of this the writer is not certain.

the Republic's delegation state that he gave them the impression that he was the agent of the State Department, with full power to make the Department's policy in Indonesia, and that the American Congress had little interest in the Indonesian question. Soedarpo Sastrosatomo, an extremely well-informed Indonesian representative in Washington, arrived in Batavia in late April and tried to convince the Republic's delegation that the American Congress was closely watching events in Indonesia and was sympathetic to the Republic's position, and that the State Department's action concerning Indonesia was closely circumscribed by the attitude in Congress. According to members of the delegation, Cochran belittled Soedarpo's report, indicating that it would be futile to rely on Congress for support. He emphasized to them, they declare, that what American support they could count on would be no more than what he, himself, would be able to convince the State Department it should extend. Also, they state that he was insistent that they conclude an agreement with the Dutch before the General Assembly held its debates on the Indonesian question, depreciating the effectiveness of any support for the Republic that these debates might elicit and maintaining that discussion of the dispute by the General Assembly would merely prolong it and let it get it out of control.

In pressing the Republic to accept the agreement with the Dutch which he advocated, Cochran, according to members of the Republic's delegation, gave his verbal guaranty that the United States would "stand behind" a transfer of sovereignty by the Netherlands to Indonesia. In addition, they state, he gave them the strong impression that if they did so they could expect substantial American economic support following the transfer of sovereignty. However, Cochran made clear to them, these Indonesians affirm, that if they refused to accept the agreement which he sponsored—a solution which the Dutch had already indicated was acceptable to them—it would no longer be at all certain that the United States would give effective support towards a Netherlands transfer of sovereignty to the Republic.

Though there was great reluctance on the part of the delegation and the leaders of the Republican government whom they consulted to accept the solution proposed by Cochran, the feeling among them was that he spoke for the United States and that unless they acceded to his proposals any real American support for the Republic might be lost. They did not doubt the Republic's ability ultimately to win Indonesia's full independence from the Dutch without outside help. However, they felt that American support could result in this being attained much sooner, at the saving of many Indonesian lives, and without entailing the risk of plunging Indonesia into a political and economic chaos such as they feared might be the consequence of a lengthy struggle, a chaos which might continue long after the Dutch had been driven out of Indonesia. They felt that the concessions to the Netherlands that Cochran was asking them to make were dangerous in that they might make possible an Indonesian federal state to which the Netherlands could make a formal transfer of sovereignty but over which the Dutch would still be able to exert a critical degree of indirect control. However, most of them believed that such a chance had to be taken in order to gain American support. Though a majority of the Republic's delegation finally agreed to accept Cochran's proposals and on May 6 won the concurrence of Soekarno and Hatta, one of its key members, Mohammad Natsir, who a little more than a year later was to emerge as Prime Minister, resigned in protest.

On May 7 the agreement which Cochran had sponsored and which was to be known as the Roem-Van Royen Agreement was formally accepted by the Republican and Netherlands delegations. Under this agreement the Republican government did not itself pledge implementation of the three Dutch demands as a prerequisite to permission for its return to Jogjakarta. But the next thing to this was agreed to. President Soekarno and Vice-President Hatta gave "their personal assurances" that they favored in conformity with the Security Council's Resolution of 28 January 1949 and its directive of 23 March:

(1) Issuance of an order to the Republican armed adherents to cease guerilla warfare;
(2) Co-operation in the restoration of peace and the maintenance of law and order; and
(3) Participation in a Round-Table Conference at the Hague with a view to accelerating the unconditional transfer of real and complete sovereignty to the United States of Indonesia.

President Soekarno and Vice-President Hatta undertake that they will urge the adoption of such a policy by the government of the Republic of Indonesia as soon as possible after its restoration to Jogjakarta.[61]

For all practical purposes, then, Van Royen had won the concessions he had demanded on April 21 as prerequisites to the Republic's return to Jogjakarta—prerequisites, it is to be observed, that the Security Council had not called for. According to the Republican view it had

[61] U.N., S/1373, p. 15.

won the Dutch much more. For though the seven-point statement of Van Royen was headed by Netherlands agreement as to the return of the Republic to Jogjakarta, there were included among the other six points items which were seen as important defeats for the Republic's position. Though the Netherlands agreed that the Republican government should exercise control over the residency of Jogjakarta, it did not undertake to return any other area to Republican control. The area it was returning was slightly smaller than the state of Rhode Island and was a small fraction of the territory which the Dutch had overrun.

Republican officials were to continue to function in those areas of Java and Sumatra where they were still doing so (i.e., where the Dutch military control did not extend), but except for Jogjakarta there was no mention of the Netherlanders' evacuating their own administrations from the areas of the Republic which they had overrun. Though both sides agreed to discontinue military operations, this undertaking in conjunction with the freezing of areas of administrative control (other than Jogjakarta Residency) seemed to Republicans to confirm all the latest Dutch conquests other than the small area around their capital, while depriving the Republic of the right to continue its successful guerrilla warfare aimed at driving the Dutch from these areas.

The Netherlands undertook to "release immediately and unconditionally all political prisoners arrested by them since 17 December 1948 in the Republic of Indonesia." The majority of Republican political prisoners captured since that date were thereby released. However, this undoubted advantage to the Republic was reduced by a maneuver of the Netherlands military commander in Indonesia, who on May 10 reclassified political prisoners who had been captured after December 31 as "criminals" and thus outside the category qualified for release.

One of Van Royen's points stated that the "Netherlands Government favors the existence of the Republic as a state to take its place in the United States of Indonesia," and it was stipulated that the Netherlands would "refrain from the establishment or recognition of *negaras* [states] or *daerahs* [territories] on territory under Republican control prior to 19 December 1948 and from the expansion of *negaras* and *daerahs* affecting the said territories." However, it was also stipulated—and this was a major defeat for the Republic—that, when a provisional representative body for the whole of Indonesia was established, only one-third of the representation therein would go to the Republic.[62] The re-

[62] U.N., S/1373, p. 49.

mainder would go to the congeries of Dutch-sponsored states and special territories.

Thus the long-expected, U.N.-supervised plebiscites in the Republican areas which the Dutch had overrun in their first military action in the summer of 1947 were no longer even mentioned.[63] The regimes which the Dutch had unilaterally established in these areas were in effect confirmed and were to represent them in the federal state that was to receive the Netherlands transfer of sovereignty.[64]

Though the more reactionary elements in the Netherlands appeared to be outraged at the Roem-Van Royen Agreement, and though Beel resigned his post as High Representative of the Crown in protest against it, most Dutch opinion seemed to be well satisfied with it. Netherlands officials in Batavia generally appeared pleased with the agreement and indicated a belief that, despite the promised return of the Republican government and leaders to Jogjakarta, the Indonesian federal state to which sovereignty would be transferred would possess a government of which they approved. This outlook appeared to be paralleled in the government's official statement to the Netherlands Parliament regarding the agreement made by the Minister of Overseas Territories on May 12.[65] The BFO was reported as greeting the agreement with "joyful feelings" and expressed its confidence that "on the basis of the present results there can be fruitful negotiations, resulting in an early and adequate settlement of the Indonesian dispute." [66]

[63] It was also pointed out that though the population of the Republican-controlled areas prior to Dec. 19, 1949, was at least 40% of that of all Indonesia, the Republic was to get only one-third of the representation in the provisional representative assembly. (The population of Republican-controlled areas prior to the Dutch military action of mid-1947 was approximately 80% of that of the whole of Indonesia.)

[64] The fact that the plan which Mr. Cochran himself had attempted to introduce (unsuccessfully) in Sept., 1948, as a basis for negotiations between the Republic and the Netherlands also called for the Republic's being restricted to one-third representation in the provisional federal government which he envisaged probably had convinced Republican leaders that they would have to give in on this point since the American and Belgian members of the Commission formed a majority aligned with the Netherlands viewpoint.

[65] As to whether or not the government's new policy varied from that of Mr. Beel's anounced before Parliament on Feb. 16, this statement read: "The government has adhered to its course in the direction of the aims then stated, but . . . in the course of the voyage towards that aim it has permitted itself some deviations which have neither been announced nor foreseen. If the government should be blamed for this, I would remark, still following this metaphor, that the captain is master of his ship but of neither the seas nor the winds" (N.E.I. Government Information Service, Batavia, A.E. 1121, May 12, 1949). Beel's successor, A. H. J. Lovink, arrived in Batavia on June 2.

[66] *Keng Po,* May 9, 1949. (It was unclear from this communiqué whether the opinion expressed was that of the whole BFO or merely that of its majority.)

However, among many of the Republican leaders responsible for signing the agreement there was grave concern and uneasiness that the action they had taken might prove to be a fatal mistake. The general reaction among the educated Republican element in Indonesia was one of great depression and a belief that an important defeat had overtaken the Republican cause. Among many of them the feeling was that expressed by the pro-Republican newspaper, *Merdeka*, that this was not only a defeat, but a defeat which could not be eradicated.[67]

It was generally believed among educated Republicans that the Roem-Van Royen Agreement had been engineered through strong American pressure on the Republican leaders. Among them there was a strong tendency to criticize their leaders for having accepted it. Some of them maintained that the terms of the agreement called for a surrender of Indonesian interests which, when coupled with past concessions made by the same leaders under U.N. and particularly American pressure, added up to such a total capitulation to the Dutch as to seriously discredit these leaders. This linking of these Republican leaders with America in conjunction with the fact that they were known to be anti-Communist tended to steer opposition to the agreement into anti-American, pro-Communist channels.[68]

Had it not been for the fact that an alternate, non-Communist channel of opposition to the agreement was opened up by Sjahrir's Indonesian Socialist party this drift would probably have been on a much larger scale than it was. Despite the safety valve for opposition sentiment provided by the Indonesian Socialist party's strong opposition to the agreement, the nationalist-Communist Partai Murba's backing increased significantly as a result of the widespread dissatisfaction. Many believed that the increase in support for Darul Islam in some areas was also a consequence.

Dissatisfaction with the agreement among Republican troops was widespread, particularly among those who had evacuated their guerrilla strongholds some fifteen months before under the terms of the Renville Agreement. Why, indeed, might they ask, had they ever done so? On May 19 and 27 Dutch authorities announced successive increases in the activity of Republican guerrillas.[69] There was considerable specu-

[67] *Merdeka*, May 8, 1949.

[68] For the most part the channel was provided by the nationalist-Communist Partai Murba rather than the more Stalinist-oriented PKI. Not until May 28 did the leaders of the Republic's two largest political parties, the Masjumi and the PNI announce that their parties would back the Roem-Van Royen Agreement.

[69] U.P. dispatches from Batavia, May 19, 27, 1949.

lation in Batavia as to whether this mounting guerrilla pressure against the Dutch reflected hostility to the Roem-Van Royen Agreement or whether it was merely a continuation of the increase that was already noticeable before the agreement.

On June 14, Sjafruddin Prawiranegara finally made clear the position of the Republican Emergency Government in a broadcast from his Sumatran headquarters. His government would support the Roem-Van Royen Agreement, but only under the following conditions: (1) the Republican army was to stay in the positions it then occupied; (2) the Dutch army was gradually to be withdrawn from the positions it occupied; (3) restoration of the Republican government to Jogjakarta was to take place unconditionally; and (4) Republican sovereignty over Java, Sumatra, Madura and surrounding (offshore) islands was to be recognized by the Netherlands in conformance with the Linggadjati Agreement.[70] As if to make clear the support of the Republic's troops for this pronouncement, two days later a Dutch army communiqué reported a "serious increase in guerrilla activity." [71]

The mounting tide of Republican military [72] pressure was noted with concern by Netherlands civil and military officers.[73] It made a strong impression on BFO delegates in Batavia. Presumably it was also noted by the American State Department.

At the same time the continuing authority of the Republican government over its troops was impressively demonstrated. On June 18, the Sultan of Jogjakarta, under orders from the Republican Emergency Government, issued a cease-fire order to all Republican troops in the residency of Jogjakarta preparatory to the evacuation of Netherlands troops in the area. The order was observed. On June 30 the last Dutch soldier withdrew from Jogjakarta Residency, and Republican army units took over without any major incident and without the "Communist disturbances" which so much of the Dutch press had been pre-

[70] Aneta dispatch, Batavia, June 15, 1949.

[71] U.P. dispatch from Batavia, June 16, 1949.

[72] "Guerrilla pressure" would be a misleading term since much of the activity of Republican armed groups was on a battalion scale, frequently involving more than a battalion.

[73] The writer noticed considerable difference in the outlook of Dutch army officers with whom he spoke in January as compared to those he spoke with in April and May. Whereas most of those he talked with in January appeared to have high morale and were certain of a quick victory, this attitude was not encountered among most of those with whom he talked in the later period. For the most part they could see no end in sight, making clear their belief that there were not enough Netherlands troops to do the job that was expected of them and frequently showing a rather alarmed respect for the aggressive courage of the Republican troops.

dicting as a certainty. The Communists were nowhere in evidence for the very good reason that their armed strength was too weak for them to even think of intruding.

Six days later Soekarno and the other long-interned Republican leaders entered Jogjakarta triumphantly to a thunderous popular acclaim. On July 13 the Republican cabinet held its first meeting since the launching of the Dutch attack seven months before. At the same time Sjafruddin Prawiranegara handed back the mandate that Soekarno and Hatta had then given him as head of the Emergency Government.[74] The Working Committee of the Republican Parliament was soon reconvened, and after a week's debate it was clear that its majority would support the Roem-Van Royen Agreement; but it was insistent that the terms laid down by Sjafruddin be met.[75]

Increasingly during the spring of 1949 the Federalist leaders, both the delegates to the BFO and the leaders of the several federal units, had become impressed with the power of the Republic's armed forces and the dogged nonco-operation of its civilian population with the Dutch. It became evident to them that the Dutch were able to secure control over only a part of the post-Renville Republican area and that even in those parts which they controlled they were unable to get Indonesians to participate in governments under Dutch sponsorship. To almost all of the Federalist leaders it had become clear that a federal Indonesian state which did not include the Republic could never be viable. Yet it was obvious that the Republic would never enter such a federal state except on its own minimum terms.

Moreover the power displayed by the Republic against the Dutch had brought the majority of Federalist leaders to believe that maintenance of their own positions would be determined quite as much by reaching agreement with this Republican power as with the power of the Netherlands. If one came from the states of East Java, Pasundan, or Central Java, where Republican forces controlled as much of the area as did the Dutch, it was impossible to reason otherwise. The Republican control of lesser, but substantial, areas of East Sumatra and South Sumatra probably brought even their strongly anti-Republican

[74] In the new cabinet, Hamengku Buwono IX, Sultan of Jogjakarta, who had previously been Minister Without Portfolio, was made Minister of Defense, a post previously filled by Hatta in addition to the post of Prime Minister.

[75] The majority's backing was thus clear in a formal sense on July 25, but had been expected for some time. The Indonesian Socialist Party was still opposed to the agreement and refused to take part in these debates. The Murba Party in registering its opposition to the Agreement described it as "a *fait accompli*."

leaders to realize that some sort of agreement with the Republic had
to be reached.

This inability of the Dutch to enforce their own political decision
in Indonesia and the progressively defensive posture of their armed
forces there was, undoubtedly, the most important reason for the increasing defection by Federalist leaders from the Dutch camp during
the late spring and early summer of 1949. However, also of great importance was the growing dissatisfaction of many of them with the
character of the "autonomy" and "self-government" that the Dutch
had granted them. Most had consented to work with the Dutch in the
expectation that they would be something more than window dress-
ing for what continued to be a very complete form of Dutch control.
Some had thought that when they could demonstrate to the populations of their areas a real measure of autonomy from Dutch control, they
might be able to expect some significant amount of popular backing.
However, the Indonesian leaders of even the "advanced" state of East
Indonesia, after nearly two and a half years of "autonomy," had pitifully little to show. In none of these federal units had the Dutch-
sponsored Indonesian leaders won the support of a majority of the
Indonesian inhabitants. In every one it was clear that the majority of
the population still looked to the officials of the Republic for leadership.

However opportunistic some Federalist collaborators of the Dutch
might be, however great the importance others attached to their aristocratic prerogatives, they were all nationalists; they all resented Dutch
domination. All were dissatisfied with the failure of the Dutch to
transfer the powers they had been led to expect would be transferred
to them. Many were acutely bitter and resentful because of this. Originally many of these Federalists had appeared to welcome the prospect
of the maintenance of a camouflaged Dutch military power in Indonesia following the transfer of sovereignty. But they had envisaged
the Dutch-officered "state security battalions" which answered this
description as buttressing administrations headed by Indonesian Federalists who had been granted real power.

Such power had not been relinquished by the Dutch, and these Indonesians were increasingly skeptical that it would be. By many the
announcement of the Dutch on March 30 that the strength of these
security battalions would be increased by 18,000 men was seen as a further indication that Dutch control would be maintained after the transfer of sovereignty. The drastic reorganization of the constitution of

East Indonesia and the introduction of the new election law there were interpreted by many Federalists as a Dutch maneuver to insure the more complete amenability of East Indonesia to Netherlands control following the transfer of sovereignty. The fact that by the elections held under this new law in the early summer of 1949 a parliament was returned which contained fewer pro-Republican representatives than the previous one seemed to confirm these fears.

To the many Federalists who had become disillusioned and embittered by their unfruitful relationship with the Dutch and who feared that the projected transfer of sovereignty by the Dutch to a federal Indonesian state would mean little real change in that relationship the Roem-Van Royen Agreement opened up a new possibility. This agreement appeared to many of them to lay the basis for a strategy whereby they could play off the Republic and the Dutch against each other and secure their aims without coming under the dominating influence of either. In return for supporting the Republic's position against the Dutch at the projected "Round-Table Conference" at the Hague they might be able to exact from the Republican leaders guaranties which would protect their own interests and positions. If they could secure such agreement, there would be less need to rely upon Dutch military and police power to keep in check the large pro-Republican majorities among the populations of their states and special territories. What was needed was Republican acquiescence to a governmental system for Indonesia that would guarantee the maintenance of the already-established federal units, grant them real autonomy, and insure the Federalist representatives so strong a position in the central government as to make certain their ability to defend the autonomy of these federal units. It was apparently with this strategy in mind that the majority of BFO delegates entered into talks with the leaders of the Republican government in mid-July.

From July 19 to 22 in Jogjakarta and from July 30 to August 2 in Batavia were held the inter-Indonesian conferences between delegations representing the Indonesian Republic and the BFO. As a result of these, a number of important concessions were made by each party. The BFO Delegation acknowledged that the envisaged federal Indonesian state would be receiving its sovereignty both from the Netherlands and the Republic of Indonesia. Also it was agreed to establish a "National Preparatory Committee" composed of representatives of the Republic and the BFO in order "to co-ordinate all preparations and activities which have to be undertaken during or after the Round-

Table Conference . . . a central organ in maintaining liaison between the Republic and the BFO." Though the undertaking was later not always adhered to, the BFO agreed that the constituent states of the federal government would not possess separate armed forces. In addition, the BFO made clear its support of the Republic's demand for a real and unconditional transfer of sovereignty without political or economic strings.

In return the Republican delegation agreed that the constitution for the new Indonesian state to be drawn up at the Round-Table Conference at the Hague, would provide for a governmental system giving the Federalists and their states what appeared to be a very strong position. Not only were the fifteen federal units which the Dutch had established to have two-thirds of the representation in the House of Representatives in the new government. In addition there would be a Senate composed of two representatives from each federal unit. Thus, this body would have thirty members from the states established by the Dutch and two from the one other federal unit of the projected United States of Indonesia, namely, the Republic. It was agreed that this Senate would have co-legislative powers with the House of Representatives in respect to all matters "concerning the relations between the central government of the Republic of the United States of Indonesia and the component states, or in matters concerning the relations between the states." Moreover, the Senate itself had the right to determine whether or not legislation fell into these categories. Only by a two-thirds majority could the House override a decision of the Senate.[76]

On August 1, 1949, a cease fire was finally agreed between the Netherlands and the Republic, to be issued simultaneously by both parties on August 3, and going into effect on August 11 in Java and on August 15 in Sumatra. Thereupon the Republican and BFO delegations, headed respectively by Prime Minister Hatta and Sultan Hamid of West Borneo, departed for the Hague, where the Round-Table Conference concerning the transfer of sovereignty was to commence on August 23.

Changes in the attitudes of both the Netherlands and American governments favored the Republican negotiators at this conference. These changes appeared to result primarily from the same factor that had been the chief reason for the change in attitude among the majority

[76] The powers which it was agreed the Senate should possess represented a compromise between the positions of the two delegations. The Republic was opposed to having any Senate at all, while the BFO initially insisted that the Senate be more powerful than the House of Representatives.

of BFO members, namely, the unsuppressible Republican resistance. More and more Netherlanders had become convinced that the military effort which their country could mount in Indonesia was not powerful enough to enforce a political settlement. Prolongation of the fighting meant not only a continuation of the destruction growing out of such fighting, but also a continuation of the conscious Republican scorched-earth policy, the planned destruction of Dutch plantations, sugar factories, etc. It was clear to many Dutch businessmen that if indeed the Netherlands army ever was able to attain full control over the country, by that time there would be little left of the billion-and-a-quarter-dollar Netherlands investment there. With many business interests in the Netherlands now adding their weight to that of liberal elements, particularly represented by the Labor Party, the domestic pressure on the government to transfer sovereignty to Indonesia, though perhaps not representative of the majority of Netherlands public opinion, had considerably increased.

The tendency for the Netherlands government to move in this direction was increased by renewed pressure from the American government. Indonesian leaders believe that by the time of the Hague Conference the State Department was completely convinced that the Dutch could not enforce a political decision in Indonesia by military means. They believe that it had also become convinced that if the Republic's delegation did not bring back genuine independence from the Hague Conference popular confidence in the Republican leaders would be gravely undermined and the prospects of communism in Indonesia much stronger.

During the two-month period preceding the Hague Conference, the same Senators who had previously urged suspension of ECA aid to Holland continually prodded the State Department to make sure that real and unfettered independence was transferred to Indonesia. As late as mid-June neither Senator Brewster nor Senator Graham had realized that there was widespread dissatisfaction among Indonesian Republicans with the Roem-Van Royen Agreement and that a number of its provisions were very unfavorable to the Republic. When they were apprised of this however, they indicated that they would utilize this information.[77]

[77] Upon the writer's informing Senator Brewster of these facts the Senator requested him to draw up a memorandum giving the Indonesian Republican reaction to the Agreement and analyzing it as to the effect of its clauses. Brewster stated he intended to utilize this memorandum promptly and that it would be of great help to him. Copies of this memorandum were given to a number of other senators including Graham and Vandenberg.

By the time the Hague Conference convened, the American government appeared to Indonesians to have reached the point where it unequivocally insisted upon the granting of full and untrammeled independence to a federal Indonesia wherein the Republican element
would be strongest, and appeared prepared to exert very considerable pressure to attain that end. Indonesian Republican delegates who
attended this conference were of the opinion that for the first time in
the history of the Indonesian independence movement as much or more
American pressure was being applied upon the Dutch to bring them
to make concessions to the Republican point of view as was being
applied upon the Republic to make concessions to the Dutch.

THE HAGUE (ROUND-TABLE) CONFERENCE

From August 23 to November 2, 1949, at The Hague, the delegations of
the Netherlands, the Republic of Indonesia, and the Federal Consultative Assembly (BFO) met together and, with important assistance
from the United Nations Commission for Indonesia, finally hammered
out an agreement. This provided for the unconditional and complete
transfer of sovereignty by the Netherlands no later than December
30, 1949, of the entire territory of the former Netherlands East Indies,
except for Western New Guinea, to the Republic of the United States
of Indonesia, a federal government formed of the Republic of Indonesia and the fifteen political units established by the Dutch. The provisional character of this Indonesian government was established by
a draft constitution drawn up by the Republican and Federalist delegates to the conference on the basis of the agreements reached between
their representatives in the inter-Indonesian conferences held in Jogjakarta and Batavia in late July and early August. (Within this federation the territory of the Republic of Indonesia, by far the largest
constituent unit, was to possess post-Renville, pre-December 1948 boundaries.[78] The transfer of sovereignty to this Indonesian government was
to be immediate, with no period of Dutch-chaperoned interim government such as had originally been envisaged.

The character of the Netherlands-Indonesian Union established
by the Hague Agreement was undoubtedly a disappointment for
that majority of Netherlands opinion which favored a "tight" or

[78] Each constituent state of the Indonesian federation was to be given the opportunity to ratify or reject this constitution. Should any state so prefer, it had the
right to negotiate with the United States of Indonesia and the Netherlands for a
special relationship ("Agreement on Transitional Measures [Hague Agreement],"
art. 2, par. 2). For an account of the provisions of this constitution, see Ch. XIV.

"heavy" union.[79] In fact this Union was largely a paper institution without real substance and powers. Primarily it was an agreement for mutual consultation on matters of common interest. Though the Queen of the Netherlands was designated as "the head of the Union," as such the Queen had absolutely no powers and was merely to effectuate "the spirit of voluntary and lasting co-operation between the partners." [80] All of the lengthy provisions for co-operation between the two partners must be read in the light of the first article of the Union Statute which is the clearest, most succinct description of the Union's character. This reads: "(1) The Netherlands-Indonesian Union effectuates the organized co-operation between the Kingdom of the Netherlands and the Republic of the United States of Indonesia on the basis of free will and equality in status with equal rights. (2) The Union does not prejudice the status of each of the two partners as an independent and sovereign State."

The only really substantive provisions of the Union Statute were for a permanent Union secretariat, the holding of conferences of a group of cabinet ministers from the two governments at least twice a year, and a Union Court of Arbitration. These conferences were to work out those details of the settlement not covered by the Hague Agreement and to provide the principal channel for voluntary co-operation in problems of mutual interest. All decisions of such ministerial conferences were to be unanimous and to require endorsement by the parliaments of the two countries.[81] The Union Court of Arbitration was charged with the settlement of legal disputes arising out of the Union Statute, other agreements between the two countries, and joint regulations (i.e., decisions taken by the Conference of Ministers and endorsed by the two parliaments). Both countries agreed to comply with and implement its decisions. It was to be composed of three members appointed from each country for terms of ten years. Its decisions were to be taken by majority vote. In cases where the votes were equally divided the court was to request the President of the International Court of Justice, or another mutually agreeable international authority, to appoint a person of another nationality as a seventh member of the court to take part in a renewed consideration of the dispute and in the decision thereon.[82]

[79] See B.H.M.V[lekke]., "Settlement in Indonesia: The Final Phase," *The World Today*, Jan. 1950, p. 34.

[80] *Union Statute* [Hague Agreement], art. 5, par. 1; art. 6.

[81] *Ibid.*, arts. 7–10.   [82] *Ibid.*, arts. 13–19.

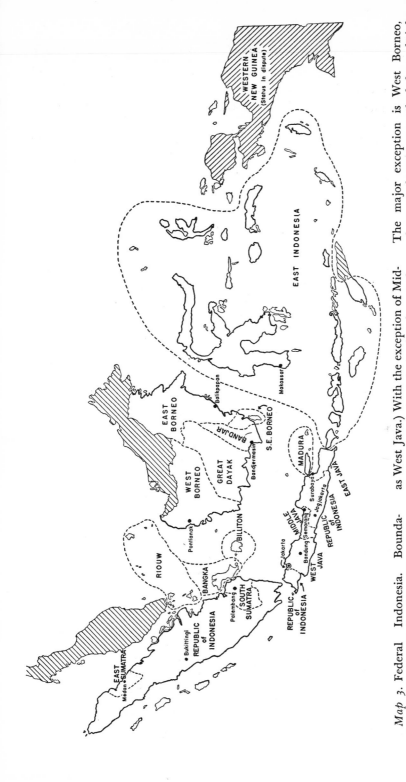

Map 3. Federal Indonesia. Boundaries shown are of the Republic of the United States of Indonesia on December 27, 1949. (Pasundan is designated here as West Java.) With the exception of Middle Java, whose boundaries date from early March, 1949, all approximate the boundaries of fourteen or more months previously.

The major exception is West Borneo, whose southwest corner had for a brief period been detached to form the short-lived autonomous area of Kota Waringen.

Explicit regulations, under the Hague Agreement, provided for the withdrawal of Netherlands troops (KL—Royal Netherlands Army) from Indonesia "within the shortest possible time" following the transfer of sovereignty. Pending their withdrawal these troops, along with those of the KNIL (the Dutch colonial army), were to be restricted to designated military areas, where responsibility for military law and discipline among them was to rest with their own Dutch officers. These troops were not to be used for military operations unless so requested by the government of the Republic of the United States of Indonesia. The KNIL and the federal security battalions were to be "reorganized," part of their personnel to be absorbed into the army of the Republic of the United States of Indonesia, part to enter the service of the Netherlands army (and thus be dispatched to Holland) and the remainder to be demobilized.[83]

Under the terms of the Hague Agreement the Republic of the United States of Indonesia (R.U.S.I.) undertook to recognize and restore "the rights, concessions and licenses properly granted under the law of the Netherlands Indies (Indonesia) and still valid on the date of transfer of sovereignty" and restore to "the rightful claimants" the "actual exercise of their rights." [84] It is also agreed to make available the possibility "for an extension, a renewal, or the granting of rights, concessions and licenses" required for the operation of "existing and new enterprises and estates" except where this was deemed to be "in contravention of the public interest, including the general economic policy of the Republic of the United States of Indonesia." [85]

[83] "Regulations on the land forces in Indonesia under the Netherlands command after the transfer of sovereignty," *Hague Agreement,* ch. ii, arts. 9–15, 20, 32. (It was stipulated that reorganization of the KNIL and security battalions was to take place "within a period of six months from the day of the publication of the conditions of enlistment in the armed land forces of the Republic of Indonesia" (art. 31, par. 1).

[84] "Financial and Economic Agreement," *Hague Agreement,* sec. A, art. 1, par. 1. The R.U.S.I. government, however, reserved the right to conduct an investigation "in respect of important rights, concessions and licenses granted after 1 March 1942 which may influence the economic policy of the Republic of the United States of Indonesia. . . ." This probably referred primarily to rights and concessions granted by the Netherlands Indies regime during the period 1947–49. With respect to this reservation account was to be taken of the public interest in those cases where plantations had been turned over to the population by the Japanese authorities for the growing of food, a rather widespread phenomenon, and also of certain private properties which had been temporarily requisitioned for government service in the public interest. Also it was specifically stated that the abolition of the antiquated and long-resented conversion rights that sugar plantations had enjoyed in the Jogjakarta and Surakarta residencies would be maintained.

[85] *Ibid.,* art. 4.

The agreement stipulated that "expropriation, nationalization, liquidation, compulsory cession, or transfer of property rights" were to take place "exclusively for the public benefit, in accordance with the procedure prescribed by law, and, in the absence of an agreement between the parties, against previously enjoyed or guaranteed indemnity to be fixed by judicial decision at the real value of the object involved, in accordance with provisions to be prescribed by law." [86]

Regulations in the field of labor relations, housing, and other social welfare measures concerning labor were to be applied equally against Netherlands and Indonesian business enterprises in Indonesia. In all such enterprises at the "earliest possible period eligible Indonesians" were to be brought into their "direction (and management) and staff." Training courses were to be established "with the objective that after a reasonable period, the predominant part of the leading staff personnel of the enterprises will consist of Indonesian nationals." [87]

The R.U.S.I. agreed to grant "most favored nation" treatment to the Netherlands and recognized "that the special interests of Netherlands nationals and corporate bodies within Indonesia will be fully taken into account." However, any suggestion implicit in this sentence that the Netherlands would enjoy a more favored position than other countries seemed to be nullified by the preceding sentence which stated: "Foreigners of all nations will have equal rights in the participation of trade with Indonesia and in the economic activity and industrial development of that country." Though the R.U.S.I. undertook to subject the interests of Netherlands nationals and corporate bodies to "no discrimination," it made clear that this commitment did not prejudice "the right of the Republic of the United States of Indonesia to make such regulations as are necessary for the protection of national interests or economically weak groups." [88]

With respect to trade policy a relatively important concession was gained by the Dutch, the the R.U.S.I. undertaking to take over and implement the trade agreements to which the preceding Netherlands Indies regime had been committed.[89] Continuance of these favored the Netherlands as against Indonesia. However, the Republican and Federalist delegations to the Hague Conference felt that Indonesia could afford to make this concession since these agreements extended only to

---

[86] *Ibid.,* art. 3. Compensation was to be paid within three years unless an arbitration board made up of one member appointed by the R.U.S.I. government, one selected by the claimant, and a third selected mutually by these two ruled otherwise (*ibid.,* sec. B, art. 18, par. 8).

[87] *Ibid.,* art. 12.   [88] *Ibid.,* art. 11.

[89] *Ibid.,* sec. C, art. 21, par. 7; and art. 22, par. 4.

October, 1950. It was agreed that the two parties would discuss possible alterations of the agreement during the first quarter of 1950 to take effect in October. However, when the time came (at the first Ministerial Conference) the R.U.S.I. found itself in a very weak bargaining position since it was then in the process of negotiating a badly needed loan from the Netherlands. Thus the R.U.S.I. was obliged to extend these agreements for another year. Indonesian resentment because of this was increased by the fact that after the Hague Agreement had been signed and just a week before the transfer of sovereignty the Dutch amended these trade agreements in a way even more favorable to the Netherlands and less favorable to Indonesia.

From the Indonesian point of view the two greatest concessions made to the Netherlands under the Hague Agreement concerned the debt assumed by the R.U.S.I. and the status of New Guinea. The question of the debt became of central importance soon after the conference was opened. In the first meeting the Netherlands delegates made clear their contention that, as long as the Netherlands remained the biggest creditor of Indonesia (and given the magnitude of the Netherlands claim it seemed probable that this condition would last for a long time), the R.U.S.I. government should not change the financial and economic laws and regulations it was inheriting from the Netherlands Indies regime without the agreement of the Netherlands.

From the outset the Republican delegation adamantly refused to yield to this claim and received backing in its position from the United Nations Commission for Indonesia. The Republican counterproposal (supported by the BFO Delegation) [90] was finally accepted. This called for prior consultations with the Dutch on all matters of monetary and financial policy where the interests of the Netherlands were concerned, so long as the Netherlands remained the R.U.S.I.'s creditor.[91] This did not commit the R.U.S.I. to accept Dutch advice in these matters, but it did, in the view of the Indonesian negotiators at least, mean an important advantage for the Dutch not possessed by any other country. For thereby they would be informed of R.U.S.I. financial and monetary policies before they were put into force and could take steps in anticipation of them.

Soon after the conference was under way, it was clear that its success

[90] In general the BFO Delegation gave the Republican delegation very strong support during the conference, sometimes being even less disposed to compromise than several members of the Republican delegation.

[91] *Hague Agreement,* sec. B, art. 19.

or failure would, to an important extent, be determined by how the issue of the public debt of the Netherlands East Indies regime was resolved. The basic view of the Dutch was that all debts of that government as of the moment of transfer of sovereignty should be taken over by the government of the Republic of the United States of Indonesia. Initially they demanded that it take over a total debt of 6,100,000,000 guilders ($1,732,400,000), consisting of an external debt of 3,100,000,-000 guilders and an internal debt of 3,000,000,000 (the internal debt having been created by the issuance of government paper money, bank notes, and government bonds).

The Dutch maintained that only the external debt could be a subject of discussion and that the internal debt was completely a matter for the future Indonesian government to solve. From the external Netherlands East Indies debt (by far the larger part of which was owed to the Netherlands) the Dutch stated that they were prepared to deduct 500,000,000 guilders, thereby leaving an external debt of 2,600,-000,000 guilders to be added to the internal debt of 3,000,000,000 or a total indebtedness of approximately 5,600,000,000 guilders.

If the Indonesian delegations would accept this, the Dutch stated that they would waive their claim for a say in the future economic and financial policy of Indonesia; they would then be satisfied, they stated, with prior consultations, leaving the ultimate decision to the Indonesians. However, they demanded that repayment of these loans be guaranteed by: (1) reserving a percentage of the proceeds in foreign exchange of Indonesian exports each year toward repayment of the debt; and (2) placing the revenues of the annual Indonesian tin production in escrow with a Dutch bank to be used toward amortization and interest on this debt in case the amount from Indonesian exports was insufficient.

Opposed to this viewpoint was that of the Indonesian delegates (both Republicans and Federalists) that while there was no objection to assuming all debts incurred prior to the Netherlands' surrender to the Japanese in March 1942, reservations were made with respect to all debts incurred thereafter. Their position was that, with regard to debts incurred afterwards, only those debts should be taken over which pertained to expenditures which had been of benefit to the Indonesian people. Consequently the Indonesian delegates made clear that they refused to bear the burden of either the direct or indirect costs incurred by the Netherlands' military actions against the Republic of Indonesia.

Proceeding on the basis of this reasoning, the Indonesian delegations, following the lead of the brilliant chairman of the Republican Delegation's Economic and Financial subcommittee, Dr. Sumitro Djojohadikusmo, came to a conclusion which reportedly astonished and shook the Netherlands Delegation. This was that the new Indonesian state would not be in debt to the Netherlands, but rather that the Netherlands would owe it more than 500,000,000 guilders.

The Indonesians reasoned as follows: The cost of Dutch military expenditures in Indonesia since 1945 they calculated at approximately 3,500,000,000 guilders (not including the maintenance of a normal peacetime army and the normal cost of government). Such expenditure on an effort to crush the Republic of Indonesia was, they maintained, something that the Indonesian people and the new Indonesian state could not be held responsible for and had to be rejected. Subtraction of this sum of 3,500,000,000 guilders from the figure of 6,100,000,000 guilders (which the Netherlands claimed the new Indonesian government would owe) left a total of 2,600,000,000 guilders owed by Indonesia to the Netherlands.

However, these Indonesians maintained that at least 2,240,000,000 guilders of the Netherlands military expenses incurred in the efforts to defeat the Republic had been raised in Indonesia, largely by internal money creation in Indonesia. This sum, the Indonesians claimed, represented a claim of the future Indonesian government against the Netherlands government. Thus out of the total internal debt of Indonesia amounting to 3,000,000,000 guilders, the Indonesians held that their new government should be responsible for only 760,000,000 guilders (i.e., 3,000,000,000 minus 2,240,000,000 guilders). Of the remainder of the 3,500,000,000 guilders expended by the Dutch in their military campaigns against the Republic, the Indonesians calculated that 1,260,000,000 was chargeable to the external debt of Indonesia, the preponderant part of which had been owed directly to the Netherlands. This indebtedness for military expenditure they likewise refused to pay and held that it should be subtracted from the total Indonesian external debt of 3,100,000,000 guilders and borne by the Netherlands itself. Thereby they calculated the legitimate external debt of Indonesia to stand at 1,840,000,000 guilders. Of this sum, however, 140,000,000 represented Indonesia's debt to third countries and only 1,700,000,000 guilders represented that part of this external debt due the Netherlands.

Thus, the Indonesian delegations wound up their calculations with the conclusion that the Netherlands owed Indonesia 2,240,000,000 guilders (its share of the Indonesian internal debt), while the new Indonesian state would owe the Netherlands 1,700,000,000 guilders (the legitimate part of its external debt, i.e., that part not ascribable to Dutch borrowing for military efforts against the Republic). Thereby they concluded the Netherlands was in debt to Indonesia to the amount of 2,240,000,000 guilders minus 1,700,000,000 or 540,000,000 guilders.[92]

With the submission of these Indonesian counterproposals the negotiations on the debt position were broken off, none of the delegations or UNCI (United Nations Commission for Indonesia) seeing a solution. The point of view of the Indonesian delegations was that the transfer of sovereignty should not be held up over this issue and that the final decision as to the distribution of the liabilities of the Netherlands East Indies government between the Netherlands and Indonesia should be worked out by a debt commission, including the representative of a third party, perhaps from the World Bank or UNCI. They held that the final debt settlements between the United States and the Philippines and between Great Britain and India had been worked out after the transfers of sovereignty had been made, and saw no reason why the same practice should not obtain between the Netherlands and Indonesia. However, the Dutch were not prepared to agree to this, and it was clear that the debt issue would have to be worked out first if the conference was not to break down.

It was the desire of both Indonesian delegations to resolve this impasse by calling in the UNCI as the third party with them and the Netherlands, and between the three (the two Indonesian delegations constituting a single party) to arrive at a compromise on the question of the distribution of the Netherlands East Indies debt. However, rather than the UNCI as a whole filling the position of arbitrating third party on the envisaged debt commission, Mr. Cochran, the American member of UNCI, according to Indonesian delegates to the conference, "forced his way" into this position himself as the sole representative of UNCI. According to Indonesian delegates this action was strongly resented by both the Indonesian delegations and by the Australian representative on UNCI, who along with one of the key Republican delegates very nearly resigned in consequence.

In general the Republican delegation always preferred to have the Australian delegate to UNCI, Mr. Thomas K. Critchley, participate in negotiations, not only because of Australia's sympathy for the Indo-

---

[92] These calculations were submitted by the Indonesian delegations during the first week of October.

nesian position, but also because they believed he had a much greater knowledge of Indonesia than either the American or Belgian delegates on UNCI. These qualities of Mr. Critchley, the Indonesians felt, would more than balance the presence on the full U.N. Commission of the Belgian member. The weight of a powerful sector of world opinion —with, if need be, debates in the General Assembly—would, they believed, strengthen the hand of the Australian member in the Commission's arbitration of the debt issue. They feared that the desire of the United States to strengthen the Dutch economy would bring Cochran to recommend a debt settlement much more favorable to the Netherlands and correspondingly more unfavorable to Indonesia than the full UNCI would be likely to countenance. Apparently this was the opinion of the Netherlands government, too, because, according to Indonesian delegates, Cochran had already secured the approval of the Netherlands Delegation to serve as sole third-party mediator before he approached the Indonesians with this suggestion.

Cochran, the Indonesian delegates state, insisted that the debt commission of which he was to constitute the third member have powers of arbitration. This, they say, meant that he would himself have full power to establish whatever debt settlement corresponded with the maximum concession the Dutch were prepared to make; they believe that this is precisely what happened. Moreover, though Cochran would be sitting on the debt commission as "a representative of UNCI," this, the Indonesian alleged, would be pure fiction since his status had been agreed upon by the Netherlands and Indonesian delegations beforehand without any consultation with UNCI and at Mr. Cochran's own personal initiative. They felt he could not be considered as anything other than a representative of the American State Department in this capacity, and they were sure his function would be so interpreted in Indonesia. As one Indonesian delegate observed at the time: "Any result coming from such a commission would be interpreted as exclusively an American solution; this would create a breeding ground in Indonesia whereby the Communists could make strong political capital."

However, American support for the Indonesian position at the Hague Conference had thus far been important, and the new Indonesian state's dependence upon promised American economic assistance was envisaged as being great. Thus the majority of the Indonesian delegates were reluctant to contest Cochran's unofficial request for this vital position. If they did so, they feared American support at the conference might be less and that the prospects of American economic assistance would become dim.

The Indonesian delegations had realized that as the price of a transfer of sovereignty they would have to go a considerable way toward meeting the Dutch position with regard to the Netherlands East Indies debt. They had been prepared to agree to a figure of 3,400,000,-000 guilders, but no more. However, both Cochran and the Netherlands Delegation insisted upon a substantially higher figure, and finally on October 24 the Indonesian delegations agreed that the new Indonesian state would take over debts totaling approximately 4,300,000,000 guilders (nearly $1,130,000,000) from the Netherlands East Indies government. Of this, 3,000,000,000 guilders composed the entire internal debt of the colonial government.[93] Of the external debt of 1,291,000,000 guilders assumed, 871,000,000 made up the consolidated debt to the Netherlands and the remaining sum—420,000,000 guilders—was owed to other countries.[94] However, Indonesia was not obliged to provide the Netherlands with any lien on its revenues as insurance that its debt to the Netherlands would be paid.

To many Indonesians the magnitude of this debt seemed an unfair burden to be placed upon the shoulders of an Indonesia which had suffered such extensive devastation from three years of Japanese occupation and a subsequent four years of warfare against the British and the Dutch. However it may have been regarded in Washington, Cochran's part in the resolving of the debt impasse, in the opinion of Indonesian delegates, did a great deal to detract from the good will which the American position, and his capable representation of it, had won with respect to the other issues that had arisen at the conference. The conviction that they were being forced to pay for a major share of the Netherlands military operations against the Republic could not but disappoint and embitter Indonesians. The 900,000,000 guilder disparity between the maximum debt that they had been prepared to shoulder and that which they were finally obliged to pay did not appear to many of them to be appreciably compensated for by the $100,000,000 American loan which Cochran several months later, as America's first ambassador to Indonesia, informed them he had arranged. (This, it was noted, was less than a third of the 900,000,000

[93] See the *N.Y. Times*, Oct. 25, 1949, p. 5.

[94] U.N. Commission for Indonesia, "Special Report to the Security Council on the Round Table Conference," S/1417 (Nov. 10, 1949), p. 34. In addition, the new Indonesian state took over the rights and liabilities under existing agreements for items in the external floating debt to the maximum of 268,500,000 guilders.

guilders; it was a loan, and one which had to be repaid with interest.)

After the debt settlement the final issue remaining in the path of successful completion of the conference was that of New Guinea. The western half of this huge island had formed a part of the Netherlands East Indies. The Netherlands contended that ethnically and culturally this area was not part of Indonesia and that there was no reason why it should be transferred to the new Indonesian state. The Indonesians, particularly the Federalist Delegation, were adamant in their contention that it was an integral part of Indonesia and that sovereignty over it should be transferred along with the rest of Indonesia.

The top Netherlands officials in Indonesia and considerable public opinion in the Netherlands favored transfer to Indonesia of this great undeveloped area. However, the Dutch cabinet, evidently with good reason, was convinced that if New Guinea was not retained it might be impossible to muster the necessary two-thirds vote (requisite to change the Netherlands Constitution) in both houses of Parliament to get the Hague Agreement ratified. Netherlands New Guinea was poor and cost some 10,000,000 guilders a year to administer. The profits to Netherlanders from its oil fields nowhere approached this figure. Dutch business and financial interests were generally not interested in retaining New Guinea. The Dutch cabinet did not feel impelled to retain it on materialistic grounds. Psychological reasons connected with the dynamics of Dutch nationalism counseled its retention. These were difficult to define, but probably, as some Netherlanders remarked, New Guinea's retention served as a symbol to indicate that the Netherlands had emerged from the conference in a position of strength, as well as a symbol indicating that the Netherlands was still an Asian power.

Finally this last impasse encountered by the conference was resolved by a compromise formula of the UNCI. This called for the *status quo* (i.e., Netherlands control and administration) in western New Guinea being maintained "with the stipulation that within a year from the date of transfer of sovereignty to the Republic of the United States of Indonesia the question of the political status of New Guinea be determined through negotiations" between the Netherlands and the R.U.S.I. With the concurrence of the two parties with this compromise, the various agreements reached during the conference were signed on November 2 by the Republican and Federalist Indonesian delegations and by that of the Netherlands.

After a long and bitter debate in which criticism was primarily directed against the amount of debt assumed by Indonesia and against the disposition of western New Guinea, the Provisional Parliament of the Republic of Indonesia (the KNIP) on December 14 ratified the agreements reached at the Hague Conference, the other fifteen constituent states of the projected United States of the Republic of Indonesia having completed their individual ratifications shortly before. On December 21 both houses of the Netherlands Parliament ratified the agreement, but in the First Chamber by a margin of only one vote over the two-thirds minimum necessary (thirty-four to fifteen). On December 27, 1949, the Netherlands formally transferred sovereignty over the whole of the former Netherlands East Indies minus western New Guinea to the new Republic of the United States of Indonesia. On the same day the capital city which had been called Batavia took once again its old Indonesian name, Jakarta.

Despite the Soviet Union's vetoing two Security Council resolutions praising the transfer and the UNCI's role in the negotiations, and assertions by its delegate and that of the Ukraine that the transfer merely cloaked the continuance of a disguised, American-backed Dutch control,[95] real sovereignty and its substantive attributes had been transferred. The new Indonesian state was fully independent.

During the next few weeks most of the major world states accorded *de jure* recognition to Indonesia. Within five months Soviet Russia and Communist China had followed suit, and shortly thereafter Indonesia was admitted into the United Nations as that organization's sixtieth member.

[95] *N.Y. Times,* Dec. 14, 1949, p. 1.

❧ CHAPTER XIV ❧

The Unitarian Movement

WITH the transfer of sovereignty, the primary objective of the Indonesian revolution had been won. However, before the Indonesian people's focus of attention began to shift from the political to the socio-economic, there was one final major development in the political sphere. This was the "unitarian movement," a development which during the first seven months of 1950 completely overshadowed all others.

The movement was energized by the almost immediate popular reaction against the primarily Dutch-created federal political order with which the Hague Agreement had endowed the new Indonesian state. Until this vestige of the repudiated neo-colonial order had been shaken off, many Indonesians would not feel that their newly won political independence was complete. It was this reaction against and liquidation of the inherited federal system and its replacement by a unitarian form of government that constituted what the Indonesians referred to as the unitarian movement.

Helpful to an understanding of this development is a knowledge of the federal Draft Constitution which from December 27, 1949, until its supercession some seven months later by a unitarian constitution governed the new Republic of the United States of Indonesia (Republik Indonesia Serikat) or R.U.S.I. as it was generally called. The Constitution of the R.U.S.I. provided for a federation composed of sixteen constituent states. By far the largest of these member states was the Republic of Indonesia with its population of more than 31,000,000 and embracing almost the same area it had under the terms of the

Renville Agreement. The other fifteen constituent states were the puppet or semipuppet states (*negaras*) and special territories (*daerah istimewas*) originally set up by the Dutch, ranging in population from about 100,000 to 11,000,000. (See Map 3.)

Each of these sixteen constituent states of the R.U.S.I., regardless of its population, was represented by two senators. Every senator was appointed by the local government of the constituent state which he represented, being selected from a list of three candidates proposed by the R.U.S.I. House of Representatives.[1] On matters "referring particularly to one, several or all participant territories or parts thereof, or concerning the relation between the Republic of the United States of Indonesia" and the constituent territories the R.U.S.I. Senate (made up of these thirty-two Senators) held co-legislative authority with the House of Representatives. The Senate could initiate legislation concerning these matters, and its agreement was required for all legislation in this sphere unless at a meeting of at least two-thirds of the members of the House of Representatives two-thirds of that number should oppose the Senate decision.[2]

The R.U.S.I. House of Representatives was made up of 150 members, fifty from the Republic of Indonesia and one hundred from the fifteen Dutch-created states according to their respective populations. It was provided that of the total membership at least nine, six, and three members respectively represent the Chinese, European, and Arab minorities. Each of the sixteen political units was free to decide on the manner of selecting its representatives, whether by election or appointment.[3] The House of Representatives had the right to introduce legislation and the concurrence of at least half of its quorum (the quorum being 50 per cent of total membership) was required to pass any legislation.[4]

The "Government" (President plus one or more ministers) exercised co-legislative power with the House on all matters and with the Senate as well in those matters coming within the compass of its authority. It could introduce legislation, and its approval was required for all legislation. The President was the "Head of the State" and commander in chief of the army, and was elected by the House and Senate in joint session. With the concurrence of these two repre-

---

[1] Draft Constitution of the Republic of the United States of Indonesia, art. 81.

[2] *Ibid.*, arts. 127–132.

[3] *Ibid.*, arts. 98–100, 109, 110. Within one year elections were scheduled to be held throughout Indonesia for these positions (art. 111).

[4] *Ibid.*, art. 108.

sentative bodies the President appointed a committee of three for the purpose of forming a cabinet. In accordance with the recommendations of this committee the President appointed the Prime Minister (who had to be one of these three) and the other ministers.[5]

According to Article 139, one that assumed great importance in the liquidation of the constituent states: "The Government on its own authority and responsibility has the right to enact emergency laws for the regulation of such matters of federal governing power as demand immediate provisions on account of urgent circumstances." Thereupon such regulations had to be presented to the House of Representatives for its approval. However, the right of initiative with respect to these emergency laws lay exclusively with the Government, and in any case they were operative until disapproved by the House.[6]

The power to amend the Constitution was lodged with the House and Senate. A quorum of two-thirds of the membership of each was required when this matter was under consideration. To make any constitutional change a two-thirds majority of both quorums or three-fourths of that of the House alone were required.[7]

On December 16, 1949, eleven days before the actual transfer of sovereignty, a joint meeting of the House and Senate unanimously elected Soekarno as President of the R.U.S.I. Instead of three, he appointed four cabinet *formateurs,* two Republicans—Mohammad Hatta and the Sultan of Jogjakarta—and two Federalists from the Dutch-sponsored states—Anak Agung Gde Agung (from East Indonesia) and Sultan Hamid II (from West Borneo). The Cabinet that emerged was headed by Hatta as prime minister and included eleven Republicans and five Federalists. The membership of Hatta's cabinet, one which was to endure until September 6, 1950, included:

Ministry		*Party*	
Prime Minister	Mohammad Hatta	Nonparty	(Republican)
Foreign Affairs	" "	"	"
Internal Affairs	Anak Agung Gde Agung		(Federalist)
Defense	Hamengku Buwono IX (Sultan of Jogjakarta)	Nonparty	(Republican)
Finance	Sjafruddin Prawiranegara	Masjumi	(Republican)
Economic Affairs	Djuanda	Nonparty	(Republican)
Education	Abu Hanifah	Masjumi	(Republican)
Labor	Wilopo	PNI	(Republican)
Justice	Supomo	Nonparty	(Republican)
Transport and Irrigation	H. Laoh	PNI	(Republican)

[5] *Ibid.,* arts. 68, 69, 74, 127–131.   [6] Art. 140.   [7] Art. 190.

Ministry		Party	
Social Affairs	Kosasih		(Federalist)
Religion	Wachid Hasjim	Masjumi	(Republican)
Health	Johannes Leimena	Christian	(Republican)
Information	Arnold Mononutu [8]		(Federalist)
Without Portfolio	Mohammad Roem	Masjumi	(Republican)
" "	Hamid II		(Federalist)
" "	Suparmo		(Federalist)

The federal system of government bequeathed by the Hague Agreement remained intact for only a scant six weeks and thereafter began progressively to disintegrate under the mounting pressure of a widespread movement for its replacement by a unitarian form of government. Actually, though this has not been too well understood by some people, the terms of the Hague Agreement's "Charter of the Transfer of Sovereignty" were not a legal bar to such a course. They are short and worth quoting:

Article 1

(1) The Kingdom of the Netherlands unconditionally and irrevocably transfers complete sovereignty over Indonesia to the Republic of the United States of Indonesia and thereby recognizes said Republic of the United States of Indonesia as an independent and sovereign state.

(2) The Republic of the United States of Indonesia accepts said sovereignty on the basis of the provisions of its Constitution which as a draft has been brought to the knowledge of the Kingdom of the Netherlands.

(3) The transfer of sovereignty shall take place at the latest on 30 December 1949.[9]

The remaining article of the document (Art. 2) dealt exclusively with New Guinea.

It is important to note that the transfer of sovereignty was *complete* and *unconditional*. Consequently there is no justification for interpreting the second paragraph as a condition of the transfer of sovereignty. Obviously an unconditionally sovereign state has the legal right to change its own constitution as it sees fit. Certainly it has the right to change a draft constitution. Thus the federal pattern with which the Hague Agreement endowed the new Indonesian state was not by the terms of the agreement inviolable and sacrosanct.

[8] Though he had been a member of the parliament of the state of East Indonesia, Mononutu had been head of the pro-Republican faction there and was considered to be much more of a Republican than a Federalist. Of the five cabinet members designated as Federalists actually only Anak Agung and Hamid II strongly favored a federal form of government.

[9] U.N., Security Council, "Appendices to the Special Report to the Security Council on the Round Table Conference," S/1417, add. 1, p. 66.

However, to many outside observers the unitarian movement appeared to develop with unnecessary haste and disorder and with a rather cavalier disregard for legal amenities and the spirit, if not the actual content, of the Hague Agreement. But if one looks behind the juridical façade of the federal system of government imposed upon Indonesia by that Agreement, the unitarian movement must seem not only entirely natural, but also healthy. Indeed Indonesia would be politically and socially sick if this development had not taken place. For, as has been seen in the previous chapters, the federal system begun by Van Mook and continued by his successors was essentially Dutch-created and Dutch-maintained. By most Indonesians it had been seen as an instrument of Dutch control and an obstacle to the attainment of their independence. To keep this system meant for them the retention of an unwelcome legacy of their colonial past and the maintenance in power of many Indonesians who had worked with the Dutch for ends which appeared selfish and opposed to the struggle of the Republic, people who in nearly every case enjoyed little backing from the populations of their areas.

Within the federal R.U.S.I. the old Republic of Indonesia remained virtually autonomous. Not only was its internal administration independent of the federal capital at Jakarta (formerly Batavia), but many civil servants in such states as Middle Java, East Java, and Pasundan looked to its capital, Jogjakarta, rather than to Jakarta for their orders. Frequently this resulted in a confusing "double administration" with two sets of civil servants attempting to administer the same territory. The already-great prestige of the old Republic as the successful champion of Indonesian independence tended to increase because of the relatively high level of law and order, administrative efficiency, and absence of corruption maintained within its area as contrasted with the other constituent states of the federation.[10]

The great majority of Indonesians were profoundly dissatisfied with the federal system with which they had been saddled by the Hague Agreement. In all the fifteen Dutch-created states this discontent soon began to manifest itself in spontaneous and widely based popular demands for a scrapping of what was conceived to be an alien-imposed federalism and for the liquidation of these states and their merger

[10] It is worth noting, too, that Soekarno and Hatta never resigned as President and Prime Minister of the Republic of Indonesia and that those who functioned in their place, Mr. Assaat and Dr. Halim, held the titles of Acting President and Acting Prime Minister respectively.

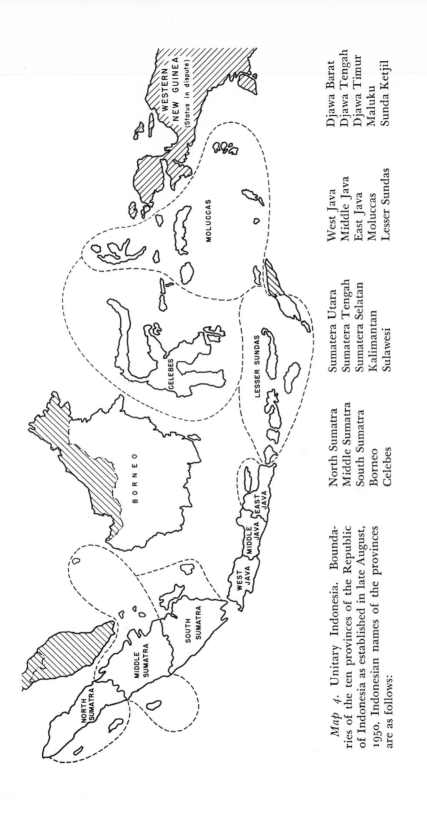

Map 4. Unitary Indonesia. Boundaries of the ten provinces of the Republic of Indonesia as established in late August, 1950. Indonesian names of the provinces are as follows:

North Sumatra	Sumatera Utara	
Middle Sumatra	Sumatera Tengah	
South Sumatra	Sumatera Selatan	
Borneo	Kalimantan	
Celebes	Sulawesi	
West Java	Djawa Barat	
Middle Java	Djawa Tengah	
East Java	Djawa Timur	
Moluccas	Maluku	
Lesser Sundas	Sunda Ketjil	

with the old Republic. Open encouragement was given these movements by the government of the old Republic and by Soekarno and
other leading Republicans in the R.U.S.I. government. As Dutch military and police authority were withdrawn from these states, and as
the several thousand strongly pro-Republican political prisoners were
released from their jails, the force of the unitarian movement became
overwhelming and met with real resistance only where large numbers
of Dutch colonial troops, the KNIL (Koninklijke Nederlandsche
Indische Leger—Royal Netherlands Indies Army), had not been demobilized and opposed it.

Not only that major part of the population which was unitarian in
sentiment but also many sincere advocates of a federal political system
backed this movement. Though advocating a federal system, the latter group wished Indonesia to have its own home-fashioned pattern
of federalism, not an artificial legacy of their old colonial master. In
general they preferred to wait upon the decision of an elected all-
Indonesian Constituent Assembly to determine whether or not Indonesia was to be federal and according to what pattern.

Such people recalled that within the Republic there had been a steady
trend toward decentralization,[11] and few were much impressed by
the assiduously fostered Dutch argument that unification meant Javanese domination. They were aware that Soekarno was half-Balinese,
that every prime minister the Republic had had down through and
including Hatta had been Sumatran, that only five out of the sixteen
members of the R.U.S.I. cabinet were Javanese, and that in the old
Republic's parliament representation was weighted strongly against
Java as compared to the areas outside.

Moreover, the federalism which they advocated was a limited one
and conditioned by the fact that Indonesia possessed far fewer educated people than necessary for the adequate staffing of even a modest
central government. The tremendous reduplication of functions inherent in the federal system of autonomous, unbalanced units (ranging
in population from 100,000 to over 30,000,000) bequeathed by the
Hague Agreement was not, they realized, in harmony with the fact
that Dutch colonial rule had provided Indonesia with an educational
system that as late as 1940 made possible the yearly graduation from

[11] One of the last acts of the Republican government before the second Dutch
military action was in this direction. On Dec. 6, 1948, it passed a law providing for
the establishment of an autonomous province of East Java.

high school of only 240 Indonesian students from a total Indonesian population of 70,000,000.

By the terms of the Hague Agreement the KNIL (colonial army), a force of 65,000 men, was to be dissolved by July 26, 1950. Actually the process was much slower than had been anticipated. Even as late as that date, 17,000 of this number had not been demobilized,[12] and not until June 4, 1951, was it officially announced that the process had been entirely completed.[13] By July 26, 1950, some 26,000 KNIL troops had been incorporated into the armed forces of the R.U.S.I., 18,750 had been demobilized in Indonesia, and 3,250 had departed for the Netherlands.[14]

Though most of the officers in the KNIL were Dutch or Eurasians, the majority of its troops were recruited from the Christian Indonesian areas of the eastern part of the archipelago, particularly Amboina, the Minahassa area of north Celebes, and Timor. Soldiers from these areas were given a substantially higher rate of pay than the relatively small number of Javanese, Sundanese, and other Indonesian soldiers in the KNIL. Many of their Dutch and Eurasian officers had taken pains to convince them that in an Indonesia dominated by Republican elements they would not only lose their higher rate of pay, but that they would likewise lose their army pensions on retiring. It had also been frequently drilled into them by these officers that in an Indonesia where the Republic was dominant their own Christian areas would be controlled by the Mohammedan Javanese.

Thus many of these soldiers had serious misgivings about the sort of future they could expect after demobilization, whether they were absorbed into the armed forces of the R.U.S.I. or returned to civilian life. A number of them already felt or were easily persuaded that maintenance of a federal system of government was the course best calculated to protect their interests. A small number of Dutch and Eurasian officers and Indonesian political leaders in some of the federal states helped convince them of this. Thus in particular in East Indonesia (within the confines of which were Amboina, the Minahassa, and

[12] U.N., Security Council, "Report dated 28 July 1950 from the United Nations Commission for Indonesia addressed to the President of the Security Council Concerning the Dissolution of the Royal Netherlands Indonesian Army, and the Netherlands Army High Command in Indonesia," S/1663, p. 2. At the time of transfer of sovereignty there were approximately 80,000 troops of the Royal Netherlands Army and 65,000 troops of the Royal Netherlands Indies Army in Indonesia (*ibid.*, p. 1).

[13] Aneta, June 4, 1951.   [14] U.N., S/1663, p. 2.

Timor) still-mobilized KNIL units as well as demobilized KNIL personnel who often possessed arms were a force opposing the unitarian movement.

Though this was the case in East Indonesia and to a lesser extent in East Sumatra, a quickly suppressed, but extremely dangerous revolutionary coup in Pasundan (West Java) by KNIL elements (both demobilized and active were involved) had the effect of accelerating the unitarian movement. By discrediting the Pasundan government and demonstrating the weakness of the federal units in dealing with these powerful anti-R.U.S.I. as well as anti-Republican forces, it gave the unitarian movement an additional justification.

Apparently at least by mid-November, 1949, Captain Paul ("Turk") Westerling, recently demobilized from the KNIL and the officer chiefly responsible for the calculated killing of large numbers of civilians in south Celebes in late 1946, had begun organizing a force made up principally of demobilized KNIL troops. A number of Netherlanders including two former police inspectors were included in his group. He and his officers entered into contact with some of the KNIL and KL (*Koninklijke Leger,* Royal Netherlands Army) troops still garrisoned in Bandung, chief city in Pasundan.

According to the Indonesian Ministry of Defense, Westerling's force approached Bandung on the evening of January 22, 1950, and was augmented by regimental shock troops of the Royal Netherlands Army stationed in Bandung. This total force of about 800 heavily armed men, of whom the ministry's communiqué estimated that about 300 were soldiers of the Royal Netherlands Army, entered Bandung on the morning of January 23. Sharp fighting ensued during which sixty men of the smaller R.U.S.I. unit quartered there were killed.[15] Westerling's forces occupied most key points within the city for part of the day, but were finally prevailed upon by Major General Engels, commander of the KL garrison of Bandung, to leave the city.

On January 26, Westerling's troops began to filter into Jakarta, apparently with the purpose of launching a major *coup d'état.* Before they could reorganize, however, they were discovered and after some brief skirmishes were driven out. Plans for this operation later found by the R.U.S.I. government indicated that the objective of the infiltration into the capital was a swift coup whereby it was planned to kill Sultan Hamengku Buwono IX, the Minister of Defense; Mr. Ali Budiardjo, Secretary-General of the Ministry of Defense; and Col.

[15] Communiqué, R.U.S.I. Ministry of Defense, Jan. 24, 1950.

Simatupang, the acting Chief of Staff, and to kidnap the remainder of the cabinet. According to R.U.S.I. sources, it later developed that Sultan Hamid II of West Borneo, one of the leading Federalists and a member of the cabinet, had masterminded the whole affair, with Westerling acting as his military arm. Upon the evidence of others involved in the coup, Hamid was arrested on April 5 and jailed. Government sources reported that on April 19 he confessed to having attempted to overthrow the R.U.S.I. government through Westerling's attempted coup of January 26 and through a later attempt on February 15 involving a projected attack on Parliament (not carried out because as a precaution a battalion of R.U.S.I. troops had been quartered nearby). After mid-February Westerling's dispersed forces appeared to melt away, and on February 26 he was arrested in Singapore after having been flown to Malaya in a Netherlands military plane.

The Westerling affair did serious harm to Indonesian-Dutch relations. Indonesians were outraged by the involvement of some Netherlands army officers in the affair, and they felt that the Netherlands army high command was seriously delinquent in its ability to keep control over its own troops. The belief that certain officials of the Pasundan government had made "arrangements" with Westerling, and the fact that a number of Dutch members of its still partly Dutch-officered police force had deserted to him, did great damage to the position of the Federalists. Following the later allegations against Hamid, one of their chief champions, their position became even more difficult.

Immediately there arose a widely based demand, which the R.U.S.I. government leaders encouraged, that the leaders of the Pasundan government be removed. On February 8, the R.U.S.I. cabinet drafted an emergency law calling for the transfer of the powers of the Pasundan government to a State Commissioner appointed by the central government. On the following day Wiranata Koesoema, *Wali Negara* (State Head) of Pasundan, transferred his powers to Sewaka, the newly appointed R.U.S.I. Commissioner for Pasundan.

Once started, the movement for implementing the unitarian idea spread rapidly. On February 10, the Representative Council of the state of South Sumatra voted to transfer the powers of the State to the R.U.S.I. government. The movement quickly entered this phase in most of the constituent states. The general tendency, however, was for dissolution of the states and their amalgamation into the old Republic rather than into the R.U.S.I. itself.

This formula was not resisted by most of the R.U.S.I. leaders. The tide of nationalist feeling was so strong that even the overwhelming majority of the members of the R.U.S.I. Senate, including many who had been strong Federalists, appeared to believe that either objective wisdom or the interests of their own political futures counseled that they go along with the R.U.S.I. House of Representatives and government in passing an emergency law, based on article 139 of the Constitution, which made legal the dissolution of those constituent states whose governments so requested and their amalgamation into the old Republic of Indonesia. Such a law was passed on March 7, 1950, and two days later, following votes of approval in the R.U.S.I. House, the requests of the governments of East Java, Central Java, and Madura for dissolution and merger into the Republic of Indonesia were approved. The requests of Pasundan and other states followed in short order and were quickly approved. By the end of March, only four states—West Borneo (headed by Sultan Hamid), East Sumatra, East Indonesia, and the now much expanded Republic of Indonesia remained as constituent states within the R.U.S.I.

In the state of West Borneo, especially after the discrediting of Hamid, there developed an increasing demand of the population (culminating in a general strike in its capital of Pontianak) for its dissolution and merger into the Republic. Upon the recommendation of a Government Commission sent to investigate conditions in West Borneo, the R.U.S.I. House of Representatives on April 22 voted fifty to one to endorse this demand.

In East Indonesia shortly after large popular demonstrations urging its liquidation and merger with the Republic and a motion to this effect by pro-Republican elements in its parliament, freedom of political assembly was again suspended and a number of strongly pro-Republican leaders who were not members of its parliament were jailed by order of Soumokil, the state's Minister of Justice.

Most of the troops stationed in East Indonesia were KNIL units. Some of them, including the principal armed force in the area of Makassar, capital of East Indonesia, were ex-KNIL units which had recently been absorbed into the R.U.S.I. army. Among these units there developed an increasing uneasiness over the rapid course of the unitarian movement. When on April 5, 1950, they learned that some 900 ex-Republican troops sent by the R.U.S.I. government from Jakarta were about to land at Makassar it must have seemed to many of them that the old order in East Indonesia was about to collapse. The landing of these troops would shift the balance of military power in the area in favor of the pro-Republican unitarian elements. There is some evidence that Soumokil and a few other leaders of the East Indonesian state helped convince them that this was their last opportunity to act. Before the Republican troops could land, about two companies of ex-KNIL troops under the command of Capt. Andi Aziz captured the few ex-Republican R.U.S.I. troops in Makassar and seized control of the city. They then drew up artillery and forced the R.U.S.I. troop transports in the harbor to sail away.

Aziz stated that he was acting to defend the state of East Indonesia. However, the East Indonesian government, except for a few of its members, refused to indorse his actions. Nevertheless it was powerless to stop him. On April 13, President Soekarno branded Aziz an insurgent, stating: "Whether East Indonesia, East Sumatra, or the Jogjakarta Republic remain autonomous states is no concern of the armed forces." He called on the R.U.S.I. armed forces to restore order in South Celebes. Sukawati, the president of East Indonesia, affirmed that his government had had absolutely nothing to do with Aziz's revolt and had given it no assistance. On the fourteenth Aziz agreed to go to Jakarta for talks with the R.U.S.I. government. Here he was summarily arrested. On April 21, newly landed R.U.S.I. army units entered Makassar without encountering resistance.

With the balance of military power thus changed, the East Indonesian cabinet of Prime Minister Diapari found itself no longer able to muster a majority in parliament and was forced to resign. It was replaced by a pro-Republican cabinet headed by Mr. Putuhena. In Makassar and the surrounding territory of South Celebes an Emergency Government was set up responsible directly to Jakarta. Political prisoners were released from jail, and a state of martial law was declared. With the shift in the balance of power, pro-Republican guerrilla elements based in the hills now felt strong enough to launch attacks on towns where some of the local aristocratic elements who had worked most closely with the Dutch headed the local administrations. This often involved sharp fighting with KNIL units still stationed in these areas. Though the Emergency Government decreed that "All officials of the princely states, local rajahdoms, and other local governments should continue their duties as a matter of routine," it at the same time seemed to give tacit encouragement to their removal by

stating: "The administration of the princely states should be democratized and . . . the princes adapt themselves to the new course of events
in line with the wishes of the people." [16]

Occasionally the guerrillas in freeing political prisoners from the
jails let ordinary criminals out as well. Many of these, as well as some
opportunistic guerrilla leaders, exploited the situation to enrich themselves or build up their own power. As a result, it was several months
before R.U.S.I. military authorities in co-operation with the more
responsible guerrilla leaders were able to establish a reasonable degree
of law and order in South Celebes. In late February, 1951, agreement
was finally reached between the Indonesian government and the principal leader and spokesman for the 14,000 guerrillas of South Celebes,
Kahar Musakar, for the incorporation of a major part of them into
the army and the demobilization of the remainder. (Later, after partial demobilization, this agreement was to fall through.)

In the meantime Soumokil had fled further east in East Indonesia to
the island of Amboina. According to R.U.S.I. government sources he
was transported there in a Netherlands army bomber. Under the leadership of Soumokil and several local political and military leaders, the
South Moluccas Council, which it should be noted had originally been
constituted during the period of Dutch occupation, proclaimed the
independence of the territory (*daerah*) of the South Moluccas.[17] The
council stated it had taken this action because East Indonesia had
been unable to maintain its position as a constituent state of the R.U.S.I.
and because the actions of the R.U.S.I. with respect to East Indonesia
were in conflict with the terms of the Hague Agreement.

Amboina, by far the most populous island of the South Moluccas,
for over a century had been the chief recruiting ground for the KNIL.
A large percentage of the families on the island wére supported by a
father or brother who was either active in the KNIL or drawing a
pension for past service. Despite assurances of the R.U.S.I. government to the contrary, there was a widespread fear that liquidation of
the KNIL would result in a loss of employment or pension for the
breadwinners of these families. In addition, the precolonial culture of
Amboina had been more completely lost than that of almost any other
area in Indonesia and there was less consciousness of kind based on

[16] Proclamation of the Emergency Government of Sulawesi Selatan (South Celebes),
May 3, 1950.

[17] The South Moluccas had been one of the 13 *daerahs* of the State of East Indonesia.
It included the islands of Amboina, Buru, Ceram, and the Uliassars. It had a population of about 450,000 and its capital was Ambon (on Amboina).

cultural affinity with the Javanese and Sumatran matrixes of the Indonesian independence movement than was true of such East Indonesian *daerahs* as South Celebes, North Celebes (Gorontalo), Bali, or the North Moluccas.

Thus for reasons of economic and prestige insecurity (because of uneasiness about the future of KNIL soldiers) and because of cultural differences, particularly religious (well over half the population of Amboina being Christian), a large part of the population of Amboina was undoubtedly disposed to support the rebellion. However, there is no way of telling whether this was a majority of the population of Amboina or not. From the outset the South Moluccas Republic was a military state governed principally by military law with a considerable degree of compulsion being exercised by military elements including a number of active KNIL officers. At the very beginning of the rebellion the special correspondent of the Dutch-owned Aneta News Service learned from Netherlands military sources in Jakarta that "the Royal Netherlands Indies Army troops stationed at Amboina are backing the Moluccas proclamation of independence." Its dispatch of April 26, 1950, went on to state: "Chief of Staff General van Langen of the Netherlands Army in Indonesia wired Commander in Chief General Buurman van Vreeden today that despite persistent efforts to keep the Indonesian members of the KNIL on Amboina under military discipline he was unable to do so." [18] Whether much of that part of the population of Amboina which appeared to support the rebellion did so freely or was dragooned into doing so, it is impossible to say. In most of the islands of the South Moluccas outside of Amboina it was, however, clear that the preponderant majority of the population had no interest in the rebellion, and in a number of them there was no dissident movement whatsoever.

At first the R.U.S.I. authorities sought to negotiate with the dissident regime. However, the mission it dispatched headed by Dr. Johannes Leimena, a distinguished Republican Ambonese who was Minister of Health in the R.U.S.I. cabinet, met with failure. The rebel leaders refused to enter into negotiations unless recognized as representatives of an independent state. This being inadmissible from the R.U.S.I. government's point of view, it was forced to undertake military measures. The number of active and demobilized KNIL troops on Amboina was considerable and they fought well. Several months of

[18] R.U.S.I. sources maintained that General van Langen himself attended the flag-raising ceremony for the "Republic of the South Moluccas" held in Amboina.

bitter fighting took place before the back of the rebellion was broken. Not until mid-November, 1950, was organized military resistance on Amboina finally overcome.

A further deterioration in Indonesian-Dutch relations was a consequence of the Amboina rebellion. Since the Netherlands government was responsible for KNIL units until they were demobilized, it was felt in Indonesian circles that the Netherlands was to an important extent responsible for events in Amboina. Illustrative of this point of view was a Ministry of Defense communiqué made shortly after the outbreak of the rebellion which stated: "Armed units falling under the responsibility of the Netherlands government have forced some politicians to announce the proclamation of the so-called South Moluccas Republic and they subsequently made arrests and committed killings." Indonesians were dissatisfied with the Netherlands military authorities' apparent unwillingness to do more than dismiss the mutinous Ambonese KNIL units from the army. They pointed out that violation of military orders usually called for courts martial and punishment.

In the meantime the unitarian movement was proceeding at a rapid rate elsewhere. As early as April 21, the President of East Indonesia, Sukawati, had announced that his state was prepared to become part of a unitarian state if the Republic of Indonesia agreed to be absorbed along with East Indonesia in such a state. The groups which wished to see East Indonesia constituted as a republic separate from the R.U.S.I. were, he said, small in size and number, and it could be generally said that the Indonesian people wished to remain one.[19]

However, there soon began a movement among all the thirteen member territories of East Indonesia except the South Moluccas to separate from the state of East Indonesia and incorporate themselves into the Republic of Indonesia. On April 30, the Minahassa *daerah* council with a vote of nineteen to zero, with three abstentions, decided to secede from East Indonesia and join the Republic of Indonesia. As contrasted to Amboina, it was significant at this time that in Minahassa, also a KNIL stronghold, all troops of the KNIL were confined to their barracks. Later that day the *daerah* of North Celebes followed the example of the Minahassa and during the course of the next few weeks all the other *daerahs* of East Indonesia except the South Moluccas followed suit.

In a conference from May 3 to 5, Mohammad Hatta, President Sukawati, and Dr. Mansur, head of the state of East Sumatra, reached

[19] Aneta report from Makassar, April 21, 1950.

agreement on the establishment of a unitarian state. On May 13 the Provisional Council of East Sumatra endorsed this decision but stipulated that it wished to join the projected unitarian state via the R.U.S.I. and not via the Republic of Indonesia. Despite strong pressure from a large part of East Sumatra's population for amalgamation via the Republic, Prime Minister Hatta staunchly supported the position of the state's Provisional Council. He felt, with justification, that the situation within the state was too delicate to admit of such a course. Amalgamation with the Republic might well have provoked the former KNIL soldiers of the still existent East Sumatra Security Battalion to undertake an adventure such as had occurred in Amboina.[20]

After several weeks of negotiations between the leaders of the R.U.S.I. government and those of the Republic of Indonesia agreement on the formation of a unitarian state was finally reached on May 19, 1950. The introduction to the agreement read:

The Government of the Republic of the United States of Indonesia which in this case also acted with a full mandate on behalf of the Governments of the State of East Indonesia and the State of East Sumatra, on the one side, and the Government of the member state, the Republic of Indonesia, on the other side . . . hereby declare: (1) that we agree to implement in co-operation the formation of a Unitarian State as a materialization of the concept of the Republic of Indonesia aimed at in the Proclamation of the 17 August 1945. . . .[21]

The agreement provided that the provisional constitution of the unitarian state "shall come into being through revision of the R.U.S.I. Provisional Constitution in such a manner that it shall contain the essentials of the Constitution of the Republic of Indonesia, including: (a) Article 27, (b) Article 29, and (c) Article 33, and additionally appropriate sections of the Provisional Constitution of the R.U.S.I." Since these three articles of the Republican Constitution were so stressed it is important to note them. They read:

Article 27
(1) All citizens have the same status in law and in the government and shall, without exception, respect the law and the government.

---

[20] Likewise the position of the PKI was strong in East Sumatra. It had been chiefly responsible for a bloody uprising against local aristocratic elements in early 1946, and there was widespread fear that if fighting broke out some similar development might take place.

[21] Charter of Agreement Between the Governments of the United States of Indonesia and the Republic of Indonesia.

(2) Every citizen shall have the right to work and to expect a reasonable standard of living.[22]

Article 29

(1) The State shall be based upon belief in the God of all Mankind.

(2) The State shall guarantee the freedom of the people to profess and to exercise their own religion.

Article 31

(1) Economy shall be organized co-operatively.

(2) Branches of production which are important to the State and which affect the life of most people, shall be controlled by the State.

(3) Land and water and the natural riches therein shall be controlled by the State and shall be exploited for the greatest welfare of the people.[23]

In attempting to describe the right of property ownership more fully than had been done in either of the constitutions, the Agreement stated that "the Provisional Constitution shall contain an article laying down the basic principle that 'the right of property is a social function.' " [24] In other words the property owner was expected to use his property in a way which was in harmony with the interests of society.[25]

Other major provisions of the Agreement concerning the new unitarian state were the following:

(a) The Senate was to be abolished.

(b) A provisional parliament for the new state was to be formed from the

22 The R.U.S.I. Constitution merely stated that "Every citizen according to his ability has the right to *available* work (art. 27; italics the writer's).

23 The rendering of these three articles follows the official English translation of the Constitution originally published in the *Voice of Free Indonesia*, Oct., 1945.

24 The phrase is *Hak milik itu adalah suatu funksi sosial*, and a literal translation would be: "The right of property exists as a social function." In the unitarian constitution that emerged later this phrase was added to the existing article concerning property in the R.U.S.I. Constitution. The original reading which was carried over into the new unitarian constitution was: "Everyone has the right to own property individually as well as in association with others. No one shall be deprived arbitrarily of his property" (art. 26 of both the R.U.S.I. Constitution and the new unitarian constitution).

Par. 1, art. 27 of both constitutions reads: "Expropriation of any property or right for the general benefit cannot take place except with indemnification and in accordance with regulations as established by law."

25 The official interpretation of this statement as given by the Minister of Justice, Professor Soepomo, shortly after promulgation of the unitarian constitution was: "The social function of property is fundamental and must be interpreted so as to mean that property may not be used to harm society" ("Elucidation to Act. no. 7, 1950, on the revision of the Provisional Constitution of the Republic of Indonesia converting this into the Provisional Constitution of the Unitary Republic of Indonesia," *Supplement* to the *R.U.S.I. Gazette*, no. 37).

combined memberships of the R.U.S.I. House of Representatives and the Working Committee [26] of the KNIP (provisional parliament of the Republic of Indonesia) with such additional members as might be appointed by the President "after consideration by the two governments."

(c) A provisional constitution for the new state was to be drawn up by an "Assembly for Changing the Constitution" made up of the House of Representatives of the R.U.S.I. and the Working Committee of the KNIP.

(d) A constituent assembly to be elected as soon as possible thereafter, "on the basis of one member for every 300,000 inhabitants with due consideration for a fair representation of minorities," which would frame a final constitution.

(e) Soekarno would be president of the new state.

(f) The cabinet of the government of the new state would be responsible to its parliament.

(g) Pending the introduction of new legislation by the unitarian state existing acts and regulations were to remain in force "with the understanding that wherever possible, the laws of the member-state, the Republic of Indonesia, shall be adhered to."

There followed a period of two months during which the representatives of the R.U.S.I. House of Representatives and of the Republican KNIP met together to work out a draft for the unitarian constitution. By July 20, they had completed their task and presented their draft to the R.U.S.I. House and Senate and the Working Committee of the KNIP for approval. It had been agreed that these bodies could not amend the draft, but could only approve or disapprove it. After more than three weeks of discussion general agreement was finally reached. On August 14, the R.U.S.I. Senate endorsed the draft by a unanimous vote, and the R.U.S.I. House did so by a vote of ninety to eighteen. The Working Committee of the KNIP ratified the document by a vote of thirty-one to two with seven abstentions. The following day, August 15, 1950, President Soekarno signed the draft bill and with the countersignature of Prof. Soepomo, Minister of Justice of the R.U.S.I., the bill was promulgated as the Provisional Constitution of the Republic of Indonesia.

The very name of the new State—Republic of Indonesia—symbolized a return to the unitarian pattern of the old Republic of Indonesia and a triumph of the nationalism which it represented. More than anything else the change from the federal R.U.S.I. to the new unitarian Republic represented the desire of the population to shake off the legacy of Dutch colonial rule. For despite the full sovereignty en-

[26] The 47-man ad interim agent of the KNIP.

joyed by the R.U.S.I., the preponderant majority of the Indonesian population saw its federal structure as Dutch-imposed and a relic of colonialism. For them the liquidation of federalism meant the final triumph of the Republic of Indonesia proclaimed in August, 1945.

The constitution of the new unitarian state is explicitly provisional and, indeed, is designated as the Provisional Constitution of the Republic of Indonesia. However, the general expectation is that the final version which emerges following the deliberations of the projected constituent assembly will be very close to it.

The present provisional Unitarian Constitution is essentially a revision of the R.U.S.I. Constitution so as to harmonize more completely with that of the old Republic of Indonesia, incorporating (with certain amendments) the Charter of Agreement of May 19 between the government of the R.U.S.I. and that of the old Republic. The most important of these amendments was the decision not to have the President appoint additional members to the new state's House of Representatives, but rather to incorporate the membership of the R.U.S.I. Senate and the Republican High Advisory Council into it along with the memberships of the R.U.S.I. House and the Working Committee of the Republican KNIP.[27]

Thus the membership of the single-chambered legislature of the new state, its House of Representatives, was made up of 237 members, 147 from the House of Representatives and 31 from the Senate of the R.U.S.I., 46 from the Working Committee of the KNIP, and 13 from the High Advisory Council of the Republic of Indonesia.[28] This first House of Representatives of the new unitarian state is considered temporary and is later to be replaced by one based upon country-wide elections.[29] A second amendment to the charter was that providing for the ratio of members to the projected Constituent Assembly to be 1 to every 150,000, rather than 1 to every 300,000 inhabitants.[30]

Except for its unitarian organization and the elimination of the Senate [31] the general pattern of government established by the unitarian

[27] The Provisional Constitution of the Republic of Indonesia, art. 77; see also "Elucidation to Act. No. 7, 1950," loc. cit.

[28] At the time of their fusion all these four constituent bodies had memberships slightly smaller than their maximum. The R.U.S.I. House of Representatives had an authorized membership of 150; the R.U.S.I. Senate, 32; Republican Working Committee, 47; and the High Advisory Council, 18. As far as the writer knows, unfilled positions arising from death or resignation were the reason for this discrepancy.

[29] See art. 56.

[30] "Elucidation to Act. No. 7, 1950," loc. cit.

[31] Sentiment for provision for a senate within the unitarian state was considerable

constitution is close to that of the R.U.S.I. It provides that legislative authority be shared between the Government (President plus cabinet) and the House of Representatives. Both can introduce legislation; and presidential decrees (including those concerning the President's authority over the armed forces) require the assent of both.[32] The Government possesses the right to enact emergency laws on its own authority. However, they must be approved by the House of Representatives at its next sitting; otherwise they lapse.[33] The cabinet as a whole as well as each minister individually is responsible to the House of Representatives. Even during the period that it is provisional (i.e., before general elections are held) the House has the right to compel the cabinet or ministers individually to resign.[34]

Thus there are actually three lodgments of power: the President, the cabinet, and the House of Representatives. All ordinary legislation requires the immediate approval of all three. Emergency legislation requires the immediate approval of President plus cabinet and ultimate sanction by the parliament, though it is operative pending obtainment of that sanction. However, this interim need not be long, for the House can assemble not only whenever requested by the Government but also whenever at least one-tenth of its membership so desires.[35] Moreover, since the cabinet is responsible to the House, it would be unlikely to approve such legislation unless reasonably sure of later securing the House's approval.

The President's [36] power is considerable. In addition to sharing in

---

enough to give reason to believe that when the projected constituent assembly frames the final and definitive constitution there is some chance that one will be provided for. Sjahrir's party pressed for its establishment in the unitarian government both for the purpose of acting as a brake on overhasty legislation and in order to give representation to cultural differences.

[32] Art. 89–95.   [33] Art. 96–97.

[34] Art. 83. These points are not made clear in Art. 83 itself, but are made explicit in the official "Elucidation" to the Constitution ("Elucidation to Act. No. 7, 1950," *loc. cit.*).

[35] Art. 65.

[36] Soekarno was elected President of the unitary state by the Assembly for Changing the Constitution (R.U.S.I. House of Representatives plus the Working Committee of the KNIP [Parliament of the old Republic]), and the Charter of Agreement of May 19, 1950, between the R.U.S.I. and the old Republic specifically stipulated that he was to be President of the unitarian state they agreed to establish. With respect to the election of the President the provisional unitarian constitution states only: "The President and the Vice-President are elected in accordance with rules to be laid down by law" (art. 45). "For the first time," this articles continues, the Vice-President is appointed by the President upon the recommendations submitted by the House of Representatives. Shortly after the formation of the first unitarian

the legislative power he has the right to dissolve the House of Representatives and call for new elections.[37] Also the President "forms the ministeries" and "appoints one or more Cabinet *formateurs*" who in turn appoint the other cabinet ministers,[38] in conformity, of course, with the wishes of the majority of the House of Representatives. Since the President if he so wishes has the option of appointing only one cabinet *formateur,* he can, therefore, appoint the Prime Minister— subject, of course, to the approval of a majority of parliament.

Though the provisional unitarian Constitution is not federal, the governmental apparatus which it provides for is not monolithic. It stipulates that "the division of Indonesia's territory into large and small autonomous territories and the organization of their administration shall be established by law, observing and considering the principles of consultation and representation in the system of government of the state" and that "the territories shall be given the largest possible measure of autonomy, to manage their own local government." [39]

Soon after promulgation of the new Constitution the territory of Indonesia [40] was subdivided into ten provinces. These are Sumatera Utara (North Sumatra), Sumatera Tengah (Middle Sumatra), Sumatera Selatan (South Sumatra), Djawa Barat (West Java), Djawa Tengah (Middle Java), Djawa Timur (East Java, including Madura), Kalimantan (Borneo), Sulawesi (Celebes), Maluku (The Moluccas), and Sunda Ketjil (The Lesser Sundas—Bali, Lombok, Sumbawa, Sumba, Flores, Timor, etc.). Though by mid-1951 some administrative decentralization had developed along provincial lines, no great amount of substantive governmental decentralization had yet occurred. Undoubtedly this was partly a consequence of the monopoly of attention still being absorbed by the pressing problems of the central government and its inability to release sufficient personnel to staff adequately the provincial administrations. It was, however, also to an important extent a consequence of the fact that these provincial administrations had not yet been granted the power to raise sums of any consequence through local taxation.

On August 22, 1950, a week after the establishment of the new

---

government Mohammad Hatta secured the support of a large majority of the House of Representatives as well as that of Soekarno for this post and became the new state's first Vice-President.

[37] Art. 84.   [38] Art. 50 and 51.   [39] Art. 131.

[40] Which is regarded as encompassing "the territory of the former Netherlands Indies." "Elucidation to Act. No. 7, 1950," *loc. cit.* Thus western New Guinea is considered included.

unitarian state, President Soekarno instructed Mohammad Natsir, chairman of the Leadership Council of the Masjumi to form a new cabinet. The cabinet announced by Natsir on September 6, symbolized the liquidation of the old federalism and the fulfillment of the unitarian movement. It contained only one former Federalist [41] and all of its key posts were occupied by former Republicans. It was based upon a coalition which derived its principal strength from the Masjumi, the largest party in parliament (having 50 of its 237 seats).

Other parties participating in Natsir's cabinet were: the Persatuan Indonesia Raja (PIR), eighteen seats; the Partai Sosialis Indonesia of Sjahrir, sixteen seats; the Fraksi Demokrat (Democratic Faction), eleven seats; the Parindra (Partai Indonesia Raja—Greater Indonesian Party), nine seats; the Partai Katolik (Catholic Party), eight seats; Partai Nasional Indonesia Merdeka (Independent Indonesian Nationalist Party), six seats; the Partai Sarekat Islam Indonesia (PSII), five seats; and the Partai Kristen (Christian Party), four seats. In addition more than half of the twenty-four nonparty members of parliament supported Natsir's cabinet.

The principal party in opposition to the new cabinet, the PNI, had refused to enter it because offered fewer portfolios than it felt entitled to. It held forty-one seats in parliament, while the other chief opposition group, the block of PKI-led, pro-Stalinist parties, controlled twenty-nine seats.[42] Not in the government, but relatively neutral in position, were the Partai Buruh (Labor Party) headed by S. M. Abidin, seven seats, and the Barisan Tani Indonesia (Indonesian Peasants' Corps), five seats.

Except for the fact that it did not have the support of the PNI, Natsir's cabinet was a strong one. Most of its members were experienced and highly respected men, the majority of whom—particularly those in the most important posts—held political and social views which were close to his. Natsir and his Minister of Finance, Sjafruddin Prawiranegara, were the two principal leaders of the Religious Socialist group within the Masjumi, and Mohammad Roem, who had been recalled from his post of High Commissioner to the Netherlands to fill the post of Minister of Foreign Affairs, was also a leading member of this group.

[41] M. A. Pellaupessy, Minister of Information.

[42] Of these the PKI had 8; the Front Buruh (Labor Front), 7; the Partai Buruh Indonesia (Indonesian Labor Party led by Sakirman), 5; the Partai Kedualatan Rakjat (People's Sovereignty Party led by Luat Siregar), 5; and the Partai Sosialis (Socialist Party), 2. The Partai Murba had only 3 representatives in Parliament, considerably less than its strength in relation to the other parties.

Two others holding important posts, Sumitro Djojohadikusumo (previously Economic Minister Plenipotentiary to the United States), Minister of Commerce and Industry, and Tandiono Manu, Minister of Agriculture, were members of Sjahrir's Indonesian Socialist Party and held socio-economic views fairly close to the Religious Socialists. Most of the other important posts were in the hands of nonparty men of proven ability. Among them was Hamengku Buwono IX, Sultan of Jogjakarta, who held the position of Deputy Prime Minister. His work in increasing internal security as Minister of Defense in Hatta's out-going cabinet had enhanced his already great prestige. In Natsir's cabi-net he continued to devote himself primarily to this task. The other functions of the Ministry of Defense were taken over by Dr. Halim, a nonparty man close in his outlook to Sjahrir and until then Acting Prime Minister of the old Republic of Indonesia. The Minister of Interior, Mr. Assaat, had a closely similar approach to social prob-lems and had won much prestige as acting President of the old Re-public and before that as Chairman of the KNIP and its Working Committee.

The membership of Natsir's cabinet (September 6, 1950 to March 20, 1951) was as follows:

Ministry		*Party*
Prime Minister	Mohammad Natsir	Masjumi
Deputy Prime Minister	Hamengku Buwono IX	Nonparty
Internal Affairs	Assaat	Nonparty
Foreign Affairs	Mohammad Roem	Masjumi
Defense	Abdul Halim [43]	Nonparty
Justice	Wongsonegoro	PIR
Finance	Sjafruddin Prawiranegara	Masjumi
Trade and Industry	Sumitro Djojohadikusumo	Indonesian Socialist Party
Agriculture	Tandiono Manu	Indonesian Socialist Party
Communications and Transport	Djuanda	Nonparty
Education and Culture	Bahder Djohan	Nonparty
Public Works and Re-construction	Johannes	PIR
Health	Johannes Leimena	Christian Party
Labor	Pandji Suroso	Parindra
Social Affairs	F. S. Harjadi	Catholic Party
Religion	Hadji Wachid Hasjim	Masjumi
Information	M. A. Pellaupessy	Democratic Faction
State	Harsono Tjokroaminoto [44]	PSII

Some of the parties participating in Natsir's cabinet, it will be noted, were new and had not been in existence during the period of

[43] Resigned because of ill-health on Dec. 8, 1950. (His duties were taken over by Natsir and Hamengku Buwono.)

[44] Resigned, because of opposition of his party to the cabinet, on Dec. 18, 1950.

Hatta's R.U.S.I. cabinet. In fact they all emerged during or immediately following the establishment of the expanded Parliament of the new unitarian state.

The largest of these newly-established parties was the Fraksi Demokrat (Democratic Faction). It was a rather loose coalition of representatives from Celebes, the Moluccas and Lesser Sundas, most of whom had when members of the R.U.S.I. House and Senate belonged to no political party. It enrolled a large number of former civil servants, including a number of administrative officials closely tied to the local aristocracies of the Lesser Sundas and some parts of the North Moluccas and southern Celebes.

The second largest of the new parties, the Parindra (Partai Indonesia Raja—Greater Indonesian Party) was based largely upon the prewar members of the party of the same name who had not already elected to join the PNI. They were drawn primarily from Java, Celebes, and the Lesser Sundas, and were for the most part civil servants previously belonging to no political party and whose position with respect to political and social problems appeared to be approximately midway between that of the PIR and the PNI.

The smallest of the new parties, the Partai Nasional Indonesia Merdeka (Independent Indonesian Nationalist Party) was a right-wing splinter that had detached itself from the main body of the PNI. According to its leaders, its defection resulted in part because of the PNI's drift to the left and what they termed its "indecisive policy." This was, however, probably more a result of the dissatisfaction of its leaders with their subordinate positions within the PNI and their attendant lack of success in attaining the governmental positions which they sought. In their own terms their action was "a revolt against the trust company of the old guard." Several months after the formation of the Natsir cabinet they changed the new party's name to that of Partai Rakjat Nasional (National People's Party).

❧ CHAPTER XV ❧

Achievements and Prospects

CONSUMMATION of the unitarian movement marked the close of the Indonesian revolution, or at least of its dominantly political phase. With the formation of the Natsir Government a new emphasis emerged which was more socio-economic than political. A number of important political problems remained, in particular those relating to Western New Guinea, maintenance of an independent foreign policy, internal security, organization of local government, and drawing up of election laws. Although these did command much attention from the new government, it was obliged to focus its attention even more on the urgent socio-economic problems which had been held in abeyance for so long by the priority of the struggle for national independence.

Before discussing some of the principal socio-economic problems confronting the postrevolutionary government, it would be worthwhile to note some of the outstanding achievements of the Indonesian revolution. Its general psychological impact had been tremendous. While bringing about a basic change in the political status of Indonesia, the revolution brought with it significant and widespread changes in the character of the Indonesian people. During the six-year period, 1945–1950, their sense of personal and collective dignity, self-respect and self-confidence had grown enormously. This change was greatest among the educated urban dwellers and next among the laboring population in the towns and on the estates. But to an important degree it had affected most of the peasant population as well. Thereby an energy and creativeness in tackling socio-economic as well as political problems was released among the Indonesian population which was surprising to many older-generation Indonesians as well as to many Netherlanders.

It was among the younger generation that this change in character appeared most marked. During the crucial years 1945–1949 the most dynamic element in the revolution was the educated sector of Indonesian youth. Without its energization the Indonesian revolution could not have succeeded. In addition, quite apart from its vanguard role in activating the revolution, circumstances dictated that it play an important role in staffing the revolutionary governmental administration and the revolutionary army. This stemmed primarily from the paucity of upper- and middle-rank Indonesian civil servants trained by the colonial regime and the accompanying lack of any sizable Indonesian professional or commercial middle class from which men could have been recruited whose experience might have qualified them to fill many of these posts. To make up for the deficiency the revolutionary regime had no alternative but to turn to the only possible remaining source of such personnel, the educated youth—in particular, college and high-school students. Therefore this element staffed a major part of the middle and upper-middle echelons of the governmental offices and of the upper and upper-middle ranks of the army of the new Indonesian state.

As a result of the heavy responsibilities it shouldered and the initiative forced upon it, Indonesian youth in general, but particularly its educated element, developed the qualities of self-confidence and enterprise to a degree which distinguished it from its counterpart of a decade before. This characteristic was most marked among the young men, but it extended to women as well. Indeed, the revolution brought a significant increase in the already-substantial social status and activities of Indonesian women in general. A number of high administrative posts in the government were filled by them, and the percentage of women in parliament was greater than in most Western European countries and in the United States Congress.[1]

The political achievements of the revolution were not limited to the attainment of independence from the Netherlands and the ending of colonial status. In addition the revolution wrought profound changes in the internal political articulation of the country. At the national level, a constitutional type of government was established which gave promise of taking firm root. It is true that the parliaments of both the revolutionary and postrevolutionary governments were made up of individuals

[1] Although it is probable that general elections will reduce this percentage, it is indicative of increased public acceptance of women in such positions.

who did not owe their office to free popular elections. The parliaments were, however, roughly representative of public opinion and exercised real power. Moreover, the large majority of the individuals composing them were sincerely dedicated to the principles of representative democracy and most of them were eager to have the existing parliament yield place to one based upon nationwide free elections.

Less well known, but of great importance, were the political achievements at the village level. Here the example set by the enlightened and progressive young Sultan of Jogjakarta, Hamengku Buwono IX, was, with some variations and adaptations to meet local conditions, being followed increasingly throughout most of Java and to a lesser extent in other places. Among the most important of the reforms introduced by the Sultan was that providing for election of all village officials under a franchise covering all inhabitants over the age of eighteen.[2] (Under the colonial regime only the village headman was elected; he then appointed the other village officials. The franchise had been limited to landowners, and sometimes colonial officials interfered in the elections, in some cases appointing the headman.) Under the Jogjakarta system the village council, Madjelis Desa, was elected under a similar franchise and was made up of representatives from each group of four to five contiguous households. Anyone over the age of eighteen, whether or not a landowner, was eligible for this office. In turn, the Madjelis Desa (averaging about four hundred members) elected a People's Representative Council (Dewan Perwakilan Rakjat) averaging about thirty members. The village legislative and executive organs were separated. Should a difference arise between the Representative Council and the executive officers of the village, collectively known as the Executive Council (Pamong Desa), the dispute was referred to the Madjelis Desa for resolvement. Whether or not such a dispute developed, the Madjelis Desa was required to meet at least once every three months to review the actions of the Representative Council and Executive Council, both of which were responsible to it. In addition, a general administrative rationalization was achieved, with the smaller adjacent villages being merged.[3] This resulted in a pooling of resources so that their facilities for education, irrigation, credit, etc. could be more effectively utilized.

Finally, throughout wide areas of Indonesia the revolution had had a

[2] The writer had an opportunity to observe this electoral process during the course of a brief investigation of local government in the Daerah Istimewa (Special District) of Jogjakarta in Dec., 1948.

[3] The 796 villages of the Daerah Istimewa of Jogjakarta were reduced to 375.

direct physical impact upon the village which stimulated the political consciousness of its inhabitants and shook up the social relationships among them. Naturally this was particularly great in those extensive areas where fighting had occurred, and it was probably greatest in Java. In many parts of the island the previous depletion of the able-bodied male population initiated under the Japanese occupation with the drafting of forced labor and the formation of a native militia was increased by the extensive recruitment for the Republic's armed forces. This tended to relieve the pressure on the land in many villages temporarily. It often resulted also in additional responsibility for women, there being more female than male landowners in some communities. Likewise, new responsibilities had to be assumed by boys in their early teens.

Those forced laborers who, after having been uprooted for several years and suffering great hardships, lived to return to their villages in 1945–1946 could not but come back with a stronger national consciousness and with quickened political pulses. As the armed forces were partially demobilized under the rationalization programs of 1948 and 1950, there streamed back to the villages many young men whose political consciousness and self-confidence were much greater, and whose parochialism was much less, than before they had left home. Probably it was to a large extent because of this that the younger generation began to participate in the political life of the village so much more actively than had previously been the case.

One important result of these developments and of the impact of the revolution as a whole on the villages was the very considerable turnover among officials there. Those village officials who had served their communities well during the periods of Netherlands and Japanese rule generally continued to hold the confidence of these communities and were maintained in office. But probably a considerably greater number were replaced by new officials. Thus, the internal political change attending the Indonesian revolution was not merely one of an exchange of governing elites at the top, with an Indonesian nationalist elite replacing the old alien colonial elite. The change penetrated deeply into Indonesian society.

In the socio-economic sphere, as well as in the political, considerable change accompanied the revolution. Some of this was a result of the conscious effort of the revolutionary government, but much was not.

At the village level, a system of *gotong-rojong* (mutual help) pioneered by the Sultan of Jogjakarta among the villages of the five regencies of the Daerah Istimewa of Jogjakarta had by late 1948 begun to be sponsored by local authorities in several other regencies of Republican-controlled Java. Under this system the funds from a 10 per cent tax levied on the incomes of rich villages within the regency were used to subsidize its poor villages. Of the money raised 20 per cent was used as a direct grant to help support the costs of administration in the poor villages. The remaining 80 per cent was lent the latter at an interest rate of 2 per cent per annum. As these sums were repaid to the rich villages, they were used by them to develop village-owned industries.

During the course of the revolution some modest beginnings were made by the central government on projects providing for reasonable agrarian credit and the establishment of peasant co-operatives. However, very little was achieved, primarily because of the military situation and the government's desperate financial straits. In general a sizable gap remained between announced government intentions and their implementation.

Largely as a result of conscious governmental policy, the status and bargaining position of labor were considerably strengthened during the revolutionary period. Initially in part a consequence of the government's desire to counter a burgeoning anarcho-syndicalism with a more socially responsible trade-union organization, this policy resulted primarily from the lasting dedication of many of the government's top leaders to the long-submerged interests of Indonesian labor. Thus, during the revolution a substantial Indonesian trade-union organization developed.

In addition, during the course of the revolution important developments in the socio-economic sphere took place quite independently of government action. The programs of the Masjumi in Kediri and elsewhere to provide land to deserving landless peasants, to organize peasant co-operatives, and to provide credit at low rates to poor merchants have already been described. Probably the most important of these developments, one which has been very much overlooked, was the widespread redistribution of wealth which occurred. In the agrarian field this was often almost revolutionary in scope. Basically it was a result of the tremendous inflation, the complete lack of governmental action adjusting the land tax to the inflation,[4] and the very limited measures taken by the government to adjust peasant debts to it. The same land tax was paid by the peasant in Republican territory in 1947 and 1948 as in 1941. Yet

----

[4] Government legislation substituting an income tax for the land tax had been drafted and was scheduled to go into effect at the beginning of 1949, but the Dutch attack made this impossible.

he was receiving over fifteen times as much money per kilo of rice in 1947 as in 1941 and more than sixty times as much by mid-1948. In effect, then, the peasant in Republican territory had virtually no land tax to pay.

Some measures were attempted by the government to adjust standing debts to the inflation, but these efforts were extremely limited and fell far short of their mark. As a result, a major share of peasant indebtedness was wiped out under the inflation. In addition, the peasantry in many areas had a tendency to view the Indonesian Chinese as aligned with the Dutch. Many of these peasants tended to identify the Chinese with the old colonial order and to see the revolution as directed against them as well as against the Dutch. Because of this, the peasants were often reluctant to repay both their inflation-lightened monetary debts and their more substantial debts in kind to those who had been their chief sources of credit, the itinerant Chinese moneylenders (*tjina mindering*). In general Republican officials showed no disposition to enforce the collection of these debts, and as a result in many places an outright repudiation of debts to Chinese creditors occurred. Thus, during the course of the revolution there was a great decline in the indebtedness of probably a majority of the peasantry in Republican Java and Sumatra.

Also estate (plantation) laborers generally fared relatively well in most areas of Republican-controlled Java and Sumatra. Except in that minority of cases where the government undertook to operate the estates, such laborers were usually free to move onto the rich estate lands and farm them, growing food crops for their own benefit. Frequently peasants from adjacent areas who owned no land or an inadequate amount of land also farmed land on these estates.

Whereas the course of the revolution saw a socio-economic adjustment which in general favored the peasantry of Republican Java and Sumatra, concurrent with this was an adjustment which was distinctly unfavorable to the majority of the middle-class and white-collar groups within the Republic. Their level of living sank to a point where most of their members suffered from grossly inadequate food and housing, a substantial number being dangerously undernourished.[5] An undoubted majority of them, while better dressed, ate considerably less than the average peasant. Urban labor often fared poorly too, but generally its

[5] The government attempted to meet this problem through price control measures and making rice stipends available to civil servants at well below cost. However, these efforts were both inadequate and belated.

level of living did not fall as much as did that of these other two urban groups.

Thus, in the socio-economic sphere the revolution had a strong leveling effect upon an indigenous society whose differentiation in this sphere was already much less than that in most other Asian countries.

Insofar as socio-economic extremes tend to create political unrest, this added leveling of Indonesian society, particularly as it occurred in the agrarian sector, probably tended to increase its political cohesion. In addition, this process probably reinforced the already substantial homogeneity of outlook among most Republican leaders with regard to the socio-economic aims and program of the new state. Indeed, this similarity of outlook was one of the most important and unique attributes of postrevolutionary Indonesia, an advantage held by few of the newly emergent states of Asia, and by none of them, except perhaps Burma, to the same degree.

The beginning of the postrevolutionary period found the leaders of all important political groups, except for the Communists, dedicated to the achievement of roughly the same sort of socio-economic system, namely, a mixed economy—co-operative, socialist, and capitalist—with primary emphasis on the co-operative sector. Secondary emphasis was ultimately to be placed on the socialist portion. However, it was generally agreed that the importance of the capitalist sector of the economy would remain substantial for some time to come, both because of the desirability of temporarily maintaining, if not augmenting, foreign capital investment and as a result of the inability of the state to move directly much farther into the economic sphere because of the small number of Indonesians sufficiently trained for staffing socialistic enterprises. A somewhat greater difference of opinion existed regarding long-term aims, especially as to how much emphasis was to be put on increasing the socialist at the expense of the capitalist sector of the economy. However, the goals envisaged by the principal non-Communist parties and the most influential nonparty individuals for at least the next decade were remarkably close.

These outlooks resulted to a large extent from the fact that in Indonesia, in contrast to most newly emergent Asian states, almost none of the political leaders held any vested interest in the existing socio-economic *status quo*. The concentration of landownership in Indonesian hands was relatively slight, and few Indonesians with much political influence had an important stake in the existing system of agrarian relationships. Moreover, Indonesia's leadership was almost entirely without capitalist roots, and only a very few politically influential Indonesians had a vested interest in the capitalist sector of the economy. The fact that this sector was almost exclusively the domain of Westerners and Chinese reinforced the socialistic penchant of many Indonesians. Even those few leaders who did not espouse some variant of socialist ideology agreed that since the country had virtually no Indonesian capitalists or private capital, the only feasible way to protect its people from exploitation by the strong and experienced non-Indonesian capitalist elements was for the government to intervene in economic life either through advancing credit for the organization of co-operatives or, where necessary, by direct participation entailing government ownership.

This homogeneity of outlook among Indonesia's postrevolutionary leadership extended also to basic political principles. The preponderant majority of that leadership, the principal exceptions being the Communists and some leaders of Darul Islam and the PIR, were dedicated to political principles and practices which were roughly the same as those aspired to in the Western democracies. Also reinforcing the prospects for democratic political development were the widespread quality of a relatively high degree of ideological and religious tolerance among the Indonesian population and the vitality of their resurgent and expanding village democracy.

Although most of Indonesia's postrevolutionary leaders espoused roughly the same political principles as did most leaders in the United States and the democracies of Western Europe, this did not entail a common international orientation. A conviction of paramount importance among Indonesian leaders was that their country should pursue an independent foreign policy tied to neither the American-Western European nor the Soviet power bloc, but that Indonesia should follow whatever course between them seemed best suited to her own interests and to what she conceived to be the interests of international peace. This strong desire for an autonomous international role stemmed primarily from Indonesia's own conditioning within the international community. In the first place, the outlook of her leaders was a reaction to her long history of colonial subjection; as in other recently freed ex-colonial countries there was a great sensitiveness to any kind of international relationship that might be interpreted as subservience to an outside power. Secondly, Indonesians had been keenly disillusioned with both the United States and Soviet Russia during the course of their revolutionary struggle; the policies of both of these powers toward Indonesia during the critical years 1946–1949 appeared to them to be much more actuated by calculations of narrow self-interest than by the principle of self-determination for subject peoples.

The necessity of organizing a new and effective state administration coupled with an extensive program of socio-economic change required that the postrevolutionary Indonesian government be a strong one. A basic question was whether it would prove possible to develop such strength while at the same time promoting a democratic system of government. Although the Republic's leaders were sincerely devoted to the attainment of both objectives, some of the most prescient among them feared that the temptation might become strong to resort to authoritarian methods in order to attain the requisite governmental strength.

One of the greatest impediments to the development of democratic political practices was the still-surviving authoritarian tradition and the related habit of dependence upon orders from above. Although among wide sectors of the population these qualities had become significantly weakened by the impact of the revolution, most of the Indonesian population still expected their leaders to solve their problems for them.

Despite its awakened national consciousness and the much increased vigor of its political life at the village level, peasant society was still not effectively linked with the national government in a mutually activated and mutually responsive relationship. The existing relationship was still predominantly a one-way affair—from the top down. Those ties between the village and the national government which were substantial were still primarily through the medium of personalities rather than political parties represented in the national parliament. So long as these parties floated as vague shapes above the peasant masses with either few or no real lines of contact between them, a two-way relationship between the village and the national representative body could not be developed. Without such a relationship, an authoritarian articulation of government could not be avoided, and a true representative democracy would not be possible.

No great progress in this direction was likely to be made until national elections were held, and the extent of such progress would depend to an important extent upon the character of the system of elections introduced. Though adequate preparation for such elections would necessarily take time, there was a danger that some political parties and individuals might out of self interest covertly delay them longer than was good for the new state's political health.

There were several other conditions which would probably influence significantly the extent to which Indonesian society moved away from its authoritarian past and towards a genuinely democratic political system. Among these, and in particular important for giving its people the necessary sense of actual participation in the political process, would be that of governmental decentralization. There was some danger that the justified repudiation of the artificial, alien-imposed federal structure inherited from the Dutch might create a groundless, long-standing prejudice against decentralization per se. However, there was a real need for a considerable number of governmental functions of predominantly local importance becoming the responsibility of local representative bodies and locally elected executive officers. Many governmental functions could not feasibly be so decentralized because of the prohibitive expense involved or because of the paucity of civil service personnel. However, a number of them could without seriously raising these problems. Among these was the police system. Once fully elected local representative bodies had ben established, it would undoubtedly be healthier politically to decentralize the police system, thereby making it more directly accountable to the citizenry. Though the postrevolutionary government appeared to be moving in the direction of decentralization of some governmental functions, there was danger that implementation of this program might be seriously prejudiced by a failure to provide sufficient local fiscal autonomy.

Another influential condition would be the ability of nontotalitarian political parties to attract the support of organized labor, the demobilized soldiers, and those important elements of educated Indonesian youth not included within these groups. The extent to which the dynamic energies of Indonesian youth, particularly its educated sector, were kept from flowing into totalitarian channels would be contingent to an important extent upon the effectiveness of the government in providing it with opportunities for socially constructive work at least roughly commensurate with the abilities it had demonstrated during the revolution.

The potentials of authoritarian and democratic forms of government in Indonesia would also be influenced by the character of the new state's program of socio-economic reconstruction. Its scope and tempo would be important in determining whether or not the pressures generated by the devastation of the economy, the popular expectation of a rapid postrevolutionary rise in the level of living, and the widespread demand for a more socialized economy could be contained in nonauthoritarian political channels. If the scope of the program which the Republic's leaders undertook to carry out were too limited, or the pace too slow, they might forfeit their popular backing, and those more disposed to employ authoritarian techniques might replace them at the helm of government. The speed and scope with which its leaders moved forward, however, would be to a critical extent dependent upon the amount of capital available to them. So long as world conditions continued to create a heavy demand for Indonesia's chief exports, sufficient domestic capital probably could be accumulated without the necessity of applying any great governmental pressure on the population. But should that demand appreciably diminish and should it also then prove impossible or unfeasible to make up for this loss through borrowing abroad, a major problem would arise. In order then to accumulate sufficient domestic capital for the full maintenance of its program the government might well be obliged to force the population to cut its level of living severely. This would require very strong measures, and it would be doubtful whether the government could put them through without its own character becoming considerably more authoritarian in the process. However, if the volume of foreign trade attained by Indonesia in 1950 could be sustained over the next five or ten years, this problem might not arise, at least not in so acute a form. For in this case the government's program for socio-economic development might have by then so strengthened and balanced the economy that even should the market for its leading exports seriously contract it would be able to raise sufficient domestic capital without forcing a program of austerity upon the population.

Whatever the case, if in attempting to solve their great postrevolutionary problems the Indonesian people were able to demonstrate the same qualities which they had shown in their struggle for political independence, their chances of success appeared strong.

Acknowledgments

MUCH of the material presented here could not have been gathered had it not been for the generous assistance of a great many of the people with whom the author had the good fortune to become acquainted while he was in Indonesia. Within the Republic he was particularly indebted to President Soekarno; Mohammed Hatta, Vice-President and then concurrently Prime Minister; former Prime Minister Soetan Sjahrir; Hadji Agoes Salim, then Minister of Foreign Affairs; Ali Sastroamidjojo, then Minister of Education; Mohammad Natsir, then Minister of Information; and Mohammad Roem, then Chairman of the Indonesian Delegation to the U.N.'s Committee of Good Offices. All of them gave generously of their time to the author during a period when they were particularly hard pressed by their important duties.

A similar debt is owed by the author to the following for their helpful assistance: Abikusno Tjokrosujoso, Ali Budiardjo, Hamid Algadrie, Abdul Gafar Pringgodigdo, Abdul Karim Pringgodigdo, the late Ratu Langie, Roeslan Abdulgani, Maria Ulfah Santoso, Subadio Sastrosatomo, Mohammad Saubari, and R. P. Selosoemardjan. The author wishes to acknowledge also the extensive help given him by members of the staffs of the Ministry of Information, in particular Hanan and Hilman, and of the Ministries of Economic Affairs, Education, and Foreign Affairs, especially Darmanto.

Among the many additional people to whom the author is indebted for assistance received in the Republic, he would in particular like to express his thanks to the following: Jo Abdurachman, Abu Hanifah,

481

Assaat Gelar Datuk Mudo, Baswedan, Didi Djajadiningrat, Professor Djokosutono, Ismojo, Koemoro, Jo Kurianingrat, Johannes Leimena, Nuradi, Ratmoko, Sjafruddin Prawiranegara, the late Amir Sjarifuddin, Monsignor Soegiopranoto, Soemardi, Sutomo Tjokronegoro, Achmad Subardjo, Sudarsono, Sukiman Wirjosandjojo, Sukrisno, Sunarjo, R. P. Soerachman, the late Suripno, Suwito, Kaslan A. Tahir, Wongsonegoro, and Mohamed Yunus.

While in the Netherlands-controlled areas of Indonesia, the writer received the appreciated assistance of Lt. Governor-General Hubertus J. van Mook; his Chief of Cabinet, P. J. Koets; and Abdoelkadir Widjojoatmodjo, as well as of the Regeerings Voorlichtings Dienst and its staff—in particular Messrs. Bajetto, Hubrecht, Scheren, Seret, and Wansink. Likewise he is grateful for the assistance given him by the Leger Contacten office of the Royal Netherlands Army and the office of Nefis dealing with the Japanese occupation.

Among the numerous other people to whom the writer is indebted for help received in Netherlands-controlled areas, he would like to mention the following:

In Batavia—Zainal Abidin, Herman and Hennie Buitenhuijis, Chen Tey Sue, Donald Davies, B. M. and Herawati Diah, Erna Djajadiningrat, Willard Hanna, Hamengku Buwono IX, Injo Beng Goat, Johannes, Jusuf, Gratimah Kartalegawa, John Ketcham, Wim Latumeten, Harold Nelson, Karl Neys, Taufik Salim, Sanjoto, Soedjono, Richard Stuart, Thio Thiam Tjong, and Wirjawan.

In Celebes—Arnold Mononutu, Anak Agung Gde Agung, Andi Burhanuddin, A.I.A. Pesik, Mayor Polak, Soh Lian Tjie; also D. A. Gerungan, Jacques W. Levij, Abdul Madjid, C. B. J. Mantouw, Andi Masarapi, Jan Maweikere, Pantouw, Jakin Permata, W. Reinstra, the Sultan of Tidore, Tjokorde Gde Rake Sukawati, Soumokil, Pastor Sondakh, Andi Sultan Daeng Radja, Tan Tek Heng, Teng Tjin Leng, and A. B. H. Wawuruntu.

In Bali—Hans Snelleman, Hans Harten, Manuaba, Theo Mejer, Made Mendera, Gusti Ketoet Ngoerah, Nonja Gusti Bagus Oka, Ide Anak Agoeng Gde Oka, I. G. Panetje, Ida Bagus Pidada, and Poetoe Wirja.

In East Java—Djaswadi Suprapto, Djoewito, Dominé Hildering, Indrakoesoma, Dominé Iskander, Murdjani, and Charles van der Plas.

In Madura—Mohamad Mahfoed, Oemar, Roeslan, Suparmo, Tjakranigrat, M. Zainalalim, and leaders of Madura branches of Pandura Rakjat Indonesia and Gaboengan Peladjar Indonesia.

In West Java—R. B. K. E. Djajadiningrat, R. Djumhana, Hasan Natanegara, Kosasih, Adil Poeradiredja, R. Soejoso, Soemarno, R. A. A. Soeriakartalegawa, Male Wiranata Koesoema, Muharam Wiranata Koesoema, and R. A. A. M. Wiranata Koesoema.

In Bangka, Semarang, and Palembang—M. Jusuf, Mas Sjarif, J. C. Verkerke, Zainal Abidien, Sinaga, Slamet Tirtosoebroto, Kiaji Hadji Azhari, and R. Hanan.

The following individuals and groups also rendered important assistance:

Republican Indonesian representatives in the United States—in particular, L. N. Palar, Soedarpo Sastrosatomo, Soedjatmoko Mangoendiningrat, Sumitro Djojohadikusumo, Ismail Thajeb, and Basoeki Djatiasmoro.

Many of the foreign correspondents in Batavia—in particular, Arnold Brackman of United Press, Henk van Maurik of the Gelderlander Pers, Quentin Pope of the *Chicago Tribune,* and Chris Scheffer of the *Nieuwe Rotterdamse Courant.*

Members or former members of the United Nations' Committee of Good Offices on the Indonesian Question and its secretariat—in particular, T. K. Critchley, Lieutenant Colonel Dewar, Frank P. Graham, Myra Jordan, John Lindsey, Colonel William Mayer, E. A. Roberts, and Philip Trezise.

In addition, the author wishes to thank Charles Wolf, Jr. for his helpful comments on the first four chapters and the following for their likewise helpful remarks pertaining to one or more of these four chapters: Willard Elsbree, Claire Holt, Nobutaka Ike, Harold Isaacs, Paul Kattenburg, Victor Purcell, Arthur A. Schiller, and the members of the Political Science Seminar at the Johns Hopkins University.

Finally the author wishes to thank the following for permission to quote extracts from their publications: The University of Chicago Press and H. A. R. Gibb, *Modern Trends in Islam; Commonweal* (December 31, 1949), a letter from Bishop Soegiopranoto; The John Day Company, and Soetan Sjahrir, *Out of Exile; Harper's Magazine* (March, 1946) and F. E. Crockett, "How the Trouble Began in Java"; The Institute of Pacific Relations and Charles Wolf, Jr., *The Indonesian Story; The New York Times* (December 26, 1948) and Arthur Krock, "Capital in a Dilemma on Indonesian Policy"; *Pacific Affairs* (December 1949) and Takdir Alisjabana, "The Indonesian Language—By-Product of Nationalism"; Presses Universitaires de France, Snouck Hurgronje's *Politique Musulmane de la Hollande;* and Soetan Sjahrir, *Onze Strijd.*

Index

484

Date Due

JAN 19		
OCT 9		
OCT 22		
NOV 23		
FEB 15		
May 31, 1966		
	WITHDRAWN	

Demco 293-5